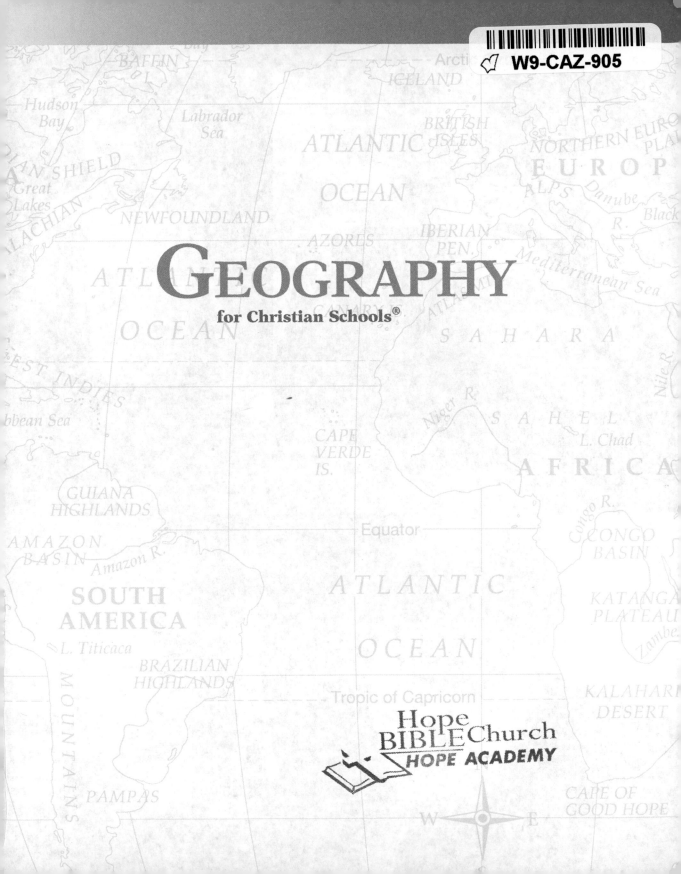

GEOGRAPHY

for Christian Schools®

Hope
BIBLE Church
HOPE ACADEMY

BJU Press

GEOGRAPHY

for Christian Schools®

Second Edition

Michael D. Matthews, M.Ed.
Ron Tagliapietra, Ed.D.
Pam Creason, M.Ed.

Bob Jones University Press
Greenville, South Carolina 29614

GEOGRAPHY for Christian Schools®
Second Edition

Michael D. Matthews, M.Ed.
Ron Tagliapietra, Ed.D.
Pam Creason, M.Ed.

Contributing Writer
  Hal C. Oberholzer II, M.A.

Produced in cooperation with the Bob Jones University College of Arts and Science and Bob Jones Academy.

for Christian Schools is a registered trademark of Bob Jones University Press.

© 1998 Bob Jones University Press
Greenville, South Carolina 29614
First Edition © 1987 Bob Jones University Press

ISBN 1-59166-420-9

15 14 13 12 11 10 9 8 7 6 5 4 3 2 1

CONTENTS

READY REFERENCE TO MAPS

Pronunciation Guide

The pronunciation key used in this text is designed to give readers a self-evident, acceptable pronunciation for a word as they read it from the page. For more nearly accurate pronunciations, consult a good dictionary.

Syllables with primary stress appear in LARGE CAPITAL letters. Syllables with secondary stress and one-syllable words appear in SMALL CAPITAL letters; for example, *Afghanistan* appears as (af GAN uh STAN). Where two or more words appear together, hyphens separate the syllables within each word; for example, the *Rub al Khali* appears as (ROOB ohl KHAH-lee).

Most sounds are readily apparent. Here are the possible exceptions:

SYMBOL	EXAMPLE	SYMBOL	EXAMPLE
g	get = GET	th	thin = THIN
j	gentle = JEN tul	*th*	then = *TH*EN
s	cent = SENT	zh	lesion = LEE zhun
a	cat = KAT	i-e	might = MITE
ah	cot = KAHT	eye	icy = EYE see
ar	car = KAR	oh	slow = SLOH
aw	all = AWL	ou	loud = LOUD
a-e	cape = KAPE	oy	toil = TOYL
ay	paint = PAYNT	u	some = SUM
e	jet = JET	uh	abet = uh BET
ee	fiend = FEEND	oo	crew = CROO
i	swim = SWIM	*oo*	push = POOSH

I sing the mighty power of God,
That made the mountains rise;
That spread the flowing seas abroad,
And built the lofty skies.
I sing the wisdom that ordained
The sun to rule the day;
The moon shines full at His command,
And all the stars obey.

I sing the goodness of the Lord,
That filled the earth with food;
He formed the creatures with His word,
And then pronounced them good.
Lord, how Thy wonders are displayed,
Where'er I turn my eye:
If I survey the ground I tread,
Or gaze upon the sky!

There's not a plant or flower below,
But makes Thy glories known;
And clouds arise, and tempests blow,
By order from Thy throne;
While all that borrows life from Thee
Is ever in Thy care,
And everywhere that man can be,
Thou, God, art present there.

Isaac Watts, 1674-1748

UNIT I

The World as God Made It

CHAPTER 1

GEOGRAPHY: FINDING OUR PLACE IN THE WORLD

The Lord by wisdom hath founded the earth; by understanding hath he established the heavens. (Prov. 3:19)

Bible verses such as the one above remind us that God created our world. Every mountain and valley is exactly where He wanted it to be. This planet did not "just happen." As we behold the earth's amazing design and provisions for life, our hearts should praise the Creator.

For thus saith the Lord that created the heavens; God himself that formed the earth and made it; he hath established it, he created it not in vain, he formed it to be inhabited: I am the Lord; and there is none else. (Isa. 45:18)

Isaiah tells us that God made the earth to be a home for man, and He supplied it with abundant resources for us to use and to enjoy. Every day man is learning more about the earth and its resources. Man uses this knowledge to help him provide for his physical needs and to build great civilizations. His challenge is to use the earth's resources in a way that honors the Creator.

WHAT IS GEOGRAPHY?

History and geography are both necessary to help us understand the world around us. Unlike history, which is the study of *time*, geography is the study of *place*. The basic tool of geography is a map, just as the basic tool of history is a time line. It is not enough, however, just to memorize a list of dates and places. Beyond the questions of when and where, we want to know how and why. Geography helps us to learn not only where places are but also how they differ and why.

Branches of Geography

The word *geography* comes from two roots meaning "earth" *(geo-)* and "description" *(-graphy).* In other words, geography is a detailed description of the earth, especially its surface. Geography has two main branches: *physical geography* (the study of the earth and its resources) and *human geography* (the study of man as he lives on the earth and uses its resources). These two main branches are divided into dozens of smaller branches, such as climatology, oceanography, and demographics.

There are two ways to study the many branches of geography. *Systematic geography* examines one branch of geography at a time, tying together examples from every region of the world. For example, a chapter entitled "Urban Geography" might discuss New York City, London, and Tokyo. *Regional geography,* on the other hand, examines only one region of the world at a time, tying together all the branches of geography. For example, a chapter entitled "The Far East" might cover the major cities there as well as the climate, mountains, and history.

This book combines both approaches. Chapters 2-5 are a general, systematic study of the whole world, with two chapters on physical geography and two chapters on human geography. Once you see the big picture and learn the basic terms of geography, you will spend the rest of the year studying the unique features of individual countries and regions.

History of Geography

Ancient Views of the Earth   Ever since the Lord commanded Noah to replenish the earth, Noah's descendants have been exploring and mapping the unknown. Early mapmakers supplied kings with maps to plan wars, to open new trade routes, and to build new cities. The earliest surviving map is a clay tablet from the Babylonian empire around 2300 B.C. It is a simple map that depicts rivers and mountains.

The Greeks were the first ancient people to study the earth extensively. Early seafarers wanted to learn all about their trade routes and the people with whom they traded. Alexander the Great, who rose to power in 336 B.C., dreamed of conquering the world. After defeating Persia, he hired surveyors to accompany his army on a four-year journey "to the ends of the earth." His march into unexplored central Asia and India greatly expanded the horizons of Greek knowledge about world geography. But his homesick army, ten thousand miles from home, mutinied and forced him to turn back.

The Greeks were also inspired by natural curiosity. The first great geographer was a Greek mathematician named **Eratosthenes** (ER uh TAHS thuh NEEZ), who lived three centuries before Christ's birth. He summed up Greek understanding of the world in a book entitled *Geography*. In fact, he was the first man to use the word *geography*. Like many Greek philosophers of his day, he believed the world was a sphere. He even calculated its circumference. A century later another Greek philosopher named Hipparchus (hih PAHR kus) made it easier to locate places on maps by drawing a **grid** (a regular pattern of intersecting vertical and horizontal lines).

The Romans borrowed their mapmaking techniques from the Greeks. With their vast empire, they emphasized practical maps to help them to build roads and to rule efficiently. The most famous geographer in the Roman Empire was **Ptolemy** (TAHL uh mee), who lived in the second century after Christ. He promoted a geocentric (earth-centered) theory, which states that the sun, stars, and planets revolve around the earth. Ptolemy's amazing map of the world pictured land from Britain to China. Both his map and his theory of the universe remained unchallenged for almost fourteen centuries.

The Age of Exploration   The translation of Ptolemy's works in the early fifteenth century revived Europe's interest in maps and helped to spark the Age of Exploration. Sea captains developed maps of the stars and charts of the winds to help them plot new sea routes to reach the spices, gold, and jewels of the Orient. After studying Ptolemy's map (which greatly exaggerated the size of Asia), an ambitious young man named Christopher Columbus decided that he could take an easy shortcut to the

Ptolemy's map of the world (second century A.D.)

Orient by sailing westward. Instead, he discovered a new, uncharted world—America.

At the same time, scientists were learning more about the earth's place in the universe. In 1543 **Nicolaus Copernicus** published a lengthy work arguing that the earth revolves around the sun. His revolutionary belief became known as the heliocentric (sun-centered) theory.

Along with these advances in science, the art of **cartography** (mapmaking) reached a new height. **Gerhardus Mercator** of Flanders published a map in 1569 that became the standard of excellence. His

Eratosthenes' Measurement of the Earth

Eratosthenes of Cyrene (ca. 276 B.C.–ca. 195 B.C.) had many talents. For instance, he drew an early map of the world, and he compiled a catalog of the stars. In mathematics he is famous for devising a method for finding prime numbers, known as Eratosthenes' sieve. He also directed the world-famous library at Alexandria. But his best-known achievement was his calculation of the circumference of the earth—seventeen hundred years before Columbus discovered America.

To achieve this great feat, Eratosthenes measured the length of shadows at noon on the first day of summer. The sun was at its height in the Egyptian city of Syene (modern Aswan), casting no shadow. But five hundred miles to the north at Alexandria, it cast a measurable shadow. Eratosthenes then drew two imaginary lines from these cities to the center of the earth. Calculating the angle between these lines, he found that Alexandria was approximately one-fiftieth of the earth's circle (a 7.2° angle) north of Syene. Thus, the earth's circumference was fifty times the distance between the two cities.

Finally, Eratosthenes calculated fifty times the 500-mile distance between the two cities. He concluded that the distance around the earth is about 25,000 miles. Today, over two thousand years later, satellite measurements have proved that Eratosthenes was amazingly close to the actual 24,860-mile circumference.

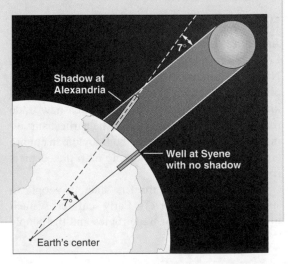

Shadow at Alexandria

Well at Syene with no shadow

7°

7°

Earth's center

Ten-Millionth of the Distance to the Equator

During the Middle Ages a confusing system of measurements arose in Europe based on thumbs, elbows, feet, and other varying standards. After the rediscovery of Greek learning, French scientists wanted a better, more "rational" standard for describing the world around them. They decided to survey the entire meridian running from Dunkirk (the northernmost city on the coast of France) all the way to Barcelona (a southern city on the coast of Spain). Based on this survey they calculated the distance from the North Pole to the equator. One ten-millionth of this distance was called a *meter.*

France's proud accomplishment proved to be terribly inaccurate. (It was short by about two thousand meters, or 0.02 percent.) The definition of the meter was soon changed from its relationship to the earth to the length of the platinum bar that the Frenchmen had forged. Today's meter has an even more precise definition: the distance light travels in a vacuum in 1/299,792,458 of a second. Obviously, it no longer has any relationship to a measurement of the earth's surface.

well-designed grid enabled seafarers to plot their courses in a straight line. His system is still used today. The maps of this period were beautifully illustrated with sea creatures, ships, and other designs to fill in the large areas about which geographers had no information.

The Modern Age   As European kings began to colonize and conquer the rest of the world, they demanded maps with more and more detail. European kingdoms, led by France, also commissioned extensive surveys of their own lands. These new maps included symbols for **topography** (detailed land features, including their heights) to help generals move their armies more quickly. When England became the world's leading sea power in the eighteenth century, it also became the world's leading mapmaker.

As modern nation-states began gathering more information about their climates, populations, and resources, they produced *thematic maps* to display their abstract findings. The United States was late in joining the map race. Since World War II, however, America has been producing hundreds of maps for its troops stationed around the world. The development of airplanes and satellites made it possible to create better, more detailed maps than ever before. The U.S. Geological Survey (USGS), founded in 1879, has created a wealth of detailed maps. Radar and infrared satellites have now mapped the ocean floors and the frigid poles.

Even though cartographers have produced very detailed and accurate maps of the earth, exploration continues. The jungles teem with millions of species that have never been cataloged. Millions, or even billions, of undiscovered animal communities dot the ocean floor. Despite many famous expeditions, many mountain peaks have never been climbed. Immense caves remain hidden, never trodden by human feet.

◎ SECTION REVIEW

1. Define *geography.* What are its two main branches?
2. Who were the two greatest ancient geographers? What did they contribute to geography?
3. What contributions from the Age of Exploration are still used today?
4. What characteristics of modern maps distinguish them from maps of the ancient world and of the Age of Exploration?
   ♀ Why has the United States become the leading mapmaker in the world?

THE GEOGRAPHIC GRID

A mistake would mean certain death. Navy vessels waited impatiently as the *Apollo 11* command module slammed into the upper atmosphere, moments before splashdown in the open sea. Were NASA's calculations correct?

The *Apollo 11* moon mission was the greatest adventure of the twentieth century and the climax of thousands of years of human exploration and learning. "Far more than three men on a voyage to the moon," observed Astronaut Buzz Aldrin, "this stands as a symbol of the insatiable curiosity of all mankind to explore the unknown."

After the walk on the moon, the return trip went smoothly. When the astronauts splashed down in the Pacific Ocean, 950 miles southwest of Honolulu, they were rescued quickly. How did the rescue ship find them so easily, even though they were surrounded by water and could not see any landmarks? They used the imaginary lines of the *geographic grid,* which divide the globe.

Hemispheres

Since the earliest times, geographers have divided the earth's sphere into two halves, calling each half a **hemisphere.** The line that divides the earth between the north and south is the **equator.** The half below the equator is called the Southern Hemisphere. The half above the equator is the Northern Hemisphere.

The *Apollo 11* astronauts landed in the Northern Hemisphere. If the earth were flat, NASA could have located them above the equator using feet and miles. But the earth is not flat; it is round. It is easier to locate points on a circle using *degrees* (°). NASA needed only two measurements to pinpoint the astronauts: degrees of latitude and degrees of longitude.

Degrees of Latitude

The first measurement that NASA needed was degrees of **latitude.** Imaginary lines run east and west around the earth. They form circles that are parallel to the equator and are therefore called **parallels** of latitude. We find latitude by measuring the angle of these circles from the equator.

How do we label latitudes? Consider the farthest point from the equator—the North Pole. If we draw an imaginary angle from the center of the earth, with one ray pointing to the equator and the other ray pointing to the North Pole, the angle drawn will be a 90° angle. Thus, the farthest parallel

Lines of Latitude

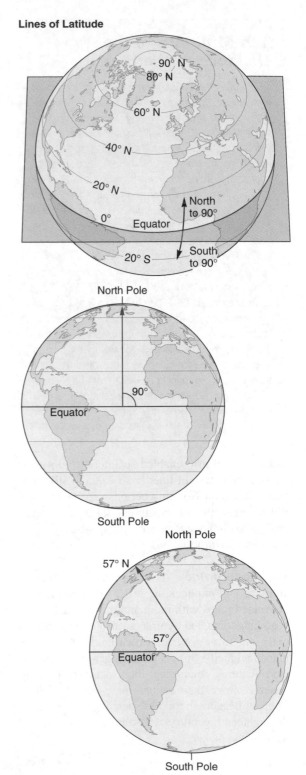

from the equator is 90° N. (The symbols N and S indicate the hemisphere the latitude is in.) All other points are closer to the equator (and must be less than 90°). For example, at an angle 57° north of the equator we find the latitude 57° N.

The distance from one degree of latitude to the next is about sixty-nine miles. But that is still not precise enough to find an astronaut floating in the middle of the ocean. We divide every degree of latitude into sixty *minutes* ('), each minute just over one mile apart. Furthermore, every minute is divided into sixty *seconds* ("), each about one hundred feet apart. A bronze marker at Meade's Ranch in eastern Kansas has been carefully measured as having a latitude of exactly 39°13'26.686" N. This location is correct to the very inch. It is used as a basis for mapping all latitudes in North America.

Degrees of Longitude

Even if NASA determined the latitude of the returning astronauts, it would need to know the point on that latitude line where the module splashed down. To find that point, they would need to know the **longitude.** Imaginary lines of longitude, called **meridians,** run north and south, stretching from pole to pole. But there is no equator running north and south from which we can measure these lines. Therefore, one of the meridians has been designated the **prime meridian** from which all others are measured. The prime meridian (0°) extends through Greenwich, England, just outside of London. Scientists there at the Royal Observatory made the original calculations for modern meridians. Their meridian became the basis of all other longitude measurements.

Like lines of latitude, meridians are measured in degrees, minutes, and seconds. However, there is one major difference: the highest degree is 180, not 90. Why? The farthest point from the prime meridian is halfway around the world. Half of a full circle is 180°. All other points are closer to the prime meridian and must be less than 180°.

The 180° meridian lies directly opposite the prime meridian and is actually a continuation of the same line. Together, these lines form a **great circle.** A great circle cuts the earth into two equal parts, or hemispheres. Every meridian except 0° and 180° is labeled as east (E) or west (W) depending on the hemisphere in which it lies.

The bronze marker at Meade's Ranch has a longitude of 98°32'30.506" W. With the help of such exact readings, NASA easily found the astronauts' command module.

Lines of Longitude

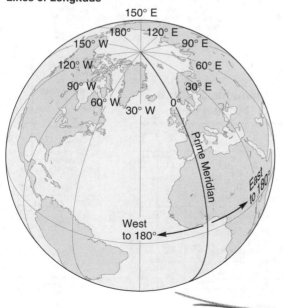

MAP PROJECTIONS

Globes show information about the earth's surface with almost perfect accuracy. Both are spheres, and both can be divided easily with lines of latitude

Surveying America's Back Yard

Any family who owns a home or land has an important legal document showing its exact boundaries. Every time someone purchases property, he must pay a professional to **survey,** or measure, the land. Landowners keep a copy of their survey map with their other legal papers.

To mark plots of land, surveyors in most areas refer to a grid set up under the Land Ordinance of 1787. As the United States acquired new territory, surveyors went out into the wilderness to measure **principal meridians** and base lines. (The map shows the dates that these lines were surveyed.) With these two

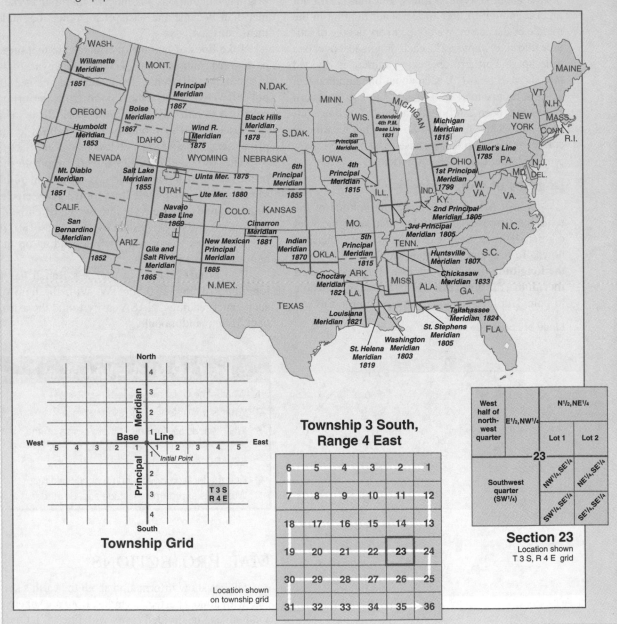

Township Grid

Township 3 South, Range 4 East

Location shown on township grid

Section 23
Location shown
T 3 S, R 4 E grid

lines as reference points, the government subdivided the land into a series of smaller and smaller squares. Surveyors first divided the land into townships that were six miles square. They further divided townships into sections, quarters, and acres.

Surveyors had two main instruments at their disposal. One was a portable instrument called a *theodolite,* which measured horizontal and vertical angles to help in mapping the contour of the land. The other instrument was *Gunter's chain,* named after its English developer. This chain was sixty-six feet long and was divided into one hundred metal bar links. An area of land ten chains long and one chain wide equaled one **acre.**

Surveyors measure small plots of land by a process called *metes and bounds* (short for "measurements and boundaries"). Originally, the surveyor had only a Gunter's chain and a compass. He would locate many landmarks, such as streams, fences, trees, or stakes; and he often added many of his own stone markers. He then used his compass to determine the exact direction of each line from one marker to another. Modern equipment makes this procedure a little simpler, but the process remains much the same.

For surveying large areas, surveyors now use sophisticated equipment such as lasers and computers. Aerial photography and information from satellites also aid in the construction of modern survey maps.

and longitude. Globes are useful, but they are difficult to carry in a briefcase or fit into a textbook.

Flat maps are much more useful than globes and can show much greater detail. Any method used to "project" the earth's round surface onto a flat map is called a **map projection.**

The Problem: Distortion

When the globe is transferred onto a flat map, a serious problem occurs. The earth's surface is not a flat rectangle like a sheet of paper. It does not "flatten" without **distortion.** There are four features of a globe that we try to avoid distorting on a flat map:

1. area
2. shape
3. distance
4. direction

Usually a flat map will distort two or three of these features while minimizing or eliminating the other distortions. No flat map of the world can be accurate in all four ways—area, shape, distance, and direction.

Consider the problem that manufacturers have in printing a globe. They must print the outer layer on a flat surface and then glue it to the globe. A typical globe is covered by twelve paper strips called **gores.**

How accurate is this map? *Areas* of land and water are accurate, and compass *directions* are fairly accurate. *Distances* also appear to be accurate—an inch equals the same number of miles on every gore. But we would find it awkward to measure distances between gores. The *shapes* have the most obvious distortions because of all the gaps.

Gores

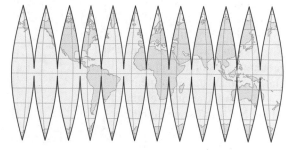

9

Imagine how difficult it would be to draw the shape of Asia using this map as a guide! Even though the gore map is fairly accurate in three respects, it is obviously not very useful as a flat map.

Solutions to the Problem

In an effort to solve the problem of distortion, cartographers have developed three basic types of map projections. These projections—cylindrical, conic, and planar—get their name from the geometric surface onto which the globe is projected.

Although maps are drawn using mathematical equations, we can picture what takes place with the help of an imaginary globe made from wire. The wires represent lines of latitude and longitude. At the center of the globe, an imaginary light shines out onto the map surface.

Cylindrical Projections   Most world maps use a variation of the **cylindrical projection.** First we roll a sheet of paper around the wire globe in the shape of a cylinder. Next we trace the shadows cast by the light, and then we unroll the paper to get a flat map.

Mercator's Projection The first important cylindrical projection was published by Mercator in 1569. Not until the second half of the twentieth century was it replaced.

On a Mercator map all lines of latitude and longitude appear straight. This feature means that compass *directions* are always constant. (North is always toward the top, east to the right, etc.) *Shapes* are also accurate. *Areas* and *distances* are increasingly distorted, however, the farther away you move from the equator. Greenland appears larger than the continent of South America, even though it is only one-eighth its size.

Cylindrical Projection

Mercator

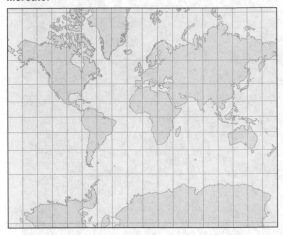

Goode's Interrupted Projection There are several popular variations of the cylindrical map. Maps that cut and flatten the earth like an orange peel are called **interrupted projections.** The map made from gores is an example. It remains in one piece, but the image is "interrupted" with gaps or cuts.

The most popular of these maps is Goode's interrupted projection. This projection is useful because the *areas* remain fairly accurate and the *shapes* of continents are less distorted than shapes on the gore map. Unfortunately, Goode's projection distorts *distances* and all north-south *directions*.

Goode's

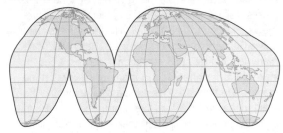

Robinson's Projection Popular for textbooks is Robinson's projection. It combines the best elements from the other projections. Its greatest advantage is that it minimizes all four types of

Robinson

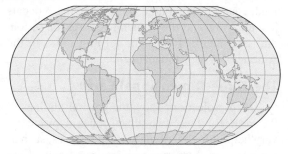

distortions. True, everything is distorted, but only by a little bit. Almost every world map in this textbook uses Robinson's projection.

Azimuthal Projection

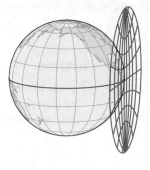

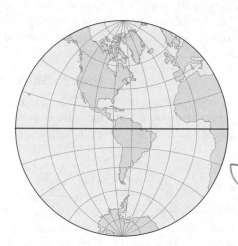

Conic Projection

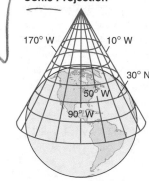

170° W   10° W

30° N

50° W

90° W

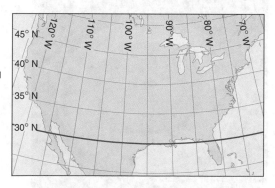

Azimuthal Projections Cylindrical projections, such as Mercator's, Goode's, and Robinson's, are all good for world maps. But planar and conic projections work better on smaller-scale maps.

The planar projection, also called an **azimuthal projection,** uses a flat plane instead of a cylinder. To make the projection, we place a flat sheet of paper on an imaginary wire globe, touching only one point. The shadows traced on this paper form an azimuthal map. The map is most accurate in the center but becomes increasingly distorted near the edges. Therefore, it is useful for compact areas, such as South America and Antarctica, where land is surrounded by water.

Conic Projections To make a **conic projection,** we place a cone-shaped piece of paper on an imaginary wire globe. After tracing the shadow onto the cone, we open and flatten the cone to make a conic projection. Unlike the planar projection, which touches a single point, the cone touches an entire line of latitude. The conic map is most accurate where the cone touches the line. Away from that line the features become gradually distorted. Thus, it is most useful for showing wide regions, such as the United States.

Choosing a projection is very important when displaying the whole world or a large region of the world. However, mapmakers do not worry much about projections of small areas, such as cities. Distortions are virtually undetectable on maps of such small areas.

11

SECTION REVIEW

1. What are the four types of distortion on flat maps?
2. Define an interrupted projection. Give two examples.
3. What is the main advantage of a Mercator projection?
4. Which projection does this textbook use for world maps? which projections for smaller-scale maps?
   💡 What projection would you use to show the nation of Russia?

MAP RELIEF

It was a simple plan. Attack the rebels from three directions and join at Albany, in the process cutting the colonies in half and crushing the rebellion. The plan seemed certain to succeed, at least while British general Gage sat in Boston, sipping his tea and looking at the map on the table. But the campaign soon ran into trouble. Gage had not known about the rough terrain in upper Maine. There British general Burgoyne's army became hopelessly entangled in the heavy forest. Continental troops, familiar with their own land, easily trapped him. In one day the redcoats lost an army, and the French had a reason to join the rebel cause. It was the turning point in the American War of Independence.

The Three-Dimensional Earth

Map projections show the general outlines of the earth. But these two-dimensional maps are not very helpful in describing surface features, such as mountains and valleys. Soldiers, road crews, and backpackers all need detailed information about the third dimension, *altitude*.

Any type of map that shows surface features is a physical map because it shows physical things. Physical maps that show specific changes in elevation are called relief maps. **Relief** refers to the height and depth of land features. Many relief maps include water features, such as rivers, and man-made features, such as dams.

How to Show the Third Dimension

There are many ways for relief maps to show the third dimension of the earth's surface. Early maps included ink drawings of hills and mountains

Bench Marks

In describing elevation, a surveyor refers to distance above sea level. What does he do when he cannot see the sea? He relies on special monuments called "bench marks," which have been placed in key spots around the world giving the exact altitude of the location. If you have ever hiked to the peak of a mountain, you might have seen a bench mark. It looks like the head of a large nail.

So how did surveyors measure the original bench marks? Although the details are complex, the theory is simple. A surveyor stands in a place where he can see the ocean with a telescope (on his theodolite). By measuring angles, he can calculate the altitude of his position and nail a marker. Then he moves farther inland and views his first marker. On and on it goes. The surveyor carries an altimeter, too, to check his altitude. The *altimeter* measures air pressure, which becomes lower as you move up in elevation.

In the past, government surveyors hacked through dense woods to get a clear line of site. The work was difficult and time consuming. Now surveyors use satellites as reference points, making their work easier and more precise.

to show upper elevations. "Raised relief" maps, such as plaster models, are literally three-dimensional. Recent advances in technology, such as computers, satellite images, and aerial photography, have made it possible to use colors to indicate different altitudes. On most color relief maps, green represents land near sea level. Yellow or light brown represents a slight rise in land. Dark brown, gray, or white indicates mountains.

Contour Lines The lines that separate colors on a relief map are called **contour lines.** Each line shows all points on the map with a given altitude. (For this reason, the line is also known as an *iso-line; iso-* means "equal.") Look at the world map on page 1. What elevation is represented by each of the five contour lines? The relief maps in the rest of this book will use these same contour lines.

Contour Intervals The difference in elevation between two contour lines is called the *contour interval.* On the world map, notice that the contour intervals are all different. The smallest interval, shaded green, is two hundred meters. That means that the change in elevation from the line at sea level to the next line is two hundred meters. Each of these intervals is shaded a different color.

Reading Relief Maps Look at the upper drawing below. It gives a picture of what one region might look like to a camera, but it is not a map. This drawing cannot show distances, directions, or the shapes and areas of the land. The bottom diagram below shows the comparative elevations of a cross section of the same landscape. It does not, however, give any information about the other dimensions.

Three Views of a Landscape

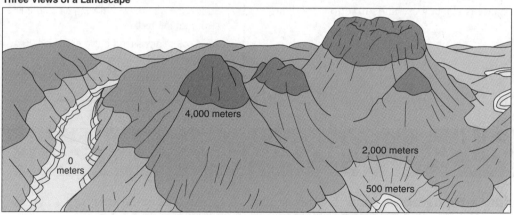

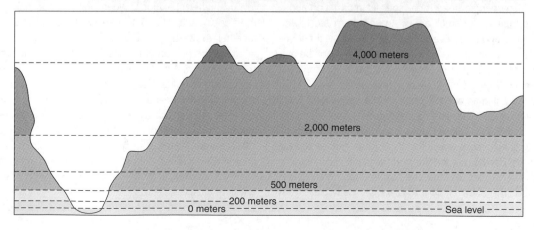

13

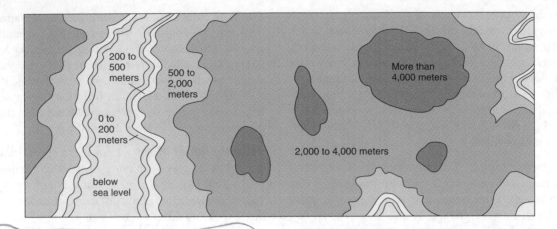

The relief map gives accurate information about all three dimensions. With it we can visualize the landforms and compare the elevations of those landforms. Relief maps also show us the general shapes, areas, distances, and directions of landforms.

SECTION REVIEW

1. What is the term for a map that shows the altitude of land features?

2. Explain the difference between a contour line and a contour interval.

3. What color shows land between 0 and 200 meters? *green*

 What color shows land below sea level? Why is this color never next to the sea?

Geographer's Corner

Reading a Topographic Map

Many people need more specific information about the topography of small areas. Among them are hikers, engineers, and land developers. Their solution is the topographic map. To someone who has never seen one before, it looks like a bunch of irregular lines with no apparent meaning. A trained map reader, however, can quickly visualize the entire terrain of a place. With a topographic map, a lost hiker can easily find his way again.

Unlike the colored relief maps in your textbook, topographic maps give all the contour lines at regular intervals. On the map on the next page, the contour interval is twenty feet, and the one-hundred-foot intervals are labeled. The direction of the slope is usually clear from the terrain around it. The land obviously slopes upward toward higher elevations. Where the lines are far apart, the slopes are gentle. But in areas where they are close together, the land rises steeply.

This is a portion of a United States Geological Survey (USGS) map of a part of northern Pennsylvania. The right side of the map lies along the seventy-seventh meridian. The left side lies near a longitude of 77°2'30" W.

The map includes some standard symbols. Two exact altitude measurements are found at the bench marks (BM). Natural features, such as creeks and ponds, appear in blue. Green areas indicate woods. The map also shows highways, houses, and other buildings and marks a cemetery with a cross.

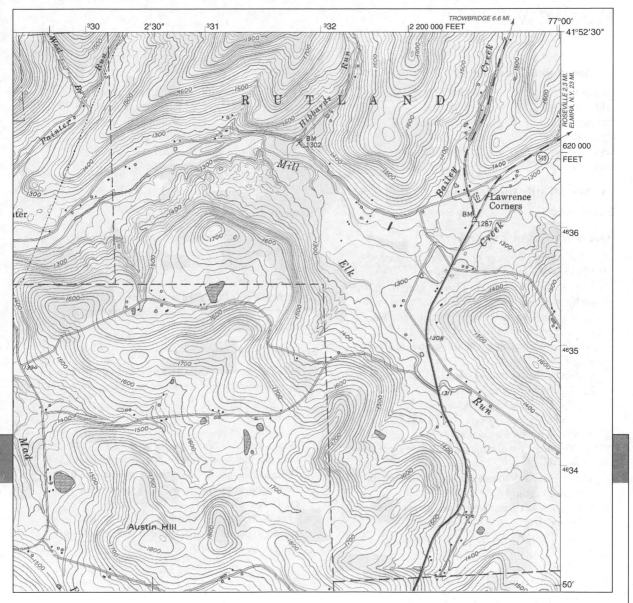

Use the information on this map to answer these questions:

1. What is the altitude for the bench mark at Lawrence Corners?

2. Is Austin Hill the highest point on the map?

3. What creek flows northwest through a wide valley and empties into Mill Creek?

4. If two inches on the map equals one mile, how far is Austin Hill from Lawrence Corners?

5. What is the latitude for points along the top of the map?

💡 Can you see Austin Hill if you are standing in Lawrence Corners? Draw a picture of what you would see when looking in that direction.

REVIEW 1

Can You Define These Terms?

geography	latitude	survey	cylindrical projection
grid	parallel	principal meridian	interrupted projection
cartography	longitude	acre	azimuthal projection
topography	meridian	map projection	conic projection
hemisphere	prime meridian	distortion	relief
equator	great circle	gore	contour line

Can You Identify These People?

Eratosthenes   Ptolemy   Copernicus   Mercator

How Much Do You Remember?

1. What are the two main branches of geography?
2. Who was the first great geographer?
3. Explain the difference between geography, cartography, and topography.
4. How are modern maps better than ancient maps? What characteristics have not changed?
5. Answer each question with the word *latitude* or *longitude*.
   a. Which runs north and south?
   b. Which runs east and west?
   c. Which is called a parallel?
   d. Which is given in degrees from 0 to 90?
   e. Which is called a meridian?
   f. Which always lies an equal distance from the next line?
6. Why do lines of latitude stop at 90° but lines of longitude extend to 180°?
7. What bodies of water are located at these points on the globe? (See p. 1.)
   a. 80° N, 80° E
   b. 28° N, 110° W
   c. 20° S, 150° E
8. Why do all flat maps of the earth contain distortions?

9. What is the main advantage of each projection?
   a. Goode's
   b. Mercator's
   c. Robinson's
10. What is a relief map? How are the relief maps in your textbook different from USGS topographic maps?

What Do You Think?

1. What are the main differences between these three maps from different periods of history?
   a. Ptolemy's
   b. Mercator's
   c. Robinson's
2. Why were mapmakers able to define the equator over two thousand years before the prime meridian?
3. What advantages does the Goode's projection have over Robinson's projection? Why do you think this textbook prefers Robinson's projection?
4. Why do most relief maps have a color scheme similar to the one in this textbook, rather than some other color scheme?

CHAPTER 2

THE EARTH'S SURFACE

O Lord my God, thou art very great; . . . who stretchest out the heavens like a curtain: who layeth the beams of his chambers in the waters: . . . who laid the foundations of the earth, that it should not be removed for ever. (Ps. 104:1-5)

The psalmist reminds us that God is responsible for the formation of the earth and of all that it contains. The Lord laid the foundations of the earth as well as of the sky and ocean deeps.

THE EARTH'S HISTORY

God's work in the earth's history can be divided into four phases: the Creation, the Flood, the modern world, and the future world. We cannot understand the modern world without understanding its past and its future. According to the apostle Peter, however, mankind is "willingly" ignorant of God's intervention in every phase of the earth's history:

For this they willingly are ignorant of, that by the word of God the heavens were of old, and the earth standing out of the water and in the water: whereby the world that then was, being overflowed with water, perished: but the heavens and the earth, which are now, by the same word are kept in store, reserved unto fire against the day of judgment and perdition of ungodly men. (II Pet. 3:5-7)

The Creation

Earth's history begins with the Creation. Genesis 1 describes how God gave the earth light, atmosphere, land, and seas. A mature world appeared within six days, filled with soil, tall trees, and croaking frogs—not just bare rocks, seeds, and tadpoles.

Modern scientists ignore God's record in Genesis. They believe that the lands and seas resulted from natural forces working over billions of years. They assume that only the forces acting on the earth now are those that have shaped the earth. If a river is carving a canyon at a rate of one foot every century and the canyon is now one hundred feet deep, scientists assume that it took ten thousand years to carve the canyon. This view is called **uniformitarianism.** People who hold this view are unwilling to recognize the existence of a powerful Creator, who made all things for a purpose and who will judge His creation.

The Flood

Christians believe the earth's features were changed by a **cataclysm** (the New Testament word for the Flood). Evolutionists say that a universal flood, as described in Genesis 7, could not have happened because such floods are not occurring today. But this conclusion is based on biased reasoning. Scoffers are "willingly ignorant," Peter said. Evolutionists stubbornly reject the Flood in spite of the evidence all around us.

Flash floods, like this one in Hawaii, continue to shape the landscape.

Rock layers on a butte near Sedona, Arizona

Only a universal flood could unleash the forces necessary to shape the world we see today. The impact of the Flood was staggering. Its waters fell for forty days from the heavens but also sprang from the "fountains of the deep" and covered the earth to a height of fifteen cubits (about twenty-two feet) above the highest mountains. Noah remained in the ark for over one year before the Flood waters subsided. During that time waves and water pressure reshaped the earth's surface. Dead plants, animal bodies, soil, and rocks washed from one area to another. Much of this material came to rest in layers.

The Flood waters also softened the earth's surface greatly. Evidence indicates that over one thousand years passed before the land dried completely. Rocks were not fully hardened and were easily broken, folded, or eroded. Earthquakes, volcanoes, and floods had a great impact on the earth's surface. The receding floodwater created great inland seas that later spilled over and washed away whole mountains. Magnificent formations, such as the Grand Canyon, formed quickly. Because the earth's surface has now hardened into rock, we do not see such massive erosion anymore.

Also, the climate took a long time to stabilize after the Flood. The large amount of water in the air formed thick clouds that blocked the sun's heat. Water froze at the poles. In some places, hundreds of feet of snow may have fallen each year. Many Creationists believe that huge glaciers covered

Bryce Canyon's pinnacles were left by erosion.

northern Europe, Canada, and the northern United States. Evidence of glaciers can still be seen. This "ice age" may have lasted for hundreds of years. Glaciers still cover the continent of Antarctica in the south and the island of Greenland in the north.

SECTION REVIEW

1. What are the four main phases in the history of the earth's surface? What does the Bible say about each phase in II Peter 3:5-7?

2. What is uniformitarianism? What biblical view better explains the changes in the world's land formations?

3. Why did the earth become unstable after the Flood?

💡 How is mixing cement a useful way to explain the softness of the earth after the Flood but its hardness today?

THE EARTH TODAY

The sea is his, and he made it: and his hands formed the dry land. (Ps. 95:5)

God has divided the earth into three parts: the **atmosphere,** the covering of air that surrounds our planet; the **lithosphere** (LITH uh SFEER), the solid part of the earth; and the **hydrosphere** (HYE druh SFEER), the water on the earth's surface. This chapter will examine the land and the water. The next chapter will discuss the atmosphere.

The Land

Lithosphere literally means "rock ball." The earth is a round ball nearly eight thousand miles in diameter. We think of the earth's surface as very rough. But when astronauts viewed it from the moon, the earth appeared as smooth as the surface of an apple.

Layers of the Earth

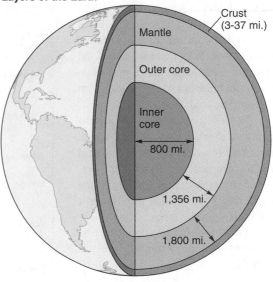

Crust (3-37 mi.)

Mantle

Outer core

Inner core

800 mi.

1,356 mi.

1,800 mi.

Layers of the Crust

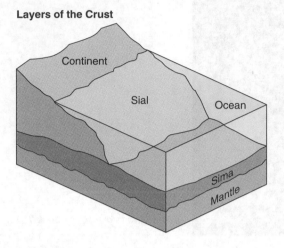

The Earth's Layers The lithosphere seems to be divided into several layers. The thin outer skin is called the **crust.** The crust consists mainly of two layers. The bottom layer of basaltic rock, called *sima,* spreads over the whole earth. Above the sima are the oceans and slabs of granitic rock, called *sial,* which are many miles thick. Where these slabs rise above the ocean, they form our continents.

Earthquakes give tantalizing hints about the secrets that lie below the earth's crust. In 1909 scientists noticed that earthquake waves change speed below the crust. They proposed that the waves were entering a different layer of hot, fluid material, called the **mantle.** Earthquake waves move faster through the hot, dense mantle than through the cold crust.

Waves from earthquakes indicate that there is also a **core** beneath the mantle, divided into a liquid outer core and a solid inner core. After studying the magnetism of the earth and its powerful gravity as it interacts with the moon, many scientists conclude that the core must be made of two heavy metals, iron and nickel.

The Continents The total surface area of the earth is 197 million square miles. Of that total, 29 percent, or 57 million square miles, is land; and the rest is ocean. All of the land surface is divided between islands and continents, but distinguishing them is a little tricky. **Continents** are the main landmasses of the earth; **islands** are landmasses surrounded by water. But aren't some continents completely surrounded by water? The other main difference is *size.* The smallest continent (Australia) is over three times larger than the largest island (Greenland).

There are six continental landmasses: North America, South America, Africa, Australia, Antarctica, and Eurasia. Eurasia, however, is often considered two continents, Europe and Asia. The Ural Mountains, shown on the world relief map on page 1, divide Europe from Asia. Can you see why Europe's status as a continent is disputed by geographers?

If the oceans were a little lower, the largest islands of the world would all become part of the nearby continents (on the slab called *sial*). We call these areas **continental islands.** Can you find the

CONTINENT	AREA (SQ. MI.)	PERCENT OF WORLD'S LAND	HIGH POINT	LOW POINT
Asia	17,129,000	29.7	Mt. Everest 29,028 ft. (Nepal)	Dead Sea −1,296 ft. (Israel)
Africa	11,707,000	20.0	Mt. Kilimanjaro 19,340 ft. (Tanzania)	Lake Assal −510 ft. (Djibouti)
North America	9,363,000	16.3	Mt. McKinley 20,320 ft. (Alaska)	Death Valley −282 ft. (California)
South America	6,886,000	12.0	Mt. Aconcagua 22,834 ft. (Argentina)	Salinas Grandes −131 ft. (Argentina)
Antarctica	5,500,000	9.6	Vinson Massif 16,067 ft.	Sea level
Europe	4,057,000	7.0	Mt. Elbrus 18,510 ft. (Russia)	Caspian Sea −92 ft. (Russia)
Australia	2,942,000	5.1	Mt. Kosciusko 7,316 ft. (New South Wales)	Lake Eyre −52 ft. (South Australia)

The earth appears as a blue gem in the blackness of space.

ten largest islands and the continents to which they belong? (See the map of the sea floor on page 635.) In contrast, **oceanic islands** rise from the ocean floor (the lower layer of the crust called *sima*).

The Oceans

The earth is unique in the solar system. Scientists have not found evidence of liquid water on any other planet or moon. Yet water covers 71 percent of the earth's surface, amounting to over three hundred million cubic miles. Even though 97 percent of the water lies in oceans, traces of water can be found on almost every square inch of land.

He gathereth the waters of the sea together as an heap: he layeth up the depth in storehouses. (Ps. 33:7)

Largest Islands

ISLAND	LOCATION	AREA (SQ. MI.)
Greenland	Atlantic Ocean	840,000
New Guinea	Pacific Ocean	306,000
Borneo	Pacific Ocean	280,100
Madagascar	Indian Ocean	226,658
Baffin	Arctic Ocean	195,928
Sumatra	Indian Ocean	165,000
Honshu	Pacific Ocean	87,805
Great Britain	Atlantic Ocean	84,200
Victoria	Arctic Ocean	83,897
Ellesmere	Arctic Ocean	75,767

OCEAN	AREA (SQ. MI.)	PERCENT OF WORLD OCEAN	LOWEST POINT
Pacific Ocean	70,000,000	50	Mariana Trench 35,840 ft.
Atlantic Ocean	36,000,000	25.5	Puerto Rico Trench 28,232 ft.
Indian Ocean	29,000,000	20.5	Java Trench 23,376 ft.
Arctic Ocean	5,400,000	4	Eurasian Basin 17,881 ft.

There are four principal bodies of water in the world: the Pacific, the Atlantic, the Indian, and the Arctic Oceans. All the world's seas, gulfs, and bays belong to one of these oceans. Continents generally mark the borders of each ocean. If you look at the world map, however, you will see that the divisions are not always clear. The oceans flow into each other. For this reason, the whole system is sometimes called the **world ocean.**

The oceans provide man with many blessings—distributing heat from the sun, providing water for rain clouds, and guarding nations from foreign invasion. Ocean waters teem with tasty fish and pearl-producing clams. The most obvious bounty of the sea is its salt. Salt has many uses; it is a seasoning for and preservative of food, a curer of

Earth's Fresh and Salt Water

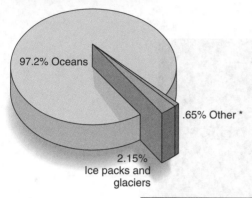

* Other	
Ground water	.62%
Freshwater lakes	.009%
Saltwater lakes	.008%
Soil water	.005%
Vapor	.001%
Streams and rivers	.0001%

leather, and a chemical used in refrigeration, soap manufacturing, and other industries.

If mankind could drink ocean water and pump it into his parched fields, it would solve many of his worst problems. But the high concentration of salt—about 3.5 percent of the total volume of seawater—is harmful to crops and land animals. Swallowing too much salt water leads to a quick, painful death from dehydration. Irrigating farmland with ocean water stunts the growth of plants and quickly makes the land unproductive.

SECTION REVIEW

1. What are the three divisions of the earth?
2. What two layers lie under the crust? Mantle Core
3. What is the difference between an island and a continent?
4. What are the seven continents? Which one is often considered part of another continent? Europe/Asia
5. Why is it difficult to find the boundary between oceans?
6. What are the four oceans?
7. Does any continent touch all four oceans?

MAJOR LANDFORMS

O beautiful for spacious skies,
For amber waves of grain,
For purple mountain majesties
Above the fruited plain!
America! America!
God shed His grace on thee,
And crown thy good with brotherhood
From sea to shining sea!

God's world is filled with a beautiful variety of land formations. Every slight variation in the landscape is called a **landform.** Geographers have classified the major landforms into three categories: mountains, plains, and plateaus. Each category has played a unique role in human civilization.

Mountains

Mountains stand high above the surrounding landscape. How do geographers distinguish them from hills? Hills are generally smaller than mountains, but no set elevation distinguishes the two. Rather, local usage of the terms is the deciding factor.

Pikes Peak towers above the rolling prairie of eastern Colorado. It stands alone as a single mountain. When many mountains appear together, such as the Rocky Mountains, the formation is called a **mountain range.** Pioneers crossing Colorado could see the towering Rockies days before they reached them. The Rocky Mountain range is a system so large that it contains ranges within ranges.

The highest mountain range in the world is the Himalayas. The name means "Abode of Snow." The highest peak, Mount Everest, is called *Chomolungma,* meaning "Sacred Mother of the Waters." Farmers many miles away depend on the rivers that flow from the melting snows of Mount Everest and other peaks of the Himalayas.

Mountains play a major role in the world. In addition to influencing weather, climate, and vegetation, they have influenced the pattern of human settlement. Many cities have arisen near mines, which burrow deep into the belly of mountains. Other cities lie in the fertile valleys of mountain ranges, where they are protected from extreme

Mount Elbert, Colorado, is the highest peak in the Rocky Mountains.

weather. But in most cases, mountains are too cold or infertile for extensive human settlement.

Mountain ranges also hinder travel and contact between people. Populations living in the mountains can easily hide from attack, and social changes are slow to reach them. As you study the United States and other countries, you will see how cultures, languages, dialects, and national borders are often defined by mountain ranges. Can you name the most famous mountain range on each continent?

Plains

In contrast to mountains, **plains** are wide areas of level land. Some famous plains lie in coastal areas, such as land along the Gulf of Mexico. These are called *coastal plains.* But low elevation does not define plains. Plains can be found at high elevation too. Nestled among the Andes Mountains of

Plains often have rolling hills.

South America is the Altiplano, which averages twelve thousand feet above sea level. Plains are not totally flat, either. For instance, the Great Plains of North America has many rolling hills.

Plains are the most valuable landform for farmers. Rivers bring water and sediments down from the mountains, and deposits, called **alluvium,** settle in the flat plains. Alluvium is often rich in nutrients that enable farms to produce large quantities of food. For this reason, plains are the "breadbaskets" of many nations.

Alluvial plains are often named after the river that flows through them. For example, the Congo Basin is an alluvial plain named for the mighty Congo River. Can you name other famous plains on each continent?

Plateaus

In addition to "purple mountain majesties above the fruited plain," Americans have a third landform, even though they may not sing about it. **Plateaus** are wide areas of relatively flat land, like plains, but they rise abruptly above surrounding lands. Steep cliffs or slopes mark at least one edge of a plateau. Indeed, plateaus are often called *tablelands* because their surface is sometimes elevated on four sides like a tabletop.

The surfaces of plateaus are much more varied than plains, often including hills, mountains, and deep canyons. The Grand Canyon cuts through one of North America's largest plateaus. The most rugged plateaus of the world are often called *highlands*. Plateaus can occur at almost any elevation. The highest is the Tibetan Plateau, which lies on the northern border of the Himalayan Mountains in Asia.

Plateaus generally have poor soils and few resources except grass for grazing animals. Indeed, many of the world's deserts are located on plateaus. Can you name a famous plateau or highland on each continent?

Along with the three basic landforms, there are many specific landforms associated with different landscapes. We will learn more about them as we study individual countries.

A plateau rises abruptly from the plain.

Geographer's Corner

Reading a Diagram

Below is a list of common geographic terms that are often confused because their definitions are so similar. But a diagram of a make-believe landscape makes it easier to see how these terms are related to each other.

Use the information on the diagram to find the ten terms described below.

1. Like a peninsula, it is a landform that sticks out into the sea, but it has a distinct point.
2. Like a valley, land rises above it on all sides, but the sides are close together and steep.
3. Like a hill, it has a slope, but the slope is limited to one side.
4. Like a mesa, it is a hill with a flat top, but it is smaller.
5. A special category of river mouth, it is made of sediment in the shape of a fan.
6. A special category of river mouth, it is subject to tidal changes.
7. Like a reef, it is a ridge near the shore that rises up from the ocean floor, but it rises above the surface.
8. Like a strait, it is a water passageway between larger bodies of water, but it is wider.

9. Like a bay, it is a body of water open to the sea, but it is usually larger and its opening is narrow.

💡 What geographic features can also be the "source" of a river?

Some Common Geographic Terms

Bar A ridge of sand or gravel built along the shore by tides or currents

Bay A partially enclosed area of water with a wide opening to the sea

Butte A hill with a small, flat top and sloping sides; common in dry regions

Canyon A narrow, deep gash in the earth with steep sides; gorge

Cape A point of land extending into a body of water

Delta A deposit of sediment at a river's mouth, usually appearing in the shape of a triangle

Escarpment A steep slope or long cliff between two level areas at different altitudes

Estuary A long, wide river mouth that rises and falls with tides

Gulf A large, partially enclosed area of water that often has a narrow opening to the sea

Common Geographic Terms

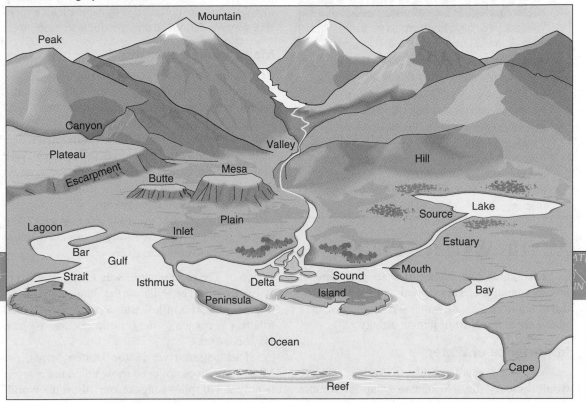

Hill   A small but visible rise in land elevation with slopes on all sides

Island   A piece of land completely surrounded by water

Isthmus   A narrow portion of land connecting two larger land areas

Lagoon   A shallow body of water separating land from nearby sandbars or coral reefs

Lake   A totally enclosed body of water with no outlets other than rivers

Mesa   A hill with a large, flat top and steep sides

Mountain   A landform that stands high above the surrounding landscape

Mouth (of a river)   The opening of a river where it empties into another body of water

Peak   A high point on a mountain

Peninsula   An area of land surrounded by water on three sides

Plain   A wide, level area of land

Plateau   A large area of land that rises above surrounding areas; tableland

Reef   A ridge below the surface of the ocean that rises up from the ocean floor near the shore

Sound   A long, wide stretch of water that is a passageway between larger bodies of water or that leads inland from the ocean

Source (of a river)   The spring, lake, or other point from which a river originates

Strait   A narrow waterway joining two larger bodies of water

Valley   A long, low area of land between higher land

AT THE WATER'S EDGE

Like landforms, bodies of water play a major role in human life. This section will show how the three main bodies of water—rivers, lakes, and seas—are at the heart of human activity.

Importance of Water

Without a ready supply of fresh water, we would quickly die. No human being lives more than a short walk away from fresh water. But fresh, clean water is scarce. Less than 3 percent of the earth's water is fresh, and over two-thirds of that water is locked up in polar ice caps and in glaciers. Most of the rest of the water is underground. The remaining water, in lakes and rivers, is a precious resource, essential to the growth and survival of our cities.

Large bodies of water often provide inexpensive "highways" for travel and trade. When settlers first arrived in America, they clustered along the coast and rivers rather than moving into the mountains. It was much cheaper to ship foods by water than to transport them overland. Ships could carry ten wagons worth of goods for the same price as one cart pulled over the mountains. Food on ships arrived at the marketplace much sooner; the food cost less and was fresher. Even today, water transportation is by far the least expensive way for nations to ship products to each other.

Major Bodies of Water

Rivers Water is in constant motion. Unless something gets in its way, water will eventually flow to the ocean. Small streams flow into rivers, which in turn flow into even larger rivers. Rivers that "feed" other rivers are called **tributaries.** The main river and all its tributaries are called a **river system.** Many of the world's great river systems flow over two thousand miles from their *headwaters* (or source) to their mouth.

But what are the "greatest" river systems? The answer is not as easy as it might seem. There are several ways to compare rivers.

Length The most obvious way to compare rivers is by length. The Nile is the longest river, an impressive 4,160 miles. But depending on which tributary is chosen as the headwaters, the Amazon may be longer.

The longest river in the United States, the Mississippi, does not even show up on the chart. It is only 2,340 miles long, or twelfth in the world. But this figure ignores the length of its longest tributary, the Missouri River, which is even longer than the main trunk of the Mississippi. Measuring from the headwaters of the Missouri adds another 1,600 miles to the Mississippi-Missouri River, increasing its rank to fourth place. Even this number ignores the tributaries that feed the Missouri.

Longest Rivers

RIVER	LOCATION	LENGTH (MI.)	DISCHARGE (CU. FT./SEC.)	DRAINAGE AREA (SQ. MI.)
Nile	Africa	4,160	110,000	1,293,000
Amazon	South America	4,000	6,350,000	2,722,000
Chang (Yangtze)	Asia	3,964	1,200,000	756,000
Huang He (Yellow)	Asia	3,395	52,900	288,000
Congo	Africa	2,718	1,458,000	1,314,000
Amur	Asia	2,744	438,000	716,000
Lena	Asia	2,734	547,000	961,000
Mackenzie	North America	2,635	400,000	711,000
Mekong	Asia	2,600	500,000	307,000
Niger	Africa	2,590	215,000	730,000

Mississippi River Basin

Discharge   Another way to compare rivers is by their flow of water—the discharge. The Nile is a virtual trickle compared to the mighty Amazon. It would take fifty rivers the size of the Nile to match the volume of water that flows out of the Amazon. The volume of water is so great that the Amazon River remains fresh and drinkable two hundred miles out into the ocean. European explorers, after a long trip across the salty Atlantic, could dip their buckets into the ocean and enjoy a drink!

Drainage Area   A third way to compare rivers is by the size of the **drainage basin,** the total land area drained by the main river and its tributaries. The Nile's drainage basin is smaller than the Amazon's, is mostly dry, and has few tributaries. In contrast, the Amazon River drains a rain forest that covers 40 percent of the continent of South America. The Missouri River has the fifth largest drainage basin (1,244,000 sq. mi.).

Navigability   Another way to compare rivers is by their depth. How far can ocean-going vessels

travel before they hit rocks and rapids? In the very heart of America, steamboats ply the Missouri River over one thousand miles from the ocean. Barges rely on deep, **navigable rivers** for carrying

The Amazon River discharges 6.35 million cubic feet of water every second.

27

Barges ply the Mississippi River as far inland as Minneapolis, eighteen hundred miles from the ocean.

Largest Lakes

LAKE	LOCATION	AREA (SQ. MI.)	DEPTH (FT.)	VOLUME (CU. MI.)
Caspian Sea	Asia	143,244	3,363	19,035
Superior	North America	31,700	1,330	2,916
Victoria	Africa	26,828	270	637
Huron	North America	23,000	220	827
Michigan	North America	22,300	750	1,161
Aral Sea	Asia	14,900	923	80
Tanganyika	Africa	12,700	4,823	4,659
Baykal	Asia	12,162	5,315	5,581
Great Bear	North America	12,096	1,463	529
Nyasa	Africa	11,150	2,280	2,009

food, coal, lumber, and other goods from their distant sources to coastal cities. The Mississippi River and its tributaries include over fifteen thousand miles of navigable water, the second largest inland water route in the world. The volume of trade on the Amazon, the only river system longer than the Mississippi, pales in comparison.

Rivers have played a central role in the history of almost every nation. Historically, explorers have used these waters as roads to the interior. The first men ever to cross the continent of North America, Lewis and Clark, journeyed up the waters of the Missouri River into the Rockies and then down the Columbia River to the Pacific Ocean. Many pioneers who came after them also settled near these rivers.

Most cities were founded beside rivers. For example, St. Louis sprang up at the point where boats floating down the Missouri entered the Mississippi River. Even where rivers are too shallow for travel, they provide drinking water, irrigation, fish, game, and recreation. The birthplace of almost every great civilization, such as ancient Egypt, was somewhere along a river. Hindus still worship the Ganges River, the lifeline of modern India.

Lakes   Bodies of water fully enclosed by land are called **lakes.** Cities are often located on the shores of lakes because lakes provide fish, drinking water,

transportation, and recreation. Lakes make it possible for some cities to be built deep in the interior of continents.

The Great Lakes of North America is the largest system of freshwater lakes in the world. It includes the largest freshwater lake—Lake Superior. (Lake Huron and Lake Michigan are among the five largest freshwater lakes.) Once home to the Woodland Indians, the Great Lakes support many world-class cities, such as Chicago.

Other continents have important freshwater lakes too. Lake Titicaca, high in the Andes Mountains, is the largest lake in South America and the highest navigable lake in the world. It is the

Chicago, America's third largest city, was founded on Lake Michigan.

In the News

Wetlands

Areas of stagnant water, often referred to as bogs, swamps, moors, fens, muskegs, or marshes, are collectively known as **wetlands.** They are not actually bodies of water, but neither are they dry land. Wetlands most often form in lowland areas near coasts, rivers, and lakes, where water cannot drain away. Water saturates the ground of these areas and often collects to form murky pools a few inches deep. Wetlands are often at sea level.

Wetlands can be categorized into three basic divisions according to their appearance and vegetation. **Bogs** describe spongy areas that look dry but are covered with wet organic materials. These soggy lands may have formed over the top of old lakes, and a layer of water may remain below the surface. Sometimes walking on a bog is dangerous because the land is not stable and may shake or open and swallow those who tread on it (a "quaking bog"). Mosses commonly grow in bogs, but few other plants survive. The mosses may collect and form a thick layer of dead organic matter called peat. In some areas of the world, such as on the British Isles, peat is cut, dried, and burned for fuel.

The second type of wetland is a **marsh.** A marsh has visible standing water, and the main kinds of vegetation growing in marshes are grasses and small water plants that survive with their roots submerged in water. The Florida Everglades is a very large marsh.

Swamps are the third type of wetland. Like marshes, they are covered by standing water. The basic difference is that swamps are dominated by large trees, and marshes are not. Cyprus, mangrove, and willow trees grow in swamps with their roots reaching down through the mire. Alligators, snakes, and other wild animals can make swamps and marshes mysterious and somewhat scary places.

Unusual forms of plant life thrive in wetland areas, and so do insects and water animals. Mosquitos, which reproduce abundantly in murky water, have been such a menace that man has tried to drain many wetland areas. In recent years, however, remaining wetlands are becoming preserved areas because of their scenic beauty and their endangered plant and animal life. They also aid in flood control and water storage. It is also believed that they provide the nursery for much of the world's food chain, and they effectively filter pollution from the water.

Wetlands are in the news because of the conflict between private property and government regulation. Landowners have spent large sums of money to purchase prime coastal land, but government regulators have rejected their plans to build on their property or to fill in mosquito-infested pools. Part of the debate concerns something as basic as the definition of a *wetland*. Early laws regulating wetlands defined them as places where water stands for at least seven days in the year, but property owners want to raise the number to twenty-one. Conservatives have proposed laws to compensate property owners for the value of the land that is lost as a result of government regulations.

💡 What issues are at stake on each side of this debate: the individual's right to own land versus the government's obligation to promote the "general welfare"?

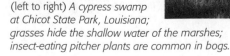

(left to right) *A cypress swamp at Chicot State Park, Louisiana; grasses hide the shallow water of the marshes; insect-eating pitcher plants are common in bogs.*

legendary birthplace of the Incas. Africa's Lake Chad has been the heart of great empires in central Africa. In east Africa is Lake Victoria, the largest lake on the continent and the second largest freshwater lake in the world. Millions of Africans live on its shores.

The deepest lake and the largest lake are both on the Asian continent. Lake Baykal, over one mile deep, holds almost as much fresh water as all the Great Lakes combined. But its surface area is relatively small. Because Siberia's cold winter freezes the lake for several months each year, it is known more for its freshwater seals than for any human inhabitants.

The Caspian Sea is the world's largest lake. Unlike Lake Superior, its water is salty. While the water in freshwater lakes is kept clean by rivers or other outlets that carry dissolved minerals downstream, a few drainage basins of the world have no outlet to the ocean. Waters collect at the lowest spot, called a depression. The Caspian Sea is actually *below* sea level. As the water evaporates, minerals are left behind. Though rare, these salt lakes are often large and famous. The Dead Sea, which is 28 percent salt, is the saltiest lake in the world.

Many modern cities have created their own man-made lakes by damming rivers. New York City, the largest city in the United States, built a lake in the Catskill Mountains—over one hundred miles away—to help supply its people with water. Dammed lakes have two additional benefits: generating electricity and controlling river flooding.

Sailing the Seven Seas

Seas are arms of the ocean partially enclosed by land. Seas can vary greatly in size, and some even have seas within seas. If you look at the Mediterranean Sea on a map, for example, you will find seven arms in the north. The ancient peoples called these the "seven seas." The Greek and Roman empires arose on their shores.

Sailors prefer carrying people and goods on the smaller seas. The shores block some of the most violent storms that batter ships on the "open" sea. Larger seas, such as the Mediterranean, can be very dangerous. You may recall the storm that threatened

Superfreighters being unloaded at a shipyard

to sink Jonah's ship and another storm that wrecked Paul's prison ship.

In addition to safe routes for travel, ships need safe places to anchor while they load and unload. A sheltered body of deep water next to the shore is called a **harbor.** The water needs to be deep enough so that the ships do not run aground. The shore needs to encircle enough of the sea to shelter ships from winds and waves that might otherwise drive them into the rocks or sand. Good harbors are rare. The key to the success of America's original colonies was their harbors. Boston, New York City, Philadelphia, and Charleston quickly became world-class cities because of their great harbors. Port cities (or *ports*) are cities with harbors.

Largest Seas

SEA	LOCATION	AREA (SQ. MI.)
Philippine Sea	Pacific Ocean	2,700,000
Coral Sea	Pacific Ocean	1,850,000
Arabian Sea	Indian Ocean	1,492,000
South China Sea	Pacific Ocean	1,148,500
Weddell Sea	Atlantic Ocean	1,080,000
Caribbean Sea	Atlantic Ocean	971,400
Mediterranean Sea	Atlantic Ocean	969,100
Tasman Sea	Pacific Ocean	900,000
Bering Sea	Pacific Ocean	873,000
Bay of Bengal	Indian Ocean	839,000

FORCES THAT CHANGE THE EARTH'S SURFACE

He putteth forth his hand upon the rock; he overturneth the mountains by the roots. He cutteth out rivers among the rocks; and his eye seeth every precious thing. (Job 28:9-10)

The earth's surface is constantly changing. Since the Flood, two basic processes continue to shape the earth. Internal forces (earthquakes and volcanoes) push rocks up, and external forces (wind and water) break rocks down. Both forces help to create the mountains and other landforms we see today.

Internal Forces—The Plate Theory

Earthquakes and volcanoes are evidences of powerful forces at work inside the earth. No one has ever observed these internal forces, and they are not perfectly understood. But scientists have found some clues. For a long time they have known that volcanoes and earthquakes are clustered along distinct lines on the earth's surface. Recently, using sonar, scientists discovered that these lines continue under the oceans. The ocean floor is scarred by lines of deep trenches and high ridges.

Based on this evidence, scientists in the 1960s proposed that the crust is broken up into pieces, called plates. According to the **plate tectonics theory,** the plates crash into one another and pull apart, releasing energy from the earth's interior and causing earthquakes and volcanoes.

Some Creationists consider this theory useful. They suggest that the earth's crust broke into sections during the Flood, when "all the fountains of the great deep [were] broken up" (Gen. 7:11). Other Creationists reject this theory as unnecessary. They emphasize that the theory is used to explain away evidence of the worldwide scope of the Flood, such as the widespread distribution of fossils in every continent, including Antarctica.

Tectonic Activity   The movement of the earth's surface is called **tectonic** (tek TAHN ik) **activity.** The two most noticeable evidences of tectonic activity are faulting and folding.

Faulting   **Faults** are deep cracks in the earth's surface where two pieces of land have moved in different directions. Although the movement is

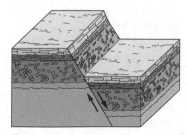

Fault

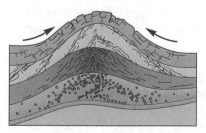

Fold

A rock fold

A fault

rarely more than a few inches, faulting can devastate life and property. The highest land displacement ever recorded—nearly fifty feet—took place during the great Alaska earthquake of 1964.

Folding   The other notable evidence of tectonic activity is folding. Just as a piece of paper will bend when you push the edges toward the center, so rock can bend upward when it is pushed from both sides. **Folds** today move at rates of less than a few feet a century.

Many mountains appear to have been formed by faulting and folding. The Sierra Nevada of the western United States offers a classic example of *fault mountains*. Its highest peak, Mount Whitney, is almost three miles above sea level. Folding is evident in the Himalayas, the Rockies, and the Alps. Some of the best *fold mountains* are in the Appalachians of

the eastern United States, where several ranges roll together like the folds of an accordion.

Both fault mountains and fold mountains are called *deformational mountains* because tectonic forces appear to have "deformed" the rocks that were already on the surface. But no one has ever seen a mountain formed by tectonic activity. Perhaps they appeared during the upheaval of the Flood, or perhaps God created them this way.

Pangaea, Laurasia, and Gondwanaland?

Scientists have extended the plate theory to help them explain the evolution of the continents. By putting the pieces of the earth together like a puzzle, it appears that all of the continents could have been joined together in one huge land mass. Scientists assume that the continents must have "drifted" to their present position.

The **continental drift theory** claims to explain events that supposedly occurred over hundreds of millions of years. After comparing fossils and landforms on different continents, scientists concluded that all of the continents were once linked into one supercontinent, called Pangaea, 220 million years ago. The islands then drifted into two large landmasses, called Laurasia (Asia and North America) and Gondwanaland (Africa and Antarctica). Later, Europe broke from North America and India broke from Africa, both crashing into Asia. South America split from Africa, and Australia split from Antarctica.

Some scientists even theorize what the pieces of land looked like before they joined into the supercontinent Pangaea. These same scientists reject God's account of the Creation because it requires "blind" faith!

There is no firm proof for such a large-scale "continental drift," but if any drift has occurred, we know that it happened in just a few thousand years, not billions of years.

Whatsoever the Lord pleased, that did he in heaven, and in earth, in the seas, and all deep places. (Ps. 135:6)

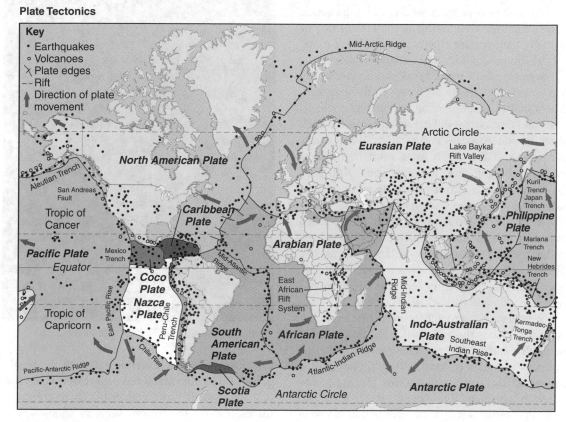

Plate Tectonics

Key
- • Earthquakes
- ○ Volcanoes
- X Plate edges
- -- Rift
- ▲ Direction of plate movement

Mid-Arctic Ridge

Arctic Circle

Eurasian Plate

Lake Baykal Rift Valley

North American Plate

Aleutian Trench

San Andreas Fault

Tropic of Cancer

Kuril Trench
Japan Trench

Philippine Plate

Mariana Trench

New Hebrides Trench

Pacific Plate

Mexico Trench

Equator

Coco Plate

Nazca Plate

Mid-Atlantic Ridge

Arabian Plate

East African Rift System

Caribbean Plate

Mid-Indian Ridge

East Pacific Rise

Tropic of Capricorn

Peru-Chile Trench

Chile Rise

South American Plate

African Plate

Indo-Australian Plate

Southeast Indian Rise

Kermadec-Tonga Trench

Pacific-Antarctic Ridge

Scotia Plate

Atlantic-Indian Ridge

Antarctic Circle

Antarctic Plate

Let's Go Exploring

1. Which plates are named after continents?

2. Where do the lines of continents follow the borders of plates?

3. Where are there many dots but no borders of a plate?

4. Where are there borders of a plate but no dots?

💡 Where are two plates clearly moving in opposite directions? Why is this border a ridge and not a trench?

Volcanic Forces Another mountain-building force is still active today—volcanoes. Volcanoes *deposit* new lava on the earth's surface, which hardens into *depositional mountains*. In 1943 a fourteen-hundred-foot mountain appeared in a Mexican farmer's cornfield as the result of a volcano. In 1963 a mountain rose out of the sea near Iceland. It now stands five hundred feet above the water and is a mile long. The world's largest active volcano is Mauna Loa, atop the island of Hawaii. This island is the tip of a massive volcano that rises 33,476 feet from the sea floor. That is a greater height than Mount Everest!

External Forces

Landforms do not remain the same. External forces wear away the landforms that internal forces have pushed up.

Weathering Although rock may seem solid and unmoving, it is constantly weakened by the action of **weathering.** Weathering is the breakdown of rocks by temperature changes, water, plant roots, and the formation of ice and mineral crystals.

Some kinds of rocks break down more easily than others. Rocks with layers are easily separated. Others shatter under extreme temperature changes. Pores and cracks that collect water break the rock when the water freezes and expands. When plants take root and grow, the roots exert tremendous pressure, causing more disintegration. Additionally, natural acids (from plants, decaying matter, and rain) can dissolve some rocks.

After Noah's Flood, water would have washed away soft rocks and sediment, leaving behind harder rocks. Unusual rock pillars, such as The Hunter in the American West, are made up of volcanic rock that apparently remained after the surrounding sedimentary rock washed away.

Weathering is crucial to life on the earth because it enriches the soil. *Soil* is the thin layer of the earth's surface where plants grow. Weathering produces particles of sand, silt, and clay (called **sediment**) that mix with **humus** (decayed substances produced by living organisms) to form soil. Farmers carefully study their soils to find out what fertilizers will make the land most productive.

The Hunter, a weathered pillar at Bryce Canyon, Utah

Erosion While weathering refers to the breakdown of rock into small pieces, **erosion** is the natural removal of those materials. There are many forces that cause erosion, such as wind, waves, glaciers, and running water.

Glaciers descend into the sea at Glacier Bay, Alaska.

Tides eroded this sea stack in New Brunswick.

Wind carries away sand and soil. Wind erosion is strongest in dry areas, particularly deserts. Sand dunes in the Sahara Desert rise fourteen hundred feet in some places and cover several square miles. Windstorms ruined American farmers throughout the Great Plains during the Dust Bowl of the 1930s. "Black blizzards" of choking dust darkened the skies as far away as New York.

The slow movement of frozen water also causes great change, especially in cold regions. **Glaciers,** large masses of moving ice and snow that have collected over time, flow downhill under the pull of gravity. Like gigantic bulldozers, glaciers push and scrape the earth in their paths. Apparently glaciers were very active during an ice age. When

they receded to their current locations, they left behind hills of debris, known as *terminal moraines.* Two famous moraines extend across the entire length of Long Island, New York.

Waves erode the seashore, creating sea caves and sea arches. Waves deposit sand off the shore to make sandbars or whole islands at the mouth of a bay. Tourists flock to the many barrier islands on the east coast of the United States.

The waters wear the stones: thou washest away the things which grow out of the dust of the earth. (Job 14:19)

The most powerful force of erosion is running water. It quickly flows through soil and soft rocks, carrying away materials as it goes. During floods, water can carve deep gullies. But water's slow action over years can be just as devastating. Farmers are constantly battling to keep water from eroding their *topsoil,* the productive surface of the soil that is richest in humus.

SECTION REVIEW

1. What evidence supports the plate tectonics theory?
2. What are the two most notable types of tectonic activity?
3. What is the difference between weathering and erosion?
4. List four forces that cause erosion.
5. What does weathering help to produce that is essential for life on the earth?

💡 The text mentions two types of mountains: deformational (from earthquakes) and depositional (from volcanoes). There is a third type, called an "erosional mountain." Based on what you have read, how was this type of mountain formed?

REVIEW 2

Can You Define These Terms?

uniformitarianism	plain	wetland	fault
cataclysm	alluvium	bog	fold
continent	plateau	marsh	continental drift theory
island	tributary	swamp	weathering
continental island	river system	sea	sediment
oceanic island	drainage basin	harbor	humus
world ocean	navigable river	plate tectonics theory	erosion
landform	lake	tectonic activity	glacier
mountain range			

Can You Locate These Natural Features?

atmosphere   hydrosphere   mantle

lithosphere   crust   core

How Much Do You Remember?

1. What two formative events in the earth's history occurred only once and will never occur again? How do these events contradict uniformitarianism?
2. Name the parts of the earth.
   a. three "spheres"
   b. three layers of the lithosphere
   c. two layers of the crust
   d. seven continents
   e. four oceans
3. Distinguish the items in each list.
   a. mountain, plain, plateau
   b. river, lake, sea
   c. river length, discharge, drainage area
   d. bog, marsh, swamp
4. A series of connected mountains is called a mountain range; a series of connected rivers is called a _____.
5. Match each of these physical features with the record it holds.

   1. Amazon   a. longest river
   2. Asia   b. highest discharge
   3. Caspian   c. highest mountain
   4. Everest   d. largest ocean
   5. Greenland   e. largest lake
   6. Nile   f. largest island
   7. Pacific   g. largest continent

6. What is tectonic activity? What are the two most notable types?
7. What are weathering and erosion? How do they work together to shape the earth's surface?

What Do You Think?

1. What evidence contradicts these popular theories: uniformitarianism and plate tectonics?
2. What major landforms are in your area?
3. Can we classify the ocean as a large lake?
4. Why do some geographers consider the Arctic Ocean a sea, not an ocean?
5. Look at the map on page 33. Are earthquakes likely to occur in your area?
6. What future cataclysms will change the earth's surface?

CLIMATE

Before God created the sea and dry land, which you studied in the last chapter, He created the light and the atmosphere. They are just as essential to life on earth.

And God said, Let there be light: and there was light. . . . And God called the light Day, and the darkness he called Night. And the evening and the morning were the first day. (Gen. 1:3-5)

Light is the "fuel" that drives the earth's "engines." It supplies energy for plants to grow, and it warms the sea and land.

And God made the firmament, and divided the waters which were under the firmament from the waters which were above the firmament: and it was so. And God called the firmament Heaven. And the evening and the morning were the second day. (Gen. 1:7-8)

The atmosphere is a blanket of air around the earth. It provides much more than the air we breathe. It is part of the earth's "plumbing system" that distributes heat to the remote corners of the globe and draws ocean water back up to the mountaintops. Without the constant movement of heat and water, the continents would become dry dust, the equator would be a boiling inferno, and the polar oceans would be ice cubes.

The first half of this chapter will explain the two basic aspects of the earth's plumbing system: the movement of heat and the movement of water. The last half of the chapter will show how heat and water, put together, define climate. The chapter ends with a brief description of the vegetation associated with climate.

HEAT IN MOTION

The record high temperature was recorded at Azizia, Libya, in 1922 when the mercury climbed to 136°F (58°C). In 1983 the temperature at Vostok, Antarctica, dipped to a record low of -129°F (-89°C). Fortunately, few places experience anything near these extremes. God has designed three main systems to distribute heat over the earth: seasons, winds, and ocean currents.

Seasons

While the earth remaineth, seedtime and harvest, and cold and heat, and summer and winter, and day and night shall not cease. (Gen. 8:22)

The sun is the source of nearly all the heat energy that warms the earth. The most obvious evidence of the sun's influence is the seasons. When you hear the word *seasons,* you probably think of the four seasons—spring, summer, fall, and winter. But people in other countries think of other kinds of seasons. Near the equator, where the air is always warm, there are two seasons, rainy and dry. Near the poles, where the air is always cold, the major seasonal change is six months of constant darkness, followed by six months of a "midnight sun." All of these changes can be considered seasons.

Why does the earth have seasons? The answer is related to the slant of sunlight and the tilt of the earth's axis.

Direct and Slanted Sunlight
The land near the equator receives more sunlight than land near the poles. Near the equator, the sun's rays strike the earth directly. There are more rays heating each square inch of gas in the atmosphere. Because the sunlight travels a shorter distance through the atmosphere, more rays reach the surface. In the polar regions, on the other hand, the sun's rays are always slanted. The gas in the air absorbs most of

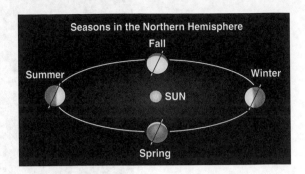

the rays' heat energy before it reaches the ground. Thus, the poles are much colder than the equator.

Tilted Axis
For every three hundred miles you travel toward the poles, the average temperature drops about 3½°F. If the earth stood perfectly straight, the temperature would drop gradually from latitude to latitude, but it would remain constant at each line of latitude.

But this is not the case. The earth's axis is tilted 23½°. Sunlight strikes the earth at different angles at different times of the year. As the earth rotates, different parts of the earth receive more (or less) sunlight. When the North Pole is exposed to the sun, more sunlight and warmth reaches the Northern Hemisphere. When the earth moves to the other side of the sun, more sunlight reaches the Southern Hemisphere. Note that the axis itself does not wobble back and forth—it always points toward the fixed North Star. But the direction of the tilt appears to change as the earth revolves around the sun.

Direct and Slanted Sunlight

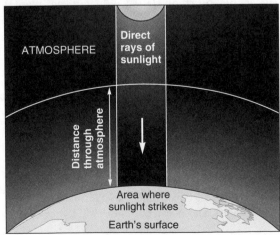

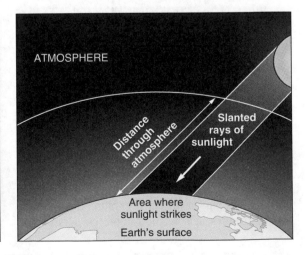

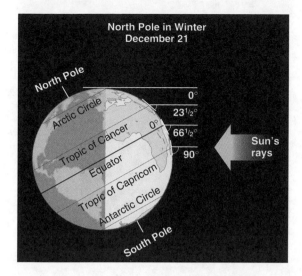

North Pole in Winter
December 21

North Pole

Arctic Circle

Tropic of Cancer

Equator

Tropic of Capricorn

Antarctic Circle

South Pole

0°
23½°
66½°
90°

Sun's rays

and 23½°. Because the sunlight is always direct, or nearly so, this zone has very warm temperatures continuously. It is usually called the **Tropics.**

In the **middle latitudes** (those latitudes between 23½° and 66½°), the sunlight is nearly direct half of each year. This creates seasonal changes from warm summers to cool winters. These regions do not have the constant heat of the Tropics; neither do they have the extreme cold of the poles. Thus they are called the **Temperate Zones,** or *mesothermal* (*meso-* "middle" + *thermal* "heat") zones.

During the long winter nights in the high latitudes (above 66½°), sunlight is always either very slanted or nonexistent. These **polar regions** can be called *microthermal (micro-* "small") zones because they receive a small amount of sunlight.

SECTION REVIEW

1. Why does latitude affect temperature?
2. What causes the changes of seasons?
3. What are the boundaries of the Tropics?
   💡 Do the Tropics have four seasons?

Once a year the North Pole reaches its maximum exposure to the sun. The direct rays of the sun never shine north of the line of latitude called the **tropic of Cancer** (23½° N). When the South Pole experiences maximum exposure to the sun, the line of direct rays is in the Southern Hemisphere as far south as the latitude 23½° S. This line, called the **tropic of Capricorn,** is the southern limit of direct rays from the sun.

The tilt of the earth has an even more obvious consequence near the poles. Not only do the poles never get direct sunlight, but they also sit in complete darkness for a few months each year. On the day that the South Pole experiences maximum exposure to the sun, no sunlight illuminates the land above 66½° N. This limit of complete darkness is called the **Arctic Circle.** The corresponding limit in the Southern Hemisphere is called the **Antarctic Circle.**

Latitude Zones The angle of sunlight and the tilt of the earth explain why different latitudes have different seasons. There are three distinct *latitude zones.* The low latitudes lie between the equator (0°)

Latitude Zones

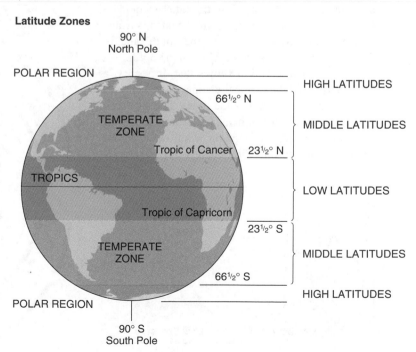

90° N
North Pole

POLAR REGION

HIGH LATITUDES

66½° N

TEMPERATE ZONE

MIDDLE LATITUDES

Tropic of Cancer   23½° N

TROPICS

LOW LATITUDES

Tropic of Capricorn

23½° S

TEMPERATE ZONE

MIDDLE LATITUDES

66½° S

POLAR REGION

HIGH LATITUDES

90° S
South Pole

39

Winds

The sun's energy is always in motion, even after it reaches the earth's atmosphere. The air carries heat between latitude zones and within each zone. What we call *wind* is ultimately caused by the movement of air that has been heated by the sun.

Hot and Cold Air Masses When a large area of air has a similar temperature and moves together, we call it an **air mass.** As the sun warms air molecules near the earth's surface, they become very energetic and begin to rise. A warm air mass rises like a five hundred-mile-wide hot-air balloon. As the air cools in the upper atmosphere, the molecules become less energetic and cluster together, forming a cold air mass. The cold air becomes heavy and sinks.

Warm and cold air masses move over the earth in a regular pattern. A permanent warm air mass sits over the Tropics, where the rays of the sun are direct. At the same time, a cold air mass sits over the polar regions. Warm air is constantly rising at the equator and moving to the cold polar regions. As air cools over the poles, it falls and moves back toward the equator. If the sun were the only factor affecting the circulation of air, the pattern would be like the illustration. In the United States, surface winds would always blow to the south, and in South America winds would blow to the north.

The next illustration shows that, in reality, a large portion of the tropical air mass loses its heat and falls before it reaches the poles. The air drops in the middle latitudes near 30°. Some of the air moves back toward the equator, while the rest continues moving toward the poles. As the air travels

Hurricanes are caused by rapid heating and cooling in the Tropics.

along the surface, it hits frigid air from the poles at about 60° latitude and rises again. Some of this air continues its journey until it finally reaches the frigid pole. Here the air drops a second time. The polar air begins moving back toward the equator. As a result of this cycle, the earth has *three* moving cells of air from the equator to the poles.

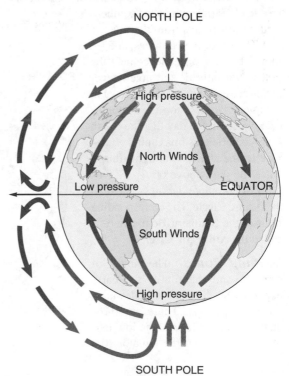

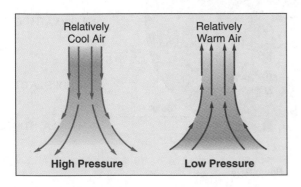

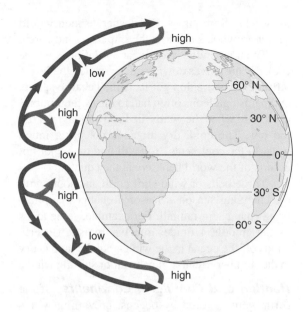

The wind goeth toward the south, and turneth about unto the north; it whirleth about continually, and the wind returneth again according to his circuits. (Eccles. 1:6)

Coriolis Effect

If no other factors affected the circulation of air, the pattern would be like the illustration above. In the United States winds would blow north; but in northern Canada and in southern Mexico, winds would blow south. In reality, few winds blow north or south. The rotation of the earth around its axis greatly influences wind direction. The effect of this rotation is known as the **Coriolis effect.**

The Coriolis effect is somewhat difficult to visualize. You do not feel the earth moving, but in fact it is moving quite rapidly, about one thousand miles per hour at the equator and five hundred miles per hour at 30° latitude. The rotation "yanks" the land out from under the wind. The wind continues to flow straight, but the land beneath it veers away. To people standing on the earth, however, the wind appears to veer away. Air moving north appears to veer off in a northeasterly direction, and air moving south appears to veer off in a southwesterly direction.

Wind Belts

The movement of warm and cold air masses, combined with the Coriolis effect, explains the basic movement of heat around the earth. Winds flow in three belts that circle the globe. These belts influence the world's climate and have also influenced the exploration and conquest of the world.

The hot Tropics have the most powerful prevailing winds. Tropical islands are famous for the constant warm winds that blow over the beaches. These winds are called **trade winds.** (The word *trade* once meant "a regular path.") Columbus used these steady winds to carry his ships west to the New World. European sailors called them the "northeast trades." They named winds after the direction they came *from,* not the direction they were going. Their main concern was to locate winds to fill their sails.

The prevailing winds that blow over the middle latitudes are called the **westerlies.** Westerlies are important because they bring warm air up from the Tropics to lands far to the north, such as Europe. Less powerful than the trade winds, westerlies still helped Columbus and other explorers to sail back east to Europe from the New World.

Jet Streams

Jet streams are fast currents of wind that flow at high altitudes. Most jet streams are about thirty miles above the earth. The paths of the streams may be up to three hundred miles wide, and some winds within the streams may reach speeds of up to three hundred miles per hour.

Jet streams occur where cold polar air meets warm equatorial air. They curve and writhe like a five-thousand-mile-long snake. Seasonal changes in temperature and air pressure help to propel them. Scientists are trying to understand the significant effect that jet streams have on weather. For example, winter jet streams looping down from Canada pull Arctic air as far south as Texas.

Man has harnessed the jet stream for a purpose other than weather prediction. Airplanes flying in a jet stream can increase their speed by nearly one hundred miles per hour and can save fuel in the process.

Near the poles is a third belt of prevailing winds, called *easterlies.* They are significant because they bring frigid air into Canada and Russia, freezing the lakes and coastal waters.

Between these belts of wind, the surface winds are calm. The major movement of air is either upward or downward. In the calm area near the equator, where hot air moves upward, clouds constantly pour rain over lush rain forests on the continents. Sailors crossing the Pacific Ocean in the Age of Exploration called this nonwindy belt the **doldrums** because they often floated motionless

for weeks. Sometimes, the desperate men would get into rowboats and tow the ship to a windy area.

The nonwindy regions near 30° latitude, where cool, dry air moves downward, are called the **horse latitudes.** This region got its name because sailors on Spanish galleons often had to throw their horses overboard when the winds died and animal feed ran too low. The cold, dry air does not bring much water to the continents. You will find the major hot deserts of the world here, *not* at the equator.

These belts of wind shift north and south with the changing seasons. Seasonal changes can also bring changes in rainfall. For example, some areas in the middle latitudes receive moist, westerly winds off the ocean in the winter, but the land is dry in the summer because of calm air or shifting winds.

Heating and Cooling of Continents If the earth were covered by oceans, prevailing winds would consistently flow in the pattern you have just studied. These patterns *do* prevail over the wide open waters of the Pacific. But the presence

Prevailing Winds

Sargasso Sea

The Sargasso Sea is surrounded by water, not land. Christopher Columbus discovered this "sea" on his journey across the Atlantic Ocean. It is a region of slow currents that move through mats of seaweed surrounded by the faster Gulf Stream and North Equatorial Current. The three-mile-deep sea covers two million square miles—an area larger than all of the states east of the Rocky Mountains. The waters are very warm and salty but also clear to depths of over three thousand feet. On the west end of the sea, the lonely island of Bermuda rises up from the ocean floor. Eels from North America and Northern Europe return to Bermuda's rivers to breed.

The sea is named after the sargassum plant, a floating seaweed that reproduces abundantly from cuttings. Mats of sargassum can cover an acre. The sargassum fish, shaped and colored to look like a piece of seaweed, finds haven here. Early, fanciful books pictured ghost ships marooned in thick mats of seaweed. But sargassum does not deserve its dangerous reputation.

Common High Pressure Systems in July

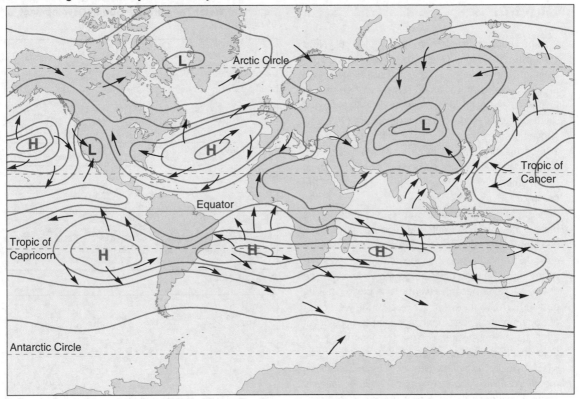

of continents affects wind patterns just as much as latitude and the earth's rotation around a tilted axis.

Because land absorbs heat much more quickly than water, hot air masses develop over the interior of continents in the summer, drawing surface winds toward them. The hot, rising air is called a **low pressure** zone. The wind at the edge of these whirling air masses, called cyclones, moves in a circular pattern. This circular movement at the edge of the cyclone explains why winds blow from the southeast in the eastern United States, but they blow from the opposite direction on the west coast.

When winter comes, this pattern reverses. The interior cools quickly, and the cold air blows outward. This cold, heavy air is called a **high pressure** zone. The whirling winds at the edge move in the opposite direction of cyclones, so they are called *anti*cyclones.

In sum, there are three major factors that influence wind direction: latitude, the earth's rotation, and continents. Taken together, these factors give a three-dimensional understanding of the earth's wind patterns. The heating of low latitudes explains why winds move from the equator to the poles. The earth's rotation around a tilted axis explains why winds veer (Coriolis effect). And the heating of the continents explains why winds can travel in opposite directions at the same latitude.

Ocean Currents

Like the atmosphere, the oceans absorb heat from the sun. Because water holds heat much longer than the air, the oceans are even more reliable than the wind in distributing heat. Temperature differences create warm and cold **ocean currents** that circle the globe, following a pattern very similar to the

El Niño

An interesting phenomenon called **El Niño** (Spanish, "the Little One") has been blamed for weather changes around the world, including drought in southeastern Africa, an extremely wet season in California, and even Mississippi flooding. El Niño is a slight increase in surface water temperature (1° to 6°C above normal) over a wide region in the Pacific. It usually occurs once every three to seven years. The National Weather Service suspects that El Niño's effect on weather may be second only to changes in the seasons.

After years of satellite surveys, oceanographers believe they have discovered El Niño's point of origin near the Easter Islands (two thousand miles west of central Chile). It begins when the normal high pressure zone drops slightly in pressure. As the trade winds die down, the water becomes warmer and begins moving eastward. The water eventually reaches the west coast of South America, veers north, and then spreads out at the equator. These waters can reach as far north as the Columbia River in Washington State. The whole cycle, which usually lasts between twelve and eighteen months, can wreak havoc on normal weather patterns. There is evidence that a similar warm current arises periodically in the Indian Ocean.

Pattern of Water Temperature During Development of El Niño

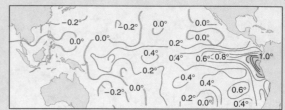

March-May

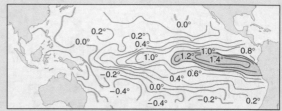

August-October

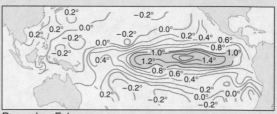

December-February

prevailing winds. Water is heated near the equator and moves toward the poles. Cold water from the poles sinks and returns to the equator. The presence of continents causes the most obvious variations between these ocean currents.

The prevailing winds help to propel surface currents. But ocean currents move slower than winds. The normal speed is under ten miles per hour. The slowest currents are called *drifts*. In special cases, however, currents may move very fast. The narrow, strong *Gulf Stream* begins in the Gulf of Mexico and moves at speeds of over sixty miles per hour. It does not weaken until it spreads out near the polar region, becoming the North Atlantic Drift.

The currents flow in circular patterns called **gyres** (JI rez). These gyres had both benefits and hazards for early oceangoing ships. Near the outer edge of the gyres, the water moved rapidly. But near the center the water became dangerously calm.

The constant circulation of heat in the oceans keeps tropical water from becoming too warm for sea life, and it keeps polar water from freezing solid. Ocean currents also influence the amount of rain that enters the air and falls on the continents. The coast of Chile is a barren desert because the cold Peru Current flows nearby. But Brazil's coast is a tropical rain forest, supplied by the warm Brazil Current. We will study more about this role of ocean currents in the next section.

WATER IN MOTION

Mount Waialeale in Hawaii receives almost *forty feet* of rain per year. In contrast, there is no record of rain in the Empty Quarter (Rub Al Khali) of the Arabian Peninsula. Few places ever see anything near these extremes. The same systems that distribute heat over the land also help to distribute life-giving water.

He causeth the vapours to ascend from the ends of the earth; he maketh lightnings for the rain; he bringeth the wind out of his treasuries. (Ps. 135:7)

Major Ocean Currents

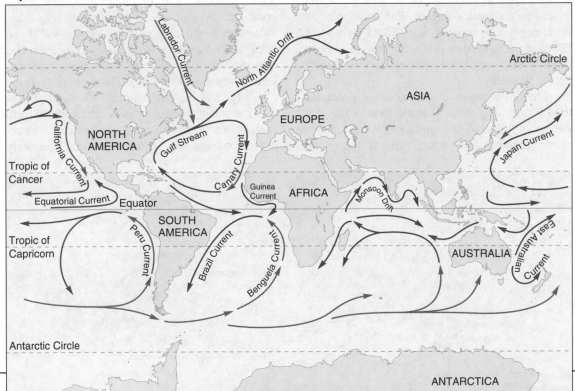

Let's Go Exploring

1. What warm current begins in the Tropics of North America and ends near Europe?

2. Do any warm currents flow past the west coast of South America?

3. List all of the *named* currents in the Pacific Ocean. Which are warm and which are cold?

💡 Can you guess the currents that Magellan's ship followed from Europe on the first trip around the world?

Different States of Water

Water appears in three forms—solid (ice), liquid, and gas (water vapor). Ocean water must change form before it reaches plants and animals on land. This change begins as ocean water absorbs heat. When the water absorbs enough heat, it changes into an invisible gas, called water vapor. This process is called **evaporation.** When water vapor loses heat, it changes back to a liquid, suspended in clouds as water droplets. The process of water's change from a gas to a liquid is called **condensation.**

Warm winds carry water vapor into the interior of the continents. Warm air can hold a lot of water vapor, or **humidity,** because hot molecules are very active. This humidity is not useful, however, until it returns to the earth's surface. The point at which water begins condensation is called the **dew point.** When the temperature drops suddenly, the water vapor loses energy, condensation occurs, and water falls to the earth.

The fall of water to earth is called **precipitation.** Most precipitation is in the form of rain. But water can fall in solid form too. A sudden change in temperature causes water vapor to freeze into crystals, lose energy, and fall to the earth as snow. Sometimes water turns into sleet or hail before it falls.

For he saith to the snow, Be thou on the earth; likewise to the small rain, and to the great rain of his strength. (Job 37:6)

Hydrologic Cycle

If there were no precipitation, all rivers would eventually dry up, and most life on land would cease. The Lord has established a water cycle that continually replenishes the soil, plants, lakes, and rivers. This cycle is called the **hydrologic cycle.**

Each year an estimated 110,000 cubic miles of water evaporates into the air from oceans, lakes, ponds, rivers, and creeks. Another 15,000 cubic miles is believed to evaporate from the soil. Even plants add water vapor to the air by a process called *transpiration* (giving off water vapor through leaves, stems, and flowers). These are the sources of nearly all of the water vapor in the atmosphere.

The water vapor eventually returns to the earth somewhere. Although most precipitation occurs over the oceans (about 80 percent), approximately

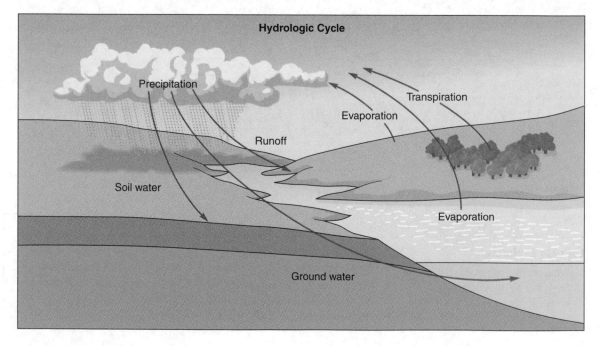

Hydrologic Cycle

Precipitation

Transpiration

Evaporation

Runoff

Soil water

Evaporation

Ground water

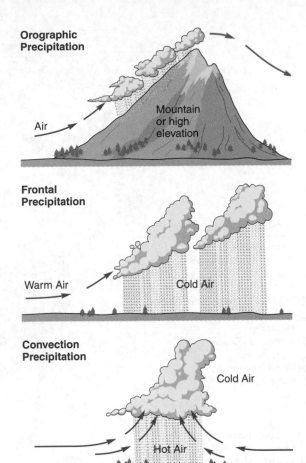

Orographic Precipitation

Frontal Precipitation

Warm Air   Cold Air

Convection Precipitation

Cold Air

Hot Air

Air

Mountain or high elevation

25,000 cubic miles of water fall on land. The water stays on the earth's surface for only a brief time. Some runs off into rivers or lakes. Some seeps through the soil to become **ground water.** Ground water is like a slow-moving river under the ground. Eventually, however, all water returns to the oceans or evaporates, completing the cycle.

Precipitation

There are three situations that cause a humid air mass to cool down and to produce precipitation. Each situation is described below.

Orographic Precipitation   The presence of mountains contributes to precipitation. When a warm mass of humid air passes over a mountainous area, the air moves upward and cools rapidly. Water vapor condenses into droplets, clouds form, and precipitation quickly follows. Because mountains are often bitterly cold, snow and sleet are common. This precipitation is said to be **orographic.** The word *orography* comes from two words, *oros* ("mountain") and *-graphy* ("description").

Orographic precipitation is common where mountain ranges rise close to the ocean or big lakes. Large amounts of water enter the air, and prevailing winds drive the water over the mountains. The land beyond the mountains is usually very dry because little water vapor survives the trip. This effect is obvious on the climate map on pages 48-49. The portion of the West Coast of the United States at the foot of the Coastal Mountains, receives the most rainfall in North America; but the prairies east of the Rockies are hot and dry. If you look for the other major highlands—Andes, Alps, Himalayas, Atlas Mountains, and the Great Dividing Range—you will see that the land on one side of the mountains has a dry climate, and the other side is wet. The dry side is called the *rainshadow.*

Frontal Precipitation   Another important cause of precipitation is the meeting of cold and warm air masses. The warmer air is lighter, so it rises above the cooler, denser air as if it were moving over a mountain range. Rain or snow falls along the line where the two air masses meet. The line is called a **front.** For precipitation to occur, the warm air mass must have water vapor that it picked up over an ocean or large lake. Frontal precipitation is common in the eastern United States, where warm air masses move in over the Gulf of Mexico and the Great Lakes.

Convection Precipitation   A third cause of precipitation is **convection,** the rise of warm air over a hot surface. In the heart of continents, the land cools at night and then heats up rapidly under the summer sun. The hot air is sometimes trapped beneath a cool air mass. When the warm, light air breaks through the cool air above, it rushes upward and cools quickly. Precipitation falls immediately and often violently. Lightning and hail may accompany such storms. Brief, local thunderstorms are common in the heart of the North American continent.

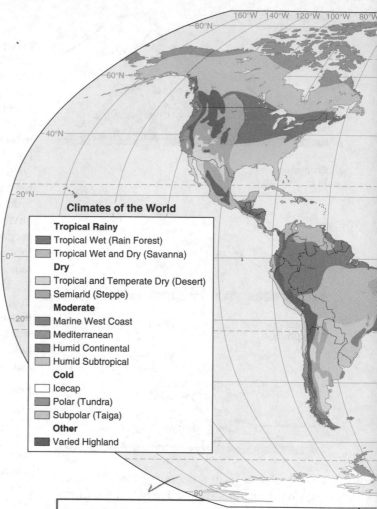

Climates of the World

Tropical Rainy
- Tropical Wet (Rain Forest)
- Tropical Wet and Dry (Savanna)

Dry
- Tropical and Temperate Dry (Desert)
- Semiarid (Steppe)

Moderate
- Marine West Coast
- Mediterranean
- Humid Continental
- Humid Subtropical

Cold
- Icecap
- Polar (Tundra)
- Subpolar (Taiga)

Other
- Varied Highland

SECTION REVIEW

1. What is the difference between condensation and precipitation?
2. Explain how dew point is related to precipitation.
3. Define the hydrologic cycle.
4. What are the three main situations that contribute to precipitation? Which one is most obvious on a climate map?

💡 Both sides of mountains on the East Coast of the United States are wet. But the mountains in California are wet on the west side and dry on the east side. Why? (Hint: Look at the maps of prevailing winds and currents on pages 42 and 45.)

CLIMATE

The amount of heat and water that reaches each region of the world determines its basic climate. **Climate** is the typical weather in a region over a long period of time. Daily changes in weather seldom determine what lives there or whether the region is good for man. Even a year of record lows or highs in temperature or rainfall does not make much of a difference. Climate refers to long-term weather patterns that often remain stable for hundreds of years.

The climate of a region is based on whether it gets too much or too little water or heat. There are twelve major divisions of world climates, classified under five broad categories. This classification system will be used on the climate maps and in the text throughout the rest of your textbook.

Tropical Rainy

Two climates occur in the warm Tropics, where the rainfall is extremely heavy. Trees grow in the *tropical wet* areas where rain falls all year (averaging ten inches per month). Only grasses

Let's Go Exploring

1. For each type of climate, give the continent where it appears most.
2. What is the most common climate at the equator? at the Arctic Circle?
3. Where is a humid subtropical climate most common, on the east coast or on the west coast of continents?

💡 Why do deserts almost never occur on the equator?

grow in the *tropical wet and dry* areas. With only about a half inch of rain during the winter months, trees cannot survive the dry season.

Dry

Everyone is familiar with *deserts,* where annual precipitation is ten inches or less. Lack of water, not high temperatures, creates deserts. Deserts are often called **arid** regions; *arid* means "lacking moisture." Deserts can occur at any latitude, cold or hot. The ice-covered interior of Greenland is technically a desert!

There is a second type of *dry* area. *Semiarid* regions receive a few more inches of rainfall than deserts and therefore can support grasses. Pioneers once called the Great Plains of the United States "the Great American Desert," but large parts of it are actually semiarid grassland, where wheat and other grains now grow.

Sagebrush covers several dry western states.

Cold

Even though some regions receive sufficient rainfall, they are too *cold* to support many kinds of plants. Nothing grows on the world's two *ice caps* in Antarctica and Greenland, which have a thick layer of ice that never melts. Although *polar regions* are cold all year round, plants grow for a brief period in the middle of the summer, when some of the snow cover melts. *Subpolar regions* are

49

not as severe in the summer, permitting hardy evergreen trees to grow. Winters are bitterly cold in all three regions, averaging less than 0°F (–18°C).

Moderate

Most of the world's good farmland and major civilizations are located in the four climate regions with *moderate* rainfall and temperatures. All four climates occur in the middle latitudes, or Temperate Zone. *Humid subtropical* refers to lands just above the Tropics that receive about fifty inches of rain during the year, mostly in the hot, rainy summer. The richest farmland in the world is located here, where farmers raise some of the most valuable

crops, such as cotton and tobacco in the southern United States.

The other three moderate climates are named after the regions where they occur in Europe: the continent, the Mediterranean Sea, and the west coast. The *humid continental* region extends far into the interior of the Eurasian continent. Rainfall is adequate but irregular because of the distance it must travel from the ocean to reach the land. Winters are colder here than in any other moderate region.

The *mediterranean* climate is named after the land beside the Mediterranean Sea. Little water falls during the summer, so the land supports few crops without irrigation.

Geographer's Corner

Climographs

Climate charts, or **climographs,** combine two important pieces of information about the climate of a city: the average temperature and the average total precipitation during each month. Climographs help us to visualize what life is like in the city. But keep in mind that these graphs show averages. Daily temperatures may exceed 100°F, and monthly rainfall may be as low as 0 inches.

Use the information on these two climographs to answer these questions:

1. About how much rain does Miami receive during July?

2. What is the average temperature in New York City during July?

3. Which city has fairly constant temperatures throughout the year?

4. Which city has a definite rainy season?

5. During which months would freezing temperatures be common in New York City?

6. Which city has the longest growing season?

   ♀ In which months would New York City probably have more precipitation than Miami?

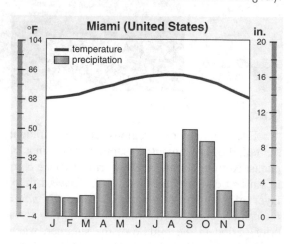

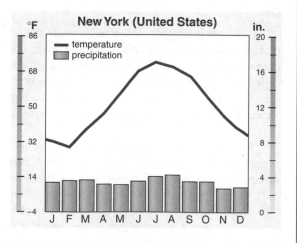

The last moderate region, *marine west coast,* covers most of Western Europe. Warm ocean currents bring warm, moist air that blows over the coast and provides a nice, steady rain. The rain is heavier in the winter than in the summer—about six inches per month compared to three inches.

Varied Highland

At the equator in South America, jungles thrive at sea level. But high up in the mountains, snow covers the ground all year round. If the top of a mountain gets more direct sunlight, however, shouldn't it be warmer than the base of the mountain?

There is another principle at work on mountains. It is related to the density of molecules in the air. There are many gas molecules near sea level, where the pull of gravity is greatest. These molecules hold much heat. As the altitude increases, however, the air becomes thinner and holds less heat. For every one thousand feet in altitude you travel up a mountain, the temperature drops about $3\frac{1}{2}°F$. This is called the **lapse rate.** If the temperature at sea level is 65°F, you can expect it to be 30°F at the peak of a ten-thousand-foot mountain. Climbing the mountain has the same effect as traveling three thousand miles toward the cold poles.

SECTION REVIEW

1. What is the difference between climate and weather?
2. What does *arid* mean?
3. What are the four types of moderate climate? What are the main differences between them?
4. How does altitude affect temperature?
  - Why are there no *moderate* climates in the Tropics, even though they receive lots of sun and rain?

VEGETATION

And God said, Let the earth bring forth grass, the herb yielding seed, and the fruit tree yielding fruit after his kind, whose seed is in itself, upon the earth: and it was so. . . . And the evening and the morning were the third day. (Gen. 1:11-13)

After God created the sun and atmosphere, He commanded the earth to be fruitful and multiply. The type of plants, or **vegetation,** that grows in each region depends on the climate. If you compare the vegetation map and the climate map, you will see that the regions are very similar. Differences between the two maps are caused by local variations in soil, mountains, and rivers.

He causeth the grass to grow for the cattle, and herb for the service of man: that he may bring forth food out of the earth. (Ps. 104:14)

A vegetation map shows us much more than the types of plants that live in a region. It is also an "animal map." The types of animals that live in a region depend on the types of plants they find there to eat. The word *biome* describes any large region where distinct populations of plants and animals are found living together. The unique characteristics of each biome help to explain why human cultures are so different. Biomes influence how people make a living, what they eat, and even what their homes look like.

There are three basic biomes: forests, grasslands, and wastelands. Within each biome are many variations.

Forests

And out of the ground made the Lord God to grow every tree that is pleasant to the sight, and good for food. (Gen. 2:9)

Wherever trees are the predominant plants, the region is called a *forest.* Because trees require a large amount of water, most forests are found in rainy climates.

Tropical Rain Forest Tropical rain forests are found in the Tropics, where many kinds of trees and animals proliferate. Teak, mahogany, and ebony are a few of the giant trees found here. The branches and leaves spread out to form a large canopy, over one hundred feet above the forest floor. Millions of species of insects scurry across the forest floor. The trees protect the thin soil from being washed away by the heavy rains. The forests are good for logging but not for farms. The primitive people who live in

Tropical rain forest in Puerto Rico

these humid forests often build tree houses or temporary leaf huts.

Shrub Forest Much different from rain forests are shrub forests. They occur in the mild mediterranean climate, where the dry summers do not provide enough rain for trees to reach great heights. Gnarled trees are widely scattered in search of water. Dense bushes, or shrubs, are common. This biome is sometimes called *woodlands* or *chaparral* (from a Spanish word meaning "dense thicket").

Coniferous Forest Conifers (KAHN uh furz) produce their seeds in a cone. Coniferous forests grow in the cold, harsh subpolar climates where most other trees cannot survive. Water does not evaporate as quickly from their needle leaves as it does from broad leaves. Nearly all needle-leaf trees stay green throughout the year and are known as evergreens. Pines and firs are among the most well known types.

Thick brush is typical of chaparral.

Vegetation of the World

Forest
- Rain Forest
- Deciduous Forest
- Coniferous Forest
- Shrub Forest (Chaparral)

Grassland
- Tropical Grassland (Savanna)
- Temperate Grassland (Steppe)

Wasteland
- Desert
- Tundra
- Highland
- Ice Cap

Wood from these trees is useful for pulp in paper, but the wood produces too much soot to be burned and is very soft. Limited coniferous forests are found in warm, rainy climates near the coast where the soil is poor. Examples include the giant redwoods of California and pine forests in Florida.

Coniferous forest in Montana

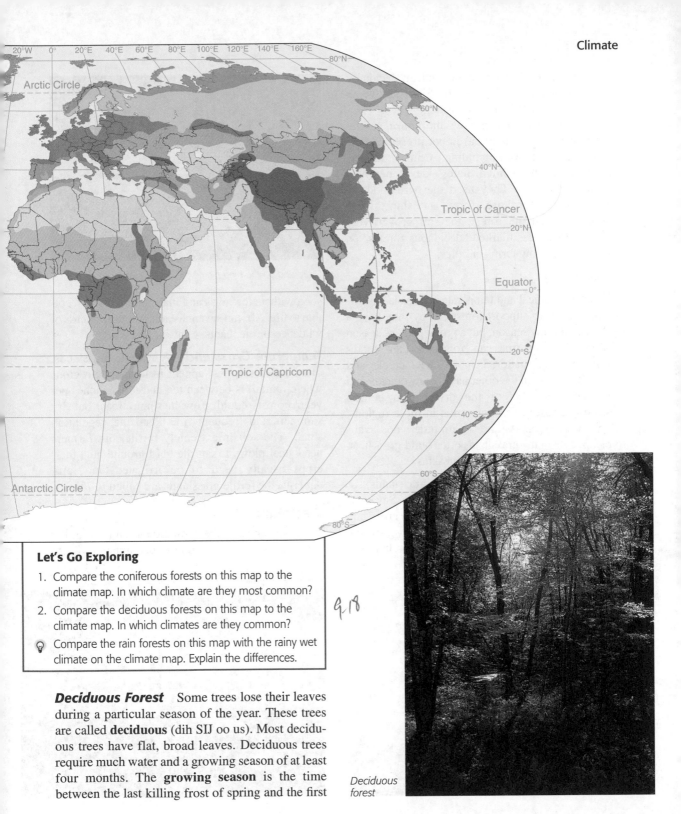

20°W 0° 20°E 40°E 60°E 80°E 100°E 120°E 140°E 160°E

80°N

Arctic Circle

60°N

40°N

Tropic of Cancer

20°N

Equator 0°

20°S

Tropic of Capricorn

40°S

60°S

Antarctic Circle

80°S

Let's Go Exploring

1. Compare the coniferous forests on this map to the climate map. In which climate are they most common?

2. Compare the deciduous forests on this map to the climate map. In which climates are they common?

💡 Compare the rain forests on this map with the rainy wet climate on the climate map. Explain the differences.

9.18

Deciduous Forest Some trees lose their leaves during a particular season of the year. These trees are called **deciduous** (dih SIJ oo us). Most deciduous trees have flat, broad leaves. Deciduous trees require much water and a growing season of at least four months. The **growing season** is the time between the last killing frost of spring and the first

Deciduous forest

53

killing frost of fall. Common broadleaf, deciduous trees include maple, oak, and elm. Such hardwoods are good for construction and heating.

Your vegetation map shows the *natural vegetation* that grows if mankind is not present. Many great civilizations—including China, France, England, and the United States—developed near deciduous forests. They used the hardwoods to build homes, furniture, forts, and ships. Once settlers cleared the forest, the soil proved very fertile. Most areas marked "deciduous forests" on your map are now farms or cities.

Grasslands

Many tropical and temperate regions lack sufficient rainfall to support forests. They may have a substantial rainy season, but a prolonged dry season follows. Although trees can grow under these conditions, they are scattered, mostly near creeks and rivers. Grasses, on the other hand, grow quickly and produce seeds before the dry season comes. Because grasses are so common in these regions, they are called **grasslands.** With little wood available, people in the grasslands often build grass huts, sod houses, or tents from animal skins.

Tropical Grassland Tropical grasslands, or **savannas,** occur in warm tropical regions. Savannas are natural "parks" with beautiful, open scenery and only a few scattered trees. Some grasses grow ten feet high in the rainy season, but the scorching sun

Grassland on the high plains of South Dakota

soon withers the grass and makes it highly susceptible to fire. African savannas are famous for herds of wildebeests, elephants, giraffes, and lions.

Temperate Grassland Temperate grasslands, often called **steppes,** appear in temperate regions where rainfall is between ten and thirty inches per year. Forests could grow in some areas, but dry summers and frequent fires keep the vegetation small. The soil is extremely fertile, but farmers need steel plows to cut the hard ground, and their crops usually need to be irrigated. In North America the fertile grasslands are called *prairie.*

Wasteland

Some areas of the earth are barren most of the year because of low amounts of precipitation. These

Savanna below Mt. Kilimanjaro in Kenya, Africa

Cacti in an Arizona desert

Mountain Vegetation

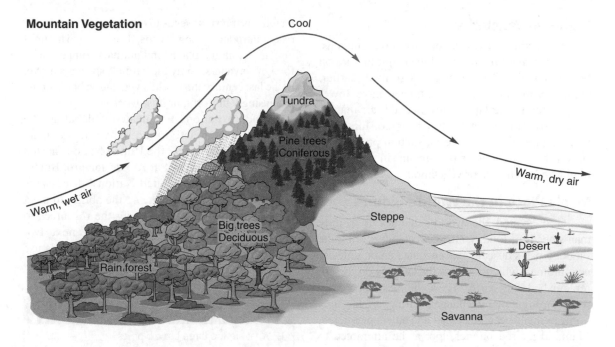

Cool

Tundra

Pine trees
Coniferous

Warm, dry air

Warm, wet air

Big trees
Deciduous

Steppe

Desert

Rain forest

Savanna

areas are called *wastelands.* Yet whenever rain falls or snow melts, these wastelands become a colorful sea of blooming life. The people who live here, such as Eskimos and Aborigines, have developed special survival skills as hunters and herders.

Desert   Two kinds of plants can grow in deserts. Some conserve water efficiently. Cacti are the most common of the succulent plants that store water in their stems and leaves. Other kinds of plants come to life quickly, produce seeds, and die in the brief period following each rain shower. A surprising variety of animals, such as the Gila monster and kangaroo rat, can survive in this extreme biome.

Tundra   The cold regions near the poles called **tundra** support only limited vegetation. Snow covers the ground most of the year. Precipitation, mainly in the form of snow, is light. During the short summer, only the top three feet of the soil thaws. Shallow-rooted plants, such as mosses, lichens, and grasses, grow in the soggy soil. The rest of the soil is **permafrost,** soil that remains frozen all year long. Not even coniferous trees can grow in the tundra.

In the summer the melting snow collects into many mosquito-infested bogs and lakes. The standing water does not evaporate quickly because the air is too cool, nor does the permafrost absorb it. When winter comes, the water freezes and a white blanket of snow returns. Herds of caribou and reindeer migrate to the tundra during the summer. Only a few hardy animals, such as musk oxen, hares, and wolves, remain all year round.

Tundra on Baffin Island, Canada

Highland Vegetation

Many kinds of vegetation grow on mountains. In fact, it is possible to see all the major biomes on one mountain. Two factors, described earlier, explain why. First, higher altitudes have lower temperatures (the lapse rate). Second, air masses passing over the mountain drop their moisture (orographic precipitation). The illustration on page 55 shows the general areas on a mountain where you might find each type of vegetation.

Man's Place in the World's Biomes

God created the world's biomes to supply man's needs of food, shelter, and clothing. After the Flood, Noah's descendants encountered completely new biomes, which arose as the animals on the ark replenished the earth. These biomes apparently went through many changes during an ice age. Some animals became extinct and others prospered. Mankind altered biomes, too, as he attempted to make the earth more productive. Modern cities cover ancient swamps. Green, irrigated fields dot the deserts. Domesticated animals, such as horses, cows, chickens, and pigs, are on every continent. Foods, such as potatoes, corn, and tomatoes, which were first discovered in the New World, are now grown worldwide.

Unfortunately, the growing human population has had a severe impact on the environment. When merchants transport seeds to other lands, they run the risk of introducing new weeds, diseases, and harmful insects. As native plants and animals compete with foreign "invaders," only the hardiest species survive. In the last century the world's vegetation has become increasingly uniform, or *homogenized.*

Modern nations are heatedly debating the effects of human activity on the world's climate and vegetation. In 1992 the United Nations hosted a historic Earth Summit at Rio de Janeiro, Brazil. The key word in the United Nations' discussions was *sustainable development,* "the ability to meet present needs without depleting the resources to support future generations." In the next two chapters, we will look more closely at man's use of the land.

◎ SECTION REVIEW

1. What are the three basic biomes?
2. Contrast coniferous and deciduous forests.
3. What are the two types of grasslands? What is the main distinction between them?
4. Why is tundra considered a wasteland?
5. What two conditions cause mountain vegetation to vary?
   - Should every country strive for sustainable development?

REVIEW 3

9-19 + Study
9.20 Test

Can You Define These Terms?

air mass	evaporation	front	conifers
Coriolis effect	condensation	convection	deciduous
trade winds	humidity	climate	growing season
westerlies	dew point	arid	grassland
low pressure	precipitation	climograph	savanna
high pressure	hydrologic cycle	lapse rate	steppe
ocean currents	ground water	vegetation	tundra
El Niño	orographic	biome	permafrost
gyres			

Can You Locate These Features?

tropic of Cancer	Antarctic Circle	Temperate Zones	doldrums
tropic of Capricorn	Tropics	polar regions	horse latitudes
Arctic Circle	middle latitudes		

How Much Do You Remember?

1. What effect does each of the following have upon the temperature of a region?
   a. latitude
   b. altitude
   c. distance from the ocean
2. What are two other names for the middle latitudes?
3. What causes air masses to rise or fall?
4. How does the Coriolis effect influence winds?
5. What is the basic cause of all precipitation? Under what three conditions does precipitation usually occur?
6. Why are trees more common in areas with wet climates?
7. A pine tree is which of the following? Give all correct answers.
   a. a needle-leaf tree
   b. a broadleaf tree
   c. a conifer
   d. deciduous
   e. evergreen
8. What is permafrost? In which climate region is it found?

What Do You Think?

1. How would the world be different if the earth did not rotate on its axis?
2. How would climate be different if the earth's axis were not tilted?
3. In your opinion, what is a perfect climate?
4. Find your home on the climate map. How does your geographic setting affect the climate?
5. What kind of natural vegetation is most common near your home? Why?
6. Why are most deserts located near the horse latitudes?

Cumulative Review

1. What are the two main branches of geography?
2. Explain the difference between latitude and longitude.
3. What two formative events in the earth's history occurred only once and will never occur again?
4. Name the seven continents and four oceans.
5. What are the basic differences between the Tropics, the middle latitudes, and the polar regions? Identify a climate that is associated with each region.

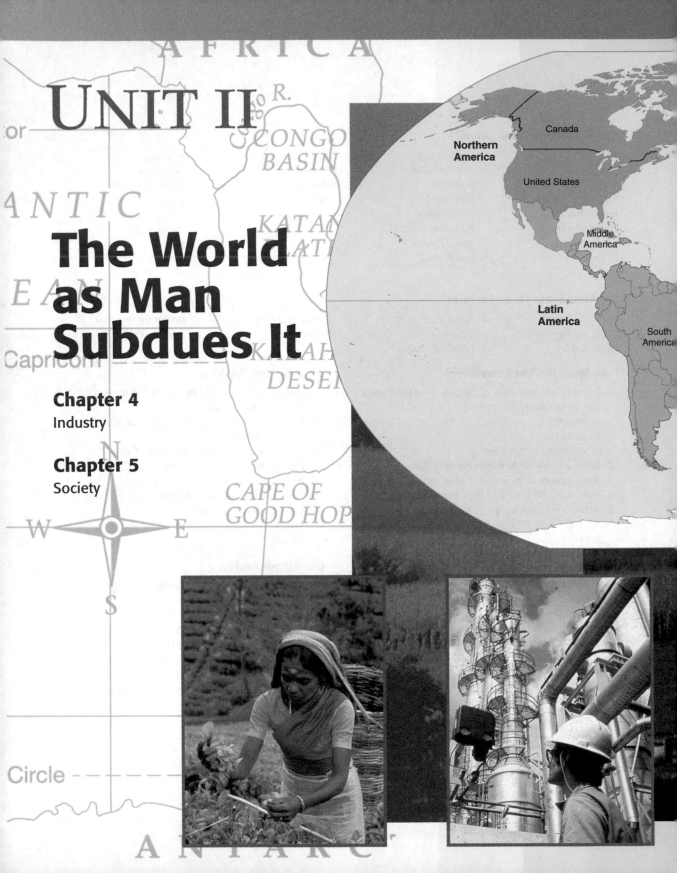

UNIT II

The World as Man Subdues It

Chapter 4
Industry

Chapter 5
Society

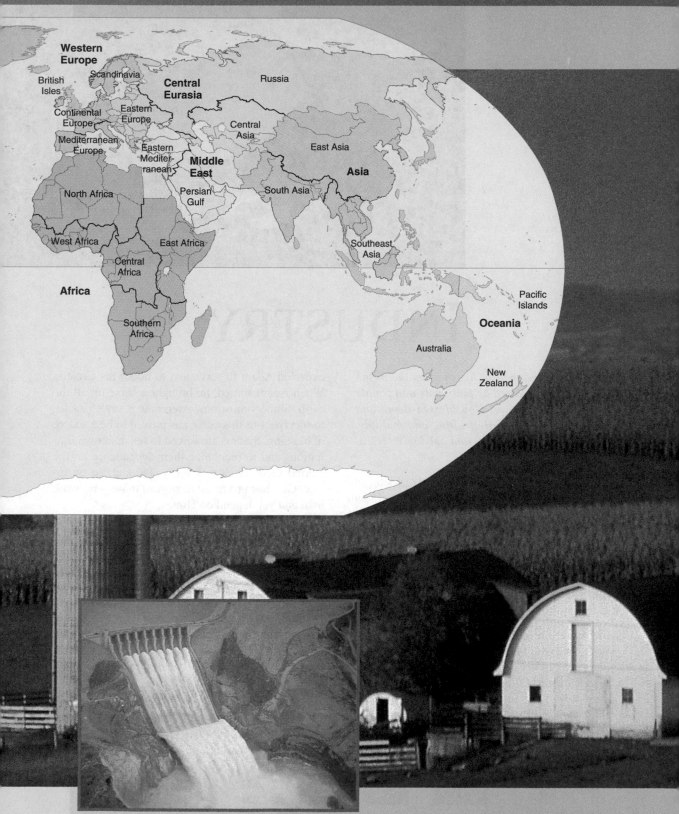

Western Europe

British Isles

Scandinavia

Central Eurasia

Russia

Continental Europe

Eastern Europe

Central Asia

East Asia

Asia

Mediterranean Europe

Eastern Mediterranean

Middle East

North Africa

Persian Gulf

South Asia

West Africa

East Africa

Southeast Asia

Central Africa

Pacific Islands

Africa

Oceania

Southern Africa

Australia

New Zealand

INDUSTRY

So God created man in his own image, in the image of God created he him; male and female created he them. And God blessed them, and God said unto them, Be fruitful, and multiply, and replenish the earth, and subdue it. (Gen. 1:27-28)

Geography is not simply the study of land and climate, plants and animals. It is the study of man, the apex and ruler of God's creation. In His first words to Adam, the Lord gave him an order, or *mandate,* to subdue the earth. The **dominion mandate** required Adam and his descendants to study the earth and to use it wisely. The rest of this textbook will focus on people and their efforts to subdue the earth.

Cursed is the ground for thy sake; in sorrow shalt thou eat of it all the days of thy life. . . . In the sweat of thy face shalt thou eat bread, till thou return unto the ground; for out of it wast thou taken: for dust thou art, and unto dust shalt thou return. (Gen. 3:17, 19)

Mankind is not the final master of Creation. God made Adam in His own image, and He expected Adam to serve and to honor his Creator. When Adam sinned, he brought a curse on all the earth. Sinners must now overcome many obstacles to survive. But this curse has proved to be a source of blessing. Sinners are forced to see their own limitations and to recognize their dependence on the eternal God (Eccles. 3:9-13). Throughout Scripture, God has promised to reward those who work hard and yet depend on Him.

The word *industry* is often used to describe man's "hard work" to make a living. Although there are many types of jobs, or industries, the basic categories have been around since the beginning of time. The U.S. government has developed a Standard Industrial Classification (SIC) system. Every job can be classified under one of the categories in the chart on page 61. This chapter will examine each industry in turn, and it will close by showing how industry contributes to the wealth of nations.

PRIMARY INDUSTRIES

All industries fall under one of three divisions: primary, secondary, or tertiary. **Primary industries** are the most basic industries of all. They take

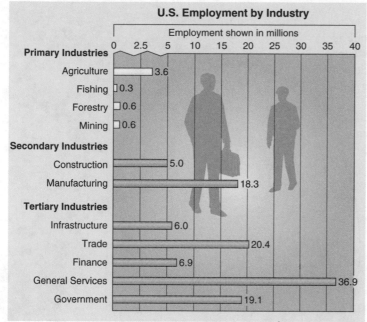

U.S. Employment by Industry

Employment shown in millions

Primary Industries	
Agriculture	3.6
Fishing	0.3
Forestry	0.6
Mining	0.6
Secondary Industries	
Construction	5.0
Manufacturing	18.3
Tertiary Industries	
Infrastructure	6.0
Trade	20.4
Finance	6.9
General Services	36.9
Government	19.1

As part of the dominion mandate, God gave Adam control over every animal and plant in the world. God intended for Adam to tend the environment that He had created. The Lord Himself planted the first garden, filling it with the most beautiful plants and the most delicious foods. Gardening is intended to make the world both more productive and more beautiful.

Contrary to the view of evolutionists, man did not have to discover how to plant seeds and how to domesticate animals. God taught Adam to be a gardener, and his two sons specialized in the two major branches of agriculture: farming and animal husbandry. Cain tilled the ground, and Abel kept sheep.

If you look closely at the world land-use map, you will see that almost all land is used for agriculture. By comparing this map to the climate map on pages 48-49, you will see a clear pattern. First, notice that crops are raised in the moderate climates. Second, in the semiarid climates, herds of animals are raised. Third, little or no agriculture takes place in the two most extreme climates—the rainy tropics and the cold arctic. Here widely scattered bands of people pursue *primitive* activities, such as hunting, fishing, and gathering berries. They must make good use of their marginal land to eke out a meager living.

materials from the earth needed for food, clothes, and shelter. Primary industries include agriculture and mining.

Agriculture

God said unto them, . . . have dominion over the fish of the sea, and over the fowl of the air, and over every living thing that moveth upon the earth. And God said, Behold, I have given you every herb bearing seed, which is upon the face of all the earth, and every tree, in the which is the fruit of a tree yielding seed; to you it shall be for meat. (Gen. 1:28-29)

Cornfield in Indiana

Cornfield in Nigeria

Farming The first main branch of agriculture is farming. Throughout the ages, farming has supplied most of man's food. Planting seeds provides a much more reliable food supply than hunting wild animals and gathering fruits.

In the past, most farmers produced only enough food to meet the needs of their own households. They made their own clothes, furniture, and homes. These farmers were **subsistence farmers.** Some subsistence farmers raised a **cash crop,** such as rice or corn, to sell. But the money barely bought enough to keep food on the table, and the household still made most of its own belongings. Billions of people still live by subsistence farming.

In the eighteenth century a revolution took place in Europe and the United States. Farmers began applying science and machinery to increase their yield. **Commercial farmers** were able to raise large cash crops for profit. Modern industrial cities depend on this steady supply of food from commercial farms.

All farmers, whether subsistence or commercial, face the same challenges. Drought, insect plagues, and disease can wipe out their crops. Windstorms, hail, and floods can devastate fields. In many places irrigation has reduced the threat of drought, insecticides have limited the threat of insects, and breeding has improved crop yields and resistance to disease. But one major problem remains: loss of soil. Wind and water can wash soil and nutrients away, while certain crops can deplete the soil of nutrients such as nitrogen. As you study each country, you will see how farmers are dealing with these challenges.

Animal Husbandry The second main form of agriculture is animal husbandry. Like farming, animal husbandry can be divided into two types: subsistence and commercial.

Subsistence husbandry, known as **nomadic herding,** is common in rugged mountains and dry areas where regular farming is difficult. Jabal, a descendent of Cain, became the "father of such as

Land Use of the World

- Commercial Farming
- Subsistence Farming
- Manufacturing and Trade
- Ranching
- Nomadic Herding
- Forestry
- Subpolar Primitive Activity
- Tropical Primitive Activity
- Limited Activity

Let's Go Exploring

1. Which continent is used almost entirely for commercial farming and manufacturing?

2. Which continent has the largest proportion of subsistence farming?

3. What type of activity is most common along the equator?

4. On which continent is ranching predominant?

5. Which hemisphere has most of the world's forestry, north or south?

6. What three continents have most of the world's manufacturing and trade?

What type of activity is always found beside every manufacturing area? Why?

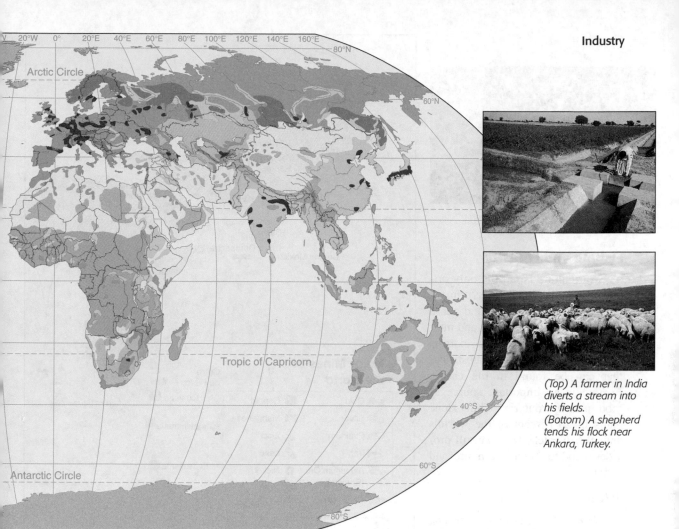

(Top) A farmer in India diverts a stream into his fields.
(Bottom) A shepherd tends his flock near Ankara, Turkey.

dwell in tents, and of such as have cattle" (Gen. 4:20). Because large herds of animals quickly consume the vegetation in an area, nomads must move constantly in search of fresh pastures.

Many nomads became raiders and conquerors, famous for their toughness and skill with horses. Among them were the Huns of Central Asia, the Sioux Indians of North America, and the Masai of East Africa. They often built their homes of animal skin because it was lighter than wood and more readily available in the grasslands.

In the eighteenth century Europeans developed a second method of animal husbandry called *ranching*. Wealthy landowners let their herds and flocks roam freely on vast tracts of land. In early America,

ranchers let their cattle run free on the "open range" (government land that no one claimed). Ranchers periodically rounded up their cattle to be branded or to be shipped to market. Sheep owners rounded up their sheep to shear the wool.

SECTION REVIEW

1. Who gave the dominion mandate? To whom was it given?
2. Name the two major divisions of agriculture.
3. Define *subsistence farming*.
4. Explain the difference between ranching and nomadic herding.
- Which type of agriculture did Abraham use?

Modern machinery aids in logging industries.

Fishing and Forestry

Agriculture is not the only primary industry. Three other primary industries have been around for a long time: fishing, forestry, and mining. Each of these industries extracts **natural resources** (useful substances that can be found in the earth). *Fishing* is an important source of food in many countries. China alone hauls in 20 percent of the world's annual fish catch. *Forestry* still provides wood for homes, furniture, and paper.

Mining

Mining has far surpassed fishing and forestry in importance. Modern countries spend great sums of money mining three resources: metals, nonmetal minerals, and fossil fuels.

Metals Underneath a thin layer of soil, the earth's crust is composed mainly of rock. Rocks contain a combination of several **minerals** (solid crystals that occur naturally and have a definite chemical composition). Scientists have identified about three thousand different minerals, but only about one hundred are common.

Metals are the most important type of mineral because of four useful properties. They are shiny, malleable (able to be hammered into sheets), ductile (able to be drawn into wire), and conductive (able to conduct electricity). Metal axes, pots, and other tools last longer and work better than tools made from

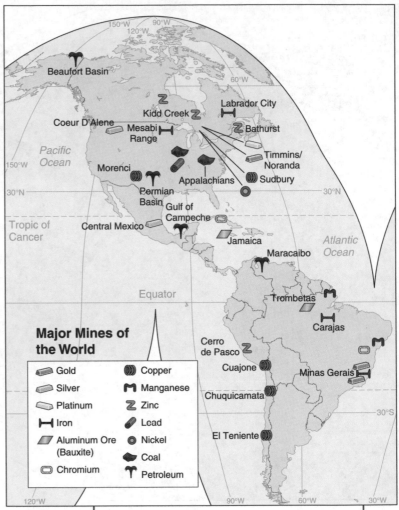

Major Mines of the World

Gold	Copper	
Silver	Manganese	
Platinum	Zinc	
Iron	Lead	
Aluminum Ore (Bauxite)	Nickel	
Chromium	Coal	
	Petroleum	

Let's Go Exploring

1. Which continent lacks gold and silver mines?
2. Find the region of South Africa that produces the most gold in the world.
3. Which continents lack coal?
4. What types of metals are mined near Broken Hill? Mt. Isa?
5. Name the two famous bauxite mines in Australia.
6. What important metal ore is mined in the island of Jamaica?
   Does any continent have a mine for every metal?

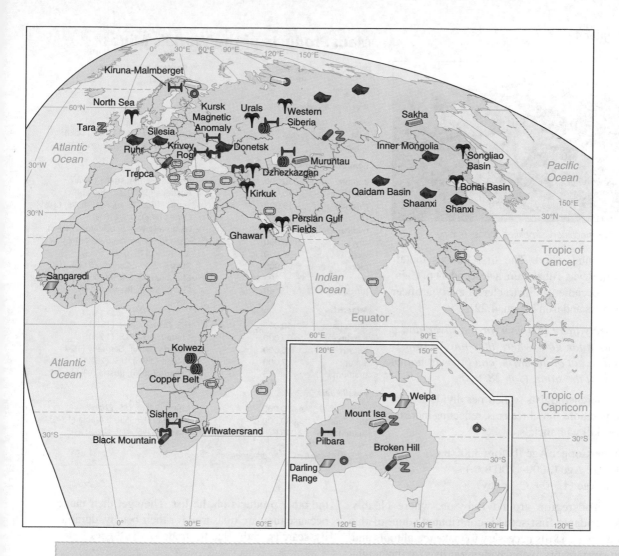

Map labels: Kiruna-Malmberget, North Sea, Tara, Atlantic Ocean, Ruhr, Silesia, Krivoy Rog, Trepca, Kursk Magnetic Anomaly, Urals, Western Siberia, Donetsk, Dzhezkazgan, Muruntau, Kirkuk, Ghawar, Persian Gulf Fields, Sakha, Inner Mongolia, Songliao Basin, Qaidam Basin, Shaanxi, Bohai Basin, Shanxi, Pacific Ocean, Indian Ocean, Equator, Tropic of Cancer, Sangaredi, Atlantic Ocean, Kolwezi, Copper Belt, Sishen, Witwatersrand, Black Mountain, Tropic of Capricorn, Weipa, Mount Isa, Pilbara, Broken Hill, Darling Range

Green Revolution

Ever since Adam planted his first seed, farmers have been trying to improve their crop yields. Wheat, the most important grain in the ancient world, once produced only a few small kernels on each stalk. Careful breeding over centuries nearly doubled its yield by the seventeenth century. Genetics and other methods of modern science have accelerated these improvements. In the 1960s the world's industrial nations sponsored the greatest effort in human history to increase crop yields in poor countries. It was so successful it became known as the *Green Revolution*.

The Green Revolution focused on human *staples*—the essential "bread and butter" of every society. The world's three main staples are wheat, rice, and maize (corn). About 500 million tons of each staple is grown every year. Modern science has created new varieties of wheat that produce over sixty kernels, and these kernels are larger, hardier, and more disease-resistant than ever before. Rice yields have made similar, dramatic improvements. While the world's population has doubled in the past forty years, the yield of staples has increased even more. India, where 1.5 million people died from malnutrition in 1943, now raises a surplus of grain that it sells abroad.

Yet no amount of science can eliminate the challenges of feeding the world. Diseases and insects have become resistant to modern chemicals. Scientific farming has drawbacks too. It is expensive, and it requires large amounts of fertilizers and insecticides that may cause long-term harm to people and wildlife.

Heavy machinery simplifies copper mining.

Main Products of the World's Mines

PRODUCT	ANNUAL PRODUCTION*	LEADING PRODUCERS (% TOTAL)
Precious Metals		
silver	16	Mexico (15%), U.S. (12%)
gold	2	South Africa (28%), U.S. (14%)
platinum	0.3	South Africa (50%), Russia (42%)
Common Metals		
iron ore	550,000	Brazil (19%), Australia (14%)
aluminum	20,000	Australia (38%), Guinea (14%)
chromium	13,000	South Africa (35%), Kazakhstan (30%)
copper	10,000	Chile (19%), U.S. (18%)
manganese	8,000	Ukraine (24%), South Africa (19%)
zinc	8,000	Canada (17%), Australia (14%)
lead	4,000	Australia (17%), U.S. (14%)
nickel	1,000	Russia (26%), Canada (21%)
tin	200	China (21%), Brazil (16%)
tungsten	40	China (59%), Russia (16%)
Minerals		
phosphates	150,000	U.S. (31%), China (15%)
nitrates	95,000	China (19%), U.S. (14%)
potash	26,000	Canada (28%), Germany (16%)
sulfur	12,000	Poland (33%), U.S. (26%)
uranium	45	Canada (20%), Russia (9%)
Fossil Fuels		
coal	4,600,000	China (24%), U.S. (20%)
petroleum	3,000,000	Russia (15%), Saudi Arabia (13%)
natural gas	2,000,000**	Russia (31%), U.S. (24%)

* 1,000 Metric tons   ** Cubic meters

stone and wood. The first famous metal-worker was Tubal-cain, a descendent of Cain, who became "an instructer of every artificer in brass and iron" (Gen. 4:22).

Surely there is a vein for the silver, and a place for gold where they fine it. Iron is taken out of the earth, and brass is molten out of the stone. (Job 28:1-2)

Archeologists sometimes divide ancient civilizations into three eras, reflecting increasing skill with metals.

Stone/Copper Age (before 3000 B.C.)
Bronze Age (3000-1200 B.C.)
Iron Age (1200 B.C.–today)

The region around Babylon, where Noah's descendants first settled, contributed some of the most basic skills necessary to make metal tools and fine ornaments. Nebuchadnezzar lived at the height of Babylonian splendor. In a dream, God showed him that succeeding world empires would not match the golden splendor of his reign. But God further revealed that later empires would make superior weapons of war from less valuable metals (Daniel 2).

Gold of the Babylonians (605-538 B.C.)
Silver of the Persians (538-332 B.C.)
Bronze of the Greeks (332-31 B.C.)
Iron of the Romans (31 B.C.–A.D. 476)

Precious Metals   The modern production of gold, silver, and platinum is small, if measured in tons. But these *precious metals* are far more valuable than the other products on the list. They get their name because they are treasured for their beauty, durability, scarcity, and value for trade.

Common Metals   *Common metals* get their name because they are mined in great quantities from the earth's surface.

Three of the common metals have been used since ancient times: copper, lead, and iron.

Copper is a "native metal," like silver and gold, that can be found in pure nuggets in the earth's crust. Copper was once used to make weapons, but it is very soft. Over 60 percent of the copper mined today is used in the electrical industry because it is the least expensive conductor of electricity.

Lead does not occur alone in nature. Like most metals, it must be extracted from an *ore* (minerals composed of several different elements). Lead is combined with sulfur in an ore called galena. A wood fire is hot enough to melt lead. Because it is such a soft metal, artists originally used lead to cast statues. Lead is now the main ingredient in car batteries.

People in the ancient world extracted iron too, but the process was very difficult and expensive. The temperature had to be very high (2,795°F), and the refined ore often contained many impurities (traces of other elements). In 1784 Britain developed a process of "puddling" (stirring) iron ore to take out the impurities. This strong, versatile metal became useful for making cannons, bridges, trains, and other modern machines. More iron is mined each year than all other metals combined.

Aluminum is the second most common metal on earth. The metal was once considered a precious stone because it was so difficult to separate out of its ore, **bauxite.** The bond holding the elements together in bauxite (hydrogen, oxygen, and aluminum) is so powerful that a process of separating them was not discovered until 1886. This process, using electrical currents, is still used today. Aluminum's light weight and resistance to corrosion make it ideal for warehouses, cars, and other machines.

Alloys The four metals you have just studied—copper, lead, iron, and aluminum—are useful by themselves. Early in history, man learned that he could also combine metals to form **alloys.** The remaining six common metals on the mining chart—chromium, manganese, zinc, nickel, tin, and tungsten—are not

Sheets of galvanized steel

usually used by themselves but are combined with one or more of the first four metals.

The first useful alloys were made with copper. Copper and tin form *bronze,* from which we get the term the Bronze Age. This pliable metal could be made into beautiful statues, weapons, and tools that were stronger than copper. Near the time of Christ, the Romans learned to make *brass* by combining copper and zinc. It is useful in making objects with intricate designs, such as musical instruments. Bronze and brass are often confused with one another because they both have a yellow color common to all copper alloys.

Steel is the world's most important alloy. It is formed by combining iron with the carbon in coal. Early civilizations knew how to produce this metal, but the process was even more difficult and unreliable than ironmaking. In 1856 Henry Bessemer devised a better process. First he shot a jet of air into molten iron to rid it of impurities. Then, by adding coal and manganese, the iron turned into a tough steel. Nearly all the world's iron ore is now turned into steel. In a sense, the Iron Age has become "the Steel Age."

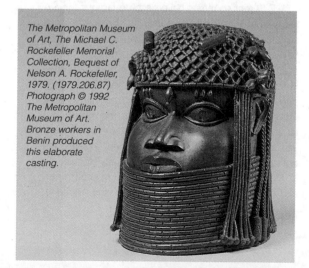

The Metropolitan Museum of Art, The Michael C. Rockefeller Memorial Collection, Bequest of Nelson A. Rockefeller, 1979. (1979.206.87) Photograph © 1992 The Metropolitan Museum of Art. Bronze workers in Benin produced this elaborate casting.

Nonmetal Minerals Metals are not the only useful minerals that God has provided. Many other kinds of minerals have played an important role in industry.

Limestone is formed mainly from calcite (calcium, carbon, and oxygen). When crushed and mixed with clay, limestone makes a powder called cement. Adding sand to cement produces mortar. Adding crushed rock to cement makes concrete, the most widely used building material in the world.

Sulfur is another versatile mineral known since ancient times. It has many modern uses. Combined with charcoal and potassium nitrate, it makes gunpowder. Sulfur is also used to process petroleum and steel, to produce fertilizer, to vulcanize (improve the strength and texture of) rubber, and even to make matches.

Several other minerals have been used since early history. Clay, a finely ground rock, is baked into bricks. Craftsmen shape clay into plates, cups, and bowls. Sand melted with limestone and soda ash makes glass for windows and bottles. Granite, marble, slate, and sandstone are cut to build monuments and decorative buildings. Halite, which we know as salt, seasons and preserves food. Graphite is a black, powdery mineral used to make the "lead" in pencils.

At the beginning of the nineteenth century, farmers learned that various common minerals could be added to the soil to make it more *fertile* (able to produce crops). Commercial farms have come to depend on three types of **fertilizers:** phosphates, nitrates, and potash. They contain the most important nutrients that the soil needs—phosphorus, nitrogen, and potassium. Bags of fertilizer sold at your local hardware store show the percentage of these nutrients. If the bag says 5-10-10, it contains 5 percent phosphorus, 10 percent nitrogen, and 10 percent potassium.

A few minerals contain uranium, a mineral fuel that was used first in atomic bombs in 1945 and soon afterward in nuclear reactors. Its high radioactivity makes it very harmful to the human body.

Fossil Fuels For thousands of years man relied on animals, wind, water, wood, and manpower for

Carved ivory

Cut gems

Precious Gems

From earliest times, children have picked up pretty stones lying on the ground. Soon kings began mining and hoarding these mineral treasures we call "precious gems." On every continent, gems are popular adornments and symbols of wealth. Because of its small size and great value, the gem was once a form of currency, especially when long caravans journeyed to distant lands.

Asians value gems mostly for their weight, so they polish the large stones and keep them in their original irregular shape. Westerners, on the other hand, cut the gems to enhance their color and symmetry. Lapidaries (gem cutters) chip small slivers from the stone to leave flat surfaces called facets. The facets reflect light to make the gem sparkle. The largest diamond ever discovered originally weighed 3024.75 carats (1 carat = 200 milligrams or .007 ounces). The queen of England had it cut into nine large diamonds for the British crown jewels.

Different countries have become famous for certain gems. Turquoise, prized for its sky-blue color, is popular in the western United States. The Chinese have carved jade for almost three thousand years. Australia is the biggest producer of rainbowlike opals. Emeralds, second only to the ruby in value, are mined primarily in Colombia. Rubies and sapphires come from the mines of Burma. Diamonds, the most popular of all gems, are excavated in South Africa. They were first discovered there in 1867 when a salesman noticed some children playing with "pretty stones."

There are two kinds of gems: inorganic (minerals) and organic (products of plants and animals).

Offshore oil rig in the Gulf of Mexico

energy to plow fields, to make products, and to travel. Only in the last two hundred years has man realized the potential of another great energy resource beneath his feet—**fossil fuels.** Coal, petroleum, and natural gas are technically not minerals but are the remains of living things. Apparently the Flood waters trapped plants and animals beneath layers of sedimentary rock. The pressure changed this *organic matter* (remains of living things) into

The organic gems include pearls (from oysters), amber (from fossilized tree resin), jet (from fossilized driftwood), coral (from the skeletons of tiny sea animals), and ivory (from tusks of elephants and other animals). Most inorganic gems apparently formed as volcanic lava forced its way upward through small cracks in the earth and superheated the minerals nearby. Rubies and sapphires came from aluminum oxide, and diamonds came from carbon. Man has tried to produce artificial gems by simulating the heat and pressure of volcanoes, but the quality is not as good as that of natural gems.

The Bible records many references to gems. The twelve stones on Aaron's breastplate (Exod. 39) may have led to the sixteenth-century tradition of birthstones for each month. Europeans mistakenly believed gems were magical and brought good luck. Revelation 21 tells us that God will build the foundation of the New Jerusalem with twelve layers of different gems.

its present form. These fossil fuels have drastically changed our way of life.

Coal is a solid rock. It occurs in different grades, or levels of quality, depending on the amount of heat produced per pound. The Chinese burned coal for heat over one thousand years before the time of Christ. In the late eighteenth century Europeans discovered its potential to make steam for steam engines. Later it was used to make coke, a necessary ingredient in steel. Coal is now used to generate most of the world's electricity.

Petroleum is a liquid fossil fuel. Noah used a thick form of petroleum, called *pitch,* to cover the ark. The ancient Chinese used petroleum that had seeped into pools on the earth's surface. The first commercial oil well was not drilled until 1859. At first Americans extracted kerosene for lamps and threw the rest of the oil away. But scientists soon realized that petroleum packs much more energy than coal. The invention of gasoline engines turned petroleum into the most important mining product in the world.

Located in many underground oil pools is a fossil fuel in gaseous form called **natural gas.** Many scientists believe that it is a by-product of the process that formed petroleum. Although burned off as waste at the first oil wells, it has become a useful fuel for heating furnaces, water heaters, dryers, and ovens.

Early oil wells near Titusville, Pennsylvania

SECONDARY INDUSTRIES

Primary industries do not change the form of natural resources. For example, they produce grains of wheat and beef on the hoof, not sacks of flour and hamburgers. **Secondary industries** take **raw materials** (natural resources that have been extracted by primary industries) and change them into a useful form. There are two types of secondary industries: construction and manufacturing.

Construction

Mankind has used a variety of natural resources in construction. Cain built the first city, but the Bible does not say what materials he used (Gen. 4:17). The first great structure mentioned in Scripture is the Tower of Babel, made of mortar. Egyptians used cut stone to build the pyramids, and the Romans used cement to build great coliseums. In the 1850s engineers learned how to reinforce concrete with steel, making possible modern dams, bridges, and skyscrapers. In later chapters you will see specific examples of these architectural wonders of the world.

Manufacturing

For most of human history, people made their clothes, bowls, and tools at home. The word *manufacture* originally meant "to make by hand." As cities grew, some individuals specialized in making certain products. Cities had bakers, tailors,

and candlestick makers. In the past two centuries, "cottage industries" have been overshadowed by large factories. **Manufacturing** now refers to big businesses and machines that turn raw materials into new products.

Industrial Revolution The discoveries and inventions between 1750 and 1850 made modern industries possible. This period of radical change is known as the **Industrial Revolution.** It started in the textile industry of Britain. Just prior to the revolution, the British people raised their own sources of wool and flax and turned it into clothes by hand with simple tools. Many hours of work went into the production of just a few yards of finished cloth. Finally, inventors developed machines that simplified and quickened production. When the steam engine came along to run the machines, the revolution took off and never stopped.

Industry experienced a "second revolution" in the second half of the nineteenth century. Exciting discoveries in chemistry, physics, and biology made this revolution possible. The application of modern science to industry is called **technology.** The key technological breakthrough was harnessing electricity. Gasoline engines, telegraphs, and telephones were also invented. These resources gave industries new freedom to place factories anywhere they wanted. Modern technology also spawned whole new industries, such as the automobile and airplane industries.

Textile machines in Britain sparked the Industrial Revolution.

Geographer's Corner

Flow Charts

Many complicated steps are involved in manufacturing a product. Flow charts show the general movement, or flow, of products through production. Below is a flow chart for the most important raw material in the modern world: petroleum. When refined, it yields a wealth of important fuels and other chemicals.

To understand how each product is made, you must carefully follow the steps in the flow chart. The refining process begins with the heating of **crude oil,** the dark liquid that comes out of the ground. Different chemicals separate from the oil as they reach their boiling temperature. Lighter chemicals boil first and appear at the top of the flow chart. The heaviest chemicals appear at the bottom.

The colors show the three processes that change the product as it moves through the plant. *Distillation* evaporates a liquid mixture into gases to separate chemicals. *Extraction* removes chemicals from a liquid mixture through filters. *Chemical processes* add chemicals that change the form of the product.

Around 45 percent of crude oil is turned into gasoline, 7 percent into jet fuel, 7 percent into diesel fuel, and 27 percent into fuel oil (fuel burned by electric companies and home heaters). The remaining heavy products are turned into lubricating oils, wax, and asphalt. Notice that some light chemicals are extracted from kerosene. These are shipped to other manufacturers, who convert them into **petrochemicals,** such as plastics, synthetic rubber, fibers for textiles, dyes, medicines, fertilizers, paints, and perfumes.

Use the information on the flow chart to answer these questions.

1. What is the heaviest product on the chart (from residues)?
2. What chemical must be extracted in refining jet fuel?
3. What two products require a blender?
4. Name three products that do not need to go through any chemical treatment.
5. What is the only example of a chemical that returns to the stage it came from?

💡 Why do fuel oils appear *twice* as a final product?

Petrochemicals

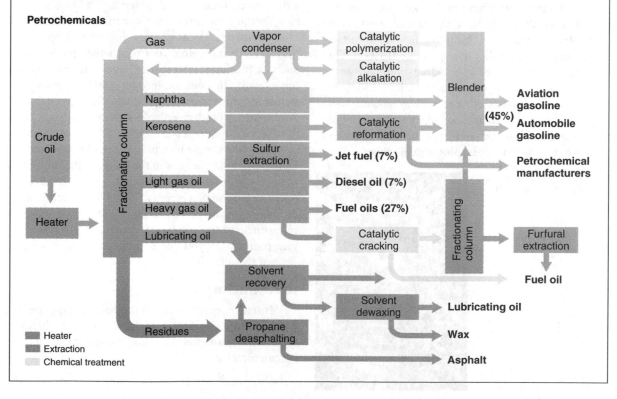

Heater
Extraction
Chemical treatment

In the second half of the twentieth century, manufacturing entered a third period of revolution. It has been called the Computer Age, the Electronics Age, or the "Information Revolution." New high-tech industries, such as computer-chip makers, use the most advanced discoveries of science and engineering. Robotics and computers have made industries so efficient that fewer people are needed to work in factories producing basic manufactured goods. Most people are free to find jobs outside the farm and factory in our *postindustrial society*.

Durable and Nondurable Manufacturing

Manufacturing industries are divided into two types, depending on the lifespan of their products. Nondurable manufacturing makes products that generally last less than a year. They include most of the inexpensive products necessary for life. Nondurable products come from eight primary sources: food, tobacco, leather, rubber, chemicals, fossil fuels (petrochemicals), wood pulp (paper), and textiles (fibers, such as wool and cotton, that can be woven).

Durable manufacturing makes products that last more than a year. They include most of the products needed for building homes, furniture, machines, and other equipment. Most durable products come from five sources: lumber, stone, clay, glass, and metals. Many of these industries take the products of other secondary industries and further improve them. For example, automobile manufacturers shape steel from steel industries and combine it with textiles, plastic, and rubber.

Honda manufactures cars in Marysville, Michigan.

SECTION REVIEW

1. What are the two types of secondary industries? How are they similar?
2. Explain the difference between raw materials and natural resources.
3. What do we call the changes in industry from 1750 to 1850? What industry was the first to experience these changes?
4. What is technology? Give an example of a high-tech industry.
💡 Identify the three revolutions in industry. What changes did each of them bring to daily life?

TERTIARY INDUSTRIES

Only half a million American adults are miners, and fewer than four million Americans work on farms. Even the number of manufacturing jobs has shrunk to below twenty million. Workers in these primary and secondary industries provide all the country's needs for food, construction materials, and manufactured products. The rest of America's workers—nearly four out of five—are employed in a third type of industry called tertiary industries.

Tertiary industries are sometimes called service industries because they produce services. *Services* are intangible (not touchable) products, such as teaching, advertising, truck driving, and auto repair. In contrast, primary and secondary industries produce *goods* (products you can touch). All industries produce either goods or services.

Service industries are the vital link between goods and the people who need them. Goods would be useless if they just sat in the fields, at the mines, or at the factories. Service workers are involved at every step of human activity. The U.S. Department of Labor recognizes five categories of service jobs: infrastructure, trade, finance, general services, and government. Do you know anyone who works in *each* of these fields?

Infrastructure

Infrastructure refers to the basic energy and equipment needs of all industries. There are three types of infrastructure: utilities, transportation, and communication.

Utilities   *Utilities* provide basic services, such as electricity, gas, water, trash collection, and sewage disposal. Governments own most utilities, or they control the prices that utilities can charge.

Electric and gas utilities produce the energy that runs modern industries and heats homes. About 90 percent of the world's energy comes from fossil fuels, followed by dammed water (hydroelectricity), and uranium (nuclear fuel). Most energy is converted into electricity. Electricity is measured in **kilowatt hours (kWh)**—the amount of work done by one thousand watts in one hour. It requires one kWh to burn ten 100-watt bulbs for one hour. The United States is the world's leading producer and consumer of electricity.

Transportation   Industries have three basic choices when transporting products and people: water, land, and air. These modes of transportation have undergone major changes in the last two centuries.

Water Transportation   Mankind has used water for cheap transportation throughout history. Noah's descendants built the first great civilizations along the mighty rivers of the world. But river routes have some obvious limitations. Shallow water limits the distance boats can travel, and rivers are often far from mineral resources. In the nineteenth century

The Corinth Canal in Greece

industrial nations attempted to overcome these limitations by building a vast network of canals. Railroads eventually became more important, but flat-bottomed barges are still common on the old canals. They carry almost 10 percent of all U.S. freight, particularly coal and metal ores.

Unlike rivers, the ocean remains vital to world transportation. Gas-powered ships transport everything from avocados to zinc. Some ships have large holds (open cargo areas below deck) to carry bulky materials, such as grain, coal, and ores. Other ships carry manufactured goods in twenty-foot-long box crates, which can be loaded and unloaded quickly. A new class of one-thousand-foot superfreighters is transforming the shipping industry. A small crew of fifteen men can handle up to six thousand containers. Oil supertankers, another type of merchant ship, are the largest ships ever built.

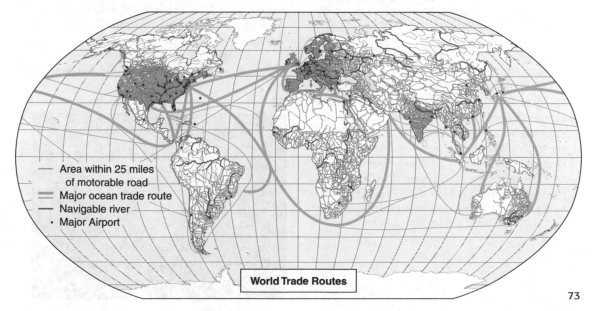

- Area within 25 miles of motorable road
- Major ocean trade route
- Navigable river
- Major Airport

World Trade Routes

Alternative Sources of Energy

Man has always looked for new ways to produce more with less energy. Modern industry would have been impossible without the development of fossil fuels. But fossil fuels are a **nonrenewable resource** that will run out some day. Countries also worry about the pollution caused by fossil fuels.

Nuclear power plant in North Carolina

Sources of Energy in the United States

92.5% Nonrenewable Energy

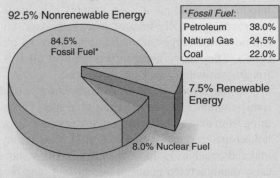

84.5%
Fossil Fuel*

Fossil Fuel:	
Petroleum	38.0%
Natural Gas	24.5%
Coal	22.0%

7.5% Renewable Energy

8.0% Nuclear Fuel

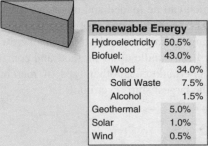

Renewable Energy	
Hydroelectricity	50.5%
Biofuel:	43.0%
Wood	34.0%
Solid Waste	7.5%
Alcohol	1.5%
Geothermal	5.0%
Solar	1.0%
Wind	0.5%

Nuclear Fuel. World War II spawned the next great innovation in energy—nuclear fuel. Splitting atoms can create enough heat to drive steam turbines to make electricity. This resource promised to solve all of man's energy needs because atoms are every-where. In reality, nuclear power has serious drawbacks. Nuclear fission uses dangerous, radioactive minerals. Government officials have done a terrible job keeping down costs and disposing of radioactive waste. In the late 1980s industrial nations decided to stop building new nuclear power plants.

Renewable Resources. Before the Arab nations cut off their supply of oil to the United States in 1973 causing an energy crisis, 98.5 percent of the energy needs in the United States were met with oil, coal, and natural gas. After the crisis, the government began studying **renewable resources,** such as water and sunlight. Renewable fuels have a virtually unlimited supply and produce relatively little pollution. Modern technology is making great strides in reducing the cost of developing renewable energy.

Hydroelectricity. The most important source of renewable energy is moving water. The Romans

Shasta Dam harnesses water power in northern California.

Fossil Fuels. The most remarkable event in the history of energy was the harnessing of steam in the eighteenth century. Early steam engines used coal, but most engines now use petroleum. In 1884 scientists learned how to turn steam into a new type of energy—electricity. Coal, petroleum, or natural gas heats water to make steam; the steam turns wheels, called tur-bines, to generate electricity. Fossil fuels still provide 84.5 percent of the energy in the United States.

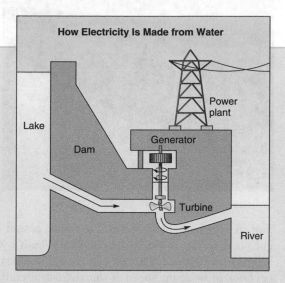

How Electricity Is Made from Water

invented the first water wheel two thousand years ago. The same year that scientists learned to make electricity from steam, they also learned to turn turbines with dammed water. The United States has now dammed most of its major rivers to take full advantage of the country's potential for hydroelectricity.

Biofuel. Plants have been used for fuel ever since Adam first built a fire. America has begun experimenting with waste products from farms and city garbage. Over a hundred electric power plants are fueled with municipal wastes, 40 percent of which is paper and its derivatives. In addition, over a thousand power facilities burn wood to generate electricity, mostly in the Northeast and Northwest.

Experimental "wind farm" in southern California

Geothermal. In some places, geothermal energy (heat from the earth) can produce enough steam to drive turbines or to heat houses. The United States accounts for most of the world's geothermal power, and most of that is produced at one installation located about sixty miles north of San Francisco. Geothermal energy is among the most polluting, releasing gases and corrosive chemicals.

Solar. The sun is the greatest source of energy in the universe. But scientists have not yet found an economical way to harness that energy. The cost of heating water directly by the sun is three times the current rate for conventional sources. The cost of converting sunlight directly to electricity on metal chips (solar cells) is almost ten times the cost of using fossil fuels. In isolated areas, solar heat is sometimes the best choice, but solar energy has a long way to go.

ENERGY SOURCE	COST OF 1 KILOWATT HOUR OF ELECTRICITY
Nonrenewable Energy	
Natural Gas	4¢
Petroleum	5¢
Coal	5¢
Nuclear	7¢
Renewable Energy	
Hydroelectric	3¢
Biofuel	7¢
Wind	8¢
Geothermal	8¢
Solar Heat	12¢
Solar Cell	35¢

Wind. One of the major untapped resources is wind. The Arabs introduced the windmill to Europe in the twelfth century. Modern windmills have been built in several windy areas of the world. Experts estimate that as much as 20 percent of U.S. electrical needs could be supplied by wind. But in most cases wind generators would take up too much area to be practical.

Renewable sources of energy are still too expensive to compete with fossil fuels. But costs of nonrenewable resources are climbing, and these resources will not last forever. Oil reserves may last another century, and coal another 250 years. One thing is certain: industries in a free market will buy the least expensive energy resource, whatever that becomes.

Land Transportation Merchants need ways to carry goods across land. Trade by caravan has a long history because it is relatively easy to travel across flat plains. The invention of the steam engine revolutionized land transportation. In the last half of the nineteenth century, steam locomotives began carrying large quantities of goods at amazing speeds across continents. Railroads provide reliable, year-round transportation and still account for around 40 percent of inland freight in the United States.

The invention of gasoline engines introduced a new mode of transportation. After World War II, cars and trucks outpaced railroads in importance. Nearly one-quarter of U.S. freight travels on trucks and other commercial vehicles. More dramatic is the almost complete reliance on cars for human transportation. Americans own more passenger cars than any other nation. They also have the lowest ratio of persons per car.

While few new rails have been laid in the past century, new roads are paved every day. The United States has more paved roads than any other country. However, paved roads are a more common sight in small, densely populated countries like Holland.

Air Transportation Airplanes are the fastest form of transportation on earth, and they are least

Trains often carry lumber from the Pacific Northwest.

limited by geographic features. The fastest passenger plane in the world is the *Concorde,* built by England and France. This jet can fly 1,550 miles per hour, or twice the speed of sound. Such aircraft have made once-popular ocean liners obsolete.

Because of its great expense, however, air travel is practical only for transporting people and small cargo, such as mail. The United States leads the world in commercial aviation. Its passenger planes fly nearly ten times more *passenger-miles* than any other country. (One passenger-mile represents one passenger transported one mile.) The United States also has the largest number of airports in the world.

Communication Communication is a form of transportation. It does not transport goods or people,

Common Transportation Statistics

COUNTRY	RAILROAD MILES	CARS	PERSONS PER CAR	MILES OF PAVED ROADS	DENSITY OF PAVED ROADS	AIRPLANE PASSENGER-MILES	AIRPORTS
Australia	23,947	9,000,000	2	503,000	0.17	38,000,000,000	400
Bangladesh	1,796	150,000	836	9,700	0.17	1,800,000,000	13
Brazil	17,027	12,000,000	14	1,030,000	0.31	20,000,000,000	139
Canada	43,579	13,200,000	2	180,000	0.05	27,000,000,000	301
China	36,266	2,900,000	417	620,100	0.17	31,900,000,000	113
Egypt	2,950	1,200,000	54	18,700	0.05	3,900,000,000	14
France	21,046	24,400,000	2	237,000	1.13	42,200,000,000	61
Germany	27,303	40,500,000	2	142,000	1.03	35,300,000,000	28
India	38,789	3,500,000	27	894,000	0.73	10,900,000,000	66
Italy	11,775	30,000,000	2	188,000	1.62	19,700,000,000	31
Japan	16,460	44,700,000	3	702,000	4.81	73,700,000,000	73
Mexico	12,772	14,600,000	7	66,000	0.87	11,900,000,000	83
Russia	95,634	10,500,000	14	461,000	0.07	40,500,000,000	75
United Kingdom	10,905	24,300,000	2	237,000	2.51	86,400,000,000	50
United States	149,040	135,000,000	2	2,210,000	0.60	510,600,000,000	834

but ideas and information. Communication industries can be divided into two broad categories, based on the medium used to pass on information: print media and electronic media.

Print Media Written language has been around for a long time, perhaps since Adam's day. Until two hundred years ago, private couriers carried most of the world's *personal communication,* such as letters and packages. Since then, national governments have taken over most of the world's postal services. The United States Postal Service delivers over two hundred billion pieces of mail each year, over one-third of the world total. The Universal Postal Union, established in 1875, regulates international mail to make sure that it is delivered. The United Nations now operates this agency.

In the early days, the primary means of **mass communication** were speeches and lectures given in one place to a large audience. The invention of the printing press in 1456 enabled individuals to share ideas and discoveries with the masses. The **publishing industry** prints the three major forms of publications: books, newspapers, and magazines.

European monarchs feared the power of publishers and strictly controlled what they could write.

A web press mass-produces textbooks.

Common Communication Statistics*

COUNTRY	NEWSPAPERS	PHONES	RADIOS	TELEVISIONS
Australia	258	500	1,250	500
Bangladesh	16	2	48	6
Brazil	45	77	400	208
Canada	189	588	1,000	667
China	23	33	185	188
Egypt	64	45	303	109
France	237	556	900	588
Germany	317	500	900	556
India	21	78	83	40
Italy	105	435	833	435
Japan	576	500	900	667
Mexico	113	100	256	164
Russia	267	170	345	370
United Kingdom	351	500	1,430	435
United States	228	625	2,000	835

* All figures per 1,000 population

After gaining independence in 1783, the United States became one of the first countries to guarantee freedom to the press. Steam engines made it possible to print "penny papers" quickly and cheaply in the early nineteenth century, making daily information available to even the poorest citizen.

Electronic Media In earlier times, people came up with some ingenious methods of rapid, long-distance communication, including flags and smoke signals. In the 1830s Samuel Morse discovered a whole new medium for communicating ideas—electricity. Sending messages through electronic impulses is called **telecommunications.** The three major modern telecommunications industries are telephone, radio, and television.

The telephone was patented in 1876 by the American inventor Alexander Graham Bell. It allowed people to talk directly, rather than in Morse code. In 1920 RCA (Radio Corporation of America) began the first commercial radio broadcasts. Regularly scheduled television broadcasts began in London sixteen years later. Radio and television have become the dominant mass media of the world. Unlike print media, they transmit sound and pictures that even illiterate adults and young children can enjoy. The United States has more telephones, radios, and televisions than any other country.

The "space age" brought radical changes to personal and mass communications. Since Russia launched the first satellite in 1957, over 4,600 satellites have been successfully boosted into space. Signals can be transmitted instantly around the world, without the need for cable connections. Computer modems allow people at any corner of the globe to exchange any form of media—text, sound, and pictures—with a keystroke. The old distinctions among communications industries are breaking down.

Trade

Someone needs to sell the products of primary and secondary industries. This is the job of *trade industries.* They buy and sell natural resources and manufactured goods. **Wholesale businesses** buy goods in large quantities from producers to sell in smaller quantities to other businesses. **Retail businesses** sell goods directly to the customer.

Finance

Modern industry would have been impossible without the rise of modern banking. Bankers, insurance companies, real estate agents, and investment firms help people to buy property, goods, and services. Finance industries make money available to help other industries grow.

General Services

Many other tertiary industries sell "support" services. They repair machines and also keep people healthy and happy while they do their work. They include maids, mechanics, engineers, lawyers, computer programmers, researchers, amusement park attendants, nurses, teachers, and zookeepers.

Government

The fifth form of tertiary industry is government. Most government employees, such as policemen, work for cities and states. The national government employs soldiers, lawmakers, judges, and *bureaucrats* (government officials who carry out the laws).

◎ SECTION REVIEW

1. What is another name for tertiary industries?
2. List the five kinds of tertiary industries.
3. What vehicle is most common for transporting (a) freight across the ocean, (b) freight within the United States, and (c) people within the United States?
4. What do we call the industry that prints information for mass communication?
5. What are the three types of telecommunications industries?

💡 Are department stores, such as Wal-Mart, retail or wholesale businesses?

THE WEALTH OF NATIONS

The earth's resources are not evenly divided among the nations. Each nation must make difficult choices about the best way to develop and distribute goods and services. The study of these choices is called **economics.**

Who Makes the Choices?

The Creator owns all the earth's resources. Mankind is merely His steward, placed in charge of the creation to develop its resources for His glory. Every system for making economic choices should be evaluated on this standard.

Capitalism It takes money to build industries. The term for this money is **capital.** Capital pays for the three ingredients of every industry: (1) raw materials, (2) workers (labor), and (3) buildings and equipment (*also* called capital).

During the Industrial Revolution, two basic economic systems arose for spending capital: capitalism and socialism. Most Western countries follow **capitalism.** Private individuals or corporations build most industries. They risk their own capital in hopes of making a profit. Anyone can start a business and attempt to profit financially. Another name for this economy is a **free market** because businesses freely

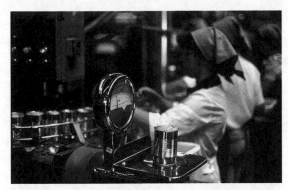

Both workers and capital are essential ingredients at a canning factory in Greece.

compete in the marketplace for buyers with little interference from the government.

The leaders who take risks and start businesses are known as *entrepreneurs,* or "captains of industry." In 1997 the wealthiest capitalist in the world was Bill Gates, an entrepreneur in the computer-chip industry, whose personal fortune exceeded $10 billion. He had more wealth than most kings.

Seest thou a man diligent in his business? he shall stand before kings; he shall not stand before mean men. (Prov. 22:29)

Socialism Many capitalists are infamous for their greed and selfishness. They do not make decisions to honor God or to serve their fellow man. In fact, they sometimes argue that serving their own self-interest is the best way to serve the interests of the rest of society. During the nineteenth century, opponents of capitalism developed an alternative system called **socialism.**

Under socialism, the government owns the major industries and promises to make production decisions for the welfare of society. In this *command economy,* the government determines where industries are built and what they produce. In the most extreme form of socialism, called *communism,* the government owns everything. In socialist economies few businessmen are willing to take risks with capital because the profit goes to the government.

The number of socialist governments mushroomed in the first half of the twentieth century. But socialist leaders ended up making choices to enrich themselves at the expense of their own people. Making choices to benefit the group proved just as wrong as making choices for selfish interests. Both systems ignored God.

Mixed Economies Between 1989 and 1991, socialist governments fell like dominoes in Eastern Europe and the Soviet Union. Most of these nations adopted a *mixed economy* that combines elements of capitalism and socialism. Private citizens can own property and businesses, but the government closely regulates their choices.

How Nations Measure Wealth (GDP)

Most people think wealth is the ownership of things, such as cattle, corn, and coins. But real wealth is the ability to *produce* new things. Consider the biblical example of Jacob. He was wealthy, not because of the size of his flocks and herds, but because the animals produced plenty of offspring each year to feed and clothe his growing family. The more a country produces each year, the more things its people can eat and enjoy that year.

The most common measurement of the wealth of nations is **Gross Domestic Product (GDP).** GDP is "the monetary value of all the goods and services produced for sale within a country's borders over the course of a year." Economists add up the value of the products produced by all the primary, secondary, and tertiary industries. Look at the definition of GDP again. It is the *gross* (total) value of all *products* (goods and services) made by *domestic* (home) workers in one year.

The total GDP means very little, however, until it is compared to the number of workers who produced those products. A more meaningful measurement is **per capita GDP** (the average value of products produced by each person in the country). This measurement shows how much each person is producing each year. In other words, it shows each worker's *productivity,* on average.

COUNTRY	POPULATION	GDP	PER CAPITA GDP
Bangladesh	125,000,000	$145,000,000,000	$1,130
Luxembourg	422,000	$10,000,000,000	$24,800

This chart compares the productivity of Bangladesh and Luxembourg. The GDP of Bangladesh is much greater than that of Luxembourg. At first glance, Bangladesh seems more productive. After you consider the number of people who produce the goods, however, you can see the low productivity of Bangladesh's industries. Bangladesh has three hundred times as many people as Luxembourg. Each Luxembourger produces goods and services valued over twenty times greater than a Bangladeshi.

A high per capita GDP does not always mean a country has a lot of industry or that the average worker makes a lot of money. Several rich countries, such as the United Arab Emirates and Qatar, have a high per capita GDP because primary industries ship valuable exports (oil in this case), but rich sheiks and bureaucrats pocket the money. The average citizen receives little benefit from the oil sales.

SECTION REVIEW

1. What measurement shows the productivity of each person in a nation?
2. What is another name for money that is invested in business equipment?
3. Explain the main difference between capitalism and socialism.
   ♀ A nation with 12 million people produces $20 billion in goods and $4 billion in services each year. What is its per capita GDP?

Distribution of Wealth Among Nations

Socialist countries view the world as a pie with a limited supply of wealth that must be cut into equal pieces to feed everyone. They imitate Robin Hood, who stole from the rich and gave back to the poor. In truth, the world's supply of wealth is

Countries with the Highest per Capita GDPs

1. United States		$27,900
2. Luxembourg		$24,800
3. Norway		$24,500
4. Canada		$24,400
5. United Arab Emirates		$24,000
6. Singapore		$22,900
7. Switzerland		$22,400
8. Liechtenstein		$22,300
9. Australia		$22,100
10. Denmark		$21,700
11. Japan		$21,300
12. Qatar		$20,820

unlimited. Industrial countries do not steal to become rich; they make new wealth that did not exist before. They turn iron ore into automobiles, silicon into computer chips. Their industries just keep making bigger pies and more of them.

Developed and Developing Countries The effective use of raw materials, labor, and capital is called *development*. Economists actually have a way to measure the value that manufacturers add to raw materials. If the original metals in a sports car are worth $500 and the final car is worth $30,500, then the **value added** is $30,000. The United States is responsible for nearly one-third of the world's value added by manufacture (over $1 trillion each year).

Development translates into power. Countries with productive economies can afford to buy weapons and influence neighbors with their money. Seven countries produce over three-fourths of all value added by manufacture. The leaders of this **Group of 7 (G-7)** meet each year to resolve economic and political disputes.

Members of the Group of 7 are **developed countries.** Developed countries have a wide range of industries that take full advantage of their people's skills. Most citizens enjoy the financial benefits of this development, reflected in a high per capita GDP.

Why are China and several other big nations not accepted in the Group of 7? They have a high national GDP and many factories, but they are considered **developing countries.** Their GDP is high by

Developed and Developing Countries

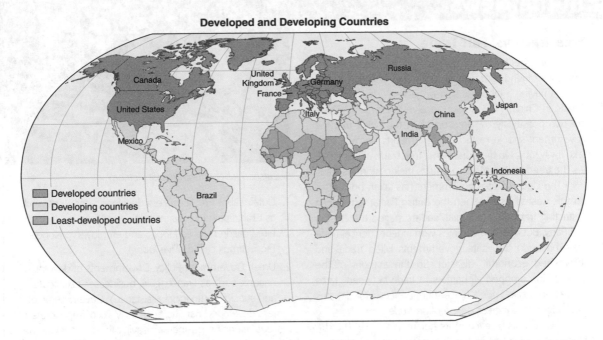

Developed countries
Developing countries
Least-developed countries

virtue of their large population, but the per capita GDP is very low. These developing countries have not yet taken full advantage of their people's skills.

Division of Labor The best evidence of a nation's development is "division of labor." This concept is illustrated in *The Wealth of Nations,* the most influential book on capitalism ever written. Adam Smith opens the book with a famous description of how ten workers in a pin factory, each specializing in a different stage of pin making, can produce forty-eight thousand pins a day, but individuals working separately can produce only a few dozen pins at most. The more that workers can use their unique, God-given talents for specialized jobs, the more productive a nation will be.

The division of labor is highly sophisticated in developed nations. Rather than everyone working on subsistence farms, workers can choose from among hundreds of thousands of different occupations. Most of these jobs are in tertiary, or service, industries. Developing nations, on the other hand, have few jobs available in service industries. The chart shows an example of the difference between the labor force in Bangladesh and Luxembourg.

Countries with the Highest GDPs

COUNTRY	GDP (BILLIONS OF DOLLARS)	POPULATION	PER CAPITA GDPs
1. United States*	$7,265	267,955,000	$27,900
2. China	$3,500	1,210,005,000	$2,500
3. Japan*	$2,679	125,717,000	$21,300
4. Germany*	$1,452	84,068,000	$17,900
5. India	$1,409	967,613,000	$1,500
6. France*	$1,173	58,040,000	$18,670
7. United Kingdom*	$1,138	58,610,000	$19,500
8. Italy*	$1,089	57,534,000	$18,700
9. Brazil	$977	164,511,000	$6,100
10. Russia	$796	147,987,000	$5,300
11. Mexico	$721	97,563,000	$7,700
12. Indonesia	$711	209,774,000	$3,500
13. Canada*	$694	29,123,000	$24,400

belongs to G-7. Russia is an unofficial member.

COUNTRY	AGRICULTURAL LABOR	INDUSTRIAL LABOR	SERVICE LABOR
Bangladesh	65%	14%	21%
Luxembourg	3%	32%	65%

In the News

Free Trade vs. Fair Trade

Your father has just lost his job making jackets. Meanwhile, your friends are rushing to the mall because a retail store is having a fabulous sale on jackets. The labels say "Made in China." How do you resolve this tension? There are two possibilities. *Protectionism* is the belief that the government should restrict foreign imports because they take away jobs. On the other hand, **free trade** allows retailers the freedom to sell any products their customers want.

The United States government has taken both sides on this heated issue. When the British Parliament began restricting free trade, colonial leaders staged the Boston Tea Party. But after the colonies won independence, trade wars between the state governments killed trade and threatened economic disaster. So the authors of the Constitution dropped all barriers to trade between states (called *domestic trade*). Since then, protectionist debates have raged in Congress over *foreign trade*.

Protectionism reached its height in the 1920s. The United States raised a high wall of tariffs to protect its industries from European industries, which began rebuilding after the ravages of World War I. The tariffs ended international trade and hurt the economy. Since World War II free trade has become popular among capitalist nations. They held several rounds of talks to draw up rules for trade. These rules became known as the General Agreement on Tariffs and Trade (GATT). Tariffs fell from 40 percent to 5 percent, and the volume of worldwide trade exploded.

Countries with common interests have been negotiating *regional free trade agreements,* which drop trade restrictions within a region but keep a wall of protective tariffs against outsiders. The earliest and most far-reaching regional agreement was the European Union (EU), whose roots go back to 1951. Its members have torn down trade barriers within Western Europe, while keeping up barriers to Eastern Europe and Asia. The Association of Southeast Asian Nations (ASEAN) was formed in 1967. In 1993 Mexico joined Canada and the United States in the North American Free Trade Agreement (NAFTA).

But Americans became increasingly disillusioned with low tariffs. Most businessmen were willing to compete in a free market, but not if the foreigners had unfair advantages. Supporters of *fair trade* argued that the United States was losing jobs and exports because of the following practices.

Sweatshop labor in Communist Vietnam

1. Unfair Labor Practices. Less developed countries, such as China, paid low wages to workers *(cheap labor),* hired children *(child labor),* and employed prisoners (sometimes called *slave labor*).

2. Unfair Government Policy. Governments of developed nations, such as France, gave businesses *tax breaks* and *subsidies* (financial assistance). Governments of less developed nations, such as Mexico, imposed *few regulations* on businesses, saving them money at the cost of poor working conditions and pollution.

3. Unfair Pricing. Businesses in Japan and other developed countries sometimes *dumped* products, such as computer chips, at prices below costs. Their low prices were designed to drive American companies out of business.

4. Piracy. The worst practice was the theft of ideas and products. Foreign businesses made copies of designer clothes, such as Levi's jeans, and put *false labels* on them. Other businesses made *unlicensed copies* of music, computer programs, and books without paying royalties.

In 1987 the United States and 117 other countries entered a new round of GATT negotiations to find a way to stop these unfair trade practices. Seven years later they concluded the largest trade negotiations in history by establishing the **World Trade Organization (WTO),** a permanent body with one representative for every nation. The WTO replaced GATT. Individual countries no longer had the final say in their trade policies. In essence, free trade turned into "managed fair trade" under the direction of international bureaucrats.

What issues are at stake on each side of this debate? Do you think the United States should withdraw from the WTO?

The division between developed and developing countries is not always so clear-cut. Brazil, which has a growing number of industrial and service industries, does not really belong in the same category as the poor agricultural country of Bangladesh. The world's poorest countries—with a per capita GDP around $2,000 or less—belong in a separate category of "underdeveloped" or "least developed" countries. Unfortunately, these countries have little promise of development in the next few decades.

The Hope of Prosperity What makes some countries rich and others poor? This is not an easy question to answer.

Possessing natural resources is not essential to riches. Japan's industries have thrived even though its islands lack natural resources. On the other hand, the Democratic Republic of Congo's mines are rich in resources, but its per capita GDP is one of the lowest in the world.

A far more important factor in wealth is labor. People are a resource, not a drain on the economy. The more hard workers a country has, the more possibilities it has for creating new wealth. Hard work includes a willingness to study, to learn, and to try new things. The Bible clearly states that stealing, cheating, and mistreating others diminishes wealth, but God blesses hard work.

Wealth gotten by vanity shall be diminished: but he that gathereth by labour shall increase. (Prov. 13:11)

Proverbs also states that the Lord blesses righteous living. The word *righteousness* means "following a rule or standard." The main factor in wealth is God, who blesses righteous living and judges sinners. The question of the wealth of nations, which has puzzled economists for centuries, is best answered this way.

Righteousness exalteth a nation: but sin is a reproach to any people. (Prov. 14:34)

So why do wicked men and wicked countries prosper? The Lord exalts whom He will. Babylon was "a golden cup in the Lord's hand" (Jer. 51:7), destroying Jerusalem in 586 B.C. and carrying the Jews away as captives. But the ill-gotten wealth of the wicked Babylonians was fleeting. God eventually judged this empire for its sin. No nation will escape divine judgment in the end.

Blessed is the nation whose God is the Lord. (Ps. 33:12)

While "the love of money is the root of all evil" (I Tim. 6:10), money itself is not evil. Wealth—and the ability to enjoy it—is a gift of God (Eccles. 5:18-20). The Lord gave mankind resources to serve God and others, not to serve himself. True wealth is found in heaven, not on earth, and is available to everyone (Matt. 6:19-20).

Trade Wars

Some countries have tried to produce everything they need without buying or selling from other countries. In 1961 the Communist leader in Albania isolated his country in every way possible. As a result, Albania became the poorest country in Europe. In contrast, the world's wealthiest nations are also the biggest trading nations.

She is like the merchants' ships; she bringeth her food from afar. . . . She maketh fine linen, and selleth it; and delivereth girdles unto the merchant. (Prov. 31:14, 24)

God meant for people to trade. The virtuous woman of Proverbs 31 bought and sold goods to provide for the needs of her house. Throughout history, nations have depended on trade to acquire the raw materials that they lack. The United States, though rich in resources, must import 100 percent of its bauxite, manganese, and graphite. It also must import most of its industrial diamonds (98%), platinum (88%), tungsten (84%), chromium (82%), tin (81%), and nickel (64%). Without these metals, assembly lines for airplanes and other critical industries would come to a halt.

Trade is essential for more than exchanging raw materials. Every industry needs a **market**—people or businesses that buy their products. **Exports** are the primary and secondary goods shipped to other countries. **Imports** are all the goods received from other countries. Countries measure international trade in terms of the monetary value of exports and imports. The difference between these two values is called the *balance of trade.*

Occasionally countries have disputes over trade. Sometimes conflicts lead to war, but countries have other weapons at their disposal. **Tariffs** are taxes on imports and exports. If the United States places a high tariff on Japanese automobiles, sales of Japanese cars drop and domestic sales increase. Another weapon is an *embargo* (ban on exports). Arab nations used an oil embargo in the 1970s to drive up the price of oil and to hurt the U.S. economy.

SECTION REVIEW

1. What is another name for the least developed countries?
2. What term is used for the people who want to buy a product?
3. What are import and export taxes called?
   In what sense is every nation a "developing country"?

REVIEW 4

Can You Define These Terms?

dominion mandate
industry
primary industry
subsistence farmer
cash crop
commercial farmer
nomadic herding
natural resource
mineral
metal
bauxite
alloy
fertilizer

fossil fuel
coal
petroleum
natural gas
secondary industry
raw material
manufacturing
Industrial Revolution
technology
crude oil
petrochemicals
tertiary industry
infrastructure

kilowatt hour (kWh)
nonrenewable resource
renewable resource
mass communication
publishing industry
telecommunications
wholesale business
retail business
economics
capital
capitalism
free market
socialism

Gross Domestic Product (GDP)
per capita GDP
value added
Group of 7 (G-7)
developed country
developing country
market
export
import
free trade
World Trade Organization (WTO)
tariff

How Much Do You Remember?

1. Label each of the following as primary, secondary, or tertiary industries.
   a. a local drug store
   b. a peach orchard
   c. a toaster factory
   d. a petroleum refinery
   e. a hot dog stand at a ball game
   f. a copper mine
   g. a local fire department
   h. a commercial airline company
2. What three fertilizers are most important for crops?
3. List the three fossil fuels. What state is each found in?
4. Name five products taken from petroleum.
5. Give the leading product in each category (ranked by tons).
   a. precious metals
   b. common metals
   c. building materials
   d. fertilizer
   e. fossil fuels
6. Give the three phases of the Industrial Revolution and their approximate time periods.
7. List the five major categories of tertiary industries. Give an example of each.
8. How did railroads change transportation? Why have passenger trains declined?
9. Give three examples of mass communication.
10. Why does China have a high GDP but a low per capita GDP?
11. What is the most important factor in the wealth of a nation: raw materials, capital, or labor?

What Do You Think?

1. Name the occupations of five adult friends or relatives. Tell whether their jobs are part of a primary, secondary, or tertiary industry.
2. Why is concrete such a useful building material?
3. How would your life change if God had not made petroleum?
4. What technology was not around when you were younger?
5. What is the most common industry in your area?
6. Why are some countries poor even though they have valuable raw materials?
7. Read Exodus 34:21. Explain why this command was difficult to obey. What was God teaching about man's first priority in life?
8. Read Revelation 13, which predicts one world economy controlled by a tyrant. What characteristics of modern society are making this possible? Does this danger mean Christians should oppose advances in industry and technology?

CHAPTER 5

SOCIETY

A man's life consisteth not in the abundance of the things which he possesseth. (Luke 12:15)

So far you have studied the physical world and how people meet their physical needs. But there is an unseen spiritual world that is far more important to study if you are to understand man's place in the world. The physical world and all its riches will pass away, but the spiritual world will endure forever.

The Lord made Adam in His image and gave him an eternal soul. His main purpose in life was to walk with God and to serve Him. However, he was not supposed to serve God alone. The Lord declared that Adam would need the help of other people.

It is not good that the man should be alone; I will make him an help meet for him. (Gen. 2:18)

Geography includes the study of **society,** the relationships among human beings. God is explicit about the purpose of society. In all earthly relationships, people are to reflect the image of their Creator, who is Father and King. Society is an outward manifestation of the unseen spiritual world.

The development of society is an integral part of man's duty to subdue the earth. The Lord told the first couple, Adam and Eve, to fill the earth with people. The Lord repeated this **cultural mandate** to Noah and all his descendants.

Be fruitful, and multiply, and replenish the earth. (Gen. 1:28; 9:1)

CULTURE

When people hear the word *culture,* they usually think of daily life—clothing, food, sports, customs, music, literature, art, and crafts. But **culture** involves much more. It is society's total "way of life," including all its traditions and institutions. *Traditions* are the products of human thought and deeds that society passes down from one generation to the next. *Institutions* are the formal organizations that society uses to transmit traditions.

Culture Regions

As people spread over the earth, they developed many different cultures. The term *culture* refers not only to human society as a whole but also

Population of the World Culture Regions

REGION	POPULATION	AREA (SQ. MI.)	POPULATION DENSITY (PER SQ. MI.)
Northern America	297,000,000	7,500,000	40
Latin America	496,000,000	8,800,000	56
Western Europe	387,000,000	1,400,000	276
Central Eurasia	436,000,000	9,304,000	47
Asia	3,202,000,000	8,005,000	400
Middle East	291,000,000	2,838,000	104
Africa	685,000,000	11,315,000	61
Oceania	29,000,000	3,300,000	9

to the distinctive way of doing things that is easily recognizable and associated with definable regions or groups of people. A **culture region** is a human society that shares the same basic culture.

Maps make it easier to study complex information about people, just as they make it easier to study physical relief. The *culture map* at the beginning of this unit, pages 58-59, shows the eight main culture regions of the world.

While individual countries change names, grow, shrink, or cease to exist, the world culture regions remain fairly constant. If you learn the characteristics of these regions, you will be well equipped to understand events in your lifetime, no matter what happens to individual countries.

The boundaries of the world regions are similar to the continents, but not the same. What differences can you find? The main exception is on the world's largest continent, Eurasia. It is divided into four distinct culture regions. Two of these regions, *Central* Eurasia and the *Middle* East, sit at the crossroads of the world. Both have been the focus of conflict throughout history.

In this textbook a separate unit is devoted to each world culture region. Christians study other cultures for several reasons: to praise the Creator for the gifts He has given to men, to profit from the good example of others, and to beware of bad examples. Though sin has marred God's image, every culture reflects some of His attributes, including an appreciation of beauty, concern for order, a moral sense, and creative genius. You need to be looking for these spiritual things as you study the cultures of the world.

Within each world region are many **subregions** that display increasingly similar characteristics. Northern America, the first region you will study, consists of two large subregions, the United States and Canada. These subregions are further

Colombian woman

Scottish man

Filipino girl

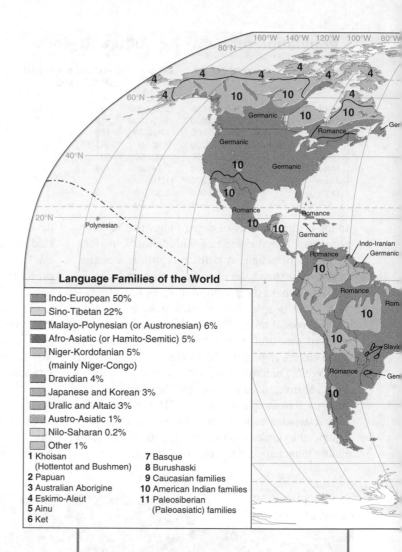

Language Families of the World

- Indo-European 50%
- Sino-Tibetan 22%
- Malayo-Polynesian (or Austronesian) 6%
- Afro-Asiatic (or Hamito-Semitic) 5%
- Niger-Kordofanian 5% (mainly Niger-Congo)
- Dravidian 4%
- Japanese and Korean 3%
- Uralic and Altaic 3%
- Austro-Asiatic 1%
- Nilo-Saharan 0.2%
- Other 1%

1 Khoisan (Hottentot and Bushmen)
2 Papuan
3 Australian Aborigine
4 Eskimo-Aleut
5 Ainu
6 Ket
7 Basque
8 Burushaski
9 Caucasian families
10 American Indian families
11 Paleosiberian (Paleoasiatic) families

broken down into even smaller sub-regions within the chapters.

Language—the Foundation of Culture

After the Flood, the descendants of Noah had one language and one culture. God commanded them to spread over the earth, but they wanted to stay together in a single society. So they moved down from the mountains of Ararat to build a city on the fertile plain of the Euphrates River (Gen. 11:1-4). The people began building a worship center to promote their wicked, man-centered culture.

Behold, the people is one, and they have all one language; . . . and now nothing will be restrained from them, which they have imagined to do. Go to, let us go down, and there confound their language, that they may not understand one another's speech. (Gen. 11:6-7)

Babel's man-centered system of thinking is called **humanism.** Humanists believe that humans can solve their own problems and bring world peace by working together. Humanists ignore man's basic problem, which is not conflict among men but spiritual conflict with God. Everyone faces the wrath of God and will be cast into an everlasting hell unless he is reconciled to his Creator. In love and mercy, God visited the city at Babel and divided the people's language so that no single culture would rule the world.

God did not scatter people randomly. The descendants of Shem, Ham, and Japheth spread abroad "after their families, after their tongues, in their lands, after their nations" (Gen 10:5, 20, 31). Each family spoke a common language and traveled as a unit. These families became the founders of the ancient culture regions. The Bible gives a catalog of these regions in Genesis 10.

Let's Go Exploring

1. What language family appears on every continent?
2. List all the language families that appear on the continent of Africa.
3. Which continent has the largest number of language families? How many?
4. Look at the eight culture regions on pp. 58-59. List what appears to be the main language family in each region.
5. Look at the physical map on p. 1 and the climate map on pp. 48-49. What climates and land features are most often associated with "other" languages? Why?

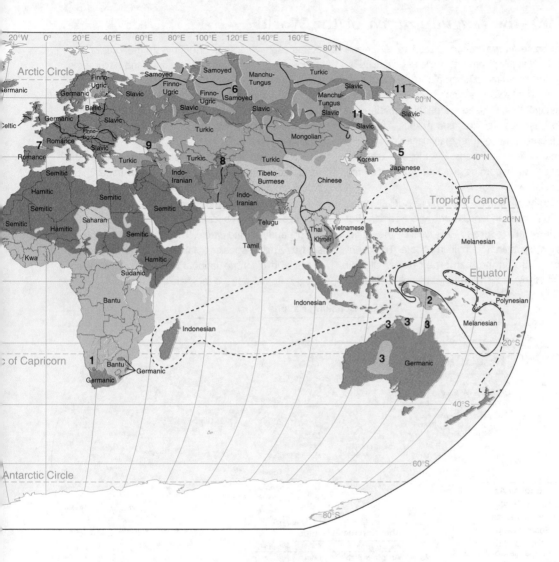

Spoken Languages Wherever mountains, oceans, and deserts prevented people from talking to one another, new languages and cultures developed. Approximately sixty-six hundred languages are spoken in the world today. Agreeing on a total is difficult, however. Speech patterns within a single language often vary considerably, in which case each speech pattern is called a **dialect.** But sometimes different languages are so similar that they are mutually understandable—speakers of Portuguese can understand Spanish with little difficulty.

Linguists recognize ten major **language families,** groups of languages that share many common characteristics. Ninety-nine percent of all people speak a language under one of the ten major families. The most prominent is the Indo-European family. Indo-Europeans account for half of the world's total population. Linguists believe the Indo-European family originated in a region somewhere between India and Europe. The modern boundaries of this and other language families reflect mankind's fascinating history of exploration, wars, and migration.

89

English—the *Lingua Franca* of the World

The phrase *lingua franca* is Latin for "Frankish language." It originally referred to the language used by the court of the Frankish emperor Charlemagne (742?–814). The word has come to describe a common language that is used by people of different nations in business, science, and politics. Since the Tower of Babel, many different languages have been used in international relations. But the one that has come closest to becoming a *lingua franca* of the world is English.

Three other languages have more *native speakers* than English—Mandarin, Hindi, and Spanish. But English is the leading *second language* of the world, learned by more than 157 million people. The countries colored blue on the map expect nearly all their students to study English in public school. Over forty countries have also made English the *official language* used in government meetings and documents. India, which has sixteen major languages spoken by over one million people each, has made English an "associate official" language. The United Nations uses two main languages for its primary documents— English and French.

Native peoples in many British colonies learned a simplified version of English for work and trade. These *pidgin languages* were a colorful combination of local words and English words with a basic grammar. In some cases, pidgin became the native language of the people and is called *creole.* The words for many items sold by English-speaking nations, such as *telephone, jeans,* and *cigarette,* appear in nearly all other languages, from Japanese to Swahili.

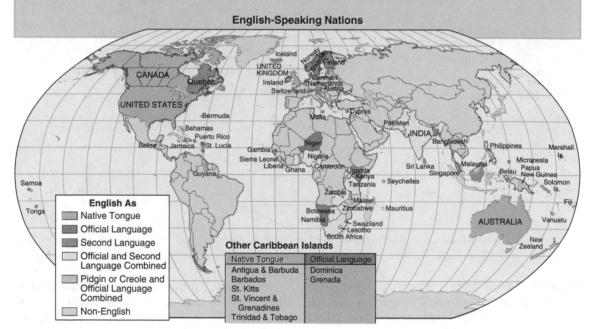

English-Speaking Nations

Language families are divided into *language subfamilies.* For example, "Germanic" is a major subfamily of the Indo-European family. It includes German, English, Swedish, and Norwegian. Another major subfamily is the "Romance" languages, descended from Latin—the language of the ancient Romans. It includes Spanish, French, and Italian.

Written Languages No one is born with culture. It is taught. Language is the primary instrument for transmitting culture to the next generation. The ability to speak and to reason distinguishes man from the animal world. Man's speech imitates his Maker, who communicates through His written Word, the Bible, and through His living Word, Jesus Christ (Heb. 1:1-2).

Most-Spoken Languages

LANGUAGE	NUMBER OF SPEAKERS (MILLIONS)
Mandarin (China)	999
English	487
Hindi (India)	457
Spanish	401
Russian	280
Bengali (India)	204
Arabic	195
Portuguese	186
Malay-Indonesian	164
French	126
Japanese	126
German	124

Literacy is an important goal in every country, including Indonesia.

Primitive societies rely on word of mouth to transmit culture. But advanced societies have written languages to keep more accurate and complete records. The first known written language was developed along the Euphrates River. The form of writing called *cuneiform* made letters by pressing mud tablets with a wedged reed, called a stylus. Writing allows the rapid spread of culture.

Few people had enough time and money to learn how to read and write until recently. Ever since a German named Gutenberg invented moveable type in the fifteenth century, the opportunity to read and write has spread to the common people. The complexity of modern, industrial society has made literacy a necessity. (**Literacy** is the ability to read and write a language.) Before 1900, less than 10 percent of the world's population were literate. Now around 75 percent of the world's people are literate. Most developed countries have a literacy rate of over 95 percent.

SECTION REVIEW

1. What is culture?
2. Name the eight culture regions of the world.
3. Why is language the foundation of culture?
4. What is a language family? Which language family has the most speakers?
5. Why is literacy important in modern societies?
   💡 Is humanism a religion?

Institutions That Transmit Culture

Every society has many institutions that transmit culture. The proper goal of all institutions is to help people to glorify God. But Adam's sin separated man from God, and it marred every relationship among mankind. Ever since then, society has struggled to subdue not only the earth but also the evil in human hearts.

By studying cultural institutions we can see how well society is accomplishing God's purposes. God has put in every heart a knowledge of the spiritual world and of man's obligations to the Creator (Rom. 1:19-20; 2:14-15). Man is without excuse.

But human institutions have diverged from their purpose of glorifying God to two extremes: glorifying the group or glorifying the individual. Although world culture regions have many differences, in general, Eastern institutions worship the group, and Western institutions worship the individual.

The Family   The foundation of society is the family. The Lord instituted the home in the Garden of Eden, before sin ever entered the world. He created Eve to be Adam's "helpmeet." At their marriage, the Lord gave them the pattern of a godly home.

Therefore shall a man leave his father and his mother, and shall cleave unto his wife: and they shall be one flesh. (Gen. 2:24)

Family life teaches traits that both parents and children need—how to obey, how to serve, how to lead, and how to love. Most importantly, parents pass on wisdom to their children. The apostle Paul instructed fathers to bring up their children "in the nurture and admonition of the Lord" (Eph. 6:4).

Every society honors the central role of the family. Western societies focus on the **nuclear family—**

a man, his wife, and their children. Eastern societies typically focus on the **extended family**—the nuclear family plus grandparents, uncles, aunts, and cousins. Every balanced society honors elders and nurtures children, and it emphasizes the central role of the parents.

But fallen societies have taken family responsibilities to extremes. Eastern cultures often worship ancestors, and husbands seek more than one wife *(polygamy)*. In contrast, Western cultures overemphasize the rights of individuals, leading to broken families—aborted and illegitimate children in the name of womens' rights, and divorce in the name of human rights.

Religion To love God is man's true purpose in life. Jesus said that this Great Commandment should guide all other human behavior (Matt. 22:37).

Broadly speaking, *religion* is a person's set of beliefs about his purpose in life. Everything he does, whether he thinks about it or not, is designed to accomplish that purpose. Most people belong to an organized religion. It provides them with both a set of beliefs and a formal code of conduct that regulates how members should live and worship together. Religion guides all other expressions of

Religions of the World

RELIGION	NUMBER OF MEMBERS
Christian	1,927,953,000
Roman Catholic	968,025,000
Protestant	466,397,000
Orthodox	217,948,000
Other (Mormon, etc.)	275,583,000
Eastern	1,489,313,000
Hindu	780,547,000
Buddhist	323,894,000
Chinese	230,391,000
Japanese	2,844,000
Other (Sikh, Baha'i, etc.)	151,637,000
Islamic	1,100,000,000
Sunni	913,000,000
Shiite	176,000,000
Other	11,000,000
Tribal	121,967,000
Jewish	14,117,000

culture, including holidays, dress, and even food preparation.

The world's cultures have fallen from the worship of the one true God into different forms of idolatry. Eastern cultures tend to worship the state, or the group. You may remember the story of Nebuchadnezzar, who built a golden idol and demanded that all his subjects worship him. Many Eastern cultures, such as Islamic nations, still have an "official religion" that society expects its members to follow. Communist nations in the Far East, such as North Korea, have developed "leadership cults" that worship the ruler as the savior of the people.

Western cultures tend more toward religious liberty. (For example, the ancient Greeks chastised Alexander the Great when he made himself a god to solidify his rule over the conquered Persians.) Western societies allow freedom of worship as long as each religion obeys general public laws. Unfortunately, Western governments tend toward radical individualism, failing to govern the conduct of their people by moral standards of right and wrong. Too often these governments allow every man to do as he chooses.

The religion map on pages 94-95 shows the religions that now dominate the world. People ask, "There are so many religions. How can I know which one is true?" God instituted only one religious institution—the church. God's church is open to people of every culture who turn to Jesus Christ as their only hope of salvation. Christianity alone offers salvation freely by grace based on Christ's finished work two thousand years ago at Calvary. All other religions are human inventions that demand human works in order to enter heaven.

I am the way, the truth, and the life: no man cometh unto the Father, but by me. (John 14:6)

Statistics usually label as *Christian* anyone who believes that Jesus Christ is Lord. They do not attempt to make the distinctions that Christ Himself makes. Christ says that many people who call Him "Lord" and do amazing works in His name will be cast into everlasting fire (Matt. 7:21-23). Christ

Missions

The Great Commission

"Does God want me to be a missionary?" Many young Christians ask themselves that question. The "Missions" boxes in this book will survey different types of missionary service. They also show how a knowledge of geography prepares Christians to serve God, whether by becoming a missionary or by supporting missionaries.

There are three reasons every Christian should be willing to go to the mission field. First, God has commanded His people to be witnesses for Him. Christ said that if you love Him, you will obey His commands (John 14:15). He repeated the *Great Commission* five times to stress its importance: Matthew 28:18-20; Mark 16:15-16; Luke 24:46-48; John 20:21; and Acts 1:8.

Second, God's people show their love for Jesus by following His example. Throughout His ministry, Jesus shared the gospel (Matt. 4:17). The early apostles followed that example. "For the love of Christ constraineth us," Paul said, to be "ambassadors for Christ," pleading with sinners to be reconciled to God (II Cor. 5:14-21).

Third, God's people show love for others by leading them to safety (Jude 22-23). Every year over thirty million people die, many never having heard the gospel. North America has only 5 percent of the world population but probably half of all Christian workers. If more Christians went abroad, more people would have an opportunity to hear the gospel and to escape eternity in hell.

In one sense, every Christian is supposed to be a missionary. Every Christian has the responsibility to share the gospel and to maintain a good testimony (Col. 4:5-6). However, Christians often distinguish *home missions*

Even high school students have opportunity to take short-term mission trips, such as these teens helping in Jamaica.

(missions in one's own country) and *foreign missions.* According to Acts 1:8, the first Christian missionaries began at home in Jerusalem and Judea and then reached out to their neighbor Samaria and on to the farthest parts of the world.

But ye shall receive power, after that the Holy Ghost is come upon you: and ye shall be witnesses unto me both in Jerusalem, and in all Judea, and in Samaria, and unto the uttermost part of the earth. (Acts 1:8)

Full-time missionaries have a deep love for and desire to obey the Holy Spirit and His Word. The initial prompting to this type of service is often called the "call to missions." Memorize Acts 1:8 and ask the Lord whether He is calling you to missions.

---

said of "Christian" religions that twist His fundamental teachings,

In vain they do worship me, teaching for doctrines the commandments of men. (Matt. 15:9)

Volunteer Community Organizations The community gives individuals a sense of identity and purpose greater than self. Societies have many community organizations, where people

make most of their friends and spend most of their time. These volunteer organizations include businesses, schools, churches, sports teams, and concert halls. They allow people an opportunity to fulfill their most basic responsibility—to love their neighbors.

For all the law is fulfilled in one word, even in this; Thou shalt love thy neighbor as thyself. (Gal. 5:14)

The Nation After God divided the languages at Babel, nations arose to transmit culture. A **nation** is a large group of people with a common history and language who have developed a strong sense of identity. Even after a nation loses control of its homeland, it often retains its identity. For example, Israel remained a nation even after foreigners drove the Hebrews out of the Promised Land. Today we often call the Kurdish people of the Middle East a "nation," though they are divided among five separate countries.

> *[God] hath made of one blood all nations of men for to dwell on all the face of the earth, and hath determined the times before appointed, and the bounds of their habitation. (Acts 17:26)*

Definition of Terms According to this verse in Acts, God has directed the settling of all the ethnic groups, or nations, of the world. The Greek word translated "nation" is *ethnos,* from which we get the word *ethnic.* The English word *nation* comes from a Latin root meaning "born." All these words share the idea of a "common birth."

Nation is often confused with related words. *Nation* refers primarily to people, but *country* refers to the land of the people, and *state* refers to the institution that governs the people. A *tribe* is a large group who share a common ancestor and is usually governed by elders.

A **nation-state** is a nation of people that has established its own government, or state. When one nation conquers other nations beyond its borders, it creates an **empire.** Governments that rule over many nations are called *multinational states.*

Religions of the World

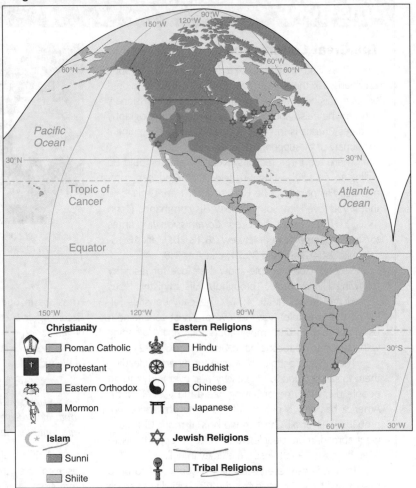

Political Maps A *political map* shows the boundaries that a state has drawn around its people regardless of common culture. The world map is divided into 185 states. Each state has *sovereignty,* the unlimited authority to run affairs within its own borders. Sovereign states come in all shapes and sizes. The smallest is Vatican City, situated on six acres inside the city of Rome, Italy. The largest state is Russia, which spans two continents and encompasses about one hundred ethnic groups.

A few territories that claim independence and run their own governments are not officially recognized by most other states. The Chinese island of

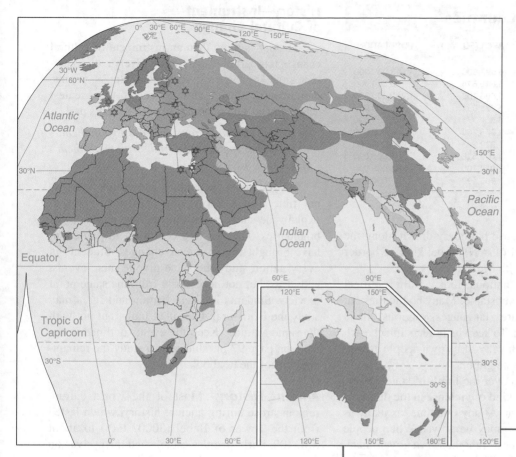

Let's Go Exploring

1. How many Jewish centers are located in North America?

2. Do any major religions appear on every continent? If so, which one?

3. Which continent has the largest number of religions?

4. Which branch of Islam covers the least area?

Look at the eight culture regions on pp. 58-59. List what appears to be the main religion in each.

Taiwan is the best example. Even though Taiwan has run its own affairs for over fifty years and has one of the biggest economies in the world, China refuses to allow it a seat in the United Nations, and most nations have sided with China.

Political boundaries are a fundamental feature of culture maps because they mark the limit of a state's authority over the lives of its people. People in two neighboring countries may share many culture traits, but they follow completely different laws. Some political boundaries follow the twists and turns of *natural boundaries,* such as rivers and mountains. Other **geometric boundaries** connect geometric points or follow lines of latitude or longitude. Most of the U.S. border with

Ten Largest Countries

COUNTRY	AREA (SQ. MI.)	POPULATION
1. Russia	6,592,800	148,000,000
2. Canada	3,849,674	29,000,000
3. China	3,696,100	1,210,000,000
4. United States	3,675,031	268,000,000
5. Brazil	3,300,171	165,000,000
6. Australia	2,966,200	18,000,000
7. India	1,222,243	968,000,000
8. Argentina	1,073,518	36,000,000
9. Kazakhstan	1,052,100	17,000,000
10. Sudan	966,499	33,000,000

Canada is a geometric boundary drawn along the forty-ninth parallel (49° N). What kind of border does Texas share with Mexico?

As you study nations, look for the political boundaries that are unstable. Many boundaries cut across natural features, languages, religions, ethnic groups, or climates. To keep its borders intact, each state must win the loyalty of its own people as well as the respect of its neighbors.

Disagreements over the limits of state authority breed the worst kind of violence in the drama of human history—war. At any one time, as many as thirty or forty states may be at war. When people within a state's borders fight their own government, it is called a **civil war.** The most common goals of a civil war are to replace the ruler or to separate from the state. *International wars* occur when independent states fight each other.

History—Instrument of Cultural Change

History is more than an instrument of cultural change; it is part of every culture. Every nation celebrates the key events in its history. Books, poems, monuments, music, and art recall the greatest achievements and tragedies of each nation's past.

He increaseth the nations, and destroyeth them: he enlargeth the nations, and straiteneth them again. (Job 12:23)

As you know, geography is the study of space, not time. But a knowledge of history helps to explain the shape of culture regions and national boundaries. The last two centuries, in particular, have brought revolutionary changes. Students in every nation study the same pivotal men, events, and ideas, but not necessarily from the same point of view. Students in Great Britain and India may study the British raj who ruled India, but not with the same attitude! Keep the events outlined in the table on page 97 in mind as you study the remaining units of the textbook.

Ancient History   Most of the world culture regions arose during ancient history, which lasted from the Tower of Babel (3000? B.C.) to about A.D. 400. Early peoples established themselves on every continent and developed their various religions and governments. Little is known about these early peoples or the wars they fought among themselves.

The Parthenon symbolizes the birth of Western civilization.

◎ SECTION REVIEW

1. What is the basic difference between Eastern and Western institutions?
2. What is a nuclear family? an extended family?
3. What are the five major religious groups?
4. How does true Christianity differ from all other religions?
5. Name two common types of political boundaries.
   ♀ Which of the world's 185 states shares borders with the most other states?

THE MAJOR PERIODS IN HISTORY	SIGNIFICANCE
Ancient History: Foundations (3000? B.C.–A.D. 400)	
1. Cradles of Civilization	First cultures and religions are established.
2. Spread of European Civilization	
Greek Empire	Greece establishes Western philosophy.
Roman Empire	Rome establishes Latin culture and law.
Spread of Christianity	The gospel "turns the world upside down."
Medieval History: Invasions and Conquests (400-1500)	
1. Nomadic Invasions from Central Eurasia	Barbaric peoples migrate to current locations in Europe.
2. Islamic Conquests from the Middle East	Islamic religion and Arab peoples spread across the Middle East.
Modern History: Empires of Western Europe (1500-today)	
1. Age of Exploration	Western Europe establishes colonies in the Western Hemisphere and Australia.
2. Age of Imperialism	Western Europe imposes new governments and boundaries on Asia, Africa,
3. Loss of Empire	and the Middle East.
World Wars I and II	European empires disappear.
Cold War	Soviet Union and the United States become the two world superpowers.

The map of modern languages gives fleeting hints about this murky past. Some nations—and the languages they spoke—apparently were once widespread but have been driven to extinction. Others survive in isolated mountain areas. The Basques in northern Spain and the Caucasians in the Caucasus Mountains have no known relationship to any other language families.

Ancient nations with superior technology and military tactics began to conquer nations beyond their borders, creating empires. Early empires were centered at the four great "cradles of civilization"—the Sumerians on the Euphrates River, the Egyptians on the Nile River, the pre-Aryans on the Indus River, and the Chinese on the Yellow River.

Although the Greeks and Romans were latecomers in the empire game, they left a profound imprint on the world. Their philosophers' ideas became the foundation of Western civilization, which now dominates the earth.

Medieval History During the medieval period of history, the Huns, Mongols, and other tribes from Central Eurasia invaded Europe and Asia, raiding and pillaging. They threw some ancient empires into turmoil and completely destroyed others. Arabs in the Middle East converted to Islam and embarked on one of the most far-reaching conquests in history. The spread of Islam continued under Turkish tribes. By the time the conquests were over, Islamic rulers sat on thrones from Spain to Southeast Asia.

The advance of these conquerors pushed other tribes out of their original territories. During this time, many tribes moved into Western Europe. The Franks settled in France and the Anglo-Saxons settled in England.

Worried about constant raids, medieval lords and their subjects became increasingly dependent on each other for survival. They developed a complex system of mutual obligations, called *feudalism*. In return for services to their lord, the people received protection from invaders. Feudal systems developed in several regions of Europe and Asia.

Modern History Modern history begins around 1500, when a series of European nations became the most powerful rulers in the world. The spread of European power falls into two broad historical periods: the Age of Exploration and the Age of Imperialism.

In the Age of Exploration, Europeans used oceangoing ships, compasses, and guns to explore and conquer the newly discovered regions of the Western Hemisphere. Although they found native peoples (including the empires of the Aztecs and Incas), Europeans considered these lands unclaimed, uncivilized, and open to settlement. Adventurous Europeans established new communities, called *colonies,* which supplied the mother country with raw materials and bought finished goods from the mother country.

The second period of conquest was the Age of **Imperialism.** In the eighteenth and nineteenth centuries, Europeans fought each other to establish empires over the peoples of Asia, Africa, and the Middle East. The map below shows all the nations that were ruled by Europeans at some time in their history. In many cases, these nations have adopted a European language and European ideas about government and industry.

Even as European emperors were fighting to increase their power, radical philosophers were planting the seeds that eventually brought an end to

The storming of the royal prison, the Bastille, marks the beginning of the French Revolution, July 14, 1789. This day is still celebrated as a national holiday in France.

European imperialism. Philosophers during the eighteenth-century **Enlightenment** argued that the government's power does not come from "the divine right of kings" but from the "will of the

Former European Colonizers

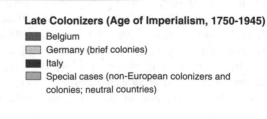

Early Colonizers (Age of Exploration, 1450-1750)

- ■ Denmark
- ■ England
- ■ France
- ■ Netherlands
- ■ Spain
- ■ Russia
- ■ Portugal

Late Colonizers (Age of Imperialism, 1750-1945)

- ■ Belgium
- ▨ Germany (brief colonies)
- ■ Italy
- ▨ Special cases (non-European colonizers and colonies; neutral countries)

people." Thomas Jefferson, the author of America's Declaration of Independence, was among these enlightened thinkers.

Europeans lost control of their colonies in the Western Hemisphere first. The thirteen American colonies broke away from England, winning independence in 1783. They were followed by the French colony of Haiti and then by the Spanish and Portuguese colonies in the New World.

Enlightened ideas soon shook the foundations of Europe itself. During the French Revolution (1789-99), the people of France executed their king. Their revolutionary armies threatened the other capitals of Europe. Eventually a popular general named Napoleon Bonaparte took the reins of power. He built a vast empire and helped to spread revolutionary ideas across the European continent.

Although Europe's monarchs eventually defeated Napoleon, their empires on the continent were never secure again. A new movement called **nationalism** sprang up among the nations they ruled. These nations had learned from France the enlightened concept that every nation has a right to establish its own government. This view threatened every European empire because each was, by definition, a multinational state.

As Europe's monarchs used their armies to quell revolutions in Europe, they continued their drive for larger empires abroad. Their competition climaxed in World Wars I and II. These wars devastated the European imperialists. One by one their colonies won independence, either by mutual agreement or by revolt. Between the end of World War II (1945) and the end of the Cold War (1991), the number of countries in the world jumped from 70 to 185.

Out of the ashes of World War II arose two *superpowers*—the Soviet Union and the United States. The United States supported free enterprise and democracy, while the Soviet Union wanted to establish world communism by force of arms. They fought a long and bitter struggle, called the Cold War. In 1991 the "evil empire" (as President Reagan called the Soviet Union) crumbled. The United States, "an empire of ideas," reigned supreme.

The Future Seeing the prosperity of Western nations, poorer countries have begun borrowing extensively from Western culture. For instance, American blue jeans and athletic shoes are worn on the streets of many nations. Businessmen on every continent wear suits and ties. The rapid rise of cities and mass communication has aided this **cultural convergence,** a growing similarity among cultures.

Unfortunately, modern cultures often borrow the worst along with the best, including divorce, abortion, materialism, and sensual music. The apostle Paul warned that these perilous times would come. Second Timothy 3:1-6 perfectly describes popular Western culture, including self-love, pride, rebellion against parents, love of pleasure, and a constant increase in information without ever finding the truth. Paul warns Christians that human society will resist the truth and persecute all who live godly in Christ Jesus (II Tim. 3:8-12).

But Christians know they have the only answer. It lies not in humanistic efforts to perfect the present world but in a miraculous redemption from the death of this world. By the blood of Christ, God offers each person from every nation an opportunity to become a new creature, with a new body, a new family, a new city, a new heaven, and a new earth. Most importantly, anyone can enter God's kingdom, ruled by Jesus Christ, the King of kings and Lord of lords. His children enter a totally new "way of life."

Thou [the Lamb] wast slain, and hast redeemed us to God by thy blood out of every kindred, and tongue, and people, and nation. (Rev. 5:9)

SECTION REVIEW

1. What are the three major periods of history? During which period was European culture established in the Western Hemisphere?

2. What is another term for empire building?

3. What philosophical movement helped to bring an end to Europe's empires?

💡 Read Matthew 10:16-42. Why did Jesus say that His followers would be hated of all men? Why does the gospel bring division?

Sports

Soccer—the World Sport

The most popular team sport in the world is football. Americans call it soccer, but other nations call it *football* or *association football*. To avoid confusion with American football, Americans use a corruption of the abbreviation "assoc." to describe this world sport.

Many cultures in history, including ancient China, have played a variety of football games. Team competitions helped to develop manly skills and to develop bonds among future warriors. England was the first to write down modern soccer rules in 1848. The world soccer organization is the Fédération Internationale de Football Association or FIFA. Begun in 1904 with seven nations, it now has over 150 member nations.

Every four years, FIFA organizes the World Cup, the most exciting championship competition in the world. Each member nation of FIFA forms an all-star team, which competes with teams from other nations. After several qualifying tournaments, the best thirty-two teams compete at the World Cup site. The defending champion and the host country's team receive automatic bids. It is estimated that over one billion people worldwide listen to media broadcasts of the final match. Only seven nations have ever produced a world-champion team. The members of the winning team are considered national heroes.

Belgium battles Saudi Arabia in a 1990 World Cup soccer match.

YEAR	WINNER	SCORE	OPPONENT	LOCATION
1930	Uruguay	4-2	Argentina	Montevideo, Uruguay
1934	Italy	2-1	Czechoslovakia	Rome
1938	Italy	4-2	Hungary	Paris
1950	Uruguay	2-1	Brazil	Rio de Janeiro
1954	W. Germany	3-2	Hungary	Bern, Switzerland
1958	Brazil	5-2	Sweden	Stockholm, Sweden
1962	Brazil	3-1	Czechoslovakia	Santiago, Chile
1966	England	4-2	W. Germany	London
1970	Brazil	4-1	Italy	Mexico City
1974	W. Germany	2-1	Netherlands	Munich
1978	Argentina	3-1	Netherlands	Buenos Aires
1982	Italy	3-1	W. Germany	Madrid
1986	Argentina	3-2	W. Germany	Mexico City
1990	W. Germany	1-0	Argentina	Rome
1994	Brazil	3-2	Italy	Pasadena, U.S.

DEMOGRAPHY

The study of human populations and their characteristics is called **demography.** Societies use three basic methods to gather demographic information. *Vital statistics* are official records of births, marriages, divorces, and deaths. **Censuses** are official government counts of the entire population within the nation's boundaries. *Surveys* are counts of small samples of the total population. Surveyors and census takers collect information about age, marriage, family size, education, and so on.

Vital Statistics

The word *vital* means "related to life." Vital statistics are the "life signs" of a society. Like a doctor taking a pulse, nations seek statistics about the life and health of their people. The greatest enemy of every society is the pall of death. The two basic vital statistics are (1) the rate of natural increase and (2) life expectancy.

Natural Increase   Countries measure population increase by comparing the number of births to the number of deaths each year. The number of children born per one thousand people is called the **crude birthrate.** The United States has a crude birthrate of about 15 (15 live births for every 1,000 people). If new babies were the only factor in

Population Growth Statistics			
COUNTRY	CRUDE BIRTH-RATE	CRUDE DEATH RATE	RATE OF NATURAL INCREASE
Australia	14	7	0.7%
Bangladesh	30	11	2.0%
Brazil	20	9	1.1%
Canada	13	7	0.6%
China	17	7	1.0%
Egypt	28	9	1.9%
France	11	9	0.2%
Germany	9	11	−0.2%
India	25	9	1.6%
Italy	10	10	0.0%
Japan	10	8	0.2%
Mexico	26	5	2.1%
Russia	11	16	−0.5%
United Kingdom	13	11	0.2%
United States	15	9	0.6%

population growth, the population would increase by 1.5 percent each year. But demographers must also calculate the number of people who die each year per 1,000 people, called the **crude death rate.** The U.S. crude death rate is about 9. Subtracting the number of deaths from the number of births (15 − 9) gives the **rate of natural increase.** It is 6 per 1,000 or 0.6 percent.

Humanists are discouraged by high death rates and high growth rates. Their ultimate goal is to end human suffering and to limit the growth of humans on the earth. They want to bring down the world's growth rate, now about 1.75 percent, to match the low rate in Western societies. In fact, the population is shrinking in some Western nations.

But the Bible gives a completely different perspective on birth and death. Suffering and death are essential to God's design for this fallen world (Gen. 3:16); and bearing children is a sign of God's blessing, as families obey God's cultural mandate. In the midst of sorrow and death, children offer hope of new life. (See Psalm 127.)

Life Expectancy   Before the Flood, people lived long lives; Methuselah, for example, lived a record 969 years. But after the Flood, life expectancy declined rapidly. By Moses' day, **life expectancy**

Extended families are typical in the Orient.

(the number of years a person can expect to live) had fallen to seventy years.

The days of our years are threescore years and ten; and if by reason of strength they be fourscore years, yet is their strength labour and sorrow; for it is soon cut off, and we fly away. (Ps. 90:10)

Around 1650, however, the growth in world population began to increase. Over the next two hundred years, the world's population doubled (from five hundred million to one billion). Eighty years later, the population doubled again. By 1975, the world population had reached four billion and was adding nearly one billion people every decade.

Advances in technology and medicine have done much to increase world population. Better crops and new vaccinations have practically eliminated the effects of malnutrition and some common diseases that once took countless lives. In the twentieth century, life expectancy in the United States increased from forty-seven to seventy-six years. The statistics are even better for women, who usually outlive men. (In the United States, seventy-nine is the average life expectancy for women, seventy-three for men).

Health improvements are most apparent in the declining death rate among children, called **infant mortality.** Infant mortality is measured by comparing the number of live births to the number of infants who die in their first year. Before the Industrial Revolution, nearly half of all babies died before they reached their first birthday. Today only 3 percent of all infants die (30 infant deaths per 1,000 live births) before their first birthday. Infant mortality in the United States is only 0.7 percent.

Infants lack immunity from many common diseases.

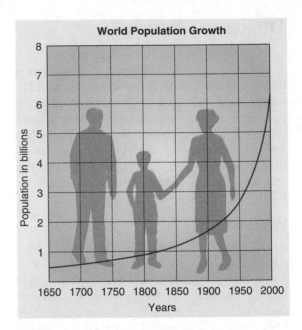

World Population Growth

Despite modern advances, science still faces many obstacles in man's quest to increase his life expectancy. Four thousand years ago, Moses managed to live 120 years. The first person on record to surpass this age was Madame Jeanne Calment of Arles, who died at age 122 in 1997.

SECTION REVIEW

1. What do we call the study of human populations and their characteristics?

2. What two statistics are used to compute the rate of natural increase of a population?

3. What are the main reasons for recent increases in life expectancy?

💡 What is the growth rate for world population? If the world population were six billion this year, what would it be next year?

Community Statistics

Vital statistics help us to understand the life of a typical family in each nation. Nations are also interested in communities—groups of families who live and work together. The growing population of communities indicates a healthy society.

Thomas Malthus on Overpopulation

Thomas Robert Malthus (1766-1834) grew up in what is called the Age of Reason. Many people at that time believed that man could make his society perfect. Malthus attacked this idealistic view by preparing a new economic theory based on the harsh realities at that time in Britain.

In *An Essay of the Principle of Population As It Affects the Future Improvement of Society* (1798), he argued that man will never escape misery and poverty. According to his formula, population increases in geometric progression (2, 4, 8, 16 . . .). Food supplies, however, increase only in simple arithmetic progression (2, 3, 4, 5 . . .). The only checks on population growth are sin, misery (such as war, famine, and disease), and self-restraint. Because of this idea, the people of that day began to believe that the world population must quit growing. Widespread famine would soon prevail as agriculture ceased to provide enough food.

Malthus immediately influenced political and economic theories. Economists began to discourage charity and to justify subsistence wages for labor. The English Poor Laws, which gave temporary relief to poverty-stricken families, were abandoned because they "worsened" misery by delaying it. People believed that public works for the unemployed should provide a living more terrible than the living of the working poor.

Great Britain soon discovered that Malthus's predictions were not entirely accurate. He had not treated

Impoverished family in Africa

the facts very scientifically. Neither was he aware of all the changes that the Industrial Revolution was bringing. Before he died, a new wave of economic optimism swept over Britain. But whenever the economy periodically declines, Malthus's theory again becomes popular. Today many Malthusian societies are prophesying the end of mankind unless we take drastic measures to curb the rising world population, especially in India and China. But the problem is not as grave as they say, and sins such as abortion and mercy killing are certainly not the solutions.

Urbanization No hard and fast rule discriminates among the different types of communities. Usage varies regarding what constitutes a city, town, or village. For simplicity, demographers have divided populated areas into two broad categories: *urban areas,* which have a large number of buildings in a small area, and *rural areas,* which have few buildings in a large area. According to the arbitrary definition of the U.S. Census Bureau, rural communities have a population of less than five thousand, and cities have a population of above five thousand.

Ten Largest Cities

CITY	POPULATION
1. Tokyo, Japan	26,959,000
2. Mexico City, Mexico	16,562,000
3. São Paulo, Brazil	16,533,000
4. New York City, U.S.	16,332,000
5. Bombay, India	15,138,000
6. Shanghai, China	13,584,000
7. Seoul, South Korea	12,609,000
8. Los Angeles, U.S.	12,410,000
9. Calcutta, India	11,923,000
10. Buenos Aires, Argentina	11,802,000

Rural and Urban Population

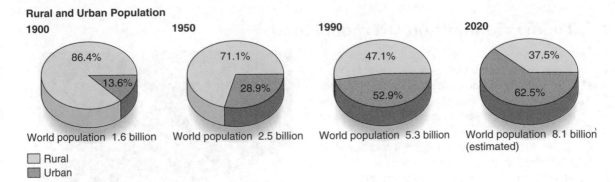

1900	**1950**	**1990**	**2020**
86.4% / 13.6%	71.1% / 28.9%	47.1% / 52.9%	37.5% / 62.5%
World population 1.6 billion	World population 2.5 billion	World population 5.3 billion	World population 8.1 billion (estimated)

☐ Rural
☐ Urban

The size and number of communities have increased throughout most of history. Since the Industrial Revolution, however, the move to urban areas has become a virtual stampede, as people have left their farms and small villages to seek opportunities in big cities. Two hundred years ago, 95 percent of Americans lived on farms, but now fewer than 5 percent do. The growth of urban areas at the expense of rural areas is called **urbanization.** Nearly 80 percent of Americans, and over 45 percent of the world population, live in an urban area.

The rise of large cities in the last century has been amazing. In 1900 only two cities—London and New York City—had a population over two million. Now over two hundred cities fit this category, and more are added almost every year. The map on pages 106-7 names the cities whose populations exceed *five* million. How many cities are shown? How many are in the United States?

Cities in developing countries are growing rapidly and will soon overtake older, established cities in developed countries. By the year 2020, no U.S. cities are likely to remain on the list of the largest urban areas in the world.

Population Density Crowding has been a serious problem since early in history. Abraham and Lot were forced to separate because their herds and servants had become so large that "the land was not able to bear them" (Gen. 13:6). The land can support only so many farms and herds. Even in modern industrial cities, where people can buy their basic needs from afar, crowding is still a concern. City leaders must work hard to provide adequate services such as sanitation and hospitals.

Population density is the average number of people who live on each square mile (or kilometer) of land. For example, the average density in Egypt

Ten Most Populous Countries

COUNTRY	POPULATION	AREA (SQ. MI.)	PERCENT ARABLE LAND	POPULATION DENSITY (PER SQ. MI.)	PHYSIOLOGICAL DENSITY (PER SQ. MI.)
1. China	1,210,000,000	3,696,100	10%	327	3,270
2. India	968,000,000	1,222,243	55%	729	1,440
3. United States	268,000,000	3,675,031	20%	72	365
4. Indonesia	210,000,000	741,052	8%	283	3,540
5. Brazil	165,000,000	3,300,171	7%	50	714
6. Russia	148,000,000	6,592,800	8%	22	281
7. Pakistan	132,000,000	307,374	23%	389	1,870
8. Japan	126,000,000	145,850	13%	861	6,650
9. Bangladesh	125,000,000	56,977	67%	2,200	3,270
10. Nigeria	107,000,000	356,689	31%	300	968

Geographer's Corner

Cartograms

You have learned how some map projections give an unusual shape or size to land areas. Although such distortion is unavoidable, it is usually unwanted. This map, however, intentionally distorts the sizes and shapes of the different countries. Actually this is not a map, but a graphic picture of world population. *Cartograms* use geometric shapes to compare populations of different countries. This cartogram also uses color to compare per capita GDP. Use the information to answer these questions.

1. What two countries appear to have the largest populations?
2. What South American country has the largest population?
3. Which appears to have the largest population: Australia, Japan, or Canada?
4. What appears to be the most typical per capita GDP on each continent? (List Asia and Europe separately.)
5. What African country has the highest per capita GDP?
   ♀ Find the most populous country that has a per capita GDP above $6,000.

World Population and GDP

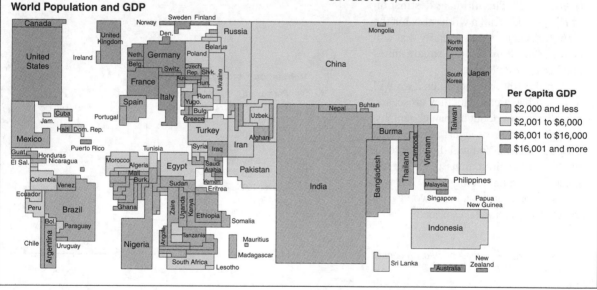

Per Capita GDP
- $2,000 and less
- $2,001 to $6,000
- $6,001 to $16,000
- $16,001 and more

is about 168 Egyptians on every square mile of land. France has about the same population as Egypt, but its density is 276 per square mile because it has only one-half the area of Egypt.

Population density is a fairly good measure of crowding, but people are not spread evenly across the landscape. They generally cluster around good farmland. Nearly all the Egyptian people live in a narrow band of land along the banks of the Nile River and in the Nile Delta. Thousands of square miles of this desert country are virtually uninhabited.

Demographers have developed an even more accurate way to measure how dense the population is. They take into account the amount of **arable land** (land that can be used to plant crops). Out of a total of 386,660 square miles of land, Egypt has only about 14,000 square miles of arable land. By comparing the total population to the arable land, demographers find the **physiological density.** Egypt's physiological density is over five thousand people per square mile. Unlike Egypt, France is covered with a large percentage of arable land (32 percent),

105

and its physiological density is under one thousand. This statistic also indicates that the lower the physiological density is, the easier it is for each nation to feed itself.

Humanists are worried about the increasing size of cities, the loss of wilderness, and the decline in rural societies. But the Bible has a different perspective on urbanization and population density. God meant for the earth to be subdued. He provided Israel with walled cities in the Promised Land, and He made provisions to ensure that the land would not return to its wild state (Deut. 7:22). The ultimate destination of His people is not a wilderness but the New Jerusalem, a massive city that will cover some four million square miles and be filled with people.

In the following chapters, we will look at urban areas, why they arose, and what they show about human geography. Studying rural areas is just as interesting for geographers. You will discover some of the natural limitations that God has placed on human settlement. You will also see some of the natural wonders in which every nation takes pride.

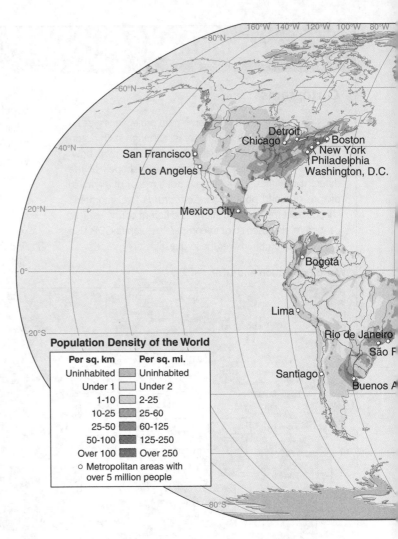

Population Density of the World

Per sq. km		Per sq. mi.
Uninhabited		Uninhabited
Under 1		Under 2
1-10		2-25
10-25		25-60
25-50		60-125
50-100		125-250
Over 100		Over 250

○ Metropolitan areas with over 5 million people

El Salvador has the highest population density in the Western Hemisphere.

SECTION REVIEW

1. Why have rural populations decreased in most developed countries?
2. What term describes the growing trend of populations to migrate to cities?
3. What is population density?
   - Calculate the physiological density of Belgium, which has a population of 125,340,000, an area of 11,787 square miles, and 24 percent arable land.

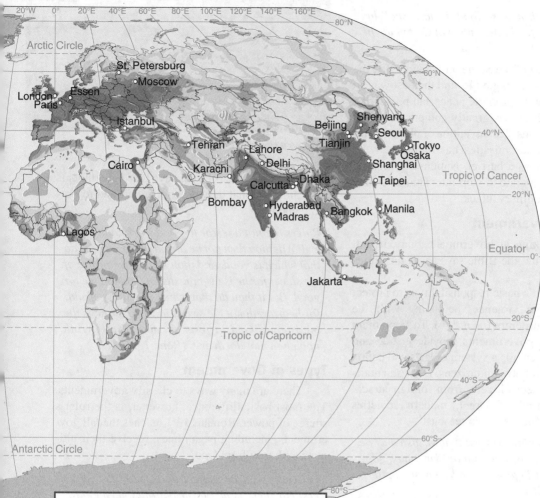

Arctic Circle

St. Petersburg
Moscow
London
Essen
Paris
Istanbul
Tehran
Cairo
Lahore
Karachi
Delhi
Calcutta
Dhaka
Bombay
Hyderabad
Madras
Beijing
Shenyang
Tianjin
Seoul
Tokyo
Osaka
Shanghai
Taipei
Bangkok
Manila
Lagos

Tropic of Cancer

Jakarta

Equator

Tropic of Capricorn

Antarctic Circle

60°N
40°N
20°N
0°
20°S
40°S
60°S
80°S

Let's Go Exploring

1. Which inhabited continent lacks any area with a population density above 250?

2. Which continent has people in every area (no uninhabited area)?

3. Where are the three largest concentrations of people in the world?

4. Which continent has the most cities with populations above five million?

○ Compare this map to the climate map on pp. 48-49. What climates are most common for areas of high population density (above 250)? for low population density (under 2)?

POLITICS: THE GOVERNMENT OF SOCIETY

Before the Flood, mankind turned away from God's rule to **anarchy** (no government). Every man apparently did what he wished. As a consequence, sin filled people's thoughts, and violence filled the earth (Gen. 6:11). When the waters receded and Noah stepped off the ark, God demanded the formation of *government,* the rule of man over man. He gave rulers the power of life and death for one primary purpose: restraining violence. By executing murderers, the government showed respect for the value of human life.

Whoso sheddeth man's blood, by man shall his blood be shed: for in the image of God made he man. (Gen. 9:6)

Since the fall of the Soviet empire in 1991, the United States has struggled to find the best way to use its leadership to promote peace and prosperity. Modern technology has greatly complicated relations among nations. The invention of planes, computers, and nuclear missiles has diminished the value of borders as a barrier. Nations are seeking new ways to cooperate to stop international crime, espionage, and military attack.

Duties of Government

Before looking at government today, it will help to know what the Bible says about the duties of government.

Government's basic responsibility is to protect its citizens from violence, beginning with the execution of murderers (Gen. 9:6). To implement this obligation, governments provide justice and defense. *Justice* entails a system of laws and courts to settle disputes between citizens. *Defense* entails an army to protect citizens from foreign attack. Like the children of Israel, modern societies demand a ruler for these two reasons:

We will have a king over us; that we also may be like all the nations; and that our king may judge us, and go out before us, and fight our battles. (I Sam. 8:19-20)

These F-18 Hornets in the Canadian navy are designed to land on aircraft carriers.

Parliament House at Canberra, Australia

In Romans 13:1-4 Paul says that governments have an additional duty, to punish evil and to promote good.

Rulers are not a terror to good works, but to the evil. Wilt thou then not be afraid of the power? do that which is good, and thou shalt have praise of the same: for he is the minister of God to thee for good. But if thou do that which is evil, be afraid; for he beareth not the sword in vain: for he is the minister of God, a revenger to execute wrath upon him that doeth evil. (Rom. 13:3-4)

Types of Government

There are many ways to classify governments. The most basic difference, however, is the ruler's source of power. Romans 13:1 teaches that all governments, including pagan ones, receive their ultimate authority from God.

Let every soul be subject unto the higher powers. For there is no power but of God: the powers that be are ordained of God. (Rom. 13:1)

Authoritarian Government Authoritarian governments hold power by claiming an authority higher than the people they govern.

Monarchies are an authoritarian form of government. Monarchs, usually kings or queens, receive their authority by birth. An **absolute monarch** rules as he pleases. Although monarchies were far more common in the past than they are now, a few absolute monarchies still exist, especially in Islamic countries.

Another type of authoritarian government is a **dictatorship.** A dictator is a person who rules by

Queen Noor was an American citizen before her marriage to King Hussein I of Jordan.

the authority of the military. Often, as in the case of Napoleon, he rises to power with public support. Some dictatorships are ruled by a small group. Dictators usually establish their own political party and allow no opposition to their actions. Dictatorships are common in developing countries.

The most extreme form of authoritarian government is a **totalitarian government.** These governments believe they should make decisions about every detail of their people's lives for the good of the whole. Citizens must get permission before they can travel within the country, change jobs, or even hold peaceful meetings. China is the largest country ruled by a totalitarian government. The leaders of the Chinese Communist Party have tremendous military power behind them to back their rule. Although the people vote, they must vote for members of the Communist Party.

Many authoritarian governments claim to be democracies that rule in the interest of the people, but the test of a true government "of the people" is free, fair, and regular elections. Very few countries enjoy this privilege. The people may have elections in an authoritarian government, but the leaders use their authority to limit opposition parties or to delay or cancel elections.

Elected Government In contrast to authoritarian governments, elected governments rely on the consent of the people to keep their position. The word *democracy* is often used to describe elected governments. *Democracy* originally described a government in which the whole population ruled. The first *direct* or *pure democracies* arose in the ancient Greek city-states. Every adult male citizen could vote on every law and issue that came before the government. Modern nations are too large for

pure democracies. Today's democracies are *indirect* or *representative* democracies. The people have an opportunity to vote for politicians of their choice, to voice their opinions, and to run for office if they wish.

One of the most common forms of modern democracy is a limited or **constitutional monarchy.** The people have limited the power of the monarch by law. He functions more as a figurehead. The real power belongs to an elected legislature. The most powerful leader of the elected assembly supervises the writing of laws and heads the bureaucracy that executes the laws.

The other major type of representative democracy is a **republic.** Unlike constitutional monarchies, republics elect their national leader, generally known as the president, who supervises the bureaucracy while the legislature writes laws. You will be studying the first modern republic—the United States—in the next chapter.

SECTION REVIEW

1. What is anarchy?
2. What is government's basic responsibility?
3. Where does an absolute monarch obtain his authority? a dictator? a president?
4. What is the main difference between a pure democracy and a representative democracy?
5. What are the two most common forms of modern democracies?
- Is it possible for a dictatorship to have a democratic form of government?

International Relations

Every nation is concerned about its relations with other nations. The set of principles that guides international relations is called *foreign policy.* Governments have two alternatives to resolve disputes: war or negotiation.

What king, going to make war against another king, sitteth not down first, and consulteth whether he be able with ten thousand to meet him that cometh against him with twenty thousand? Or else, while the other is yet a great way off, he sendeth an ambassage, and desireth conditions of peace. (Luke 14:31-32)

The Threat of War   Nations can influence their neighbors through *foreign aid* (gifts of money, goods, or technology to foreign nations). But the most obvious way to influence neighbors is the threat of military attack.

Nations constantly evaluate their military strength and the strength of their potential enemies to see whether they can defend themselves against attack. There are many ways to measure military strength. The *active troop strength* (number of full-time soldiers in uniform) is the most common measurement, but it can be misleading. With less than fifty thousand men, Alexander the Great defeated a Persian army of over one-quarter million men. His soldiers relied on high discipline and superior tactics to win. The best measurement of modern military strength is its yearly *defense spending* on military technology. By this measurement, the United States is now the only superpower in the world.

Frequently, powerful nations vie for cultural and political leadership over their weaker neighbors. These powerful nations consider their weaker neighbors their *sphere of influence*—the nations that they want to influence. You cannot understand events in each of the world's culture regions without appreciating who are the big dogs and who are the underdogs.

Since the United States is now the world's only superpower, its sphere of influence circles the globe. It has built military bases and stationed troops in almost every region to help it "project power" for the benefit of its allies. A capitalist nation that thrives on trade, the United States believes the spread of freedom and capitalism is a vital *national interest* that should guide its foreign policy.

The first concern of U.S. foreign policy is the seven world powers that spend the most on military technology and have the most influence on world politics. They are, by region, Russia (in Central Eurasia); France, the United Kingdom, Germany, and Italy (in Western Europe); and China and Japan (in East Asia). Almost every other nation consults them when making foreign policy decisions.

The United States is also concerned about *militarized states,* which have a large number of soldiers and spend a large percentage of their GDP on weapons. Militarized states may be poor, but they are very dangerous. War can break out on their borders at any moment. You will be studying more about militarized states as you study each cultural subregion.

A third area of concern is the nations that oppose the role of the United States as a superpower and that reject democracy and capitalism. The most dangerous of these nations are **rogue nations** that ignore some of the most fundamental principles of international relations. They willingly use chemical weapons, terrorism, or any other means necessary to increase their power. The two most common types of rogue nations are Communist countries, such as China, and radical Muslim nations, such as Iran.

Negotiating Peace   *Diplomacy* is the art of negotiating agreements between nations. Formal agreements between nations are called *treaties*. To avoid war, nations have two kinds of treaties to

Ten Largest Armies in the World

COUNTRY	ACTIVE TROOP STRENGTH	DEFENSE SPENDING ($, BILLION)	DEFENSE SPENDING AS PERCENT GDP	TROOP STRENGTH PER 1,000
1. China	2,930,000	29	2.7%	2.5
2. United States	1,550,000	270	4.2%	5.8
3. Russia	1,520,000	98	21.5%	9.3
4. India	1,150,000	7	2.8%	1.4
5. North Korea	1,130,000	6	26.6%	52.0
6. South Korea	633,000	14	3.3%	16.6
7. Pakistan	587,000	3	5.6%	4.2
8. Vietnam	572,000	1	2.5%	11.7
9. Iran	513,000	5	3.5%	8.4
10. Turkey	508,000	5	5.6%	13.0

negotiate. They can talk to their enemies and sign a peace treaty. Or they can make strong *military alliances* with their friends, agreeing to help each other in case of attack.

For most of its history the United States followed the advice of its Founding Fathers to avoid "entangling alliances." But the tragedy of two world wars and the threat of Communism to world peace has forced it to change its foreign policy. It has made military alliances with at least forty countries. In the 1940s it took the lead in creating two significant *international organizations:* NATO and the UN.

The North Atlantic Treaty Organization (**NATO**) is the most powerful and successful alliance in history. In 1947 the United States joined Canada and most of the free nations of Western Europe in establishing NATO. Its arsenal of nuclear weapons, tanks, and soldiers was so intimidating that the Soviet Union never once set foot in Western Europe. NATO never fired a shot during the Cold War.

The **United Nations** (UN) is the other ambitious international organization formed in the wake of World War II. The United States completed the

Civil war has destroyed many towns in Croatia, which broke away from Yugoslavia at the end of the Cold War.

negotiations in 1945. From past experience, most members knew that the UN would not stop war. But they wanted a neutral place where they could negotiate peaceful solutions to disputes. Representatives from the members of the UN meet in the General Assembly to vote on agreements. But the five major Allies of World War II—the United States, the United Kingdom, France, China, and the Soviet Union (now Russia)—hold the reins of power. They are the five permanent members of the **Security Council.** Any one of them can *veto* (vote down) decisions of the General Assembly. In this way, the United States ensures that the UN cannot make important policies without U.S. support.

The UN has proved to be much less successful than NATO. Because of the Soviet Union's veto power, the UN has been helpless to intervene in dozens of bloody wars that the Soviets supported around the world. America's military alliances and resolve, not the UN, helped bring about the final collapse of the Soviet empire.

George Bush, when he was president of the United States, hoped that a "new world order" would emerge from the collapse of Communism. But his vision did not materialize. In 1991 civil war engulfed the multinational state of Yugoslavia on Europe's southern border. The bloodshed between 1991 and 1995 was the worst in Europe since World War II. It seemed that every action taken by NATO, the UN, or the United States only worsened the situation.

Flags of many nations fly on the grounds of the United Nations Building in New York City.

Red Cross

The Red Cross is one of the most widely recognized volunteer organizations in the world. With over 250 million members, it shows mankind's willingness to make sacrifices to relieve the sufferings of others in times of war or natural disaster.

The Red Cross has its headquarters in Geneva, Switzerland. Its universally recognized symbol—a red cross on a white field—is based on the flag of Switzerland. Each nation organizes its own society, which agrees to follow the general guidelines of the headquarters. The United States has nearly one Red Cross chapter for every county. Muslim countries also have a relief agency. Their flags use a Red Crescent.

The Swiss businessman Jean Henri Dunant (doo-NAHN) founded the Red Cross in 1863 after he witnessed the carnage of the battle of Solferino in 1859. At a Red Cross meeting in 1864 various nations drew

The Red Cross provided aid to Kurds fleeing Iraq's tyrant Saddam Hussein.

up the *Geneva Conventions,* a treaty establishing basic rules for treating wounded soldiers and prisoners of war. Although the original focus of the Red Cross was assisting victims of war, it has expanded its activities to include collecting blood, reuniting families, assisting during natural disasters, and distributing medicine and relief goods to needy nations.

Yugoslavia's civil war has revealed some of the serious flaws in the Enlightenment concept of the nation-state. Two competing principles are working against each other. According to the principle of **self-determination,** all peoples have a right to vote for the type of government they will have. But if self-determination were taken too far, almost every sovereign country would be in danger. Few countries are true nation-states, consisting wholly of one kind of people. If every minority voted to become independent, most nations would lose their **territorial integrity** (defensible borders).

When four ethnic minorities in Yugoslavia voted to become independent in 1990 and 1991, the Western nations recognized their independence, in spite of protests from the Serbs, the most powerful ethnic group in Yugoslavia. But when minorities in the new republics voted to break away and rejoin the Serbs, Europe refused to recognize their right to self-determination. Do you see the inconsistency?

The Enlightenment failed to recognize that God in His sovereignty has established each government. People need to learn to live together despite their differences. It is foolish to believe that self-determination will bring peace. The root problem is man's sinful heart, which does not change based on where people live or how they govern. The only solution to world strife is a miraculous change of heart, which is the realm of Christ, not human kings.

SECTION REVIEW

1. What is the best measurement of the military strength of a nation?
2. List the eight world powers that have the most influence on world politics.
3. What is a rogue nation?
4. Name the most successful military alliance in history.
5. How can the five permanent members of the Security Council control the policies of the UN?
  - Could the UN have solved Yugoslavia's problems peaceably?

REVIEW

Can You Define These Terms?

society
cultural mandate
culture
culture region
subregion
humanism
dialect
language family
literacy
nuclear family
extended family
nation

nation-state
empire
political boundary
geometric boundary
civil war
imperialism
Enlightenment
nationalism
cultural convergence
demography
census

crude birthrate
crude death rate
rate of natural increase
life expectancy
infant mortality
urbanization
population density
arable land
physiological density
anarchy
absolute monarchy

dictatorship
totalitarian government
democracy
constitutional monarchy
republic
rogue nation
NATO
United Nations
Security Council
self-determination
territorial integrity

How Much Do You Remember?

1. How many culture regions are in the world? What region are you in?
2. What is the most widespread language family in the world?
3. Why did God establish the institution of the family? nations? Give Scripture references.
4. Explain how the Enlightenment has influenced modern government.
5. Show how the rate of natural increase is derived for the United States.
6. Why has the world's population increased dramatically since 1650?
7. Explain the value of calculating physiological density.
8. What country has the largest area? the largest population?
9. What type of government do most Communist countries have?
10. Which of the following terms describe the government of the United States?
    a. elected government
    b. rogue nation
    c. republic
    d. dictatorship
    e. pure democracy

What Do You Think?

1. Was there written language before the Flood?
2. Why do some demographers classify Christianity as a "Western religion," just as they call Buddhism an "Eastern religion"? Are they correct?
3. Use a map of your state to find all of its natural and geometric boundaries.
4. Is the United States a true nation-state?
5. Why are death rates relatively high in some developed countries?
6. List as many examples as you can of specific medical advances that have increased life expectancy.
7. Consider your own city or a city near you. What advantages might attract rural people and what problems might they find?
8. Why do most rogue nations have authoritarian governments?
9. If you were president of the United States, what culture region would worry you the most? Explain your answer using your knowledge of politics.

Cumulative Review

1. What are the two main branches of geography?
2. Explain the difference between latitude and longitude.
3. What two events in the earth's history occurred only once and will never occur again?
4. Name the seven continents and the four oceans.
5. What are the basic differences between the Tropics, the middle latitudes, and the polar regions? Identify a climate that is associated with each region.
6. Define primary, secondary, and tertiary industries and give an example of each.
7. List six major statistics used by demographers to describe the population of a country. Explain the value of each.
8. List the eight culture regions of the world.

UNIT III

Northern America

CHAPTER 6

THE NORTHEASTERN UNITED STATES

The United States ranks fourth among the nations of the earth in physical size, and third in population. Yet it is the richest and most prosperous nation in history. It owes its success partly to a combination of hard-working people, rich farmland, abundant resources, and good climate. Its variety of lands and peoples is unmatched by any other nation.

The United States is divided into four main regions—the Northeast, the South, the Midwest, and the West. The Northeast has a special place in the hearts of Americans. Visitors from all over the nation come to see reminders of America's early history. Nine of the original thirteen colonies were in the Northeast. Monuments remind Americans of the many ways that the Northeast has contributed to this nation's greatest treasure—liberty.

True freedom is a gift from the Lord. God tells Christians to use their liberty not selfishly but for the good of all.

For, brethren, ye have been called unto liberty; only use not liberty for an occasion to the flesh, but by love serve one another. (Gal. 5:13)

NEW ENGLAND

The six states at the far northeast corner of the United States are very small—all six could fit inside Missouri. Yet they have played a big role in the nation.

The explorer John Cabot claimed this region for England in 1497. He called it **New England.** Closer to the British Isles than any other part of the United States, its shores were easily reached by ships sailing across the Atlantic. At least nine out of ten people in New England are descendants of Englishmen. The first settlers were proud of their British heritage. They created a "New" England by following the best traditions from "old" England.

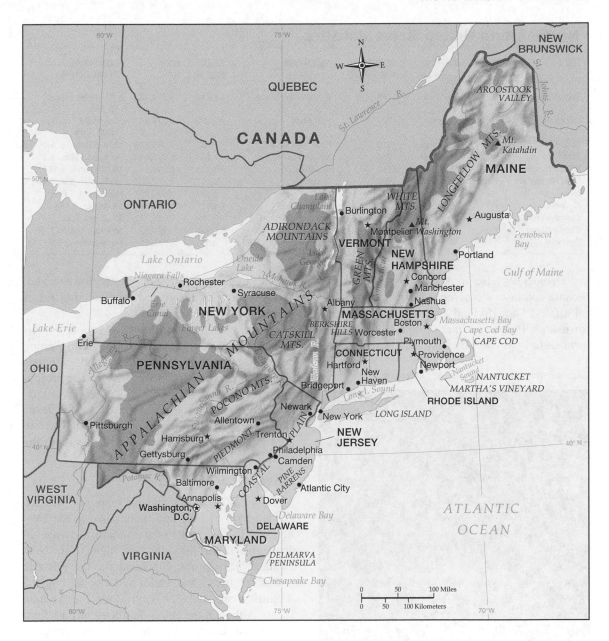

Many families trace their family tree back to the very first English settlers.

Because the wide ocean separated these colonies from the mother country, freedom flourished in New England. Liberty took root in three important areas—business, politics, and religion.

Capitalism developed in New England because settlers were able to start businesses with little interference from the crown. From the first year they arrived, these tough, pioneering souls set an example of hard work and an independent spirit.

Northeastern United States Statistics

STATE	P.O. CODE	CAPITAL	DATE OF STATEHOOD	NICKNAME	AREA (SQ. MI.)	POP.	HIGH POINT, ELEVATION (FT.)
Connecticut	CT	Hartford	1788	Constitution State	52,423	3,274,238	S. slope Mt. Frissell, 2,380
Delaware	DE	Dover	1787	First State	2,489	724,842	Ebright Rd. (Tower Hill), 448
Maine	ME	Augusta	1820	Pine Tree State	35,387	1,243,316	Mt. Katahdin, 5,267
Maryland	MD	Annapolis	1788	Old Line State	12,407	5,071,604	Backbone Mtn., 3,360
Massachusetts	MA	Boston	1788	Bay State	10,555	6,092,352	Mt. Greylock, 3,487
New Hampshire	NH	Concord	1788	Granite State	9,351	1,162,481	Mt. Washington, 6,288
New Jersey	NJ	Trenton	1787	Garden State	8,722	7,987,933	High Point, 1,803
New York	NY	Albany	1788	Empire State	54,471	18,184,774	Mt. Marcy, 5,344
Pennsylvania	PA	Harrisburg	1787	Keystone State	46,058	12,056,112	Mt. Davis, 3,213
Rhode Island	RI	Providence	1790	Ocean State	1,545	990,225	Jerimoth Hill, 812
Vermont	VT	Montpelier	1791	Green Mountain State	9,615	588,654	Mt. Mansfield, 4,393

Democracy also took root in New England because colonists were free to run their own political affairs. They divided land into districts called **townships.** Property owners within each township met regularly to vote on community matters. Many

Tourists flock to Vermont to enjoy its fall colors.

old meeting halls still stand at the town center. Today townships are joined together into larger political units called counties.

America's greatest liberty—*freedom of religion*—also took root in New England. Fleeing persecution by the Church of England, colonists wanted to worship God as they chose. The preaching of the gospel allowed many colonists to discover the true liberty that is found only in Jesus Christ. Christian principles guided social life in the colonies. Church steeples still dominate the skyline of every New England town.

Lower New England

If you look at the physical map, you will see that a series of hills and mountains divide New England from the rest of the nation. Because no deep rivers cut through this high wall, New England has always depended on the Atlantic Ocean for travel and trade. Settlements hug the **Atlantic seaboard** (the land along the Atlantic coast). Although the entire Northeast has a humid continental climate, New England is not very good for farming. New England's winters are cold, and the growing season is short.

New England is divided into three types of terrain: lowlands, uplands, and mountain ranges. The *lowlands* are a narrow strip of coastal plains. The **New England uplands** is a low, rocky plateau that rises above the coastal lowlands. Farther

Boston lighthouse

Mayflower Compact (an agreement to make laws to govern themselves).

Plymouth never became a major port, however. The best harbors in New England were north of Plymouth, on Massachusetts Bay. Thousands of Puritans who migrated to America in the 1630s built homes on this bay. You can still see dock workers busily unloading materials from all over the world. The main port, **Boston,** soon became the largest city in New England. It is the capital of the Bay State.

Bostonians led in the colonies' decision to break with England. When the king began violating their rights, the colonies united in a long, bloody **War for Independence** (1776-83). What youngster has not heard thrilling stories of the Boston Tea Party, Paul Revere's midnight ride, and Lexington's "shot heard round the world"? Visitors can still see where many of these events occurred, along Boston's "Freedom Trail." This walking tour ends at the top of Bunker Hill, the first and bloodiest major battle in the War for Independence.

Most of the state's population live on the coastal plain on the eastern part of the state. Boston and its neighboring cities have built many industries on these lowlands. The state's most famous body of water, Walden Pond, is west of Boston. On this beautiful pond the early naturalist Henry David Thoreau lived alone for two years and then wrote a novel about his experiences. The swampy plain south of Boston produces almost one-half of the nation's cranberries.

inland, several mountain ranges rise within the Appalachian Mountain system.

The New England uplands cover most of the three "lower" states—Massachusetts, Rhode Island, and Connecticut. The soil is often too rocky for profitable farms, even along the large stretches of coastal lowlands. Past glaciers exposed the underlying rock and made the soil shallow. Most good farmland arises in the river valleys. Deep harbors have allowed large cities to thrive on trade and fishing.

Massachusetts Massachusetts played a leading role in this nation's founding. The first New England colony was built by the **Pilgrims,** who landed near Plymouth Rock on December 26, 1620. Their courageous struggle to build a new life on the savage frontier inspired every American who came after them.

The Pilgrims laid the foundation for self-government in America. It came as a result of a navigational error by the captain of the *Mayflower.* He landed at Plymouth Harbor hundreds of miles north of his intended destination in Virginia. Before going ashore, the men on the *Mayflower* signed the

Harvard University, at Cambridge near Boston, was the first college built on North American soil (1636).

The coastal plain includes Cape Cod and many islands. Cape Cod is a long peninsula that curls like a fishhook into the Atlantic. Its beautiful sandy beaches are now protected as a national seashore. Two islands south of Cape Cod are famous: Martha's Vineyard and Nantucket—once the whaling capital of the world. Whaling was a uniquely American industry. Whalers plied the seven seas and battled the elements in search of precious whale oil. *Moby Dick* tells the fictional story of Captain Ahab, who sailed from Nantucket to find the Great White Whale. Ferry boats now take visitors to museums and historic buildings on these islands.

The two remaining areas are the central uplands and the western hills and mountains. The New England uplands run through the heart of Massachusetts. The fertile Connecticut River valley divides this low plateau into eastern and western portions. West of the plateau are the **Berkshire Hills,** a low range of the Appalachians. The scenic hills are covered with maple, ash, and birch forests that turn beautiful colors in the fall. On the western line of the state are the narrow Taconic Mountains, which form the border between Massachusetts and New York.

Rhode Island: Religious Freedom

The American Industrial Revolution began at Slater's Mill on the Blackstone River near Pawtucket, Rhode Island.

Expelled from Massachusetts by Puritans, Roger Williams went to an area southwest of Boston where several others had already gone. Williams helped to settle disagreements among these refugees and founded the Rhode Island colony. The capital, Providence, was named in honor of God's provisions. Though the smallest colony, Rhode Island made a vital contribution to the nation: the colonists became outspoken on religious freedom.

Rhode Island has the most independent spirit of any northeastern state. Its people burned a British vessel in protest long before the events of Lexington and Concord, and they renounced British rule on May 4, 1776—two months before the Declaration of Independence. It was also the last of the original thirteen colonies to ratify the Constitution. Religious freedom attracted settlers of many faiths, including Jews.

The Cradle of American Industry was located at the town of Pawtucket, just north of Providence. Slater's Mill became the first major industry in the nation, in 1793. A young English laborer named Samuel Slater, who had secretly memorized the plans of an English cloth factory, reproduced the design after he moved to Rhode Island. As a result, England's firm grip on the textile industry was broken. The looms wove *textiles* (cloth). **Textile mills** in New England once produced more cloth than any other place in the world, and they are still important to Rhode Island.

Rhode Island is sandwiched on the coast between Massachusetts and Connecticut. It has no mountains and sparsely populated uplands in the northwest. Most people live on the coastal plain along Narragansett Bay. The capital, Providence, is the second largest city in New England. Its harbor is protected by many offshore islands. The name of the state comes from the largest of these islands, Rhode Island. The America's Cup yacht races are held each year near this island.

Connecticut: The Constitution State

Connecticut is nicknamed the Constitution State for two reasons. It was the first colony to write a constitution (1639). A **constitution** is a set of laws describing and limiting the government's power. Its second contribution came when the states met in 1787 to draft a national constitution. Connecticut offered the **Great Compromise** that resolved a debate that threatened to break up the meeting. This "middle-sized" state proposed a **bicameral system** with *two* law-making bodies that share power: the Senate, where small states have the same votes as large states; and the House, where large states receive more votes equal to their population.

The people in Connecticut enjoy a high standard of living despite the state's lack of natural resources. In fact, its per capita income—over $32,000 per person—is higher than any other state's. Connecticut owes much of its success to Yankee ingenuity. Skilled inventors and businessmen have started thousands of manufacturing plants. Samuel Colt invented the Colt revolver. Eli Whitney, the inventor of the cotton gin, built a musket factory in Connecticut based on the new concept of **mass production.** Workers made gun parts from molds, all identical, rather than handmaking each gun one at a time. Virtually every factory on earth now uses this money-saving technique.

Most of Connecticut consists of hilly uplands. (A narrow strip of lowlands lies on the coast, and a few Taconic Mountains dip down from Massachusetts.) The English settlers built their first cities on the broad, fertile valley of the **Connecticut River,** which cuts the state in half. Hartford, the state's capital and largest city, is located on the Connecticut—the longest river in New England. Although it has many industries, Hartford is most proud of its role as the Insurance Capital of the World. Ship owners first started these insurance companies to protect themselves from the high risk of their cargo sinking in the ocean.

Several small towns on the Connecticut River experienced the first and most famous revival in American history. **Jonathan Edwards,** the greatest early American preacher, delivered a sermon that students still study in school today, entitled "Sinners in the Hands of an Angry God." His written account of a revival in his church (1735) was read throughout the colonies and helped to spark the first Great Awakening.

Many ports arose in Connecticut along Long Island Sound. Long Island, the largest island on the Atlantic seaboard, protects the Connecticut coast from Atlantic storms. (Long Island belongs to Connecticut's western neighbor, New York.) A rivalry with Boston inspired the port city of New Haven to build Yale University—the second college in the Northeast. Another port, Groton, became the submarine capital of the world. Groton launched the first modern submarine. It also produces most of the nation's nuclear subs and is a

The fastest clipper ships of the nineteenth century were built at the shipyards of Mystic Seaport, Connecticut. A museum there displays several vessels, including the last wooden whaling ship.

submarine base. Near Groton is Mystic Seaport. Once a whaling center in New England, it has been restored as a popular tourist spot.

◎ SECTION REVIEW

1. List the three basic freedoms that took root in New England.
2. What three basic types of terrain are found in New England? Which lower state lacks mountains?
3. Find the largest city in each state of lower New England. Explain how geography helped these cities to grow.
4. Name one tourist site and one product associated with each state in lower New England.
5. Why is Connecticut called the Constitution State?
💡 Why did Connecticut's main cities arise on a river, not on the coast?

Upper New England

Upper New England refers to the three northernmost New England states. Though small, these states are much larger than the lower three states. Several factors have hindered settlement, however. Upper New England has the highest mountain range in the Northeast. Glaciers exposed rocky soils, making farming difficult. The mountains not only block travel; they also shorten the growing seasons. Instead of seeing sprawling cities, one sees moose browsing in remote ponds.

Mountains truly dominate upper New England. All three states have mountains that rise above the **timber line,** the altitude at which the climate is too cold for trees to grow. Only one other state east of the Mississippi (New York) has mountains above the timber line. Everything above the timber line is called the **alpine zone** because the climate and stunted vegetation is similar to that in the Alps. Without trees and other obstructions, climbers can enjoy spectacular views but have no protection from fierce winds and storms.

New Hampshire: Live Free or Die

New Hampshire is the only Upper New England state that was one of the thirteen original colonies. As the ninth state to ratify the Constitution of the United States, its vote put the Constitution into effect. It also has traditionally hosted the first presidential primary in election years. These contributions explain why the state proudly claims the motto: "Live Free or Die."

The **White Mountains,** known for their white peaks and Christmas tree farms, dominate the northern region of the state. Tourists flock to ski resorts in winter and to covered bridges and rock formations in summer. The most famous rock formation, the Old Man of the Mountains, resembles the side of a face and has become a symbol of the state.

The Presidential Range is the most famous range in the White Mountains. The highest peaks are named after presidents, including Mt. Washington, Mt. Adams, Mt. Quincy Adams, Mt. Jefferson, Mt. Madison, Mt. Monroe, Mt. Pierce, and Mt. Eisenhower. Most of these exceed five thousand feet in elevation. A few peaks in the Franconia Range, such as Mt. Lincoln and Mt. Lafayette, also rise this high.

Local highways wind through several **notches** in the White Mountains. A notch is a low place on a ridge or mountain range through which a road can pass. The cuts in the ridges look as though a huge axe "notched" them out. Other regions call these low spots a *pass* or a *gap.* Many tourists stop at Franconia Notch to view the Old Man of the Mountains.

Mount Washington has a snow cover early in the fall.

Sports

Popular Trails

Perhaps the most spectacular hike east of the Rocky Mountains is the Knife Edge Trail in Maine. The mile-long trail, five to twenty feet wide, follows a ridge on the top of Mount Katahdin. The entire ridge, whose sides drop two thousand feet to the wooded valley, is well above timber line.

The Northeast was the birthplace of the nation's most famous trail—the Appalachian Trail. In 1921 Benton MacKaye, who had traveled the entire length of the Green Mountains, published plans for a chain of trails through the Appalachian Mountains. Another backpacker, Earl Shaffer, became the first man to hike the entire route in 1948, even before it was completed. Congress declared it a "national scenic trail" in 1968, along with trails on the Pacific Crest and on the Continental Divide. The Appalachian Trail runs two thousand miles across fourteen states, from Mt. Katahdin in Maine to Springer Mountain in Georgia. Every year hundreds of "through hikers" devote over half a year of their lives walking the entire length of the trail.

Many consider the Knife Edge Trail the most spectacular trail in the eastern states.

Horseback riding and mountain biking are also popular in the mountains of the Northeast—in the Whites of New Hampshire, the Greens of Vermont, the Poconos of Pennsylvania, and the Catskills and Adirondacks of New York. The Great Smoky Mountains are a famous destination for horseback riders in the South, and the Sierra Nevada are popular in the West.

The highest peak in the White Mountains is Mt. Washington (6,288 ft.), the only mountain in the Northeast that exceeds six thousand feet. Because it stands at a junction of weather systems, it has terrible weather. In April 1934, its weather station clocked a world-record wind speed of 231 miles per hour. In winter, snow accumulates to a depth of fifteen feet. The winds and storms have earned it the dubious distinction of having the "worst weather in the world." Tourists can ride the cog railway or drive to the summit to experience life in the alpine zone.

Most people live in the southern part of the state. The state's major industrial centers arose in this region—Nashua, Manchester, and the capital, Concord. Most of the south is New England uplands. One famous solitary mountain, Mt. Monadnock, rises above the landscape. The word **monadnock** has come to describe any rocky peak standing alone.

Only eighteen miles of New Hampshire's border touches the ocean. Portsmouth is the state's only major seaport. It is located on a narrow strip of coastal lowlands.

Vermont: The Green Mountain State

Vermont was once part of New York and New Hampshire. For many years, settlers from

Vermont has 115 covered bridges, more than any other state.

Church steeples and fall leaves characterize Vermont's countryside, such as this scene in the village of East Orange.

so well that the state became Norman Rockwell's preferred location for painting. Vermont boasts over one hundred covered bridges. Visitors come from all corners of the nation to view Vermont's most wonderful feature—the brilliant colors of autumn leaves.

Vermont has the lowest population in the Northeast for a couple of reasons. Like other New England states, it has little good farmland. Since the state is landlocked, Vermonters cannot make a living from fishing or trade. Instead they make the most of their mountain resources. The city of Barre is the nation's greatest producer of granite. Fair Haven quarries several colors of slate, and Proctor is famous for marble. The state is most known, however, for its maple syrup. Farms are covered with acres of ancient sugar maple trees. The Indians taught the early settlers how to gather maple sap and turn it into sugar and syrup.

The **Green Mountains,** extending from north to south, comprise most of Vermont's portion of the Appalachian Mountains. These high mountains are named for their evergreen carpets. Tourists ride gondolas or drive a toll-road to the top of Mt. Mansfield, Vermont's highest mountain. Because only five peaks exceed four thousand feet, this mountain offers a rare opportunity for Vermonters to see the alpine zone.

Valleys border the state on the east and west. The Connecticut River begins near Canada and forms the eastern boundary between Vermont and New Hampshire. Lake Champlain sprawls over the western border. This large lake is famous for sightings of Champ, the Vermont version of the Loch Ness monster. These two valleys—along the Connecticut River and Lake Champlain—support most of the state's population.

Maine Maine is the largest New England state. In fact, the other New England states could all fit within its borders. Yet Maine was not one of the thirteen original colonies. It was a frontier owned since 1677 by the Massachusetts colony. Citizens in the region resisted the Stamp Act of 1765 and later captured a British ship near Machias in the first naval battle of

both colonies argued over who owned the mountainous land between them. Finally the mountain settlers decided to form their own militia in 1770, called the Green Mountain Boys. They drove out the settlers from New York and refused to recognize the government in New Hampshire. The tough Green Mountain Boys captured Britain's Fort Ticonderoga (1776), an early victory in the War for Independence. Vermont declared itself an independent republic on January 15, 1777. After fourteen years of independence, Vermont became the first state to join the union after the original thirteen.

Though it is the only landlocked state in New England, Vermont displays all the other New England hallmarks. Its church steeples, barns, dairy farms, and hillside villages represent New England

the Revolutionary War. Maine was occupied by Britain during the war, and it later suffered from repeated raids during the War of 1812. Maine gained statehood in 1820.

Cities in Maine are small. Portland, the only large city, is the closest port in America for ships sailing to and from Europe. Most of Maine's coast is rocky, contrasting sharply with the beaches of the rest of the Atlantic states. The fifteen-hundred-foot Cadillac Mountain is the highest point on the entire Atlantic Coast between Labrador in Canada and Rio de Janeiro in Brazil. It is part of Acadia National Park, the first national park in the East and the only national park in the Northeast. Quoddy Head, a rocky cape extending into the Atlantic, is the easternmost point of the United States (longitude 66°57′ W).

Tourists visit the state to see its many ocean attractions. At the docks you can watch lobstermen unloading lobster pots. Maine lobster is world famous—the most valuable seafood catch worldwide. Boat rides will take visitors far out into the ocean to watch large whales surfacing. Others go to the islands off Penobscot Bay, which have America's only colonies of puffins outside Alaska. These funny birds, sometimes called "sea parrots," have colorful beaks like parrots and orange webbed feet like ducks.

North and west of the state are the Longfellow and White Mountains. These are the northernmost ranges of the great Appalachian Mountain system, which stretches from Maine to Alabama. The highest peak in the Longfellow Mountains is Mt. Katahdin. Its horseshoe ridge offers spectacular alpine scenery.

Wilderness covers much of Maine's mountain and upland area. Indeed, the Pine Tree State has the largest wilderness region east of the Mississippi. Its trees produce most of the nation's toothpicks—one hundred million every day. The trackless northern border with Canada was disputed until 1842. Fighting between lumberjacks almost sparked a war. Building forts with spade and shovel was the only action in the so-called Aroostook War. The fertile **Aroostook Valley** is now the nation's second largest producer of potatoes.

Mount Katahdin is the highest mountain in Maine and the start of the Appalachian Trail.

SECTION REVIEW

1. Define *alpine zone*. What four Eastern states have an alpine zone?
2. What mountain range is associated with New Hampshire? with Vermont?
3. What are notches?
4. Name the highest mountain in each upper New England state. What do these peaks have in common?
5. Name one main product associated with each state in upper New England.
6. Vermont's countryside displays all the hallmarks of a New England state. Name at least five of these hallmarks.

💡 Why does Maine have the lowest per capita income in all of New England?

THE MIDDLE ATLANTIC

The five states midway between New England and the South are called the Middle Atlantic states. This region's "middle" location on the Atlantic seaboard explains why it has a such a mixture of climate and culture. Unlike New Englanders, who are proud of the unique traits of their region, no people identify themselves as "Middle Atlanticers." Most consider themselves Easterners, but a few call themselves New Englanders or Southerners.

Swedes, Finns, and Dutch were the first to settle the Middle Atlantic. Large groups of Irish, Germans, and Italians have also settled here. Such **diversity** is just as much a trait of America as is its English heritage. People are free to develop their God-given talents, and the whole nation benefits in the process. America has been called "the most culturally diverse nation in the world." The following graph shows the ancestry of Americans, according to the latest census.

The Middle Atlantic is divided into three major geographic regions. (See map on page 147.) The Atlantic Coastal Plain is a flat, fertile area near the sea. The **Piedmont** is a low plateau with hills, slightly higher than the coastal plain. Beyond the Piedmont rise the various ranges of the Appalachian Mountains. A few states extend west beyond the mountains to the Appalachian Plateau and the Great Lakes Plain.

A geographic feature called the Fall Line explains why the Middle Atlantic has become known for its big cities. The **Fall Line** is the edge of the Piedmont, where the land drops to the coastal plain. As rivers plunge over this line, they form rapids and waterfalls that block ships. In colonial days, farmers and trappers in the interior carried food and furs overland to the Fall Line, where they were loaded onto ships and taken to distant ports. Many large cities sprang up on the Fall Line to handle this trade. Cities also used the water to turn water wheels for their industries.

New York

Albany, the capital of New York, is known as the Cradle of the Union. Here in 1754 Benjamin Franklin presented the first formal plan to unite the colonies against their common enemies—the French and the Indians. During the War for Independence, the British believed they could destroy the American rebellion by capturing Albany. One out of every three battles in the war was fought on New York soil.

During the nineteenth century New York became a "melting pot" where millions of immigrants experienced liberty for the first time in their lives with nobody telling them where to live, where to work, or how to worship. The Statue of Liberty, a symbol of the nation, still greets nearly one hundred thousand foreign immigrants who arrive each year.

A Megalopolis New York City is the largest city in the nation. Its total population, seven million, is more than double that of the second largest city, Los Angeles. It also has a higher population *density* than any other city—over twenty-three thousand people per square mile! This great mass of people makes things happen. New York City has more cultural attractions than any other city in the nation.

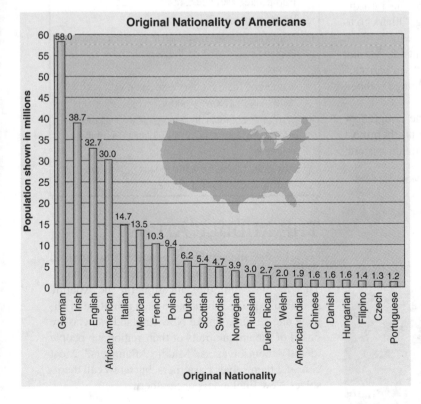

Original Nationality of Americans

Population shown in millions

German 58.0, Irish 38.7, English 32.7, African American 30.0, Italian 14.7, Mexican 13.5, French 10.3, Polish 9.4, Dutch 6.2, Scottish 5.4, Swedish 4.7, Norwegian 3.9, Russian 3.0, Puerto Rican 2.7, Welsh 2.0, American Indian 1.9, Chinese 1.6, Danish 1.6, Hungarian 1.6, Filipino 1.4, Czech 1.3, Portuguese 1.2

Original Nationality

The Fall Line

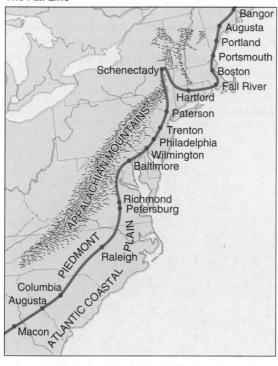

The population of New York City has outgrown the city limits. People have moved to nearby towns and communities called **suburbs.** When we talk about a city, we often mean both the city and its suburbs, called the **metropolitan area.** The metropolitan area for New York City includes suburbs in four states and exceeds 19.5 million people!

Most of New York's skyscrapers rise above the south end of Manhattan Island.

Statue of Liberty

The Statue of Liberty, the tallest statue ever built, has inspired millions of immigrants seeking freedom in America. Lady Liberty is dressed in flowing robes, chains of bondage lying at her feet, while her right hand raises the torch of freedom. Seven rays on her crown radiate freedom to all nations. Her left hand carries a law book, inscribed with the date July 4, 1776.

The people of France spent $400,000 to build the statue. They wanted to give the American people a gift to commemorate their first one hundred years of independence, which France helped them to win. The statue, first conceived in 1865, was built in France and then disassembled for shipment. An American architect completed its magnificent pedestal on Liberty Island. President Cleveland dedicated the statue on October 28, 1886.

From toe to crown, Lady Liberty stands 111 feet high. The outstretched arm and torch add another 40 feet. The iron framework was designed by Alexandre Gustave Eiffel, who later created the Eiffel Tower in Paris. The three hundred copper sheets that cover the iron frame are now weathered, giving the 225-ton statue its green color. Though Lady Liberty does not stand as tall as the Motherland Statue in Russia, the 154-foot pedestal adds enough height to make it the tallest ever built. The statue's nose alone is the size of a person. Each year two million visitors ascend a 171-step spiral staircase to view New York harbor from an observation point inside the crown.

A **megalopolis** (meaning "great city") is a combination of several metropolitan areas that have run into each other. Almost the entire northeastern seaboard has become one big megalopolis. A continuous chain of cities runs from Boston to Washington, D.C., with New York City at its heart. Four of the top seven metro areas in the United States are in this megalopolis: New York City (first), the Washington-Baltimore metro area (fourth), Philadelphia-Trenton (fifth), and Boston (seventh). This is the most densely populated area

127

in America. It was the first megalopolis in the world, and it is still growing.

The Upstate New York is a big state—the biggest in the Northeast. Even though half the population lives in New York City, the city occupies only a small fraction of the state's area at the mouth of the Hudson River. The rest of the mainland is called **Upstate New York** or the Upstate. Upstate New Yorkers are not part of the New York metropolitan area, and they distinguish themselves from the "downstate."

Population Density of North America

Let's Go Exploring

1. Where is the largest single area with a population density over 250 per square mile?

2. Does any part of the Northeast have a population density under two per square mile?

3. Is any part of the United States "uninhabited"?

4. Where is the only purple area outside the United States?

💡 Where in the United States can you find a population density over 250 per square mile *not* near any major bodies of water?

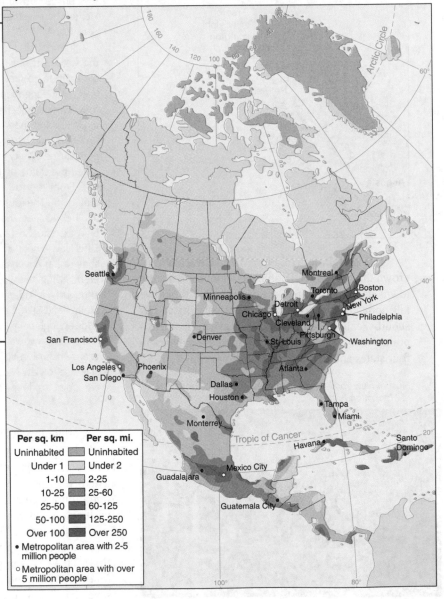

Per sq. km	Per sq. mi.
Uninhabited	Uninhabited
Under 1	Under 2
1-10	2-25
10-25	25-60
25-50	60-125
50-100	125-250
Over 100	Over 250

• Metropolitan area with 2-5 million people

○ Metropolitan area with over 5 million people

The Big Apple

New York City is the largest city in the United States. For many years it was the largest city in the world. Although other cities are now larger than New York, it remains a leader in business, finance, fashion, and the arts.

The mayor of New York City is responsible for more people than the governors of *forty-three* states! New York City's five districts, or **boroughs** (BUR oze), are almost as famous as the city itself. Have you ever heard of Manhattan, Brooklyn, Queens, Staten Island, and the Bronx? Only the Bronx lies on the mainland of New York State. The other four boroughs are spread across three islands.

Manhattan, the central part of the city, stands on an island at the mouth of the Hudson River. The Dutch discovered this harbor—the best harbor on the East Coast of North America. In 1626 they bought the island from the Indians for about twenty-four dollars worth of trinkets. The Dutch called their town New

Times Square, New York City

Amsterdam after their own capital, Amsterdam, the best port in Europe. (The name was later changed to New York in honor of the Duke of York, who captured the colony for England.)

Now Manhattan Island houses over 1.5 million people. During work days, over 3 million people earn their living on the island. To accommodate so many, Manhattan has many skyscrapers. The skyline includes the Empire State Building, once the tallest building in the world, and the twin towers of the World Trade Center.

Manhattan's street names are known worldwide. Banks, stock exchanges, and other financial institutions line Wall Street. Theaters line Broadway. Fifth Avenue is famous for department stores and fashion shops. Advertising agencies have offices along Madison Avenue, and impressive office complexes and apartments rise beside Park Avenue. Central Park, a large open area of trees, ponds, paths, museums, and art galleries, provides a haven from the crowded streets and buildings of the city.

Toll bridges and tunnels have replaced most of the ferry boats that once brought people to the islands. However, the Staten Island Ferry still carries sightseers from Manhattan to Staten Island. The ferry passes by Liberty Island, where the Statue of Liberty raises her torch above the harbor. The Verrazano Narrows Bridge, which joins Staten Island and Long Island, has the longest suspension span on the North American continent.

New York has many ethnic neighborhoods, such as Cuban, Greek, Irish, and Puerto Rican. China Town is a popular tourist area in south Manhattan. The largest population of Jews outside of Israel lives in Brooklyn. Greenwich Village, originally settled by Bohemians, is now famous for art shops, bookstores, curio shops, and cafes. Most immigrants in the 1990s have come from Latin American countries, such as Jamaica and Haiti. Immigrants from the Dominican Republic make up the largest ethnic neighborhood in the city.

Of course, in such a large city, some neighborhoods are miserable slums where criminals threaten the residents daily. Only a few small churches preach the true gospel. Regardless of wealth or background, all New Yorkers need to accept the Lord Jesus Christ as their own personal Savior. Pray for New York City.

The Upstate includes the most important valley in the Northeast. Look at the map on page 117. The **Hudson River** and its main tributary, the **Mohawk River,** provide the only northern gap through the Appalachian Mountains. This green valley gave the state access to the West (any land beyond the Appalachians). At the time of the American Revolution, however, the Mohawk Indians had large towns and forts all along the Mohawk River. They refused to sell land to the Whites. Their power was broken when they joined Britain's war against the colonies. Most fled to Canada, but a few thousand still live on reservations in New York today.

Two technological achievements helped settlers to settle the Upstate quickly. In 1807 Robert Fulton steered the first steamboat *up* the Hudson River to Albany, making two-way trade possible. In 1817 New York began constructing the famous **Erie Canal** in the Mohawk Valley, making it possible for boats to travel all the way from Albany to the Great

Lakes. The Erie Canal was a marvel of engineering. It turned New York City into the trade capital of the world. The state's second and third largest cities are located at the other end of the Erie Canal system— Buffalo, on Lake Erie, and Rochester, on Lake Ontario.

Few people live in the mountains that run through the heart of Upstate New York. The Mohawk Valley divides the mountains into two main ranges. South are the low Catskill Mountains. Rip Van Winkle supposedly slept on these hills for twenty years. North are the high **Adirondack Mountains.** They boast two 5,000-foot peaks and over forty 4,000-foot peaks. The twelve highest peaks reach the alpine zone. The Adirondacks have been the site of the Winter Olympics twice at Lake Placid. This vast, empty wilderness is part of the largest state park in the nation.

New York and Pennsylvania are the only two northeastern states that have large sections west of the Appalachian Mountains. There we find the

Geographer's Corner

Map Scale

It is impossible to show all the important details of New York City on a single map. If a cartographer tried to show the streets of Manhattan on a map that shows all five boroughs, the map would look like a big black blob. A mapmaker must always choose the best *map scale* to show the details he wants to emphasize.

A map scale is the small bar on the edge of the map that looks like a ruler. Find the map scale on the three maps.

Use the information on the three scales to answer these questions.

1. On which map does one-half inch equal one mile?

2. Which map gives you directions to Wall Street?

3. Which map shows all the suburbs of New York City?

4. What river runs between Manhattan and the Bronx?

5. Which borough has the John F. Kennedy International Airport?

6. About how long is Long Island?

♀ What is the total land area of Manhattan Island?

Northeast Megalopolis and Nearby Metropolitan Areas

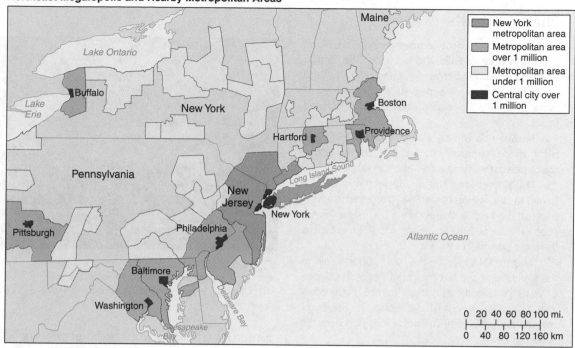

■	New York metropolitan area
■	Metropolitan area over 1 million
□	Metropolitan area under 1 million
■	Central city over 1 million

City's Five Boroughs

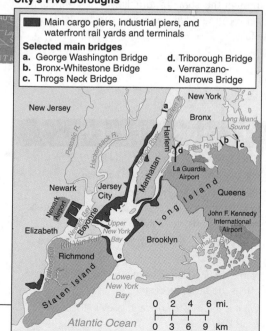

■ Main cargo piers, industrial piers, and waterfront rail yards and terminals

Selected main bridges
- **a.** George Washington Bridge
- **b.** Bronx-Whitestone Bridge
- **c.** Throgs Neck Bridge
- **d.** Triborough Bridge
- **e.** Verranzano-Narrows Bridge

Manhattan: The Heart of New York City

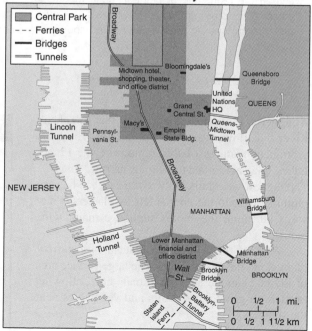

■	Central Park
- - -	Ferries
▬▬	Bridges
═══	Tunnels

Niagara Falls

Perhaps the most famous waterfall in North America is **Niagara Falls.** It is located on the Niagara River, which flows between Ontario, Canada, and western New York. It serves as part of the international boundary between Canada and the United States.

Niagara Falls is really a combination of falls. Goat Island divides the river into two falls. On the United States side of the island is the American Falls. It is more than 1,000 feet long and is 182 feet high. On the Canadian side is Horseshoe Falls. It received its name because the brink is shaped like a horseshoe. Horseshoe Falls, about 2,600 feet long and 173 feet high, is the more powerful of the two.

Niagara Falls may be the most powerful falls in the world. Someone has estimated that 500,000 tons of water go over the falls every minute. Put another way, 114 million gallons fall over Horseshoe Falls every minute, and another 6 million gallons flow over the American Falls.

Niagara Falls is a favorite tourist attraction. It has earned the reputation of being a "honeymooner's paradise" because so many newlyweds visit this breathtaking site. At night, multicolored spotlights

Niagara Falls is the most powerful waterfall in the Northern Hemisphere. The average water flow is 212,000 cubic feet per second. American Falls is shown here.

shine on the falls, adding to the beauty of the falling water. Tour boats take riders on the river below the falls through the spray of tumbling water. Although they get wet, the riders see some spectacular views of the falls.

Allegheny Plateau, named after the Allegheny River that flows *west* into the interior. The most prominent features of this region are the Finger Lakes. Glaciers carved these long, narrow "fingers." The highest waterfalls in the Northeast can be seen plummeting into the gorges left by glaciers. Vineyards all along the shores support a major wine industry.

West of the Allegheny Plateau is a narrow plain along the Great Lakes. The large surface area of the lakes moderates the climate here, allowing farmers to grow many fruits and vegetables near the shore.

◎ SECTION REVIEW

1. What is diversity? What role did New York play in bringing diversity to the United States?
2. Describe the three major geographic regions found in the Middle Atlantic. What two other geographic regions are found in New York?
3. Distinguish *city, suburb, metropolitan area,* and *megalopolis.*
4. Name the five boroughs of New York City. Which one is the business center?
5. What is the most important valley in the Northeast? Why?
♀ Why is New York City called the Big Apple?

Life on the Delaware River

The **Delaware River** forms the long boundary between Pennsylvania and New Jersey. Although it rises in New York and empties into the ocean in the state of Delaware, the river has exerted its primary influence on Pennsylvania and New Jersey. The distinct culture of the Delaware Valley is reflected in everyday words. For example, they eat "hot cakes" rather than "griddle cakes" or "pancakes."

Pennsylvania The nation's two most important documents—the Declaration of Independence and the Constitution—were signed at the Pennsylvania State House. This historic building, renamed Independence Hall, sits in downtown Philadelphia. The Liberty Bell is just across the street. Every year the United States celebrates the signing of the Declaration of Independence, July 4, 1776, on Independence Day. Pennsylvania also has a national cemetery in the town of Gettysburg, commemorating those who died in the nation's only civil war (1861-65). Thousands of Pennsylvanians and other troops died at Gettysburg, the bloodiest battle ever fought on the North American continent.

The state's largest city, **Philadelphia,** is located on a magnificent harbor on the banks of the deep Delaware River. The most populous city in colonial America, it still ranks fifth largest. The founder, William Penn, carefully planned the streets and parks of the old city with a grid pattern that has been imitated by many other cities.

Philadelphia was built in the wooded Piedmont at the southeastern corner of Pennsylvania. Quakers from England were the first occupants. They named the city from two Greek words meaning "city of brotherly love." Laws guaranteeing freedom of religion attracted many religious minorities, such as the Amish and the Mennonites of Germany. Americans still enjoy their products—the twisted pretzels of the Pennsylvania Dutch, Philadelphia cream cheese, and fine Amish furniture. Most of all, Americans enjoy chocolate from the town of Hershey, which has the largest chocolate factory in the world.

The Liberty Bell is on display at a historic park in Philadelphia, Pennsylvania.

Low Appalachian Mountains cut through the center of the state. The Pocono Mountains are a scenic subrange that extends east to the border of New Jersey. Like New York, Pennsylvania stretches beyond the Appalachians to the Allegheny Plateau. Two large rivers—the Monongahela and the Allegheny—drain water from this plateau. These two rivers meet to form the Ohio River—the easternmost extension of the vast Mississippi River drainage basin. Ships can load goods on these navigable waters and ship them almost two thousand miles to the mouth of the Mississippi.

Located at the vital junction of the Allegheny and Monongahela Rivers is the city of Pittsburgh. It boasts the nation's largest steel industry. Both iron ore and coal are used in the making of steel. Hard coal, or **anthracite coal,** is best for making steel because it burns longer and makes less smoke than soft coal. Only five states in the nation have

The Amish

The Amish religious sect broke away from the Mennonites in the 1690s over a difference of opinion about church discipline. Jacob Amman, a Swiss Mennonite bishop, strongly believed that members who were excommunicated from the church should be avoided completely, or "shunned."

The Amish fled to North America around 1720 during a time of general religious persecution in Europe. At the invitation of William Penn, they first settled in eastern Pennsylvania. The largest concentration of Amish today is found on the fertile farmland of Lancaster County, Pennsylvania. Large communities of Amish are also located in the states of Ohio, Indiana, Illinois, and Iowa. At this time, there are virtually no Amish remnants in Europe.

The Amish people are known for their simple lifestyle and the self-sufficiency of their communities. Amish doctrine emphasizes living apart from the world and close to the soil. Their plain clothing symbolizes their nonconformist way of life. Amish women wear simple homemade black dresses and bonnets. Traditionally, the men wear hats and do not shave their beards.

Farming provides the livelihood for most Amish families. They are generally excellent farmers, even though most of them refuse to use modern farm equipment. The Old Order Amish, the most conservative branch of the sect, strictly avoid electricity and automobiles. It is not uncommon for them to till the soil with horse-drawn plows and to rely on horses and buggies for transportation. Although they avoid many mechanical conveniences, Old Order farmers do not hesitate to use fertilizers and pesticides. Amish farms must be productive in order to support their large families.

Amish settlements are made up of church districts that are both self-contained and self-governing. The members meet in each other's homes, since there are no church buildings. The services are conducted in a mixture of German and English, commonly known as Pennsylvania Dutch. The Amish baptize only adults, when they join the church. Amish do not force their children to join the church. However, they continue to "shun" members who leave—excluding them from many of the activities of daily life.

Amish people still use horse-drawn carriages in Pennsylvania.

The Pennsylvania Dutch descended from German immigrants who came to America in the eighteenth and nineteenth centuries. These people were called "Dutch," not because they were from the Netherlands, but because the German word for "German" is *Deutsch*. Americans simplified the pronunciation when describing these settlers.

deposits of anthracite coal. Pennsylvania has the nation's most extensive hard coal deposits. (See the map of America's coal fields on page 161.)

The Great Lakes Plain at the extreme northwest are the only lowlands in the state. The city of Erie on Lake Erie is the state's only port on the Great Lakes. Pennsylvania has inland sea ports on all three eastern waterways: the Atlantic Ocean, the Mississippi River, and the Great Lakes.

New Jersey Nearly one hundred battles were fought in New Jersey during the War for Independence. Each year people reenact George Washington's crossing of the ice-choked Delaware River to surprise a British outpost at Trenton on Christmas Day, 1776.

Most of New Jersey's population lives on the east side of the state, across the bay from New York City. A string of cities stretches from this end of the state west to Trenton, the capital. Trenton is located on the Fall Line of the Delaware River, the western boundary of the state. This heavily industrialized region is part of the northeastern megalopolis.

Coastal plains cover all of New Jersey south of the Fall Line. Port cities process the nation's largest clam catch. Atlantic City has the world's most famous *boardwalk* (an oceanfront sidewalk made from wooden planks). Park Place and other street names in the game Monopoly came from Atlantic City. The **Pine Barrens,** a wooded and boggy wilderness, covers one thousand square miles of the coast. Tales abound of campers lost in the dense woods and of sightings of the legendary Jersey Devil.

New Jersey's climate is warmer than much of the Northeast, and its soil is extremely fertile. The warm, moist air from the Gulf Stream creates a humid subtropical climate. New Jersey was nicknamed the Garden State because of its many small farms and roadside produce stands. Farmers raise common garden crops such as beans, tomatoes, green peppers, and melons. Their farms are called **truck farms** because they can easily ship fresh products to the big cities by truck. The state also has many greenhouses for growing roses, orchids, lilies, poinsettias, geraniums, and chrysanthemums.

The Piedmont covers most of the rest of the state. Truck farms and greenhouses appear in the Piedmont as well as in the coastal plains. The only mountainous area is Kittatinny Ridge of the Appalachians, which extends down into the northwest corner of the state.

Washington Crossing the Delaware, *by Emanuel Gottlieb Leutze, The Metropolitan Museum of Art, Gift of John Stewart Kennedy, 1897. (97.34) Photograph © 1992. George Washington crossed the ice-clogged Delaware River and surprised British soldiers at Trenton, New Jersey.*

1. What religious group founded Pennsylvania? Why did so many other groups settle here?

2. Name a major Pennsylvania port on each of the three great Eastern waterways.

3. What major industries are found in Pennsylvania and New Jersey?

4. Why is New Jersey called the Garden State?

💡 Why did Philadelphia become the largest city in the American colonies?

Two Border States

Maryland and Delaware are border states, located between the Northeast and the South. They once had much in common with the Southern states—large plantations, wealthy slaveholders, and a Southern drawl. But during the Civil War, both Maryland and Delaware remained in the Union, while the Southern states seceded. Both states have since become an integral part of the great megalopolis of the Northeast.

The two border states share much in common. Both have a humid subtropical climate and rich soil, associated with the South. Both share land on

the **Delmarva Peninsula,** the largest peninsula in the Northeast. The peninsula gets its name because it contains parts of three states: *Del*aware, *Mar*yland, and Virginia (*Va.*). Unlike most northeastern regions, this wide coastal plain has rich soil. Small towns and farms are scattered across the peninsula. Most large cities, however, have grown up along the rivers that flow into the two bays on either side of the peninsula—the Delaware Bay and the Chesapeake Bay.

On the Delaware Bay Delaware is proud of its nickname: the First State. It was the first state to ratify the constitution. Earlier at Dover, the young nation had hammered out its first plan of government, the Articles of Confederation (1778).

Lutherans built the Old Swedes Church in Wilmington, Delaware, in 1698. Now occupied by Episcopalians, it is the oldest active Protestant church in North America.

Mason-Dixon Line

The Mason-Dixon Line is the most famous state boundary line ever surveyed in America. Two surveyors, Charles Mason and Jeremiah Dixon, spent three years (1765–68) settling the disputed border between Pennsylvania and Maryland at parallel 39°43′17.6″ N. Later, the line was extended west to mark the border between Pennsylvania and Virginia (modern-day West Virginia). Many of the original milestones still stand at the border.

During the debates in the early nineteenth century that led to the Civil War, Congress divided the nation at the Mason-Dixon Line. This parallel marked the northern limits of slavery. As a result, the Mason-Dixon line became a symbol of the differences between the North and the South.

Delaware, located on the Delaware Bay, is the nation's second smallest state. It lies almost entirely on the eastern side of the Delmarva Peninsula. With just over twenty-five thousand people, the capital, Dover, is the only large town located on this peninsula. Swedish colonists first settled the area, which they called New Sweden. They were the first settlers to build log cabins. Logs were much quicker to prepare than the English-style sawed boards that the Puritans had been using. Log cabins became the standard style of home on the frontier.

Only a small strip of Piedmont crosses the northern tip of Delaware, near the mouth of the Delaware River. The state's largest city, Wilmington, is located here. Wilmington has so many chemical plants, especially Du Pont, that it is known as the Chemical Capital of the World. The state's low taxes and minimal regulations have attracted many large banks to Wilmington.

On the Chesapeake Bay

Maryland is nicknamed the Old Line State in honor of the line of brave soldiers who fought at the Battle of Long Island (August 27, 1776). While the rest of the Continental Army was fleeing in headlong retreat, a small line of crack Marylander troops stepped forward to halt the advancing redcoats. Seven times the tiny line pressed forward, until it was overwhelmed by the enemy. Only a handful of the "immortal" Marylanders survived, but they saved Washington's army. Maryland later sacrificed land for the nation's capital. (Virginia also contributed land, but it was not needed and later became the city of Arlington.)

Although no Revolutionary battles were fought in Maryland, the state has two famous battle sites from other wars. During the War of 1812, the British attempted to capture Fort McHenry, on Baltimore Harbor. Francis Scott Key, a Maryland citizen, witnessed the night-time bombardment. He was so moved at seeing the American flag still flying in the morning that he composed what later became the national anthem, "The Star-Spangled Banner." Another famous site is Antietam, near Sharpsburg. More American soldiers died there in

The Great Falls of the Potomac mark the Fall Line near Washington, D.C.

one day of the Civil War (September 17, 1862) than on any other day in the nation's history.

All of Maryland's large cities are located on its extensive coastal plain. Many rivers flow through this rich farmland into the **Chesapeake Bay.** This vast, deep bay—the largest in the United States—cuts the state nearly in half. Its salt waters provide much of the nation's clams and crabs for supermarkets. Annapolis, the state capital, touches the bay. Naval officers train here at the U.S. Naval Academy.

Baltimore, Maryland's largest city and primary seaport, is an industrial center on the bay. Baltimore became the nation's first railroad center in the early nineteenth century, handling goods shipped from the West on the Baltimore-Ohio railroad. Tom Thumb, the first major train to be tested in the United States (in 1830), was stationed in Baltimore. The world's first telegraph line, running from nearby Washington, D.C. to Baltimore, carried Samuel F. B. Morse's first telegraph message, "What hath God wrought?"

Maryland, first settled by European Catholics, has a great diversity of peoples. The suburbs of Baltimore and Washington, D.C. have sprawled into each other to form a single metropolitan area. The Baltimore suburbs have also spread north through Wilmington and Philadelphia to link Baltimore with the Northeastern megalopolis.

Maryland has the most unusual shape of any state in the Northeast. Look at the map on page 117. Notice the east border on the Delmarva Peninsula. The west border is just as unusual. Which borders are natural and which are political? The narrow strip of land that extends deep into the continent is called a **panhandle** (any long, narrow strip of a state). Maryland is only two miles wide at its narrowest point in the panhandle! Maryland's panhandle extends past the Appalachian Mountains into the Allegheny Plateau.

The District of Columbia

Our study of the Northeast ends appropriately at the national capital, Washington, D.C. This city is not part of any state, but an independent district run by Congress. For this reason, it is called the *District* of Columbia (D.C.). Every year leaders from all fifty states of the Union gather here, along with their families and tens of thousands of staff members.

To protect the American people from power-hungry rulers, the founders of the United States established a unique form of government, called a **federated republic.** A *republic* is a government run by elected representatives of the people. A *federation* divides powers between state governments and a national government. The founders further weakened the national government by dividing its powers among three separate branches: Congress, which passes laws; the president, who enforces laws; and the Supreme Court, which interprets the laws.

Washington, D.C. stands on Capitol Hill overlooking the Potomac River. The city planners laid out a city in the wilderness both beautiful and

The Statue of Freedom has crowned the Capitol dome since 1863.

The United States	
Capital	Washington, D.C.
Area (sq. mi.)	3,675,031
Population	267,954,767
Natural Increase	0.6%
Life Expectancy	76
Literacy Rate	96%
Per Capita GDP	$27,607
Population Density	72

efficient. Parks and trees line the roads. The city roads look like the spokes on a wheel radiating from the central hub. The central park area, called the National Mall, is surrounded by beautifully designed government buildings. Its layout makes Washington among the most beautiful capitals in the world.

There are six important government buildings in the Washington area. The most important are the White House, where the President lives; the Capitol building, where Congress meets; and the Supreme Court Building. Paper money is printed at the Bureau of Engraving and Printing. The Federal Bureau of Investigation (FBI) Building is the headquarters for this crime-fighting bureau. Every

Washington Monument is the highest structure in the capital. A few visitors climb the 898 steps to the top, but most ride the elevator.

Constitution, and the Bill of Rights. You can also visit the Library of Congress, the National Aquarium, the U.S. Botanic Garden, and the National Arboretum (a tree garden).

The most famous monument in the capital is the Washington Monument, a 555-foot tower that offers splendid views of the city. It honors **George Washington,** the first president and greatest hero in United States history. Every year on President's Day, Americans honor Washington. Few other nations can claim such a leader who sacrificed personal ambition to promote the freedom of his people.

The city has many other monuments and memorials. Jefferson Memorial and the Lincoln Memorial house massive statues of these honored presidents. The city preserves two other historical

Lincoln's statue is the highlight of the Lincoln Memorial in Washington, D.C.

morning some twenty-three thousand employees show up at the Pentagon, headquarters of the United States armed forces. The Pentagon is located across the Potomac in Arlington, Virginia. This five-sided structure is the largest office complex anywhere on earth.

Besides the government buildings, this city offers the nation's greatest collection of national museums and national monuments. The **Smithsonian Institution** houses the largest museum in the nation. It includes fourteen buildings plus the National Zoo. The buildings house everything from Alexander Graham Bell's first telephone to the Wright Brothers' plane. The tattered flag mentioned in "The Star-Spangled Banner" hangs on one wall. The capital also has the National Archives, which preserve the nation's founding documents—the Declaration of Independence, the monuments for President Lincoln, who steered the nation through the Civil War: the Ford Theater, where he was shot, and the Peterson House across the street, where he died. A memorial to Theodore Roosevelt sits on an island in the Potomac. Across the Potomac is Arlington National Cemetery, the final resting place of many soldiers from America's wars. Its most famous monuments are the Tomb of the Unknown Soldier and the Eternal Flame. The National Mall has another war memorial that names every soldier who died in the Vietnam War (1954-75).

In spite of the Northeast's great history, it is struggling with the problems that face all great civilizations—drugs, divorce, and crime. Abortion has been legalized in the name of "freedom of choice." Many churches and universities have become famous for *attacking* the absolute truths of Scripture. Five major false religions began in the Northeast by leaders who found "new" interpretations of the Bible (Jehovah's Witnesses, Christian Science, Adventism, Mormonism, and Unitarianism). Unitarianism took root in Boston—once the heart of Puritan territory—right after the War for Independence. Unitarians reject the deity of Christ, believing that God is one person, not three. In 1933 many Unitarian leaders led in drafting the *Humanist Manifesto,* a radical document that denied the existence of human sin and that affirmed mankind's ability to make himself perfect. Although few Americans claim to be humanists, most are humanists in practice.

The only lasting solution to these problems is a return to the beliefs on which America was founded. God gave a solemn warning to His people after they arrived at the Promised Land, and their failure is a lesson for Americans today:

Beware . . . lest when thou hast eaten and art full, and hast built goodly houses, and dwelt therein; and when thy herds and thy flocks multiply, and thy silver and thy gold is multiplied, and all that thou hast is multiplied; then thine heart be lifted up, and thou forget the Lord thy God, which brought thee forth out of the land of Egypt, from the house of bondage; . . . and thou say in thine heart, my power and the might of mine hand hath gotten me this wealth. (Deut. 8:11-14, 17)

SECTION REVIEW

1. Why are Maryland and Delaware called border states?

2. What two bays are located on either side of Delmarva Peninsula?

3. Name the major geographic regions in Delaware and Maryland.

4. Explain how the Constitution is designed to protect Americans from power-hungry rulers.

5. Who is the greatest hero in United States history? Why?

- Why are there no large cities on Delmarva Peninsula?

REVIEW 6

Can You Define These Terms?

township
Atlantic seaboard
textile mills
constitution
bicameral system

mass production
timber line
alpine zone
notch
monadnock

diversity
suburb
metropolitan area
megalopolis
borough

anthracite coal
truck farm
panhandle
federated republic

Can You Locate These Natural Features?

New England uplands
Berkshire Hills
Connecticut River
White Mountains
Green Mountains

Aroostook Valley
Piedmont
Fall Line
Hudson River

Mohawk River
Adirondack Mountains
Niagara Falls
Allegheny Plateau

Delaware River
Pine Barrens
Delmarva Peninsula
Chesapeake Bay

Can You Explain the Significance of These People, Places, and Events?

New England
Pilgrims
Boston
War for Independence

Great Compromise
Jonathan Edwards
New York City
Upstate New York

Manhattan
Erie Canal
Philadelphia
Baltimore

District of Columbia
Smithsonian Institution
George Washington

How Much Do You Remember?

1. Compare and contrast the basic features of New England and the Middle Atlantic.
   a. geography
   b. climate
   c. cultural diversity
   d. industries
   e. cities
2. Which state made each of these contributions to America?
   a. Liberty Bell
   b. first college
   c. first constitution
3. What two northeastern states were *not* among the original thirteen colonies? Why?
4. Make a chart of the eleven northeastern states. On the left column write the state name. Then make four more columns for the main mountain range, river, port, and products/industry. Some cells will be blank.
5. Why were so many cities founded on the Fall Line?
6. What geographic features made Massachusetts the leading state in New England? What made New York the leading state in the Middle Atlantic area?

7. What three mountain ranges in the Northeast contain peaks above five thousand feet? What other range in the Northeast reaches the alpine zone?
8. Name the five major rivers of the Northeast. What major cities are on each river?

What Do You Think?

1. What does the Bible mean by *liberty* in Galatians 5:13? Can the government provide this type of liberty?
2. Why do you think God has blessed America with freedom and prosperity?
3. What bad consequences occur in business, politics, and religion when freedom is used selfishly?
4. Does diversity have any disadvantages?
5. What northeastern state has no connection to the megalopolis? Why?
6. Have Americans lost some of the liberty they once enjoyed? Explain your answer.
7. What can you do now to protect liberty in America?

141

CHAPTER 7

THE SOUTHERN UNITED STATES

The South has contributed much to the greatness of the United States. Since colonial days, Southern leaders fought to make the states free and independent. Among the early heroes were Thomas Jefferson, who wrote the Declaration of Independence, and George Washington, who helped to make the dream of independence a reality.

Over 650,000 Americans died in the **American Civil War** (1861-65), the bloodiest war in the nation's history. Military parks and national monuments across the Southern states remind the nation about the issues raised by this war. Southerners believed that they were fighting to preserve **states' rights,** the right of independent states to run their own affairs, which included slavery. They believed they could leave the Union if the federal government became overbearing. Northerners, in contrast, believed that the states did not have a right to dissolve the Union. Abraham Lincoln and other leaders accepted the right of Southern states to retain slavery in their own lands, but they argued that slavery was a moral evil that the nation could not allow to spread. In an address to the Republican Party in 1858, Lincoln showed from Scripture that nations cannot remain divided on such issues:

If a kingdom be divided against itself, that kingdom cannot stand. And if a house be divided against itself, that house cannot stand. (Mark 3:24-25)

The South was devastated by the war, and it struggled for decades to recover. Its old way of life had disappeared forever. After years of bitterness and strife, Southern leaders of all races have finally begun working together to make a new, better way of life. Even after all the changes, the South has not lost its distinct culture. Southerners are known for their *conservativeness,* holding on to traditional values and opposing rapid change.

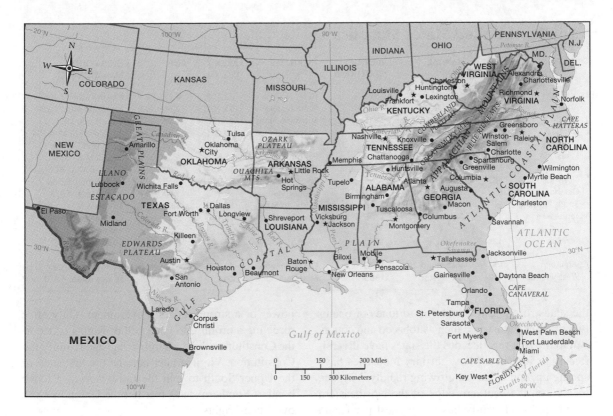

THE UPPER SOUTH

Unlike the plains in the Lower South, mountains dominate large portions of the Upper South. The five states of the Upper South have mountains that exceed four thousand feet. As in Upper New England, the mountains have played a major role in the region's history.

Tobacco States of the Atlantic

Virginia and North Carolina were among the original thirteen colonies, founded on the Atlantic seaboard. The Appalachian Mountains in the west kept early settlers on the Piedmont and the wide **Atlantic Coastal Plain.** North Carolina has more Atlantic coastline than any of the other original colonies, and Virginia's shoreline is second.

The warm climate and fertile alluvial soil make these two Atlantic states ideal for growing tobacco. They are still at the heart of America's tobacco belt. Because of the abundance of farmland, settlements are more dispersed than in the Northeast. The multitude of small towns is a trademark of the South.

The twentieth century has brought many changes to the South. For centuries the economy of

War Between the States

- Union States
- Confederate States
- Border States
- Territories

Southern United States Statistics

STATE	P.O. CODE	CAPITAL	DATE OF STATEHOOD	NICKNAME	AREA (SQ. MI.)	POP.	HIGH POINT, ELEVATION (FT.)
Alabama	AL	Montgomery	1819	Heart of Dixie	52,423	4,273,084	Cheaha Mtn., 2,405
Arkansas	AR	Little Rock	1836	Natural State	53,182	2,509,793	Magazine Mtn., 2,753
Florida	FL	Tallahassee	1845	Sunshine State	65,756	14,399,985	Britton Hill, 345
Georgia	GA	Atlanta	1788	Peach State	59,441	7,353,225	Brasstown Bald, 4,784
Kentucky	KY	Frankfort	1792	Bluegrass State	40,411	3,883,723	Black Mtn., 4,139
Louisiana	LA	Baton Rouge	1812	Pelican State	51,843	4,350,579	Driskill Mtn., 535
Mississippi	MS	Jackson	1817	Magnolia State	48,434	2,716,115	Woodall Mtn., 806
North Carolina	NC	Raleigh	1789	Tar Heel State	53,821	7,322,870	Mt. Mitchell, 6,684
Oklahoma	OK	Oklahoma City	1907	Sooner State	69,903	3,300,902	Black Mesa, 4,973
South Carolina	SC	Columbia	1788	Palmetto State	32,008	3,698,746	Sassafras Mtn., 3,560
Tennessee	TN	Nashville	1796	Volunteer State	42,146	5,319,654	Clingmans Dome, 6,643
Texas	TX	Austin	1845	Lone Star State	268,601	19,128,261	Guadalupe Peak, 8,749
Virginia	VA	Richmond	1788	Old Dominion	42,777	6,675,451	Mt. Rogers, 5,729
West Virginia	WV	Charleston	1863	Mountain State	24,231	1,825,754	Spruce Knob, 4,861

the states rose and fell with the fortunes of one or two primary industries, such as tobacco and cotton. But in the past few decades the states have **diversified** their industry. Many tertiary industries have sprung up, and cities are growing rapidly. Virginia, located on the southern edge of the Northeastern megalopolis, currently has the highest per capita GDP in the South.

Virginia, the Mother of States

Virginia, a large state on the border between the Northeast and the South, has always played a central role in American history. At the time of the American Revolution, Virginia was the largest state in the Union, claiming lands west to the Mississippi and northwest to the Great Lakes. Although it gave up its claims, Virginia retained sufficient size and wealth to be a leader in the nation. Eight American presidents were born in this state, including three Founding Fathers— George Washington, Thomas Jefferson, and James Madison. Their plantation homes have become major visitor centers, especially Jefferson's Monticello and Washington's Mount Vernon.

Virginia staunchly defended independent states. "Give me liberty or give me death!" shouted Virginia's Patrick Henry in 1765. The state almost did not approve the Constitution because it feared the power of a strong federal government. Only after receiving a promise to get a Bill of Rights added to the Constitution did the Virginia legislature ratify the Constitution. Virginia later became the first state in the Upper South to join the *Confederacy,* a loose bond of Southern states that left the Union in 1861 over states' rights.

Most of the fighting in the Civil War focused on the capture of Richmond, Virginia, the Confederate capital. Virginia supplied the South with its greatest general, **Robert E. Lee.** This brilliant leader and Christian gentleman won the respect and admiration of Americans on both sides of the conflict. Indeed, President Lincoln offered Lee supreme command of the Union armies, but Lee prayerfully chose to defend his homeland instead. After the Civil War, Virginia became the first state to elect a black governor, a tribute to its openness to change.

The Tidewater   Virginia and Maryland share the coastal plain along Chesapeake Bay. Many broad, swift rivers flow down the mountains into the plain. Because tides flow in and out of the wide river mouths, the coastal plain is called the **Tidewater.** Dismal Swamp, on the border with North Carolina, is typical of the swampy, southern Tidewater.

The James is the main river on the Tidewater. Jamestown, the first permanent English settlement

The restored capitol in Williamsburg, Virginia, where the House of Burgesses met for eighty-one years (1699-1780). Among its most famous members were Thomas Jefferson, Patrick Henry, and George Washington.

on the continent, was founded in 1607 on a swampy island in the James River. The colonists struggled to survive by exporting tobacco, America's first cash crop. In 1619 Jamestown established the House of Burgesses, the first representative government in America. The colony bought its first slaves the same year.

The nearby town of Williamsburg soon became the capital of the colony. Over eighty original buildings still stand at Williamsburg, the oldest surviving British buildings in the New World. Williamsburg's College of William and Mary is the oldest college in the South and second oldest in the nation. Many visitors come to see Yorktown on a peninsula east of Williamsburg, where George Washington trapped Cornwallis's army and ended the Revolutionary War.

On a deep harbor at the mouth of the James River is Norfolk, Virginia's largest metropolitan area. Norfolk has the busiest naval base in the nation because of its strategic location at the mouth of Chesapeake Bay, guarding access to the national capital.

The Piedmont   Virginia's Piedmont runs through the center of the state from the Fall Line to the Appalachians. Richmond sits on the James River, upstream from Williamsburg, at the Fall Line. More Civil War battles were fought in Virginia than

in any other state. The most-visited of Virginia's national battlefields are in the piedmont at Richmond, Petersburg, Fredericksburg, and Manassas. Appomattox Court House, where the South surrendered on April 9, 1865, is a national historic park.

The Appalachians   Appalachian Mountains extend along Virginia's western quarter. The beautiful Blue Ridge Mountains rise first above the Piedmont, and farther west the Allegheny Mountains rise.

Between these two ranges is the fertile **Shenandoah Valley.** This broad valley was the colonists' early gateway to the frontier. It provided grazing land for pioneers who left the Atlantic coast. Daniel Boone explored a route through the southern end of the valley into Tennessee and Kentucky. By 1800 over two hundred thousand pioneers had poured through the Cumberland Gap. The southern word *gap* corresponds to the word *notch* used in the Northeast. Typically not as steep and deep as notches, gaps look more like chips than axe cuts in the ridges.

North Carolina   North Carolina, fearful of losing its rights, was the last Southern state to approve the Constitution. North Carolina contributed more troops to the Confederate cause than any other state. Over one-quarter of all Civil War casualties were North Carolinians.

Outer Banks   North Carolina has a proud history that goes back to colonial days. The early settlements along the Atlantic Coastal Plain were small because they had few deep harbors. A chain of **barrier islands,** created by silt deposits, lines the coast. Cape Hatteras was once called the Graveyard of the Atlantic because it claimed so many ships.

The narrow barrier islands, called the **Outer Banks,** are popular beaches today. Two of the nation's ten protected seashores are on the Outer Banks. A national memorial at Kill Devil Hill, near the village of Kitty Hawk, honors the flight of the first powered airplane. The Wright brothers chose the Outer Banks because of the high winds that sweep across the shore.

Industries in the Piedmont Most of the state's major cities are located in the Piedmont. Many cities, like Raleigh, developed along the Fall Line. Cities closer to the mountains have been growing rapidly in recent years, now that highways, not water wheels, are the most important factor in modern industry. The textile industry of the Northeast moved South in the 1930s to take advantage of cheap labor. Charlotte, the largest city in the state, is now the national leader in the wholesale textile trade. The textile industry became the basis for many other diversified industries.

Agriculture remains important to the state's economy. North Carolina leads the nation in turkey and sweet potato production. The state's tobacco crop is the largest in the nation. The Piedmont city of Winston-Salem is known for its cigarette production.

Mountain Attractions The mountains at the western end of the state have many attractions. Asheville, the highest major city in the eastern United States, lies between the Blue Ridge Mountains and the main Appalachian range.

The Appalachian ranges of North Carolina include the highest mountains in the eastern United States. Grandfather Mountain (5,964 ft.) has spectacular views. Forty mountains in the central ranges exceed six thousand feet in elevation, and fifteen are higher than Mount Washington. The highest peak of all is Mount Mitchell (6,684 ft.), just north of Asheville in the Black Mountains.

The mountain forests provide valuable hardwoods for the industries that manufacture furniture. North Carolina leads all other states in sales of wood furniture. The mountains support a few commercial mines. North Carolina's emerald mining, however, is exceptional, especially for the United States. Several tourist areas permit visitors to mine emeralds, sapphires, and rubies on their own.

The Appalachians explode with color in the fall. Unlike the Northeast, the South's mountains have no alpine zone. Dense deciduous forests grow on the lower slopes, giving way to coniferous forests on the summits. Coniferous forests near the timberline are often called **subalpine** forests. North Carolinians call their summits **balsams** after the

Whitewater Falls, 411 feet high, is the highest of North Carolina's five hundred waterfalls.

local name for red spruce and Fraser fir. Visitors to Mount Mitchell must climb an observation deck to see above the trees.

Another feature of the mountains is the Cherokee Indian Reservation. The Cherokee were the first Indians to accept European culture and the first to adopt a writing system. They have one of the South's few reservations east of the Mississippi River. Their nightly outdoor drama, *Unto These Hills,* is the most famous Indian drama in the nation. It recounts their forced march west on the Trail of Tears. President Andrew Jackson ordered the army to expel the Indians from their homes, and many died on the hard march west. After years of entreaty, some were allowed to return; and others, who had never left their North Carolina home, came out of hiding.

The Nantahalas, mountains near the Georgia border, are famous for waterfalls. Transylvania County, the "Land of Waterfalls," has several hundred falls. Rainfall here, near the junction of North Carolina, Georgia, and South Carolina, is heavier than at any other place in the South or in the Northeast. From what you have learned about mountains and precipitation, can you explain why?

SECTION REVIEW

1. What role did Virginia and North Carolina play in the Civil War?

2. What physical features characterize these two states?

3. How have the tobacco states diversified their economies?

4. Explain the local terms *balsam* and *gap*.

5. What state has the ten highest mountains in the eastern United States?

💡 What are some of the reasons that it took the South a long time to recover from the Civil War?

Beyond the Appalachians

All but three southern states with **Appalachian Mountains** have coastlines and the Piedmont where most of the population settled and prospered. The three interior states have not been so fortunate. Like Vermont in the Northeast, West Virginia, Kentucky, and Tennessee have struggled to make a living from the rough mountains. The mountainous parts of these states are a major part of a larger region known as **Appalachia.** Appalachia is famous for mountain traditions, folk music, and arts and crafts; but it is also known for its poverty.

All three states share two geographical features: the Appalachian Mountains and a rugged region west of the mountains, the Appalachian Plateau. In West Virginia, the plateau is called the *Allegheny Plateau.* In Kentucky and Tennessee, it is called the **Cumberland Plateau.**

These states have old ties to the South. Kentucky and West Virginia were once part of Virginia, and Tennessee was once a county of North Carolina. Pioneers from these coastal states settled

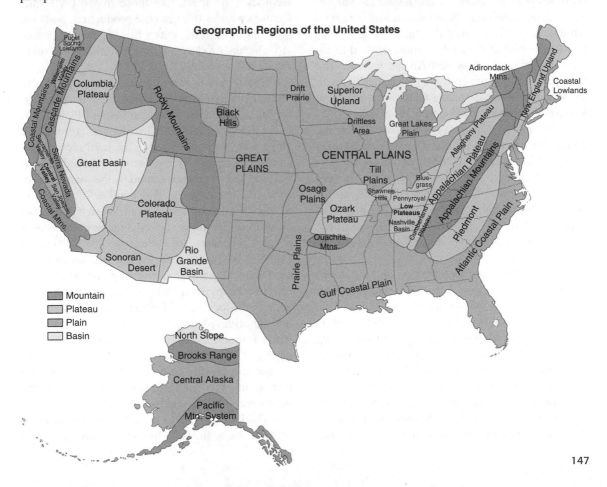

Geographic Regions of the United States

Mountain
Plateau
Plain
Basin

lands beyond the mountains. Tennessee and Kentucky were the second and third states to join the original thirteen states of the Union (after Vermont).

West Virginia, the Mountain State

At the beginning of the Civil War, West Virginia was part of Virginia. Robert E. Lee's most skilled subordinate, General Thomas "Stonewall" Jackson, came from this area. Like other Southern states, West Virginia supported states' rights. However, settlers in the mountains of western Virginia disliked paying taxes to the Tidewater cities without receiving help for roads and schools. When Virginia seceded in 1861, the western counties declared the vote void and created an independent state, Kanawha. The region suffered numerous Civil War battles as the North and South fought for control—the town of Romney changed hands fifty-six times. West Virginia became a state in 1863.

The Appalachian Mountains and the rugged Allegheny Plateau cover the entire state. Just to build an airport at the capital, engineers had to cut off some mountaintops and fill the valleys. The Mountain State is the epitome of Appalachia, with the second lowest per capita GDP in the nation. It also has the lowest population in the South.

The rugged Allegheny Mountains lie on the eastern border with Virginia. The steel arch bridge over New River Gorge is the second highest bridge on the continent. The historic town of Harpers Ferry is at the tip of the eastern panhandle, in the Shenandoah Valley. The abolitionist John Brown, hoping to start a slave revolt in 1859, seized the federal arsenal at Harpers Ferry. But he was captured and hanged.

Most of the state's population and industries lie west in the valleys of the Ohio and Kanawha Rivers, which cut through the low mountains of the Allegheny Plateau. Charleston, the state capital, is in the Kanawha Valley. Wheeling and Parkersburg are in the Ohio Valley. Manufacturers in Parkersburg produce most of the nation's glass marbles, made from silica sand that is mined nearby.

The state is most known for its coal mines, which produce low-grade **bituminous** (soft) coal. Wyoming leads in coal production, but it cannot beat West Virginia's storied past. Long hours and low pay have aggravated the dangerous life of the West Virginia miner. In 1907 a single mine explosion killed 361 workers. Because of its dependence on one product—coal—the state has had a roller-coaster economy that rises and falls with prices. The state is struggling to diversify its economy.

Kentucky, the Bluegrass State

Kentucky was the birthplace of both Civil War presidents, Abraham Lincoln and Jefferson Davis. Lincoln moved to Illinois, a Northern state, but Davis stayed in Kentucky. As a border state in the war, Kentucky sent troops to both sides. But it remains strongly Southern in culture and dialect.

The Rugged East   The Appalachian Mountains and Cumberland Plateau, which lie in eastern Kentucky, are much like those in West Virginia. Kentucky ranks third in coal production, and coal provides most of the state's fuel for electric power. Appalachia produces more coal than any other region of the country.

The terrain is very rugged. Cumberland Falls, on the Cumberland River, is one of the most powerful falls in the East. The Cumberland Plateau has many overhangs and other unusual rock formations. Huge holes have appeared in the hard rock ridges, sometimes caused by river erosion (called *natural bridges*) and sometimes caused by the weathering of rocks (called *arches*). The number of arches in Kentucky is second only to Utah. When boulders fall away from the hillside, overhangs or shelter caves result. Overhangs are called *rock houses* on the Cumberland Plateau because the Indians formerly used many of these large overhangs as houses.

The Pennyroyal Plateau, named after a small herb, is the local name for Kentucky's portion of a low interior plateau west of the Cumberland Plateau. (See the map of U.S. geographic regions, page 147.) Farmers grow tobacco throughout the region; only North Carolina produces more tobacco than Kentucky. The hilly northwest provides the state's second major coal-mining area.

The Pennyroyal is a **karst** region, where water seeping through soft limestone has produced

Mammoth Cave

Mammoth Cave is by far the longest cave in the world. (The second longest, in Ukraine, is only a third as long.) Winding passages lead to many underground wonders.

Some passages are bare, but others have amazing formations. Large *columns* are formed by stalactites and stalagmites that meet. The largest column in Mammoth Cave rises 192 feet. *Flowstone draperies,* such as Frozen Niagara, are mineral formations that look like waterfalls flowing down the walls. In other places, black pits drop beyond sight, the deepest plummeting 105 feet. Underground lakes and rivers have enough room for boats to move around. Shallow water in *rimstone pools* displays limestone pearls. Eyeless fish, crickets, and crayfish move around in the silent darkness of the cave.

Mammoth Cave became a national park in 1936, but its location was known for centuries prior to that. Arrowheads and other Indian artifacts have been unearthed at the entrance. During the War of 1812, saltpeter was mined at the cave for gunpowder.

The first map of the cave was made in 1835, but the "end" of Mammoth Cave eluded **spelunkers** (cave explorers) for over a century. By 1972 the explorations had increased the mapped portions of Mammoth Cave from eight to fifty-six miles of passages. In 1972 a team of spelunkers made the greatest discovery in cave history. While exploring the nearby Flint Ridge system,

Frozen Niagara is the most famous of the flowstone draperies in Mammoth Cave, Kentucky.

which had eighty miles of known passages, the team discovered a new passage joining the Flint Ridge and Mammoth Cave systems. The total mapped length of the Flint-Mammoth Cave system is now over 325 miles.

---

sinkholes, underground streams, and caverns. The world's largest cavern is Mammoth Cave, with many passages and exotic cave formations.

The Bluegrass   The **Bluegrass** region, in northern Kentucky along the Ohio River, takes its name from the blue flower of a local grass. It has the best soil and shipping routes in the state. Among the first settlers was Daniel Boone, who founded Boonesboro after blazing the Wilderness Road from Cumberland Gap across the Cumberland Plateau.

Rich grasslands have enabled Kentucky to produce many famous horses. The state breeds and sells more thoroughbred horses than any other region in the nation. Prizewinning racehorses have run in the Kentucky Derby annually since 1875, at Churchill Downs near Louisville.

The Purchase   Kentucky's far west, the Purchase, is part of the low plain that runs along the Mississippi River. Its name comes from Andrew Jackson's purchase of the area from the Chickasaw Indians in 1818. Swamps and lakes lie in the flood plains. A peninsula called the Land Between the Lakes is a popular national recreation area.

 Tennessee   More Civil War battles were fought in Tennessee than in any

Denominations

Tennessee is known for more than music. Memphis and Nashville are the headquarters of the four largest non-Catholic denominations in the United States listed in the table. Each one represents a major doctrinal division in American Protestantism.

A *denomination* is an officially organized group of churches that follow the same teachings, or doctrine. The U.S. tradition of religious freedom and individualism helps to explain why it has so many denominations—over twenty thousand.

Cultural divisions have affected the location of denominations in the United States. Baptists are most common in the South, particularly in the coastal plains. Methodists are most common in the border states and in the Appalachian Mountains. The debate over slavery divided the nation and denominations as well. Southern Baptists and Southern Methodists split from their Northern counterparts in the 1840s. (Northern Baptists are now known as American Baptists. The Methodists eventually rejoined to form the United Methodist Church.)

Black Churches Baptist, Methodist, and Pentecostal denominations in the South eventually split along racial lines. Some black denominations have splintered as a result of divisions among their own leaders. The largest of these denominations is the National Baptist Convention, USA.

TOP-TEN DENOMINATIONS	MEMBERSHIP (MILLION)
1. Roman Catholic Church	60.2
2. Southern Baptist Convention	15.6
3. United Methodist Church	8.6
4. *National Baptist Convention, USA	8.2
5. *Church of God in Christ	5.5
6. Evangelical Lutheran Church in America	5.2
7. Presbyterian Church (USA)	3.7
8. *African Methodist Episcopal	3.5
9. *National Baptist Convention of America	3.5
10. Lutheran Church–Missouri Synod	2.6

* black denominations

Mainline Denominations Yet another series of splits resulted from the Darwinism and humanism that invaded the Northeastern churches in the late nineteenth and early twentieth centuries. Many denominational leaders accepted evolutionary theory and made efforts to "modernize" the gospel. Their churches became known as *mainline denominations*. Most of the nation's oldest denominations turned to Modernism. The two exceptions are the Southern Baptists and the Lutheran Church–Missouri Synod, whose members continue to fight over Modernism to this day.

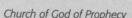
Church of God of Prophecy

Methodist church

Baptist church

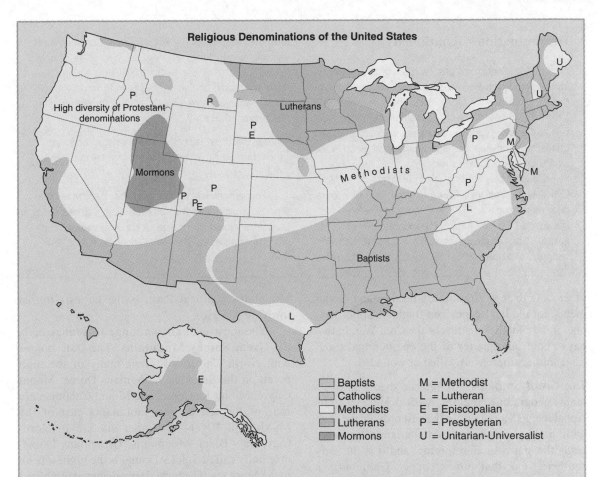

Religious Denominations of the United States

High diversity of Protestant denominations

P

P

Lutherans

P

E

Mormons

M e t h o d i s t s

P

P

P

E

L

M

M

P

P

L

U

U

Baptists

L

E

☐ Baptists	M = Methodist
☐ Catholics	L = Lutheran
☐ Methodists	E = Episcopalian
☐ Lutherans	P = Presbyterian
☐ Mormons	U = Unitarian-Universalist

Evangelicals Desiring to defend the *fundamental* doctrines that all true Christians believe, **Fundamentalist** churches broke away from their liberal counterparts in the early twentieth century. Many of these churches became independent rather than creating new denominations.

Fundamentalists never fully settled the question of how to combat Modernism. In the late 1940s a number of leaders openly rejected the militant tactics of their fellow Fundamentalists. This breed of "new" Evangelicals argued the need to build bridges to the mainline denominations. Over time, more and more denominations joined the New Evangelicals, or **Evangelicals,** as they now call themselves. The organization that became their umbrella was the National Association of Evangelicals (NAE), founded in 1942. It

now includes over eighty denominations and fifteen million people.

Pentecostals and Charismatics Pentecostalism arose in the early twentieth century. These congregations stress the Holy Spirit's gifts given at Pentecost. They adopted flamboyant worship styles, including raised hands, clapping, and shouting. The leading branches are the Assemblies of God and its counterpart among blacks, the Church of God in Christ.

In the 1960s, the morals of the country reached a breaking point, the various Evangelical and Pentecostal movements appeared to be losing their influence, and the mainline churches entered a period of steady decline. At this time the Charismatic movement appeared. The name **Charismatic** first applied to people

Denominations—continued

in mainline denominations who sought to speak in tongues and to experience the other spiritual gifts, or *charisma* (Greek: "gifts"), described in the New Testament. Eventually, many Charismatics founded independent churches and denominations. Pentecostals and Charismatics now are the largest Protestant group in the world—over 400 million strong.

Despite their efforts, all four major divisions of Christianity admit their failure to stem the rapid moral decline in America. To spread the gospel more effectively, many argue that everyone who believes the gospel should join together, even if some believers happen to belong to a mainline denomination that promotes false teaching. But the Great Commission is very plain. It includes making *disciples* of all people, teaching them all the truths that Christ taught. The Bible commands believers to separate from any religious leader who preaches a gospel that contradicts that preached by Paul.

If any man preach any other gospel unto you than that ye have received, let him be accursed. (Gal. 1:9)

Fundamentalists quote plain biblical commands to separate from disobedient brothers (e.g., II Thess. 3:6). Christians should evangelize God's way, without compromise, and let God give the increase (I Cor. 2:4-5; 3:6).

other state except Virginia. Battle sites and monuments dot the landscape. The Battle of Shiloh was one of the bloodiest battles of the Civil War. In two days about one-quarter of the one hundred thousand soldiers there were killed or wounded.

The Great Smokies Tennessee shares all of its main geographic regions with Kentucky. The Appalachian Mountains in the east provide the state with mineral resources and tourism. Tennessee leads the states in zinc mining, and it is the only southern state that mines copper. Gatlinburg, a mountain town at the entrance to the Great Smoky

The Great Smoky Mountains of Tennessee and North Carolina take their name from the clouds that hover above the peaks. The Cherokees called them Sha-cona-ge, or "place of blue smoke."

Mountains National Park, is the largest "tourist town" in America.

The most well known range in Tennessee is the **Great Smoky Mountains.** The state border with North Carolina follows many of the high points in the Smokies. Clingmans Dome, Mount Guyot, Mount Le Conte, and Mount Chapman are four of the ten highest mountains east of the Mississippi River—the other six are in North Carolina's Black Mountains. Clingmans Dome, originally called Smoky Dome, is the highest peak in the Smokies. The term **dome** designates a broad rounded mountaintop. A famous folksong "On Top of Old Smoky" refers to Clingmans Dome.

River Cities Most major cities in Tennessee arose on the great rivers that drain west of the Appalachians. General Ulysses S. Grant's campaign to defeat the Confederacy began with the capture of two crucial forts on the Cumberland and Tennessee Rivers. These tributaries of the Mississippi give oceangoing ships access to Tennessee's heartland.

The big cities of Knoxville and Chattanooga lie on the banks of the **Tennessee River** where it cuts through the Cumberland Plateau.

Farther west are Nashville and Memphis, the largest cities in the Upper South. Nashville, the state capital, arose on the low plateau west of the

Cumberland, called the Nashville Basin. **Memphis,** the largest city, lies on the western Mississippi border. Ships pass through Memphis on their way north to Minneapolis on the Mississippi River or west to Kansas City on the Missouri River or east to cities on the Ohio River.

The **Tennessee Valley Authority** (TVA) regulates the Tennessee River and its tributaries in seven states. The original goal of this major government-run industry, begun in 1933, was to stop flooding and to provide rural communities with inexpensive electricity for homes and industry. Now TVA has three nuclear power plants, eleven coal-fired plants, and twenty-nine hydroelectric plants. These facilities help make the United States the world leader in electricity production.

SECTION REVIEW

1. Which Southern states never seceded during the Civil War?

2. List the major geographic regions shared by Kentucky and Tennessee.

3. Compare and contrast the Blue Ridge and the Great Smoky Mountains.

4. Name a product that each interior southern state leads the nation in producing.

5. Explain arches and rock houses. How do they differ from natural bridges? What geographic region is famous for each?

💡 Why does Appalachia's economy lag behind that of other regions'? What cultural riches does it offer?

THE LOWER SOUTH

The **Deep South** refers to the southernmost states along the Atlantic and Gulf coasts. The entire South enjoys a humid subtropical climate, but the Deep South gave the region its reputation for warm weather. The South's regional reputation rests as much on the plantations of the southern coastal plains as on the interior mountains. Books by popular southern writers, such as Margaret Mitchell's *Gone with the Wind,* have celebrated the fabled Old South, with lingering images of slow-paced plantation life before the Civil War.

King Cotton once ruled the entire economy of the Deep South. Boats loaded with cotton once crowded the rivers and ports of Southern cities. Dependence on a single cash crop brought the South great wealth, but it hurt the region in many ways. Fortunes rose and fell with the whims of world cotton prices. As cotton depleted the soil in the eastern states, planters were forced to move farther and farther west. Worst of all, picking cotton required large numbers of workers, primarily slaves.

Few Southerners grew rich on cotton and slavery. Most white Southerners were middle-class farmers. But the men who held the positions of leadership—the slaveholders, merchants, and politicians—made their wealth from cotton. They believed that the abolition of slavery would ruin their livelihood. When radical abolitionists began supporting the violent overthrow of slavery, the states of the Lower South were the first to secede from the Union.

The Deep South has been the focus of the nation's efforts to reconcile the concerns of the white majority and the large black minority. Thirteen percent of the nation is black, but blacks make up over 25 percent of the population in every state of the Deep South. (Maryland is the only other state with this large of a percentage of blacks.) Mississippi has the largest percentage of blacks, more than 36 percent of the state total. The **civil rights movement** of the 1960s brought minority issues to the forefront of the nation, but the passage of federal laws has failed to resolve all the problems. Diversifying the economy and improving job opportunities have done far more to improve race relations.

Colonial States of the Lower South

Of the thirteen original colonies, South Carolina and Georgia were located the farthest south. Their ports on the Atlantic seaboard became major colonial cities, rivaling Boston and Philadelphia.

 South Carolina South Carolina has several historic sites from colonial days and more battle sites from the Revolutionary War than any other state. But most Americans know the state for its role in the Civil War. It was the first state to secede, and the only one to give unanimous approval to secession. The legislature voted for secession on December 20, 1860. Four months later, Confederate troops fired the first shots of the Civil War at Union troops at Fort Sumter in Charleston's bay.

South Carolina's war sacrifices were great: one-quarter of the state's army died, and the capital, Columbia, was burned. The cotton economy was ruined, and recovery took decades. South Carolina, like its neighbors, eventually turned to textile industries.

Colorful mansions line the Battery at Charleston, South Carolina. Palmettos, the state tree, frame these historic houses.

The Low Country Charleston, first settled in 1670 on the mouth of the Ashley and Cooper Rivers, has been a bustling seaport for centuries. Tourists come from all over to enjoy its beaches and to view its grand mansions along the waterfront. Historic plantations near Charleston, which once grew rice, are now preserved as gardens. The city has been called the Jewel of the South.

Bordered by numerous barrier islands, much of the coast has alligator-infested swamps. Farther inland, Four Holes Swamp provides boardwalks for sightseers.

The Up Country The capital, Columbia, is located on the Fall Line where the coastal plain meets the Piedmont. Congaree Swamp near Columbia has the largest stand of virgin forest in the state and many of the state's largest trees. It is also famous as the hideout of the Swamp Fox, Francis Marion, a Revolutionary War hero.

Above the Fall Line, the Piedmont extends across most of the rest of the state. The fastest-growing region of the state is the combined metropolitan areas of Greenville and Spartanburg, on

the highway between the large industrial cities of Charlotte, North Carolina, and Atlanta, Georgia. The textile industry of South Carolina centered in this region is second only to that of North Carolina. This area is also known for its peach orchards. South Carolina produces more peaches than its neighbor Georgia, the self-proclaimed Peach State.

Low mountains in the northwest corner are the beginning of the Blue Ridge Mountains. These are part of the Appalachian Mountain system, but locally they are referred to as the Foothills. The Foothills Parkway, which winds through this area,

African American Minority Population

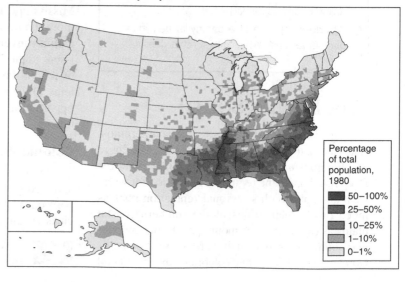

Percentage of total population, 1980

- ■ 50–100%
- ■ 25–50%
- ■ 10–25%
- □ 1–10%
- □ 0–1%

Sports

White-Water Rafting

The many swift white-water rivers of the South attract rafting enthusiasts from all over the world. Ocoee River in Tennessee was the site of the 1996 Olympic competitions for the various river sports. The Chattooga River, which divides northern Georgia and South Carolina, is famous in films. Other popular places are the Nantahala River of North Carolina, the Big South Fork River of Kentucky and Tennessee, and the Buffalo River of Arkansas.

Rapids are rated for difficulty on a scale of one to six. *Class one* rapids are easy enough for any novice rafter. The classes are for rapids—calm waters are not rated. *Class six* rapids are the most dangerous rapids that nevertheless

Families have fun on the Class 2 rapids of North Carolina's Nantahala River.

Experienced rafters take on the Class 5 rapids at Pillow Rock. It is one of many tough sections on the Gauley River of West Virginia—the South's toughest run.

are technically navigable. Only experts risk their lives in such difficult waters. Gauley River in West Virginia is one of the most challenging. High waterfalls, such as Niagara, are usually not rated, though some performers have gone over in barrels and other contraptions.

While canoes are fine for calm rivers, rafts and kayaks are best for white water. Canoes made of metal or wood are heavier and slower than inflated rafts of rubberized nylon. Kayaks are the smallest and lightest river crafts. Typically, kayaks are for individuals, and rafts are for parties of five or six.

has been voted one of the nation's top eight scenic drives.

Georgia Georgia has many reminders of its suffering during the Civil War. The Battle of Atlanta and Sherman's March to the Sea left charred ruins on a sixty-mile-wide path of destruction. The state is best known, however, for the efforts of **Martin Luther King Jr.,** a black preacher whose name became synonymous with civil rights in the 1960s. His **march on Washington** in 1963 attracted a million Americans to the nation's capital to demand equal rights for blacks. His most

famous speech, "I Have a Dream," inspired the nation with the hope that

one day on the red hills of Georgia the sons of former slaves and the sons of former slaveowners will be able to sit down together at the table of brotherhood. . . . I have a dream that my four little children will one day live in a nation where they will not be judged by the color of their skin, but by the content of their character.

Five years later King was assassinated, but his dream lives on. King is now honored by a national holiday.

Okefenokee Swamp

Alligators lurk in the southeast corner of Georgia at Okefenokee Swamp, the largest and most famous swamp in America. Okefenokee harbors alligators, deer, otters, bears, raccoons, opossums, and bobcats. Like most swamps in the United States, Okefenokee is a *cypress swamp.* Cypress trees are tall trees with knobby roots, called knees, that poke up out of the water. Spanish moss hangs from the trees and water snakes lurk in the dark waters. Many visitors canoe through the swamp, but popular tourist areas have boardwalks that make it easy to enjoy the swamp on foot.

Visitors can take canoe trips lasting as long as five days through the channels of Okefenokee Swamp, Georgia.

The nation's other famous swamps are all cypress swamps of the South. Louisiana has the most swamps, many of which lie along the Atchafalaya River. Dismal Swamp, which now covers 350 square miles in Virginia and North Carolina, was once the largest cypress swamp in America; but George Washington and other plantation owners drained the water to farm the rich soil.

Georgia is the largest state of the thirteen original colonies. A wide coastal plain covers the southern half of the state. Georgia's Atlantic coast is much like South Carolina's. It is protected by numerous barrier islands and has several marshes and swamps. The state's first settlement and main port is Savannah. It was Sherman's final destination on his destructive March to the Sea.

The southern plains of Georgia lead the nation in the production of peanuts and pecans. Peanuts, or "goobers," became important in the twentieth century as a soil-enriching alternative to cotton. Georgians eat them raw, boiled, or ground as peanut butter; but they also sell the peanut oil to be used in salad dressings, soap, paint, cosmetics, and nitroglycerin. Peanut shell powders are used in plastics, abrasives, and wallboard. A peanut farmer and former Georgia governor named Jimmy Carter, known for his religious devotion and trademark smile, was elected president in 1976.

Atlanta, the state capital, lies in the piedmont region of central Georgia. Atlanta boasts the South's highest skyscraper, the Nations Bank building, over one thousand feet high. Only five other cities in the nation have skyscrapers this high. Atlanta is proud of its high-tech image. In 1996 it hosted the Summer Olympics, hoping to throw off the South's image as a backward region of the nation. The Coca-Cola museum reminds visitors that the world's most famous soft drink began in Atlanta. Nearby rises the most famous landmark of the piedmont, **Stone Mountain,** a

Atlanta's Nations Bank is 1,023 feet high. Atlanta is one of only six American cities with skyscrapers over one thousand feet.

A popular landmark in the South, Stone Mountain, Georgia, displays three famous Confederate leaders.

solitary mountain, or monadnock of granite, with a huge carving of three Civil War heroes—Robert E. Lee, Stonewall Jackson, and Jefferson Davis—on horseback.

The Appalachian Mountains cover north Georgia. Georgia's four thousand-foot peaks are unique among the states of the Lower South. The three highest peaks, Brasstown Bald, Rabun Bald, and Blood Mountain, all offer beautiful views. Not quite as high, Springer Mountain is the beginning of the Appalachian Trail. The discovery of gold in Georgia's mountains near Dahlonega in 1828 sparked the nation's first gold rush, long before the forty-niners headed to California.

Gulf States

The warm waters of the **Gulf of Mexico** touch the southern coasts of five states, from Florida to Texas. Several rivers flow through the fertile **Gulf Coastal Plain** in these states. The histories of two Gulf states, Alabama and Mississippi, are closely tied to each other. Both were part of the Mississippi Territory. After Andrew Jackson's defeat of the Creek Indians at the Battle of Horseshoe Bend in 1814, settlers moved in rapidly. The state of Mississippi split off in 1817, and Alabama followed two years later.

Mississippi and Alabama share a chain of offshore islands along their coasts. These are farther offshore than the barrier islands of Georgia and South Carolina, leaving a large body of open water, or a sound. This protected shipping lane, the Gulf Intracoastal Waterway, extends west all the way into Texas and east into Florida.

Alabama, the Heart of Dixie

Another name for the Confederate states is *Dixie*. The term was popularized by the 1859 song "Dixie's Land." Alabama claims to be the Heart of Dixie. The secessionists drew up the constitution for the Confederate States of America at Montgomery. The same convention chose Montgomery as the first Confederate capital and elected a provisional president and vice president.

Alabama later became the main focus of the civil rights movement. Montgomery is known for a

Cotton fields in Alabama

SECTION REVIEW

1. The Old South produced what famous crop? What other products are South Carolina and Georgia known for now?
2. What are the three main geographical regions in Georgia and South Carolina?
3. Name the two main colonial cities on the South Atlantic.
   ♀ Columbia, South Carolina, has the only capitol that still flies a Confederate flag (under the state and national flags). Why is there a debate about honoring this Civil War symbol?

Dr. Martin Luther King Jr., a Baptist minister, won the Nobel Peace Prize in 1964 for his efforts toward racial equality.

yearlong **bus boycott** (1955-56) by blacks who refused to ride the public buses after police arrested Rosa Parks. The tired seamstress refused to give up her seat and move to the back of a bus to make room for a white male patron. The boycott's leader was a little-known preacher named Martin Luther King Jr.

The Gulf Coastal Plain covers more than half the state and includes the major port city of Mobile at the mouth of the Alabama River. The state capital, Montgomery, lies in a strip in the plain called the Black Belt, where the rich, black clay soil is conducive to farming.

The southern end of the Appalachian range is in northeastern Alabama at Cheaha Mountain, a crest of Talladega Mountain. Mountainous plateaus cover the state west of the Appalachians. In the 1960s the National Air and Space Administration (NASA) chose the northern city of Huntsville to develop technology for sending the *Apollo* spacecraft to the moon. High-tech industries have since surpassed the importance of cotton in the "Rocket City." Huntsville's Space and Rocket Center displays the largest collection of space missiles and equipment in the world.

Mississippi, on the Father of Waters

Mississippi was the second state to secede from the Union, and it suffered one of the worst sieges in history. The Union effort to take Vicksburg involved all aspects of warfare. Naval ironclads clashed on the Mississippi River while cannons fired from the protected bluff above. Armies met in the field several times as General Grant drew a noose around the city. A forty-seven day siege finally forced the starving people to surrender. Lincoln considered the victory even more important than the Battle of Gettysburg, which the North had won a day earlier. After taking Vicksburg, the Union controlled all forts along the Mississippi, cutting the Confederacy in two. "The Father of Waters again flows unvexed to the sea," Lincoln exulted.

Almost the entire state is coastal plain. (Alabama's low interior plateau crosses into Mississippi's extreme northeast corner.) The **Mississippi River** and its tributaries dominate the coastal plain. Floodwaters have deposited rich sediments on the river's wide flood plains, called the **Mississippi Valley.** Farmers grow cotton near the Mississippi and in the Black Belt, which the state shares with Alabama. This rural state, with the lowest per capita GDP in the nation, has tried to diversify its industry. Manmade ponds now produce the largest number of catfish sold in the nation.

Florida, at the Meeting of Waters

Florida is not quite the same as other Deep South states. It is the only state in the country with coasts on both the Atlantic Ocean and the Gulf of Mexico. Unlike the other states of the Deep South, it was once a Spanish colony, ceded to the United States in 1819 after a long and turbulent history. In addition to the continuing influence of Spanish-speaking immigrants from the Caribbean, Florida is a popular vacation spot and retirement center for Americans from all over the country. The state has the highest population and per capita GDP in the Deep South.

Florida had been a state for only sixteen years when it voted to secede from the Union in 1861. Tallahassee was the only capital of the Deep South that did not fall to Union troops.

The Panhandle Florida's topography is flat. A panhandle stretches west along the continent for

American Dialects

Hundreds of languages are spoken in the United States today, but English is the most common. In fact, the United States has the largest English-speaking population in the world. Technically, American English is only a variation of the Standard English spoken in London, England. But Americans look to the Midwest (or *Midland English*) to find *Standard American.* Since the invention of radio and television, every American has become familiar with the standard speech.

Nevertheless, there are some striking variations from Standard American. The most striking is *Southern English,* and the other is *New England English.* Southerners' and New Englanders' distinctive accents, vocabularies, sounds, and word orders are easily recognized but not easily understood by people from elsewhere in the country. Within the South and New England are many variations. But as you move West, these variations become less distinct.

One of the most interesting things about the dialect map is what it shows about the history of the United States. As Americans moved westward from the coast, they brought their speech patterns with them. What impact did the Appalachian Mountains have on the spread of languages? Where did the settlers of the Northwest come from?

Not all dialects are divided by physical regions. Many black Americans speak a *social dialect* among themselves, but then they use Standard English at school and in the workplace.

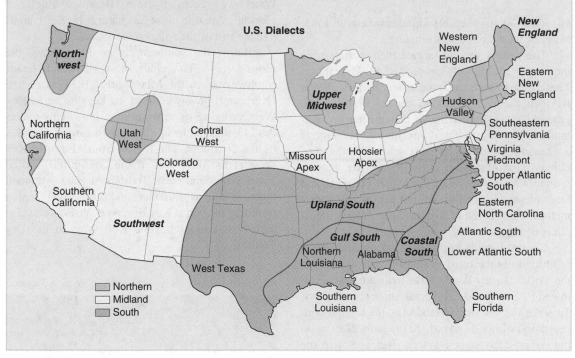

U.S. Dialects

New England
Western New England
Eastern New England
Hudson Valley
Southeastern Pennsylvania
Virginia Piedmont
Upper Atlantic South
Eastern North Carolina
Atlantic South
Lower Atlantic South
Southern Florida

North-west
Upper Midwest
Northern California
Utah West
Central West
Missouri Apex
Hoosier Apex
Colorado West
Southern California
Southwest
Upland South
Gulf South
Coastal South
Northern Louisiana
Alabama
West Texas
Southern Louisiana

☐ Northern
☐ Midland
☐ South

225 miles—over halfway to the Mississippi River. The panhandle includes the state capital, Tallahassee. Most of Florida, however, is a large peninsula jutting southward.

The Peninsula On the northern Atlantic coast is Jacksonville, the largest city in the state. Nearby is St. Augustine, the oldest European-settled city in the United States. Ponce de Leon landed here in

Florida's orange groves produce over twelve million pounds of oranges annually. All the other forty-nine states combined produce only one-half of this amount. Brazil is the only country that produces more oranges than Florida.

1513, and Spanish settlers founded the city in 1565. Many of its old buildings remain.

The state's second largest metropolitan area includes the cities of Tampa and St. Petersburg. These cities share the state's best harbor, Tampa Bay, on the Gulf coast in central Florida. The ground here is slightly higher than the marshy wetlands to the south. The "Sunshine State" enjoys a growing season of at least seven months. The climate and soil support vast orange groves. Florida produces three-fourths of the nation's oranges and leads in grapefruits, lemons, tangerines, and watermelons. This region is also the nation's largest producer of sugar cane.

Central Florida has many attractions. The city of Orlando is the most visited recreational area in the world. Disney World is the main attraction, followed by Sea World, Universal Studios, and others. To serve the visitors, Orlando has the highest concentration of hotels anywhere on earth. Nearby on the Atlantic coast is Daytona Beach, where the Daytona 500 car races are run, and Cape Canaveral, where space shuttles and rockets are launched.

The Marshy South   Most of the land south of Lake Okeechobee is marshy. The most well known marshland is in the 1.5-million-acre **Everglades,** with exotic animals found nowhere else in the United States. But along the coast the marsh gives way to mangrove swamps and one large area of cypress swamp called Big Cypress. Most of the population lives along the east coast in Miami. **Miami** is the largest metropolitan area in the Lower South. Fort Lauderdale is a sister city in the metropolitan area. Palm Beach and Miami Beach are two famous suburbs with beachfront property. Since the Communist dictator Fidel Castro took over Cuba in 1959, thousands of Spanish-speaking immigrants have fled to Miami, transforming the ethnic makeup of the city.

Since the Gulf meets the Atlantic in South Florida, two great shipping lanes meet near Key West: the Gulf Intracoastal Waterway extending from the tip of Texas, and the Atlantic Intracoastal Waterway reaching from Boston. Much of Florida's Atlantic coast has natural barrier islands like the rest of the Atlantic seaboard.

Below the southern tip of Florida are the Florida Keys. This chain of small islands heads southwest from the Miami area. Bridges on the Overseas Highway connect the keys as far as Key West, crossing more water than land. This makes the 113-mile highway the longest bridge complex on the continent. The region from Miami to Key West is the only part of the contiguous United States with coral reefs. Tourists in glass-bottomed boats, as well as snorkelers and scuba divers, enjoy watching the fish at Key Biscayne. Visitors can also take boat cruises beyond Key West to the Dry Tortugas.

Marsh grass dominates the Everglades in southern Florida.

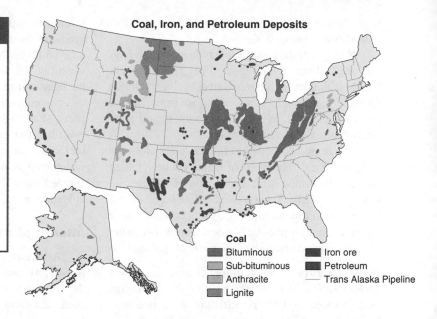

Coal, Iron, and Petroleum Deposits

Coal
- Bituminous
- Sub-bituminous
- Anthracite
- Lignite
- Iron ore
- Petroleum
- Trans Alaska Pipeline

THE SOUTH CENTRAL STATES

The four South Central states lie west of the Mississippi River. They joined the Union much later than the Deep South. These frontier states still have vast forests.

"Black gold"—oil—is the most important product from this region. Oil rigs exploit the oil fields underground, and offshore oil wells rise above the Gulf of Mexico. Texas leads the states in oil production. Texas, Louisiana, and Oklahoma are also the top three states in natural gas production. The United States ranks second worldwide in natural gas production, and third in oil production.

An oil well at Electra, twenty-five miles west of Wichita Falls, Texas

The economy of the oil states has traditionally risen and fallen with the world price of oil. But these states are diversifying into many fields, including computers and other high-tech industries.

Louisiana, at the Mouth of the Mississippi

The cotton plantations that once lined the Mississippi's alluvial plain clearly identify Louisiana's place within the Deep South. Louisiana joined the first six states at the Montgomery convention that formed the original Confederate States of America. Civil War battles in this state focused on the Union effort to capture forts along the Mississippi. David G. Farragut, a brilliant Union naval commander, bypassed the isolated forts at the mouth of the Mississippi River and sailed straight to New Orleans. The loss of the city, the South's largest city and most important seaport, was an early blow from which the Confederacy never recovered.

Cajun Country The slow-moving streams that meander across Louisiana's low coastal swamps are called **bayous.** These swampy areas have few places where people can drive, let alone live. The

161

state, however, leads the nation in the harvest of fish, shrimp, and oysters.

Nearly one-half million people along the bayous are **Cajuns** (KAY juhnz). They speak French, but their dialect has changed over the years, much as American English has changed from British English. The Cajuns are skilled hunters and trappers of alligators in the bayous.

The region belonged to France long before the British arrived. The heart of Cajun country, called *Acadia,* is named after the region of Maine and Canada where the French lived before being driven out by Britain in the mid-eighteenth century. Spicy Cajun cooking is popular on local menus. If you are ever in Cajun country, be sure to try alligator.

New Orleans French influence extends to **New Orleans.** The state's biggest city, New Orleans was founded in 1718 by citizens of France long before the rural Cajuns settled in the bayous. The French Quarter is the most famous part of the city. The elite society, a mix of French and Spanish descent called Creoles, has left its mark on New Orleans cuisine. Many cafes offer an okra stew called *gumbo* and a spicy seafood dish called *jambalaya.* Roman Catholicism, the most prominent religion in France, remains a strong influence in the city. **Mardi Gras,** celebrated before the fasting of Lent, brings the city alive with parades and festivities. Jazz festivals are the city's other major cultural event. Unfortunately, the party spirit promotes debauchery and open vice.

New Orleans stands on a narrow strip of land between the Mississippi River and Lake Pontchartrain. A canal connects the two bodies of water for shipping. Lake Pontchartrain is the largest lake in the state. Cars crossing the 29.6-mile Pontchartrain Causeway—the nation's longest bridge over open water—completely lose sight of land for eight miles!

The Delta The Mississippi River dominates Louisiana in the east, and the Red River dominates Louisiana in the west. The **Red River** joins the Mississippi north of Baton Rouge. This region's

salt mines make Louisiana the nation's leading salt producer. Near the **confluence** (where the rivers meet) both the Mississippi and Red Rivers begin to wash out into several different branches that form the **Mississippi Delta.**

Louisiana has four of the nation's ten busiest ports. (Lake Charles, in Cajun country, is ranked twelfth.) Two of these four are in New Orleans, including the nation's busiest port of all, through which over two hundred million tons of goods are shipped annually. Upstream are the other two ports, at Plaquemine and at Baton Rouge, the state capital.

Interior States

Arkansas and Oklahoma are closely linked in geography and history. They lie in the interior of the continent and thus lack coasts. Both have low mountain ranges unrelated to the famous Appalachians or Rockies. Oklahoma Territory was once administered from a town in Arkansas.

Arkansas, the Natural State

Arkansas seceded from the Union when President Lincoln called for troops to fight the Confederacy. When Little Rock fell in 1863, Confederates set up a new state capital in southwest Arkansas at Washington. For nearly two years the state had two capitals.

Arkansas advertises itself as the Natural State, with scenic mountains and forests covering over half the state. It has always been one of the least populous states—with fewer people than all other southern states except West Virginia. Reflecting efforts to diversify its industry and to attract new business, Arkansas has begun advertising itself as the Land of Opportunity.

Arkansas has two major geographic regions. The Lowlands cover the southeastern half of the state. They consist of the Gulf Coastal Plain and the Mississippi Flood Plain, where Arkansas grows more rice than any other state. The **Ozark Plateau** covers the northwestern half of Arkansas. This region of low mountains provides the largest share of the nation's chickens.

Geographer's Corner

Road Maps

Lines of latitude and longitude provide a geographic grid that helps us to find any spot in the world. State maps use another type of grid, usually given as letters and numbers. An *index* gives a specific letter and number for each location. The *map legend* explains several symbols on the map, such as types of roads. Using the information on the road map of southern Louisiana, answer these questions.

1. What is the index number of Thibodaux?
2. How many lanes link Thibodaux and Raceland?
3. What is the southernmost city on the grid? What type of road must you take to reach it?
4. Find the mouth of the Mississippi. Are any major cities located here?

Find the shortest route from New Orleans to Thibodaux. How many miles is it?

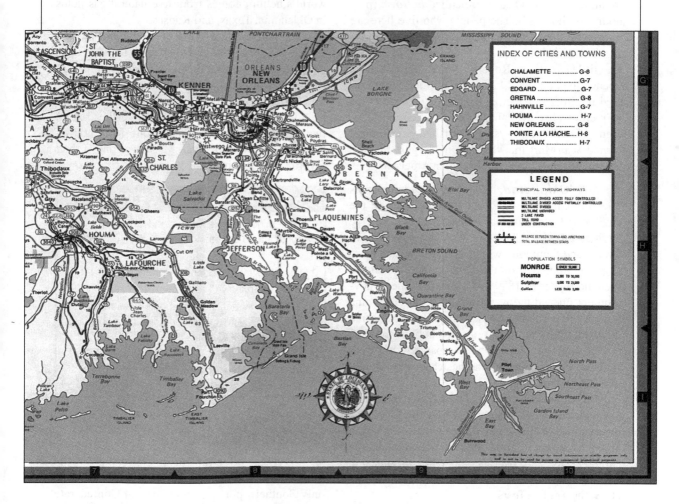

The state capital, Little Rock, is located where the Arkansas River runs down the plateau into the Mississippi Flood Plain. Mineral waters from nearby Hot Springs are famed for their supposed healing power. The southwestern section of the state has the nation's best diamond field. Although the diamonds are too sparse for commercial mining, visitors can dig for a small fee.

The Arkansas River cuts through the Ozark Plateau, separating the Ozark Mountains in the north from the Ouachita (WASH ih TAW) Mountains in the south. The wooded ravines between mountains in the Ozarks are called *hollows* (pronounced "hollers"). The people who live here are known for their crafts and country living.

The northwest corner of the state is famed for the little town of Rogers, where Sam Walton opened the first Wal-Mart store. Walton revolutionized retailing in America by making a wide range of merchandise available to small cities. His efficient distribution system satisfied customers, turned Wal-Mart into the nation's largest retailer, and made "Sam" the richest man in America.

Oklahoma The word *Oklahoma* is Choctaw for "Red People." During the Civil War, Oklahoma was Indian territory. The Five Civilized Tribes (Cherokee, Chickasaw, Choctaw, Creek, and Seminole) were forcibly relocated there from the Southeast on the Trail of Tears march. In the land rushes of 1889 and 1893, the federal government opened the western half of the Oklahoma territory to homesteaders seeking 160 acres of free land, but the eastern half remained Indian land. The two portions sought statehood separately but were refused. The Indians and homesteaders eventually united to form a single state.

Oklahoma has over 250,000 Indians, more than any other state. Some churches on the Cherokee reservations still use old Bibles written using the alphabet invented by Sequoyah. Tahlequah, the capital of the Cherokee Nation, offers a museum, a re-created Indian village, and an outdoor drama about the Trail of Tears.

Oklahoma shares two geographic regions with Arkansas on its eastern border—the Gulf Coastal Plain and the Ozark Plateau. But the Central Plains cover most of the state. The state's capital, Oklahoma City, is here. The Central Plains become higher and more rugged toward the west.

The Great Plains cover the western part of the state and have a higher elevation than any of the mountains in eastern Oklahoma! This flat, treeless area often reminds travelers of scenes from Wild West films. As in other parts of the Great Plains, sorghum is a valuable crop grown for grain, animal feed, and broom fibers. The region's most important product, however, is helium. Most of the world's helium comes from five natural gas fields in Oklahoma, Texas, and Kansas.

The panhandle portion of the Great Plains is called No Man's Land because it was once unclaimed by surrounding states. The border of Kansas had already been established, and the slave state of Texas could not include land north of the Missouri Compromise line (1820). For this reason the panhandle became a hideout for outlaws. Robber's Roost, near Black Mesa, was one of their favorite places to hide.

◎ SECTION REVIEW

1. What minorities in Louisiana and Oklahoma contribute to the ethnic diversity of the United States?

2. What geographic regions do Oklahoma and Arkansas share?

3. What main product are the South Central states known for? Name another product from Louisiana, Arkansas, and Oklahoma.

♀ List the main arguments for and against grouping the South Central states together as a single cultural subregion.

The Lone Star State

Texas pride runs deep. Galveston was the pride of Texas in the Civil War. It was the only Southern port that remained in Confederate hands at the end of the Civil War. Texas was the largest state in the Union until Alaska joined in

1959, and it still has the biggest cities in the South. For several years after it won independence from Mexico, Texas was an independent republic—thus its nickname, the Lone Star State.

Texas is centrally located on the border between Mexico, the South, the Midwest, and the Southwest. As a result, it has a wide variety of geographic regions, cultures, and industries. The eastern part of the state has large forests and cotton plantations, like other southern states. But the arid west has features typical of the American Southwest. The four main geographic regions of the state are the Gulf Coastal Plain, the Central Plains, the Great Plains, and the Rocky Mountains.

The Gulf Coast   The long coastal plain is the most important region in Texas. Its chain of barrier islands, which includes Padre Island, is part of the Intracoastal Waterway, a shipping lane for Houston, Corpus Christi, and Texas City. These cities have three of the nation's ten busiest ports. **Houston** leads the nation in imports and is one of only six cities in the nation with skyscrapers over one thousand feet high. The height of the Texas Commerce Center is tenth in the nation and second in the South.

The eastern coastal plain has fertile soil that Southerners found excellent for cotton crops. Texas leads the nation in cotton production. Along the Louisiana border are numerous swamps. The largest is Big Thicket, a natural reserve so dense that it is impassable.

Austin, the capital, is located where the Gulf Coastal Plain rises into the Central Plains. When Texas built its capitol in 1888, it made sure the building was taller than any other state capitol, and it was even taller than the national capitol by seven feet. Austin is home to several high-tech computer companies, such as Texas Instruments.

San Antonio, just southwest of Austin, far exceeds Austin in population. Half the people in this old Spanish town have a Spanish background. Evidence of Spanish culture is everywhere in the city, Texas's biggest tourist destination. San Antonio is most noted for the Alamo, an old Spanish mission that reminds visitors of Texas's former status as a

Remember the Alamo! On March 6, 1836, an army of five thousand Mexicans attacked 187 Texans, including Davy Crockett and Jim Bowie. The defenders gave their lives, but not before killing over fourteen hundred Mexicans.

Spanish territory and its effort to win independence. The brave stand by the defenders gave other Texans time to gather their forces. Their valiance inspired Texans to fight for liberty under the battle cry "Remember the Alamo!"

Big Ranches and Big Cities on the Central Plains   Longhorn steers can still be seen in the hilly Central Plains as far west as the Texas panhandle. Texas longhorns are a symbol of Texas, the nation's leader in the production of beef; but ranchers have found better breeds to replace the tough, thin longhorns that survived the famed cattle drives of the 1880s.

If you consider the population within city limits, Texas has three of the ten largest cities in the nation: Houston ranks fourth, Dallas ninth, and San Antonio tenth. Dallas and Houston also have the ninth and tenth largest metropolitan areas in the nation. The Dallas metropolitan area, located on the Central Plains, is boosted by its sister city, Fort Worth. Whichever way it is figured, Dallas and Houston are the two largest cities in the entire South.

Dallas was founded on the Trinity River by settlers who hoped the river would be navigable. But the hope proved vain. Dallas, however, has plenty of other means of transportation today. The Dallas/Fort Worth Airport, which handles over fifty

Cowboys brand their calves to prove ownership.

million passengers a year, is the world's second busiest airport (after Chicago's O'Hare Airport). Cities on the plains rely on roads and airplanes for transportation because, like the rest of the arid Southwest, the rivers are muddy and shallow.

The Great Plains   The Great Plains extend from the Mexican border in the south to the panhandle in the north. This hot and dry region is treeless. The treeless plain in the south is known locally as Edwards Plateau, and the western plain in the panhandle is known by the Spanish term *Llano Estecado* (meaning Staked Plain). The state's best oil fields are here, and the soil is irrigated for crops. The rangelands, which are good for sheep, make Texas the nation's leader in head of sheep.

The Low Rockies   The western wing of Texas is a portion of the Rocky Mountains. The mountains are low for the Rockies, only eight thousand feet, but they are far higher than any other mountains in the South or Midwest. The highest peaks are in the Guadalupe Mountains on the border with New Mexico. Big Bend National Park has high peaks, deserts, and deep gorges along the Rio Grande, which set the West apart from the humid swamps of east Texas.

El Paso is the major city in Texas's far western Mountain Time Zone. It epitomizes the dry climate of the rugged western mountains. The name of the city is Spanish for "The Pass." The Spanish language also gave us the word *mesa* ("table"), used for small plateaus in the area. The river running by the city, the **Rio Grande,** means "Great River." Texas has numerous Latin Americans in all its border cities. A bridge crosses the Rio Grande to the largest city on the Texas border, Ciudad Juárez, Mexico. Most Mexican food enjoyed around the United States is really a modified version called Tex-Mex.

SECTION REVIEW

1. Why is Texas a southern state? In what other region can it be classified?
2. What are the four main geographic regions of Texas?
3. How is Texas geography similar to the geography of the Atlantic states? What would correspond to the Fall Line?
4. Of which products is Texas the leading producer?
   ♀ Is state pride a good thing?

REVIEW

Can You Define These Terms?

states' rights	subalpine	spelunker	dome
diversify	balsam	Fundamentalist	bayou
gap	bituminous	Evangelical	confluence
barrier island	karst	Charismatic	

Can You Locate These Natural Features?

Atlantic Coastal Plain	Cumberland Plateau	Gulf of Mexico	Red River
Tidewater	Bluegrass	Gulf Coastal Plain	Mississippi Delta
Shenandoah Valley	Great Smoky Mountains	Mississippi River	Ozark Plateau
Outer Banks	Tennessee River	Mississippi Valley	Rio Grande
Appalachian Mountains	Stone Mountain	Everglades	

Can You Explain the Significance of These People, Places, and Events?

American Civil War	Deep South	Atlanta	New Orleans
Robert E. Lee	civil rights movement	bus boycott	Mardi Gras
Appalachia	Martin Luther King Jr.	Miami	Houston
Memphis	march on Washington	Cajun	Dallas
Tennessee Valley Authority			

How Much Do You Remember?

1. List all of the states that have a significant number of the following ethnic minorities.
   a. Indian
   b. French
   c. Spanish
2. What state has the largest percentage of blacks?
3. Put these events in chronological order: march on Washington, bus boycott, American Civil War.
4. What are the two main parts of the coastal plain?
5. Give the main geographic features of the following regions.
   a. Upper South
   b. Lower South
   c. South Central states
6. Match the products associated with each cultural subregion. (Products can be used more than once.)
   (1) Upper South   a. tobacco
   (2) Lower South   b. cotton
   (3) South Central states   c. coal
                              e. fruit
                              f. oil

7. For every southern state, give a major product *not* on the list above.
8. Why is it good for a state's economy to diversify?

What Do You Think?

1. Is regionalism good for a nation?
2. Is slavery sinful? Is secession sinful?
3. Was the civil rights movement a good solution to the racial divisions in the South?
4. Are you proud of your state? Why?
5. Why does the South have no megalopolis like the Northeast? Look at the population map on pages 106–7. Where is one most likely to arise?

CHAPTER 8

THE MIDWESTERN UNITED STATES

Americans call the north central region of their nation the **Midwest.** How can it be both Middle and West? This odd term reminds the nation of its frontier heritage. After the Revolutionary War, the wild, unsettled "West" lay just beyond the Appalachian Mountains. The promise of cheap farmland earned the young nation a reputation as the "land of opportunity." Settlers flocked to the frontier from the original thirteen states.

The Midwest became the "Middle" after the United States acquired lands on the Pacific coast. The Midwest has become the hub of transportation that links the rest of the nation—the Northeast, South, and West. The Midwest is also the breadbasket of the nation, providing almost half of its agricultural products. Midwestern speech even sets the standard for national broadcasts.

The flat **Central Plains,** which cover all twelve midwestern states, lack the spectacular peaks of the other regions. But God has given the region a subtle beauty that is often overlooked by motorists in a hurry. Checkered farms give a perfect picture of peace and prosperity. Midwesterners find simple pleasures in fishing trips to remote wooded lakes, breathtaking sunsets that seem to go on forever, and fireflies dancing at dusk among the "amber waves of grain."

The Midwest has profoundly influenced the character of the nation. Unlike the original colonies, which were settled by foreigners and aristocrats, everyday American families packed up and moved to the Midwest, where they struggled to survive against the basic elements of nature. While the original colonies allowed only wealthy landholders to vote for congressmen, frontier states generally adopted **universal manhood suffrage,** the right of every adult man to vote, regardless of his wealth, education, or beliefs. County fairs, courthouses, and capitols throughout the Midwest honor the "common man."

God has a special purpose for any man who will serve Him only. The world at large may not appreciate a man's work, but God promises great rewards to such a person, greater than the riches of kings, philosophers, and mighty men.

For ye see your calling, brethren, how that not many wise men after the flesh, not many mighty, not many noble, are called: but God hath chosen the foolish things of the world to confound the wise; and God hath chosen the weak things of the world to confound the things which are mighty. (I Cor. 1:26-27)

THE GREAT LAKES STATES

Not a single state in the Midwest touches the ocean. Before the invention of railroads and cars, Midwesterners wanting to travel and trade relied on the two great drainage basins in North America—the Mississippi River Basin and the Great Lakes.

As you learned in Chapter 2, the five **Great Lakes** make up the largest body of fresh water in the world. No other nation has a similar interconnected series of lakes that cut deep into the interior of the continent. Five midwestern states have rich farmland and major port cities on the Great Lakes Plain.

This land was inhabited mostly by Indians and trappers until after the Revolutionary War, when the Continental Congress organized the land into the **Northwest Territory.** Congress established a wise pattern for settling the frontiers and then preparing them to join the Union as free and equal states. Surveyors divided the land into townships six miles square. Each township was divided into thirty-six sections, or lots. (See map on page 8.) Farmers could buy a lot for as little as $1 an acre ($640 total). One lot was reserved for each township's local government, which could sell the lot to build schools.

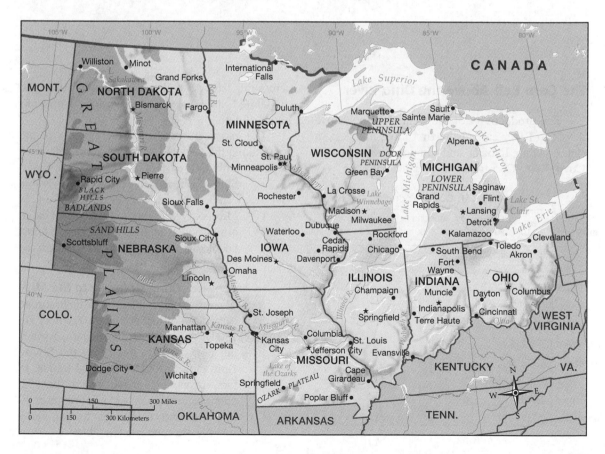

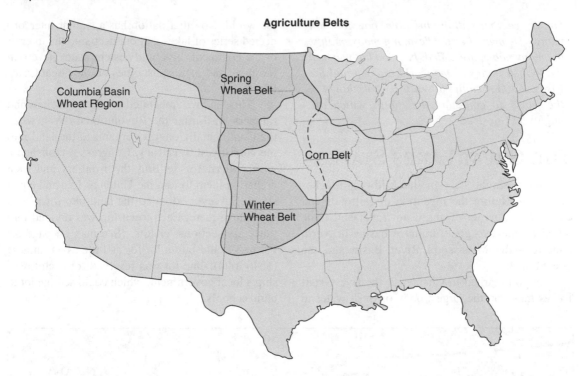

Agriculture Belts

Columbia Basin Wheat Region

Spring Wheat Belt

Corn Belt

Winter Wheat Belt

The Corn Belt Above the Ohio River

The productivity of the Central Plains above the Ohio River earned the first three midwestern states—Ohio, Indiana, and Illinois—the title of the **Corn Belt.** Cornfields now extend all the way across this latitude to Nebraska. They have helped the United States become the world's largest exporter of corn.

The early settlers entered the territory in the south along the **Ohio River.** The Ohio is the most important tributary east of the Mississippi River. Ships from as far east as Pennsylvania could travel downriver to the Gulf of Mexico. Over eighty million tons of cargo is transported annually on the Ohio, almost double the amount that passes through the Panama Canal.

Ohio, Gateway to the Midwest Ohio was the first state carved out of the Northwest Territory (in 1803). As the easternmost state, bordering both the Northeast and the South, Ohio closely follows national trends. In fact, researchers have found that the opinions of Ohioans are most representative of the nation. For this reason, many surveys are conducted in Ohio.

Top-Ten Corn-Producing Countries

Corn (millions of metric tons)

Country	
U.S.	187.3
China	112.0
Brazil	33.0
Mexico	16.0
France	12.3
Argentina	10.7
Romania	9.9
India	9.8
Italy	8.4
Yugoslavia	8.3

Midwestern United States Statistics

STATE	P.O. CODE	CAPITAL	DATE OF STATEHOOD	NICKNAME	AREA (SQ. MI.)	POP.	HIGH POINT, ELEVATION (FT.)
Illinois	IL	Springfield	1818	Prairie State	57,918	11,846,544	Charles Mound, 1,235
Indiana	IN	Indianapolis	1816	Hoosier State	36,420	5,840,528	Hoosier Hill, 1,257
Iowa	IA	Des Moines	1846	Hawkeye State	56,276	2,581,792	Sterler Farm, 1,670
Kansas	KS	Topeka	1861	Sunflower State	82,282	2,572,150	Mt. Sunflower, 4,039
Michigan	MI	Lansing	1837	Great Lakes State	96,705	9,594,350	Mt. Arvon, 1,979
Minnesota	MN	St. Paul	1858	North Star State	86,943	4,657,758	Eagle Mtn., 2,301
Missouri	MO	Jefferson City	1821	Show Me State	69,709	5,358,692	Taum Sauk Mtn., 1,772
Nebraska	NE	Lincoln	1867	Cornhusker State	77,358	1,652,093	Panorama Point, 5,424
North Dakota	ND	Bismarck	1889	Peace Garden State	70,704	643,539	White Butte, 3,506
Ohio	OH	Columbus	1803	Buckeye State	44,828	11,172,782	Campbell Hill, 1,549
South Dakota	SD	Pierre	1889	Coyote State	77,121	732,405	Harney Peak, 7,242
Wisconsin	WI	Madison	1848	Badger State	65,499	5,159,795	Timms Hill, 1,951

Ohio remains a leader in the Midwest. It has the second highest population in the region (just behind Illinois). Ohio State University, the first school of higher learning in the Midwest, is the largest university in the nation. Ohio rivals Virginia as the nation's Mother of Presidents. Seven presidents hailed from the state. The first, Ulysses S. Grant (1869-77), became president after helping the Union win the Civil War.

Ohio has long been a leader in industry. It produces more iron and steel than any other state except Indiana. Thomas Edison, the self-taught inventor of the light bulb and phonograph, was born in Ohio. Ransom Eli Olds, the Father of the Automobile Industry, is another native son of Ohio. He built the first automobile factory—the Olds Motor Works—in Detroit, Michigan, in 1899. The Wright brothers worked out of their bike shop in Dayton, Ohio, before testing their airplane designs at Kitty Hawk, North Carolina, in 1903.

Most of the state's population lies in the northern plains along Lake Erie, called the Great Lakes Plain. Upstate New Yorkers and New Englanders settled in Cleveland and Toledo after the completion of the Erie Canal in 1825. Both lake cities retain close ties to the northeastern megalopolis.

Good farmland covers the west of the state on the *till plains*. **Till** is deep fertile soil left by the glaciers that apparently dug out the Great Lakes. On the southwest border is Cincinnati, the second largest city on the Ohio River after Pittsburgh, Pennsylvania. Columbus, the state capital, lies on the till plains in the center of the state.

Few industries arose east of Columbus on the Appalachian Plateau, which runs along Ohio's border with Pennsylvania and West Virginia. The hills provide coal for manufacturing, but they are not very good for farmland. The industrial city of Akron lies in the north near Cleveland. B. F. Goodrich's manufacturing plant made Akron famous for tires and other rubber products. The nation's two other great tire manufacturers—Firestone and Goodyear—also started in this city.

Indiana The Midwest is proud of its prize product, **Abraham Lincoln,** the most beloved president after George Washington. Born in Kentucky, he grew up in the backwoods of Indiana near Evansville and later moved to Illinois at age twenty-one. Midwesterners respect the qualities that made Lincoln great—hard work, honesty, intelligence, ready wit, and love of country. After losing every major political contest he entered early

Great Serpent Mound

The Ohio and Mississippi Rivers were the center of vanished Indian cultures that arose long before Columbus ever discovered America. These civilizations (ca. 500 B.C.–A.D. 1600) built magnificent **Indian mounds.** Every state along the Mississippi and Ohio Rivers has Indian mounds. Ohio's most famous ruin is the Great Serpent Mound, on the till plains northeast of Cincinnati. This beautifully designed snake winds thirteen hundred feet from tail to head. An egg is clasped in the serpent's jaws.

Any mound shaped like an animal or bird is called an *effigy mound.* Most effigy mounds are located in Wisconsin, near Sheboygan and West Bend. Several others were built in northeast Iowa at Effigy Mounds. The origin of these mounds has been a subject of debate. Why did ancient people work so hard to pile up these dirt hills—the most spectacular ancient ruins east of the Rockies?

The "mound builders" most often built *burial mounds.* Animal shapes are rare. Most mounds are geometric shapes. Ohio has the most well known burial mounds, dating from around the time of Christ. The Hopewell sites have several circles, squares, and octagons, which range in area from twenty to fifty acres.

Serpent Mound winds almost one-quarter of a mile in southern Ohio near Locust Grove.

The largest burial mound is not in Ohio, however, but in Minnesota—the Grand Mound at International Falls.

Thousands of small, flat-topped *temple mounds* were commonly used in religious ceremonies. The earliest are dated circa A.D. 700. They appear to be imitations of the pre-Aztec pyramids in Mexico and Central America. Among the sixty-five Cahokia mounds near St. Louis is the highest mound, Monk's Mound, a pyramid rising one hundred feet. The largest of the temple mound complexes is Emerald Mound, located at Natchez, Mississippi.

in his career, Lincoln persevered to become president of the United States. His life's story inspired the dream that any boy can grow up to become president.

Indiana, sandwiched between Ohio and Illinois, has the smallest area of any midwestern state. But it has big cities and major manufacturing centers. Gary is Indiana's leading port on Lake Michigan. Farther inland on the Great Lakes Plain is Fort Wayne, which makes trucks, cars, mobile homes, recreational vehicles, and boats. Nearby Elkhart leads the nation in the production of brass musical instruments.

Till plains cover most of the state. Indianapolis, the third biggest city in the Midwest, lies on the White River in the till plains at the center of Indiana. Its 2.5-mile Motor Speedway hosts the most famous car race in the nation, the Indianapolis

500. Near Memorial Day each year, the world's best drivers endure a grueling five-hundred-mile-long race to the finish.

Southern Indiana is a hilly plateau that extends up from Kentucky's Pennyroyal Plateau.

Abe Lincoln lived on this land during his boyhood years from 1816 to 1830. The reconstructed farm is now a national memorial near Lincoln City, Indiana.

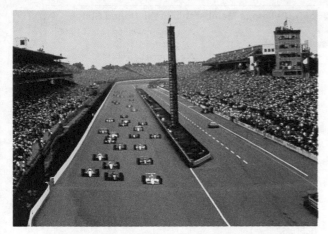

Four hundred thousand fans watch the Indianapolis 500, considered the largest one-day sporting event in the world.

Evansville, the largest city in the area, is the state's major port on the Ohio River. A historic attraction northwest of the city is New Harmony, an early experiment in communal living, where liberals from the East tried to build a perfect society with all living in "harmony" as equals. Greed, selfishness, and laziness ruined the project after only two years.

Illinois, Land of Lincoln Lincoln's career as a lawyer began in Illinois. The only house he ever bought is preserved as a national historic site near the state capital, Springfield. Visitors can also see the church he attended, the capitol where he served, and his tomb. The Land of Lincoln has become the central state of the Midwest, with the largest population, the largest city, and the largest railroad center and airport.

The Prairie State Pioneers in the eastern states of Ohio and Indiana had to clear vast forests to make room for their farms. But in Illinois they discovered a great **prairie,** rolling plains with high grasses that spread across the western half of the Midwest. This land does not receive adequate rainfall to support forests.

The fertile prairie has made Illinois the second highest producer of corn and the leader in soybeans. In 1837 John Deere invented the first steel plow that could cut the tough prairie sod. His manufacturing plant in Moline made it "the farm-equipment capital" of the nation. The mechanical reaper, which Cyrus McCormick began manufacturing in Chicago in 1847, opened the way to large-scale commercial farms in America. Peoria is the headquarters of Caterpillar, Inc., which produces earthmoving machines. It is such a typical American city that opinion pollsters and companies go there to test new products. Politicians today, when considering how to vote on controversial issues, ask, "Will it play in Peoria?"

Southern Illinois is very different from the Central Plains that cover the rest of the state. The Shawnee Hills is a low interior plateau typical of neighboring southern states. The canyons and rock formations of Shawnee National Forest are quite scenic. Bald Knob Cross, a manmade cross standing 111 feet high on a hill near the Mississippi River, is the largest monument to Christ in the nation.

The southernmost tip of the state, where the Ohio meets the Mississippi River, is part of the Gulf Coastal Plain. In some ways, the port of Cairo is like a town of the South. Nearby Horseshoe Lake is typical of southern cypress swamps. The lake marks the northern limit of cypress trees along the Mississippi River.

The Second City In 1850 **Chicago** was a tiny town on the outskirts of the Northwest. But the steady advance of the railroad changed everything. Chicago stood at the key junction between the railroads and ships that carried primary goods from the West and manufactured goods from the East. The population exploded as immigrants poured into the city, many of them staying rather than continuing farther west. Until Los Angeles surpassed it in 1990, Chicago ranked as the second largest city proper in the nation.

In spite of the nickname, the Second City was never an imitation of New York. It has its own distinctive styles. Chicago-style hot dogs go heavy on the mustard and onions, and Chicago-style pizza is in a pan with lots of toppings. The bygone days of Al Capone add to its unique flavor. Irish immigrants who moved in from Boston never forgot their roots. During the festive St. Patrick's Day celebration each year, Irish Catholics dye the Chicago River green.

Missions

Target Groups

As in so many other things, the Midwest reflects the nation's typical views on religion. Surveys indicate that almost every American believes in God and heaven, three-fourths believe in hell, two-thirds believe in the Devil, and one-third believe the Bible is the literal Word of God. While the percentage of weekly churchgoers is highest in the South and lowest in the Northeast and West, it is near the national average in the Midwest (38 percent).

The Midwest is also a crossroads of religions. Not only does it have churches from every major denomination, it also has temples and synagogues from every major world religion. This includes Eastern religions. Swami Vivekenanda of India brought Hinduism to America in 1893 at a major conference in Chicago which drew religious leaders from around the world. Bahai's national headquarters, a beautiful nine-sided temple, is in a suburb of Chicago.

Because of its size and diversity, Chicago has been a magnet for various Christian ministries. Chicago's most renowned religious figure is **Dwight L. Moody,** who moved there from Boston in 1856 hoping to strike it rich. But he soon gave his life to serving the city's poor. He started the first big Sunday schools in Chicago, and he was a promoter of the Young Men's Christian Association (YMCA). Moody later won fame as an evangelist. His large citywide campaigns in the 1870s set an example for every *urban evangelist* of the twentieth century. Moody's church and Bible institute are still active to this day. Another of Chicago's famous ongoing ministries, Pacific Garden Mission (founded 1877), reaches inner-city alcoholics and outcasts.

Most of these ministries have a "target group," a special segment of the whole population they are trying to reach. They follow the pattern of the apostle Paul, who ministered in busy cities where people came from all around the world (I Thess. 1:8).

In the 1980s some Evangelical churches began taking polls to find out what would attract more people from a "target audience" to their churches. Using this approach, a leader in the church-growth movement built the nation's second largest Protestant congregation in a suburb of Chicago. Some of their own supporters called it "entertainment evangelism." Unlike the statisticians in this movement, the apostle Paul reminded Timothy that Christians must preach the same message to all groups. Paul warned

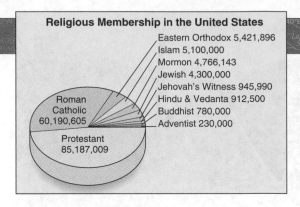

Religious Membership in the United States

Roman Catholic 60,190,605
Protestant 85,187,009
Eastern Orthodox 5,421,896
Islam 5,100,000
Mormon 4,766,143
Jewish 4,300,000
Jehovah's Witness 945,990
Hindu & Vedanta 912,500
Buddhist 780,000
Adventist 230,000

against the temptation to adjust the message to please the hearers.

Preach the word; be instant in season, out of season; reprove, rebuke, exhort with all longsuffering and doctrine. For the time will come when they will not endure sound doctrine; but after their own lusts shall they heap to themselves teachers, having itching ears. (II Tim. 4:2-3)

Has the Lord burdened your heart to share the gospel with a special group—the deaf, the blind, orphans, the sick, college students, the homeless, soldiers, foreign immigrants, Indians? Regardless of the group you want to reach, most full-time missionaries need several years of preparation, including practical experience helping local ministries, a diploma from a Christian college or Bible institute, and often a master's degree from seminary. Next comes deputation, a time to seek financial backing and prayer support from individual churches. The more you understand mission work, the better you can pray for other missionaries and prepare yourself to go.

Pacific Garden Mission

In 1871, the Chicago Fire burned a third of the city, including every public building except the old water tower. Not to be stopped, the hard-working midwesterners rebuilt their city following one of the best plans for a city its size in the nation. "Chicago style" is a distinctive type of office building imitated by many other cities. Later, Frank Lloyd Wright developed the modern "Prairie style" of architecture. His unusual homes and large buildings are designed to blend with the landscape. Twenty-five famous Wright homes, including his own home and studio, are major tourist stops in Chicago's Oak Park suburb.

Chicago invented skyscrapers. Although New York's skyscrapers surpassed Chicago for many years, the Second City regained the lead with the Sears Tower in 1974. Over fourteen hundred feet high, it is still the highest skyscraper in the nation. New York and Chicago are the only U.S. cities with skyscrapers taller than twelve hundred feet, and each city has three. Chicago's other two are the Amoco Building and the John Hancock Center. Visitors enjoy spectacular views from the observation decks on top of both the Sears and Hancock buildings.

Chicago's metropolitan area curls around Lake Michigan, from Gary, Indiana, in the east to Kenosha, Wisconsin, in the north. Des Plaines, the birthplace of McDonalds Restaurants, may be the most well known suburb of Chicago. Like New

The 110-story-high Sears Tower in Chicago, Illinois, was the world's tallest building at its completion in 1974. It is still the tallest in the Western Hemisphere and second tallest in the world.

York City and the northeastern megalopolis, Chicago is the hub of the Great Lakes megalopolis, which stretches north to Milwaukee and east to Detroit.

Chicago is the transportation capital of the nation, with hubs for every type of travel. Its inhabitants have always shipped goods on Lake Michigan. The city later became the railroad capital of the world when connections were completed to San Francisco in 1869. Six major interstates converge in Chicago. O'Hare International Airport has been the world's busiest airport for more than forty years.

An elevated railroad, called the Loop, runs through the downtown area of Chicago.

SECTION REVIEW

1. What are the two great drainage basins of North America?
2. Who is the most beloved president from the Midwest?
3. Name the main products of Ohio, Indiana, and Illinois.
4. What term describes a rolling plain with high grasses?
5. Why is Chicago called the Second City? Does the nickname fit?
- Does universal manhood suffrage present any potential problems?

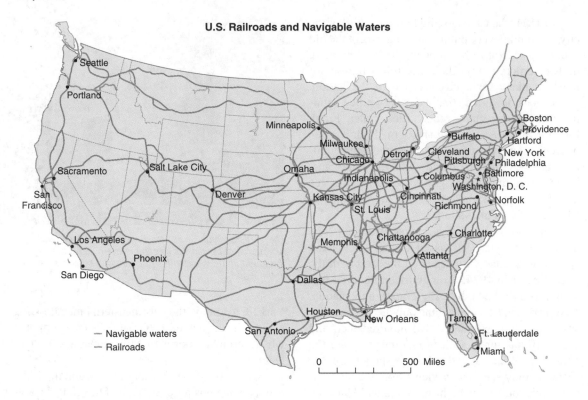

U.S. Railroads and Navigable Waters

— Navigable waters
— Railroads

0   500 Miles

The Dairy Belt of the Far North

Michigan and Wisconsin were the last states created from the Old Northwest Territory. The land is not as good for farms, partly because of the cold and partly because of the soils. Unable to produce more valuable crops, farmers grow hay and raise herds of dairy cattle on pastureland. The **Dairy Belt** stretches all the way across the northern Great Lakes region, from Vermont and New York in the east to Minnesota in the west. Wisconsin wins the prize for the most dairy cattle, but Minnesota does not lag far behind. Wisconsin's dairy industry leads in all three major dairy products: milk, butter, and cheese.

Michigan, the Great Lakes State

Michigan is the only state with shoreline on four Great Lakes. Its very name, taken from the local Indians, means "great lake." **Lake Michigan,** the only Great Lake located entirely within the United States, divides the state in two. The lake flows through the Straits of Mackinac (MACK uh NAW) into Lake Huron and the rest of the lake system. The two parts of Michigan, known as the Lower Peninsula and the Upper Peninsula, are linked by Mackinac Bridge, the "Big Mac."

The Populated Lower Peninsula Michigan is the largest state in the Midwest, and it is third in population (after Illinois and Ohio). Most of the dairy farms and cities lie on the Lower Peninsula. Although the Great Lakes Plain covers the whole peninsula, the best land is in the south.

Detroit, the second largest city in the Midwest, lies on the eastern shore of the Lower Peninsula, where Lake Huron runs into Lake Erie. Detroit is the Automotive Capital of the World. Here Henry Ford invented the modern assembly line, which revolutionized manufacturing. America's "Big Three" car manufacturers—General Motors, Chrysler, and Ford—have headquarters in Detroit.

Lansing, the state capital, is located west of Detroit. It has the oldest **land-grant college** in the nation—Michigan State University. In 1862 the federal government granted all states and territories thirty thousand acres of federal land to pay for at least one public college specializing in the study of "agriculture and the mechanic arts." Large land-grant, or "A & M" colleges, arose all over the Midwest.

The western shore of the Lower Peninsula is less populous than the east. Sleeping Bear Dunes is the most beautiful of many sand dunes on Lake Michigan's shore. The moderating effects of the lake on the weather allow fruit trees to thrive—in fact, Michigan leads the nation in cherry production.

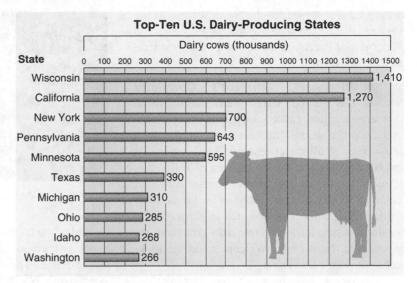

Top-Ten U.S. Dairy-Producing States

Dairy cows (thousands)

State	Dairy cows (thousands)
Wisconsin	1,410
California	1,270
New York	700
Pennsylvania	643
Minnesota	595
Texas	390
Michigan	310
Ohio	285
Idaho	268
Washington	266

Island of the Wolves

North of Michigan's shore lies Isle Royale, the largest island in Lake Superior. No motor vehicles are allowed on the fifty-mile-long island. No one lives on the island except for those at a lodge at one end and at a campground and inn at the other. Since it can be reached only by ferry, the island is the most remote national park in the Midwest.

The island has several creeks, bays, offshore islands, and thirty inland lakes. Along with many birds and freshwater fish, this amazing park supports a diversity of mammals, including beavers, red foxes, snowshoe hares, rabbits, and squirrels. Scientists come to observe the unique ecosystem, which is a haven for a large moose herd and timber wolves.

How did all the large mammals get there? Apparently, some swam or drifted on logs, while others came on the ice that forms in bitterly cold winters on Lake Superior.

The main western city, Grand Rapids, is located on the rapids of the Grand River. It is known for fine furniture made from the state's plentiful forests. Testimony to the city's Dutch Reformed roots is its four large Christian book publishers—the so-called Netherlands Quartet: Zondervan, Baker, Eerdmans, and Kregel. A lesser known city below Grand Rapids is Battle Creek, the Cereal Capital of the World. It is the headquarters of America's two great cereal processors, Post and Kellogg's.

Wilderness of the Upper Peninsula The Upper Peninsula is sparsely populated. Its northern shore touches **Lake Superior,** the largest and westernmost of the Great Lakes. Swamps, waterfalls, and cliffs line the eastern shore. The naturally golden waters of Tahquamenon Falls roar down the most powerful waterfall in the Midwest. (The Midwest's *highest* waterfall is in neighboring Wisconsin.)

While the eastern half of the Upper Peninsula is considered part of the Great Lakes Plain, the western half rises into the **Superior Uplands,** a plateau that continues west into Minnesota. Geologists believe that glaciers, leaving rich deposits on the southern till plains, left this plateau almost bare of soil. The coniferous trees of the **North Woods** cover the uplands. Of the two hundred falls in the Upper

Peninsula, most appear in the North Woods. At the western edge of the state are the rugged peaks and wilderness of Porcupine Mountains, the largest state park in the Midwest.

Wisconsin, America's Dairyland

The United States leads the world in cheese production and consumes more ice cream than any other nation. Wisconsin accounts for about one-quarter of all the cheese produced nationally, and it ranks high in the production of ice cream, dried milk, yogurt, and cottage cheese. Although ice-cream cones were invented in St. Louis, Missouri, malted milk was invented in Racine, Wisconsin. The state has nearly one dairy cow for every two people. No wonder Wisconsin has the nickname America's Dairyland.

Wisconsin has been at the forefront of increased voting rights for the common man. Throughout the nineteenth century party leaders, or "bosses," picked the candidates who ran for state and national offices. The people had no choice in the names of the Republicans or Democrats who appeared on the ballots. Crying "No more boss rule," the people of Wisconsin passed the first law in 1903 requiring **primary elections.** Under this system, the people vote directly for each party's candidates. Today, every state has adopted some form of primary elections.

Most of Wisconsin's dairy farms and cities lie in the fertile Great Lakes Plain of the eastern half of the state. Milwaukee is the state's largest city, located on Lake Michigan. Dairy products testify to the city's North European roots, but so does its beer. The city leads the nation in beer production and takes pride in its breweries, even naming a professional baseball team the Milwaukee Brewers. But God's Word promises woe to those who distribute alcoholic beverages.

Woe unto him that giveth his neighbor drink. (Hab. 2:15)

The western half of Wisconsin is divided between the Superior Uplands in the north and the Driftless Area in the south. Forestry and paper manufacturing is an important industry in the Superior

Boat trips along the Wisconsin River enjoy the scenery of the Wisconsin Dells.

Upland of the northwest. Over eight thousand lakes tempt fishermen hungry for northern pike and muskellunge. The highest of many waterfalls in Wisconsin's North Woods is Big Manitous Falls, with a 162-foot drop.

The hilly Driftless Area, though part of the Central Plains, appears not to have been scraped by glaciers. The poor soil supports few major farms. The scenic Wisconsin River winds through high wooded cliffs, known as the Wisconsin Dells, near the western border of the state.

SECTION REVIEW

1. What strait divides Michigan in two?
2. What plateau is part of the Dairy Belt?
3. Name the four Great Lakes that touch Michigan.
4. Name the most important products for each state.
   Can you think of any possible disadvantages of direct primaries?

THE HEARTLAND

In 1803, while most of the Northwest Territory remained unsettled, President Thomas Jefferson had an opportunity to buy even more unsettled land farther west. France agreed to sell the vast **Louisiana Purchase** for only $15 million. It more than doubled the size of the nation.

This region is America's geographic heartland. Geographers and demographers have located five geometric "centers" in the former Louisiana Purchase. The geographic center of the North American continent is east of Minot, North Dakota. The geographic center of the fifty states is near the western border of South Dakota. The center of the forty-eight lower states lies in northern Kansas. Meade's Ranch in eastern Kansas is the geodetic center of the United States, from which surveyors begin measurements. Finally, the center of America's population distribution is northeast of Rolla, Missouri.

In many respects, this region is America's cultural heartland. The Central Plains are less populated, and major cities are fewer. A greater proportion of the people live in small towns and farms, or they work in scattered cities that process farm products. From *Tom Sawyer* to *Little House on the Prairie,* the western plains provide many pictures of common American life. **Americana** refers to geography and culture that is considered typical of America.

The former Louisiana Territory is also America's agricultural heartland. Six of the top ten corn-producing states are here. (The other four states of the Corn Belt lie in the former Northwest Territory.) Three of the top wheat-producing states are here too.

The Upper Mississippi Basin

Just as the Great Lakes serve a central role in the eastern half of the Midwest, the Mississippi River plays a central role in the heartland. The upper Mississippi River officially begins on the placid waters of Lake Itasca in Minnesota. Beginning as a stream only two feet deep, it gathers water as it runs along the eastern border of the heartland. Among the tributaries that flow into the Mississippi from the West are the Minnesota, Iowa, and Missouri Rivers. The first two are relatively short, but the Missouri River brings water all the way from the Rockies. The biggest cities in the heartland arose near where these tributaries joined the mighty Mississippi.

The Louisiana Purchase included the mouth of the Mississippi and all the **Mississippi River Basin**

west of the main branch. But at the time of the purchase, no one knew just how far the claim extended. No white man had ever surveyed the upper reaches of the Mississippi's western tributaries. Jefferson commissioned Lewis and Clark's western expedition (1804-6) to find the edge of America's new land at the headwaters of the Mississippi's main western tributary—the Missouri River.

Missouri, Gateway to the West

Missouri is a good illustration of the heartland pattern of scattered farm communities and **nodal cities.** Look back at the population map in Chapter 6, page 128, to find these cities. Farmers live around small hamlets that may have fewer than a hundred people. Rural farmers may take trips once a week to nearby towns. On special occasions they travel to a big city. Nodal cities process farm goods into flour, beef, and pork, and other finished products. The two main nodal cities in Missouri are St. Louis in the east and Kansas City in the west.

Nodal Cities on the Missouri River St. Louis was the first major city of the heartland, founded where the **Missouri River** flows into the Mississippi. Lewis and Clark started their western expedition here. The Gateway Arch at St. Louis, the largest monument in the nation, marks the spot where thousands of pioneers launched into the western frontier.

The Missouri-born novelist Samuel Clemens, better known by his pen name, **Mark Twain,** celebrated famous scenes from frontier life on the Mississippi River. He spent his childhood in the small town of Hannibal, north of St. Louis; and as a young man, he piloted steamboats up and down the Mississippi. Mark Twain described many of his childhood escapades in *The Adventures of Tom Sawyer.* A more serious novel is *The Adventures of Huckleberry Finn,* which recounts Huck Finn's trip down the Mississippi River with an escaped slave. It is sometimes called the first modern American novel, written as a first-person account by a typical American boy speaking in his own nonstandard dialect.

The Gateway Arch is a monument to the opening of the western frontier.

Kansas City arose farther up the Missouri River, where it is joined by the Kansas River. Like Twain's Mississippi, the Missouri River has much Americana. Kansas City hosts the largest livestock show in the nation—the American Royal. This nodal city has one of the nation's largest flour mill industries. The metropolitan area includes Independence, where the Oregon Trail began. Farther north is St. Joseph, the beginning of the pony express route.

The Ozarks   The populated part of the state lies in the Central Plains. The sparsely populated Ozark Plateau covers the southern half of the state, which it shares with the southern state of Arkansas. Lake of the Ozarks is an especially popular tourist destination. Silver Dollar City displays the crafts and talents of the hill people. The area has the most productive lead mines in the country. Cotton is grown in a small area of the Gulf Coastal Plain at the southeast corner of the state, known as the "Bootheel."

Thomas Hart Benton, the most well known "regionalist" painter in America, was born in a small town at the southwest corner of Missouri. His paintings and bright murals depict many scenes of frontier life. Benton was commissioned to paint murals for the statehouse in Jefferson City and for the Harry S Truman Library in Independence.

The state is proud of President **Harry S Truman,** born in a tiny southern town near Springfield. A short, unimposing man with thick glasses, he was never expected to rise to the presidency. But the death of Franklin D. Roosevelt catapulted him to the highest office in the crucial year of 1945. As president, he earned a reputation as a hard driver who took responsibility and kept his word. A sign reading "The Buck Stops Here" sat on his desk. Truman decided to drop the atomic bomb on Japan to end World War II, and he later refused to back down to Soviet threats during the Cold War. His spirited come-from-behind victory in 1948 surprised the nation, including the newspaper editors who printed a story assuming he had been defeated.

Iowa, Hogs and Corn   Iowa produces 7 percent of the nation's entire food supply. It produces more corn than any other state—about 20 percent of the nation's total. It also raises about one-quarter of the nation's hogs, slaughtered to make ham, sausage, and bacon. Iowa has four times as many hogs as people!

On the west side of the state is Sioux City, Iowa's main port on the Missouri River. The chief port on the Mississippi River in the east is Davenport. President Herbert Hoover's home is just west of Davenport. He is famous for urging "rugged individualism," not government programs, to overcome the Great Depression that hit the nation in 1929.

The state's capital and largest city, Des Moines, is located on the Des Moines River in the middle of the state. A nearby tourist attraction is the Amana Colonies, founded in 1855 by a religious sect of German immigrants who wanted to follow a rural communal lifestyle. Today, the villagers own their own restaurants, museums, and craft shops that attract many visitors.

Iowa is completely covered by Central Plains but has three distinct parts. The southern and western

Top-Ten U.S. Corn-Producing States

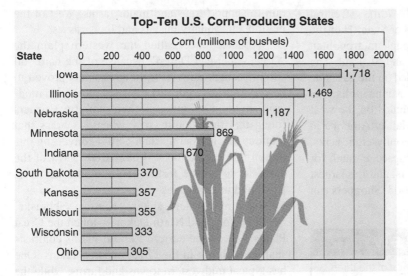

State	Corn (millions of bushels)
Iowa	1,718
Illinois	1,469
Nebraska	1,187
Minnesota	869
Indiana	670
South Dakota	370
Kansas	357
Missouri	355
Wisconsin	333
Ohio	305

edges of the state are till plains. The large north central region has some of the most fertile soil in the world in a region called Drift Prairie. Like till, **drift** is deep soil possibly deposited by glaciers. The third type of Central Plain is the hilly Driftless Area along the northeastern border. It has no drift and poor soil. **Bluffs** (steep riverbanks) overlooking the Mississippi River are the primary nesting areas for bald eagles, the emblem of the nation's freedom and strength.

Minnesota, Land of Ten Thousand Lakes

Minnesota is the second largest midwestern state, behind its Great Lakes neighbor Michigan. The tall tales of Paul Bunyan symbolize the tough lumberjacks who braved the cold North. Twenty-five-foot statues of this friendly giant appear near the towns of Bemidji, Brainerd, and Akeley. Several statues of Paul Bunyan also appear in Michigan.

The North Woods

The lonely North Woods cover the northeastern half of the state, from Lake Superior to the Lake of the Woods. Minnesota shares the North Woods with Michigan, and it shares the Lake of the Woods—the largest of its fifteen thousand lakes—with Canada. On the north end of Lake of the Woods is Northwest Angle, the northernmost spit of land in the forty-eight lower states. Can you find Northwest Angle on the map on page 169? The only way to reach this Indian Reservation without leaving the United States is by boating across Lake of the Woods.

Duluth is the major port on the Great Lakes. It was originally founded to serve the fur traders who trapped on the lakes, and it later became a center for lumber. With the rise of modern industry, it became the distribution center for the iron mines in **Mesabi Range** southwest of Duluth. This hilly region in the Superior Uplands has the leading iron ore producing mines in the nation. The ore is shipped to Pittsburgh and manufacturing cities on the Great Lakes. A three-mile-wide, open-pit mine is known as the Grand Canyon of Minnesota.

Split Rock Lighthouse is the most famous lighthouse on Lake Superior and perhaps in the Great Lakes system. It was built in 1910 on scenic cliffs one hundred feet high, near Two Harbors, Minnesota.

Twin Cities on the Central Plains Central Plains cover the rest of the Gopher State. Half the state lives in the Twin Cities, a single metropolitan area consisting of Minneapolis and St. Paul. The state capital, St. Paul, was founded on the east side of the Mississippi River; and Minneapolis, the largest city in the state, was founded on the west side of the river. The massive Mall of America in suburban Minneapolis covers seventy-eight acres. It has 4.2 million square feet of space, enough for four hundred stores, eight theaters, and the largest indoor amusement park in the world. Shoppers can even ride a roller coaster.

⊚ SECTION REVIEW

1. Name the main nodal cities in each of the three states of the upper Mississippi basin.
2. In what two ways was Missouri a gateway to the West?
3. What is a drift plain? Is it fertile?
4. Give an example of Americana in Missouri, Iowa, and Minnesota.
5. Name the most important product of each state.
   ♀ Compare and contrast the roles of Missouri and Illinois in the life of the Midwest.

The Great Plains

Motorists driving on the Central Plains toward the Rockies feel like they are continuing across monotonously level land. But the western part of their trip will take them through the **Great Plains.** Unlike the Central Plains, the Great Plains slope gradually upward so that the western end at the foot of the Rockies is four *thousand* feet higher than the eastern end.

One visible sign that you are entering a new plain is the climate and vegetation. The Great Plains are more arid than the Central Plains. Dry prevailing westerlies, which blow down the Rockies, do not pick up much moisture until they reach the one-hundredth meridian. Here, at the border between the Great Plains and the Central Plains, the annual rainfall reaches twenty inches—enough rain to support trees and major farms. West of the meridian lie squatty bushes and low grasses.

Pioneers once called the western plain the "Great American Desert" because of the hard soil and infrequent rains. But the grasslands proved to be very fertile, requiring only steel plows and modern irrigation to unleash their bounty. Farmers found that they could grow wheat—a grass that requires much less rain than corn—converting this region into the nation's **Wheat Belt.** Most of the cities arose on the fertile banks of the Missouri River and its tributaries.

Four midwestern states—Kansas, Nebraska, South Dakota, and North Dakota—touch the Great Plains. Life in the eastern Central Plains contrasts sharply with life in the Great or High Plains. One has typical midwestern towns and farms, while the other often has oil fields, cattle, and ranches. The frontier spirit still lives in these four states, the last in the Midwest to gain statehood.

Kansas, Wheat Kansas is known as the Sunflower State because it leads the nation in sunflower seed production. But its most important crop is wheat. Kansas leads the nation in *winter wheat,* which is planted in the fall, grows for a short time before it is blanketed by snow, and then finishes growing in the spring or summer.

The till plains in the northeast are the most fertile region of Kansas. The major cities of Topeka and Kansas City, Kansas, are in the till plains on the Kansas River, a tributary of the Missouri. The

Dark storms roll across the Badlands of South Dakota.

Top-Ten U.S. Wheat-Producing States

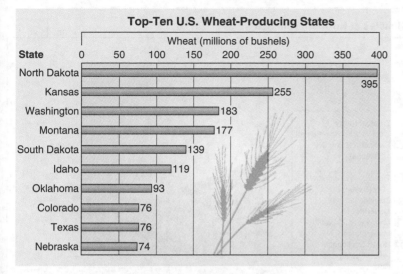

Wheat (millions of bushels)

State	Wheat
North Dakota	395
Kansas	255
Washington	183
Montana	177
South Dakota	139
Idaho	119
Oklahoma	93
Colorado	76
Texas	76
Nebraska	74

Nebraska, Cornhuskers

Nebraska is a leading farm state in spite of the uncertain rainfall and other hazards of the Great Plains, which cover most of the state. Farms and ranches cover 95 percent of the land, a higher proportion than in any other state. Farmers have wisely selected what to raise and where to irrigate to make Nebraska a perfect picture of midwestern productivity. The end of the Corn Belt lies in the east, and the most productive slice of the Wheat Belt lies in the south.

Nebraska has the most democratic state government in the United States. It is the only state with a **unicameral** (one house) legislature. Elected officials easily pass laws by majority vote, without worrying about vetoes from another house. All the other states have a **bicameral** system of two houses. Nebraska's capitol also differs from that of most states. A magnificent four hundred-foot "Tower of the Plains" rises above the middle of the capitol, topped by "The Sower," a fine bronze statue of a farmer.

One of America's great heroes came from Nebraska. **William Jennings Bryan,** a strong Christian and eloquent speaker, almost won the presidency in 1896. He was known as the Great Commoner because of his sympathy for the common man. Bryan's views won the support of a midwestern party called the People's, or Populist, Party. His famous Cross of Gold speech, given at

state's other major city, Wichita, lies in the Osage Plains on the Arkansas River. Locals call it the "r-Kansas" river. Wichita is the Airplane Capital of the World, producing the world's largest crop of private planes.

"There's no place like home" is a well-known phrase from the *Wizard of Oz.* It describes Dorothy's farm in Kansas, at the heart of Americana. Laura Ingalls Wilder, author of *Little House on the Prairie,* spent her childhood on a farm in the southeastern corner of the state. Another bit of Americana lies in the west at Dodge City. Several gunslingers were buried on "Boot Hill" in this Old West frontier town.

Kansas, in the heart of the Wheat Belt, produces more winter wheat than any other state.

Wheat-Producing Regions

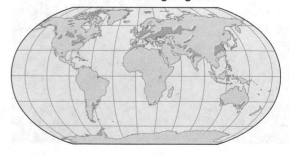

Let's Go Exploring

1. What climate is typical of the northeastern states? What is the only exception?
2. What climate is typical of the southern states? List the exceptions.
3. What climate is typical of the midwestern states? What are the exceptions?
4. What is the main difference between the climates of the west coast and the climate on the other side of the highlands?
5. What climate regions does the United States share with Canada? What climates are unique to the United States?

Based on this map, what other U.S. culture region is probably most similar to the Midwest?

Climates of Northern America

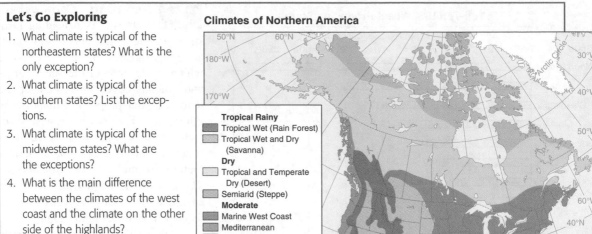

Tropical Rainy
- Tropical Wet (Rain Forest)
- Tropical Wet and Dry (Savanna)

Dry
- Tropical and Temperate Dry (Desert)
- Semiarid (Steppe)

Moderate
- Marine West Coast
- Mediterranean
- Humid Continental
- Humid Subtropical

Cold
- Polar (Tundra)
- Subpolar (Taiga)

Other
- Varied Highland

---

the Democratic Party convention in Chicago, pled with eastern bankers to relieve the poor farmers crucified "upon a cross of gold." Bryan lost his bid for the presidency, but many of his Populist goals were later passed into law.

Wagons once rumbled past Scottsbluff, Nebraska, an important landmark on the Oregon Trail.

Omaha, the state's main port on the Missouri River, lies in the eastern quarter of Nebraska in the Central Plains. The capital, south of Omaha, was named in honor of the Midwest's great hero, Abraham Lincoln. Western Nebraska's Great Plains include fertile lands on the North Platte River. Early pioneers followed this river on the Oregon Trail. Chimney Rock and Scottsbluff were important landmarks. At Scottsbluff, tourists can see actual wagon ruts and covered wagons.

South Dakota, Mount Rushmore

South Dakota produces the nation's largest crop of rye—a grass similar to wheat. However, it is most famous for Mount Rushmore, a mountain sculpture twice the height of the Sphinx in Egypt. A little-known American sculptor and his son fulfilled a vision of honoring four presidents: Washington, who founded the nation; Jefferson, who expanded the nation westward; Lincoln, who ended slavery; and Theodore Roosevelt, who won

Tornado Alley

More than seven hundred tornadoes are reported in the United States every year. It is the most tornado-prone region in the world. Most of the tornadoes strike in the Tornado Alley.

Tornadoes are usually associated with thunderstorms, where warm, moist air meets cool, dry air. In the violent clash between these air masses, the air is ripe for tornadoes. But scientists still cannot explain precisely what creates these swirling funnel-shaped clouds, which pack winds with speeds of more than two hundred miles per hour. Midwesterners often call them *twisters*.

Why are tornadoes so common in the Midwest? The heart of a continent suffers more extreme weather changes than does the ocean coast. The ground heats and cools rapidly. In the Midwest, polar air masses move down from Canada. In the spring and early

Kansas twister

summer, warm, moist air masses move north from off the Gulf of Mexico. When both masses meet, trouble follows. The main track of Tornado Alley runs northeast from the Texas panhandle to Missouri.

---

worldwide respect for the nation and who set aside parts of the West in national parks.

Like Nebraska, South Dakota has been a leader in democracy. In 1898 it passed the first laws giving the people direct power to propose and pass laws. The **initiative** allows the people to propose new laws by gathering signatures from voters. The **referendum** allows the people to vote directly on new laws, without going through legislators. About half the states now allow some form of initiative, and almost all allow referendums.

Plains and Badlands   Most of South Dakota looks similar to neighboring states. The southeast corner is till plain, which supports most of the state's farms and the state's largest city, Sioux Falls. The Great Plains extend across the west of the state. The capital, Pierre, sits in the Great Plains on the Missouri River.

The southwest corner of the state has a remote, rugged area of the Great Plains called the **Badlands,** typified by knobs, spires, rock pinnacles, windswept ridges, and isolated buttes. Deep gullies and canyons carve out the floors of the Badlands. Pioneers avoided these bleak regions, but they

became a favorite hideout for outlaws and renegade Indians.

The Black Hills   The **Black Hills** rise in the far western part of the state, a pocket of mountains towering above the sea of midwestern grasslands. These are the highest peaks east of the Rocky Mountains. The most popular peak to see is Mt. Rushmore, but Harney Peak is the highest (7,242 ft.). The Black Hills display beautiful mountain scenery—waterfalls, buffalo, and cathedral spires. The evergreen trees on the subalpine peaks contrast sharply with the surrounding Great Plains.

Deadwood is a popular Old West town in the Black Hills, reminiscent of the 1874 gold rush that sparked fighting between the U.S. cavalry and the Indians. The Homestake Mine, started in the Black Hills in 1876, still outproduces every other gold mine in the nation. White men never obtained legal claim to the Black Hills, and Sioux leaders have begun pressing claims in court. A U.S. treaty written in 1868 promised that these sacred lands would remain in Sioux hands "as long as rivers run and grass grows and trees bear leaves."

Geographer's Corner

Reading a Weather Map

The map that Americans look at the most is the weather map. This simple weather map, similar to ones on television and in the newspaper, shows two high pressure zones. Remember from Chapter 2 that high pressure comes from a cold mass of dry air that is sinking. The air moves in a clockwise pattern because of the Coriolis effect. These winds draw warm, moist air from the Gulf of Mexico into the central part of the United States. Review what you studied about weather in Chapter 2, pages 40-43, to answer these questions.

1. What kind of pressure area lies over the Great Plains?
2. What type of precipitation is falling over Kansas—orographic, frontal, or convection?
3. What kind of pressure area lies in the Southwest?
4. From what direction are most of California's winds blowing?
5. Look at the relief map of North America on page 218. What type of precipitation is probably occurring in California?

Reading a Weather Map

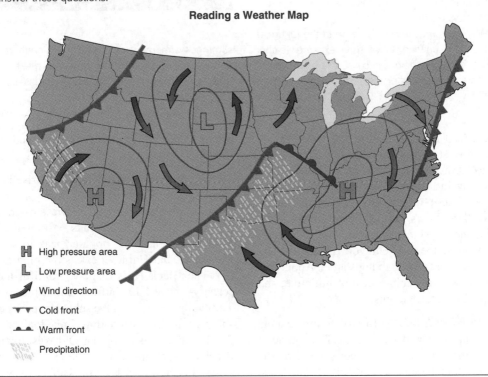

H High pressure area
L Low pressure area
➚ Wind direction
▼▼ Cold front
▲▲ Warm front
▨ Precipitation

For centuries the Sioux gathered for powwows at these sacred hills, which they called *wamaka ognaka onakizin,* meaning "the sanctuary of everything that is," where the legendary first Sioux was put on earth. Sioux Indians still gather every year in Rapid City, at the foot of the hills, for the Black Hills PowWow, where they ·reenact tribal dances and crafts.

The name of the state, *Dakota,* comes from the Sioux's name for themselves, meaning "friends." Many tribes once roamed across the Dakotas. South Dakota has nine reservations covering one-third of the state's Great Plains. The most well known is Pine Ridge Reservation, where the U.S. fought the last major "battle" with Indians at Wounded Knee Creek on December 29, 1890. The soldiers were

Mount Rushmore

Four sixty-foot-high heads gaze out from the side of a mountain in the Black Hills. If bodies had been carved for the heads, they would be the largest statues in the world. As it is, they are the largest human heads ever carved. Mount Rushmore remains the most extensive mountain carving project ever completed. A larger statue of Chief Crazy Horse on horseback is in progress atop nearby Thunderhead Mountain.

Local historian Doane Robinson got the idea for a "shrine to democracy" in 1924, and work began in 1927 under the direction of sculptor Gutzon Borglum. Sixty years old when he began, Borglum spent the rest of his life on his beloved shrine. Local miners helped him break up the granite mountain using dynamite, jackhammers, and chisels. Borglum unveiled each head as he finished it: George Washington in 1930, Thomas Jefferson in 1936, Abraham Lincoln in 1937, and Theodore Roosevelt in 1939. Borglum died two years later.

Each of the presidents' faces carved on Mount Rushmore, South Dakota, is sixty feet tall.

attempting to disarm a disgruntled band of about three hundred Indians when shots were fired. At least 153 Sioux Indians died, half of them women and children. Wounded Knee has become a symbol of the federal government's bungling relationships with America's Indian nations.

North Dakota, Peace Garden State

The International Peace Garden is a park that straddles the peaceful border between Canada and the United States. The people live the quality of life symbolized by their garden. As the least populous Midwestern state, North Dakota offers plenty of space for all. The state ranks among the highest in life expectancy.

Scandinavian immigrants from northern Europe moved into the upper Midwest and built prosperous farms and communities. Numerous festivals still commemorate their Nordic dress and heritage. The Scandinavians also brought their Lutheran religion. Just as Baptists are most common in the Bible Belt of the South, Lutherans are most common in the "Lutheran Belt" of the North. Although North Dakota does not have the most Lutherans in the United States, it has the largest percentage (37 percent), followed by Minnesota (34 percent), South Dakota (30 percent), and Wisconsin (26 percent).

The eastern half of the state, in the Central Plains, produces the largest spring wheat crop in the nation. *Spring wheat* is planted in the spring and grows rapidly in the short growing season. North Dakota also has the largest barley crop, and it vies with Kansas for the most sunflower seeds.

The Great Plains that cover the western half of the state are similar to South Dakota. Indians hold tribal ceremonies and dances at three reservations. Scenic and remote badlands are protected by Theodore Roosevelt National Park. The Garrison Dam on the Missouri River forms two-hundred-mile long Lake Sakakawea, the largest reservoir east of the Rockies and the third largest in the nation.

◎ SECTION REVIEW

1. Why are temperatures in the Great Plains more extreme than those on the coast?

2. Describe the main difference between the Central Plains and the Great Plains.

3. Give one example of the Old West in Kansas, Nebraska, and the Dakotas.

4. What is the difference between an initiative and a referendum?

5. Compare and contrast the basic geography of the Badlands and of the Black Hills.

💡 Why do you think most states have not adopted a unicameral legislature?

REVIEW

Can You Define These Terms?

universal manhood suffrage	primary elections	drift	bicameral
till	Americana	bluff	initiative
prairie	nodal cities	unicameral	referendum
land-grant college			

Can You Locate These Natural Features?

Central Plains	Lake Michigan	North Woods	Mesabi Range
Great Lakes	Lake Superior	Mississippi River Basin	Great Plains
Ohio River	Superior Uplands	Missouri River	Badlands
			Black Hills

Can You Explain the Significance of These People and Places?

Midwest	Indian mounds	Detroit	Harry S Truman
Northwest Territory	Chicago	Louisiana Purchase	Wheat Belt
Corn Belt	Dwight L. Moody	Mark Twain	William Jennings Bryan
Abraham Lincoln	Dairy Belt		

How Much Do You Remember?

1. Give the top producer among the states in each agricultural belt.
   a. corn
   b. dairy
   c. wheat
2. Describe three main differences between the Great Lakes states and the heartland.
3. Explain how each of these men exemplifies the values of the Midwest: Abraham Lincoln, Harry S Truman, and William Jennings Bryan.
4. Explain why the Great Plains are so arid.
5. Why are there so many Lutherans in the far north?
6. Which two midwestern states on the Ohio River do *not* include prairie? Why?
7. Why is wheat more common than corn on the Great Plains?
8. What is most unusual about the location of the Black Hills?

What Do You Think?

1. What is the most typical American state? the most typical American city?
2. Why do many Iowans consider the Great Plains states part of the West, not the Midwest?
3. Which midwestern state would you most like to visit? Why?
4. Is this the same as the midwestern state where you would most like to live?
5. If you could add one face to Mt. Rushmore, whose would it be?

CHAPTER 9

THE WESTERN UNITED STATES

Just as the Midwest is a land of averages, the West is a land of extremes. The landscape has the highest and lowest points in the United States, the driest and the wettest spots, the only deserts and the most productive valleys. Among the western states is the biggest and one of the smallest states, the most and least populous states, the quickest to win statehood and the last to win statehood.

Westerners do share something in common. In general, they look to the future and are not bound by ties to tradition as their brothers in the East are. The West was the last region added to the Union. In the 1840s, when the best lands were being taken on the plains, Americans turned their eyes to the far West. The belief swept the nation of America's "**manifest destiny** to overspread and to possess the whole of the continent which Providence has given us" (*New York Times,* 1845). Within a decade, Americans moved their borders past the Louisiana Purchase to include all the lands "from sea to shining sea."

In the West, Americans found riches beyond their wildest imaginations. All thirteen western states have beautiful mountain landscapes, fertile valleys, and valuable mineral resources. In ten of the thirteen western states, the first wave of settlers came during **gold rushes.** The 1849 gold rush to California boosted the population so quickly that it became a new state the following year. Few prospectors struck it rich, but almost everyone stayed, earning a living in other ways. A free and independent spirit is still evident in the West.

NATURAL TREASURES OF THE WEST

Federal Lands, Including All National Parks and Seashores

Olympic NP
North Cascades NP
Glacier NP
Mt. Rainier NP
Crater Lake NP
Yellowstone NP
Theodore Roosevelt NP
Voyageurs NP
Isle Royale NP
Pictured Rocks NL
Apostle Islands NL
Sleeping Bear Dunes NL
Acadia NP
Redwood NP
Lassen Volcanic NP
Grand Teton NP
Wind Cave NP
Badlands NP
Cape Cod NS
Point Reyes NS
Yosemite NP
Great Basin NP
Bryce Canyon NP
Rocky Mountain NP
Indiana Dunes NL
Fire Island NS
King's Canyon NP
Capitol Reef NP
Arches NP
Shenandoah NP
Assateague Island NS
Sequoia NP
Death Valley NP
Zion NP
Canyon-lands NP
Mammoth Cave NP
Channel Islands NP
Joshua Tree NP
Grand Canyon NP
Mesa Verde NP
Great Smoky Mts. NP
Cape Hatteras NS
Cape Lookout NS
Petrified Forest NP
Saguaro NP
Carlsbad Caverns NP
Hot Springs NP
Cumberland Island NS
Guadalupe NP
Canaveral NS
Big Bend NP
Gulf Islands NS
Padre Island NS
Everglades NP
Biscayne NP
Dry Tortugas NP

ALASKA

Kobuk Valley NP
Gates of the Arctic NP
Denali NP
Wrangell-St. Elias NP
Lake Clark NP
Katmai NP
Kenai Fjords NP
Glacier Bay NP

HAWAII

Haleakala NP
Hawaii Volcanoes NP

- National Parks (NP)
- National Seashores and Lakeshores (NS and NL)
- National Monuments, Preserves, and Recreation Areas
- National Forests (and Grasslands)
- National Wildlife Refuges
- Bureau of Land Management

The federal government still owns and oversees almost one-half of all western lands. With the closing of the frontier at the end of the nineteenth century, Americans wanted to preserve the nation's remaining natural treasures for future generations. The map and photo survey give only a hint of the treasures to be found in the West.

Old Faithful spouts to heights of 170 feet at regular intervals.

Geothermal Features   Yellowstone, Wyoming, was the nation's first national park. It contains one of the world's three major basins with geysers. (The other two are in Iceland and New Zealand). Popular hot springs are also in California.

Canyons   Hells Canyon is the deepest canyon in the nation. Though not as deep, Grand Canyon in Arizona is more famous as the longest and widest canyon in the world. Dinosaur National Monument, known most for its fossils and dinosaur graveyard, has the nation's third deepest canyon—the Canyon of Lodore (Utah). Spectacular gorges are popular at the Black Canyon of Gunnison, Colorado, and at the Narrows of Zion National Park in Utah. Bryce Canyon, Utah, is known for its strange rock formations.

The Snake River flows through Hells Canyon, the deepest canyon in America, which divides Oregon from Idaho.

Mountains   The Rockies are famed for peaks stretching to all horizons, as in Colorado's Rocky Mountain National Park. The highest mountain in the lower forty-eight states, however, is Mount Whitney in California's Sierra Nevada. Outside Alaska, the most majestic peaks with permanent snowcaps are in the Cascade Mountains: Mount Rainier in Washington and Mount Shasta in California. The highest and most remote mountains are in Alaska. Mount McKinley is the highest and most majestic snowy peak on the continent. The largest national park in the United States is Alaska's remote Wrangell–St. Elias National Park, which includes six of the nation's top ten peaks.

Arches   The arid Southwest has the longest arches on the planet (nine exceeding two hundred feet). Utah has the seven longest arches. The top two would span a football field: Kolob Arch (311 ft.) at Zion National Park and Landscape Arch (306 ft.) at Arches National Park. Utah also boasts the three tallest arches in the nation. Rainbow Bridge is

The Maroon Bells, two Fourteeners that soar high above Maroon Lake, are considered the most beautiful peaks in the Colorado Rockies.

Rainbow Bridge, Utah, is the tallest (209 ft.) and third longest (278 ft.) arch in the world.

first (290 ft.), Kolob Arch is second (230 ft.), and Sipapu Bridge at Natural Bridges is third (220 ft.). Utah's Arches National Park has the most arches of any area in the world.

Caves New Mexico has the most famous cave system in the West—Carlsbad Caverns, known for its great depths, huge rooms, and variety of formations. Utah has Timpanogos Cave, Nevada has Lehman Caves at Great Basin National Park, and Oregon has Oregon Caves.

Deserts Portions of America's great deserts are now protected: the Mojave Desert in California, Death Valley in the Great Basin Desert, White Sands in New Mexico's Chihuahuan Desert, and the Saguaro National Monument in Arizona's Sonoran Desert. White Sands and Death Valley have large sand dunes far from the ocean. Other big interior dunes are at Great Sand Dunes in Colorado and Kobuk Valley in Alaska. Petrified wood lies in Arizona's Petrified Forest and Painted Desert. Joshua trees, rare desert trees, are in California.

Stalactites form a hanging forest in the Fairyland portion of Carlsbad Caverns, New Mexico.

Forests Redwoods National Park in California is the most famous forest in the nation. Besides the tallest trees, California has two other records for trees: largest girth (sequoias) and oldest living things in the world (bristlecone pines). California's bristlecones are at Inyo National Forest. Nevada and Utah have bristlecones in the Great Basin and at Bryce Canyon. Olympic National Park in Washington protects a rare temperate rain forest.

Waterfalls Every Western state has waterfalls over three hundred feet high. All fourteen U.S. waterfalls above one thousand feet are in the West. The highest waterfall, ten times higher than Niagara Falls, is Yosemite Falls in California. Five other falls at Yosemite National Park are above a thousand feet, including Ribbon Falls, the highest single drop in the nation (1,612 feet). Glacier National Park in Montana sports three of the top fourteen. Hawaii has four of the top fourteen,

Redwoods, the world's tallest trees, reach heights up to 368 feet.

Tall saguaros and numerous prickly pears cover the Sonoran Desert near Tucson, Arizona.

Lava courses down the slopes of Kilauea, Hawaii's most active volcano.

and the other is a little-known fall in Yellowstone. Three areas are famous for high concentrations of major waterfalls—Yosemite, Mt. Rainier in Washington, and the Columbia River in Oregon.

Coasts   California has the only national seashore in the west at Point Reyes, west of San Francisco. Boats take visitors to see sea lions on the Channel Islands, west of Los Angeles. Oregon has the longest stretch of sand dunes on any ocean in the world. The dunes extend forty miles along the coast and range up to five miles inland. Washington's stark, rugged coasts at Olympic National Park have pounding surfs. Alaska offers the best *fjords* (deep valleys by the ocean). Cruises take sightseers to the fjords and glaciers of Kenai Fjords, Misty Fjords, and Glacier Bay.

Volcanoes   Hawaii has the most active volcanoes in the world, and they are easy to watch from a distance. The most recent volcano to erupt in the lower forty-eight states was Mount St. Helens in Washington. Craters of the Moon, Idaho, has one of the nation's largest *lava fields,* a level area where lava has cooled. You can see *cinder cones*—piles of loose volcanic ash—at Capulin Volcano (New Mexico) and at Mount Lassen (California). El Malpais in New Mexico has *spatter cones,* cones made of hard volcanic rock, and *lava tubes,* empty caves through which lava once passed to the surface.

Glaciers descend into the Inside Passage at Glacier Bay, Alaska.

After plunging 1,430 feet over the Upper Falls, Yosemite Falls continues over two more tiers for a total drop of 2,425 feet, the longest total drop in North America.

Manifest Destiny

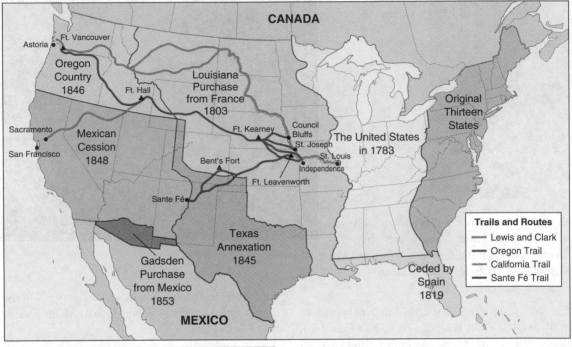

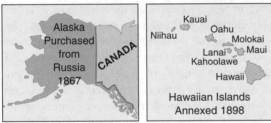

Alaska Purchased from Russia 1867

Hawaiian Islands Annexed 1898

Western states are big and not completely tamed. Nine of the ten largest states are in the West (and the other big state, Texas, is a neighbor in the Southwest). Most have small populations and lots of undeveloped public lands. Westerners have worked hard to make the land productive, cutting down forests to provide wood for homes and raising dams across rivers to provide electricity and water for irrigation. Today, however, the West is trying to preserve its remaining natural beauty in various national parks and wildernesses.

The American West has earned a reputation as the nation's playground, a place to escape from everyday life. It is home to the world's leading film industry (Hollywood) and the first and most famous theme park (Disneyland). The West offers the longest hiking and bicycle trails, the best downhill slopes for skiers, and the biggest waves for surfers. God recognizes the need for quiet places where people can rest from their labors. Vacations give an opportunity to restore strength and to marvel at God's creation.

And he said unto them, Come ye yourselves apart into a desert place, and rest a while: for there were many coming and going, and they had no leisure so much as to eat. (Mark 6:31)

THE DRY INTERIOR

Eight western states have dry climates and no ocean borders. High mountain ranges prevent moisture from reaching the interior plateaus and basins. The early pioneers dreaded crossing this region of deserts and mountains on their way to the fertile Pacific valleys. The discovery of mineral wealth

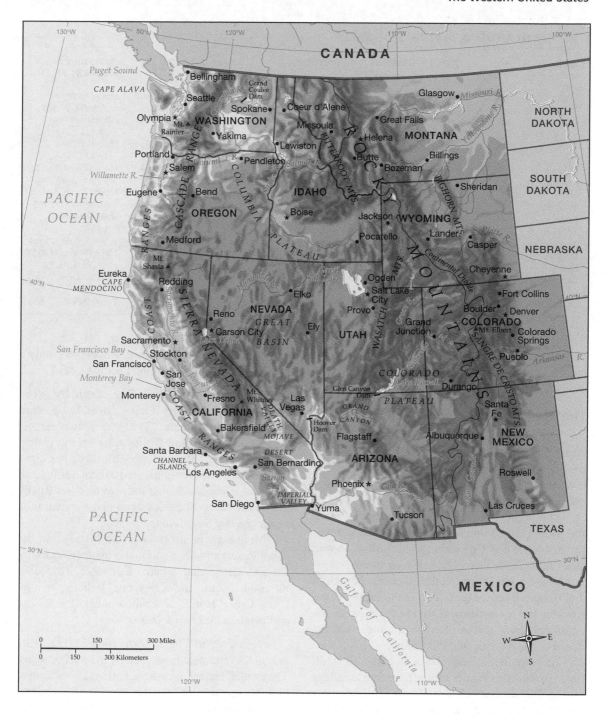

CANADA

NORTH DAKOTA

SOUTH DAKOTA

NEBRASKA

PACIFIC OCEAN

Puget Sound

CAPE ALAVA

Bellingham
Seattle
Olympia
Mt. Rainier
Yakima
Portland
Salem
Willamette R.
Eugene
Bend

Grand Coulee Dam
Spokane
Coeur d'Alene
Missoula
Lewiston
Pendleton
Columbia R.
Salmon R.

Glasgow
Missouri R.
Great Falls
Helena
MONTANA
Butte
Bozeman
Billings
Sheridan
Yellowstone R.

WASHINGTON

CASCADE RANGE

OREGON

COLUMBIA PLATEAU

IDAHO
Boise

BITTERROOT MTS.

ROCKY

Jackson
Pocatello

WYOMING
Lander
Casper
N. Platte R.
Cheyenne

Continental Divide

COAST RANGES

Medford
Mt. Shasta
Eureka
CAPE MENDOCINO
Redding
Sacramento R.

PACIFIC OCEAN

SIERRA RANGES

Reno
Carson City
Lake Tahoe

NEVADA
GREAT BASIN
Humboldt R.
Elko
Ely

Great Salt Lake
Ogden
Salt Lake City
Provo

UTAH

WASATCH MTS.

Grand Junction

Green R.

MOUNTAINS

Fort Collins
Boulder
Denver
COLORADO
Mt. Elbert
Colorado Springs
Pueblo
Arkansas R.

SANGRE DE CRISTO MTS.

San Francisco Bay
Sacramento
Stockton
San Francisco
Monterey Bay
San Jose
Monterey
Fresno
San Joaquin R.
Mt. Whitney
DEATH VALLEY

CALIFORNIA
Bakersfield
MOJAVE DESERT
Santa Barbara
CHANNEL ISLANDS
Los Angeles
San Bernardino
Salton Sea
IMPERIAL VALLEY
San Diego

Las Vegas
Hoover Dam
GRAND CANYON
Flagstaff

ARIZONA
Phoenix
Yuma
Tucson
Gila R.

COLORADO PLATEAU
Glen Canyon Dam
Lake Powell
Durango

Santa Fe
Albuquerque
Rio Grande
NEW MEXICO
Roswell
Las Cruces

TEXAS

MEXICO

Gulf of California

130°W
50°N
120°W
110°W
100°W
40°N
30°N

0   150   300 Miles
0   150   300 Kilometers

N
W   E
S

Western United States Statistics

STATE	P.O. CODE	CAPITAL	DATE OF STATEHOOD	NICKNAME	AREA (SQ. MI.)	POP.	HIGH POINT, ELEVATION (FT.)
Alaska	AK	Juneau	1959	The Last Frontier	656,424	607,007	Mount McKinley (Denali), 20,320
Arizona	AZ	Phoenix	1912	Grand Canyon State	114,006	4,428,068	Humphreys Peak, 12,333
California	CA	Sacramento	1850	Golden State	163,707	31,878,234	Mount Whitney, 14,494
Colorado	CO	Denver	1876	Centennial State	104,100	3,822,676	Mount Elbert, 14,433
Hawaii	HI	Honolulu	1959	Aloha State	10,932	1,183,723	Mauna Kea, 13,796
Idaho	ID	Boise	1890	Gem State	83,574	1,189,251	Mount Borah, 12,662
Montana	MT	Helena	1889	Treasure State	147,046	879,372	Granite Peak, 12,799
Nevada	NV	Carson City	1864	Silver State	110,567	1,603,163	Boundary Peak, 13,140
New Mexico	NM	Santa Fe	1912	Land of Enchantment	121,598	1,713,407	Wheeler Peak, 13,161
Oregon	OR	Salem	1859	Beaver State	98,386	3,203,735	Mount Hood, 11,239
Utah	UT	Salt Lake City	1896	Beehive State	84,904	2,000,494	Kings Peak, 13,528
Washington	WA	Olympia	1889	Evergreen State	71,302	5,532,939	Mount Rainier, 14,410
Wyoming	WY	Cheyenne	1890	Equality State	97,818	481,400	Gannett Peak, 13,804

changed everything. In recent years, the dry climate has attracted a host of new industries, tourists, and retirees.

The Rocky Mountain States

The Appalachian Mountains have little in common with the **Rocky Mountains,** a high wall that runs down the entire length of the North American continent. The Rockies dominate the climate, vegetation, and history of the West.

The highest chain of the Rockies runs down the four Rocky Mountain states: Montana, Wyoming, Idaho, and Colorado. Water falling on one side of the *divide* flows into one river drainage system, while water falling on the other side flows into a different river system. The main chain of the Rockies has a **continental divide** that divides the continent into rivers that flow into separate oceans—the Atlantic and the Pacific.

Early pioneers and railroads had a difficult time crossing this barrier to reach the fertile valleys on the Pacific coast. They liked to follow water routes, which passed through the lowest valleys and supplied plenty of drinking water. Find the start of the Platte River, a tributary of the Missouri

River, on the map of the West. What rivers, only a few miles away, flow into the Pacific Ocean?

Montana, Big Sky Country The treeless Great Plains cover the eastern two-thirds of Montana. The state's two largest cities, Great Falls and Billings, lie on the plains. Like other Great Plains states, Montana has cowboys, Indian reservations, and wheat farms, but Montana is almost double the size of other Rocky Mountain states. The wide open plains explain the nickname Big Sky Country.

Montana's plains have a rich history. On the Crow Reservation is a national monument marking Custer's Last Stand, where on June 25, 1876, two thousand Sioux and Cheyenne Indians, led by Chief Crazy Horse, ambushed and killed Custer and two hundred cavalrymen.

"There's Gold in Them Thar' Hills!" The western third of the state is covered by mountain ranges. The capital, Helena, lies in the eastern Lewis Range. Gold prospectors hit "pay dirt" here in 1864, calling their mining camp Last Chance Gulch. A copper mine at nearby Butte became known as the "richest hill on Earth." The state may not be the top producer

Glacial lakes reflect majestic peaks at Glacier National Park, Montana.

signs of such movement. Normally when tons of rocks move, they grind the rocks underneath and leave scrapes, buckles, and gravel. God formed these mountains to testify of His own handiwork and to confound the theories of men.

All thy works shall praise thee. (Ps. 145:10)

Two Trailblazers The Lewis and Clark National Historic Trail follows these two explorers' famous journey up the Missouri River. In Montana, Lewis and Clark discovered Great Falls, a series of five falls, the most beautiful sight they had ever seen. A dam has covered the main fall, but the visible falls are still impressive.

Continuing up the river from Great Falls, Lewis and Clark discovered the headwaters of the Missouri at Three Forks, just west of Bozeman. Here the Madison, Jefferson, and Gallatin Rivers join. Trout in these mountain rivers lure anglers from across the nation. The explorers next went west into the mountains, crossing the Continental Divide at Lemhi Pass. Then they crossed the Bitterroot Range at Lolo Pass, west of modern Missoula. Sacajawea, the wife of a hired assistant, then led the expedition to a Shoshone Indian chief, who turned out to be her brother.

Wyoming Wyoming has the lowest population of any state—some say the tumbleweeds outnumber the people! Yet like the midwestern states, it pioneered democratic reforms. The Equality State was the first to give women the right to vote. The federal government extended the right to vote to women in 1920.

The Great Plains and a portion of the Black Hills cover the eastern quarter of Wyoming. The state's largest cities—Cheyenne, Laramie, Casper, and Sheridan—lie on the plains. City life revolves around livestock and agriculture. Only Texas produces more wool than Wyoming. Cheyenne, the capital, hosts the largest rodeo in the nation—Frontier Days.

The First National Park The Rocky Mountains cover the western three-quarters of the state. Wyoming leads the nation in coal production, with

of gold and copper, but it leads in talc, vermiculite, and gem sapphires. It also has the nation's only platinum mine.

The Lewis Range has other treasures—the grizzlies and glaciers of Glacier National Park, located on the northern border with Canada. The Continental Divide passes north through the park. On one amazing peak, water flows not only east and west but also north across the *Arctic Divide* into the Arctic Ocean. Three creeks, which originate on Triple Divide Peak, are named for the ocean into which they flow: Atlantic Creek, Pacific Creek, and Arctic Creek.

Evolutionists are troubled by the unusual rock layers in the Lewis Range. The top layers should be farther down, if the evolutionary theory is correct. Evolutionists insist that tectonics squeezed the top layers out from below, even though there are no

Yellowstone's Geothermal Activity

Yellowstone has impressive waterfalls, canyons, and lakes. But most famous is the evidence of **geothermal** activity—heat under the earth that rises and creates strange features on the surface.

Water from rain and melting snows seeps deep into the soil, where it is heated by molten rock and makes its way back to the surface. In some places the rising steam bursts through cracks into the air to make *geysers*. Old Faithful, the most famous of Yellowstone's three hundred geysers, sprays steaming water over a hundred feet into the air every seventy-one minutes. Other geysers spray higher, more often, and more volume of water, but none spouts so regularly, day and night, all year long.

Yellowstone has several other geothermal features. Nearly ten thousand *hot springs* occur where underground water rises slowly to the surface and collects in steaming pools. Algae and bacteria color the pools yellow, orange, green, and blue. Many hot springs have staircases and other fabulous shapes made of *travertine*, minerals deposited by ground water. *Mud pots* result when boiling water passes through mud, causing the mud to bubble and steam. *Fumaroles* are sulphurous vents that blow heat without water.

the major coal mining area in the southwest corner of the state. Wyoming's favorite vacationland is Yellowstone National Park in the northwest corner. Yellowstone became the world's first national park, and it preserves the world's largest collection of hot springs and geysers. Yellowstone is named for the yellow cliffs in the Grand Canyon of the Yellowstone. The Yellowstone River, which begins in the park, flows through this canyon and has two large waterfalls.

Grand Tetons National Park, just south of Yellowstone, has breathtaking views of mountain glaciers above crystal blue lakes. Mountaineers enjoy climbing the craggy peaks. The Grand Teton is the state's second highest mountain.

The Grand Teton (13,770 ft.) towers over the Snake River and nearby Jackson, Wyoming.

"Wagons Ho!" Wagon trains traveling to the Pacific chose Wyoming as the best route to pass through the Rockies. Historic Fort Laramie was their last stop on the plains. Pioneers continued up the North Platte River, passing between the Bighorn Mountains and the more southerly Laramie Mountains. They usually stopped at Independence Rock, a 193-foot granite landmark, where thousands scrawled their names on "The Great Register of the Desert."

West of Independence Rock, the Continental Divide does an unusual thing. The main Rocky Mountain range splits and then rejoins leaving a basin where rain cannot drain into either ocean. The Red Desert covers this Great Divide Basin, complete with sand dunes. The early pioneers skirted the north of the desert up Sweetwater River to break through the Divide at South Pass near where the city of Lander is located today. Later the Union Pacific—the eastern end of the first transcontinental railroad—skirted south of the desert and linked up with Bitter Creek beyond the Divide.

Idaho Idaho lies west of Montana and Wyoming. The remote mountains of the Bitterroot Range cover most of Idaho's northern half and its eastern border with Montana, which squiggles along the Continental Divide. The largest wilderness outside Alaska is on the upper Salmon

Shoshone Falls, on the Snake River near Twin Falls, Idaho, is the second most powerful waterfall in the United States, dumping seventeen thousand cubic feet per second.

bombs, lava caves, lava fields, volcanic vents, and cinder cones.

Down the Snake River The great **Snake River,** a tributary of the Columbia River, winds across the plateau. At "the Niagara of the West," the Snake topples 212 feet over a cliff at Shoshone Falls. Before its waters were controlled by dams, it matched Niagara's power during rainy seasons. It is thirty feet higher than Niagara and has spectacular canyon scenery. Downstream, the Snake River winds north on Idaho's border with Oregon and Washington. This stretch, called Hells Canyon, gives rafters a thrilling white-water adventure through the deepest canyon on the continent—deeper than the Grand Canyon.

The early explorers and pioneers went down the Snake River after crossing the Continental Divide. The first white people to live in Idaho were the missionaries Henry and Eliza Spalding, who built a successful ministry for the Nez Perce Indians near modern Lewiston. Idaho's major cities are located on the Snake River and its tributaries.

Colorado, the Rocky Mountain State

Many people are surprised to learn that almost half of Colorado is flat! Its plains are among the top wheat producers in the nation.

The Plains Colorado's largest cities—Denver, Colorado Springs, and Pueblo—stand at the foot of the Rockies on the plains. A gold rush to Pikes Peak in 1858 turned Denver into a boomtown. **Denver,** "mile-high city" and gateway to the high country, has half of the state's population. Its metropolitan area is the largest in the four-state Rocky Mountain region. It is also the largest city on the Great Plains. The Denver Mint produces gold coins and stores gold worth about two billion dollars. The dome of its capitol is covered with twenty-four-carat gold leaf. Denver recently completed an airport that covers fifty-three square miles—the largest (and most expensive) ever built in the nation.

The Mountains Colorado is the centerpiece of the Rockies. It has the highest mountains, including fifty-four peaks above fourteen thousand feet. Avid

River and is called the River of No Return Wilderness. The adjacent Selway-Bitterroot Wilderness is almost as large.

The Columbia Plateau Like the Appalachian Mountains, the Rocky Mountains descend into rugged plateaus. The **Columbia Plateau** extends west of the Idaho Rockies into neighboring Washington and Oregon. It is named after the Columbia River system, which flows from the mountains to the Pacific Ocean. The plateau yields the leading potato crop in the nation.

Built from layers of basalt (a volcanic rock), the Columbia Plateau has some curious scenery. At a lava field called Craters of the Moon, visitors can see many types of volcanic features, including lava climbers learn their names and compete to "bag" all fifty-four **Fourteeners.** The barren, snowcapped peaks soar far above timberline. Although the snow usually melts in the summer, some snow-covered patches remain year-round.

Locals proudly call their state "God's Country." Tourism, a big part of the state economy, brings in about four billion dollars a year. Aspen and Vail are synonymous with powder-snow skiing. Tourists also enjoy mining towns, ghost towns, and several deep canyons. At Royal Gorge you can walk across the highest bridge in the world, overlooking the Arkansas River at the bottom.

Colorado has several major ranges. The **Front Range** in the north and the **Sangre de Cristo** (Blood of Christ) **Range** in the south form a wall in the east, towering above the Great Plains. Mount Evans and Pikes Peak are two well-known peaks in the Front Range near Denver. They are the only Fourteeners with roads to the top. On the western slopes of the Sangre de Cristo Range lie the blowing sand dunes of Great Sand Dunes National Monument.

Behind the Front Range is the **Sawatch Range,** the Backbone of the Continent. It contains the highest mountains in the Rockies. The highest is Mount Elbert—14,433 feet. Mountains in a section called Collegiate Peaks are named for

The Mountain of the Holy Cross is the only place in America that has lost its national monument status. The snow has melted in the horizontal gully near the top.

famous colleges: Mt. Harvard, Mt. Yale, Mt. Oxford, Mt. Princeton, and Mt. Columbia. Another interesting mountain, the Mount of the Holy Cross, takes its name from a cross-shaped ice field on the mountain's face. The mountain became a tourist attraction in the 1920s and remained a national monument until 1950.

The rugged maze of the San Juan Range covers southwestern Colorado. The San Juans cover the largest area in the state, over ten thousand square miles. Several portions are protected as wildernesses. Only four paved roads remain open year-round across these mountains. In the south is Durango, a town typical of the Old Southwest.

The Plateau The western one-fifth of Colorado is not part of the Rockies, but the start of a flatter plateau that extends all the way to California. Like the Columbia Plateau in the north, the **Colorado Plateau** gets its name from the river that cuts through the landscape—the Colorado River. The high plateau exceeds five thousand feet in elevation and is quite dry. Dinosaur National Monument lies on the plateau at the northwest corner of the state, while Mesa Verde lies near the southwest corner.

Visitors come from around the world to see the exotic Indian ruins on Mesa Verde (or Green Table), a high plateau in southwestern Colorado. Cliff Palace is the largest of all cliff dwellings.

The commercial center on the plateau is Grand Junction, on the Colorado River. Among the many mesas east of Grand Junction is Grand Mesa, the world's largest flat-topped mountain, with over two hundred trout-filled lakes.

◎ SECTION REVIEW

1. List four common characteristics of the West's cultural heritage.
2. Name a leading product of each Rocky Mountain state.
3. What major geographic feature is found in Idaho but not the other Rocky Mountain states? What feature is found in the other states but not in Idaho?
4. Within the Rocky Mountains, which range has the highest peaks? the most wilderness? part of a state's boundary?
💡 Why did the westward-bound pioneers choose to go through Wyoming rather than taking Lewis and Clark's route through Montana?

The Great Basin

The land immediately west of the Rockies is not all plateau. The **Great Basin** is a bowl of low, rugged land between the Columbia Plateau and the Colorado Plateau. (See the map of U.S. geographic regions on page 147.) It starts in the northeast corner of Utah and extends west through Nevada. Because it is lower than the mountains that border it on both sides, water in the Great Basin cannot drain into any ocean.

Utah   The first people to settle in Utah were the **Mormons,** a religious sect that migrated to Utah from the East. Persecuted for their practice of polygamy (marrying more than one wife), their leader, Brigham Young, finally settled beside the Great Salt Lake in 1847. He believed this valley was where God wanted his people to build Zion. **Salt Lake City,** the largest city in the state, stands near the lake. It has the main Mormon Temple as well as the state capitol. About three-quarters of the people who live in Utah are Mormons. They portray an image of strong families.

But though we, or an angel from heaven, preach any other gospel unto you than that which we have preached unto you, let him be accursed. (Gal. 1:8)

Mormons call themselves the Church of Jesus Christ of Latter-day Saints. Their founder was the "prophet" Joseph Smith. God supposedly told him that the present churches are "all wrong," their members are "all corrupt," and their doctrines are "abomination in [the Lord's] sight." An "angel" named Moroni later showed Smith a copy of the Book of Mormon on golden plates. The Book of Mormon tells about the lost tribes of Israel, who migrated to America in 600 B.C. during the Babylonian Captivity. No archeological evidence supports any names, cities, or events in the book, however.

Mormonism is the largest of the many cults that have sprung from America's cultural soil. This false religion has about ten million members, half in the United States and the rest in over 160 countries. About fifty thousand young Mormon missionaries go out to find new converts every year. ***Cult*** is not a popular word today. It refers to an offshoot of historic Christianity that aggressively seeks converts, preaches that it is the exclusive hope of salvation, and denies fundamental doctrines of the Christian faith, including

1. The sole authority of the Bible. Mormons follow new revelation in the Book of Mormon and other books.
2. The nature of the Trinity. Mormons believe God was once a man as we are now, with flesh and bones.
3. The nature of Jesus Christ. Mormons believe Jesus was one of God's sons, and His spirit brother was Lucifer.
4. The sufficiency of Jesus' sacrifice. Mormons believe the temple rituals of their priesthood are essential for salvation.

Great Salt Lake   The Wasatch Range dips down from Wyoming into Utah on the northeast border. At

The Mormon Temple at Salt Lake City, Utah, is the main center of the Mormon religion.

the base of this portion of the Rocky Mountains begins the Great Basin. **Great Salt Lake** is the largest of the stagnant salt lakes that collect rainwater in the basin. High temperatures and infrequent rains cause rapid evaporation. As portions of the lake dry up, the parched earth forms dried **salt flats.** On salt flats west of the lake—among the flattest places in the world—specialized cars have set speed records of over seven hundred miles per hour.

Early pioneers avoided the Great Salt Lake region because of its desert climate. Yet it offered a level path between Wyoming and California. The pony express (1860-61) took this route, going south of the lake to deliver mail between St. Joseph, Missouri, and Sacramento, California. Western Union followed the same path in laying the first telegraph cable across the continent in 1861. On May 10, 1869, two companies completed the first transcontinental railroad north of Salt Lake at Promontory Point. Golden Spike Monument commemorates the spike they nailed to link the two tracks.

The Colorado River   The Colorado Plateau covers the eastern half of Utah. The **Colorado River** flows down from Colorado through the plateau. Glen Canyon Dam has backed up the river to form Lake Powell, the second largest reservoir in the nation and a haven for water sports.

All five of the state's national parks are in the Colorado Basin. Arches National Park has more arches than any other place in the world. Bryce Canyon is famous for **hoodoos,** columns of

strangely shaped pinnacles and spires. One of the massive peaks in Zion National Park is called the Great White Throne because it reminds people of the final judgment seat of God.

And I saw a great white throne. . . . And whosoever was not found written in the book of life was cast into the lake of fire. (Rev. 20:11, 15)

Evolutionists believe that every layer of the **"geologic column"** appears in the right order on three regions of the Colorado Plateau—Zion, Bryce Canyon, and Grand Canyon National Parks. If evolutionary theory is correct, the layers of the earth's rocks should reflect hundreds of millions of years of geologic history. One way that evolutionists date rocks is their location in the geologic column. But one occurence does not prove a theory, and even on the plateau you have to go to all three national parks to see all the layers! Sediments are jumbled in many different orders elsewhere around the world.

Kolob Arch, at Zion National Park, Utah, is the world's longest arch, 311 feet long.

Rhyolite, Nevada, once boasted twelve thousand people. It is now a ghost town.

Nevada, the Silver State

Nevada is the heart of the dry Great Basin. Nevada's largest natural lake, Pyramid Lake north of Reno, is very salty, just like Utah's Great Salt Lake. The longest river in the state, the 290-mile-long Humboldt River, starts as a creek in the northeast and disappears into the Humboldt Sink in the west. Early pioneers traveling to California followed the Humboldt River after crossing the Rockies.

Several parallel ranges run down the Great Basin like a giant washboard. The highest mountains are in the west along the California border. Waters from the mountains make Lake Tahoe, which Nevada shares with California, a blue paradise in the desolate Great Basin.

The Silver State mines most of the nation's silver, and it leads in the production of mercury. Its gold mines equal those of other states as well. The Comstock Lode at Virginia City, a boomtown in the 1870s, yielded about one billion dollars worth of gold and silver before the vein was exhausted. The reconstructed town, between Reno and Carson City, is now a tourist attraction. The pony express passed through the capital, Carson City.

Also called the Sagebrush State, Nevada is drier than any other state, receiving less than ten inches of rainfall a year, on average. The only major river is the Colorado River, at the southern border. To solve the state's thirst for water, the tall Hoover Dam was built on the Colorado. The Lake Mead reservoir is essential, supplying water for drinking and for irrigating local farms.

While Utah is known for its Mormon religion, Nevada is known for legalized gambling and all the sin that goes with it. Las Vegas, the state's largest city, is famed for its casinos and nightclubs. The streets display more neon signs per square mile than any other place in the world. The signs make sin seem glamorous, but the pleasure of sin is soon forgotten while sin's damage may endure for eternity.

The Southwest

The American **Southwest** is bleak and dry. It stretches from western Texas and Oklahoma to southern California. America's four great deserts—the Great Basin, Sonoran, Mojave, and Chihuahuan—are in the Southwest. American Indians and old Spanish towns dominate the cultural heritage of this region. New Mexico and Arizona lie at the heart of the Southwest.

New Mexico, Land of Enchantment

The stark, mesmerizing beauty of the landscape draws tourists year-round to the Land of Enchantment.

The Great Plains on the eastern quarter of New Mexico have many spectacular features. Carlsbad Caverns, in the southeast corner, has the most beautiful caverns in the nation and the largest bat colonies. Potash, mined near Carlsbad, makes New Mexico the nation's leading producer of this

The five-story Taos Pueblo in New Mexico is the tallest and most picturesque adobe pueblo made by Indians.

Indian Reservations

Indians are proud figures in U.S. history. Their tribal names appear everywhere in history books and in geography—Massachusett, Delaware, Erie, Huron, Miami, Illinois, Missouri, Omaha, Wichita, Dakota, Cheyenne, and Shasta, to name a few. Over two million Indians still live in the United States, mostly in the West. About one-fifth of them live on reservations.

The Bureau of Indian Affairs, a division of the U.S. Department of the Interior, recognizes 328 official Indian "entities" in the lower forty-eight states, including Indian tribes, bands, villages, groups, and pueblos. Thirty-three states have reservations set aside for the Indians. This chart shows the thirteen states with over half a million acres of tribally owned land.

STATE	TRIBAL ACREAGE	NUMBER OF RESERVATIONS	INDIAN POPULATION
1. Arizona	19,775,959	23	204,000
2. New Mexico	7,252,326	25	134,000
3. Montana	2,663,385	7	48,000
4. South Dakota	2,339,531	9	51,000
5. Utah	2,286,448	4	24,000
6. Washington	2,250,731	27	81,000
7. Wyoming	1,958,095	1	10,000
8. Nevada	1,147,088	19	20,000
9. Minnesota	779,138	14	50,000
10. Colorado	764,120	2	28,000
11. Oregon	660,367	7	39,000
12. Idaho	609,622	4	14,000
13. California	520,049	96	242,000

Navajo Indian woman in Arizona

Crow Indians of Montana

Indians are struggling to make a new life in the modern world, now that they have lost their original hunting grounds and their old way of living. Unfortunately, their reservations are located on some of the most unproductive land in America. They suffer from some of the worst social and economic problems in the nation, including poverty, disease, and suicide. Many homes still lack running water. Death from alcoholism is over four times the national average.

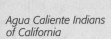

Agua Caliente Indians of California

fertilizer. The largest U.S. collection of dinosaur tracks were found at Clayton Lake in the northeast corner of the state. Capulin Volcano (extinct) rises from the plains nearby.

Northern Indian Reservations A portion of the Sangre de Cristo Range extends into northern New Mexico. This Rocky Mountain range has the highest mountains in the state, with beautiful alpine scenery and skiing. A popular attraction is the Taos pueblos, which rise five stories high.

Several reservations have been set aside on the Colorado Plateau, which covers the northwestern quarter of the state. The tribes of Southwest Indians include the Navajo, Apache, and Zuni. At the Acoma Indian Reservation is Sky City, a pueblo village high on a mesa overlooking the plateau 350 feet below. Acoma Indians have lived here for eight

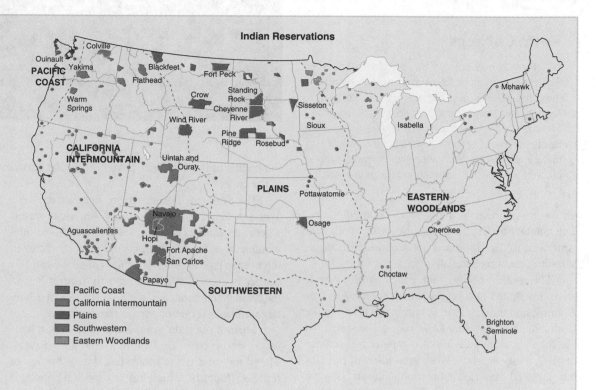

Indian Reservations

Ouinault
Colville
Yakima
PACIFIC COAST
Blackfeet
Flathead
Fort Peck
Warm Springs
Crow
Standing Rock
Cheyenne River
Sisseton
Mohawk
Wind River
Pine Ridge
Rosebud
Sioux
Isabella
CALIFORNIA INTERMOUNTAIN
Uintah and Ouray.
PLAINS
Pottawatomie
EASTERN WOODLANDS
Navajo
Osage
Cherokee
Aguascalientes
Hopi
Fort Apache
San Carlos
Papayo
Choctaw
SOUTHWESTERN
Brighton Seminole

- Pacific Coast
- California Intermountain
- Plains
- Southwestern
- Eastern Woodlands

Why are there so many problems? Liberals blame the European "invaders," who mistreated the Indians, took away their dignity, and destroyed their traditional way of life. Liberals have tried to help the Indians since the 1940s by heaping welfare on the reservations. Conservatives blame the lack of private property and mismanagement by bureaucrats in the Bureau of Indian Affairs. Conservative politicians tried to help Indians in 1988 by legalizing gambling on reservations. Although gambling has brought new wealth to many tribes, it is not the solution.

The real solution is spiritual. Indians need to take personal responsibility for their affairs and give their lives to God. As one Navajo pastor has said about outside help, "I think the Navajo has learned that someone else will do it for him. The federal government will take care of physical needs, and he'll let the churches and preachers take care of the spiritual needs. He hasn't made Christ a real part of his life yet. Until that happens, I think the Navajo will remain where he is."

hundred years, making it the oldest inhabited city in the nation.

Spanish Cities on the Upper Rio Grande

The **Rio Grande Valley** is the heart of New Mexico. The Rocky Mountain system, which peters out in New Mexico, bounds the river. Water flows down these scattered mountains into the river. This major river continues south to Texas. The upper Rio Grande provides water for irrigation in New Mexico. Among the many products in the valley are citrus fruit, cotton, vegetables, and most of the nation's hot chili peppers.

The state's three largest cities—Sante Fe, Albuquerque, and Las Cruces—lie in the Rio Grande basin. Spain founded Santa Fe far up the Rio Grande, ten years before the Pilgrims landed at Plymouth Bay. The city's Palace of Governors is the

The gaping maw of the Grand Canyon opens ten miles wide.

Four Corners

There is only one place in the United States where the corners of four states meet. A monument marks the spot where Utah, Colorado, Arizona, and New Mexico join. Four Corners is in the midst of the desert at the Navajo Reservation. By placing a hand or foot in each state, it is possible to be in all four states at once! Indian jewelry and blankets are sold at booths around the monument.

oldest government building in the United States. The Sante Fe Historic Trail shows the path that American traders followed between Independence, Missouri, and this Spanish city.

The atomic bombs that ended World War II were developed at a secret research center in Los Alamos, and the first atomic bomb was tested in the Chihuahuan Desert near Las Cruces. The state now has the densest population of computer and science experts, many of whom work in a cluster of military bases and laboratories in the mountains and deserts.

Arizona, the Grand Canyon State

The **Grand Canyon** is the centerpiece of the Colorado Plateau, which covers northern Arizona. The canyon, ten miles wide at its widest point and 217 miles long, is one of the seven natural wonders of the world. White-water rafters enjoy exhilarating trips down the Colorado River through the canyon.

At the northeast corner of the state is the Navajo Reservation, the largest reservation in the nation, which spills over into two neighboring states. The reservation offers several buttes and scenic rock formations. Some people think the Indian ruins at Canyon de Chelly (duh SHAY) surpass even Mesa Verde.

South of the Navajo Reservation are three other interesting features on the Colorado Plateau. The Painted Desert displays a rainbow of colors caused by a variety of minerals. The Petrified Forest has the biggest "forest" of its kind in the nation. A massive meteor crashed nearby to form the four-thousand-foot-wide Meteor Crater.

Fragments of the meteorite have been found buried in the crater.

The **Sonoran Desert** covers southern Arizona. The Sonoran Desert is the only American desert where the famous saguaro cacti grow. A national monument at the Mexican border protects the even rarer organ pipe cactus. Two-thirds of all the nation's copper is mined in Arizona, mostly from mines in the desolate mountains of the Sonoran Desert. Many large Indian reservations are in the desert too.

Most of the state's non-Indian population lives in the desert near the Colorado and Gila Rivers. The sunny and dry climate has drawn hordes of retirees. **Phoenix,** which has one million people, is the largest city in all of the eight interior states. High ratings for quality of life have attracted many companies to Phoenix, the "Sun City." Extensive irrigation and reservoirs support the desert metropolis. Tucson is the second largest city. A national monument near this desert city protects a beautiful area of saguaros.

SECTION REVIEW

1. What major geographic feature is shared by Utah and Nevada? How are the cultures of Utah and Nevada different?

2. What cultural characteristics are common in the Southwest?

3. Name the leading products of Nevada and each state in the Southwest.

4. What is the largest Indian reservation in the United States?

   Why did the pioneers who were headed for California travel through the Great Basin rather than through the Southwest?

Geographer's Corner

Special Climate Statistics for Cities

Here is a table showing climate statistics for a typical year in major cities of the West. Which cities are at the extremes in each category?

CITY	ELEVATION (FT.)	HIGH TEMP °F	LOW TEMP °F	ANNUAL PRECIPITATION (IN.)	FASTEST WIND (MPH)	CLEAR DAYS	CLOUDY DAYS	RAINY DAYS
Albuquerque, NM	5,311	103	16	5.7	41	151	91	50
Anchorage, AK	114	78	−15	13.8	43	61	244	93
Denver, CO	5,282	99	−7	18.7	45	130	115	94
Fairbanks, AK	436	88	−48	8.9	25	71	189	79
Lander, WY	5,557	97	−10	19.7	39	118	134	95
Los Angeles, CA	97	93	44	23.3	29	132	120	42
Phoenix, AZ	1,109	121	37	9.5	41	214	68	31
Portland, OR	21	99	16	43.3	51	66	222	134
Reno, NV	4,404	100	10	12.6	48	142	137	64
Salt Lake City, UT	4,221	106	11	16.9	43	115	160	96
San Francisco, CA	8	95	38	27.4	54	137	144	87
Seattle, WA	400	96	22	42.6	41	66	215	144

THE PACIFIC STATES

The Pacific Ocean laps the shores of five American states. While the eastern states have close cultural and economic ties with Europe across the Atlantic, the young West has been open to influences from the **Pacific Rim**—Asia, Polynesia, and the rest of the nations that touch the Pacific. Diesel ships have closed the distances between the many nations of the Pacific "lake."

All five Pacific states are mountainous, but the mountains are different in character from those of the interior states. These mountains are mostly volcanic—part of the **Pacific Ring of Fire** on the Pacific Rim. The mountains receive much more rainfall because of the moist air blowing off the Pacific Ocean.

The Golden State

 If California were still a separate republic, it would rank among the largest nations in the world—tenth in area and thirtieth in population.

Moreover, it would be the twelfth richest country! Among the fifty states, it is third in size but first in population and variety. A few hours of driving will take you from sunny beaches to alpine slopes, from the continent's lowest elevation to the highest mountains outside Alaska.

Populous Coasts With thirty million people, California almost doubles the population of the next most populous states, New York and Texas. It has more large cities than any other state—twelve over two hundred thousand and forty-six over one hundred thousand. All but six of them are in the coastal plains beside the Pacific Ocean.

Southern California There are two centers of population in California. Most of the state's cities lie in **Southern California,** which is quickly becoming a megalopolis. The greater Los Angeles area has twenty-five of the forty-six largest cities, and four others are at nearby San Diego. The region has a strong Southwest flavor, including the most productive oil wells outside Texas and Alaska.

Immigration

The United States is a nation of immigrants. Ever since the United States was founded, waves of newcomers have flooded its shores. Today this nation accepts almost as many foreigners as the rest of the world combined. The year 1996 saw a record 1.1 million immigrants *naturalized* (sworn in as citizens).

The recent wave of **immigration**—movement of foreigners into the nation—is not like the past. Most immigrants in the past came from Europe, and a strict law in 1920 limited immigration to skilled workers who had obvious talents. The recent wave began in 1965 when Congress opened the door to unskilled immigrants from undeveloped nations in Asia and Latin America. The number of immigrants from Mexico alone matches the number from the next nine leading nations combined.

This new wave has created alarm in some states. Immigrants compete for jobs, add to the cost of public education, and require medical care and welfare benefits. Concern is greatest in California, the main destination of immigrants to the United States. California is easy to reach from anywhere on the Pacific Rim. The state is particularly worried about Mexicans who cross the border illegally. In 1994 California voters passed Proposition 187, which denied public services, such as schooling and medical benefits, to illegal immigrants. In the wake of this law, the U.S. Congress doubled the border patrol and built a three-layer deep fence near San Diego. Politicians began calling for new limits on legal immigration too.

Texans are not as concerned as Californians about immigrants, even though Texas gets many immigrants from Mexico. Why not? One reason may be Texas's ties with Mexico. Its 1,248-mile border is six times longer than California's border with Mexico. Mexico accounts for 40 percent of Texas's foreign trade. In contrast, California's main partner is Japan, and Mexico is a distant fourth.

Supporters of immigration argue that the impact of immigrants is not as bad as it seems. Although unemployment is initially higher among immigrants, after ten years their income is above average. Immigrants typically take jobs that no one else wants, or they create new jobs among their own people. Only 8 percent of modern Americans are foreign-born, compared to a high of 15 percent in the early twentieth century.

Many Americans complain about the "un-American" traditions of the recent wave of immigrants. But they are no different from past waves, which required a *three-generation assimilation.* The first generation retained the old ways and language, their children learned to speak English as well as their parents' language, and finally the third generation forgot the language and traditions of their grandparents. Modern technology, especially television, is speeding this transition to two generations.

Most modern immigrants speak Spanish and are called *Hispanics.* Polls indicate that Hispanics, rather than keeping their old ways, quickly adopt American ways. Over 90 percent of Hispanics believe all U.S. citizens and residents should learn English. Hispanic immigrants are also among the leading opponents of new immigration because they fear competition for jobs.

💡 Should America place new restrictions on immigration? Why did the Old Testament require Israel to let aliens glean from the corners of fields (Deut. 24:19-22)? Why did God demand that the heathen nation of Moab accept outcasts from other nations (Isa. 16:3-4)? Explain the significance of Exodus 22:21 and Leviticus 19:33.

Hispanic Minority Population

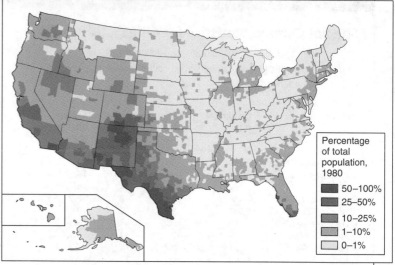

Percentage of total population, 1980

- 50–100%
- 25–50%
- 10–25%
- 1–10%
- 0–1%

The key to Southern California is **Los Angeles,** meaning the "City of Angels." It is second only to New York City in population. The metropolitan area includes four large cities in their own right: Long Beach, Santa Ana, Anaheim, and Riverside. Malibu Beach and Sunset Beach have the most popular surfing beaches outside Hawaii. Suburbs extend as far inland as San Bernardino.

America has over 250 amusement parks, more than any other nation. Entertainment is one of America's biggest exports. Few nations have the luxury and resources to devote so much energy on pleasure. Christians must beware of the many hazards of pleasure.

I will set no wicked thing before mine eyes: I hate the work of them that turn aside; it shall not cleave to me. (Ps. 101:3)

Los Angeles rivals New York City's cultural diversity. Over one hundred languages other than English are spoken, chiefly Spanish. Los Angeles actually has the second-largest Iranian population of any city in the world. Among the religions associated with Los Angeles's diverse culture is Scientology, a popular cult founded by a science fiction writer named L. Ron Hubbard in 1954. Some Hollywood actors are among its most visible followers.

San Diego, near the Mexican border, is the state's second largest city and third largest metropolitan area. San Diego has the best natural harbor in Southern California and the largest naval air station. Like other border towns, it has a major Hispanic population. Spanish influence began in 1542 when the explorer Cabrillo discovered San Diego Bay and claimed the whole of California for Spain. The first **mission** (building for Roman Catholic missionaries) was not founded until 1769 in San Diego, the cradle of California. San Diego de Alcalá Mission still stands. A total of twenty-one Catholic missions, from San Diego to Sonoma (just north of San Francisco), helped Spain to settle the state.

Los Angeles and San Diego must overcome many challenges to meet the needs of their growing populations. The Coast Ranges, just inland from the plain, trap pollutants, called *smog* (smoke fog). Steep slopes are prone to mudslides. Hot Santa Ana winds blow off the desert and cause frequent fires. An earthquake in Los Angeles on January 17, 1994, caused damage estimated at twenty billion dollars, killed fifty-one, and injured four thousand. California is the most monitored earthquake area in the nation, but scientists have much to learn about earthquake prediction and earthquake-proof construction.

Another serious challenge is lack of sufficient drinking water. So an **aqueduct,** or canal, was built to ship water from the Colorado River. Competition with neighboring states for water led to another water project in the north. The Oroville Dam on the Sacramento River brings water to Los Angeles via one of the largest aqueduct systems in the world.

The Bay Area Up the coast from Los Angeles is San Francisco Bay. Fifty miles wide, it is one of the

Trolley cars in San Francisco offer views of the famous Alcatraz Island prison in San Francisco Bay.

best harbors in the world. Eleven cities with populations above one hundred thousand are in the **Bay Area,** with San Francisco as the historic hub. Trolley cars, Chinatown, Fisherman's Wharf, and Alcatraz prison are still favorite tourist stops in the "City of Hills." The Golden Gate Bridge crosses the mouth of the bay. In recent years San Jose, at the south end of the bay, has surpassed San Francisco in population and modern high-tech industry. The core of the computer hardware industry, the San Jose area is often referred to as **Silicon Valley.**

Though free of smog and mudslides, the Bay area lies on the San Andreas Fault. The worst earthquake in the nation's history struck San Francisco in 1906, killing about seven hundred people and demolishing nearly thirty thousand buildings. Another big earthquake hit in 1989, but with much less damage and loss of life. People in other regions sometimes ask why Californians live on an earthquake fault, but every region has its own hazards, such as tornados, hurricanes, floods, and drought, which the people learn to live with.

The cities of the coastal plains are hemmed in by the **Coast Ranges.** At some places, such as Big Sur near Monterey, the mountains descend directly into the ocean. Redwood trees grow nowhere else in the world except the Coast Ranges of northern California.

The Central Valley Inland beyond the Coast Ranges lies the **Central Valley,** the best agricultural region in the West. The state got its start in the gold-filled streams of this valley. Many prospectors, however, could not find enough gold and turned to farming the rich soil for a living.

Two major rivers run through the valley and empty into San Francisco Bay. The **Sacramento River** flows through the highly fertile north end of the valley, and the San Joaquin (wah KEEN) River flows through the less fertile south end. The San Joaquin valley is only three hundred feet above sea level.

The Central Valley has a mild mediterranean climate with perfect temperatures for crops that require a long growing season. Infrequent rains,

The Golden Gate Bridge was an engineering marvel, the longest single span of its day. It still has the tallest supporting towers of any bridge.

except in the winter, mean that most farms must be irrigated.

California leads the nation in the production of numerous crops. Its vegetables include cauliflower, lettuce, onions, tomatoes, and avocados. Fruits and nuts include apricots, figs, plums, pomegranates, almonds, and walnuts. California produces most of the nation's grapes and related products, including raisins and wine. It is the only state with an olive crop, and it produces three-quarters of the lemons and strawberries consumed in the United States. California is second in two products associated with other regions of the nation: bales of cotton (behind Texas) and dairy cows (behind Wisconsin).

The United States captured California, along with the rest of the **Mexican Cession,** during the

Apricots drying near Patterson in the northern San Joaquin Valley, California

Mexican War (1846-48). Most inhabitants were Spanish at the time. One exception was John Sutter, who had built an adobe fort in the valley of the Sacramento River. The Golden State got its start in 1848, the year that the Mexican War ended, when a few gold nuggets were found near Sutter's sawmill. A year later a stampede of eighty thousand forty-niners poured into the territory—enough men to establish a state the next year. The boomtown of Sacramento, near Sutter's fort, became the capital in 1854.

The state remains known for its openness to new ideas and radical individualism. In 1969 it adopted the first "no-fault" divorce laws in the Western world, allowing a partner to break the marriage contract without showing a cause. An antitax

Land Use of Northern America

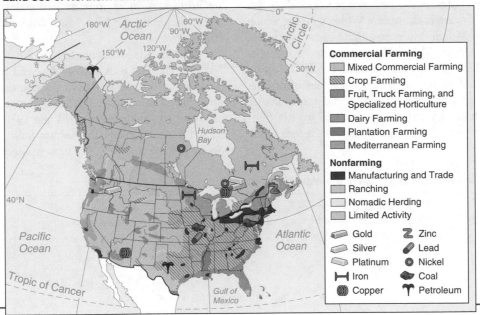

Let's Go Exploring

1. What term describes the tobacco and citrus farms of the Atlantic and Gulf coasts?

2. What type of agriculture takes place on the upper Rio Grande?

3. Is there any region of "crop farming" (wheat) west of the Rockies?

4. Outside Alaska, what are the only places in the United States with no economic activity?

5. What type of farming takes place in California but nowhere else in the United States? in Alaska but nowhere else?

Summarize the main differences between land use in the East and in the West.

movement in California led voters to pass an initiative in 1978 called Proposition 13, which required their congressmen to cut back property taxes. This "tax revolt" propelled California's Governor **Ronald Reagan,** a former Hollywood actor, to the presidency (1981-89), where he passed massive national tax cuts. President Richard Nixon was also from California.

The High Sierra The **Sierra Nevada** lies east of the Central Valley, separating the valley from the Great Basin. The Spanish word *sierra* means "mountains," while *nevada* means "snow-clad." These mountains, which include eleven Fourteeners and one hundred other peaks over thirteen thousand feet, are the highest in the United States outside Alaska.

The highest peaks are south of Lake Tahoe. Six Fourteeners are in the Mount Whitney group, which includes Mount Muir and the highest mountain outside Alaska, **Mount Whitney.** Four Fourteeners are farther north in the Palisade Peaks. Yosemite National Park has no Fourteeners but offers the highest waterfalls in the nation and a spectacular valley ringed by cliffs. El Capitan, thirty-six hundred feet high, is the largest granite cliff face in the world.

The John Muir Trail runs two hundred miles across three parks in the High Sierra, from Yosemite to Mount Whitney. It is the nation's longest wilderness trail that never crosses a road. The trail is named for **John Muir** (1838-1914), a famous American naturalist born in Scotland and reared in Wisconsin. Muir trekked across the eastern wilderness before moving to California in 1868. He discovered Muir Glacier in 1879 at Glacier Bay, Alaska, and he helped to establish Yosemite National Park in 1890. Camping with Theodore Roosevelt in 1903, he persuaded the president to set aside 148 million acres as national forests.

Muir founded the Sierra Club in 1892 and served as its first president. Today, the club is the largest environmentalist group worldwide and has used its influence to get the federal government to set aside several regions as national wilderness areas, including the John Muir Wilderness in the High Sierra.

The Cascade Mountains begin north of the Sierra Nevada. The first peak, Mount Lassen (10,457 ft.), rises east of the city of Redding above the northern tip of the Sacramento Valley. Mount Lassen is a volcano that erupted between 1914 and 1916. North of Mount Lassen broods the snowy hulk of Mount Shasta (14,162 ft.), the state's most massive peak.

Rainshadow Effect of the Western Mountains

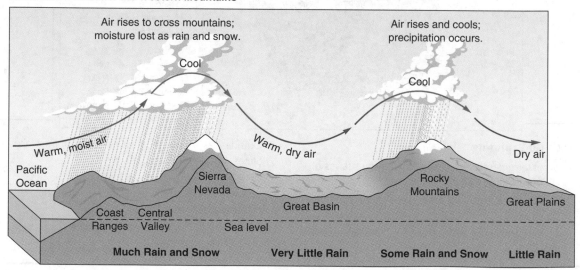

Air rises to cross mountains; moisture lost as rain and snow.

Cool

Air rises and cools; precipitation occurs.

Cool

Warm, moist air

Warm, dry air

Dry air

Pacific Ocean

Sierra Nevada

Rocky Mountains

Great Basin

Great Plains

Coast Ranges Central Valley Sea level

Much Rain and Snow **Very Little Rain** **Some Rain and Snow** **Little Rain**

Southern Deserts   Moist winds blowing off the Pacific Ocean lose their moisture when they hit the western slopes of the High Sierra. While the waters flow down the mountains to enrich the rivers of the Central Valley, almost no water reaches the eastern **rainshadow.** This explains why so many deserts lie in the Great Basin and the Southwest.

The Mojave Desert and Death Valley lie in the Great Basin region of southern California. **Death Valley,** one hundred miles east of Mount Whitney, sinks to the lowest spot on the continent—282 feet below sea level—at a salty basin called Bad Water.

The Sonoran Desert lies on California's border with Arizona. It is also called the Colorado Desert, after the Colorado River that flows down the border. The sediment at the delta of the Colorado has blocked this low area from the ocean. The desert includes the Salton Sea, 232 feet below sea level. At one time this salt-water lake was a dry salt flat, but a levee on the Colorado River broke in 1905, refilling the flat and creating the salt lake. The Imperial Valley is also in this area. Irrigation from the Colorado River has turned the desert into productive farmland.

SECTION REVIEW

1. Give three major differences between Southern California and the Bay Area.
2. List five of California's most important products. Where are they produced or mined?
3. Name the six major geographical regions of California.
4. What are the highest and lowest points in California?
5. What ranges have most of California's Fourteeners?
6. Who is the most famous American conservationist?
7. Why has Los Angeles become the most populous city in the West?

Pacific Northwest

Oregon and Washington are the heart of the Pacific Northwest. They share the beautiful Cascade Mountains, fertile valleys, and a mild climate. Heavy rains have produced lush vegetation and thick forests that are the nation's main source of lumber. To preserve the region's "utopian ecology," some radical environmentalists have called for the creation of a new country, extending from San Francisco to Alaska, called Ecotopia.

The **Cascade Mountains** are the backbone of the Pacific Northwest. This series of volcanic peaks extends from northern California into Canada. The range is well named. The high amount of rainfall creates hundreds of powerful waterfalls that cascade down the towering peaks. The Cascades have more major falls than any other region in the nation.

The narrow chain of Cascade Mountains does not compete with the broadness of the Rocky Mountains or its wealth of Fourteeners. But the Cascades have other boasts. Cascade peaks are far higher from base to crest. Mount Rainier, for instance, rises from sea level, whereas the base of the Rockies rises from the mile-high Great Plains. Unlike the Rockies, the most majestic Cascade summits have snowcapped peaks year-round. Glaciers are also more common in the Cascades.

Oregon   Oregon is less populated than either of its Pacific neighbors. With no Fourteeners and only one national park, its beauty is a well-kept secret. Oregonians like it that way. They enjoy their alpine summits and Pacific coast without the masses of people encountered at Yosemite or Mount Rainier. Oregon is a haven for wilderness enthusiasts and mountaineers.

The low Coast Ranges cover the western one-fifth of the state and sometimes descend to the sea in rocky cliffs. The coast has beaches too. Dune buggies enjoy the stretch of dunes from Coos Bay to Florence. Nearby, you can descend by elevator into Sea Lion Caves, where sea lions give birth before returning to Alaska. Seaside parks offer sea arches, rock monoliths, and rocky shores with tide pools. Cyclists enjoy the nation's most spectacular bicycle trail. Open only to bicycles, the path follows the state's four-hundred-mile-long coast.

The Willamette Valley   The Willamette (Wil LAM it) River flows through a narrow plain east of

Logging is a major industry in the Pacific Northwest.

the Coast Ranges. All the state's major cities lie in the **Willamette Valley,** which has fertile soil and mild weather throughout the year. Missionary accounts of unspoiled farmland lured pioneers on the Oregon Trail in the 1840s and 1850s.

Oregon has experimented with many new ideas in state and local government. In 1902 it became the first state to include initiative and referendum in its constitution. In 1908 it gave voters the right to *recall* (remove from office) elected officials before their term expires. Portland, the state's largest city, passed a moratorium on skyscrapers in order to preserve views of the surrounding mountains. The capital, Salem, passed the nation's first environmental laws. It required deposits on carbonated drink cans to reduce litter, and it banned smoking in public buildings and on buses.

Willamette Valley extends as far south as Eugene and Springfield, the second largest metropolitan area in the state. It has the best farmland in the state. Oregon is famous for its blackberries, blueberries, and raspberries. Other tasty fruit, such as salal, thimbleberries, salmonberries, and Oregon grape, grow wild.

The Columbia River   The Cascade Range rises east of the Willamette Valley. The only waterway that cuts through these high mountains into the Pacific Ocean is the **Columbia River.** The river gave Lewis and Clark a natural passageway to the coast, and it remains the best northern route into the interior. Visitors can view dozens of the state's most spectacular waterfalls along the Columbia River. The highest is Multnomah Falls at 611 feet.

The Cascade Mountains have many attractions too. The blue water of Crater Lake, the deepest lake in the nation, lies in a volcano's crater near Oregon's southern border. Mount Hood, just south of the Columbia River, is the most frequently climbed major peak in the nation. The deep snow on Mount Hood made it the logical site of the nation's first year-round ski resort. Evergreen forests give Oregon much of its beauty, and they also make it the nation's leading producer of wood products.

The high and arid Columbia Plateau dominates Oregon east of the Cascade Mountains. Herds of cattle graze on the grassland, and wheat fields are common near the Columbia River. Pendleton is famous for its rodeo, the Pendleton Round-Up.

A skier enjoys Mount Hood Meadows, the first year-round ski resort in America.

Precipitation in the United States

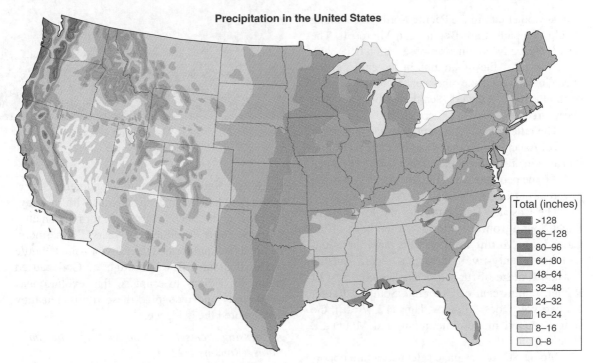

Total (inches)
- >128
- 96–128
- 80–96
- 64–80
- 48–64
- 32–48
- 24–32
- 16–24
- 8–16
- 0–8

Dams along the Columbia River produce one-third of the total hydroelectric power produced by the United States. A fish ladder beside Bonneville Dam allows salmon to continue upriver to lay eggs.

Washington Because the Pacific Coast Ranges come right up to the shore, the Northwest coast has few good ports. Most of Washington State's coastal towns are small. The northern tip of the Coast Ranges juts out into the ocean at **Olympic Peninsula.** It has the highest point in the Coast Ranges, at snowcapped Mount Olympus (7,965 ft.).

The national park on Olympic Peninsula gets the most rain of any place outside Hawaii. The rains support the nation's largest temperate rain forest on the slopes of Mount Olympus. This sparsely settled peninsula has several Pacific Coast Indian reservations. The Makah Reservation lies on Cape Alava, the westernmost point of the lower forty-eight states.

Puget (PYOO jit) **Sound,** an arm of the Pacific Ocean, pushes north of the Olympic Peninsula far into Washington State. The deep waters of

Puget Sound give Washington State its best natural harbors. Early pioneers settled on the coastal lowlands along the sound. Like the Willamette Valley, the lowlands of Puget Sound are a leader in berry production.

The city of **Seattle** lies on one of the protected harbors of Puget Sound. The largest port north of San Francisco, it does substantial trade with the other nations on the Pacific Rim. Seattle is larger

The Hoh Rain Forest in Olympic National Park, Washington, gets 140 inches of rain annually.

than any other city in the Pacific Northwest. Among its big companies are Boeing and Microsoft. The Seattle Space Needle has an observation deck with good views of the mountains in the east and the ocean in the west. Like other health-conscious cities of the Pacific Northwest, Seattle has bike lanes on every street.

The cities of Puget Sound have many descendants of Asian immigrants. Seattle's large metropolitan area includes Tacoma and the capital, Olympia. In 1996 the people elected the first Asian-American governor outside of Hawaii.

The Cascade Range divides the lowlands of Puget Sound from the interior. At the heart of the Cascades is **Mount Rainier.** This majestic mountain has twenty-five glaciers, a record outside Alaska. A maze of rugged peaks lies northeast of Ranier, reminiscent of Colorado. South of Ranier are two volcanoes: Mount Adams (12,276 ft.), the state's second highest mountain, and Mount St. Helens (8,365 ft.)

Mount St. Helens gave scientists a rare opportunity to witness a big eruption in 1980. The eruption blew 1,312 feet off of the mountain summit, killing over fifty people and destroying much property. The devastated area is now part of Mount

The 605-foot-high Space Needle offers views of Mount Rainier and of Seattle, Washington.

St. Helens National Volcanic Monument. Superheated mud laid down deep canyons with rock layers, proving that such features can form in a matter of hours, not over millions of years. Furthermore, the floods of mud formed the canyon—not the little stream that now flows through it. God caused Mount St. Helens to erupt so that evolutionists could study and recognize these truths, but they have ignored the evidence.

Professing themselves to be wise, they became fools. (Romans 1:22)

The Columbia Plateau covers the eastern part of Washington. Spokane is the second largest city in the state and the largest on the plateau. It is the hub of a region called the **Inland Empire.** This

Great Dams of the West

The largest dams in the United States cross the rivers of the West. At one time, the United States held all the records for height, size of reservoirs, and power produced. However, in recent years American engineers have been assisting other nations to harness larger and more powerful rivers.

Two great dams on the Colorado River are vital to the water supply and electricity of the Southwest. The Glen Canyon Dam created the Lake Powell reservoir in southern Utah, on the border with Arizona. The Hoover Dam created Lake Mead farther downstream on the border between Arizona and Nevada. When completed in 1936, Hoover Dam was the highest dam in the world (221 ft.), and Lake Mead was the largest reservoir. It is still the second highest dam in the United States.

Grand Coulee Dam, which harnesses the raging Columbia River in Washington, is still a world-class dam. It puts out more kilowatts of power than any other dam in the world, except Itaipu Dam in Brazil. Grand Coulee's rated capacity is 10,830,000 kilowatts of power, three times the next largest capacity of a dam in the United States. When Grand Coulee Dam became operational in 1942, it was the largest masonry structure ever built on earth, seven times larger than the Great Pyramid. The concrete at its base is 480 feet thick—wider than one and a half football fields. Its spillway is three times higher than Niagara Falls. The reservoir above the dam, named after President Franklin D. Roosevelt, stretches north into Canada.

"empire" includes the upper Columbia River and its main tributary—the Snake River. Orchards in Washington's fertile river valleys produce more apples and pears than all other states combined. Fields of wheat make Washington a leading wheat producer in the United States.

Along with Puget Sound and Willamette Valley, the Inland Empire was a main destination of the Oregon Trail. Some of the early arrivals were the Presbyterian missionaries Marcus and Narcissa Whitman, who started a mission at Walla Walla in 1836. The Whitmans sent glowing reports of the land in their appeals for missionaries. But the stream of pioneers caused resentment among the Indians. In 1847, after a measles epidemic wiped out nearly half the tribe, a party of Cayuse Indians massacred the Whitmans and other missionaries at the mission.

Today there is a wide diversity of Christian denominations and religious groups in the Pacific Northwest. Baptists and Methodists are relatively uncommon. Washington State has the largest percentage of Americans who claim no religion (17 percent), followed by Oregon (14 percent), Wyoming (14 percent), California (13 percent), and Arizona (12 percent).

SECTION REVIEW

1. Compare and contrast the Willamette Valley, Puget Sound, and the Inland Empire.
2. Give three ways that the Cascades surpass the Rockies.
3. What major geographical regions do Oregon and Washington share?
4. What is the highest mountain in the Cascades?
5. Who was the first white man to settle in the Inland Empire?

💡 Find Portland on the map. Why is it the biggest city in Oregon?

The Farthest Shores

The **contiguous** (or *conterminous*) states are the forty-eight "lower states" that connect with each other. The other two states—Alaska and Hawaii—did not gain statehood until 1959, almost fifty years after the last contiguous state (Arizona). They also have the most extreme points of land within the fifty states. The southern tip of Hawaii, Ka Lae (or South Cape), is the southernmost point of land in the fifty states (18°55′ N). Point Barrow, Alaska, on the Arctic Ocean, is the northernmost point (71°23′ N). Alaska's Attu Island (172°27′ E), actually in the Eastern Hemisphere, is the west end of the nation.

Alaska and Hawaii are among the strongest proponents of individualism in the West. In 1970 they joined New York as the first states to abolish laws against abortion, in the name of women's rights. In 1996 a judge in Hawaii ruled that homosexuals should be allowed to get a marriage license, in the name of civil rights.

Alaska, the Last Frontier Alaska is vast and remote. It is more than twice as large as the second largest state, Texas. The distance from its southeastern islands to its western islands is greater than the distance between Maryland and California. No other state is so far north, touching the Arctic Ocean. Its windswept mountains are much higher than anything in the lower forty-eight, and its glaciers are the only ones that descend to the sea. One of Alaska's national

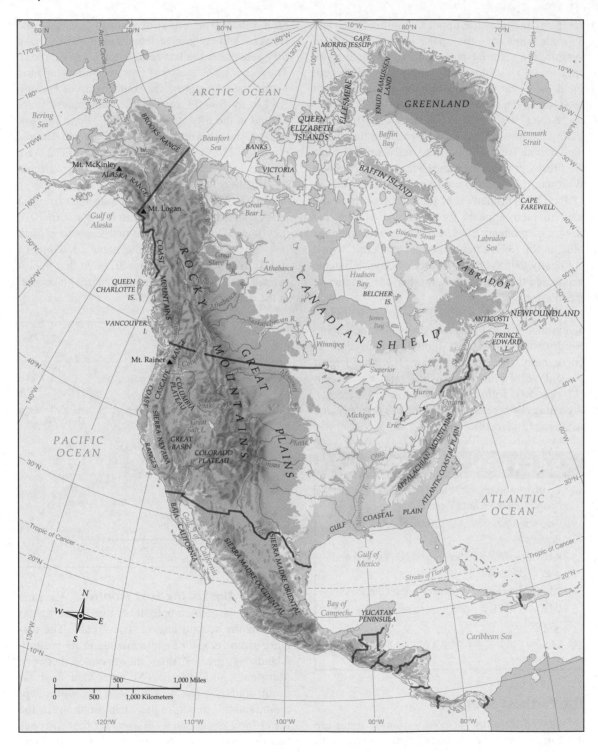

Mount McKinley is the highest mountain in North America—20,320 feet above sea level.

parks is larger than the entire state of Maryland, and it has even larger unprotected wildernesses. Alaska is truly America's Last Frontier.

Many Americans ridiculed Secretary of State William Seward when he purchased Alaska from Russia in 1867 for $7.2 million. No one laughed about "Seward's Ice Box" after the discovery of gold around Juneau in 1880. But the big gold rush came in 1896 with the discovery of gold in the Klondike region just north of Juneau. Later rushes occurred near Nome (1899) and Fairbanks (1903).

The state capital, Juneau, lies in Alaska's southeastern panhandle. Most of the panhandle is a chain of islands that extend up the Pacific coast from Washington State. Many tourists take the four-day cruise from Washington through the islands along the **Inside Passage.** They pass many places famous for totem poles made by the Tlingit (TKLINK it) Indians. After passing the capital they reach the north end of the passage at Glacier Bay, where glaciers drop icebergs into the Pacific.

Most of Alaska's people live along the Pacific coast. The ocean keeps the climate moderate with an average annual temperature of 60°F. The largest port, Anchorage, has half of the state's population and ranks among the seventy largest American cities. South of Anchorage, boat cruises go to Kodiak Island, where the largest bears in the world live.

North of Anchorage is the **Alaska Range.** It is the northern end of the *Pacific Mountain System,* which includes the Cascades in Washington and the Sierra Nevada in California. The Pacific Mountain

System rises to its greatest height in the Alaska Range. Denali National Park has the highest peak, **Mount McKinley** (20,320 ft.). The Pacific Mountain System continues west of the Alaska Range into the Pacific Ocean, where it becomes the chain of Aleutian Islands. The chain is named for the Aleut (uh LOOT) Indians.

North of the Alaska Range are the lowlands of the Yukon River and the Kuskokwim River. Temperatures range from –20 to 75°F. Fairbanks, the largest inland city in the state, lies in these lowlands. On the west coast is Nome. Located far out on the Seward Peninsula, it can only be reached by plane, boat, or dogsled. The harsh polar climate around Nome supports only mosses and grasses, typical of tundra.

The **Brooks Range** lies north of the Arctic Circle. It is the northernmost extension of the Rocky Mountains. The **North Slope,** a coastal plain along the Arctic Ocean, slopes down from the Brooks Range to the ocean. In 1977 the eight-hundred-mile-long Alaska Pipeline started carrying oil from the North Slope to Valdez on the Pacific. Alaska vies with Texas as the leading state for petroleum production.

North of the Arctic Circle the sun gets low on the horizon but does not set for many days. Temperatures often plunge to –75°F in the winter. Point Barrow is the northernmost tip of land, and the nearby town of Barrow is both the northernmost

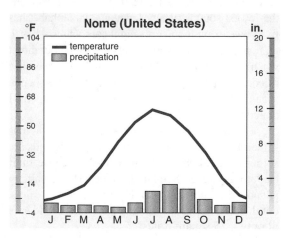

Iditarod Trail

A diphtheria epidemic struck Nome, Alaska, in 1925. Blinding snow and a thousand miles of rough terrain separated Nome from needed medicine in Anchorage. But courageous dogsled drivers stood up to the challenge and averted disaster.

Since 1973 an annual dogsled race retraces the old route. Drivers of dog teams, called mushers, prepare throughout the year for the contest. Each of the fifty contestants may stash fifteen pounds of food and supplies at twenty-five checkpoints along the route. Besides warm clothes and headlamps, each musher is responsible for the food, harnesses, and booties of his fifteen dogs. For safety, the race requires each musher to rest twenty-four hours at one of the checkpoints.

In 1995 Doug Swingley of Montana won the race in record time: nine days, two hours, forty-three minutes. He was the first non-Alaskan to win. No female has ever won, but Susan Butcher placed second in 1982, only four minutes behind the winner. The winner receives a prize of about fifty thousand dollars in cash and a new pickup truck. More importantly, his name is added to the list of winners in one of America's most challenging sports.

---

settlement and the largest Eskimo village in the nation. Tourists fly in during the summer to enjoy its eighty-two days of constant sunlight in the "Land of the Midnight Sun."

Aloha State Hawaii is the only tropical paradise among the states. Sightseers come to view the hundreds of huge waterfalls, tropical jungles, and active volcanoes. Others enjoy the native inhabitants, who have a reputation for kindness. The state nickname, *Aloha,* means "love."

Hawaii, twenty-four hundred miles from the North American mainland, is in Polynesia. The first Hawaiians were Polynesians, and many of their traditions continue—Hawaiian hulas (dances), luaus (feasts), and the giving of leis (stringed flowers). The Hawaiian language is interesting because it contains the fewest sounds of any language. Its alphabet has five vowel sounds and only eight consonants—h, k, l, m, n, p, w, and ' (the sound that catches in your throat when you say uh-oh). Hawaii is the only state once ruled by an independent monarchy, which began around the year 1800 when King Kamehameha I united the warring island tribes.

Hawaii consists of 132 islands spread across fifteen hundred miles. The eight largest islands are sometimes called the High Islands because their elevations exceed five hundred feet. The remaining islands, the Leeward Islands, consist of rock islets, coral atolls, reefs, and shoals, with a total land area of only 5.25 square miles.

Hawaii, called the **Big Island,** has almost half of the state's area. It was apparently formed by five volcanoes. Hualalai last erupted in 1801, while Kohala and Mauna Kea (13,796 ft.) are dormant. The other two, Mauna Loa (13,680 ft.) and Kilauea (4,090 ft.) are still active.

The Big Island aptly illustrates the wide variety of climates in Hawaii. Average high temperatures around 80°F attract tourists year-round to the balmy beaches. Meanwhile, downhill skiers enjoy snow-clad slopes on Mauna Kea during the winter. Trade winds bring heavy rains to the eastern side of the mountains. Hilo, the second largest city in the state, receives 138 inches of rainfall annually. Tropical rain forests make the Big Island the nation's top producer of coffee, orchids, and macadamia nuts. In the rainshadow only ten miles west from Hilo, the average rainfall is only 9.5 inches. This abrupt change from rain forest to the dry rainshadow occurs on the four largest islands.

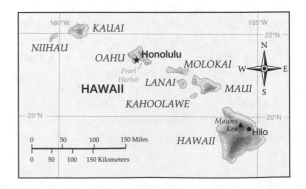

ISLANDS	AREA (SQ. MI.)	POPULATION	HIGH POINT, ELEVATION (FT.)
Hawaii	4,038	136,103	Mauna Kea, 13,796
Maui	729	107,812	Haleakala, 10,023
Kahoolawe	45	0	Lua Makika, 1,477
Lanai	140	2,410	Mount Lanaihale, 3,370
Molokai	261	3,114	Kamakou, 4,970
Oahu	608	878,249	Kaala, 4,040
Kauai	553	55,714	Mount Kawaikini, 5,243
Niihau	73	221	Paniau, 1,281

Maui has two volcanoes. Maui's nickname, the Valley Isle, comes from the great valley between the two mountains. The crater of Haleakala is twenty miles around, the largest dormant crater in the world. Several coastal towns circle the other volcano, Puu Kukui. The city of Lahaina served as King Kamehameha I's capital.

Maui has three interesting neighbors. Kahoolawe, the "Goat Island," is uninhabited except for wild goats. The military uses the island for bombing practice. Lanai, the "Pineapple Island," welcomes visitors to its plantations. Together with Maui, it produces almost all of America's pineapples. Molokai, sometimes called the "Forgotten Island," is less populated and less visited than the four larger islands. Its rugged eastern half boasts towering cliffs and the highest waterfalls in the state. A few devoted tourists consider Molokai the "Friendly Island."

Three-fourths of the state's population lives on **Oahu,** Hawaiian for the "Gathering Place." The state's capital and largest city, Honolulu, is on the island. The volcano Diamond Head dominates the skyline of the city, and Waikiki Beach lies in the shadow of Diamond Head. The home of Hawaii's monarchs, Iolani Palace, built by the "Merry Monarch" David Kalakaua (1879-82), is in Honolulu. The port at Honolulu ships many of the state's exotic exports, including mangos, papayas, and guavas. A large U.S. naval base lies near Honolulu at Pearl Harbor. A museum permits viewing of the U.S.S. *Arizona,* which was sunk by the Japanese in World War II.

Kauai is the main island beyond Oahu. Mt. Waialeale (5,208 ft.) receives about 460 inches of rain every year, making it the wettest spot on earth. The rain produces luxuriant tropical forests on the "Garden Isle." Waimea Canyon is the "Grand Canyon of the Pacific," and Wailua Falls is the most famous waterfall.

Niihau, "the Forbidden Island," is restricted to Polynesian residents. Tours permit one-hour stops. Halalii Lake, which covers 850 acres, is the largest freshwater lake in the state. In contrast to the post card pictures of Hawaii, many of the native people live in great poverty, and some openly resent the loss of their independence.

The United States has several small territories. Some lie southeast of Florida, and others are west of Hawaii. Puerto Rico has the largest size and population in the Caribbean, and Guam is the largest territory in the Pacific. You will study more about them in later chapters.

The Volcanoes of Hawaii

Mauna Loa, the "Monarch of Mountains," is the largest active volcano in the world. The volcano erupts about once every three and a half years. Mauna Loa is not a symmetrical cone, but a rounded *shield volcano* sixty miles long and thirty miles wide. The sides of the broad summit form a gently sloping oval dome.

Kilauea is the other major active volcano on Hawaii's Big Island. It lies on the southern slope of Mauna Loa. Unlike Mauna Loa, it has a larger crater, or *caldera,* two miles across, making it the largest active volcanic crater in the world. Lava sometimes spurts fifty feet into the air, creating a fantastic "curtain of fire." Mauna Loa and Kilauea are both inside Hawaii Volcanoes National Park.

◎ SECTION REVIEW

1. Name four major geographic regions in Alaska.
2. List the leading products of Alaska and Hawaii.
3. Name the highest peak in North America. What range is it in?
4. Give one distinctive fact about each island: the Big Island, Oahu, and Kauai.
   💡 What effect has remoteness had on the culture of the noncontiguous states?

REVIEW 9

Can You Define These Terms?

manifest destiny	Fourteener	geologic column	mission
gold rush	cult	Pacific Rim	aqueduct
Continental Divide	salt flat	Pacific Ring of Fire	rainshadow
geothermal	hoodoo	immigration	contiguous

Can You Locate These Natural Features?

Rocky Mountains	Colorado River	Death Valley	Alaska Range
Columbia Plateau	Rio Grande Valley	Cascade Mountains	Mount McKinley
Snake River	Grand Canyon	Willamette Valley	Brooks Range
Front Range	Sonoran Desert	Columbia River	North Slope
Sangre de Cristo Range	Coast Ranges	Olympic Peninsula	Big Island
Sawatch Range	Central Valley	Puget Sound	Oahu
Colorado Plateau	Sacramento River	Mount Rainier	Mauna Loa
Great Basin	Sierra Nevada	Inside Passage	Kauai
Great Salt Lake	Mount Whitney		

Can You Explain the Significance of These People and Places?

Denver	Phoenix	Silicon Valley	John Muir
Mormons	Southern California	Mexican Cession	Seattle
Salt Lake City	Los Angeles	Ronald Reagan	Inland Empire
Southwest	Bay Area		

How Much Do You Remember?

1. Give a major example of a primary, secondary, and tertiary industry in the West.
2. Name one leading product from ten western states.
3. Give the location and date of gold rushes in five western states.
4. List all the major rivers, mountains, and landmarks on these two trails:
   a. Lewis and Clark Trail
   b. Oregon Trail
5. Which states have a continental divide?
6. What state has the source of the Missouri River? the Snake River? the Colorado River? the Sacramento River?
7. Which state has the most area devoted to reservations? Why do you think this is so?
8. What are the three major geographic regions west of the Rockies?
9. Give the mountain peak associated with each phrase, and give the height.
   a. highest in North America
   b. highest in the Sierra Nevada
   c. highest in the Cascades
   d. highest in the Coast Ranges
   e. largest active volcano in the world
10. Where is the best evidence of a geologic column? What two other places in the West strongly contradict this evolutionary concept?

What Do You Think?

1. Read Mark 6. What is the purpose of recreation? Should Christians take long vacations? Is it okay to miss church services?
2. What is the greatest treasure that the West has to offer the United States?
3. Several politicians in Arizona want the federal government to give more land to the state so that it can develop mining and other industries. Who should have ultimate control of land in a state?
4. Should the federal government limit logging and ranching on federal lands if it endangers rare species?
5. Compare and contrast the culture of the West and the Northeast.

CANADA

The United States's northern neighbor, Canada, is the second largest country in the world. Yet it has a small population. This unusual combination offers Canada great benefits. Canadians are able to make a comfortable living and still export large quantities of raw materials.

Canada has much in common with the United States. It shares a border of 3,987 miles with America's forty-eight lower states, and it shares another 1,538-mile border with Alaska. The two nations have been at peace for over 150 years. In fact, they share the longest unfortified border in the world. Tourists and job seekers cross the borders with ease.

Canada and the United States are the richest and most industrialized nations in the Western Hemisphere. They trade more goods with each other than with any other nation in the world. The United States depends on many of Canada's raw materials, such as nickel and wood pulp, while Canada buys many U.S. manufactured goods.

Canada and the United States are like brothers in many other ways. Both nations grew from British and French roots. Both cleared settlements in a wild frontier. Both worship in churches led by Protestant preachers or Catholic priests. Large pockets of native Indians and Eskimos still live in the West and in the cold North. Canada also shares many geographic regions with the United States, from the eastern Appalachians to the western Rockies.

Canadians sometimes resent the wealth and influence of their powerful neighbor. Like brothers, Canada and the United States sometimes squabble. But they are still a family. Their bond deepened during World War II, as their young men fought side by side in Europe and Asia to defeat Hitler and other tyrants who threatened their cherished freedoms.

A friend loveth at all times, and a brother is born for adversity. (Proverbs 17:17)

THE MARITIME PROVINCES

Canada has ten provinces. The four smallest provinces, located in the eastern corner along the Atlantic coast, are known as the Maritime Provinces. *Maritime* means "bordering the sea." The smell of salt spray and the sound of crashing waves fill the air. For centuries, sailors have lived in scattered villages along the coasts, depending on the sea for their livelihood, just as their neighbors do in New England.

Newfoundland, "The Rock"

Many markers celebrate the peaceful border between the United States and Canada.

The rocky island of **Newfoundland** (NOO fun lund) and a large, rocky strip of land on the mainland together form the province known as Newfoundland. In 1964, however, the province officially adopted the name "Newfoundland and Labrador" to give both parts of the province equal honor.

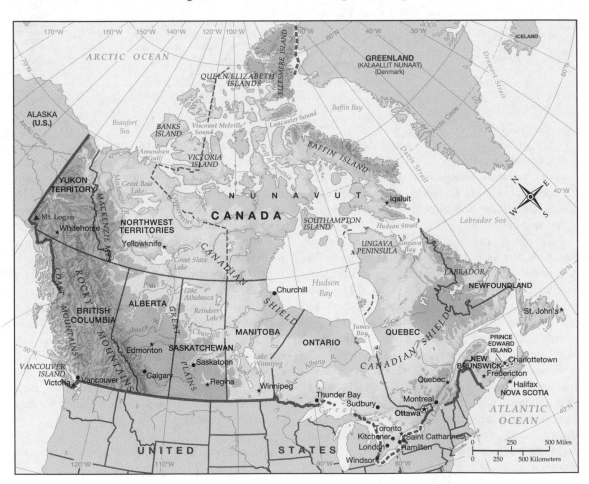

Canada Statistics

PROVINCE (SQ. MI.)	P.O. CODE	CAPITAL	DATE OF ENTRY	NICKNAME	AREA (SQ. MI.)	POPULATION	HIGH POINT, ELEVATION (FT.)
Newfoundland	NF	St. John's	1949	Britain's Oldest Colony	156,649	551,792	Mount Caubvick, 5,415
Nova Scotia	NS	Halifax	1867	Land of Evangeline	21,425	909,282	White Hill, 1,747
Prince Edward Island	PE	Charlottetown	1873	Million-Acre Farm	2,185	134,557	near Hunter River, 465
New Brunswick	NB	Fredericton	1867	Loyalist Province	28,355	738,133	Mount Carleton, 2,690
Quebec	PQ	Quebec	1867	Storied Province	594,860	7,138,795	Mount d'Iberville, 5,412
Ontario	ON	Toronto	1867	Manufacturing Heartland	412,581	10,753,573	Ishpatine Ridge, 2,275
Manitoba	MB	Winnipeg	1870	Keystone Province	250,947	1,113,898	Baldy Mountain, 2,729
Saskatchewan	SK	Regina	1905	Canada's Breadbasket	251,866	990,237	Cypress Hills, 4,816
Alberta	AB	Edmonton	1905	Sunny Alberta	255,287	2,696,826	Mount Columbia, 12,294
British Columbia	BC	Victoria	1871	Beautiful British Columbia	365,948	3,724,500	Mount Fairweather, 15,300
Yukon Territory	YT	Whitehorse	NA	Klondike Gold Rush	186,661	30,766	Mount Logan, 19,524
Northwest Territories	NT	Yellowknife	NA	Mackenzie Land	552,910	38,402	Mount Sir James MacBrien, 9,062
Nunavut	NU	Iqaluit	NA	Land of Inuit	770,000	26,000	Barbeau Peak, 8,584

A Rural Island   The island is actually the northeastern edge of the Appalachian Mountain system, part of which lies underwater. Its rocky coasts and rolling hills are covered by stunted forests.

The Vikings who settled at L'Anse aux Meadows, Newfoundland, lived in sod houses such as this one until driven off by Indians.

Beautiful fjords, gouged by past glaciers, attract many tourists to the western coast. Bird sanctuaries host puffins and millions of other nesting birds.

Most Newfoundlanders live on the island. Though the climate is cool, the Gulf Stream keeps the climate from becoming too harsh. The capital, St. John's, sits beside the world-famous **Grand Banks** fishing grounds. Here cod reigned as king for almost five hundred years. But stocks are dwindling, and in 1994 Canada temporarily banned cod fishing.

Europeans built their first settlement in the New World here—a Viking outpost dating back to A.D. 1000. The British claimed the island in 1583, but they opposed settlement, fearing that local fishermen might become rivals to British companies. Fishermen, however, secretly built winter camps in the *coves* (small, sheltered bays) that dot the

225

Grand Banks

Early explorers were astounded by the teeming fish in the Grand Banks. John Cabot first discovered these waters in 1497. In just a few years, fishing boats from many parts of Western Europe were braving the icebergs, fogs, and storms to harvest fish. Cod became the most important commercial fish, but haddock, flounder, and herring were also abundant.

What makes the Grand Banks the world's greatest fishing grounds? Off the southeast coast of

Mixing of Ocean Currents at the Grand Banks

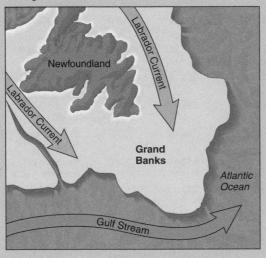

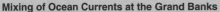
Cod fishing

Newfoundland, the continental shelf extends far out into the Atlantic Ocean. This 139,000-square-mile underwater plateau provides a perfect fish "nursery." The comparatively shallow waters, averaging six hundred feet in depth, receive plenty of sunlight. The warm Gulf Stream mixes with the icy, oxygen-rich Labrador Current, encouraging explosive growth of plankton and other fish food.

In recent decades, fishing vessels from Russia, Poland, Germany, Romania, and Japan have begun trawling these waters. To control overfishing, Canada requires all fishing vessels to obtain a license. But illegal fishing remains a serious threat to the Grand Banks's famed stocks.

island. Fishing villages sprang up long before the first official settlements in the nineteenth century. Prosperous and independent-minded, Newfoundland did not join Canada until 1949, the last province to join the federation.

Labrador The peninsula of **Labrador** on the mainland is cold all year round. The frigid Labrador Current carries Arctic water and icebergs past the coast. As air temperatures dip below -50°F in the winter, the surface of the coastal waters freeze into ice called *ballicater*. Freshly caught fish freeze almost instantly in these temperatures. Seeing how this freezing kept fish tasty for months, Clarence Birdseye first conceived of frozen food in 1915.

In spite of the cold, Labrador has stark beauty. Rocky tundra covers the north, and thick forests of spruce and pine blanket the south. Several mountain ranges have alpine summits. Mount Caubvick, the highest peak east of the Canadian Rockies, dominates the Torngat Range in the far north. The largest herd of caribou in the world migrates to Labrador each spring to calve.

Underneath Labrador's rocky mountains lie zinc and one of the largest iron ore deposits in Canada. Mines near Labrador City produce more iron than any other province. Only one American state—Minnesota—produces more iron. During the summer lumberjacks fell the evergreen trees and ship the logs to mills at the island city of

Corner Brook. These mills produce the largest quantity of *newsprint* (cheap paper for newspapers) in the nation.

Acadia

The French settled the three southernmost Maritime Provinces. They called the region **Acadia.** Here they established the first French settlement in the New World, Port Royal, founded in 1604 on the Bay of Fundy in Nova Scotia.

Henry Wadsworth Longfellow's poem *Evangeline* helped make Acadia famous. It tells of the tragic conflict between British and French settlers. Trouble started in 1621 when Scottish colonists arrived and began claiming land that the French wanted. After repeated wars, the Treaty of Utrecht in 1713 awarded the area to Britain. But disputes continued. In 1755 the British decided to resolve the problem by forcing thousands of French Acadians out of their homes and by shipping them south. Some of the Acadians settled in New Orleans, where they became known as Cajuns. Others escaped expulsion, and a few later returned to Acadia. Today, their descendants continue to speak French and follow French ways.

Nova Scotia, Land of Evangeline

Nova Scotia was once the home of large French settlements, including Grand Pré, the home of Wadsworth's character Evangeline. Today, most Nova Scotians have a British heritage. Scottish settlers named the province Nova Scotia, meaning New Scotland.

Nova Scotia is a long, narrow peninsula, surrounded by ocean except for a narrow twenty-mile strip that connects it to the mainland. Residents are never far from one of the many sandy beaches of the "Ocean Province." Canso Causeway connects the peninsula to Cape Breton Island, off the northeast corner of the peninsula. Canso Strait is the deepest water ever bridged.

The Atlantic Upland, similar to the New England Upland in Maine, dominates the landscape. A few coastal lowlands permit fruit growing and dairy farming. Forests provide many of the Christmas trees sold in Canada each year. The capital,

Halifax, is the largest city, port, and industrial area in the Maritime Provinces. Nova Scotia leads the nation in its lobster and scallop catch.

New Brunswick, the Loyalist Province

French Acadians make up 40 percent of New Brunswick's population. They represent the second largest French population of any province (after Quebec). The remainder of New Brunswick's citizens are mainly of British or Loyalist ancestry. Loyalists were American colonists who lost their homes because they supported King George III during the American War for Independence. Many Loyalists escaped to New Brunswick, the only Maritime Province that shares a border with the United States.

Most of New Brunswick is coastal lowland. Farmers in the south grow potatoes, as do their neighbors in Maine. The southwestern part of the province is Atlantic Upland, a continuation of Maine's New England Upland. The Appalachian Mountains, which extend into the northern parts of New Brunswick, are mined for lead, copper, and zinc. The forests also provide lumber.

Prince Edward Island

Prince Edward Island is a tiny island in the Gulf of St. Lawrence. P.E.I., as it is affectionately called, is the smallest Canadian province, only slightly larger

The Swallowtail Lighthouse in New Brunswick shines from an island at the entrance to the Bay of Fundy.

than the state of Delaware. Its farmland supports the highest population density of any Canadian province—about sixty-two people per square mile. Yet, because the people are so spread out, this "crowded" island is mostly rural.

Because the entire island is arable lowland, it is sometimes called Canada's Million-Acre Farm. The fertile soil has a distinct red color from rusted oxides. Leading the provinces in potato production, the province has earned the nickname Spud Island. Beef and dairy cattle also enjoy good pastureland.

The quaint villages and sandy beaches make the scenery picturesque and inviting to tourists.

House of Green Gables at Cavendish, Prince Edward Island, inspired the story of Anne of Green Gables.

Many foreigners visit the Victorian-style Green Gables House, made famous by the novel *Anne of Green Gables*. Many residents opposed the construction of a bridge to the mainland, completed in

Bay of Fundy

Situated between Nova Scotia and New Brunswick, the Bay of Fundy is the most famous bay of the Atlantic Ocean. It has the highest tides in the world. The ocean water rises and falls as much as forty-four feet every twelve hours.

Tides occur twice a day all over the world. The gravitational pull of the moon causes two bulges in the oceans. The ocean facing the moon is pulled toward it, and the ocean on the opposite side of the earth bulges away from the moon. As the earth rotates each day, every place on the earth will pass both close to the moon and opposite the moon. High tides occur during the bulges and low tides between bulges.

Irregularities in the shapes of the coast cause the height of tides to vary. Because the Bay of Fundy

gradually narrows and gets shallower as it extends north, the bay creates a natural funnel. The tides rush farther inland here than anywhere else in the world. Visitors at Moncton, New Brunswick, at the north end of the bay, can watch a two-foot-high *bore* (tidal wave) flow in from many miles away.

The tides have other interesting effects along the Bay of Fundy. The tide climbs thirteen feet up over the rapids of the St. John River, making the rapids flow backwards. Visitors come from around the world to watch the St. John Reversing Falls. Another popular destination is "the Rocks." At low tide, people walk safely onto a dry beach at the foot of towering rock formations; but at high tide the ocean surrounds the rocks, which become islands. Visitors must quickly climb ladders to avoid drowning.

Low tide at the Bay of Fundy

High tide at the Bay of Fundy

1996, because of the threat to the island's quaint lifestyle.

A majority of the islanders have a Scottish heritage. In fact, over half of the last names of the islanders begin with "Mac." Weekend festivals feature Scottish traditions such as bagpipes and kilts.

SECTION REVIEW

1. What two European countries competed for control of Canada?

2. Who is Canada's major trading partner?

3. Contrast Newfoundland with the provinces of Acadia.

4. What causes tides? Where are they highest?

5. Name a major product in each Maritime Province.

💡 List all the similarities you can find between Maine and the Maritime Provinces.

THE CENTRAL PROVINCES

Canada lies far north of the equator, where the rays of the sun provide little warmth. Furthermore, huge inland areas lack the moderating effect of the oceans. As a result, most Canadian cities are on the southern strip of the nation, where the temperatures are less severe. In fact, over two-thirds of Canadians live within one hundred miles of the United States border. The building of farms, towns, and industries along a narrow band of good land is called **ribbon development.**

If you look at the climate map on page 184, you will find that there is a band of humid continental climate along the Great Lakes and the St. Lawrence River that escapes the frigid extremes farther north. Here summer temperatures rise into the eighties and farmland remains frost-free for about six months. The two biggest and most populous provinces—Quebec and Ontario—arose in this climate on the rich southern plains and valleys. Pioneers cleared mixed forests of pine, hemlock, sugar maple, and beech to plant their farms and to found their greatest cities.

Few people live in the harsh "northland." A solid mass of hard rock, called the **Canadian Shield,** covers most of eastern Canada. The Canadian Shield (or *Laurentian Plateau*) surrounds **Hudson Bay** like a giant horseshoe. The soil is thin and very poor. It appears that past glaciers scraped and wore down the mountains and hills, exposing the bedrock. The glaciers also may have dug out the thousands of lakes and marshes in the shield. Though poor in soil, the northland has been a

Evergreen forests
Deciduous forests
Mixed coniferous and deciduous forests
Grasslands
Chaparral
Tundra
Desert plants
Barren lands

229

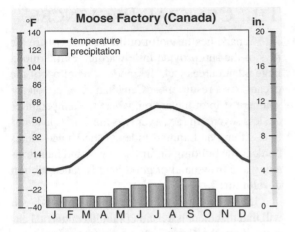

Moose Factory (Canada)

blessing to miners, who exploit rich deposits of iron, copper, nickel, gold, lead, zinc, and cobalt.

A subpolar climate dominates the Canadian Shield. Needle-leaf evergreen trees, such as spruce, fir, and pine, are about the only trees that grow, and they become increasingly stunted as you travel north. These coniferous forests, called **taiga,** cover most of the Central Provinces. Moose, beaver, and black bear live in the cool forests, and plenty of insects appear during the warm months. In the northernmost extremes, trees cannot grow at all and give way to tundra.

Quebec, the French Heartland

Canada's earliest European explorers came from France. Jacques Cartier, Samuel de Champlain, and Robert de La Salle mapped the St. Lawrence and Great Lakes regions, which they called New France.

The discovery of valuable furs of beaver, mink, otter, and muskrat lured many hardy Frenchmen during the early seventeenth century. These *coureurs de bois* (koo-RER DE BWAH, "runners of the woods") became part of Canada's folklore, much like the free-spirited woodsmen in the United States. They crisscrossed the interior lakes and frigid rivers, often carrying their canoes for miles on their backs. (The French word *portage* describes land routes used by canoe toters.)

While the French trapped furs and traded with the Huron Indians, England explored the Hudson

Bay farther north. The Hudson Bay Company, chartered in 1670, opened a thriving trade with the Algonquian Indians. As the British increased their holdings near Hudson Bay, and as the thirteen American colonies expanded, the French felt squeezed from both sides. The French and British fought sporadically until Britain won a decisive victory in the Seven Years' War (1757-63). The burning question of how to treat the French has brought trouble to Canada ever since.

Unlike America, which is often called a "melting pot" of peoples, Canada takes pride in its cultural "mosaic." The varied peoples who settled Canada have retained more of the distinct and colorful attributes of their Old World cultures. This mosaic is most apparent in Quebec, Canada's largest province. Eighty percent of the population are French speakers, who call themselves the Quebecois (KAY beh KWAH). In 1974 Quebec made French the province's sole *official language* (the language used in government records and road signs).

Cities of the St. Lawrence Valley Quebec's most productive land lies in the St. Lawrence Valley, on the southern edge of the province. The growing season is just long enough for fruits,

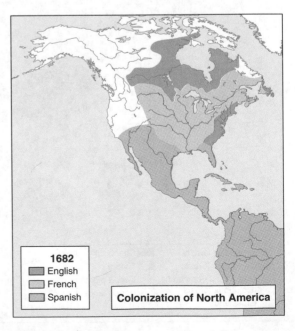

1682
English
French
Spanish
Colonization of North America

Christ Church Cathedral is an Anglican church in Montreal, Quebec, built in 1859.

vegetables, and some grains. Quebec leads the nation in dairy products, and only two dairy states in the United States surpass its butter production. Quebec also leads the nation in maple syrup. Most people in Quebec have chosen to live in this productive valley.

Quebec (Quebec City) is the capital and second largest city of the province. Founded in 1608 on a rocky bluff overlooking the St. Lawrence River, Quebec City became the cradle of French civilization in North America. Here France built the only walled city north of Mexico. By capturing this strategic fort in 1759, Great Britain effectively ended French rule in Canada. American soldiers vainly attacked the city in the winter of 1775, hoping to end British rule in North America. Today, the winding streets and beautiful old buildings give the city an old-Europe charm.

Upstream from Quebec City is **Montreal,** the largest city in the province. It sits on an island in the middle of the river. The explorer Jacques Cartier named the island Mont Réal (French for Mount Royal) after he climbed its highest point, a 770-foot-high royal "mountain." Located at the farthest navigable point on the St. Lawrence River, Montreal became the commercial center of the province. With over one million inhabitants, Montreal's city proper surpasses the population of any other in the nation. Indeed, it is the second-largest French-speaking city in the world, after Paris.

Unlike Quebec City, Montreal has a large minority of English speakers. The city has French newspapers and English newspapers, French-speaking schools and English-speaking schools, and radio and television broadcasts in both languages. To get ahead in business, many French Canadians are **bilingual** (speak two languages).

In an effort to escape the cold winters, Montreal has built a vast underground mall, with stores, restaurants, businesses, and hotels. A subway, called the Métro, carries people from one part of the underground city to the other.

Hockey is the national sport. In fact, Canadians invented hockey. During the winter, fans fill the stadium to cheer the Montreal Canadiens, a hockey team with many winning seasons. But in the summer you will find fans cheering their baseball team—the Montreal Expos.

Land's End Most of Quebec's mines are located north and west of the St. Lawrence on the Canadian Shield. Some mining, however, takes place on a peninsula east of the St. Lawrence. The Gaspé (gas PAY) Peninsula derives from a Micmac Indian word, *Gespeg,* meaning "Land's End." The mineral-rich Appalachian Mountains cover this region. It includes the highest Appalachian peak north of Maine, Mount Jacques Cartier (4,190 ft.). A portion of the Gaspé Peninsula is a protected park, with pebble beaches and sea cliffs that permit views of offshore whales.

◎ SECTION REVIEW

1. What two conditions keep temperatures cool throughout most of Canada?
2. What term describes Canada's settlement pattern?
3. What important water routes serve the two provinces of central Canada?
4. What is the Canadian Shield?
5. Which province has the largest French-speaking population?
 💡 Why are the Central Provinces more populous than the Maritime Provinces?

Saint Lawrence Seaway

The **Saint Lawrence River** is the largest Canadian river. The French explorer Jacques Cartier, who sailed up the river in 1535, called it the River of Canada. Others have called it the Mother of Canada because it conveyed Canada's early explorers, traders, and colonists. The Saint Lawrence is a vital water route for both Canada and the United States, linking the Atlantic Ocean to the Great Lakes and the interior of the continent.

Early in Canada's history, Indians and trappers brought furs from lake areas in the far north to forts on Lake Superior. The main forts were at Thunder Bay, Duluth, and Grand Portage (now a national monument in Minnesota). Large ships could sail most of the twenty-three hundred miles from Duluth to the mouth of the St. Lawrence River, but rapids and shallow water closed several stretches to ships. To make the entire seaway navigable, Canada needed to build several canals and **locks.** A lock is a section of water with gates on both sides. Ships enter one gate, the water level is changed to match the other side, and then the ships exit the other gate.

Canadians first built canals in the worst spots near Montreal. They completed the Welland Canal in 1829, using several locks to bypass Niagara Falls. The last important canal, completed in 1895 at Sault Ste. Marie, permitted ships to enter Lake Superior.

Ships on the St. Lawrence Seaway must pass through a lock at Montreal, Quebec.

During the twentieth century, the size of ships exceeded the size of the canals. So in 1954 Canada and the United States joined forces on the Saint Lawrence Seaway project. They built new canals and enlarged existing ones. By 1959 oceangoing ships could again reach industrial centers on the Great Lakes. The increased shipping of grain, wood, cars, and machinery boosted the regional economy.

The seaway is not without its limitations. Ice packs close much of the waterway during the winter. In addition, many of the newest cargo ships are too large to pass through the new locks. Despite these setbacks, the Saint Lawrence Seaway has dramatically helped both Canada and the United States.

Ontario, the Nation's Heartland

Although the province of Ontario ranks second in size, it is first in population. Canadians sometimes refer to it as the Heartland of Canada. In sharp contrast to Quebec's French heritage, Ontario's people have a strong British heritage.

Northern Ontario Few people live in Ontario's cold north. A narrow strip of swampy lowlands and coastal plains runs along the Hudson Bay. Though the Hudson Bay lowlands are not part of the Canadian Shield, they are just as stark and uninhabitable. A large portion of the lowlands is set aside as the Polar Bear Provincial Park. Some shipping takes place on Hudson Bay during the ice-free months, but little activity takes place during the long winter.

The Canadian Shield covers about half of Ontario. Though sparsely populated, this region has magnificent forests and one-quarter million lakes. The word *Ontario* comes from an Iroquois word meaning "shining waters." The lakes support large numbers of furry animals. Under the shield lie important mineral resources. Ontario leads the nation in gold and nickel mining.

Canada's Population Centers About 90 percent of Ontario's people live south of the Canadian Shield on a tiny finger of land between Lake Huron and Lake Ontario. It is the southernmost region in

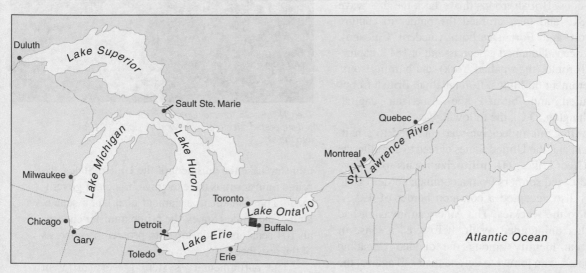

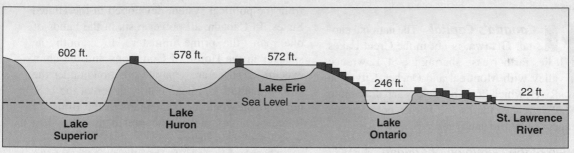

Canada. In fact, the city of Windsor lies farther south than Boston, Massachusetts. The relatively warm climate, fertile soil, and shipping advantages of the Great Lakes Plain make this region the center of Canada's industry and population.

Life here is very similar to life in the bordering U.S. dairy states. Dairy farms, orchards, vegetable gardens, and grain fields dot the countryside. Industries dominate the western shore of Lake Ontario, sometimes called the Golden Horseshoe. Its proximity to iron mines and ports enabled factories to thrive in the late nineteenth century. Ontario quickly became Canada's leading automobile manufacturer, just as Michigan became the leader in the United States. With the coming of the information age, computer industries have sprouted along the Golden Horseshoe.

One-half of Canada's twenty largest cities lie in the Great Lakes Plain. At the hub is **Toronto,** the capital of Ontario and the largest metropolitan area in the nation. Toronto is the nation's commercial center. Its stock exchange and banks handle more business than those in any other Canadian city. Five of Toronto's suburbs rank among the nation's twenty largest cities. Outside the Toronto metro area lie the busy industrial cities of Hamilton, London, and Windsor.

The Great Lakes Plain was the last place in Canada invaded by foreign troops. During the War of 1812, the United States launched two major

233

invasions. British troops drove back the first wave in 1812 and then crossed the border to capture Detroit and Fort Dearborn (modern Chicago). Americans launched a new assault in 1813, capturing Toronto (then called York) and burning some government buildings. In retaliation, British troops captured and burned the American capital, Washington, D.C., the following year.

After this indecisive war sputtered to a halt, Britain and the United States agreed to demilitarize the Great Lakes. (**Demilitarize** means to remove all forts and soldiers from a common border.) Both sides also accepted a common border of 49° N, west to the Rockies. The American invasion had another unintended result. It fostered a sense of national identity among the divided Canadian colonies, who joined to defend their soil against the Yankees.

Canada's Capital The national capital, **Ottawa,** is not in the Great Lakes Plain. It lies farther east, sharing the St. Lawrence River valley with Montreal and Quebec City. The Ottawa River, which flows by the city and drains into the St. Lawrence, marks the border between the provinces of Ontario and Quebec.

Creation of the Dominion of Canada In 1837 colonists in Upper Canada (Quebec) and Lower Canada (Ontario) rebelled against Great Britain, demanding more democracy. After putting down the rebellions, Britain combined the two colonies into one called Canada. The new Province of Canada received the right to govern its internal affairs. This union lasted until the **British North America Act** (1867) established a confederation of four provinces—Ontario, New Brunswick, Quebec, and Nova Scotia. Since then, six other provinces have joined the confederation. July 1 is celebrated in every province except Quebec as Canada Day.

The Dominion of Canada is modeled after the British parliamentary system. Canadians elect representatives to the House of Commons, a law-making body similar to the U.S. House of Representatives. The leader of the Commons becomes the prime

The CN Tower in Toronto, Ontario, is the tallest self-supported structure in the world, rising 1,821 feet into the sky.

minister. Like the president of the United States, the prime minister runs the executive branch of government. The Canadian parliament also has a senate. Unlike the United States, the prime minister chooses all 104 senators. Their job is to protect the interests of the provinces.

The parliamentary system is very different from the political system developed in the United States. In Canada, all power rests in the hands of one man—the prime minister. He is both the speaker in the House of Commons and the chief executive. These are separate positions under the U.S. Constitution. Imagine how different the U.S. government would be if members of the House of Representatives picked the president, who then selected all the senators.

Canada has voluntarily chosen to remain a member of the British Commonwealth. As a member, Canada remains loyal to the British monarch. Queen Elizabeth II of England is the queen of Canada. She serves as a ceremonial *head of state,* however, and does not interfere in Canada's internal affairs. She appoints a governor general to represent her.

Canada has a federal system of government. Ottawa shares power with the provinces. Each province has its own unicameral (one-branch)

Canada	
Capital	Ottawa
Area (sq. mi.)	3,851,790
Population	29,123,194
Natural Increase	1.2%
Life Expectancy	76
Literacy Rate	97%
Per Capita GDP	$24,400
Population Density	8

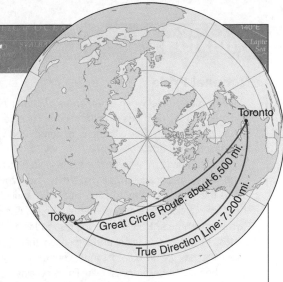

Great Circle Routes

Distances can be deceptive on maps, as you learned in Chapter 1. Pilots need a special type of projection to help them choose the fastest route between international airports.

Below is a world map with a Mercator projection. Look at the straight line between Toronto (Canada's busiest airport) and Tokyo, Japan. Does this indicate the shortest route between these two cities? No. The Mercator projection distorts distance.

Using a globe and a piece of string, you could find the shortest line between Toronto and Tokyo. It arcs north of the "straight" line on the Mercator map. If you were to extend the string all the way around the globe, you would form a great circle, cutting the globe into two equal parts. This route between Toronto and Tokyo is called a great circle route. A great circle route is always the shortest distance between two points. Airplanes usually fly great circle routes unless atmospheric conditions or political restrictions make such paths undesirable.

Because pilots cannot carry globes easily, mapmakers provide them with a variation of the azimuthal projection, discussed on page 11. These maps place one city at the center of the map and draw all lines in reference to that point. Lines of latitude appear as concentric circles around the city, and flight paths radiate in straight lines from the central airport.

Use the azimuthal projection to answer these questions.

1. Does the great circle route from Toronto to Tokyo pass through Hawaii or Alaska?

2. Do any major airports lie near the great circle route from Toronto to Tokyo?

3. If you flew a great circle route from Toronto over the North Pole, what major airport would you be heading toward?

4. What major airports would you pass over on a great circle route from Toronto to Rome?

5. What two airports are the farthest from Toronto? How far?

💡 If China closed its air space to foreign planes, what route would be fastest to Singapore?

Major Airports

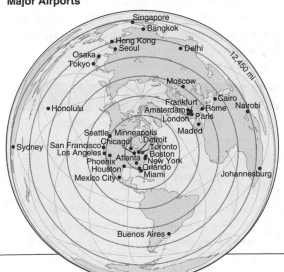

Mercator Projection

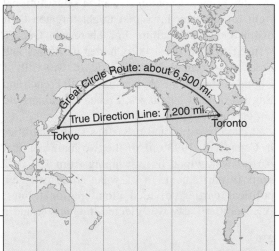

Missions

legislature and a governor called the **premier.** Like the prime minister, the premier is chosen by the legislature.

The Constitutional Crisis Canada has never suffered a civil war, but the union is extremely fragile. French Canadians want a constitutional right to veto any laws that might threaten their distinctive French culture. For this reason, Quebec refused to sign the 1982 Charter of Rights and Freedoms—Canada's equivalent of the Bill of Rights. Although the charter made both French and English official languages, French Canadians did not get the veto power.

The constitutional crisis has shaken politics in Canada. In 1993 one of the two main political parties was wiped out, dropping from 153 to 2 seats in parliament. In its wake arose two new political parties, divided along regional lines. A Separatist Party was elected in Quebec; and a Reform Party was elected by the Western Provinces, which dislike Ottawa's big government programs and special treatment of Quebec. Two years later Quebec almost passed a referendum to become a sovereign country. The vote failed, 49.4 percent to 50.6 percent, but the future of the union looks grim.

SECTION REVIEW

1. Which province has the largest population?
2. Who is the head of state in Canada?
3. Who chooses the prime minister of Canada?
4. How many provinces are in Canada's confederation?
5. To what church do most Canadians belong?
   - Compare and contrast Quebec's regionalism with the Southern states in the American union.

THE WESTERN PROVINCES

The common traits shared by the United States and Canada continue into the west. The four Western Provinces were settled much later than those in the East. In fact, vast tracts of land have so few people that they remain territories to this day. The frontier spirit lives on among western Canadians.

The 4,860-mile **Trans-Canada Highway** links the east and west. It follows the ribbon development just north of the American border. A network of railroads also crosses the continent. Only two other countries—Russia and the United States—have more rail lines than Canada. Like Alaskans, isolated people in the far north depend on airplanes for transportation.

The Prairie Provinces

The Central Plains of the United States extend northward into Canada's heartland, between the Canadian Shield and the Rocky Mountains. Temperatures in the south are comfortable in the summer. Even so, the continental heating and cooling makes the climate somewhat harsh. While summer temperatures can climb to 100°F, winter nights often drop below 0°F. Because the plains lie in the rainshadow of the Rocky Mountains, rainfall is light, with most areas receiving about fifteen inches of precipitation per year. Until man introduced steel plows, grasses covered most of the plains.

Because of the colder climate, Canada's frontier remained open long after the American frontier

Winnipeg, Manitoba, is Canada's "Gateway to the West," much like St. Louis is the gateway to the western United States.

had closed. Immigrants from Germany, Poland, Russia, and eastern Canada cautiously moved in during the late nineteenth and early twentieth centuries. Early farmers struggled each year to glean crops from the rich soil before drought, insects, and untimely frosts destroyed them. "Wait until next year" became a popular saying. During the 1930s farmers shared the misery of the Dust Bowl with America's midwestern states; Canadians call this bleak period the Dirty Thirties. Better seed and irrigation equipment have greatly improved the lot of the prairie farmer.

The Prairie Provinces have become the breadbasket of Canada. A frequent sight in these provinces are the tall grain elevators which rise up from the monotonous landscape. These "skyscrapers of the prairie" hold mounds of wheat and barley. Canada is second only to the United States as a wheat-exporting country. Canada's barley harvest is second only to Russia's, and its flax harvest is second to none.

As in the east, a few people eke out a living in the northern Canadian Shield. Scattered bands of Indians struggle to survive on isolated reserves. Lakes and streams help make the taiga and tundra beautiful in the summer, but it becomes a lonely, white wilderness in winter.

Manitoba, Gateway to the West

Two strings of lakes straddle the center of Manitoba. The larger Lake Winnipeg sits in the east, and Lakes Manitoba and Winnipegosis sit in the west. Winnipeg, the province's capital and main city, sits on the Red River, which flows into Lake Winnipeg from its source in Minnesota. The French *coureurs de bois* crossed here as they journeyed westward from the Great Lakes.

Métis, descendants of French men and Indian women, once lived off the buffalo that dotted the plains. When Irish and Scottish settlers established a farming community on the Red River in 1812, the *métis* attacked them and killed their colonial leader. After the creation of the Dominion of Canada in 1867, the *métis* rebelled again. They feared that a rush of farmers would take over their land, for which they had no title. The Red River Rebellion forced Canada to grant the local people a bill of rights in 1870 and to create Canada's fifth province.

Only the southwest portion of Manitoba, the easternmost Prairie Province, is a prairie. Its farms lead Canada in the production of flax, buckwheat, sunflowers, and peas. But not all the grassland is tilled. At Riding Mountain National Park, wolves, bison, and lynx continue to roam the meadows and scattered forests.

Most of Manitoba is covered by the unproductive Canadian Shield. The far northeast consists of swampy lowlands along the Hudson Bay, which it shares with Ontario. Churchill, the largest town in this desolate region, claims the title of "the Polar Bear Capital of the World."

Saskatchewan, Canada's Breadbasket

The other two Prairie Provinces, Saskatchewan and Alberta, were settled later than Manitoba. The *métis* were the first to settle here, moving out of Manitoba and establishing farms along the North and South Saskatchewan Rivers. When the railroads began inching west, bringing white settlers with them, the *métis* revolted again, setting up their own government. This time the Canadian government sent troops, who captured the rebel leader, Louis Riel, and hanged him. Saskatchewan did not become a province until 1905.

In the southern half of the province is the Saskatchewan Plain, a productive extension of the Interior Plains of the United States. Modern wheat farms make Saskatchewan the nation's leading wheat producer, outproducing every other province or American state. The wheat is processed at the capital, Regina, or at Saskatoon, a bit farther north. From there the wheat is transported across the nation.

A few low hills bring variety to the flat plain. The Cypress Hills, which straddle the southwest border with Alberta, have the highest point between Labrador and the Canadian Rockies. Buffalo roam the wilderness of Prince Albert National Park, a few miles north of Saskatoon.

Northern Saskatchewan is known for its wilderness and for its uranium. Taiga and tundra cover this part of the Canadian Shield, and rich deposits of uranium lie underneath the surface.

The Canadian National Railway loads wheat from a town near Edmonton, Alberta.

Canada is the world's leading producer of uranium, and over half of Canada's uranium comes from Saskatchewan.

Alberta

West of Saskatchewan is Alberta. The Great Plains extend north over the entire province, except for the southwestern mountains and the northeastern shield. Alberta leads the continent in barley production and has the most beef cattle of any province. Edmonton is the capital and agricultural center of Alberta.

The Canadian Shield enters the northeastern tip of Alberta. This region is notable for valuable oil reserves said to exceed Saudi Arabia's. Also noteworthy is Wood Buffalo National Park, established in 1922. It offers sand dunes, salt plains, boreal forests, gypsum karst formations, and river deltas at the mouth of the Peace and Athabasca Rivers. Its wild herd of three thousand wood buffalo is the largest in the world.

Calgary, the gateway to the Canadian Rockies, is Canada's second largest city (excluding

Moraine Lake is the most famous of the beautiful lakes in Banff National Park near Calgary. Banff was the first national park in Canada.

When some people think of Canada, the first thing they think of is the Royal Canadian Mounted Police, or the Mounties. Dressed in bright red jackets and mounted on horses, the Mounties symbolize the Canadian spirit.

metropolitan area). Its growth is due partly to tourism and partly to the discovery of a major petroleum field nearby. Calgary is famous for its annual rodeo, the Calgary Stampede, held in July. Skiers flock to the nearby ski resorts in the winter. The city has even hosted the Winter Olympics.

The southwestern border of Alberta follows the Continental Divide through a succession of spectacular parks in the Canadian Rockies. The southernmost national park is Waterton Lakes, which adjoins Montana's Glacier National Park. Next is Banff, and beyond that is Jasper. Another interesting place in Alberta is Head-Smashed-In Buffalo Jump near Fort MacLeod. Visitors can see where the Plains Indians stampeded buffalo herds over the cliffs to their deaths. At a campsite below the cliffs, the Indians butchered the buffalo for meat.

Beautiful British Columbia

British Columbia is the third largest and third most populous province. The only province on the Pacific Ocean, it is closely tied to America's Pacific Northwest.

The Rockies and the Pacific ranges cut the Pacific Northwest off from the rest of the continent. British ships did not sight its shores until 1778, but fur trade with coastal Indians quickly prospered. American ships arrived a decade later, exploring the Columbia River. However, the two nations could not agree on ownership. They almost went to

Sports

Calgary Stampede

Rodeos in Canada? Yes, rodeos are as popular in Canada as in the American West.

Prescott, Arizona, held the first rodeo with paid admission in 1888. Famous American rodeos include the Cheyenne Frontier Days in Wyoming, the Pendleton Round-Up in Oregon, and the National Finals Rodeo in

Calgary Stampede, Calgary, Alberta

Oklahoma City. But perhaps the biggest rodeo of all is the Calgary Stampede in Calgary, Alberta.

Guy Weadick organized the first Calgary Stampede in 1912. While not the oldest rodeo, it has been an annual event since 1919. The Calgary Stampede is most famous for its chuck wagon races.

Most rodeos have eight events, seven for cowboys and one for cowgirls. Three events require riders to sit on the backs of either untamed bucking broncos (horses) or Brahma bulls. Cowboys must hold on with only one hand while spurring the animal. These events, called roughriding, include bull riding, bronco riding, and saddled bronco riding.

The other events are timed. Cowboys compete in calf roping, steer wrestling, and steer roping, both individually and in teams. Cowgirls enjoy barrel racing—riding horses in tight curves around barrels. A few rodeos add milking contests, trick riding, fancy roping, and other events. Another favorite event is open to young people in the audience—catching a greased pig.

war in the early 1840s after American settlers began pouring into the Oregon country. Americans demanded all lands south of latitude 54°40′ N, while Britain claimed the lands north of the Columbia River. Running on the campaign slogan "Fifty-Four Forty or Fight," President Polk won the election but avoided war by accepting a compromise boundary at 49° N.

Western Cordillera   The chain of mountains that stretch from Alaska to the southern tip of South America are called the Western Cordillera. The word **cordillera** (KAWR dil-YARE uh) means "a chain of mountains." The cordillera covers most of British Columbia, except for the northeastern corner, where the Peace River valley provides some agriculture on the Great Plains.

If you look at the map of North America on page 218, you will see some important differences between the cordillera in Canada and in the United States. America's portion of the cordillera encompasses a one-thousand-mile-wide band of three mountain systems—the Rockies, the Sierra Nevada and Cascades, and the Coast Ranges. In Canada, the cordillera forms a five-hundred-mile-wide band of two systems—the Rockies and the Coast Mountains. The third U.S. system—the Coast Ranges—disappears under the ocean off Canada's west coast.

Although logging and lead mining occur in the Rockies, the biggest industry is tourism. Four national parks in British Columbia—Yoho, Kootenay, Glacier, and Mount Revelstoke—display pristine mountain beauty. Several peaks exceed ten thousand feet. The highest peak is Mount Robson (12,972 ft.).

A plateau, similar to the Columbia Plateau in Washington State, separates the Canadian Rockies from the Coast Mountains. The Coast Mountains have the highest peaks in all of Canada. Copper mines produce more copper than in any other province or state except Arizona.

Pacific Coast   The warm Japan Current gives the coast of British Columbia a marine-west-coast climate. The coast enjoys the most pleasant climate in Canada. Although winters are wet, temperatures generally stay above freezing. In the summer they

The marine-west-coast climate near Victoria, British Columbia, supports one of the world's foremost gardens: forty-nine-acre Butchart Gardens.

rarely climb above 80°F. Orchards grace the valleys, and salmon fill the rivers. Tall, dense forests of Douglas fir, red cedar, and hemlock cover the mountains. British Columbia produces more lumber and other forest products than any other province or state.

Vancouver, the largest city in British Columbia, is ideally located at the mouth of the Fraser River, which empties into the Pacific Ocean north of Puget Sound. The soil of the Fraser River valley is the most fertile in the province. The city of Vancouver began growing rapidly in 1885, after the completion of the nation's first transcontinental railroad—the CP Rail (Canadian Pacific Railway). Vancouver's deep port is the busiest in the nation. Lumber, salmon, minerals, and prairie wheat pass through Vancouver to America, Japan, and the rest of the Pacific rim. Vancouver is the third-largest and fastest-growing metropolitan area in Canada.

Off the west coast of British Columbia is an island chain that protects the Inside Passage. These islands are the tops of the Coastal Range, which continues northward from Washington's Olympic Peninsula. Because the ocean has flooded this range, it is sometimes called the **Insular Mountains.** Vancouver Island is the largest insular mountain. In fact, it is the largest island off the west coast of the American continents.

British Columbia's capital, Victoria, sits across from Vancouver on the southern edge of Vancouver Island. Victoria is one of the few Canadian cities where British Canadians have been careful to keep British traditions intact. The streets and houses appear much like those of British cities, and many of the people speak with a distinctly British accent. Evidence of British influence is everywhere, from the double-decker buses to the formal gardens. Butchart Gardens is world famous. Flowered walks and ivy-covered buildings add to Victoria's charm.

◉ SECTION REVIEW

1. Name the Prairie Provinces.

2. What is the only province on the Pacific?

3. Define *cordillera*. Which two provinces contain part of the Western Cordillera?

4. Where is Canada's mildest climate? Why is it so mild?

5. Name a product of and a national park in each Western Province.

💡 What are Canada's Coastal Mountains called after they enter the United States? Why does the name change?

Canada's Territories

Over 40 percent of Canada's land is located in its northern territories, but taken together the territories have fewer people than tiny Prince Edward Island. The obvious reason is the cold climate. Only a few Eskimo, Indians, and European Canadians brave the cold to work at reservations, trading posts, mines, and military installations.

The Eskimo and Indians are the two native peoples of Canada. Indians lived in areas south of the Arctic Circle. The Eskimo lived north of the Arctic Circle, hunting seals, walruses, and whales on the coast and caribou in the interior. Europeans called them Eskimos, or "eaters of raw meat," but they call themselves the **Inuit,** or "real men" (as opposed to all non-Eskimos).

When the Europeans arrived, they traded blankets, knives, guns, and other goods for fur and skins. The fur trade helped to establish friendly relations. The trickle of French trappers did not upset the natives, as the rush of immigrants did in America. The large country had more than enough room for everyone.

The modern Indian population totals over three hundred thousand. Ottawa has given the Indians large tracts of land as reserves, and many Indians remain on these reserves. Unfortunately, government subsidies and little opportunity for real work have encouraged alcoholism and other evils. Some Indians move to Canadian cities, but this drastic step can be a great shock to a tribal culture.

Canada's Eskimo number about twenty-five thousand. Most live in northern military and mining settlements, where they hold regular jobs. A few continue to hunt and fish, mostly with the aid of modern weapons and equipment. Rifles have replaced most harpoons, and snowmobiles are as common as dogsleds. Although the traditional Eskimo way of life is almost gone, Eskimo bone carvings and other crafts have become popular.

Yukon Territory The cold Yukon Territory, north of British Columbia and bordering Alaska, is slightly larger than California. Gold brought thousands of miners to the Klondike region in the 1890s, and mining continues to be the major activity. Today, however, lead and zinc mining have surpassed gold. The Yukon leads Canada in lead production, and it helps to make Canada the world's leading supplier of zinc.

The **Alaska Highway** (also called the Alaska-Canada Highway or Al-Can) winds through the mountains of the Yukon to connect Dawson Creek, British Columbia, with Anchorage, Alaska. The U.S. Army blazed the first rough highway as an overland route for military supplies during World War II.

The Yukon Territory has the same geographic divisions as Alaska. A narrow central valley lies along the Yukon River. Here miners established the capital, Whitehorse, the only real city between Dawson and Anchorage. The Coastal Mountains include Canada's highest mountain, Mount Logan (19,524 ft.).

Northwest Territories   This vast territory covers one-third of Canada, but only sixty thousand people live there. Nearly one-fifth of the population lives in the capital, Yellowknife. It stands beside Great Slave Lake, the deepest lake in North America. Great Bear Lake is the only lake in Canada that covers more area than the Great Slave Lake.

The **Mackenzie River,** the longest river system in North America, winds northward from the Great Slave Lake through the western part of the territory to the Arctic Ocean. It is named after Sir Alexander Mackenzie, a trapper who first explored the length of the river in 1789. Most settlements in the Northwest Territory are scattered along the Mackenzie River valley. Oil companies have found petroleum in the ice-choked Mackenzie delta.

A few forests of small evergreens grow near the Mackenzie River and the southern part of the territory, but most of the land lies above the timberline. Trapping, fishing, and the mining of lead and zinc are the major industries. The discovery of diamonds in 1991 northeast of Yellowknife has sparked the biggest mineral rush in Canada's history, even bigger than the Klondike gold rush. Over two hundred companies have staked claims around Lac de Gras.

North of the continent is one of the earth's great **archipelagos,** or island groups. Nine of these islands exceed ten thousand square miles in area. The southern islands are flat, but the northern islands are mountainous. Barbeau Peak, located on Ellesmere Island, is the highest peak in the archipelago (8,582 ft.). Most of the Arctic islands sit above the Arctic Circle. With few exceptions, these rocky, barren islands are uninhabited and covered by snow and ice throughout the year.

The Arctic islands and northern parts of the Canadian Shield have a polar or tundra climate. Winter temperatures often fall to −30°F or lower. Summer temperatures rarely climb above 50°F, and they stay above freezing for only about two months. Permafrost keeps large plants from growing, but small lichens and some other tiny plants and bushes grow in colorful profusion during summer's brief thaw.

Eskimo fishermen cut holes in the Arctic's frozen lakes.

Nunavut   On May 4, 1992, the Northwest Territories approved a plan to split the territory in April 1999 and to allow Inuit self-government. The new territory, *Nunavut* (Inuit for "our land"), includes most of the old territory, except for the westernmost Arctic islands and the Mackenzie River valley. Only twenty-eight small villages exist in this wide wilderness. The most populous town, Iqaluit (under 4,000), is the proposed capital.

Nunavut includes **Baffin Island,** the largest island in the Canadian archipelago and the fifth largest island in the world. Ten thousand glaciers creep down its sides to the sea. Iqaluit is located on Baffin Island's southernmost bay, facing the Atlantic Ocean.

SECTION REVIEW

1. Distinguish the two native peoples of Canada.
2. What industry mutually benefited the Europeans and the native people?
3. What two ranges extend through British Columbia to Alaska? Where is Canada's highest mountain?
4. Where are most settlements in the Northwest Territory?
   💡 Why did many Canadians oppose the creation of Nunavut?

REVIEW 10

Can You Define These Terms?

maritime	portage	demilitarize	Inuit
ribbon development	bilingual	premier	archipelago
taiga	lock	cordillera	

Can You Locate These Natural Features?

Newfoundland	Canadian Shield	St. Lawrence River	Mackenzie River
Grand Banks	Hudson Bay	Insular Mountains	Baffin Island
Labrador			

Can You Explain the Significance of These Places and Documents?

Acadia	Montreal	British North America Act	Vancouver
Halifax	Toronto	Trans-Canada Highway	Alaska Highway
Quebec	Ottawa	Calgary	

How Much Do You Remember?

1. Name five geographic features shared by Canada and the United States.
2. What are the four main ethnic groups of Canadians?
3. Give three major differences among the Maritime, Central, and Western Provinces.
4. Which European country first explored and claimed the land around the St. Lawrence River?
5. What kind of government does Canada have?
6. Which province fits each description?
   a. smallest in size
   b. largest in size
   c. largest in population
   d. automobile-manufacturing
   e. uranium
   f. iron
   g. potatoes
   h. flax, buckwheat, and peas
   i. butter
   j. wheat
   k. beef and oil
7. Why is each of these dates important in Canadian history: 1497, 1583, 1604, 1608, 1755, 1867, 1870, 1905, 1949, 1999? Does the United States have any similar events that are important in its history?
8. Why did fewer immigrants come to Canada than to the United States?
9. Name the two national languages of Canada.
10. Why is southern Ontario such an important region of Canada?
11. What is the largest city in Canada? the largest metropolitan area?
12. Why are Canada's territories valuable despite their cold climates?

What Do You Think?

1. How are Canadians and Americans like brothers (Prov. 17:17)?
2. What impact might Quebec's independence have on Canada? on the United States?
3. Compare and contrast the plight of the French minority in Canada to the Black and Hispanic minorities in the United States.
4. Make a list of the similarities and differences between Canada and the United States. Include geography, economy, population, cities, history, and government.

Cumulative Review

1. Explain the difference between latitude and longitude.
2. Name the seven continents and four oceans.
3. Identify a climate associated with the Tropics, the middle latitudes, and the polar regions.
4. Define primary, secondary, and tertiary industries. Give an example of each from Canada.
5. Compare and contrast the demographic statistics of Canada and the United States. Explain the differences.
6. List the eight culture regions of the world. In what region do Canada and the United States belong?

243

Mexico

West
Indies

**Middle
America**

Central
America

Guiana
Highlands

Caribbean

Brazil

**South
America**

Andes

Río
de la Plata

UNIT IV

Latin America

Chapter 11
Middle America

Chapter 12
South America

CHAPTER 11

MIDDLE AMERICA

Canada and the United States are the main English-speaking nations of the Western Hemisphere. To the south is a different cultural region we call **Latin America.** *Latin* people speak one of the languages descended from ancient Latin—Spanish, Portuguese, or French.

Latin America has two main subregions. The next chapter will examine the continent of South America, which Spain and Portugal claimed all for themselves. This chapter will cover **Middle America**—the nations and islands that lie in the "middle" between the United States and South America. Here, several empires clashed for control. Middle America has become a colorful blend of native Indians, Europeans, Africans, and Asians. Local superstition has blended with Roman Catholicism; local words have blended with Latin languages. Even the people's blood has mixed together, creating new peoples and cultures.

This mixing of peoples has not been easy. Middle America has a violent past, stretching back to the bloody wars and human sacrifices of ancient Indian empires. The European conquest of the region in the fifteenth century was no less bloody. As revolutionaries cast off their colonial powers in the nineteenth century, they tried to create prosperous democracies similar to the American republic to the north. But Middle America's reliance on guns has bred a vicious cycle of bloodshed and poverty.

For all they that take the sword shall perish with the sword. (Matt. 26:52)

Over the past century, the United States has been trying to use its influence to encourage democracy, peace, and prosperity among its southern neighbors. It wants governments that respect American property and that trade freely with American businesses.

REVOLUTION IN MEXICO

Mexico was once the crown jewel of the Spanish Empire. Its borders included Texas, California, Colorado, and the American Southwest. Even today, Mexico has the largest Spanish-speaking population in the world. It epitomizes the strengths and weaknesses of Latin American culture.

The Mesa Central, Mexico's Heartland

The vast **Mexican Plateau,** bordered by two great mountain ranges, dominates the landscape of Mexico. Most of Mexico is too dry for farming. But during the rainy season in the late spring and summer, easterly trade winds from the Caribbean Sea blow over the southern end of the Mexican Plateau, bringing adequate water for crops. This region, where the mountain ranges come together, is called the Mesa Central.

Although the Mesa Central is located in the Tropics, the high altitude keeps the temperatures relatively mild. The early Spanish explorers noticed the influence of altitude, giving different names to each **altitude zone.** They called the low tropical coasts the *tierra caliente,* or "hot lands." The best lands on the plateaus and mountain valleys they called *tierra templada,* or "temperate lands." They divided the high mountains into the *tierra fría,* or "cold lands" of the subalpine zone; the *páramo,* or the alpine zone; and the *tierra helada,* or the "frozen lands" of the permanent snow cap.

Thousands of small farms and villages cover the *bajio* (bah HEE oh), the flat western portion of the Mesa Central. Many subsistence farmers eke out a living on small plots that barely support their large families. Typical crops are corn and beans, with patches of squash and peppers.

But more and more young Mexicans are seeking work in the *bajio*'s manufacturing cities. Guadalajara, the second largest city in Mexico, stands near Lake Chapala, the nation's largest lake. León ranks among the twenty largest cities in Mexico. Those unable to find work in these cities

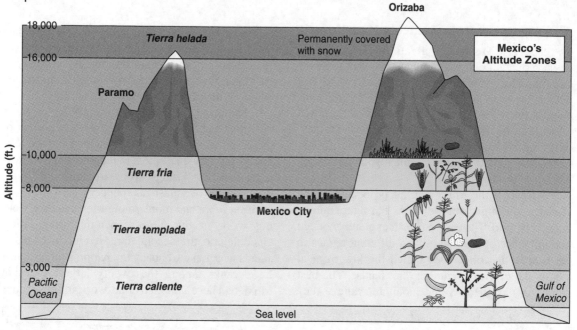

Mexico's Altitude Zones

move to the eastern part of the Mesa Central, where the capital, Mexico City, is located.

Conquest of the Aztec Capital

The Mesa Central has been the center of a series of civilizations. Ancient ruins date back to 2000 B.C. Around A.D. 500, a mysterious early people built the first city in Middle America—Teotihuacán, whose ruins still stand north of Mexico City. Tourists can climb the Temple of the Sun, which has a longer base than the great pyramids of the Egyptian pharaohs.

The **Toltec** Empire dominated the Mesa Central beginning about A.D. 900. The ruins of their capital, Tula, lie fifty miles north of Mexico City. Visitors still marvel at their temple to the rain god, Quetzalcoatl (a feathered serpent), where fifteen-foot-tall warriors still stand guard.

The **Aztecs** burned Tula around the year 1200 and founded their own capital in 1325 on an island in Lake Texcoco. The capital, Tenochtitlán, was crisscrossed by bridges and massive canals. The center of the city was a temple to the sun god, where Aztecs ritually offered human sacrifices, cutting the hearts out of their victims. At special times the priests made hundreds of sacrifices and displayed the skulls in the capital.

Then came the Spanish *conquistador* Hernando Cortés in 1519. With the aid of neighboring tribes who hated the Aztecs, Cortés conquered the mighty Aztecs with only fourteen cannon and five hundred soldiers. Today, several statues honor the last Aztec chief, Cuautémoc, who vowed never to

Early Indian Empires

▨	Maya
▨	Aztec
▨	Tarascan
▨	Toltec
▨	Inca

bow to the Spanish. No statues in all of Mexico honor Cortés, who had Cuautémoc tortured and then executed.

On the ruins of Tenochtitlán, the Spaniards built the capital of their new colony. For the next three hundred years Spanish *viceroys* ruled "New Spain" on behalf of the Spanish monarch. Catholic priests built missions and spread Roman Catholicism among the Indians. Wealthy Spanish noblemen owned most of the land and built vast ranches, called **haciendas,** which they ran like feudal manors from the Middle Ages. They forced the Indian *peónes* (serfs) to farm the land and to mine gold and copper, while they kept the profit.

Life in Mexico City **Mexico City** is the largest city in North America. Its metropolitan area, home to twenty million people, ranks among the four largest in the world. A constant stream of new people arrive each day, seeking employment. Those who cannot find housing build makeshift homes from cardboard, old tin, and other scraps. Water, sewage, and health services are inadequate in these outlying districts.

Yet, Mexicans take much pride in their city, the cultural center of the nation. It boasts Spanish colonial architecture, museums, orchestras, ballet, and drama. Although bullfighting is popular, the country's biggest spectator sport is *fútbol* (soccer).

Middle America Statistics

COUNTRY BY REGION	CAPITAL	AREA (SQ. MI.)	POPULATION	NATURAL INCREASE	LIFE EXPECTANCY	LITERACY RATE	PER CAPITA GDP	POP. DENSITY
Mexico and Central America								
Mexico	Mexico City	761,601	78,000,000	2.9%	66	74%	$2,180	102
Belize	Belmopan	8,866	156,000	1.9%	66	91%	$1,130	18
Costa Rica	San José	19,575	2,440,000	2.4%	74	93%	$5,050	125
El Salvador	San Salvador	8,260	5,390,000	3.0%	64	65%	$680	653
Guatemala	Guatemala	42,042	8,170,000	3.1%	60	50%	$1,110	194
Honduras	Tegucigalpa	43,277	4,250,000	3.5%	60	56%	$670	98
Nicaragua	Managua	50,193	3,100,000	3.9%	58	66%	$880	62
Panama	Panama	29,208	2,000,000	2.3%	71	90%	$2,110	68
West Indies								
Bahamas and Greater Antilles								
Bahamas	Nassau	5,380	226,000	2.1%	69	89%	$4,050	42
Cuba	Havana	44,218	9,780,000	0.8%	75	96%	$1,534	221
Dominican Republic	Santo Domingo	18,816	6,100,000	2.4%	63	64%	$1,160	324
Haiti	Port-au-Prince	10,714	5,400,000	1.8%	54	23%	$290	504
Jamaica	Kingston	4,232	2,290,000	1.3%	71	76%	$1,270	541
Lesser Antilles								
Antigua and Barbuda	St. John's	171	65,176	1.2%	—	90%	$5,800	381
Barbados	Bridgetown	166	256,395	0.7%	74	99%	$8,700	1,545
Dominica	Roseau	290	82,608	1.3%	77	94%	$2,100	285
Grenada	St. George's	133	94,486	2.4%	71	85%	$3,000	710
St. Kitts and Nevis	Basseterre	104	40,992	1.4%	—	98%	$3,976	394
St. Lucia	Castries	238	156,050	1.6%	66	80%	$3,000	656
St. Vincent and the Grenadines	Kingstown	150	117,580	1.4%	73	85%	$2,000	784
Trinidad and Tobago	Port of Spain	1,980	1,271,159	1.0%	68	96%	$8,000	642

Geographer's Corner

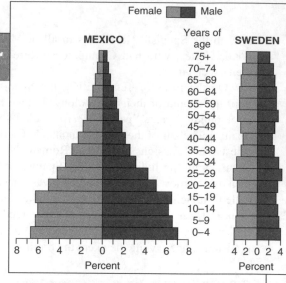

Population Pyramids

In developing countries such as Mexico, where the birthrate is high, more than half the people are under age twenty. As a result, relatively few old people live in Mexico.

Graphs called **population pyramids** vividly depict age distributions in nations. They also show the relative sizes of male and female populations. The length of each bar on the graph, from the center of the pyramid outward, indicates the percentage of the population that is male or female. For instance, male children, ages four and under, account for about 7 percent of Mexico's population; and the females at that age account for another 7 percent.

The graph for Mexico looks like a pyramid. Why is it so different from the graph for Sweden, a developed country with a low birthrate? Use the information on the population pyramids to answer these questions.

1. About how much of Mexico's population is under age ten?

2. About how much of Sweden's population is under age twenty?

3. If Sweden's population is ten million how many people are under the age twenty?

4. If Mexico's population is eighty million, how many are males from thirty to thirty-four years of age?

5. If a worker's most productive years are between ages twenty and sixty-five, which country has the largest percentage of productive workers?

💡 What would the population pyramid look like for the United States, which had a "baby boom" in the decade after U.S. soldiers returned from World War II (1945-55). What is the social impact of a bulge in the graph?

Almost every weekend, professional *fútbol* teams battle at Aztec Stadium.

At the center of Mexico City stands the largest church in the nation, the Metropolitan Church. But the most popular site among Roman Catholic pilgrims is a hill located just outside the city. There they believe the Virgin Mary appeared to an Indian peasant five hundred years ago. The brown-skinned "Virgin of Guadalupe" (GWAHD ul OOP) is the patron saint of Mexico. Every year some six million people visit the **Shrine of Our Lady of Guadalupe.** Except for the Vatican, it is the most visited site in the Catholic world.

Another part of the city, the Plaza of the Three Cultures, shows how the people equally honor both their Indian and Spanish heritages. Unlike the English colonists, the early Spaniards brought few

women and married native Indians. A unique blend of these two peoples gave birth to a third culture. Around 60 percent of Mexicans are **mestizos** (mess TEE zohs), who have a mixture of Spanish and Indian blood. The Plaza of the Three Cultures,

A matador faces an enraged bull in Mexico City.

Mexico City, the nation's leading center of culture, transportation, and business, has a modern stock exchange.

volcanoes in the world, constantly spewing sulfur. Its twin is Ixtacihuatl (17,343 ft.). Farther east rises the highest peak in Middle America, called Citlaltépetl by the Aztecs or Orizaba by the Spanish. It reaches an altitude of 18,410 feet.

The Seat of Government At the center of Mexico City is the country's main public square, known as the *Zócalo.* As is the case in most Spanish colonial cities, the square is surrounded by government buildings and a church. Here sit City Hall, the Metropolitan Church, and the National Palace, where the president and his cabinet live. Nearby is the Senate, the Chamber of Deputies, and the Supreme Court of Justice. Like Washington, D.C., the capital of Mexico is a federal district, run by the legislature.

History of Revolt Mexico's struggle to win independence from Spain began in 1810, while the Spanish king was distracted by the armies of the French emperor Napoleon. A local priest at the Mexican town of Delores called on his flock to lead a revolt. Each year on September 15, cities and villages all across Mexico begin their celebration of Independence Day with a ringing of the church bell and a recitation of the "Cry of Delores." The War of Independence ended in 1821.

From the beginning, the nation's leaders disagreed on states' rights and religious freedom. Liberals wanted a weak central government and freedom of religion, but Conservatives wanted a strong ruler and a state-supported Roman Catholic Church. The next forty years was a time of turmoil, as forty presidents rose and fell. Dissatisfied leaders often took power in a **coup** (KOO)—the sudden, illegal overthrow of the government by a military officer or government official.

Most of the early fighting took place between full-blooded Spaniards. Under the Spanish colonial system, men born in Spain, called *peninsulares,* could own estates; but any men born in the colonies, called *criollos,* were second-class citizens. The inheritors of the large estates wanted to keep everything after the revolution, but the landless believed the lands should be broken up. A

where you can see Aztec ruins, a Spanish church, and a concrete office complex, honors the modern blend of old cultures.

Although its lakes and parks are very beautiful, Mexico City has been called the worst-located city in the world. This teeming mass of humanity is packed into the broad Valley of Mexico, surrounded by mountains that trap air pollution in the valley and create a daily health hazard. No water escapes the closed valley, making the ground spongy and buildings unstable. Heavy rains bring floods and turn low areas into swamps. A chain of active volcanoes rings the southern edge of the city.

Two volcanoes tower over Mexico City. The Aztecs called the taller twin Popocatépetl (17,883 ft.), or "Smoking Mountain." Popo, as it is commonly called, is one of the most active major goal of the *criollos* was **land reform,** the "fair" distribution of land. In a region that depends on agriculture for survival, land reform became a recurring theme of revolt.

Finally, the overtaxed, landless mestizos and Indians revolted in 1910. Over one million Mexicans died during the violent revolution, which lasted until 1920. The Liberal faction won. They broke the power of the Conservatives, took over church lands, and forbade Catholic priests from entering politics. Since then, Mexico has been the only Latin American country to avoid a coup attempt.

Reforms Since the Revolution   After the revolution of 1910, the Mexican government began taking land from the wealthy and distributing it among the poor. The plots, called *ejidos,* were owned in common by the people of the village. No other nation has accomplished such a large transfer of land with relative peace.

The revolutionary constitution of 1917 established a federal government similar to that in the United States. Each of Mexico's thirty-one states has its own governor and legislature. The country also has a bicameral legislature, with a Senate and a Chamber of Deputies.

But Mexico is not a true republic. Since 1929, the Revolutionary Institutional Party (PRI) has controlled the government and used its money and power to win elections. The party chooses the candidate for president and most of the candidates for the legislature. The legislature has little real power to make laws. All power is vested in the president, who rules much as a dictator for six years. But he can serve for only one term before the party selects another candidate. Perhaps this blend of dictatorship and democracy is one reason Mexicans have tolerated the system so long.

Demands for change have increased in recent years as the PRI has become corrupt and wasteful, and its programs have failed to help the average citizen. In the late 1980s the president began encouraging more private ownership of land and other economic reforms. Economic freedoms increased demands for political freedom. PRI officials have

The Village Market and Fiesta

¡Hola! Life in the big cities of Mexico is very modern. But the rural towns and villages still retain many old ways. Villages are built around a **plaza** or public square. The Catholic church usually stands on one side, and the plaza is usually decorated with walks, flowers, and sometimes even a fountain. The plaza is the center of life in the town.

Every week on market day, the plaza bustles with activity. Some people sell their goods from covered stalls, while others sit on the pavement with their goods spread around them. Those who sit in the open may wear a *sombrero,* a wide-brimmed hat, as shade from the sun. Each person works hard during the week to have something to sell on market day, and with the money they earn they can buy corn, blankets, and other items. Indians don colorful blankets, called *ponchos,* by putting their head through a hole in the center. The different designs tell which Indian group wove them.

The goods do not have price tags, so the people barter. One party suggests a certain number of *pesos* (money) for an item, and the other makes a counteroffer to his liking. The verbal exchange continues until they agree on a price. In Mexico as in Spain, the people customarily stand right in your face, about

A mariachi band serenades diners in Mexico City

openly bought votes and cheated on ballot counts. Hoping to reduce complaints, the PRI allowed the opposing National Action Party to win a governorship for the first time in 1989. In 1997 it allowed the people to elect a non-PRI majority to run the legislature.

Vendors sell tacos and other foods in Mexico's street markets.

cakes. The fried cakes are called tortillas, unless they are fried to crispness, which makes them *tostadas*. A tortilla folded to hold other food is a *taco*, a tortilla rolled around grilled meat makes a *fajita* (fuh HEE tuh), and a tortilla stuffed and covered with chili sauce makes an *enchilada*. Cornmeal rolled up with meat and hot chili peppers makes *tamales*. When flour is substituted for cornmeal, the stuffed flour tortilla is called a *burrito*. *Frijoles* (free HOH leez), or refried beans, are the most common supplement to the tortillas. Some Mexicans like their food very hot and spicy, but this varies with different regions of Mexico.

The whole town comes alive on special celebrations called *fiestas*. On Independence Day (September 16), fireworks, special toys and decorations of tissue paper and cardboard, and *mariachi* music complete the festivities. The unusual fiesta of November 2 is the Day of the Dead (All Soul's Day), a celebration in memory of the dead. Children eat sugar skeletons and play with wind-up toy skeletons, while the men picnic in the cemetery. Nativity scenes, snow scenes, and carols celebrate the Holy Week of the Christmas season. Groups representing the Holy Family travel from home to home but are refused until they reach a prearranged home. Here, the children take turns trying to break the brightly decorated *piñata* while blindfolded. When one succeeds in breaking the papier-mâché or earthenware piñata, all of its candy, fruit, and toys spill out for the children. *Adiós.*

twelve inches away (whereas Americans like more space, about eighteen inches).

Narrow streets radiate from the plaza and are lined with homes usually made of *adobe*. Many have balconies as well as an interior courtyard called a *patio*. This inner garden of flowers and trees cannot be seen from the street, so it is a place of privacy for the family. Following the Spanish custom, everyone comes home from work in the middle of the day for the main meal. Many take a *siesta*, or nap, after the meal, preferring to eat and rest during the hottest part of the day and to work in the cool of the morning and late afternoon. Because they work in late afternoon, their evening meal is not usually served until as late as 9:30 P.M.

Most meals include *tortillas* (tawr TEE yuhz). The Mexican women grind corn into meal on a flat stone, mix it with water to make a dough, and roll it into thin

SECTION REVIEW

1. What two factors made the Mesa Central the most populous part of Mexico?

2. Name three empires that have dominated the Mesa Central.

3. What are people of mixed European and Indian ancestry called?

4. Give four reasons that Mexico City was built in a bad location.

5. How is the federal government of Mexico different from that of the United States?

💡 Why was the "unequal distribution of land" a recurring problem in Mexico, but not in the United States?

U.S. Influence in Northern Mexico

Mexico and the United States, which share a two-thousand-mile-long border, have benefited greatly from the exchange of cultures and goods. In fact, the United States is Mexico's main trading partner, and Mexico buys more American goods than any other country except Canada and Japan. Nevertheless, the relationship has been very strained at times.

Americans fought two wars against Mexico in the 1830s and 1840s before their boundary was settled. Texan settlers, who resented the laws imposed by the dictator General Santa Anna, fought the Texas War of Independence in 1835-36. The United

States fought a second war over the southern boundary of Texas. During the course of the **Mexican War** (1846-48), American armies captured the Spanish settlements in California and New Mexico, while two other armies captured the major cities of northern and central Mexico.

The United States returned in 1867, this time to chase away French troops who had landed in Mexico. The last time the United States invaded Mexico was during the Mexican revolution of 1910-20. In 1914 U.S. Marines landed at the coast to cut off arms shipments to Mexico's dictator and to help the revolutionaries. Later in 1916 General John Pershing led a U.S. army across the Texas border to track down the revolutionary leader Pancho Villa, who had been making raids in American territory. The army withdrew the following year, as the clouds of World War I turned America's attention to Europe.

Oil on the Gulf The Gulf Coastal Plain extends along the Gulf Coast from Texas all the way to the

NAFTA, Boom or Bust

In 1988 Mexico's main trading partner was the United States. But U.S.-Canadian trade was *eighty* times greater than U.S.-Mexican trade. Hoping to improve trade, Mexico asked to join a trade agreement with Canada and the United States. The North American Free Trade Agreement **(NAFTA),** signed in 1993, created the second largest free-trade zone in the world (after the European Union).

Negotiations over NAFTA stirred controversy in all three countries. Canada and the United States are industrial giants, while Mexico is an underdeveloped nation with one-twentieth the economy of the United States. Mexico had much to offer: a potentially big market, cheap workers, and inexpensive products, such as cement and farm produce. But some Americans feared "unfair" competition from Mexican companies, which had fewer regulations on working conditions and pollution. Mexican farmers feared competition from America's cheap grain.

It will take many years before we see the full impact of the NAFTA treaty. Factories in the United States have begun sending many of their parts across the border to assembly plants, called *maquiladoras* (mah KEE lah DOR ahz). Although these jobs are not fancy, they provide Mexicans with above-average wages. American workers in some low-paying jobs have lost their jobs, but employment in the trade industry has boomed.

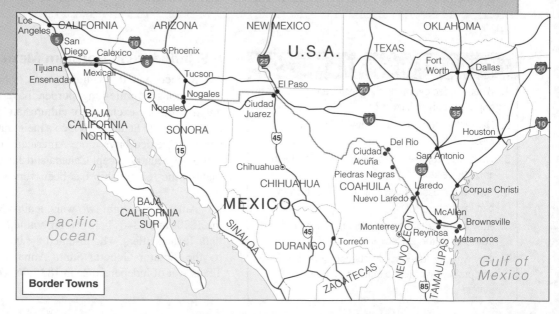

Border Towns

Yucatan Peninsula. Mexico's Gulf states have grown in importance since the discovery of reserves of natural gas and petroleum. The largest offshore oil field was discovered in the 1970s under the Bay of Campeche to the east. The sale of gas and oil to the United States is Mexico's most important source of foreign currency.

The biggest port in Mexico, **Veracruz,** lies on the Gulf Coastal Plain at the gateway to Mexico City and the Mesa Central. Goods shipped from Texas and other American Gulf States first pass through Veracruz before reaching the interior. Cortés landed his invasion force here in 1519, establishing the first Spanish settlement in Mexico. A huge American army landed at Veracruz in the Mexican War, before it marched on the capital.

Deserts, Mines, and Ranches of the Northern Plateau
Northern Mexico is very similar to the American Southwest. The *Sierra Madre,* or "Mother Range," extends down from the Rockies into Mexico. The eastern range is called the **Sierra Madre *Oriental*** ("Eastern" Mother Range). The western range is called the **Sierra Madre *Occidental*** ("Western" Mother Range). Between the ranges lies the rugged Northern Plateau.

The hot, dry winds of the subtropics, which blow across the American Southwest, also blow across northern Mexico, keeping it dry all year long. Westerlies occasionally blow off the Pacific Ocean, dropping water as they rise over the high Sierra Madre Occidental range. Except for these mountains, however, all of northern Mexico is desert and semiarid grassland. The **Chihuahuan Desert** covers large parts of the Northern Plateau. The state of Chihuahua—the largest state in Mexico—takes its name from this desert.

Irrigation permits some farming around Monterrey, Ciudad Juárez, Chihuahua, Torreón, and Saltillo. Monterrey, the most populous northern city, was the destination of American armies that invaded northern Mexico during the Mexican War. Chihuahua is a center for silver, lead, and zinc mining. Silver mines throughout Mexico make it the world's leading producer of silver. Durango also has important iron mines.

The Sierra Madre

Cattle ranching is common outside the cities. American cowboys patterned their clothing, gear, and skills after the Spanish cowboys, called *vaqueros.* The *charreria,* or Mexican rodeo, is often considered Mexico's national sport. The *charros* dress up in fine clothes as part of the ritual.

On the western edge of the Northern Plateau rises the Sierra Madre Occidental. No paved roads cross these tree-covered mountains between the U.S. border and Durango, five hundred miles south. Only one railroad, a true feat of human engineering, winds between them. The highlight of the trip is where the train crosses Copper Canyon, the Grand Canyon of Mexico. Its Basaseachic Falls is the highest in Mexico.

Gulf of California
The blue Gulf of California juts deep into the rugged, desert lands west of the Sierra Madre Occidental. Mexico's Pacific Northwest is nothing like America's Pacific Northwest. The Sonoran Desert, with its saguaro cacti, covers much of the mainland.

Four states border the Gulf of California. Two lie on the mainland, and two on the narrow peninsula of **Baja California.** The highest peak on this rugged peninsula is Devil's Peak (10,073 ft.).

Tijuana (TEE uh WAH nuh), across the border from San Diego in Southern California, is the most popular stop for American tourists visiting Mexico. Crowds haggle in the markets for good prices on silver jewelry and other souvenirs. To the east, Mexicali sits at the southern end of California's Imperial Valley. Its elevation of thirty-three feet below sea level marks the lowest point in Mexico. As in California, irrigation from the Colorado River permits large-scale agriculture. Wheat, cotton, and sesame seeds are among the most important crops.

Indians of Mexico's Southern Tropics

While the United States is most influential in the dry north, Indian culture has kept its strongest foothold in the tropical south. Southern Mexico has a rainy and a dry season, rather than the four seasons in the United States. Savannah covers the coastal areas, though it gives way to mangrove swamps in some parts. In the interior, colorful parrots, chattering monkeys, tapirs, and other exotic animals roam the lush rain forests.

Poverty of the Southern Highlands

Many Indians continue to live in the isolated valleys of the **Sierra Madre del Sur,** or "Southern" *Sierra Madre,* which runs parallel to the southern curve of Mexico's Pacific Coast. If you look at the map on page 247, you will see that the three Sierra Madre ranges join at Mexico's narrowest point, the Isthmus of Tehuantepec. From here the range continues down the coast into Central America.

The Southern Highlands is the poorest region in the country. Most American tourists see only Acapulco, "the pearl of the Pacific," where tropical beaches remind them of Hawaii. But the posh resorts stand in stark contrast to the poverty of the surrounding rural areas.

The state of Michoacán is known for the **Tarascan** Indians. Though not as famous as the Aztecs, they had a powerful empire throughout the fifteenth century. These mountain dwellers resisted Aztec attacks from the east, but they could not resist the Spanish. Many Tarascan Indians still carry on their traditional way of life. They fish, weave nets and baskets, and grow traditional Indian foods—corn, beans, squash, and chile peppers. Of the 2 percent of Mexicans who do not speak Spanish, the majority are Tarascans.

Chiapas (chee AHP uhs) is the southernmost state in Mexico. A third of the people are full-blooded Indians, few of whom speak Spanish. The state broke away from Guatemala and joined the original nineteen states of Mexico in 1824. But Chiapas has become the poorest and most unstable state in Mexico. The passage of NAFTA in 1994 sparked a rebellion among Indian farmers, who feared they could not compete with the low prices of American grain.

Although most Indians in Chiapas claim to be Roman Catholics,

Climates of Latin America

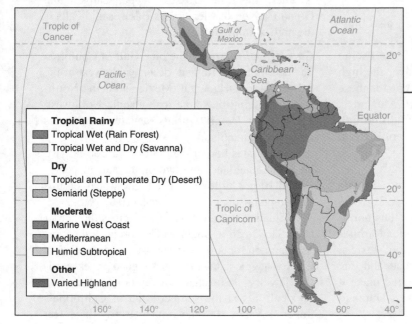

Tropic of Cancer

Gulf of Mexico

Atlantic Ocean

20°

Pacific Ocean

Caribbean Sea

Equator

20°

Tropic of Capricorn

40°

Tropical Rainy
- ■ Tropical Wet (Rain Forest)
- ▢ Tropical Wet and Dry (Savanna)

Dry
- ▢ Tropical and Temperate Dry (Desert)
- ■ Semiarid (Steppe)

Moderate
- ■ Marine West Coast
- ■ Mediterranean
- ▢ Humid Subtropical

Other
- ■ Varied Highland

160° 140° 120° 100° 80° 60° 40°

Let's Go Exploring

1. What is the most common climate on Mexico's northern border?

2. What three climates does Mexico share with most nations of Middle America?

3. What is the most common climate west of the highlands in Middle America?

4. What climates appear in South America but not in Middle America?

○ How can Mexico feed so many people even though it lacks a moderate climate?

Chichen Itza

Among the thirty major Mayan ruins that have been found in the jungles of the Yucatan, the most famous is **Chichen Itza.** This complex includes over one hundred structures, among which are a seventy-five-foot-high pyramid, the Temple of the Warriors, the tomb of the high priest, an observatory, various wells, and a ball court that is the largest in Middle America.

The high pyramid, called the Castillo (meaning "castle"), is an engineering marvel. Each side, aligned along a point on the compass, has eighteen parts for each Mayan month. Each staircase has ninety-one steps: the steps on four sides plus the top platform equal 365 days of the Mayan year. At each equinox, the shadow of a snake appears: the shadow cast by the steps forms the body and a statue provides the head.

An entrance on the north side of the Castillo leads to two oft-photographed chambers. One chamber contains an altar in the form of a reclining god, Chac Mool. The other chamber has a huge throne in the shape of a red jaguar with eyes of green jade.

The Mayas performed bloody pagan rituals. During famines, children were thrown into the seventy-five-foot-deep Well of Sacrifice to appease the rain god. Nearby stood Skull Rack and the Platforms of the Jaguars and the Eagles. Here Mayas placed human heads on stakes and sacrificed still-throbbing hearts on

Ninety-one steps ascend the pyramid El Castillo at Chichen Itza, Mexico.

bloody altars. Even at ball games, contestants were beheaded, as shown in their artwork.

Though some Mayan ruins date to before Christ, Chichen Itza does not. In fact, it did not flourish until A.D. 1000 and declined after 1224. The cause of the decline of the Mayas is a great mystery. Perhaps God, who especially hates child sacrifice, sent a judgment against the Mayas similar to the judgment that fell on Judah in the time of Jeremiah.

Because they have forsaken me . . . and have filled this place with the blood of innocents; they have built also the high places of Baal, to burn their sons with fire for burnt offerings unto Baal, which I commanded not, nor spake it, neither came it into my mind: Therefore . . . I will cause them to fall by the sword before their enemies. (Jer. 19:4-7)

they have retained many traditions from the times before Columbus. Many ancient superstitions and celebrations continue today.

Catholic villagers in Chiapas have driven over thirty thousand Protestants from their homes in recent years. Local *caciques,* "party bosses" appointed by the PRI, rule as mini-dictators. The *caciques* make their money by selling alcohol at religious festivals, but Protestants refuse to participate. Many church members are beaten, and several pastors have been murdered. Yet the gospel witness continues.

Mayas in the Yucatan The ancient Maya Indians built cities and massive pyramids in the southern jungles of Mexico, east of the Isthmus of Tehuantepec. The greatest concentration of Mayan ruins are on the **Yucatan** (YOO kuh TAN) Peninsula. This flat slab of limestone has poor soil and no rivers. The Mayas built their cities near sinkholes that drop down to subterranean streams. They considered these wells, or *cenotes,* sacred.

Although the great Mayan cities fell into decay long before the arrival of the Spanish, descendants of the Mayas remained on the peninsula. As

Spanish dominion increased, the Mayas retreated to jungle hideouts. The Indians resented Mexican rule. Twice since Mexico became independent, the Mayas have declared the Yucatan independent.

The first Spanish stronghold was built on the north shore at Mérida. It is now the largest city on the peninsula. The chief product is henequen (HEN uh kwen), a plant whose fibers sailors needed in making string, twine, and rope. Cancún, the Atlantic version of Acapulco, far surpasses Mérida in fame. Developers saw its potential as a beach resort and built the city in less than a decade, almost from scratch.

◎ SECTION REVIEW

1. What three mountain ranges dominate Mexico's geography?
2. List all the times that American soldiers have intervened in Mexican history.
3. What geographical features does northern Mexico share with the United States?
4. What countries are members of NAFTA?
5. What are the two largest tourist resorts in Mexico? What climate are they in?
 💡 Why would the northern states of Mexico support NAFTA, but the southern states oppose it?

CENTRAL AMERICA

An **isthmus,** or narrow land bridge, connects Mexico with South America. Seven small countries lie in this region, known as **Central America.** Although strung out over one thousand miles, all seven countries would fit into Texas, with enough room left for Georgia.

Central America is very similar to southern Mexico. The mountains of the western cordillera continue south along the Pacific shore. The eastern coast receives over one hundred inches of rain from trade winds blowing over the Caribbean Sea. But the Pacific Coast, which lies in the rainshadow, receives forty inches of rain. Most people live in the comfortable *tierra templada* of the highlands.

The nations of Central America are relatively poor like southern Mexico. The Pacific Ring of Fire poses the constant danger of earthquakes and volcanic eruptions. The fertile volcanic soils are the region's only important resource. Many Central Americans are subsistence farmers, growing just enough corn and vegetables to feed their families.

The Europeans introduced a new kind of farming called a **plantation economy.** Plantations require large numbers of workers to raise specialized crops, such as cotton, cacao, coffee, and bananas. These crops need many hands to tend, gather, and ship them to foreign markets. The early Spaniards forced the Indians to clear the forests and work the plantations. Later, they brought slaves from Africa. Today, the owners hire local workers.

Central America shares several other characteristics with Mexico. All the nations except Belize were Spanish colonies, and their people speak Spanish. The Roman Catholic Church is predominant. Revolutions and civil strife have racked these struggling republics.

The Central American provinces once tried to form a single, strong nation like the United States. When independence came in 1821, they joined Mexico for two years, but then they seceded and formed the United Provinces of Central America. Unfortunately, conflicts between liberals and conservatives tore the union apart after fifteen years. Occasionally, pleas to form a new union are voiced. The nations have created the Central American Common Market, but it has little power.

The United States has had a profound influence in the region. American and British warships helped to keep the region free from foreign invasion during the nineteenth century, while each nation tried to settle its political problems. At times, America has sent weapons or even troops to restore peace. Currently each nation of Central America trades more with the United States than with any other nation, including each other.

Lands of the Maya

Like southern Mexico, the four nations of northern Central America were settled long ago by

Tikal, a Mayan capital, draws tourists to Guatemala.

Indian weavers sell their goods to tourists near Tikal.

the Mayas. The **Maya** civilization dates back to about 1000 B.C. and reached its peak from A.D. 300 to 900. It crumbled about 1200.

Of all the Indian civilizations, the Mayas are the most famous because they left written records. Until recently, their hieroglyphics and number system remained a great mystery. With the help of accurate calendars on the walls of Chichen Itza and other cities, many of the inscriptions have now been deciphered. They tell of the Maya's military prowess and their sacrifices to the god Kukulcan, the Mayan version of Quetzalcoatl.

About two million descendants of the Mayas still live in the five nations of the old Mayan Empire. The jungle has reclaimed most of the Mayan cities, but the nations with Mayan ruins are working together to reclaim and protect Mayan art and architecture. They also hope to tap the region's great potential for tourism.

Guatemala, the Maya Heartland
On the Yucatan's southern border lies Guatemala, the center of Maya civilization. Tayasal, the last Mayan city, did not fall to Spanish forces until 1697. The Highland Maya lived in the mountains near the Pacific. The Lowland Maya lived on the great plain of northern Guatemala, called the Petén. The capital Tikal and most of the population

centers were in the lowlands. More than half the people of Guatemala are descendants of the Mayas, many of whom live as did their ancestors in the northern plain. The rest of the people are mestizos, called *ladinos,* who follow more Spanish traditions.

Today, Guatemala is the most populous nation in Central America. The highlands contain the largest city in Central America, **Guatemala City,** which is the capital. Plantations in the highlands produce coffee beans, while the plantations on the Pacific lowlands produce sugar cane and cotton. The highlands boast the highest mountain in Central America, Volcán Tajumulco (13,845 ft.).

After a devastating earthquake struck Guatemala in 1976, Protestant missionaries found hearts receptive to the gospel. Nearly 30 percent of the people are now Protestants, compared to an average of 6 percent in the rest of Central America. In 1991 a Guatemalan became the first Protestant elected president in Latin American history.

Guatemala was the scene of the longest-running civil war in Central America. Some 140,000 people died in thirty-five years of bloodshed before the rebels signed a formal peace accord in 1996. The conflict revolved around efforts to break up the land held by 2 percent of the population.

Belize, the Outsider
All of Belize (buh LEEZ) was once part of the Mayan Empire. In 1993 the oldest Mayan burial site was found at Cuello and dated to 1000 B.C. Lowland Maya lived in the Caribbean lowlands, a slab of limestone that extends down from the Yucatan and covers most of Belize.

Unlike the other nations of Central America, Belize was settled by the British. Forsaken by the Spanish because it lacked gold, this difficult coastland was first settled by shipwrecked British sailors in 1638. The Spanish, Caribbean pirates, and Indians tried to drive the settlers away, but they did not budge. "British Honduras" remained a colony until 1981, when it became independent and changed its name to Belize. Like Canada it remains a member of the British Commonwealth. British troops remain in the country to protect it

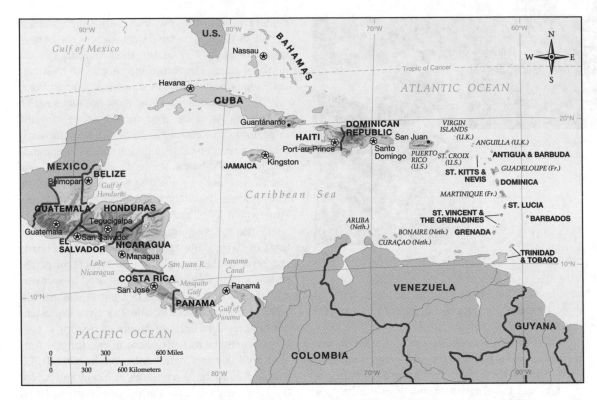

from Guatemala, which has claimed the country as its own.

In contrast to Guatemala, Belize has the lowest population in all of Central America. Only about 10 percent of the people are descended from the Maya, and another 40 percent are mestizos. The others have full or partial African ancestry. These are the descendants of slaves that the British brought to work on the plantations. Those with partial African and partial European ancestry are called **mulattoes.** A small minority are descendants of Europeans, Lebanese, Indians, and Chinese immigrants. Belize has the highest Black population in Central America.

Belize has a distinctly British heritage. About 30 percent of the people are Protestant. English-speaking tourists find Belize easy to visit. Besides Mayan ruins, they come to see the Belize Barrier Reef, the world's second longest barrier reef.

El Salvador, Land of the Volcanoes

Although El Salvador has a few Mayan ruins in the mountains, it is most famous for volcanoes. Over two dozen of them rise above the central plateau—more than in any other nation of Central America. Izalco, the Lighthouse of the Pacific, appeared in 1770, rising 7,828 feet and spitting out lava nightly for almost two hundred years.

Once the most spectacular volcano in Central America, Izalco has been relatively quiet since 1958.

El Salvador is even smaller than Belize. Indeed, it has the smallest area of any country in Central America. Yet this is the most densely populated nation on either American continent. Its capital, San Salvador, competes with Guatemala City as the largest metropolitan area in Central America.

In contrast to Belize, whose coast touches only the Caribbean Sea, El Salvador touches only the Pacific Ocean. Most people live in the central plateau between the northern mountains and the coast, where they grow coffee, the nation's major crop.

The close-knit "Fourteen Families," descendants of the original Spanish landholders, have owned most of the plantations and controlled the government of El Salvador for most of its history. Bloodshed has been common. Several **juntas** (HOON tuhs)—councils of military and civilian leaders who share power—have seized power. A civil war broke out in the 1970s over the redistribution of land. The civil war finally ended in 1992, after seventy-five thousand had died.

Honduras, the Banana Republic

The capital and largest city of Honduras, Tegucigalpa, lies in the mountains that cover most of Honduras. Most people are rural peasants, or *campesinos,* who live in one-room bamboo homes called *ranchos*. Few people live in the northeastern region of tropical rain forests and grasslands, called the Mosquito Coast, which extends down into Nicaragua. Honduras is 90 percent mestizo.

Honduras's major crop, bananas, is grown on the north Caribbean coast. In the early twentieth century, U.S. fruit companies bought large tracts of land and provided much of the nation's income. But the companies used their money to influence politics and to win special privileges. At times the U.S. government used the threat of military intervention to protect U.S. companies. Because the economy—and government—rose and fell with the price of one cash crop, Honduras earned the nickname "the banana republic." The name has been used to describe any unstable republic of Latin America.

In addition to coups, Honduras has had trouble with its neighbors. A border dispute with Nicaragua over the Mosquito Coast lasted until 1960, when the UN's World Court ruled in Honduras's favor. A border dispute with El Salvador led to war in 1969. The pretext for the four-day "Soccer War" was a controversial call at a soccer match during the World Cup. The World Court did not settle the land dispute until 1992.

Southern Crossroads of Central America

Central America has been called the Crossroads of the Americas. This is especially evident in the three southern nations

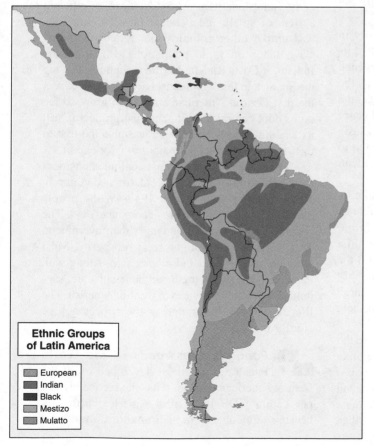

Ethnic Groups of Latin America

- European
- Indian
- Black
- Mestizo
- Mulatto

of Central America—Nicaragua, Costa Rica, and Panama. All three have both Pacific and Caribbean ports. All three are reached by a railway that links most of Central America. More importantly, all three control portions of the **Pan American Highway,** which extends from the United States to Puerto Montt, Chile, linking seventeen Latin American capitals.

Nicaragua's Bout with Communism

Because highlands cover the central region of Nicaragua, most people live in the fertile Pacific lowlands. Lake Nicaragua, the largest lake in Central America, is famed for its three volcanoes and the world's only freshwater sharks. The San Juan River flows east from the lake to the Caribbean Sea. The United States considered building a canal here in the late nineteenth century, but Nicaragua's ruler put too many restrictions in the agreement.

Although Nicaragua is the largest country in Central America, political divisions have stifled its economic potential. Americans have intervened several times. Marines landed three times in the early twentieth century, leaving only after the people elected a leader in 1933 who promised peace and friendship with the United States. But Anastasio Somoza, the general of the U.S.-trained army left to defend the republic, soon made himself president. He and his sons ruled for forty-two years.

Protests against the Somoza family sparked a civil war in the 1970s. The Communist rebels, called the Sandinista National Liberation Front, finally took over the country in 1979. For the first time ever, Communists controlled a nation on the American continent. The United States, greatly alarmed by the **Sandinistas,** began sending large amounts of money and weapons to protect Nicaragua's neighbors.

The United States also began to ship arms to the rebel **Contras,** who opposed the Communist regime. They hid out in the jungles of the Mosquito Coast along the Caribbean coast of Nicaragua and Honduras. The Sandinista leader, Daniel Ortega, grudgingly held elections in 1990. Although Ortega

lost, he retained control of the military. The main issue facing the new government was the future of land that the Sandinistas had taken from plantation owners and given to 200,000 peasant families.

Democracy in Costa Rica, Land of the Eternal Spring

While on his last voyage to the New World, Christopher Columbus named the coast south of Nicaragua's Mosquito Coast "Rich Coast" (*Costa Rica* in Spanish). The name still fits. Costa Rica has a pleasant climate that has helped give the people the highest per capita GDP in Central America. The capital, San José, which is located high in the central plateau, has springlike temperatures all year around.

The main reason for Costa Rica's wealth is its large number of private landowners. Around 95 percent of the people are direct descendants of early Spanish settlers, who developed an efficient system of small, independent farms. Costa Rica was unlike other colonies that relied on Indian slave labor on large plantations. (Most of the Indians of Costa Rica fled to the mountains, leaving the Spanish to fend for themselves.) Costa Rica was the first Central American country to grow coffee on its cool central plateau, and that product is still its leading export. Costa Rica was also the first to raise bananas, its second major crop, for export.

The country has the oldest continuous democracy in Latin America. Except for a dictator in 1917-19 and a civil war in 1948-49, the people have freely elected their president since 1889. The country has no army to endanger the government. This stability has brought great prosperity. Most families have a radio and a television. Along with Panama, it has the best education, health care, sanitation, and public services of Central America. The life expectancy is similar to the expectancy of North Americans.

Panama, Crossroads of the World

Panama is the most developed of all the Central American nations. It has the second highest per capita GDP in Central America, primarily because of income from the **Panama Canal.** Most

Panama Canal

The United States keeps separate navy fleets in the Atlantic and Pacific Oceans. During the Spanish-American War, the United States experienced great difficulty in transferring battleships from one ocean to the other. The *Oregon* sailed 12,000 miles around Cape Horn before it finally reached Cuba. Naval officers realized that a canal through Central America would cut the distance by two-thirds, to only 4,600 miles.

French engineers had attempted to build a canal across Panama in 1882, but gave up after seven years and twenty thousand deaths from tropical diseases, such as yellow fever, bubonic plague, and malaria. Before Americans tried their hand at it, they drained the mosquito-infested swamps. Construction began in earnest in 1907, with the building of the Gatun Dam that created a 163-square-mile lake. Next, came six pairs of locks. Finally, though plagued by landslides, American workers dug the Gaillard Cut, a channel across the continental divide. The S.S. *Ancon* made the first trial crossing in August 1914, and President Woodrow Wilson officially opened the $340-million canal on July 12, 1920.

The trip across Panama takes eight hours and costs about $32,000 per ship. Because of an unusual loop in the isthmus, a ship traveling from the Atlantic Ocean reaches the Pacific twenty-seven miles farther east than where it began! (Look at the map to see why.) About thirty-five ships take the fifty-mile trip each day. Why do you think the canal has benefitted every single nation in Central America?

The Panama Canal serves ships of all nations, including this vessel from Romania.

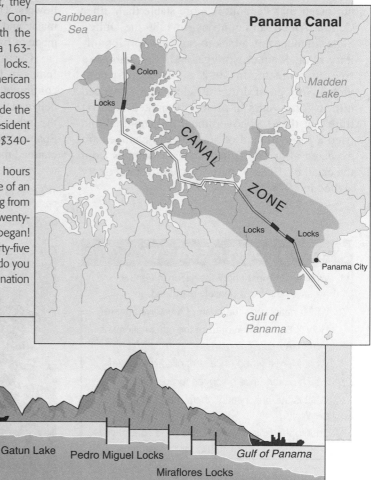

good jobs are related to operating the canal and serving the soldiers who protect it. Outside the canal zone, most people are subsistence farmers. The canal's presence has earned Panama the title Crossroads of the World.

It was here that the *conquistador* Balboa crossed the isthmus and first sighted the Pacific Ocean. After winning independence from Spain in 1821, Panama joined Colombia. Later, when Panamanians wanted to break away from Colombia, the president of the United States sent warships to help in 1903. Three months after Panama became an independent republic, the U.S. president signed a treaty to build a canal.

The presence of U.S. citizens and troops does not mean that Panama is more stable than other Central American countries. In 1989 the United States launched an attack to capture a corrupt military ruler, Manuel Noriega, and to reestablish a free government. In 1992 a Miami court convicted Noriega of drug trafficking and sentenced him to forty years in prison. It marked the first time that the U.S. government had captured and tried a foreign head of state. Major changes are expected after the United States withdraws from the canal by 1999, as part of a controversial treaty signed in 1978.

THE WEST INDIES

Between Florida and the northern coast of South America lie about one thousand islands and thousands of tiny *islets* (small, usually uninhabitable islands). These islands, the **West Indies,** together contain about twice as much land as Pennsylvania. The islands fall into three main groups: the Bahamas, the Greater Antilles, and the Lesser Antilles.

Most of the West Indies lie in the Tropics, and all have a mild climate. Rainfall averages about thirty inches annually, and temperatures remain in the 70s or 80s all year. The vegetation is lush with plenty of swaying palm trees and fragrant tropical flowers. The islanders are known for their love of music and dancing and for their colorful costumes made of light, cool cotton.

Christopher Columbus discovered the West Indies in 1492. After landing in the Bahamas, he continued to Cuba and Hispaniola. Because he believed the islands to be near India, he called them the Indies, and he called the native peoples Indians. Spanish sailors soon discovered, explored, and claimed most of the islands of the West Indies.

The fortress at San Cristóbal once guarded Spanish possessions in Old San Juan, Puerto Rico.

SECTION REVIEW

1. What is the most populous nation in Central America? the most densely populated?
2. Which nation was the heart of the Maya Empire?
3. How is Belize different from the other nations of Central America?
4. What Marxist group once controlled Nicaragua?
5. Which nation once belonged to Colombia?
6. What is the only nation where most of the people are White?

   💡 Should the United States send aid to corrupt governments just because they fight Communism?

The Bahamas

The **Bahamas,** a cluster of coral islands north of the Greater Antilles, differ from the other mountainous islands of the West Indies. Because they are formed from coral, all the islands are low, with neither mountains nor good soils.

Finding nothing of value on the islands, the Spanish did not stay. The British founded a colony in 1648, and the British navy soon became master of the whole island chain. Several thousand British Loyalists brought their slaves here after the American Revolution. As more African slaves were brought to the Bahamas, they became a large majority of the population.

As a former British colony and now a member of the British Commonwealth, the Bahamas enjoy one of the highest standards of living in the Western Hemisphere. Tax breaks have attracted international banks. In the past, fishing was the most common occupation, but tourism provides most modern jobs. In spite of its English heritage, more islanders are Baptists than Anglicans or Roman Catholics.

The Greater Antilles

In contrast to the Bahamas, the Antilles islands are the crest of an underwater mountain chain. The western "range" consists of the four largest islands, called the **Greater Antilles.** The islands are Cuba, Hispaniola, Puerto Rico, and Jamaica.

Spain used these islands as a base for exploring much of the New World. They built major ports and strongholds to protect their shipping routes. Early settlers built large sugar plantations on the islands, and later they introduced coffee, tobacco, and fruits. Most islanders on Jamaica and Hispaniola are descendants of African slaves who worked on the plantations. The people of Cuba and Puerto Rico are predominantly of Spanish descent.

Cuba With an area larger than that of Tennessee, **Cuba** is the largest and most populous island in the West Indies. It has more arable land than any other country in Central America or the West Indies. Its fertile soil and central location near Florida and Mexico have made it the most influential island in the Western Hemisphere.

Cuba is the world's third-largest producer of sugar, and sugar production is central to the economy. Most sugar cane is grown on the eastern edge of the island, which receives moist trade winds. Low central mountains block this moisture from reaching the western end. The west's wet-and-dry climate is perfect for grazing cattle and growing tobacco. Cuba's rolled cigars are world-famous.

Spain kept control of Cuba long after it lost its holdings in Central and South America. But Americans grew concerned about mistreatment of rebellious colonists in the late nineteenth century. News reports of atrocities helped to spark the **Spanish-American War** in 1898. American soldiers quickly trounced the Spanish troops in Cuba, freeing the colony except for a naval base that they kept at Guantanamo Bay. American politicians and businessmen greatly influenced the development of the new nation. However, the Cubans had trouble establishing a strong republican government. One government after another fell as dictators seized control and then were toppled.

In 1959 a Marxist rebel named **Fidel Castro** gained control of the country and established the first Communist government in the Western Hemisphere. He made the Soviet Union his major ally. Armed soldiers and secret police enforced his commands and quieted all opposition. Thousands of Cubans fled to the United States during the revolution, and others came later on flimsy rafts, hoping to cross the ninety miles to Florida before they drowned or starved.

Fidel Castro overthrew Cuba's dictator in 1959 and established his own Communist dictatorship.

Havana, Cuba

Havana, the capital of Cuba, was a thriving tourist and commercial center during the heyday of republican government. It remains the largest city in the West Indies, but it has lost its elegance. While Castro amassed a personal fortune worth over $1 billion, his people sank into worse poverty. After the Soviet Union collapsed in 1991, Cuba lost its major trade partner and source of oil. Industries closed and cities went without power for hours at a time. In the summer of 1994 Havana experienced its worst rioting since Castro took power.

Facing up to economic realities, Castro allowed small-scale private businesses, a few private markets to sell produce, and the foreign ownership of private property. But Castro failed to achieve his central goal: to reopen trade with the United States, Cuba's natural trade partner.

The Two Nations of Hispaniola Two countries occupy the island of **Hispaniola** (HIS pun YOH luh). Haiti occupies the west, and the Dominican Republic lies on the east. Although the Spanish were the first to settle this mountainous island, they gave the western third to France in 1697. France and Spain brought African slaves to both parts of the island.

Haiti The French Revolution, which engulfed France in 1791, gave slaves in the colony of Saint Domingue an opportunity to revolt against their French masters. Toussaint L'Ouverture, one of the few Black slaves who could read, used his knowledge of tactics to win victory after victory. France's effort to retake the island failed, and the republic of Haiti was declared on January 1, 1804. It was the second republic in the New World.

Sadly, Haiti has become the poorest country in the Western Hemisphere. While a French colony, Haiti was the richest colony in the Western Hemisphere, providing most of Europe's tea and sugar cane. But the revolutionaries burned the plantations and devastated the countryside. Conflicts between rival groups keep the nation in a constant state of turmoil.

A major cause of Haiti's troubles is its religion. The one characteristic that united the slaves was **voodoo,** a strange mixture of West African spirit worship, black magic, and Roman Catholicism. At the beginning of the rebellion, voodoo priests dedicated the country to Satan. Many leaders still rely on voodoo curses and bloodshed to keep power.

The people are divided into two classes: a rich minority (about 5 percent) of mulattoes and a large majority of Blacks, most of whom cannot read. Educated Haitians, particularly the mulattoes, still speak French. But the majority of the people speak a mixture of French and African words called **Creole.** "Bonjour, Blanc! (Hi, White!)" is a common greeting to foreigners seen on the street.

Haitians have suffered under a succession of violent dictators. Twice the U.S. Marines have landed on Haitian soil to restore order. The first marines came in 1915 and stayed until 1934. They returned in 1994 to restore Jean-Bertrand Aristide, a Black president who had been elected under UN supervision but who fled following a coup by Creole military officers.

Haiti's president lives in the National Palace at Port-au-Prince.

Missions

Medical Missions

For I was an hungered, and ye gave me meat: I was thirsty, and ye gave me drink: . . . naked, and ye clothed me: I was sick and ye visited me. (Matt. 25:35-36)

Do you like to help the poor and the sick? Jesus gave us an example of how to love them in Matthew 25:34-46. While some Latin American cities are very modern, others are very poor. Haiti is one of the poorest nations in the world. Only one person out of one hundred has a telephone, and one out of about three hundred has a television. Without money, the people cannot afford proper medical care: there is only one doctor per six thousand people, and the infant mortality rate is over 10 percent.

The heart of many missionaries reaches out to such needy people. They are willing to forego modern conveniences to bring help. Medical missionaries provide medical care as an opportunity to share the gospel. Christian doctors and nurses patiently work with substandard facilities. They willingly become weak to gain the weak, as Paul did, becoming susceptible to tropical diseases (I Cor. 9:22).

An American nurse ministers to tuberculosis patients at a children's hospital in Port-au-Prince, Haiti.

To the poor Haitians, even the most unfortunate American seems to live like a king. The prophet Haggai rebuked his people for living in luxury instead of building God's temple (1:4). Today, you have an opportunity to build temples in the hearts of believers (I Cor. 3:17). Are you willing to build God's house among your needy neighbors, or will you remain comfortable at home?

Dominican Republic Like Haiti, the Dominican Republic is mountainous. It boasts the highest point in the West Indies: Duarte Peak (10,417 feet). But mountains are the only characteristic the Dominican Republic shares with Haiti. The islanders enjoy a normal life expectancy, high literacy, and a better economy. In the late 1960s the Dominican Republic finally set up a stable republic with the help of U.S. soldiers.

The capital, **Santo Domingo,** is the oldest European-established city in the Western Hemisphere, founded in 1496 by the brother of Columbus. Santo Domingo vies with Havana as the largest city in the West Indies.

The African slaves mixed freely with the Spanish in the Dominican Republic, and the majority of its peoples are mulattoes. Spanish is spoken throughout the country, and Catholicism is the major religion. In addition, the people have developed a famous blend of the music and customs of Africa and Spain.

Jamaica The beautiful island of Jamaica was a Spanish colony for 150 years, until the British captured the island in 1655. But it took many years for Britain to establish complete control. The Jamaican city of Port Royal became a notorious haven for pirates.

Large numbers of African slaves once worked in Jamaica's sugar plantations, and their descendants now make up about 95 percent of the population. "Every'ting irie? (Everything all right?)" Most Jamaicans speak Jamaica Talk, a colorful English dialect that mixes many old English words and African pronunciation and grammar.

Many Caribbean countries grow sugar cane for export.

Some Jamaicans are Roman Catholic, but far more belong to Protestant denominations. Fundamentalist missionaries have had great success in recent years. But many Jamaicans follow Rastafarianism, a mix of African and Christian religion. You can spot a male Rastafarian, or "Rasta," because he does not cut his hair and ties it into tight braids, or dreadlocks.

Jamaica, which received independence from Britain in 1962, has great economic potential. Plantations still produce sugar cane. Jamaica is a center of the spice trade in the West Indies. It produces the world's finest ginger and is the leading producer of allspice (also called pimento). Large deposits of bauxite make the island the third largest supplier of aluminum ore. The parliamentary government helps the economy by promoting peace and tourism.

U.S. Commonwealth of Puerto Rico The Spanish island of **Puerto Rico** came under the control of the United States after the Spanish-American War. The people are mostly of Spanish descent. A few mestizos are the last descendants of the Arawaks, who intermarried with Whites. Puerto Rican farmers produce sugar cane and coffee, but manufacturing has become the island's chief source of income.

In 1951 Puerto Rico voted to become a **commonwealth** of the United States. Puerto Ricans are U.S. citizens with most of the privileges of other American citizens. They have their own constitution and elect a governor, but they cannot vote in presidential elections. Until recently, this drawback was balanced by their having freedom from federal taxes. An increasing number of Puerto Ricans support becoming the fifty-first state.

The Lesser Antilles

The **Lesser Antilles** are a chain of smaller islands that form the eastern boundary of the Caribbean Sea. The chain curves southward from Puerto Rico to the South American coast. Apart from tourism, fishing and farming are the main economic activities. Tropical fruits and vegetables are common crops, and some farmers also raise sugar cane, cotton, or coffee.

Lack of gold and silver made the Spanish lose interest in the Lesser Antilles, leaving them open to settlement by British, French, and Dutch colonists. The people of these islands are mostly Black descendants of early slaves. Today, most islands remain territories of the three European countries or of the United States. Eight British islands, however, gained independence between 1962 and 1983.

Leeward Islands The northern islands of the Lesser Antilles, from the Virgin Islands to Dominica, are called the **Leeward Islands.** The word *leeward* refers to an island that is sheltered from prevailing winds on the open ocean. The Leeward Islands are sheltered from many tropical storms that rip through the Windward Islands farther south and east.

Just east of Puerto Rico are the most famous Leewards—the Virgin Islands. Three major islands and about a hundred islets belong to the United States, and the rest belong to Great Britain.

Most of the remaining colonies lie southeast of the Virgin Islands. Anguilla and Montserrat are British. The Dutch control Saba, St. Eustatius, and St. Maarten. St. Martin and Guadeloupe are the main French islands. Three independent nations lie in the Leeward Islands: St. Kitts and Nevis,

The southernmost Windward nation is Grenada. It produces about three-fourths of the world's supply of nutmeg. A Cuban-backed Communist government took control of Grenada temporarily, but in 1983 the United States led a successful attack that drove out the Communists.

 Outlying Lesser Antilles The other islands of the Lesser Antilles are not part of the chain of Leeward and Windward Islands. Trinidad, nearly two thousand square miles in area, is the largest of the Lesser Antilles. Trinidad and Tobago became independent of Great Britain in 1962, making it the first independent nation in the Lesser Antilles. Barbados is the only other independent nation in the Lesser Antilles. It has by far the greatest population density in the Western Hemisphere. Yet its people vie with Trinidad and Tobago for the highest GDP in Middle America.

The famed British admiral Horatio Nelson docked ships at Nelson's Dockyard in Antigua. The three-masted ships were tipped on their sides to be cleaned and tarred.

Antigua and Barbuda, and Dominica. English is the national language of all three nations, each of which has a high literacy rate. Their economies are similar to those of the Central American nations.

   The Windward Islands The **Windward Islands** face the prevailing southeasterly winds that blow off the Atlantic Ocean. They suffer the full brunt of hurricanes. The chain runs from Martinique to Grenada. Martinique is a French territory, but the other islands are former British territories that gained independence in the 1970s. St. Lucia is the northernmost of the three nations. Most of the middle islands are owned by St. Vincent and the Grenadines.

SECTION REVIEW

1. What three island groups form the West Indies?
2. What two nations share the island of Hispaniola?
3. What two island chains form the east boundary of the Caribbean Sea?
4. What is the largest island in the West Indies? the largest island in the Lesser Antilles? the most densely populated island in the Western Hemisphere?

💡 Should the United States accept Puerto Rico as a state?

REVIEW

Can You Define These Terms?

altitude zone	land reform	*cacique*	junta
hacienda	*ejido*	isthmus	voodoo
population pyramid	plaza	plantation economy	Creole
mestizo	*maquiladoras*	mulatto	Commonwealth
coup			

Can You Locate These Natural Features?

Middle America	Baja California	Bahamas	Puerto Rico
Mexican Plateau	Sierra Madre del Sur	Greater Antilles	Lesser Antilles
Sierra Madre Oriental	Yucatan	Cuba	Leeward Islands
Sierra Madre Occidental	Central America	Hispaniola	Windward Islands
Chihuahuan Desert	West Indies	Jamaica	

Can You Explain the Significance of These People, Places, and Events?

Latin America	NAFTA	Maya	Panama Canal
Toltec	Veracruz	Guatemala City	Spanish-American War
Aztec	Tarascan	Pan-American Highway	Fidel Castro
Mexico City	Chiapas	Sandinistas	Havana
Shrine of Our Lady of Guadalupe	Chichen Itza	Contras	Santo Domingo
Mexican War			

How Much Do You Remember?

1. What are the five altitude zones common in Latin America? Which zone has the most people?
2. Compare and contrast the federal governments of Mexico and the United States.
3. Compare and contrast the hacienda and the plantation economy.
4. Name the two large peninsulas of Mexico.
5. What is the most productive and populous region of Mexico? Why?
6. What religion is prominent throughout Latin America?
7. What role has land ownership played in Latin America's political unrest?
8. Which Central American country lacks a Spanish heritage?
9. Which Middle American countries have had a Communist government?
10. Name the four islands of the Greater Antilles.
11. Name all the nations that have been occupied by U.S. troops. Why were they sent?
12. What European nation controlled the islands of the Lesser Antilles that have since become independent?

What Do You Think?

1. How does Matthew 26:52 help to explain the political turmoil in Latin America? Why have the United States and Canada been more stable?
2. Should the United States try to keep out all illegal aliens from Mexico? Why or why not?
3. Should Puerto Rico be made a state? Why or why not?
4. Should the United States have helped the Contras? Why or why not?

CHAPTER 12

SOUTH AMERICA

Though smaller than North America, South America has the same wonderful diversity of geography and cultures.

When Europeans discovered South America, it was already filled with thousands of diverse Indian tribes. Since then, the Latin culture of Europe has come to dominate the continent. Spain and Portugal signed a treaty in 1494 dividing the whole continent between them. The Treaty of Tordesillas, negotiated with the pope's help, was meant to ensure that these staunchly Roman Catholic kingdoms would win these lands for the Church.

Since winning independence in the early nineteenth century, the nations of South America have struggled to establish free, prosperous republics patterned after the United States. Unfortunately, as in Middle America, they have suffered from constant coups, wars, and revolts. South Americans have the talents and resources necessary to create thriving nations, if only they would stop looking to politicians for instant wealth. Recent events have given hope of a brighter future.

He that tilleth his land shall have plenty of bread: but he that followeth after vain persons shall have poverty enough. A faithful man shall abound with blessings: but he that maketh haste to be rich shall not be innocent. (Prov. 28:19-20)

NATIONS OF THE CARIBBEAN

Two South American nations—Colombia and Venezuela—border the Caribbean Sea and share many features with Middle America. The people are a diverse mix of descendants from native Indians, Spanish conquerors, and African slaves. More than half the people are mestizos, followed by Whites, mulattoes, Blacks, and about 1 percent Indians. Another 3 percent are *zambos* (people of mixed African and Indian descent).

Venezuela and Colombia share many geographic features with Middle America. The Western Cordillera extends into South America, where it is

South America Statistics

COUNTRY	CAPITAL	AREA (SQ. MI.)	POPULATION	NATURAL INCREASE	LIFE EXPECTANCY	LITERACY RATE	PER CAPITA GDP	POP. DENSITY
Argentina	Buenos Aires	1,068,297	35,797,536	1.2%	74	96%	$8,100	33
Bolivia	La Paz & Sucre	424,162	7,669,868	2.2%	60	83%	$2,530	18
Brazil	Brasilia	3,286,472	164,511,366	1.1%	62	83%	$6,100	50
Chile	Santiago	292,257	14,508,168	1.2%	75	95%	$8,000	50
Colombia	Bogotá	439,735	37,418,290	1.6%	73	91%	$5,300	85
Ecuador	Quito	109,483	11,690,535	1.9%	72	90%	$4,100	111
Guyana	Georgetown	83,000	706,116	0.9%	59	99%	$2,200	9
Paraguay	Asunción	157,047	5,651,634	2.6%	74	92%	$3,200	35
Peru	Lima	496,222	24,949,512	1.8%	70	89%	$3,600	50
Suriname	Paramaribo	63,037	443,446	1.8%	70	93%	$2,950	7
Uruguay	Montevideo	68,037	3,261,707	0.8%	75	97%	$7,600	47
Venezuela	Caracas	352,143	22,396,407	1.9%	73	91%	$9,300	63

known as the Andes. Although Colombia and Venezuela are located in the Tropics, altitude is the major influence on climate. Most people live in the temperate *tierra templada*.

Colonial Administration Circa 1790

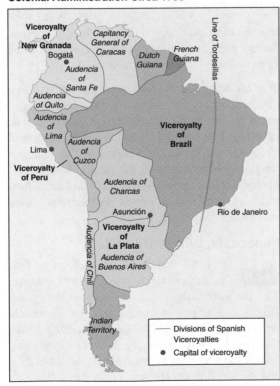

The nations of South America were once part of the elaborate colonial system that Spain and Portugal developed to govern their Latin colonies. At the top were the *viceroys,* or governors, who ruled in the name of the king. South America was divided into three separate viceroyalties. The northernmost viceroyalty, New Granada, included modern Venezuela and Colombia.

The colonial system created great resentment in the colonies. The ruling *peninsulares* from Spain treated their subjects with contempt. Their subjects included the Spanish *criollos,* or **Creoles,** born in America. The Creoles became restive and finally revolted.

The man who led the revolt was the greatest hero of Latin America, **Simon Bolívar,** "the Liberator." He was born in 1783 to a rich Creole family in Caracas, Venezuela. During a trip to Europe, he was inspired by the revolutionary fervor of the French Revolution. After a failed attempt to liberate his homeland, he fled to Haiti. Returning, he defeated the Spanish in 1819 outside the capital of New Granada (Santa Fe de Bogotá). The Battle of Boyacá liberated Colombia but not the other divisions of New Granada. Next Bolívar turned east and freed Venezuela. Finally, he turned south and liberated Ecuador. Bolívar then became the president and dictator of a united nation he called Gran (Great) Colombia. But the union broke apart a decade later.

Colombia at the Crossroads

Like Central America, Colombia is located at the crossroads of the American continents. Its one-hundred-mile-long border with Panama is South America's only tie to North America. In fact, the lowlands of Panama were once part of Colombia. Colombia also shares South America's two main geographic features—the Andes Mountains and the Amazon Basin.

Caribbean and Pacific Lowlands Colombia is unique in South America because it has coasts on both the Caribbean and the Pacific. Though the Caribbean lowlands are hot, about one-fifth of the population lives there, many working on plantations. Few people live on the swampy Pacific coast, where the average annual rainfall is four hundred inches.

The Mountainous Interior Most Colombians live in the cool valleys of the Andes Mountains. The Andes, which follow the entire west coast of South America, split into three separate ranges in Colombia and stretch northward toward the Caribbean. The western range, or Cordillera Occidental, is the lowest of the three. Next is the Cordillera Central. The easternmost range, or Cordillera Oriental, reaches into Venezuela.

The capital of Colombia, Santa Fe de Bogotá (BOH guh-TAH), lies in the Cordillera Oriental. This teeming city of five million is the cultural center of the nation. Like other Latin American cities, however, rural workers live in large slums, or *turgurios*.

The other major cities of Colombia lie along the two river valleys between Colombia's three Andes ranges. The deepest river is the Magdalena, "the lifeline of Colombia." Oceangoing ships can travel up the river far into the interior. Major oil wells operate in the Magdalena River valley. The Cauca River supports the cities of Medellín and Cali. Together with Bogotá, they form Colombia's "industrial triangle."

The Andes provide Colombia with several important products. Colombia produces one-eighth of the world's coffee on its *tierra templada*. The nation ranks tenth in world production of gold and

A statue of Simon Bolívar dominates the Caribbean port of Cartagena, Colombia.

has the only platinum mines in South America. Ninety percent of all the world's emeralds come from mines in Colombia's mountains.

The Llanos On the far side of the Andes lies a vast wilderness, one of the largest undeveloped areas in the world. These broad grassy plains, called the **Llanos** (LAH nohs), cover 60 percent of Colombia and a third of Venezuela. The *llaneros,* tough cowboys who ride the plains, are national heroes. The northernmost rivers of the Llanos flow into the Caribbean Sea, but the southern rivers flow into the Amazon River.

Venezuela, Where Oil Is King

In 1802 Venezuela became the first Spanish colony to declare independence. Like the merchants in Boston who rebelled against Britain's Stamp Act, merchants in Venezuela rebelled against Spanish laws restricting trade. Caracas (kuh RAH kus), the nation's capital, still honors the man who eventually became their liberator, Simon Bolívar. His tomb is in the city.

The War on Drugs

Colombia is famous for more than just mountain-grown coffee. Illegal drugs, especially cocaine and heroin, account for a big part of the nation's economy.

Since ancient times, farmers in the mountains of Turkey have grown opium poppies, the natural source of heroin, hashish, and all other *narcotics* (nerve-numbing drugs). Latin America began growing poppies recently to supply the growing foreign demand for heroin. While Burma remains the leading producer of opium, Colombia is quickly catching up.

Coca plants were first cultivated in the Andes, long before Columbus discovered America. The Incas chewed the leaves to reduce the effects of fatigue. Cocaine, made from coca leaves, is nature's most potent *stimulant* (nerve-stimulating drug). This hardy plant is easy to raise and yields up to four harvests in a single year. Colombia is the world leader in cocaine exports, supplying the U.S. "drug culture" that began in the 1960s.

The drug trade touches every nation on the Caribbean rim. Gangsters, called "drug lords," buy coca and opium from remote peasants, convert them into powder at remote bases, and smuggle the drugs by every possible route into the United States. Drug lords have become so rich that they almost run some countries.

The dangers of the drug trade are most obvious in Colombia, which controlled 80 percent of the world cocaine trade in the 1980s. Colombian drug lords developed sophisticated crime syndicates. They used bribes to "buy off" judges, politicians, and reporters in Colombia. When bribes did not work, the drug lords resorted to kidnapping and assassination. Assassins, called *sicarios,* worked for as little as thirty dollars. The murder rate reached fifteen times that of the United States, and homicide became the leading cause of death among adults. Medellín, the "crime capital" of the nation, experienced seven thousand murders every year.

What is the solution to the drug menace in the Caribbean? Two approaches have been tried: cutting supply (by stopping farmers and drug lords) and cutting demand (by educating and treating drug users). The United States is cooperating closely with Latin American governments. President Nixon declared a "war on drugs" in the 1970s, and President Bush later brought in the military. The U.S. military has helped to catch criminals and to find and destroy cocaine fields. Meanwhile U.S. money is helping farmers to develop alternative crops.

But after spending over $150 billion to stop the flow of drugs, the United States has been disappointed by the results. Cheap drugs are readily available on the streets of America, and demand is strong.

Some Americans have suggested the radical solution of legalizing drugs, as in the nineteenth century. They argue that once legalized, illegal drugs will lose their mystique, and government regulations can make them safer. Crime will go down because transporting and using drugs will no longer be illegal.

💡 What issues are at stake in the war on drugs? Compare the drug war to America's prohibition of alcohol in the 1920s. What does the Bible say about the role of government in regulating sinful behavior?

Cocaine is processed from coca leaves.

Coastal Mountains In Venezuela the Andes taper off into the Caribbean Sea. The people prefer to live in the mild highlands on the coastal side of the Andes. Though short compared to other mountains of the Andes, Bolívar Peak exceeds sixteen thousand feet.

Near the northwest coast of Venezuela is **Lake Maracaibo** (MAR uh KYE boh), the largest lake on the continent of South America. This shallow lake connects to the Caribbean Sea by a narrow inlet, but its water is fresh. The discovery of oil fields under the lake has made Venezuela the richest

Who Grows the Best Coffee Bean?

Coffee has become the world's most popular hot beverage, with U.S. consumers taking the lead. The ten-minute coffee break is an American ritual. But not all rituals are the same. Even the closest of friends argue over the best coffee bean.

The cultivation of the bean has a long and colorful history. According to legend, a goatherder in Ethiopia discovered coffee in the fourteenth century when his goats stayed awake all night after munching on the beans. Arab traders were the first to popularize brewed coffee. From the Arabian Peninsula, coffee plants have been transported around the world.

Coffee beans ripen on this Brazil arabica plant. After harvest, the beans are toasted at about 900°F. Toasting causes complex chemical reactions that bring out the best aromas.

Two species of coffee plants are grown on plantations. The Arabs cultivated *Coffea arabica,* exporting beans from the famous coffee port of Mocha. Arabica is now grown throughout Latin America and much of Asia. The other species is *Coffea robusta.* This robust plant thrives in the hot, rainy tropics of Africa. A robusta coffee plant produces about four pounds of beans, twice that of an arabica coffee plant.

So why doesn't everyone grow *C. robusta,* if it is so hardy and productive? The key to good coffee is

Coffee-Producing Regions

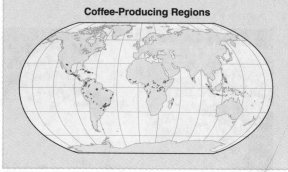

aroma, or smell. Africa's robusta plant has a cereal-like aroma. Most coffee-drinkers prefer arabica coffee. It has two popular varieties: the Milds give off a fruity aroma mixed with the smell of flowers; the Brazils have an earthy aroma with more neutral flavors.

Although Brazil leads the world in coffee production, its beans are considered inferior to those of Colombia, Brazil's main competitor. The Andean soil of Colombia is much better for flavor than the soil of Brazil. Indonesia is the third leading coffee producer. Excellent coffees are grown on the Indonesian island of Java. Coffee is sometimes even called Java.

One reason for coffee's popularity is not its aroma and flavor, but the stimulant caffeine. Unfortunately, this powerful drug is highly addictive and leads to headaches and nervousness. Mormons and conservative Muslims believe it is sinful to drink coffee. Many of the arguments against tobacco apply to coffee as well.

nation on the continent. Most of the oil is sold to the United States.

The Interior Wilderness On the far side of the Andes, Venezuela shares the Llanos with Colombia. Waters flowing off the Andes drain into the Llanos's **Orinoco** (OR uh NO koh) **River,** the

third longest river on the continent. In one strange place near the source of the Orinoco, it splits and flows into the Amazon River system. These two great river systems are the only places in the world where flesh-eating piranha hunt their prey.

The mountains that separate the Orinoco from the Amazon are called the Guiana Highlands. This

Angel Falls

With a height of 3,212 feet, **Angel Falls** is easily the highest waterfall in the world. The upper part plummets over half a mile straight down, and then it cascades down rocks for the remaining 564 feet.

The water issues through cracks in the side of the cliff, just below the top of a mesa. The springs merge as they fall, crashing on the rocks below and sending up blankets of mist and spray. The waters eventually reach the Atlantic Ocean via the Orinoco River.

Angel Falls is not named after its appearance, but after Jimmy Angel, an American pilot who spotted the falls in 1935 while flying over the remote Guiana Highlands. The region is still wild, but small planes offer air tours to view the falls.

Highest Falls

FALLS	LOCATION	HEIGHT (FEET)
Angel Falls	Venezuela	3,212
Tugela Falls	South Africa	3,110
Utigordsfossen	Norway	2,625
Mongefossen	Norway	2,539
Mtarazi	Zimbabwe	2,500
Yosemite Falls	California, USA	2,425
Esplandsfoss	Norway	2,307
North Mardalsfoss	Norway	2,149
Cuquenán Falls	Venezuela	2,000
Mardalsfossen	Norway	2,000

Angel Falls is the highest waterfall in the world.

wilderness region contains Angel Falls and Cuquenán Falls, two of the ten highest falls in the world.

12-1

◎ SECTION REVIEW

1. Why are the Andes important to the Caribbean nations?
2. What lowland wilderness do the Caribbean nations share?
3. What are the highest falls in the world?
4. On which coast are most of Colombia's ports?
5. What are the key products of each Caribbean nation?

💡 How does Colombia's geography help to explain its problems with the drug trade?

THE TOWERING ANDES

The **Andes Mountains** dwarf the mountains of North America. They form the highest mountain range in the Western Hemisphere, making them the highlight of the entire cordillera from Alaska to Chile. More than fifty peaks exceed twenty thousand feet, and at least forty of them are higher than Mount McKinley. These peaks are the highest mountains outside of Asia.

The Andes also form the longest mountain range in the world, stretching about forty-five hundred miles. These mountains divide the continent of South America. Water flowing west runs immediately into the Pacific. Water flowing east runs for many miles before it reaches the Atlantic. The Andes lie so close to the Pacific coast that in some areas the mountains slope directly down to the shore, leaving steep cliffs and jagged rocks at the water's edge. In other areas, a narrow plain lines the shore.

Because the Andean nations lie mostly in the warm and humid Tropics, the majority of the people live high in the *tierra templada*. Isolated Indians have been able to retain much of their culture. In sharp contrast to the Caribbean nations, four out of five people in Andean nations have some Indian heritage, either mestizo or full-blooded Indian. Unfortunately, the Pacific Ring of Fire threatens the mountain villages.

The hero of most Andean nations is Simon Bolívar. After liberating New Granada, he continued south to the Spanish Viceroyalty of Peru. He and his general, Antonio José de Sucre, liberated Peru in 1823. Next they marched into the third and last viceroyalty on the continent, winning independence for Bolivia.

Ecuador on the Equator

Ecuador means "equator," an apt name for this country. The equator cuts across this small Andes nation. Hot coastal lowlands cover about one-quarter of Ecuador, a much greater percentage than other Andes nations. As a result, Ecuador is a major banana and cacao exporter. The nation's largest city, Guayaquil, is a port with two million people.

The Andes cover another one-quarter of Ecuador. Chimborazo, the tallest peak, is higher than Mount McKinley. More famous is Cotopaxi (19,347 ft.), the highest active volcano in the world.

Most people live in the Andes. Quito, the capital and second largest city in the nation, lies on a high and cool plateau in the mountains. At a monument outside Quito, you can stand with one foot in the Northern Hemisphere and one foot in the Southern Hemisphere.

To the east of the Andes lies the Amazon rain forest, where few people lived until the discovery of oil in 1967. A pipeline across the Andes has turned Ecuador into the second leading oil producer in South America.

Peru, Citadel of the Inca

South of Ecuador is Peru, the largest Andes nation. The Andes ranges, which narrow to 100 miles near Quito, spread to a width of 250 miles in Peru. Eleven peaks exceed twenty thousand feet. The highest railroad in the world crosses these mountains.

The mountains are broken by the deepest canyons in the world. Colca Canyon, which slices through the west side of the Andes into the Pacific, is twice the depth of the Grand Canyon. The second deepest canyon, the Apurimac, cuts through the eastern side of the Andes. Its streams form the headwaters of the mighty Amazon River.

Peru has the highest major mines in the world. Their zinc output is fourth in the world, and their copper output is tenth. Peru's main copper mine at Cuajone is located high in the mountains near the border with Chile.

Children of the Sun A series of Indian civilizations arose along the plateaus and valleys of the Andes. The last and greatest were the **Incas,** whose name means "children of the sun." At its height, the Inca Empire controlled most of the Andes. The Incas built an amazing two-thousand-mile-long network of stone roads, some of which are still used today. The emperor's engineers dug tunnels through mountains, crossed swamps with causeways, and bridged chasms with grass suspension bridges.

Although they had no written language, the Incas invented the *quipu,* a code using strings of llama wool knotted together on a rope. The meaning of each message depended on the size and number of knots and the color of the wool. Runners relayed these knot messages to and from the capital. The emperor could send a message two hundred miles in a single day.

Cuzco was the sacred Inca capital. You can find it on the map on page 272. The streets were laid out in the shape of a puma, with the fortress Sacsahuaman forming the puma's head. When the Spanish *conquistador* **Francisco Pizarro** arrived in 1531, the empire was torn by feuds. Pizarro easily captured the Great Inca and held him for ransom,

The Galápagos Islands

South America's most famous islands are the Galápagos (guh LAH puh gus) Islands. The Spanish named them for the giant five-hundred-pound tortoises that roamed the islands. These giants provided crews with a ready source of fresh meat. The tortoises could survive in the ship's hold for a year or more without food or water.

Spanish sailors first discovered these remote islands, five hundred miles west of Ecuador, when their vessel drifted off course. The sixteen islands are dotted with volcanoes, a handful of which are still active. During the seventeenth and eighteenth centuries, English pirates buried stolen treasures on the islands. In the nineteenth century whaling ships and seal hunters visited to pick up fresh water and supplies. Their mailbox on Santa Maria Island, where outbound whalers left letters for inbound vessels, is still in use. In 1832 the islands became a part of Ecuador.

Isolation allowed many unusual animals to flourish on the islands. Although the islands straddle the equator, the cold Peru Current keeps the weather mild and dry. Antarctic animals, such as penguins and fur seals, live alongside tropical animals, such as four-foot iguanas, flamingoes, a rare flightless bird, and a mockingbird unknown elsewhere. Twenty-eight species of birds and nineteen species of reptiles are **endemic,** found nowhere else in the world. Charles Darwin used his study of Galápagos finches in 1835 to support his mistaken theory of evolution.

A land iguana sunbathes on Santa Fe Island in the Galápagos.

A Sally Lightfoot crab is one of the unusual creatures found on the shores of Floreana Island in the Galápagos.

The amazing variety of finches, each with local adaptations for highly specific needs, led Darwin to conclude that they must have evolved.

promising to let him go if the people filled a royal chamber once with gold and twice with silver. When the deed was done, however, the Spanish did not keep their end of the bargain. They killed the Inca emperor but left the city intact. Over one-quarter million Indians still live in Cuzco, making it the oldest continually inhabited city in the New World.

After plundering the gold and silver, the Spaniards forced the Incas to work in the haciendas and mines. Old racial distinctions remain strong in Peru. The upper class consists of Whites, who own the coastal plantations and hold most positions of leadership. More than 40 percent of Peruvians are mestizos, who make up the middle class. They own most farms in the Andes. Mestizos usually speak an Indian language but learn Spanish to improve their social status.

The lower classes consist of Indians descended from the Incas. Most of them speak **Quechua** (KECH wuh), the Inca language. It is the most widely spoken native language in South America. Several English words, such as *puma* and *llama*, come from Quechua. Most Indians believe they should keep their place in society. They look down on the *cholos*—Indians who learn Spanish and dress like mestizos.

Desert Coasts   The high mountain barrier of the Andes has a disastrous effect on the coastal climate of South America. Easterly winds from the Atlantic Ocean drop their moisture as they cross the Andes, leaving almost no water for the rainshadow on the western side of the Andes. The problem is compounded by the **Peru Current** (also called the Humboldt Current), which flows north from the Antarctic. The cold current keeps the air cold and dry. The Sechura Desert lies on the north coast of Peru. Irrigation is possible farther south, where swift rivers descend from the Andes.

The Modern Capital   Pizarro established his headquarters, **Lima,** on one of these swift rivers.

Machu Picchu, Last Refuge of the Incas

For centuries, the Inca stronghold of Machu Picchu remained hidden from European eyes. Legends spoke of a mountain "city in the clouds," but adventurers were baffled by the rugged terrain and tangled vegetation. Finally Hiram Bingham of Yale University set out to find Vilcabamba, the last refuge of the Incas who fled from Pizarro. The breathtaking ruins he found in 1911, just sixty miles northwest of Cuzco, continue to amaze visitors.

Machu Picchu rises precariously between two craggy peaks. Somehow Inca craftsmen carried supplies up to the five-acre plateau, 7,875 feet in the clouds. Pure white granite temples, palaces, and dwellings served about fifteen hundred people. Without mortar or iron tools, the engineers cut stones that fit together perfectly. Earthquakes of recent centuries have not been able to topple them. Dirt was hauled up from the valley to provide soil for vegetable gardens on the slopes.

No one knows what happened to the Incas who lived here. Perhaps they abandoned the stronghold when their last emperor died. Tradition says that seventy young ladies who served in the Sun Temple at Cuzco escaped to Machu Picchu and died there. An exploration after 1911 found that the last Inca refuge, Vilcabamba, was a minor outpost deep in the Amazon rain forest, not at Machu Picchu.

From the dizzying heights of Machu Picchu, cliffs drop fifteen hundred feet to the Urubamba River.

The Incas held an annual ceremony at the winter solstice to tether the sun to the hitching post (Intihuatana) at Machu Picchu, Peru.

An unknown people scraped this hummingbird figure, visible from the air, in the desert surface near Nazca, Peru.

The average rainfall at Lima is only two inches per year, but a moist cloud, called *garúa*, settles on the desert city during the winter. Lima became the nerve center of the Spanish Empire in South America. Pizarro laid the cornerstone of Lima's most famous landmark, the Cathedral. A glass case in the church allegedly contains his remains.

Lima is the capital of Peru and the largest city among the Andean nations. One-quarter of Peru's people live here. Along with beautiful Spanish architecture, it has the largest *barriadas* (BAH ree AH dahz), or slums, on the continent.

Ancient Ruins   Ruins from several ancient Indian empires dot the coastal desert. North near the modern city of Trujillo lies Chan Chan. Covering six square miles, it is all that remains of the powerful Chimu Empire of the twelfth century. Nearby, archeologists have found ruins of the earlier Moche Empire (A.D. 100-700), including burial chambers stocked with gold, silver, ceramics, and paintings.

Even more intriguing are the Nazca Lines located south of Lima. These mysterious designs, drawn by an unknown civilization in the first six centuries after Christ's birth, include condors and other animals the size of a football field. No one knew what the lines represented until pilots viewed them from the air in the twentieth century. Among the unsolved mysteries are the designs of monkeys and insects that lived, not on the Pacific, but hundreds of miles east in the Amazon forest.

La Montaña   The lowlands east of the Andes are known as *La Montaña* (mawn TAHN yuh). Water from the mountains drains into this part of the vast Amazon Basin. The city of Iquitos is Peru's largest port on the Amazon River. Oceangoing ships travel back and forth from the Atlantic, over two thousand miles away.

Few people live in La Montaña. Some isolated Indian tribes continue to resist Lima's authority. Since 1978 a Communist guerilla force, called the **Shining Path,** has been fighting the government from its bases in the jungles and mountains. The Shining Path is the most deadly rebel group in Latin American history. It has killed over twenty thousand Peruvians and destroyed $20 billion in property, including schools and hospitals.

The Shining Path uses money from coca plants to buy weapons. Coca plants are grown all along the eastern slopes of the Andes. Growing coca plants is legal, but manufacturing cocaine is not. Indians can make forty times more money by selling coca leaves than they can by selling grain.

12-2

SECTION REVIEW

1. What Andes nation lies on the equator?
2. What Indians built the biggest civilization in South America?
3. What is the oldest continuously inhabited city in the New World?
4. Explain why Peru's coast is a desert.
   💡 Why do you think Pizarro built a new capital on the coastal desert?

Landlocked Bolivia

After Bolívar freed the region known as Upper Peru, it changed its name to Bolivia in his honor. Bolivia was once a large nation. But wars with neighbors have deprived it of almost half its territory, including access to the sea. Surrounded by mountains in the west and jungles in the east, modern Bolivia is a **landlocked** nation. Its isolation has hindered the development of trade and industry.

About 60 percent of Bolivians are full-blooded Indians, who live in villages and work on subsistence farms and villages. Another 30 percent of

Camels of the Western Hemisphere

The Indians of the New World never had the advantage of large beasts of burden, such as horses, cattle, and camels, essential to the Old World. The Indians of North America had only dogs, while the peoples of the Andes domesticated four small members of the camel family, called lamoids.

The four "camels of the Andes" are the alpaca, vicuña, guanaco, and llama. Generally speaking, lamoids have long legs and necks, small heads, and large pointed ears. Unlike camels, they have no hump. The lamoids supplied the ancient Incas with wool, meat, and leather. The most useful lamoid was the large llama, which stands four feet tall at the shoulder and weighs up to three hundred pounds.

The llama is well suited for mountain life. Its lungs are used to the thin air, and its coarse and woolly hair provides plenty of warmth. It can survive on the sparse grasses and shrubs on the rocky mountain slopes. The llama can go for weeks without a drink, drawing nourishment from the food alone.

A sure-footed pack animal, the llama easily climbs the steep trails of the high mountains. It is able to travel twenty miles per day while carrying a load of up to 130 pounds. However, a llama knows its limits. When overburdened or exhausted, a llama will sit down and refuse to move. If forced to get up, it will hiss and spit foul saliva (like their camel cousins do).

Llamas occupied a special place in the Inca religion. An excavation of an ancient Inca city of Peru uncovered a large sacrifice table in the shape of a llama. Today the descendants of the Incas still find many uses for the llama. The hide is good for sandals, the hair is braided into rope, and candles are made from the fat. Even llama droppings are used as fuel.

(left) *Wild vicuñas in Peru;* (below) *Alpacas near Cuzco, Peru;* (right) *Llamas in Peru*

Bolivians are mestizos, and the rest are of European descent. They speak Spanish, while most Indians speak either Quechua or Aymara. All three are national languages.

While city life in Bolivia is very modern, rural Indians suffer from primitive conditions. Dysentery, measles, tuberculosis, and whooping cough are common because the Indians cannot travel easily to doctors in the city. Bolivians have the highest infant mortality rate and the lowest literacy rate in all of South America.

The nation's only important natural resources are in the mountains. Bolivia ranks fifth among the world's tin producers, but primitive methods hinder the mines' profitability. Farmers raise the chinchilla for fur and guinea pigs for meat.

The Altiplano Most of the nation live on the **Altiplano,** the largest of several plains that lie between the Andes ranges. The cold and windy Altiplano (or "high plain") is over two miles above sea level and covers an area almost as large as West

Virginia—twenty thousand square miles. Bolivia shares the Altiplano with Peru.

At the heart of the Altiplano, on the border between Peru and Bolivia, is **Lake Titicaca,** the second largest lake in South America. The lake helps to moderate the cold temperatures of the Altiplano, permitting agriculture. The shores of Lake Titicaca became the center of the Tiahuanaco Empire, which preceded the Incas. The Incas believed the first man and woman were created on an island in the lake.

Titicaca is the highest navigable lake in the world. Many Indian settlements dot the shore. Some Uru Indians actually live on the water itself, building islands from the totora reeds that grow

Uro Indians build reed boats and live in reed huts on manmade reed islands in Lake Titicaca.

Geographer's Corner

Cross-Sections

Topographic maps are only one way to give map-readers a three-dimensional view. Cross-section diagrams give you a side angle. By exaggerating heights, they give a good overall impression of altitudes and distance.

This diagram shows a 250-mile-wide area of the Andes that includes the Altiplano. Notice that the scale is different for altitude than it is for distance. Four miles in altitude equals about one hundred miles of horizontal distance. Without this distortion, altitude would become almost a straight line.

Use the diagram to answer these questions.

1. How tall is Mount Illampu?
2. Approximately how wide is the Altiplano?
3. What mountain rises above the city of Arequipa?
4. Which city has the lowest elevation?
5. Approximately how many feet above sea level is Puno?

💡 Where would you expect to find the most rainfall?

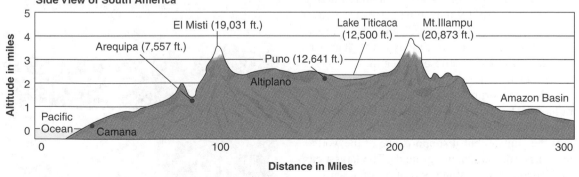

283

along the water's edge. Indians also use the versatile totora for fuel, animal food, baskets, mats, houses, and boats.

A few miles southeast of Lake Titicaca is the largest city in Bolivia, La Paz, with over one million people. Since most government offices are located in La Paz, it is considered Bolivia's capital. It is the highest capital city in the world. (The Supreme Court meets in Sucre, the official capital, located farther south in one of the many valleys of the Andes.)

The Yungas As the Andes drop in the east, ridges and valleys abound. Bolivians call this rugged region the Yungas. Farmers have transformed the fertile valleys to meet much of Bolivia's food needs. Santa Cruz and Cochabamba, in this region, are the largest cities in Bolivia after La Paz.

The Eastern Lowlands At the base of the Yungas is the Amazon Basin. These lowlands cover over half of Bolivia's land area, but few people live in the swamps and jungles.

Chile, the Shoestring Republic

The Andes Mountains form a wall three thousand miles long, dividing Chile from Argentina. Yet Chile is only one hundred miles wide. This peculiar "shoestring" of land divides into three regions: the northern desert, the Central Valley, and the southern archipelago.

The Atacama Desert The northern twelve hundred miles of Chile is covered by the **Atacama Desert,** a continuation of Peru's southern desert. The climate is so dry that some places have never recorded any rainfall. The red sands, barren rock, and salt flats give mute testimony to the Atacama's reputation as the driest desert on earth.

Limited farming is possible with irrigation in the southern portions of the Atacama, where some rains fall. In spite of the harsh conditions, a few cities manage to survive. The Peru Current may hurt the climate, but it supports one of the world's three best sardine fishing grounds. The largest city in the desert is the fishing port of Antofagasta.

People brave the scarred desert to exploit its mineral wealth. Chile has the world's only natural deposits of sodium nitrate, which is used to make explosives and fertilizer. Chile is second behind the United States in the production of molybdenum. Chile's primary resource, however, is copper. It is the world leader in copper production. Near the southern tip of Bolivia, Chuquicamata has the world's largest open pit copper mine.

The Central Valley The Aconcagua River (meaning "no water") marks the southern edge of the Atacama Desert. Three-fourths of all Chileans live south of this river in the **Central Valley.** It extends six hundred miles from Valparaíso to Puerto Montt in the south.

The Central Valley is similar to California's lush Central Valley. Both have a mediterranean climate: westerlies bring winter rains from the Pacific Ocean. Mineral deposits in both valleys have attracted miners: southeast of Santiago is the world's largest underground copper mine, El Teniente. East of the valleys are high mountains that provide ski resorts and spectacular scenery.

Chile's cold mountain valleys are unsuitable for large populations. Unlike other Andean nations, which have large Indian populations, most of Chile's population are Europeans or mestizos, who live on the coastal lowlands. One-third of the nation lives in the capital, Santiago, a modern city of over 4.5 million people.

The Atacama Desert, often called the driest desert in the world, covers northern Chile and extends into Peru as far as Paracas National Reserve.

Chile has been one of the most successful nations in South America, both economically and militarily. Chile's victory against Peru and Bolivia in the War of the Pacific (1879-83) won it possession of the mineral-rich Atacama Desert. Wealth from nitrates and copper has created a small but growing middle class in the Central Valley.

The poorer classes voted for a Marxist president in 1970, but his efforts to redistribute land ruined the economy and sparked a coup in 1973. General **Augusto Pinochet** took power and ruled with an iron hand for nearly two decades. While Pinochet relied on secret police to keep political power, he also introduced the first free-market reforms in South America. His policies turned Chile into an economic dynamo. In 1989 Pinochet allowed the people to vote on whether to continue his military dictatorship, but they chose democracy instead.

The Archipelago A rugged archipelago stretches one thousand miles to the southern tip of South America. The archipelago includes some three hundred islands.

Most of Chile's full-blooded Indians live in this region. The fierce Araucanian Indians resisted Spanish and Chilean armies for centuries, until they were defeated in 1883. Now the Indians farm or raise sheep or cattle on reservations.

Chile's archipelago is similar to Alaska's Inside Passage. Both have a mild and wet marine-west-coast climate. Forests cover the mountains and islands, but the trees are deciduous, not

Santiago, Chile

coniferous. Glaciers have carved deep gorges, and the ocean has flooded them to form fjords. National parks protect spectacular spots, such as pink granite pinnacles called the Torres (Towers) del Paine. A park that protects one hundred miles of fjord country was named for Bernardo O'Higgins, Chile's first president, who freed the slaves.

Below the southern tip of the continental land mass is the perilous **Strait of Magellan.** The first fleet to *circumnavigate* (journey around) the world, commanded by Ferdinand Magellan, passed through this strait. Until the construction of the Panama Canal, it was the main shipping route between the Atlantic and Pacific Oceans. Punta Arenas, a city of 120,000 on the strait, is the southernmost city in the world.

South of the Strait of Magellan is the large island of **Tierra del Fuego** meaning "Land of the Fire." Early explorers called it this because they saw many Indian campfires flickering near the shore. Oil rigs now dot the landscape, giving Chile precious petroleum.

A string of islands continues south from Tierra del Fuego toward Antarctica. The southernmost islet is Cape Horn. Nearby is Puerto Williams, the southernmost settlement (not city) in the world. The six-hundred-mile-wide **Drake Passage** separates Cape Horn from the frozen continent of Antarctica. It was named after Sir Francis Drake, the first Englishman to "round the Horn" and circumnavigate the earth.

The Towers of Paine pierce the sky at Torres del Paine National Park, Chile.

12-3

◎ SECTION REVIEW

1. How has being landlocked hurt Bolivia?
2. What nation has two capitals?
3. Describe two unusual features of Lake Titicaca.
4. Name the three regions of Chile.
5. What dictator helped to bring prosperity to Chile?
💡 Why do you think Chile has offered to help Bolivia by giving it access to the sea?

Silos hold soybeans for processing in Argentina.

THE RÍO DE LA PLATA

As you saw in Chile, the southern half of South America is quite different from the tropical north. The climate is colder in the mountains and more temperate in the lowlands. Few pure-blooded Indians survived the Spanish conquest.

The center of Spanish settlement in the east was the **Río de la Plata,** the widest **estuary,** or ocean inlet, on the Atlantic coast. The mighty Paraná and Uruguay Rivers flow into the Río de la Plata. These navigable rivers are the life blood of three nations—Argentina, Paraguay, and Uruguay.

The southern half of South America, including Chile and Bolivia, was once ruled by the Viceroyalty of La Plata. The great liberator of these lands was **José de San Martín.** After winning Argentina's independence from Spain in 1813, he led his army over the Andes into Chile and surprised the Spanish garrison there. After this success, San Martín sailed to Lima and helped Bolívar free Bolivia.

Argentina, the Spanish Giant

More than one million square miles in area, Argentina is the eighth largest country in the world. Although less populous than Mexico, Argentina has the largest number of Spanish speakers in South America. Almost all Argentines are of European descent (85 percent). Half are descended from Italian colonists, and a third from Spanish. Mestizos make up the remaining 15 percent of the population.

Argentina has the potential to become a leader in world affairs, but political strife has devastated the country from its very beginning. For fifty years after independence, merchants fought ranchers for control of the government. Opponents even resorted to murder and assassination.

Argentina enjoyed a brief "Golden Age" between 1880 and 1914, when European immigrants poured into the country from Italy, Spain, Austria, Britain, France, Germany, Portugal, Russia, and Switzerland. After the Great Depression of the 1930s, however, Argentina was plagued by a series of juntas. The most famous "strongman," or *caudillo,* was **Juan Perón** (1946-55). Perón and his beautiful wife, Evita, promised to help the poor workers, but they left the country in debt and economic ruin. Nevertheless, the Peronista Party remains a strong force in the country.

The Pampas Argentina's low plains around the Río de la Plata are called the **Pampas.** Most of the nation's people, industry, and agriculture are here. The plains extend south and west across central Argentina.

The Pampas are similar to the Great Plains in the American West. A semiarid climate supports vast grasslands. The soil, among the most fertile in the world, is ideal for alfalfa, wheat, and corn. In fact, Argentina exports more corn than the United States. Cattle and sheep, which graze on huge ranches called *estancias,* provide meat, hides, and wool for industries in the city.

Half of the people of the Pampas live in **Buenos Aires,** the nation's capital. It is the second

Land Use of Latin America

Commercial Farming
- Mixed Commercial Farming
- Crop Farming
- Fruit, Truck Farming, and Specialized Horticulture
- Plantation Farming
- Mediterranean Farming

Subsistence Farming

Shifting Agriculture

Nonfarming
- Manufacturing and Trade
- Ranching
- Forestry
- Limited Activity

- Gold
- Silver
- Iron
- Aluminum Ore (Bauxite)
- Chromium
- Copper
- Manganese
- Zinc
- Petroleum

Let's Go Exploring

1. What types of land use occur in both Central and South America?
2. Where does mediterranean farming occur?
3. What nation has the largest area of crop farming?
4. What is the most common type of land use in the Amazon Basin?
- Which nation has the greatest variety of land use?

The Andes Mountain system reaches its highest peaks in Argentina. Here are nine of the Western Hemisphere's ten highest peaks. The father of them all is **Aconcagua,** at 22,834 feet. Only a half dozen roads cross this rugged chain along the two-thousand-mile-long border with Chile.

San Martín mustered his army at Mendoza before leading them over the Andes into Chile. His history-making route to Santiago went through a pass called Uspallata Pass, or La Cumbre, south of Aconcagua. At the top of the pass stands the massive statue *Christ of the Andes.* Chile and Argentina fought over their border for many years before they finally reached a settlement in 1902. They built the statue

largest city on the continent. Buenos Aires is ideally located near the mouth of the Paraná River, on the Río de la Plata. The humid subtropical climate provides much more rain than the semiarid areas in the western and southern Pampas. Winter temperatures rarely drop below freezing, even in July, the coldest month in the Southern Hemisphere.

Buenos Aires is the main industrial center of Argentina. Industries process primary products from the Pampas, including meat and leather. The nation has two other industrial cities. Rosario, also on the Río de la Plata, is known for oil refineries. Córdoba, where the Pampas meet the Andes, manufactures automobiles and railroad cars.

The Andes Border   West of the Pampas lie the Andes. Steady rainfall on the eastern valleys and slopes supports several cities, including Mendoza, Salta, and San Miguel de Tucumán. But most of the Andes are remote and sparsely populated.

Christ of the Andes *marks the once-disputed border of Argentina and Chile.*

in honor of their pledge before Christ to maintain peace. The monument is similar to the Peace Garden on the border between the United States and Canada.

Patagonia   South of the Pampas is a high plateau called **Patagonia.** It rises in steplike cliffs toward the Andes Mountains. Scenic hills and canyons resemble America's Great Basin, complete with a petrified forest. Temperatures are similar to Canada's cold Maritime Provinces.

The European explorers named the region Patagonia, or "Big Feet," after the Indians, who stuffed their oversized boots with grass for insulation from the cold. Today, the Indians are gone, and most of the scattered settlers live in small coastal villages. A few inland residents raise sheep on the sparse grasses and shrubs. Their ranches are built in the canyons to protect them from the constant winds.

Northern Argentina   North of the Pampas, Argentina has two regions: Mesopotamia in the northeast and the Gran Chaco in the northwest.

Mesopotamia is named after the region of the Middle East that lies between two rivers. The western edge of Mesopotamia is the Paraná River; the eastern edge is the Uruguay River, at Argentina's border with Uruguay and Brazil. The climate is hot and humid.

West of the Paraná River is the **Gran Chaco.** Like the Pampas, it is flat and dry, but this plain is covered by shrubs and forest rather than grass. Part of the Gran Chaco, between Rosario and Tucumán, is desert. The rhea, or South American ostrich, lives on the plains. The main human occupation is harvesting *quebracho* ("ax-breaker"), a hardwood tree used for rail ties and telephone poles. Tannin from the quebracho is used in tanning leather.

Uruguay, a Pawn Between Giants

The Río de la Plata is the focus of life in the tiny nation of Uruguay. Montevideo (MAHN tuh vih DAY oh), the capital, is on this estuary. About one-half of the nation's people live in Montevideo's metro area. Another one-quarter million live in towns along the Uruguay River.

Gauchos, Cowboys of the South

The cowboys of Argentina, or **gauchos** (GOW chose), are national folk heroes. Hordes of them rode the Pampas in the nineteenth century, rounding up wild horses and cattle. Today, the few that remain work on ranches.

In the early days, the gauchos spent most of their time in the saddle. They were distinguished not only by their riding skills, but also by their clothes. Their distinctive costume included a wide silver belt, baggy trousers, and a brightly colored scarf. They were rovers, who loved the wide open spaces and freedom of the plains.

Cattle are central to the economy of Argentina.

Uruguay has the most thoroughly European population in South America, but its location between the two giants of Brazil and Argentina has made life difficult.

Past Divisions   Spain and Portugal argued for centuries over the border between their New World empires, as outlined in the Treaty of Tordesillas. When Portugal founded a colony in 1680 across from the Spanish town of Buenos Aires, Spain responded by establishing Montevideo in the same area. Spanish troops drove the Portuguese out of the colony in 1777 and made Uruguay part of the Viceroyalty of La Plata.

Uruguay's path to independence was long and complex. José Gervasio Artigas, Uruguay's national hero, attempted to free Montevideo from Spain in 1811, but Portugal intervened to stop him. When Spain later lost Montevideo to Martín's armies, Portugal again stepped in, taking Uruguay back as part of Brazil. In 1825 patriots, aided by Argentina, revolted. Brazil tried to block all shipping to the Río de la Plata. But in response Great Britain sent its warships to break the blockade, and Uruguay became an independent republic.

Present Struggles Spanish is the national language, although Portuguese is common along the border with Brazil. The economy is very much like Argentina's, but its history is less stable. Civil wars, terrorism, and foreign wars have plagued the tiny nation.

Landlocked Paraguay

Spanish explorers first visited Paraguay while searching for an alternate route to the riches of Peru. Asunción (Ah SOON SYAWN), founded on the Paraguay River in 1537, became the first capital of Spain's colonies in southeastern South America. But Spain neglected this landlocked, unproductive region. When Spain formed the Viceroyalty of La Plata in 1776, the people of Asunción disliked taking orders from the new capital at Buenos Aires. They declared independence in 1811. Dictators, civil war, and wars with every neighbor have decimated the nation. The nation did not hold its first multiparty elections until 1993.

Around 95 percent of Paraguayans are mestizos. Most are bilingual. They speak Spanish in schools, government, and commerce; but they use their native Indian tongue, Guaraní, in day-to-day life. Paraguay may be the most thoroughly bilingual nation in the world.

Like Bolivia, Paraguay is undeveloped and lacks mineral resources. Its one advantage over Bolivia is the **Paraná River,** the second longest river system in South America. Steamboats can go up the Paraguay River, a tributary of the Paraná, to Paraguay's capital. Most of the nation's population lives along the river system.

Many Paraguayans are subsistence farmers, who make their living from the rich alluvial soils of the Paraná and Paraguay Rivers. They barely grow enough crops to feed their families, cutting down forests on public lands and moving on when the

Itaipu Dam can generate more power than any other dam in the world.

soil is depleted. Most live in one-room *ranchos,* with dirt floors and no plumbing.

The Gran Chaco, west of the Paraguay River, is largely uninhabited, except for a few Guaraní Indians and Mennonites. Mennonite communities in the Chaco, started in 1926, now produce nearly one-half of the nation's dairy products.

SECTION REVIEW

1. What is an estuary?
2. Who liberated Argentina and Chile from Spain?
3. What is the second largest city in South America? Why is it so big?
4. Match each area with the associated word.

   (1) Pampas   a. Gran Chaco
   (2) Paraguay   b. plateau
   (3) Patagonia   c. gauchos

   💡 Compare and contrast Bolivia and Paraguay.

BRAZIL, THE PORTUGUESE GIANT

Brazil is the fifth largest nation in the world, and the fifth most populous. It covers half the South American continent and contains several of the continent's key geographic areas. Its wealth of resources and vibrant culture hold the promise of a great future.

Brazil is unique among Latin American nations. It is the only nation in the Western Hemisphere that once belonged to Portugal. It is also the largest Roman Catholic nation in the world. While most Brazilians remain Catholic, Protestant churches have grown rapidly in recent years, particularly among charismatic denominations that emphasize lively worship and miraculous signs.

Atlantic Coast

The Treaty of Tordesillas gave Portugal all the lands east of the **Line of Demarcation** (defined as the line of longitude 370 leagues west of the Cape Verde Islands, or about 48° W). Pedro Cabral's discovery of Brazil in 1500 affirmed Portugal's claim to the eastern tip of South America.

Because of the rough terrain and the hostile Indians of the interior, the first settlements were coastal. Like the United States, these towns were often at harbors and tied to Atlantic trade with the Old World.

Portuguese Settlers Colonists began to arrive from Portugal in 1530. While Spain was building sugar plantations in the Caribbean with the help of African slaves, Portugal built sugar plantations all along the east coast of Brazil. Within two years, São Vicente (near the southern city of Santos) became the first colony and oldest city in Brazil. Two years later, Recife was established on the northeastern tip nearest Europe.

If you look at the map of modern Brazil, you will see that Portugal settled quite a bit more of the coast than they were supposed to. In 1669 Portuguese settlers crossed the treaty line and founded Manaus far up the Amazon River. Another group of settlers founded Pôrto Alegre on the southern coast in 1740. The westward movement required a new treaty with Spain. The Treaty of Madrid, signed in 1750, gave Portugal almost all the land of modern Brazil.

Independence The French emperor Napoleon attacked Portugal in 1807, as vengeance for Portugal's aiding Great Britain. When Portugal's prince fled to Brazil, he made a city in Brazil the capital of his Portuguese Empire. This lasted until 1821, when

Iguaçu Falls

"Poor Niagara," cried the visiting wife of an American president when she first beheld Iguaçu Falls. Iguaçu Falls is about eighty feet higher than Niagara Falls and twice as wide, making it the widest waterfall in the world. Although less powerful than Niagara on most days, the rainy season turns Iguaçu into a raging torrent. Its flow has been recorded to be as high as 452,059 cubic feet per second, which more than doubles the flow at Niagara Falls.

Some 275 cataracts, separated by stony outcroppings, fall over a semicircular cliff that is 1.8 miles wide. The rushing falls plunge 237 feet into the canyons below, sending up clouds of mist in a lush jungle setting.

After the Iguaçu River flows over the Falls, it joins the Paraná twelve miles downstream. Near this point is Itaipu Dam, the largest dam in the world. Built in 1982 to harness the mighty Paraná River, Itaipu's concrete

Iguaçu Falls is the most powerful waterfall in the world.

wall is five miles long and seventy-five stories high. Brazil and Paraguay jointly constructed the amazing hydroelectric plant, which has the highest kilowatt output in the world.

he returned to Portugal and left his son, Dom Pedro, in charge.

The next year, **Dom Pedro** declared independence for Brazil and became the emperor. Brazil remained a monarchy for sixty-six years under Pedro and his son, Pedro II. The Age of Pedro II, 1840-89, is fondly remembered. He opened the door to thousands of European immigrants, and he freed the Black slaves in 1888. Freeing the slaves brought about his downfall, however. Angry slave owners, who received no money for compensation, overthrew Pedro II and declared Brazil a republic, modeling its constitution after the United States. The republic has been interrupted by periodic dictatorships and military rule.

Brazil shares borders with seven Spanish-speaking nations. The splintered Spanish Empire was no match for the united empire of Brazil. This powerful country has won a sliver of territory from every one of its Spanish neighbors. It was also the first Latin American country to develop nuclear capability, and the only one to send an army to Europe during World Wars I and II.

Modern Coastal Cities
Modern Coastal Cities   As is typical of South America, Brazil's large cities are very modern. Cars and buses fill the streets. Operas, plays, and orchestras entertain the people; and schools are excellent. Houses and apartments may be small and crowded, but they have basic appliances, such as refrigerators, toasters, and televisions.

Cities in the South   The biggest cities are in South Brazil, the nation's heartland. Most of the region enjoys a humid subtropical climate, similar to U.S. southern states. But **Rio de Janeiro,** the nation's second largest city and third on the continent, has a pleasant tropical climate on the coastal plain. Orange groves in the area make Brazil the world's leading producer of oranges.

"Rio" is considered the most charming city of the New World, much like Paris in the Old World. Dom Pedro I made Rio de Janiero his capital, and it remains the cultural center of the nation. Its harbor is internationally acclaimed, surpassing the beauty of San Francisco Bay. Sugar Loaf, a granite mountain shaped like a dome, is a famous landmark.

Life on the Northeast Coast   Most other major coastal cities of Brazil lie on the eastern "bulge," known as the Northeast. Eight state capitals, from São Luís to Salvador, are clustered together on this crowded coast. Salvador, Fortaleza, and Recife are the largest cities in the region, each with over two million people. Recife is the major industrial city of the Northeast. Farmers from the drought-stricken interior have poured into the coastal cities to find work. Most of them end up in one of the cities' huge slums, called **favelas** (fah VEH lahs).

The northeast coast has a large Black population, descended from the African slaves who once worked on the sugar plantations. Whites still own and supervise most plantations, but hired workers enjoy moderately good living conditions. In addition to sugar cane, the modern plantations raise cacoa, bananas, and cotton. Brazil leads the Western Hemisphere in producing bananas (third worldwide) and cacao (second worldwide).

The Brazilian Highlands

Above the narrow coastal plain rise the **Brazilian Highlands,** a rugged plateau that dominates the east side of the continent. Near the Atlantic coast, the highlands form a steep wall-like slope called the Great Escarpment. It reaches its highest point at 9,482 feet above sea level, at Bandeira Peak just west of Vitória.

Like the Andes, the Brazilian Highlands greatly influence river drainage on the continent. Most waters flow down the highlands into two great water systems—the Amazon in the north or

Christ the Redeemer, *a huge statue of Jesus Christ, overlooks the city of Rio de Janeiro.*

Population Density of Latin America

Let's Go Exploring

1. Where is the most densely populated region? the most sparsely populated region?

2. What regions are uninhabited?

3. What countries in Central America have *no* populated areas above 25 per square mile?

4. Does the west coast of Latin America have any region with a population density above 250 per square mile?

💡 What part of Brazil is closest to becoming a megalopolis? Why here?

Per sq. km	Per sq. mi.
Uninhabited	Uninhabited
Under 1	Under 2
1-10	2-25
10-25	25-60
25-50	60-125
50-100	125-250
Over 100	Over 250

• Metropolitan area with 2-5 million people

○ Metropolitan area with over 5 million people

the Rio de la Plata in the south. The only other major river, São Francisco, cuts east through the highlands. Paulo Afonso Falls, where the river drops toward the coast, is one of the world's five most powerful high falls.

Even though the Brazilian Highlands lie in the Tropics, the climate is not like that of the Amazon Basin. The Amazon, which straddles the equator, is rainy all year long; but heavy rains fall only half the year in the highlands farther south. Why? The Amazon always receives direct sunlight, which heats the surface and causes regular afternoon showers (by convection precipitation, which you studied in Chapter 3). But in the highlands, the direct rays of

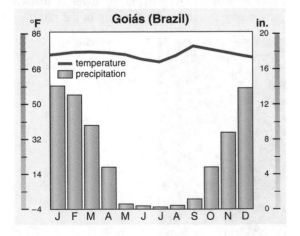

the sun shift every six months. The rainfall begins in February, when the sun shifts over the highlands. When the sun shifts back north in August, the land cools, cold air rises, and the rains cease.

Life in the Highlands Many people live in the Brazilian Highlands, where the high elevation keeps the temperatures relatively cool.

Cities in the South Two hundred miles west of Rio is **São Paulo,** the largest city in Latin America, exceeding even Mexico City in population. Including its metro area, São Paulo is the third largest city in the world (after Tokyo and New York).

São Paulo includes ethnic populations from all over the world. Liberdade, with over one million inhabitants, is the largest Japanese community outside Japan. But the minorities of Brazil, including the Japanese, Germans, and Arabs, now speak Portuguese and have adopted Brazilian culture.

São Paulo arose in one of the most fertile areas of the country. Plantations raise coffee, sugar cane,

Carnival

Carnival is the biggest festival on the Roman Catholic Church's long roster of holiday celebrations. Every Latin American country observes Carnival, but Rio de Janeiro hosts the biggest Carnival of them all. For four days and nights, Catholics party in the streets. Afterwards begins the forty days of Lent, when they are supposed to pray and fast in preparation for Easter.

Drinking, loud music, and outlandish costumes are all part of the "fun." The party ends on the final night with a grand parade along the Sambadrome, a street with grandstands built in 1984 especially for this occasion. Sadly, the Carnival shows just how wicked professing Christians can be, turning their religion into an excuse for sin. The partiers wake up in the morning just as needy and empty as they were before the party began.

Carnival at Rio de Janeiro, Brazil, may be the world's largest annual festival.

I hate, I despise your feast days. . . . Take thou away from me the noise of thy songs; for I will not hear the melody of thy viols. But let judgment run down as waters, and righteousness as a mighty stream. (Amos 5:21, 23-24)

and cotton. São Paulo's coffee has made Brazil the world leader in coffee exports. Brazil also raises more beef cattle than any other nation, many of them raised in the dry savanna around São Paulo.

The third largest city in Brazil, Belo Horizonte, is also located on the Brazilian Highlands in the southern heartland. It is the capital of **Minas Gerais,** one of Brazil's largest states. This highly industrialized state has the largest deposit of iron ore in the world. In fact, Brazil is the world leader in the production of iron ore. Minas Gerais has other mineral resources as well, including diamonds, manganese, and gold. Brazil produces more gold than any other nation in South America. Brazil also produces most of the world's finest imperial topaz.

Tropical Climates

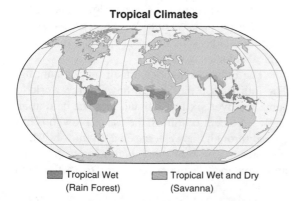

☐ Tropical Wet
(Rain Forest)

☐ Tropical Wet and Dry
(Savanna)

Poverty of the Northeast Unlike the southern heartland, the northeast portion of the Brazilian Highlands, known as the *sertão,* has poor soil and long dry seasons. While the coastal cities afford decent living conditions, the interior is a virtual desert and its people are very poor. The *sertão*'s primary crop is **cassava** (also called manioc), a root similar to a potato that can be eaten or used to make tapioca. Brazil is the world's leading producer of cassava.

The Nation's Capital, in the Remote Interior

In an effort to move some of its population westward into the interior, Brazil built Brasília in 1960. The carefully planned, modern city was carved out of the Brazilian Highland about six hundred miles from the coast. The economy of the new capital is slowly developing, but most people prefer to remain on the coast. The government of "the United States of Brazil" is a federal republic, with twenty-six states and the federal district of Brasília.

West of the Brazilian Highlands is the **Mato Grosso Plateau.** Swamps cover the plateau along the borders with Paraguay and Bolivia. Though remote, this region undoubtedly holds great potential wealth.

The Río Solimoes (light) and Río Negro (dark) join at the Meeting of the Waters to form the Amazon proper near Manaus, Brazil.

SECTION REVIEW

1. What country colonized Brazil?

2. What is Brazil's largest city? Which city is its cultural center?

3. Why are southern cities more prosperous than northeastern cities?

4. Brazil leads in world production of what three products from the Brazilian Highlands?

💡 Why did the Spanish colonies break up after independence, but not the Portuguese colonies? What advantages has unity given Brazil?

The Amazon

The **Amazon River** is the greatest river system in the world. Not only does it drain the largest area, but more water flows out of the Amazon than out of the next ten largest rivers combined. The Amazon is also the longest river by some estimates. Even the lowest figures put it within 160 miles of the Nile.

The flat basin of the Amazon River is covered by a steamy rain forest, called **selva.** Spreading over one-third of the continent, it is the largest tropical rain forest in the world. The high canopy of trees supports a host of exotic animals: the anaconda, the world's longest snake; the capybara, the world's largest rodent; colorful toucans and parrots; jaguars; tapirs; and sloths. The waters teem with electric eels, the razor-toothed piranha, the tiny but dreaded candiru, and the ten-foot-long pirarucu.

Amazon/Mississippi Comparison

Amazon River at Óbidos, Brazil:	Mississippi River at Vicksburg, Mississippi:
1½ miles wide, 200 feet deep	⅓ mile wide, 70 feet deep

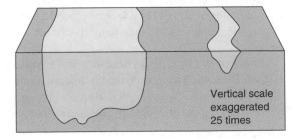

Vertical scale exaggerated 25 times

Even dolphins and sharks have appeared as far upstream as Iquitos, Peru!

Life of the Remote Indians   Few people live in the Amazon rain forest. It has a very steamy, uncomfortable climate. Temperatures hover between 75°F and 95°F throughout the year. Many areas receive over one hundred inches of rain annually.

Several small, scattered Indian tribes live deep in the forests. The forest Indians share nothing in common with the Incas. Each Indian group generally lives together in one large community structure, called a *malocas,* covered with woven palm leaves. The only significant piece of furniture is the hammock—a marvelous invention of the Amazon Indians. Sailors have adopted it the world over, and hammocks are a common sight in most homes of coastal Brazilians.

Virtually all tribes practice shifting or **slash-and-burn agriculture.** They cut down a plot of forest, burn the vegetation to fertilize the soil, and then plant manioc. In most cases, they have replaced their ancient stone tools with modern steel. The women turn the manioc into flour and store it in baskets. When the soil is depleted, they cut down a new plot. Manioc is not dense in nutrients, but it grows well in the poor, acidic soil. Europeans spread manioc to tropical colonies worldwide.

The Indians supplement their diet by hunting. The Indians use the longest bows in the world—some are over six feet tall and must be held at an angle. In recent centuries, the use of blowguns has spread through the western selva. In thick brush, it is easier to aim blowguns than bows to hit birds and monkeys. Using tubes, eight to twelve feet

Yagua Indians still use poison darts and blowguns in the remote Amazon Basin.

long, skilled blowers can hit targets as high as 120 feet in the trees. Poison darts, whose butt is made from the silky fiber of kapoc, move in deadly silence. The tribes make poison from the sap of the *strychnos* vine.

Missionaries have contacted most tribes of the selva and have stopped cannibalism. Though some Indians have accepted Christ and are learning to read, others remain bound by spirit worship and superstitious practices. Humanistic anthropologists are urging the Indians to retain their traditional lifestyle in harmony with nature. "Foreigners tell us to reject the missionaries and go back to our old ways," said one Yanomamo Christian. "But they do not have Christ in their hearts. Our old ways were evil. We will never go back."

Modern Development and Deforestation

As part of its program to develop the rich potential of the Amazon, the government has divided it into seven states. The largest and most populous states in Brazil are Amazonas and Pará. They share the land along the main channel of the Amazon River. **Amazonas,** with its capital of Manaus, governs the western half of the river. Pará, with its bustling capital of Belém on the coast, governs the eastern half. Pará is slightly smaller than Amazonas, but it has over twice the population. Five other remote states contain chunks of the Amazon Basin and are the least populated states of Brazil.

An increasing number of Brazilian settlers are moving into the rain forest, both legally and illegally, to exploit its riches—minerals, farmland, and lumber. Though a plain, the Amazon has a valuable supply of mineral resources. Pará has Brazil's second major iron ore deposit, located about 250 miles south of Belém. South America's leading bauxite and tin mines are located in the Amazon. The state of Rondônia, along Brazil's southern border with Bolivia, is the world's second largest producer of tin (after China).

Farmers have attempted to grow crops in the rain forest. A few cacao and rubber plantations thrive along the banks of the Amazon. You might think that heavy rainfall would make productive soil, but the soil is actually very thin. Insects and rapid decay deprive the soil of humus. In a process called **leaching,** constant rains dissolve nutrients in the soil and carry them away.

Increasing numbers of lumberjacks are felling the forests to extract valuable hardwoods, such as mahogany and ebony. But because the trees hold the soil in place, **deforestation** is depleting the soil, rendering the land useless for future generations. Environmentalists are also concerned about the loss of these oxygen-producing forests.

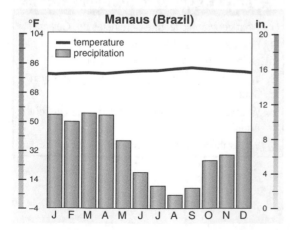

Manaus (Brazil)

°F / in. — temperature / precipitation

J F M A M J J A S O N D

SECTION REVIEW

1. What term describes the Amazon rain forest?
2. Which records does the Amazon River hold: most volume, longest river, largest rain forest, or highest waterfall?
3. Why is the soil poor in the Amazon?
4. Name the two leading cities in the Amazon Basin.
5. What mineral products come from the Amazon Basin?

   💡 Compare and contrast Brazil's settlement of the Amazon with the U.S. settlement of the West.

12-6

THE GUIANA HIGHLANDS

Tepuis dominate the Guyana Highlands on the border between Venezuela, Guyana, and Brazil.

We have come full circle in our survey of the continent. The **Guiana Highlands** (gee AN uh) is the rugged plateau that separates Venezuela's Caribbean coast from the Amazon Basin. Venezuela's world-famous Angel Falls plummets down the side of these highlands. While Spain and Portugal controlled most of South America, three other European powers founded small colonies on the coast below the Guiana Highlands. These colonies became known as the **Guianas.**

The tropical climate supports sugar cane, rice, and banana plantations along the coast. In the interior, several coffee plantations operate in the highlands, and cattle graze on some interior grasslands. The European colonists imported Black slaves to work on the plantations. After slavery was abolished in the nineteenth century, many Blacks moved inland. So the Europeans hired laborers from India and Indonesia, who brought their languages and Hindu religion.

Guyana

The westernmost colony of the Guianas was British. It became the country of Guyana in 1966, although the border with Venezuela was not yet settled. English is the national language of the republic, but Indian tribes in the remote rain forests still speak their old tongues.

Huge, block-shaped mountains, called *tepuis,* rise above the highlands in the interior of Guyana. Mountaineering is the only way to reach the flat savannas on the top. The highest *tepui,* Mount Roraima (9,219 ft.), towers above the junction between Venezuela, Guyana, and Brazil. Waters from this mountain flow south into the Amazon and north into the Orinoco. The isolated biome of Mount Roraima inspired Sir Arthur Conan Doyle to write *The Lost World* about dinosaurs and ape men cut off from the rest of the world. The first explorers, who reached the tabletop in 1884, discovered several new species of animals—but no dinosaurs.

As in Venezuela, world-class waterfalls descend the slopes of the highlands of Guyana. They include 1,600-foot-high King George VI Falls and 350-foot-wide Kaieteur.

Suriname

East of Guyana is a former Dutch colony. Dutch Guiana received independence in 1975 and changed its name to Suriname. The Dutch brought the first coffee to South America, but the modern economy depends on bauxite (aluminum ore). Suriname has the fewest people per square mile of any nation on the continent. Its population density compares to that of Canada.

French Guiana

French Guiana is the only part of the continent that is still under European control. It sends a representative to the French legislature in Paris. Its population density is even lower than Suriname's. The entire territory has fewer people than Chattanooga, Tennessee. While Cayenne is the major town, the most famous place in the territory is Devil's Island, an abandoned prison colony much like Alcatraz in San Francisco Bay.

12-7

◎ SECTION REVIEW

1. What geographic feature dominates the Guianas?
2. Besides Spain and Portugal, what European nations had colonies in South America?
3. What nation has the lowest population density in South America?
4. What is the only foreign-controlled region in South America?
💡 Why is the wildlife so unusual on the *tepuis?*

REVIEW

Can You Define These Terms?

Creole   estuary   cassava   leaching
endemic   gaucho   selva   deforestation
landlocked   favelas   slash-and-burn agriculture

Can You Locate These Natural Features?

Llanos   Altiplano   Drake Passage   Paraná River
Lake Maracaibo   Lake Titicaca   Río de la Plata   Brazilian Highlands
Orinoco River   Atacama Desert   Pampas   Mato Grosso
Andes Mountains   Central Valley   Aconcagua   Amazon River
Angel Falls   Strait of Magellan   Patagonia   Guiana Highlands
Peru Current   Tierra del Fuego   Gran Chaco

Can You Explain the Significance of These People, Places, and Events?

Simon Bolívar   Lima   Buenos Aires   Minas Gerais
Incas   Shining Path   Line of Demarcation   Mato Grosso Plateau
Cuzco   Augusto Pinochet   Dom Pedro   Amazonas
Francisco Pizarro   José de San Martín   Río de Janeiro   Guianas
Quechua   Juan Perón   São Paulo

How Much Do You Remember?

1. Match each geographic feature with its most closely associated term.

(1) Lake Maracaibo	a. Andes Mountains
(2) Strait of Magellan	b. estuary
(3) Amazon River	c. Caribbean Sea
(4) Aconcagua	d. selva
(5) Paraná River	e. Guiana Highlands
(6) Angel Falls	f. Tierra del Fuego
(7) Río de la Plata	g. Paraguay River

2. Name the three plateau regions of South America.
3. Name the three major South American river systems.
4. What role did the Creoles play in the history of South America?
5. What piece of land joins North and South America?
6. What illegal drug first came from South America?
7. Why is much of South America's Pacific coast so dry?
8. What large plain lies high in the Andes?
9. What is the most fertile grassland area in South America?
10. Which countries of South America were not settled by the Spanish?
11. Why do some tropical areas have a rainy season and a dry season?
12. Why is the soil of the selva generally poor for agriculture?

What Do You Think?

1. Give three examples from South America of the principle described in Proverbs 28:19-20.
2. Pick a city in South America where you would like to live. Describe how your life would change if you moved there. *Essay*
3. Why do environmentalists want Brazil to stop developing the selva? Should other nations have a say in Brazil's decisions? *Essay*

Cumulative Review

1. Name the seven continents and four oceans.
2. Define primary, secondary, and tertiary industries. Which industry is most prominent in South America?
3. List the eight culture regions of the world. In what region does South America belong?
4. Compare and contrast Peru, Argentina, and Brazil. Explain how each of them are representative of a different region in South America.

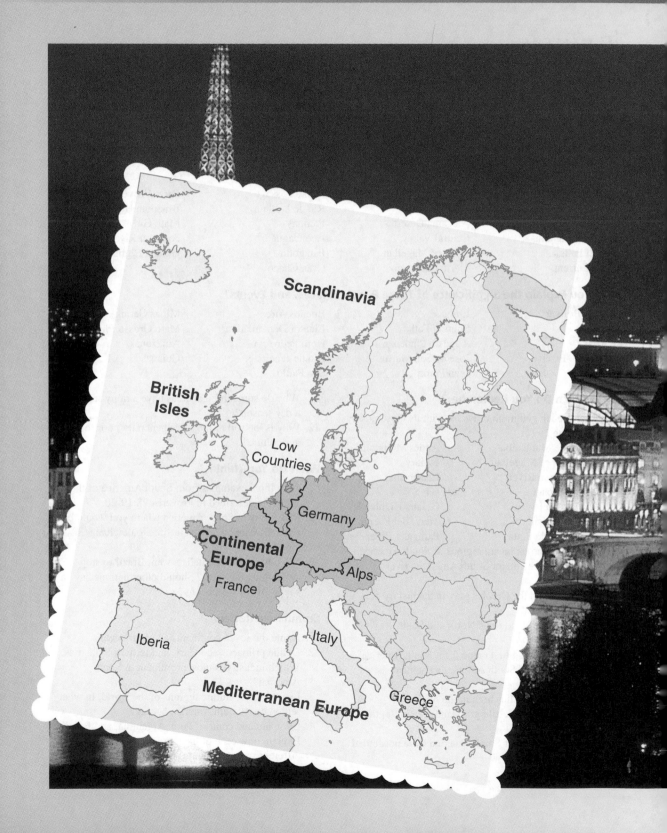

Scandinavia

British
Isles

Low
Countries

Germany

Continental
Europe

Alps

France

Iberia

Italy

Mediterranean Europe

Greece

UNIT V

Western Europe

Chapter 13
British Isles and Scandinavia

Chapter 14
Continental Europe

Chapter 15
Mediterranean Europe

13

BRITISH ISLES AND SCANDINAVIA

The Lord has blessed Europe in many ways. It is the only continent with no deserts. The good climate and rich soils support productive farms and industry. Europe has many fine harbors and deep rivers that allow flourishing trade. Indeed, Europe has been called a "peninsula of peninsulas" because it is one large peninsula on the Eurasian landmass, strewn with numerous smaller peninsulas.

Western Europe has less than 5 percent of the earth's landmass, but its people have dominated world history. Virtually every nation in western Europe has enjoyed a golden age of glory. European traditions and institutions are found on every continent. Three other continents—North America, South America, and Australia—are peopled by descendants of western Europeans.

The Lord maketh poor, and maketh rich: he bringeth low, and lifteth up. (I Sam. 2:7)

The rise and fall of European empires reveals how God controls the affairs of men. No nation or people, no matter how rich and powerful, has room for pride. The changing fortunes of northern Europe, the topic of this chapter, reminds us of this truth.

A UNITED KINGDOM

 At the heart of northern Europe is **Great Britain,** the largest island in Europe. It sits astride the major water routes of northern Europe. Off the east coast lies the **North Sea,** the main route to the peninsulas of Scandinavia. Off the west coast lies the choppy Irish Sea, between Great Britain and Ireland. South of Great Britain is the **English Channel,** a narrow body of water between the island and the European mainland.

Geographer's Corner

Time Zones

With an empire that stretched around the globe, the Royal Navy needed an accurate method to keep track of ship schedules and locations. So in the eighteenth century they established a system of twenty-four meridians, evenly spaced one hour, or fifteen degrees longitude, apart. The prime meridian was set at the Royal Greenwich Observatory, just outside London.

The system worked fine until the invention of steamships and railroads. *Local time* varied from town to town by a few minutes, based on the location of the sun. To make train schedules less complicated, all cities in England, Wales, and Scotland decided to set their clocks by one *standard time,* based in Greenwich. Every hour on the hour, Londoners hear the peal of the 13.5-ton Big Ben,

located in a clock tower high above the House of Parliament. Big Ben, first hung in 1858, has become a symbol of the British people's punctuality.

A single standard time worked fine for the British Isles, but not for the United States, which spanned a whole continent. In 1884 the United States called an international conference to develop a global system of twenty-four *time zones.* Under this system, time remains the same within each zone, but it changes between zones. The boundaries of time zones do not always follow meridians, but may zigzag across convenient boundaries.

Calculating time changes is fairly simple. Find Moscow on the map. It is three time zones east of Greenwich. If you are in Moscow and need to know the standard time

---

Until recently, merchant ships had to pass through this channel to reach the ports in northern Europe.

The island of Great Britain has three political divisions—England in the south, Wales in the west, and Scotland in the north. In 1707 these kingdoms were officially united, with one parliament, in the

William the Conqueror began to build the keep, or White Tower, in 1078. Even after walls and a moat were added, this fortress on the Thames retained the name "Tower" of London. Among the famous prisoners beheaded at the tower were Lady Jane Grey, a Protestant martyr, and Anne Boleyn, second wife of Henry VIII. Today, visitors can see the crown jewels and a collection of medieval armor there.

United Kingdom. Today the United Kingdom officially includes Northern Ireland. But sometimes you will hear the kingdom loosely called Great Britain or just Britain.

London on the Thames

The capital of the United Kingdom is **London,** one of Europe's oldest cities. Its rich history traces back two thousand years, when the Romans established a trading post named Londonium in A.D. 43.

With seven million people, London is the largest city in Western Europe. Some of history's greatest writers, artists, scientists, and statesmen have called London home. Everywhere visitors find familiar names and places. Almost every English-speaking person is familiar with novels and plays set in London.

Port of London One reason that London became such a great city is its strategic location along the **Thames River.** Oceangoing ships can easily navigate the fifty miles upstream to unload at some of the world's best ports. The Port of London Authority supervises some forty miles of wharves along the Thames.

in London, you simply subtract three hours. Now find New York on the map. Because New York City is five time zones west of Greenwich, you *add* five hours to find the standard time.

What if you are traveling and need to change your watch? Just add or subtract one hour for every time zone between you and your destination. If it is 2:00 P.M. at the Los Angeles airport and you are traveling east to Chicago, you must move your clock ahead two hours for two time zones. But if you are flying to Honolulu, two time zones west, you must set your watch back to noon.

Use the map to answer the questions.

1. Sydney, Australia, lies how many time zones east of London?

2. If it is 9:00 P.M. in Sydney, what is Greenwich time?

3. If it is 1:00 A.M. in Athens, Greece, what time is it in Tokyo?

4. If it is 10:00 A.M. in Rio de Janeiro, Brazil, what time is it in Denver, Colorado?

5. If it is 4:00 A.M. in Halifax, Nova Scotia, what time is it in Tokyo?

Why does Iceland have standard time rather than +1?

Time Zones of the World

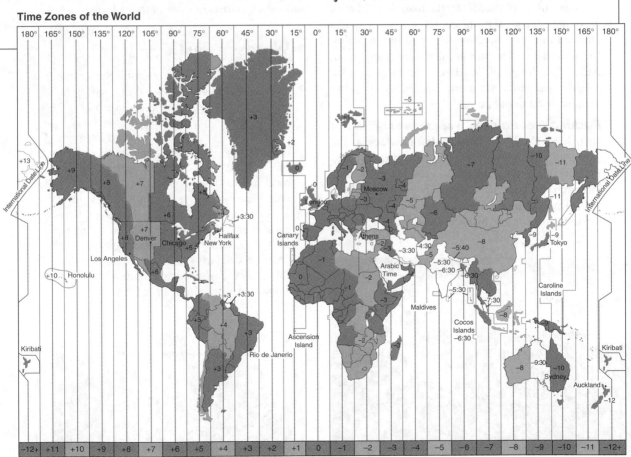

303

British Isles and Scandinavia Statistics

COUNTRY	CAPITAL	AREA (SQ. MI.)	POPULATION	NATURAL INCREASE	LIFE EXPECTANCY	LITERACY RATE	PER CAPITA GDP	POP. DENSITY
Denmark	Copenhagen	16,639	5,268,775	0.1%	78	100%	$21,700	317
Finland	Helsinki	130,559	5,109,148	0%	76	100%	$18,200	39
Iceland	Reykjavik	39,699	272,550	1.1%	81	100%	$18,800	7
Ireland	Dublin	27,137	3,555,500	0.4%	76	100%	$15,400	131
Norway	Oslo	125,050	4,404,456	0.1%	78	100%	$24,500	35
Sweden	Stockholm	173,732	8,946,193	−0.1%	78	100%	$20,100	51
United Kingdom	London	94,251	58,610,182	0.2%	77	100%	$19,500	621

The city grew in a haphazard fashion on the Thames. Westminster was originally a residence for rulers on the outskirts of the city, but it was built up and became meshed with old London. This is the heart of London. It still retains the original layout—a tangle of unplanned streets that is a driver's nightmare. From the old center, the city extends outward in every direction for up to twenty miles. In the midst of the jumble, there are many green parks, "the lungs of London." The largest parks, called royal parks, were once owned by kings but are now open to public use.

Buckingham Palace   The primary residence of British monarchs is **Buckingham Palace** at the west end of London. A royal standard is flown to indicate when the monarch is in residence. The first monarch to take up residence in Buckingham Palace was **Queen Victoria,** the longest reigning monarch in English history. During the Victorian Age (1837-1901), the British Empire reached its peak—"the sun never set on the British Empire." Buckingham Palace became the symbol of Victoria's glorious empire. The Changing of the Guard, an ancient ceremony by red-coated sentries, still wows tourists in front of the palace.

Windsor Castle

Windsor Castle is the oldest inhabited royal residence in the world. William the Conqueror built the original fortifications in 1070, overlooking the Thames River. It has grown to become the largest castle in Britain, nearly one mile in circumference.

The additions and reconstructions have left no trace of the original castle, but parts of each succeeding project remain. King Henry II built the Round Tower in 1170, and Henry III built two towers fifty years later. King George IV, who commissioned the architect Wyatville, is responsible for the appearance of most of the rest of the castle. St. George's Chapel, added in 1475, is the burial place of Henry VIII, Charles I, George IV, and several others. No changes have been made since the 1820s.

Buckingham Palace

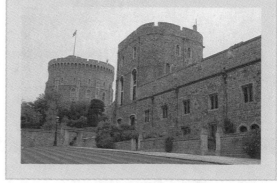

Commonwealth of Nations

British gunboats and redcoats helped to build and maintain the British Empire throughout the nineteenth century. But things began to change after World War I (1914-18). Many of the British colonies wanted independence. The British **Commonwealth of Nations** was formed in 1931 to convert the British Empire into an association of free countries. Member nations continue to work together with Britain for the good of all. The Commonwealth assists member nations in holding elections and in developing their economies. Today, over fifty nations are members of the British Commonwealth.

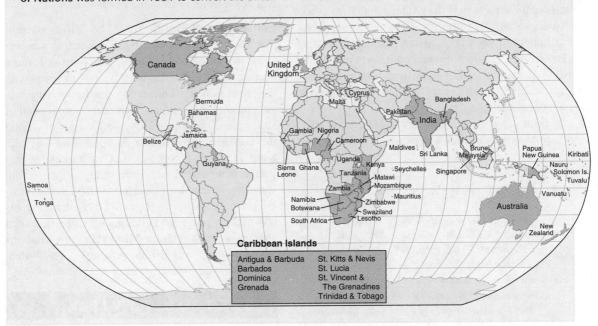

Caribbean Islands

Antigua & Barbuda	St. Kitts & Nevis
Barbados	St. Lucia
Dominica	St. Vincent &
Grenada	The Grenadines
	Trinidad & Tobago

Westminster Abbey The best-known church in Great Britain is **Westminster Abbey.** At his coronation in Westminster Abbey, the British monarch becomes the head of the Church of England, or the **Anglican Church.** The monarch appoints the archbishop of Canterbury, who becomes the nation's spiritual leader, and an archbishop of York, who serves the northern part of England. In this *episcopal* system of church government, power rests in bishops, who appoint lesser officials. Henry VIII founded the Anglican Church in 1534 when he broke from the Catholic Church over the issue of divorce. Henry eventually married six women, a record for one king!

The Anglican Church once preached the gospel. Many Protestant beliefs, including justification by grace alone and the sole authority of the Bible, can be found in the official Book of Common Prayer and in the creed, known as the Thirty-nine Articles. Unfortunately, like mainline leaders in America, Anglican leaders have rejected many biblical truths. They are even holding discussions, or *dialogs,* with the Catholic Church in the hope of reuniting the two branches of Christianity.

Parliament Across the street from Westminster Abbey are the two Houses of **Parliament,** the law-making branch of the British government. The **House of Commons** is the chief body, elected by the "common" people over age eighteen. Lively debates occur in this chamber, as MPs (Members of Parliament) make speeches, interrupt each other, argue, and shout their views on proposed laws. The other body in Parliament, the House of Lords, consists mostly of nobility who are not elected but inherit their seats. The members of this quiet chamber have little power. They can only delay the passage of new laws.

The Cabinet System   The British Parliament is called a **cabinet system** because a "cabinet" of parliamentary leaders runs the government. They work in various office buildings down the street from Parliament. A prime minister is elected by the House of Commons from among its own members. He then appoints other MPs to cabinet positions. Each cabinet minister has supreme power in his own department, or "ministry."

Forming a government is not easy, especially when no one party has a majority of MPs. When more than one party joins to form a government, it is called a **coalition government.** Sometimes several parties join together during a national emergency, such as a war. At such times they form a *national government,* giving each party one or more cabinet positions. The House of Commons must hold elections at least once every five years, but the prime minister can dissolve the cabinet and call new elections any time he chooses.

Constitutional Monarchy   The British government is still a monarchy, but the monarch's power is mostly ceremonial. The monarch hosts foreign heads of state and holds weekly conversations with the prime minister. During any deaths or changes in government, he remains as the ceremonial head of state. The British monarchy lost its power during the **Glorious Revolution** of 1688. The Catholic King James II (1685-88) was so unpopular that Parliament asked a Protestant prince from Germany to take his place. James fled and the new king signed a Bill of Rights (1689), limiting his law-making power and granting new liberties, such as freedom of speech for MPs. Many other nations have imitated Great Britain's example of a limited, *constitutional monarchy.*

British English

The British have many dialects of English, just as Americans do: Southern British English, Northern British English, Scottish English, and so on. The British Broadcasting System uses the *British Received Pronunciation* of London and the southeast. It is sometimes called King's or Queen's English.

The Standard English of Great Britain is quite different from the Standard English in America. To the British, gasoline is *petrol,* and raising the hood of a car is *looking under the bonnet.* The trunk of a car is the *boot.*

American Word	English Word
cookies	*biscuits*
biscuits	*scones*
truck	*lorry*
sink	*basin*
closet	*cupboard*
candy	*sweets*
dessert	*pudding*
elevator	*lift*
horn	*hooter*
radio	*wireless*
drugstore	*chemist*

⊚ SECTION REVIEW

1. Distinguish Great Britain from the United Kingdom.
2. Where does the queen live in London?
3. What religious group is headquartered at Westminster Abbey?
4. Which house of Parliament is more important?
💡 Compare and contrast the elected government in the United States with the one in the United Kingdom.

England, Land of Angles and Saxons

Modern Englishmen are descendants of seafaring Germanic tribes who invaded England in the mid-fifth century. The Jutes arrived first on the south coast, but the **Angles** and **Saxons** eventually divided the land between themselves. The Old English language developed from the German dialects of the Angles, Saxons, and Jutes. The name **England,** in fact, is from two Old English words meaning "Angles' land."

The Anglo-Saxons divided England into seven petty kingdoms, known as the Heptarchy. Saxons ruled the southern kingdoms of Kent, Essex, Sussex, and Wessex. (The last three names, still in use today, are contractions of East Saxons, South Saxons, and West Saxons.) The Angles divided central and northern England into the kingdoms of Mercia, East Anglia, and Northumbria. The seven kingdoms fought one another over the next few centuries.

During the ninth century, Vikings from Denmark conquered six of the Anglo-Saxon kingdoms. King Alfred of Wessex, known as Alfred the Great, retook the Danish lands in the south and became the father of modern England. Southern England again fell to invaders from Denmark in 1016. But the Danes could not hold onto their kingdom. In the turmoil that followed, William of Normandy crossed the English Channel and defeated the last Saxon king, Harold. The Battle of Hastings (1066) proved to be a turning point in history. **William the Conqueror** and his Norman knights were the last successful invaders of England. Isolated from mainland Europe, the English people developed a culture uniquely their own.

Lowlands of Southern England
England's agricultural heartland is the rolling plains and hills of southern England. The Thames River flows through the center of this region. England's crops and livestock place the United Kingdom among the world's top ten producers of barley, beet sugar, beef exports, sheep, and wool. The region also produces potatoes and wheat. England is divided into nearly fifty counties. Southern England has most of the famous ones, discussed below.

Kent on the Southeast Corner
The historic county of Kent lies in the southeast corner, just across the English Channel from France. Here the sea crashes against the forbidding white chalk cliffs of Dover. The narrowest point in the channel, only twenty-one miles wide, is called the Strait of Dover. The turbulent channel has been called England's "first line of defense" against conquering hordes on the mainland. But in fact, Britain was once the conqueror. England held large parts of the mainland until 1558, when the last British troops were driven out of Calais, a French city across from Dover.

The Downs of Sussex
West of Kent on the English Channel are the two counties of old Sussex: East Sussex and West Sussex. The city of Brighton is the heart of the region. William the Conqueror landed east of Brighton near the coastal town of Hastings.

The green countryside of Sussex has a special beauty. Two parallel ranges of rolling hills run along the interior. The South Downs run near the channel, and the North Downs run just south of the Thames. These chalk hills, called **downs,** cannot support trees but have plenty of grass for cattle and sheep.

Ports of Old Wessex
Farther west are the large lands of the former West Saxons (Wessex), once ruled by Alfred the Great. No one county is named Wessex. Instead, it was divided into many smaller districts, called **shires.** Several modern counties have retained the old shire divisions. For example, the county next to West Sussex is called Hamp*shire.*

Several good ports lie on the coast in old Wessex. The deep *Bristol Channel,* an arm of the Atlantic Ocean, extends far into the western side of the island of Great Britain. The important port of Bristol lies on deep Avon River, which flows into the channel. East of Bristol is the county of Wiltshire, where visitors can examine the prehistoric ruins at Stonehenge.

The Southwestern Peninsula
The two counties of Devon and Cornwall occupy the southwest peninsula of Great Britain. Unlike the adjacent lowlands of England, these counties consist of a low plateau with scattered granite highlands. Flaxseed, used in making linseed oil for paints and varnishes, is an important product. The United Kingdom ranks fifth worldwide in the production of flaxseed.

Stonehenge

Henge is the Saxon name for a collection of stones standing upright or laying across other standing stones. Ancient henges are visible all over the British Isles, but Stonehenge, east of Bristol, is by far the most famous. The twenty-four-foot-tall slabs of bluestone weigh up to fifty tons. The nearest possible quarry for these stones was two hundred miles away in the Prescelly Mountains of Wales. The ingenuity of the mysterious builders has given rise to tales of a race of giants or of extraterrestrial visitors.

A seventeenth-century architect believed Stonehenge was an ancient Roman temple to the god Coelus. In the eighteenth century a popular view held that druids built the place for sacrifices. Modern archaeologists have dated the ruins to before 1400 B.C., disproving both theories. (The druids arrived in the British Isles after 700 B.C.). Cremated bodies and nearby *barrows* (earth mounds over graves) suggest that Stonehenge was a necropolis, or city of the dead.

In 1963, a professor showed that a horseshoe of stones lines up with a solitary stone, called the heelstone, at sunrise of the summer solstice. Because this would aid calculation of eclipses and lunar phases, some people think Stonehenge was used for occult rites, but it may also have been a "farmer's almanac" to guide planting and harvesting of crops. God created the stars "for signs, and for seasons, and for days, and years" (Gen. 1:14).

The Moors of Devon Devon is known for Dartmoor and Exmoor, two national parks that protect moors. A **moor** is a wasteland on a high, treeless plateau. The land cannot be cultivated, although a tangle of low shrubs grow on it. Because fields of heather are so common, moors are often called *heaths.* Moors also have patches of peat bog or sphagnum moss. Most moors are farther north in the uplands of Scotland, but a few lie in the scattered high regions of England.

Devon's main port is Plymouth. The Pilgrims sailed from this port on their historic voyage to the New World.

Cornwall at Land's End Cornwall lies on the southwest tip of England. Lizard Point is the southern extreme and Land's End is the western extreme of the island of Great Britain. The isolated port of Penzance, once famous for its bustling trade in illegal goods and its pirates, lies in the bay between these two points.

Midlands, Workshop of the World North of the Thames River is the grassy plain of the **Midlands.** The Industrial Revolution started here in the eighteenth century for several reasons: easy access to iron and coal, productive farms that produced flax and wool for textiles, plentiful rivers for transportation, colonies that supplied raw materials from around the world, and political freedom that encouraged new ideas and inventions.

Rise of the Factory System Before the Industrial Revolution, most work was done at home in the *cottage industry.* But the invention of efficient textile machines, run by water and later by steam, changed rural life forever. The **factory system** brought workers, raw materials, and machinery under one roof. Rural workers flocked to the towns and cities to work in the factories. For a time, England became "the workshop of the world." But the factory system was quickly adopted by other nations in Europe.

The first major industry was in the eastern Midlands around Leicester. The focus of the Industrial Revolution later shifted to the western Midlands around **Birmingham.** The town was ideally located between the two longest rivers north of the Thames: the Severn River, which flows southwest into the Bristol Channel, and the Trent River, which flows northeast into the North Sea. It became a hub of canals and railroads, much like Chicago in the United States. Birmingham is now the second largest city in the British Isles.

Modern Socialist Debate   The growing power of miners and factory workers brought many changes to British government and politics. The government regulated factories and improved work conditions. Most adult males received the right to vote by 1884, and women received the right to vote in 1918. The greatest change came in the 1940s when the Labour Party created a welfare state. The government took direct control of several industries, a process called **nationalization.** But high taxes ruined Britain's economy. Debate over the merits of socialism continues in Britain, as in the other industrialized nations.

Northern England   Northern England includes all the counties north of the Trent River. It has some of England's most beautiful scenery—and some colorful history.

The Pennines   The **Pennine Mountains,** extending south from Scotland to the Midlands, form the backbone of England. Sherwood Forest—the fabled haunts of Robin Hood—is located at the southern tip of the Pennines, around Nottingham.

The Pennines have England's greatest deposits of iron ore. Because coal is an essential ingredient

The Chunnel

France and England have toyed with the idea of building a tunnel under the English Channel for many years. The project was even started a couple of times, but costs and problems always put an end to construction. On May 6, 1994, however, the tunnel became a reality. The project involved fifteen thousand workers and cost sixteen billion dollars. It was one of the great engineering feats of the century.

The tunnel is thirty-one miles long, linking Dover, England, to Calais, France. Twenty-three miles of the tunnel are under the ocean. Miners bored three parallel tunnels about 130 feet below the Channel floor. Digging was relatively easy because of the soft chalk marl, a sedimentary rock that is almost waterproof. Buses, cars, and trucks drive right onto the shuttles, which are one-half mile long. The entire trip through the Chunnel takes forty-two minutes and shortens Channel crossings by three and one-half hours.

The official name of the English Channel Tunnel is the Eurotunnel, but the British fondly refer to it as the "Chunnel." The tunnel benefits both trade partners, although some Englishmen still lament the end to their traditional isolation from the continent.

The Chunnel

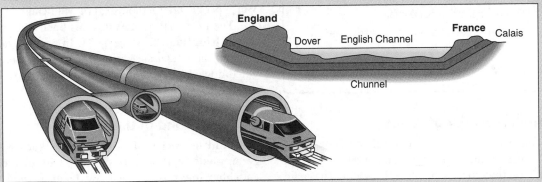

England   Dover   English Channel   France   Calais

Chunnel

in iron processing, several mining towns with nearby coal deposits boomed during the Industrial Revolution. The cities of Leeds, Sheffield, and Newcastle upon Tyne each have over one million people. In fact, they are the fourth, fifth, and sixth largest metropolitan areas in the British Isles.

Wars of the Roses   Other important cities lie in the plains on either side of the Pennines. Lancaster and York are famous for the Wars of the Roses (1455-85), a feud between two families over the English crown. The House of York, whose emblem was a white rose, fought Lancaster, whose emblem was a red rose. York is an ancient city in the east, on the **Yorkshire Plain.** York's size has been overshadowed by bigger cities on the North Sea. Downriver is Kingston upon Hull, the main fishing port on the east coast.

On the west side of the Pennine Mountains is the **Lancashire Plain.** Lancaster is now a minor city, but canals and railroads have brought industry and trade to other cities. Manchester, located at the foot of the Pennine Mountains, is the third largest metropolitan area in the British Isles. It was once the textile capital of the world. West of Manchester on a major estuary of the Irish Sea is Liverpool, England's second biggest port (after London).

◎ SECTION REVIEW

1. What river lies at the heart of Southern England?
2. In what plains did the Industrial Revolution unfold? Why there?
3. What is the "backbone of England"?
4. What are downs? moors? heaths?
5. Name the three largest metropolitan areas in the British Isles.

💡 Is nationalization a form of theft, as some conservatives claim?

The Principality of Wales

Wales occupies a broad peninsula on the western side of England. It is mostly mountainous except for a narrow coastal plain in the south. The main range is the Cambrian Mountains. The climate of Wales is mild and wet, similar to that of England, but less than 10 percent of the land is arable. Dairy cattle and sheep graze on the grassy but treeless uplands.

Cardiff and Swansea are the main ports on the south coast. Coal mines began operating in the Rhondda Valley during the Industrial Revolution. Here farm boys could earn in a short time more than their parents made in a lifetime on the farm. As the demand for coal declined, however, many mines shut down and many jobless Welshmen sailed to the United States. Today the Welsh are struggling to find alternative jobs in services, banking, and insurance.

The Welsh people descended from ancient **Celts,** who found refuge in the mountains from Anglo-Saxon invaders. One in five people still speak the Celtic dialect of Wales, along with the main language—English. The complex Welsh language is one of the world's most musical. Outsiders find it hard to pronounce and spell, however, because it has so many double consonants.

Wales joined the Anglican Church when it was first founded, but the Welsh remained open to the preaching of *nonconformists,* who refused to conform to Anglican rule. In the eighteenth century, miners and factory workers readily listened to the message of John Wesley, one of England's greatest evangelists. He rode up and down the byways of Great Britain, preaching anywhere he could find a listener, not just inside church walls. Wesley was an Anglican priest, but disagreements eventually forced him to form the Methodist Church. Most Welsh people are Methodists, not Anglicans.

The principality of Wales has been officially united with England since 1536. In spite of deep pride in their separate heritage, the Welsh people voted down a referendum for limited self-government in 1979.

Scotland, Land of the Scots

Scotland lies north of England. It is known for green **glens** (narrow valleys carved by glaciers) and blue **lochs** (deep, narrow lakes carved by glaciers). The Scots, descendants of the Celts,

United Kingdom Statistics

DIVISION	CAPITAL	DATE OF UNION	AREA (SQ. MI.)	POPULATION	HIGH POINT, ELEVATION (FT.)
England	London	1536	50,378	49,123,518	Scafell Pike, 3,210
Wales	Cardiff	1536	8,018	2,899,000	Snowdon, 3,561
Scotland	Edinburgh	1707	30,420	5,111,000	Ben Nevis, 4,406
Northern Ireland	Belfast	1801	5,461	1,610,000	Slieve Donard, 2,796
Dependencies					
Channel Islands	NA	1066	75	152,241	Jersey Island, 454
Isle of Man	Douglas	1765	227	74,504	Snaefell, 2,034

held off many invaders who tried to take their rugged and isolated homeland. Though part of the United Kingdom, Scots have preserved a culture distinctly their own.

Two figures stand out among the many Scotsmen who fought against England. Their exploits are still celebrated in statue and song. William Wallace was a fierce patriot who surprised and

Hadrian's Wall, completed in A.D. 136, protected Roman England from the northern barbarians. Seventy-four miles long and twenty feet high, it is the largest Roman ruin in Britain.

defeated King Edward I at Stirling Bridge. In spite of defeat the following year, Wallace carried on an effective guerrilla war until his capture and execution in 1305. The gallant but treacherous Robert the Bruce declared himself the rightful king of Scotland in 1306. His victory at Bannockburn in 1314 established his right to the crown.

Nationalism is growing in Scotland. In an effort to save the United Kingdom, Parliament granted Scotland its own parliament in 1997, with limited self-government and taxing authority. The Stone of Scone, Scotland's symbol of sovereignty removed to London in 1296 by Edward I, was returned to Edinburgh Castle.

The Southern Uplands   Scotland's border with England's Pennines is called the Southern Uplands. It consists of barren hilltops, fertile slopes, and foggy moors. The range that divides Scotland from England is the **Cheviot Hills** and is crowned by Hadrian's Wall, which Rome built to stop raids from the unconquered Scots north of Brittania.

Once known for their cottage industries of wool spinning and weaving, these uplands now have great woolen mills. The tweeds and sweaters made here are exported all over the world.

Cities of the Scottish Lowlands   North of the border, a belt of lowlands stretches across central Scotland. The flat lands and relatively fertile soil make it Scotland's most populated area. About 75 percent of the Scottish people are crowded around Glasgow in the west and Edinburgh in the east.

Glasgow, Scotland's largest city, is a center of industry and commerce. Oceangoing vessels stop

Edinburgh, Scotland. Edinburgh Castle is obvious in the background. Its famous occupants included Mary Queen of Scots. Her son, James VI of Scotland, moved to London after he was crowned King James I of England.

here at the mouth of the Clyde River. After union with Britain in 1707, Scottish ports were allowed to trade directly with the colonies in North America. The resulting commerce helped Glasgow to prosper. With major deposits of coal and iron in the surrounding hills, Glasgow was one of the first cities to benefit from the Industrial Revolution. At a mine nearby, James Watt developed the first efficient steam engine.

The capital city of **Edinburgh** has earned the nickname "Athens of the North" because it is a center of culture and learning. Scholars from the University of Edinburgh are highly esteemed,

Bagpipes please a crowd at a Scottish festival on the Isle of Skye, the Inner Hebrides.

especially in medicine. People from around the world attend annual festivals to enjoy many musical and dramatic productions.

Edinburgh was the home of John Knox, a fiery preacher who brought the Protestant Reformation to Scotland. Knox promoted strict moral discipline among the Scottish people, and he established the Kirk (Church) of Scotland, which has become the official church. Unlike the episcopal system of the Anglicans, the Scots developed a *presbyterian* system, which gives all powers to church elders, called presbyters, not to bishops.

Scottish Highlands North of the populous lowlands are the Grampian Mountains, the principal range of the Scottish Highlands. They include Ben Nevis, the highest mountain in the British Isles

Territorial Claims in the North Sea

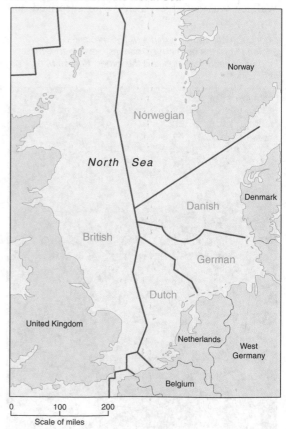

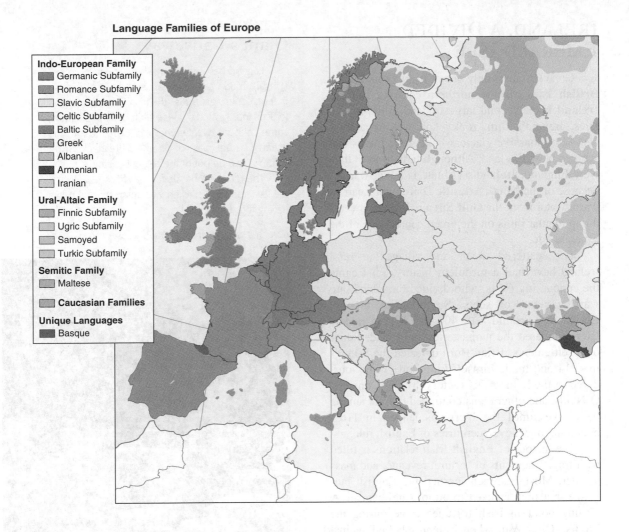

Language Families of Europe

Indo-European Family
- Germanic Subfamily
- Romance Subfamily
- Slavic Subfamily
- Celtic Subfamily
- Baltic Subfamily
- Greek
- Albanian
- Armenian
- Iranian

Ural-Altaic Family
- Finnic Subfamily
- Ugric Subfamily
- Samoyed
- Turkic Subfamily

Semitic Family
- Maltese

Caucasian Families

Unique Languages
- Basque

(4,406 ft.). North of this mountain system is a deep valley, called Glen More or the Great Glen. The Caledonian Canal cuts through this valley and includes the waters of Loch Ness. Inverness is the main city on the canal. Beyond the Great Glen are more highlands and the Hebrides Islands, where isolated people still speak a Celtic dialect.

The Scottish Highlanders were even more fierce and independent than the lowlanders. They once lived in warring *clans,* groups of related families that banded together. The Campbells, MacDonalds, Mackenzies, and other clans each adopted a unique tartan plaid design. Today clans gather from all over to participate in the Highland Games each summer. The men dress in traditional kilts and participate in events like tossing the caber, a huge tree trunk that is hefted end over end. Bagpipe music, once used to inspire warriors, plays an important part in the ceremonies.

The discovery of oil and natural gas in the North Sea has brought many jobs and economic development to the area nearby. The city of Aberdeen on the east coast is known as the "oil capital of Europe." The United Kingdom ranks seventh worldwide in the production of natural gas, although reserves are running out.

IRELAND, A DIVIDED EMERALD ISLE

Great Britain is only one of many islands in the **British Isles** off the northern coast of Europe. **Ireland** is the second largest island in the British Isles. Ireland's thin, rocky soil was apparently caused by massive glaciers—the same forces that scraped New England. Although farther north than New England, Ireland's climate is much warmer because of the **North Atlantic Drift,** which carries warm water from the Gulf Stream. Westerly winds dump regular rains on the green countryside of the Emerald Isle.

The scattered towns and villages of rural Ireland have had a turbulent history. First came the conquering Celts, who divided the island into warring clans, or septs. Saint Patrick brought Christianity around A.D. 400, but Viking raiders later plundered the monasteries and founded their own settlements. Brian Boru defeated the Vikings in 1014 and made himself king, only to be murdered in the hour of his victory. The O'Connells, O'Neills, and other clans continued to fight among themselves until the Normans landed in 1169, beginning over seven centuries of English rule.

The history of English-Irish relations is filled with tragic incidents of torture, revenge, and mass murder. Most Irishmen learned the English language, but they refused to adopt Anglicanism. A turning point in Irish fortunes came during the English Civil War, when Ireland rebelled against England and lost. The English confiscated most of their land, and the Irish became landless peasants in their own country. More than ever, the Irish ambition was to regain independence.

Northern Ireland

Northern Ireland, also called Ulster, consists of six counties on the northeast corner of the island. It is a land of rugged coasts and rolling hills. Many crystal lakes, called "loughs," dot the interior. Lough Neagh is the largest, covering over 150 square miles. The plentiful lakes and rivers provide fishermen with salmon and sea trout. Among the

Giant's Causeway

Legend has it that an Irish giant, Finn McCool (Fingal), made a pier, or causeway, out of rock so that he could walk across the Irish Sea from Ireland to Scotland. Around thirty-seven thousand columns, some of them twenty feet high, descend into the ocean on the coast of Northern Ireland. Similar columns rise up out of the sea in Scotland.

The rocks are basalt, formed from lava. When the lava cooled, it cracked into prism-shaped pillars having four to eight sides.

Natural basalt columns at Giants Causeway, Northern Ireland

region's many bays are the excellent harbors of Londonderry and Belfast.

Belfast, the capital and largest city, is an industrial city once famed for shipbuilding. Belfast shipyards built many warships and ocean liners, including the *Titanic*. Aircraft construction is now an important part of the economy. The textile mills are known for their fine Irish linen.

Ulster has a long history of independence from the rest of the island. It was a distinct kingdom from the fifth century until the Normans overthrew their king in the twelfth century. Later, clan leaders in Ulster resisted English domination more than most other Irish provinces. Ironically, their final defeat left the region depopulated and open to British settlement. The first Ulster "plantation" was planted in 1607—the same year as Jamestown was planted in Virginia. Today two-thirds of the people of Ulster are descendants of "planters" from Scotland, England, and Wales.

Most descendants of the British settlers are Protestants, evenly divided between Anglicans and Presbyterians. They are loyal British citizens. They have never forgotten the atrocities suffered in the Great Rebellion of 1641, when Roman Catholic rebels butchered Englishmen across the land, singling out the Protestant pastors for torture. Every year the Orange Day Parade is held to celebrate the Battle of the Boyne (1690), when William of Orange, the Protestant king of the Glorious Revolution, defeated James II's rebel army and ended any threat of a Catholic monarchy.

Most Irish Catholics, on the other hand, would like independence. Over the centuries England has instituted harsh measures discriminating against the Catholics, including a law that once prevented them from buying or inheriting land. A radical group known as the **Irish Republican Army** (IRA) has fought the longest and deadliest campaign of terrorism in modern European history. The IRA has set off over ten thousand bombs and killed over two thousand people. Their goal is to force the British Parliament to surrender control of Ulster. Very few Irishmen support the terrorists, but they do want independence.

The Republic of Ireland

The Republic of Ireland covers five-sixths of the island of Ireland. Over 90 percent of the population is Roman Catholic. More than any other nation in western Europe, the Roman Catholic Church continues to have a major influence on Irish culture and national identity.

Most Irishmen speak English, though they do so with a *brogue,* or soft accent. **Gaelic,** also called Irish, is their ancient Celtic language. The constitution calls it the "first official language," and street signs and official documents must be bilingual. But only one-quarter of the people speak Gaelic with "some proficiency."

The Republic of Ireland was born in violent circumstances. The radical political party Sinn Fein (shihn FAYN, meaning "We Ourselves") staged a rebellion in the city of Dublin on Easter Monday in 1916, while the British army was busy fighting World War I. The Sinn Feiners were stopped and their leaders executed. Violence continued, however, forcing the British Parliament to negotiate the Anglo-Irish Treaty in 1921, creating an Irish Free State. In 1949 the Republic of Ireland cut all ties with Britain.

The Potato Famine

In the nineteenth century Irish farmers raised potatoes as their main crop. Potatoes grow well in the poor Irish soil, and they produce a plentiful crop when conditions are right.

But in 1845, 1846, and 1848, a dreaded fungus attacked the potato fields. Spreading quickly in the moist climate, it wiped out whole fields in a matter of days. The poverty-stricken farmers had no money to afford foreign food. Hundreds of thousands sold everything they had, or they got help from family members so that they could find work abroad. But the least fortunate had to stay. Nearly one million people died of starvation during the Irish potato famine. A great wave of immigrants came to the United States at this time, settling mostly in the cities of the Northeast. These Irish-Americans brought their cultural riches to the American heritage.

The Coast Ireland has always been a land of poor, rural farms. Many young people are moving to the city in search of employment. Nearly one-quarter of the population lives in and around the capital, **Dublin.** Since the country has few natural resources, industries must process imported materials. Well-known exports include fine Waterford crystal.

The Interior A rim of mountains surrounds the coast of Ireland. Ireland ranks tenth in the mining of zinc, found in the mountains west of Dundalk. The Shannon River, which flows through the rolling plain in the center of Ireland, is even longer than the Thames. The grasslands support cattle and horses. Horse racing and related festivals are a national pastime. In the central and western parts of the island are many bogs, where the water sits without access to the ocean. Here partly decayed mosses have been compressed to form thick layers of **peat.** Since Ireland lacks coal, many people burn peat for heating and cooking.

Many giants of modern English literature were born in Dublin, including Oscar Wilde, George Bernard Shaw, and James Joyce.

> ## ◎ SECTION REVIEW
>
> 1. Compare and contrast Wales, Northern Ireland, and Scotland. Include physical geography, history, population, language, religion, and economy.
> 2. What mineral resource comes from the North Sea?
> 3. What range divides Scotland from England?
> 4. What is Gaelic?
> 5. Why do Protestants in Ulster want to remain in the United Kingdom?
> ♀ What are the arguments for and against England giving Scotland full independence?

SCANDINAVIA

Scandinavia is the Land of the Midnight Sun. Parts of this region lie above the Arctic Circle, where the sun never sets for over two months each summer, and where it never rises for two months each winter. During the sun's absence, the northern lights (aurora borealis) are visible. Norway's view is especially famous. Vacationers in Hammerfest can see the midnight sun hanging over the Arctic Ocean.

The tall people of these northern lands, with fair hair and blue eyes, are known by many names—Nordic, Norsemen, Northmen. But most names have the same root *nor,* meaning "north." Today we call them Scandinavians, from an ancient center of the Norsemen called Scandia. There are five countries in **Scandinavia:** Norway, Sweden, Finland, Denmark, and Iceland.

Viking is a Norse word meaning "inlet," a reference to the sea inlets where the Norsemen live. In A.D. 793 Vikings began to terrorize the rest of Europe. They also conquered most of England and settled on the northern coast of France (still called *Nor*mandy, land of the *Nor*mans or Norsemen). Vikings from Norway plundered Scotland, Wales, and Ireland. Vikings from Sweden (called Varangians) invaded Russia and established the first Russian cities. Vikings later discovered and colonized Iceland, Greenland, and North America (Newfoundland).

The Scandinavians fought among themselves as well as against foreigners. For a time all five Scandinavian nations were under one ruler (1397-1523). **Queen Margaret** of Denmark established this union. The union lasted until Sweden rebelled and began building its own empire in Europe.

The Scandinavians eventually converted to Christianity, but they never felt close ties to Rome. When Martin Luther started the Protestant movement in the sixteenth century, they quickly converted. Today, over 90 percent of all Scandinavians

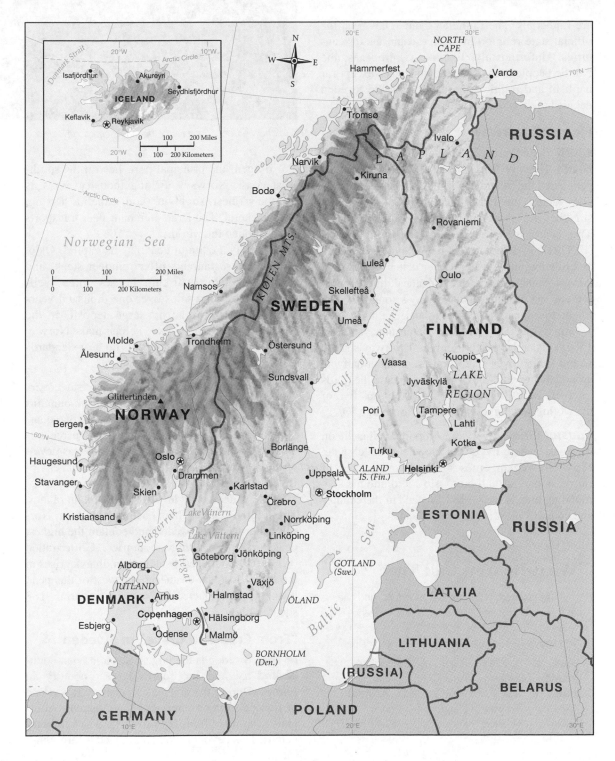

ICELAND

Denmark Strait

Isafjördhur
Akureyri
Seydhisfjördhur
Keflavik
Reykjavik

Arctic Circle

20°W
10°W

0   100   200 Miles
0   100   200 Kilometers

N
W   E
S

20°E
30°E

NORTH CAPE
Hammerfest
Vardø
70°N

Tromsø
Ivalo
RUSSIA

Narvik
Kiruna
L A P L A N D

Bodø
Rovaniemi

Arctic Circle

Norwegian Sea

Luleå
Oulo

Namsos
Skellefteå
Gulf of Bothnia

0   100   200 Miles
0   100   200 Kilometers

Molde
SWEDEN
Umeå
FINLAND

Ålesund
Trondheim
Östersund
Vaasa
Kuopio

KJØLEN MTS.
Sundsvall
LAKE REGION
Jyväskylä

Glittertinden
Pori
Tampere
Lahti

Bergen
NORWAY
Borlänge
Turku
Kotka

60°N
Uppsala
ALAND IS. (Fin.)
Helsinki

Haugesund
Oslo
Karlstad
Stockholm

Stavanger
Drammen
Örebro
ESTONIA
RUSSIA

Skien
Norrköping
Lake Vänern

Kristiansand
Linköping
Lake Vättern
Baltic Sea

Skagerrak
Göteborg
Jönköping
GOTLAND (Swe.)
LATVIA

Kattegat
Växjö

Alborg
Halmstad
ÖLAND

JUTLAND
Arhus
LITHUANIA

DENMARK
Copenhagen
Hälsingborg
BORNHOLM (Den.)

Esbjerg
Odense
Malmö
(RUSSIA)
BELARUS

GERMANY
POLAND

10°E
20°E
30°E

317

are Lutherans. The Lutheran Church has been the official state religion in all five countries for centuries. Unfortunately, like most Europeans, the Nordic people no longer attend services except for baptism and religious holidays. In 1996 Sweden decided to drop the Lutheran state church.

Fjords of Norway

Scandinavia is known for its peninsulas. Norway and Sweden share the largest peninsula, the **Scandinavian Peninsula,** with Norway facing the North Sea. Norway's coastline stretches for more than sixteen hundred miles. The coast is splintered by numerous **fjords** (FYORDZ)—long, narrow bays carved by glaciers and filled with sea water. Other major fjords are in Alaska, Patagonia, and New Zealand; but the most famous are in Norway. Norway's longest fjord, Sogne Fjord, cuts 127 miles inland.

Including all the bays, peninsulas, and the 150,000 islands, the full length of Norway's shore would stretch over 13,250 miles, or about halfway around the world. Many streams drop into the fjords to create beautiful waterfalls. Norway has five of the world's ten highest waterfalls. (See page 277.)

Coastal Cities Norway's important cities lie on the coast, where the ocean moderates the climate. Most Norwegian cities also take advantage of fjords as natural harbors. Oslo Fjord and the surrounding area is the largest lowland in the country and contains most of the arable land.

A rainbow graces Sogne Fjord, the longest fjord in Norway.

Bergen, the principal port, lies on the southwest coast. Norway's fishing industry ranks as Europe's finest, supplying cod, capelin, herring, and mackerel. The large merchant fleet transports goods around the world.

Norway's cultural center is its capital, **Oslo.** Norwegian restaurants offer reindeer steak, and the Viking Ship Museum houses three well-preserved wooden ships over one thousand years old. Oslo refines oil from large deposits in the North Sea. Oil exports have helped make Norway rich. It enjoys one of the world's highest standards of living.

The Remote Interior A high plateau covers most of Norway. Glaciers cover many mountains and have scraped the rocky surface. Only one-quarter of Norway is forested, and only 3 percent is arable. Nordic, or cross-country, skiing was developed in this wasteland. The small Norwegian city of Lillehammer hosted the Winter Olympics in 1994.

The plateau includes several mountain ranges. The **Kjolen** (CHUH luhn) **Mountains** form Norway's border with Sweden and contain the highest peaks in both of those countries. Glittertinden (8,110 ft.), the highest peak in Scandinavia, rises in the south. Jostedal Glacier to the west of this peak is the largest glacier in Norway, covering 188 square miles.

"From Cradle to Grave" in Sweden

Sweden is the largest Scandinavian country and the fourth largest country in Europe. During the seventeenth century it was one of Europe's major empires. King Gustavus Adolphus, who ruled from 1611 to 1632, was a military genius. This devout Lutheran king led an army into

---

What Do You Call Them?

A person from Germany is a German, and one from Italy is an Italian. However, one from France is a Frenchman, and one from Poland is a Pole. Do you know what to call a person from these places?

Australia	Sweden	Israel	Denmark
Ireland	Turkey	Finland	Nepal
Haiti	Japan	Peru	Switzerland
Greece	Norway	Philippines	Congo
Spain	Thailand	Portugal	Iceland

Germany when France's Catholic armies appeared on the verge of reconquering northern Europe. He greatly extended Swedish territory until his death in battle. Sweden is now known as a peacemaker. Alfred Nobel, the Swedish inventor of dynamite, used his fortune to start the annual Nobel Peace Prizes, first awarded in 1901. Sweden remained **neutral** throughout World Wars I and II, not joining either side. It later stayed out of NATO and the European Union during the Cold War.

Sweden's welfare state set the example for all other Nordic countries by providing "cradle to grave" benefits, including most major expenses from childbirth to burial. Unlike the socialists in Great Britain, the "Swedish model" was a *mixed economy* that allowed businesses to stay in private hands, but the state taxed and regulated businesses heavily. It also adopted one of the highest income taxes in the world. In the 1990s, however, the people began to see the damage this system can do to private enterprise. But change is slow in coming.

Sweden has a strong economy, based on its reputation for quality, high-tech engineering and metallurgy. Its industries make everything from ball bearings to surgical instruments. Sweden is also a major producer of automobiles, including Volvo and Saab.

Lowland South   About one-third of Sweden is lowland plains in the south. The mild climate and fertile soil make it Sweden's best agricultural region. Sweden ranks sixth worldwide for the production of oats. A low plateau in the center of the plain has poor, rocky soil that is useful for dairy cattle.

Stockholm, the nation's capital, is the largest city in Scandinavia. Covering fourteen islands and connected by fifty bridges, it is aptly nicknamed the "Venice of the North." While the North Atlantic Drift keeps nearly all of Norway's harbors ice-free year-round, many ports on the **Baltic Sea,** including Stockholm, freeze in winter. Ships enter only with the help of icebreakers.

Most of Sweden's western border is shared with Norway. In the south, however, the west coast lies along the Skagerrak and Kattegat, two arms of the North Sea. Göteborg is the second largest city in Sweden. Ice-free year-round, Göteborg has become Sweden's leading port. The Göta Canal provides the eastern ports with a year-round trade route through the interior lakes of Vänern and Vättern.

Rugged Northland   Sweden's sparsely populated Northland is considered the last frontier of Europe. Mountains line the border with Norway, and rugged hills cover the rest of the region. Rivers flow southeast through deep gorges that broaden into valleys near the **Gulf of Bothnia.** Great forests of pine and spruce cover these hills and provide timber for the pulp and sawmills on the coast. Sweden is Europe's leading producer of wood and produces about one-fifth of the world's wood pulp. The region around Kiruna is the greatest source of iron ore in all of Western Europe.

SECTION REVIEW

1. Who were the Vikings?
2. What religion is common throughout Scandinavia?
3. What peninsula contains both Norway and Sweden?
4. What mountains divide Norway and Sweden?
5. What is the largest city in Scandinavia? Why?
   Why did Sweden's welfare state prosper for many years, unlike Britain's?

Finland, Land of Ten Thousand Lakes

Finland has been independent only since 1917. Prior to that time, the Finns spent a century under Russian control and seven centuries under Swedish control. Unlike the other Scandinavians, their language and physical features are related to people from northern Russia. The difficult Finnish language is not Germanic, or even Indo-European, but Uralic. To improve their ability to trade, many Finns are learning English or German.

Finns work hard to keep their environment one of the cleanest in the world. Their love of nature is reflected in their favorite recreational activities of

Let's Go Exploring

1. What climate occurs throughout the British Isles? Which Scandinavian country does *not* have this climate?

2. What is the climate in Lapland?

3. As you move east across Europe, what does the marine-west-coast climate become?

4. What climate is most common on the southern peninsulas of Europe?

5. What are the only two countries in Western Europe with a semiarid climate?

   💡 Why is the west coast of Norway so much warmer than the eastern border?

Climates of Western Europe

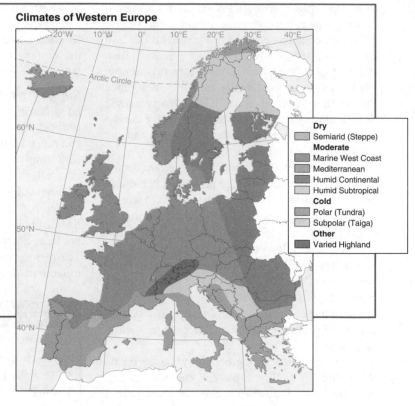

Dry	
	Semiarid (Steppe)
Moderate	
	Marine West Coast
	Mediterranean
	Humid Continental
	Humid Subtropical
Cold	
	Polar (Tundra)
	Subpolar (Taiga)
Other	
	Varied Highland

fishing, hunting, and camping. However, relaxing in a hot sauna is the national pastime. Every apartment complex has a sauna and so do many homes.

Finland's only access to the ocean is the Baltic Sea. It has a long coastline along the Gulf of Bothnia. Most of Finland's population clusters in the southern coastal lowlands. The lowlands enjoy the mildest climate and the best farmland. Only one-tenth of Finland's land is arable, but Finland's farms are self-sufficient. The ports freeze during the long winters, but the shipbuilding industry builds over half of the world's icebreakers to keep the ports open. Helsinki is the nation's capital, main seaport, and largest city. The city often hosts peace talks between warring nations.

The "Land of Ten Thousand Lakes" refers to Finland's southern interior. Like Minnesota, Finland has many glacial lakes, perhaps one hundred thousand. Thick forests cover three-fourths of Finland, and timber products account for 70 percent of its exports. The shimmering lakes and rivers are called "white coal" because the running water produces cheap hydroelectricity to run the mills and other industry.

Northern Finland contains the heart of **Lapland,** which extends into Sweden, Norway, and Russia. The regional capital is Rovaniemi. The **Lapps,** who call themselves Sami, have tended reindeer in this region for thousands of years. In summer, they take the reindeer north to feed on the moss and lichen of the tundra. In the winter, they

A few Laplanders continue to herd reindeer in the Arctic.

return south to the forests. But since many Lapps have moved to villages to work as fishermen or lumberjacks, the Lapp's nomadic customs and culture are fading.

Denmark

Denmark has been an independent country since 950 and even ruled England from 1013 to 1042. Its islands and mainland peninsula lie farther south than the rest of Scandinavia, where winters are less severe. Lacking mineral resources, the country depends heavily on agriculture and trade. Firm believers in welfare, the Danes pay one of the highest tax rates in the world. After taxes and duties are added to a new car, its cost triples!

Jutland Peninsula   The **Jutland** Peninsula extends northward from Germany and accounts for about 70 percent of Denmark's land area. Jutland is "the land of the Jutes," the Germanic people who invaded England along with the Angles and Saxons. Dunes along the west coast protect the peninsula from winds off the North Sea. A rocky plain covers the far north and a sandy plain covers the southwest. Low hills roll gently across the rest of the peninsula. Farmers grow barley and raise both beef and dairy cattle. Denmark is the world's largest exporter of butter and cheese.

The king of Denmark built Rosenborg Palace in 1618 to serve as his summer home in Copenhagen. It now houses a museum of the royal family.

Nearby Islands   About half of Denmark's people live on ninety islands east of Jutland. Hills cover the islands as on Jutland, but the deep soils are more fertile.

The capital city, **Copenhagen,** is on Denmark's largest island, Zealand. Copenhagen houses one-quarter of the country's population and is the largest metropolitan area in Scandinavia. The name Copenhagen means "merchant's harbor," and it is indeed a strategic port. The Danes are known for elegant design and fine quality in their exported furniture, machinery, and silverware.

Distant Islands   Denmark's overseas territories have included Iceland, Greenland, and the Faeroe Islands, a group of seventeen inhabited islands north of Scotland. Denmark granted Iceland independence in 1918, but retained the other islands. The Faeroe Islands and Greenland are now self-ruling provinces within the kingdom of Denmark. **Greenland** is the largest island in the world, fifty times larger than Denmark and thirteen hundred miles west of Denmark in North America. The United States offered to buy Greenland after World War II. Though Denmark refused, a U.S. radar base and weather station operate at Thule in the far north.

Eric the Red, a Viking navigator, settled Greenland with a band of Icelanders in 985. They deceptively named the island Greenland to attract settlers. In reality, 84 percent lies under an ice cap that averages almost a mile thick. Colonists settled on the southwest coast, the island's warmest region. In the fifteenth century, the entire colony perished, but the Danes resettled in the eighteenth century. Today, Greenlanders are a mixture of Eskimo and Danish ancestry. More than one-third are employed in the fishing industry.

Iceland, Land of Fire and Ice

About 650 miles west of Norway is the "Land of Fire and Ice." Large glaciers glide down the active volcanoes on Iceland. The glacier-carved fjords are reminiscent of Norway, but not the island's two-hundred volcanoes, one of which erupts about every five years. Surtsey, an island off the south coast, was created by an under-sea volcano in 1963. The most famous active volcano, Mount Hekla (4,892 ft.), was once thought to conceal the gates of hell.

As elsewhere in Scandinavia, the North Atlantic Drift flows around Iceland, warming the southern coast. Temperatures similar to those in New York City keep the ports open all year.

Icelanders are proud of their heritage. The Althing, its national assembly founded in 930, is the oldest democracy in the world. Iceland and Finland are republics, while the other three Scandinavian nations have a constitutional monarchy. The Icelandic language is the only Scandinavian tongue that remains essentially unchanged from the Viking era. Without too much difficulty, Icelanders can read the medieval chronicles of their Viking ancestors. Desiring to keep their language pure, a special committee creates new Icelandic words for such things as telephones and computers instead of adopting foreign words.

Coastal Lowlands Iceland's fjords harbor almost all the population and the island's 1 percent of arable land. The main crop is hay for the sheep,

Rising from the ocean in November 1963, the island of Surtsey now covers one square mile and rises 560 feet above the sea. Nearby Surtlinger is still active.

which in turn provide food and clothing. Potatoes and turnips also withstand the cool climate. Iceland's fishing fleet is one of the world's most modern. Nearly 80 percent of Iceland's exports are fish products.

The capital, Reykjavik, houses half the population. Geothermal energy provides heat for hot water, heated outdoor swimming pools, greenhouses, and 70 percent of the homes. The greenhouses enable Icelanders to grow flowers, tomatoes, and fruit during the long winters.

Rugged Interior Iceland is known for its rugged beauty. The barren interior plateau is twenty-five hundred feet above sea level. The plateau has the largest glacier in Europe, Vatnajökull. This glacier has more ice than all the other glaciers of Europe combined. Glacial lakes dot the region, and glacier-fed rivers create beautiful waterfalls.

Iceland has more hot springs than any other country in the world. The English word *geyser* comes from Iceland's most spectacular hot spring, the Great Geysir, which spews water almost two hundred feet high.

Most Icelanders live in small villages.

◎ SECTION REVIEW

1. What people live in northern Finland?
2. What is the major product of Finland?
3. What is Denmark's peninsula called?
4. Why did Copenhagen become a leading city?
5. What do Hekla and Surtsey illustrate about Iceland?
- 💡 Why might geographers exclude Finland from Scandinavia? Why might they exclude Iceland?

REVIEW

Can You Define These Terms?

Commonwealth of Nations	cabinet system	moor	loch
Anglican Church	coalition government	factory system	peat
Parliament	downs	nationalization	fjord
House of Commons	shire	glen	neutral

Can You Locate These Natural Features?

Great Britain	Pennine Mountains	Ireland	Gulf of Bothnia
North Sea	Yorkshire Plain	North Atlantic Drift	Jutland
English Channel	Lancashire Plain	Scandinavian Peninsula	Greenland
Thames River	Cheviot Hills	Kjolen Mountains	
Midlands	British Isles	Baltic Sea	

Can You Explain the Significance of These People, Places, and Events?

United Kingdom	Saxons	Edinburgh	Queen Margaret
London	England	Northern Ireland	Oslo
Buckingham Palace	William the Conqueror	Irish Republican Army	Stockholm
Queen Victoria	Birmingham	Gaelic	Lapland
Westminster Abbey	Wales	Dublin	Lapps
Glorious Revolution	Celts	Scandinavia	Copenhagen
Angles	Scotland	Viking	

How Much Do You Remember?

1. Put these leaders in chronological order and describe their place in English history: William the Conqueror, Henry VIII, Alfred the Great, Victoria.
2. List the countries of northern Europe that fit each description. The total number of answers is given in parenthesis.
   a. Anglican (1)
   b. Roman Catholic (1)
   c. Lutheran (5)
   d. constitutional monarchy (4)
   e. republic (3)
   f. island nation (3)
   g. peninsulas on Europe's mainland (4)
   h. frozen harbors (2)
   i. oil (2)
3. Match each part of the United Kingdom with the associated term.
   a. England
   b. Wales
   c. Scotland
   d. Northern Ireland
      (1) Anglican
      (2) Presbyterian
      (3) Methodist
      (4) downs
      (5) glens
      (6) loughs
      (7) highest peak

4. How did the United Kingdom set an example for Europe in these areas: parliament, monarchy, industry, religion?
5. Give at least one major product of each country in northern Europe.
6. What parts of the United Kingdom still speak Celtic? Why has it survived in those places?
7. Give three features shared in common by all five Scandinavian nations.

What Do You Think?

1. Give examples from the history of northern Europe that illustrate the lesson of I Samuel 2:7.
2. Why do you think the official state church is strong in Ireland but not the rest of northern Europe?
3. Do the British Isles and Scandinavia belong in the same culture region?
4. What two nations have the highest population densities in northern Europe? Why?
5. Compare and contrast the governments of Great Britain and the United States.

CHAPTER 14

CONTINENTAL EUROPE

Continental Europe refers to the main land-mass of Western Europe, as opposed to the islands and peninsulas. Much of the continent is a wide coastal lowland with a marine-west-coast climate. The countries on the continent have greatly influenced the history and culture of the world. Two of these countries, France and Germany, are members of the Group of Seven—the top seven economic powers in the world.

Without a doubt, the greatest contribution of Continental Europe has been the spread of the gospel. After the dark days of the Middle Ages, the light of the gospel shone again, first in Germany, then across Western Europe, and finally around the world. *Sola Scriptura! Sola Fide!* (Scripture alone! Faith alone!) was the cry of the Reformers, who protested the teachings of the Catholic Church. They recognized two lost truths, that Scripture is the sole authority for living and that salvation comes through faith alone. Europe's greatest days followed the **Protestant Reformation.**

The Reformation divided the continent. Today Roman Catholicism dominates the south and west, and Protestant denominations are prominent in the north. The industrious peoples of Europe have grown rich in the years since the Reformation, but they have lost their religious zeal. Few people care about doctrinal differences but simply follow the traditions and rituals of their forefathers. They have forgotten the truths of the Protestant Reformation, for which many great Christian martyrs died.

Ye were not redeemed with corruptible things, as silver and gold, from your vain conversation received by tradition from your fathers; but with the precious blood of Christ. (I Peter 1:18-19)

THE FRENCH REVOLUTION

France is the largest country in Europe. Three-fourths of the people are Roman Catholic. Although France has a few Muslims, Protestants, and Jews, most of the other French citizens claim no religion at all. The cities of France were once the center of titanic struggles between Protestants and Catholics. A Protestant nobleman, Henry of Navarre, won the war. Though he converted to Catholicism, his Edict of Nantes (1598) allowed freedom of worship among the French Protestants, known as Huguenots.

France prospered with the help of the Huguenots, but Louis XIV, a Catholic king, later revoked the Edict of Nantes in 1685. He tried to stop Protestants from spreading their faith or even from teaching their children. As a result, four hundred thousand Huguenots fled to Britain, Holland, Poland, and America, taking their skills with them. Meanwhile, France never fully recovered from the loss. In the vacuum, France became the seedbed of the Enlightenment, a philosophy in the eighteenth century that worshiped reason and challenged all traditional authority—including the authority of the Catholic Church and the divine right of kings. France suffered from constant civil unrest, which culminated in the French Revolution.

The **French Revolution** (1789-99) is the most pivotal event in modern Europe. It brought changes

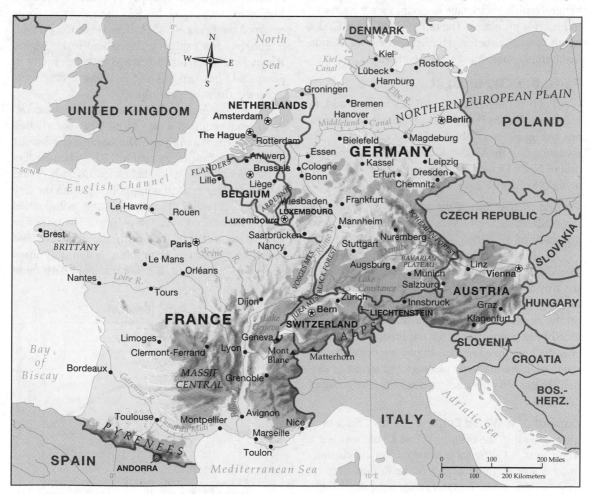

in political thought that are felt around the world today. It is this radical revolution—not the American Revolution—that inspired the violent civil wars and wars of independence fought around the world in the nineteenth and twentieth centuries. Since the revolution, Europe has been torn by unrest, civil war, and world war.

Even today in coffeehouses all across the continent, you can hear Europeans hotly debating the merits and evils of the French Revolution. Some blame Europe's problems on the Enlightenment, which broke the power of the monarchy and of the church. Others support the humanistic ideas of the Enlightenment but blame the failure of the leaders to live up to humanistic ideals. Christians know better. Neither politicians nor popes are the answer to France's problems. The only way to avoid God's wrath is to bow before His Son, repenting of sins and humbly submitting to His authority.

Paris, the City of Light

Paris is the most beautiful city in the world, at least according to Frenchmen. Among its many sites are the gardens of the Tuileries, the Louvre art museum, and the Gothic architecture of the Cathedral of Notre Dame. The view from the Eiffel Tower at night explains Paris's nickname "City of Light."

Palace of the Sun King Outside the city is the magnificent Palace of Versailles, built by the most powerful of all French kings—**Louis XIV** (1661-1715). He was known as the "Sun King" because European politics revolved around his palace during the fifty-five years of his reign. He spent so much money to build Versailles and to win glory in battles on the eastern frontier, that he bankrupted France. One of the main reasons for the French Revolution was the high taxes needed to pay his debts. Paris's continuing emphasis on pleasure and leisure is evident in the city's fame for fashion and gourmet cooking.

Capital of a World Empire Julius Caesar conquered Gaul in the century before Christ was born. The Gauls, a Celtic tribe, adopted Roman customs and became an integral part of the Roman Empire. In A.D. 486, however, the Franks conquered Gaul.

The Eiffel Tower, designed for display at the 1889 Paris Exposition to commemorate the one hundredth anniversary of the French Revolution, was the tallest structure in the world.

The modern name *France* comes from the word *Franks,* though the French continue to speak a Romance language. In 987 the feudal lords crowned the first king of France, Hugh Capet, who established his capital on an island in the **Seine River.** Today, Paris is the capital and largest city in France and has two million inhabitants. It sprawls along the river for eight miles.

The monarchy lasted nearly one thousand years and acquired a world empire that rivaled those of Britain and Spain. The last in a continuous line of thirty-four kings died in 1792, when leaders in the French Revolution beheaded Louis XVI and instituted France's first republic. Under the cry "Liberty, Equality, Fraternity," the enlightened leaders introduced a "Reign of Terror" to guillotine anyone suspected of supporting the monarchy and opposing equality. The republic lasted only three years. In the turmoil, a general named **Napoleon**

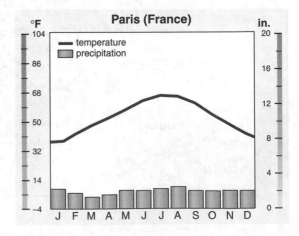

Paris (France)

Barbarian Invasions of the Roman Empire

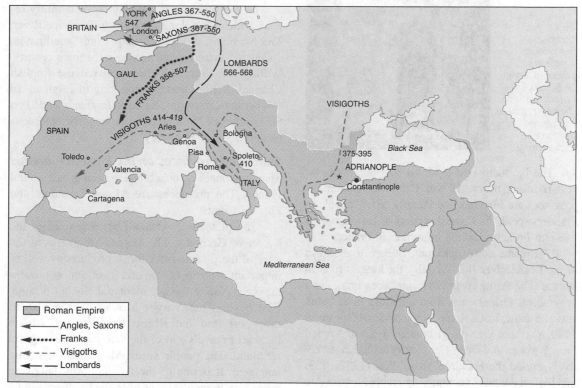

Legend:
- Roman Empire
- ← Angles, Saxons
- ◄••••• Franks
- ◄- - - Visigoths
- ◄— Lombards

Bonaparte rose to power, promising to pursue the ideals of the Revolution. Instead, he crowned himself as a new emperor and dragged Europe into more than a decade of disastrous wars against the ancient kingdoms of Europe. For a time, he controlled most of Europe, but the peoples he had "liberated" rose up against him.

Napoleon's Empire

In Napoleon's wake, France has gone through four kings and five republics. It has been a parliamentary republic since 1870. The present constitution was passed in 1958. Modern France is divided into twenty-two provinces, which are subdivided into ninety-six departments. Eight island territories and French Guiana are all that is left of a once mighty empire that spanned four continents.

Northern France

In general, northern France is lower and flatter than the southern regions. Three of the five major French rivers flow through this region.

Northern France Plains The Great European Plain extends across the north of the European continent, from France to Russia. The plains around Paris produce wheat, barley, and sugar beets. France is second only to Germany worldwide in sugar beet production. It also leads Europe in wheat and exceeds the United States in barley.

The Arc de Triomphe memorializes Napoleon's brilliant victory at the Battle of Austerlitz (1805), when he crushed a combined Austrian and Russian army.

The Northern France Plains continue northeast of Paris, along the border with Belgium. Two famous provinces are Flanders and Picardy. Many people in Flanders speak the Flemish dialect of Dutch, one of five non-French speaking minorities in France.

The plains also extend south of Paris to the basin of the **Loire River** (luh WAHR), the longest river in France. The fertile river valley produces grapes and vegetables. Orléans and Tours, both famous battle sites, lie on the Loire River. At the battle of Orléans in 1449, a sixteen-year-old girl named **Joan of Arc** led French troops to victory. Her victory at Orléans effectively ended the Hundred Years' War (1337-1453) and British dreams of conquering France. Joan of Arc is now one of the patron saints of France.

At the battle of Tours in 732, a French army under Charles Martel ("the Hammer") halted a Muslim army invading Europe from Spain. The city became a center of Protestantism early in the Reformation, but Louis XIV grew jealous of their prosperous silk industry and expelled these skilled Protestant craftsmen.

Northwest Hills of Brittany and Normandy

The far western province of France is a peninsula called **Brittany.** The north coast on the English Channel is rocky and rugged, but the south coast on the Bay of Biscay has fine beaches and major fishing villages. The best-known town is Brest, but Rennes is the administrative center.

The Celts of Brittany, like the Celts of the British Isles, withdrew to the hills during the invasion of foreign tribes. In Brittany they are known as Bretons. Bretons are trying to preserve their language, similar to Welsh, and some would like independence.

East of Brittany is the historic **Normandy** region, which runs along the coast to the Seine River. The Normans, a Viking group from Scandinavia, conquered these rugged coasts in the ninth century. William of Normandy later crossed the English Channel in 1066 and became king of England. In 1944 American troops, based in England, landed on the beaches of Normandy in the largest *amphibious* (water) invasion in history.

Contested Provinces on the Eastern Plateaus

Three provinces lie on a broad plateau in east central France. The provinces are Alsace, Lorraine, and Franche-Comté.

The plateau of **Alsace-Lorraine** touches the border of Germany. The Vosges Mountains at the edge of the plateau offer forest products as well as important deposits of iron ore. Steel centers process the ore at Nancy, the key industrial city in Lorraine. East beyond the Vosges Mountains, the plateau drops off into the **Rhine River** valley. Alsace includes France's part of the valley and offers good farmland. The people speak Alsatian, a Germanic language. It is one of the five minority language pockets in France. Alsace-Lorraine has been a bone of contention between Germany and France for centuries. Germany took it in the Franco-Prussian War (1871), but France regained it after World War I.

Some consider Chartres Cathedral the most beautiful cathedral in the world because of its twin spires and stained glass.

Geographer's Corner

Time Lines

Time lines are essential for understanding the relationship between events in different regions of the world. They are especially helpful in studying Western Europe, which has a complex history that stretches back for over two thousand years. This time line shows some of the major events in the last five hundred years.

Use the time line to answer these questions.

1. Did the Protestant Reformation begin before or after the discovery of America?

2. What occurred in England while Louis XIV was ruling France?

3. Which of these people did not live in the same century as the other three: John Calvin, Napoleon, Elizabeth I, or Martin Luther?

4. Did England have a bill of rights before the independence of the United States?

5. Which of these events did not occur in the twentieth century: World War I, the creation of the Common Market, the French Revolution, or the creation of the British Commonwealth?

💡 What events are part of church history? Choose one and summarize its impact on Europe.

Key Events in European History

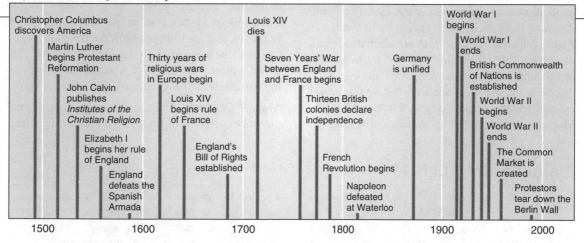

The **Jura Mountains** lie south of the Alsace-Lorraine plateau along the Swiss border. The low Jura Mountains are the dominant feature in the province of Franche-Comté. Few mountains rise above the timberline, which is around 5,300 feet. The Jurassic period in evolutionary geology is named after the Jura Mountains, which display "Jurassic" dinosaur fossils.

Southern France

Southern France has a complex geography of mountains, rivers, and lowlands. All three main regions in southern France have mountains exceeding ten thousand feet. But they each have lowland valleys and coastal plains as well, where large populations thrive.

The Alps Southeast France is a favorite vacation spot. The Alps divide France from Italy, and the border has been disputed between the two countries. **Mont Blanc** is the highest mountain in the Alps at 15,771 feet. It lies near the Italian and Swiss borders. Nearby is the deepest cave in the world, the Jean Bernard Cave, which reaches depths of about one mile below the surface.

Moderate Climates

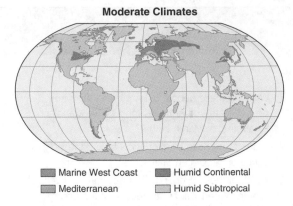

- ▨ Marine West Coast
- ▨ Mediterranean
- ▨ Humid Continental
- ▨ Humid Subtropical

The Rhone River   The water from the snowcapped Alps drains west into the **Rhone River** which flows south into the Mediterranean Sea. The valley and adjacent coasts are unique in Continental Europe because of the mediterranean climate. The region is a major producer of grapes and wine. Lyon (lee OHN), the third largest city in France, lies in the Rhone River valley. This valley, which cuts deep into France, was historically the main overland route between mediterranean Europe and Northern Europe.

Near the mouth of the Rhone River is the oldest and second largest city in France: Marseille. Marseille was founded by the ancient Greeks and became a thriving port. During the Middle Ages, it was the center of a powerful territory called Provence. The French dialect of Provence competed with Parisian French as the national standard. Paris's northern dialect, *langue d'oïl*, became dominant, however, as the power of the king increased. The southern dialect, called *langue d'oc*, can still be heard in the vicinity of Marseille.

The Riviera   Nice (NEECE), the fifth largest city in France, lies on the coast between the Rhone River and Italy. It is the center of the **French Riviera,** Europe's answer to Hawaii as a vacation paradise. The area is one of the few vacation spots in the world with year-round snow-covered mountains only a few miles away from year-round balmy beaches.

Corsica   The Alps descend into the Mediterranean Sea and form the island of **Corsica.** Corsica's mountains rise to 8,943 feet at Monte Cinto. Corsicans speak their own unique language, similar to Italian, and are trying to preserve their language. Corsica's beaches are favorite French resorts. The island's most famous native was Napoleon, whom the British called the Corsican Ogre.

Massif Central   The capitals of the four central provinces, Toulouse, Limoges, Clermont-Ferrand,

Mont-Saint-Michel

Off the coast of France in the English Channel is an unusual little isle called Mont-Saint-Michel. A Celtic temple once stood on the rock, and Benedictine monks later built an abbey that became a center of learning. King Philip II built the current fortress in the thirteenth century.

Each year a flood of tourists pass through the narrow gate that guards the entrance to the three-acre isle. They walk on the ramparts and towers that encircle the isle, climb to the fortified abbey on the 256-foot summit, and enjoy the old inns and medieval shops on the village street below.

What makes Mont-Saint-Michel so unusual is its "moat." During high tides, the raging ocean fills the mile of land that separates the isle from the coast, but the waters recede when the tide goes out. The island was a perfect fortress, which withstood all assaults during the Hundred Years War and during the religious wars of the Reformation. Since 1875, however, a mile-long dike has connected the rock with the mainland.

In addition to the abbey at the summit, Mont-Saint-Michel includes crypts, cellars, dungeons, a guardhouse, and the Hall of Knights. The knights of the Order of Saint Michel, formed in 1469, successfully defended the fortress against all attacks.

The Pyrenees are a natural boundary between France and Spain. Few passes cross these mountains.

historic cave paintings. Bordeaux (bore DOH), the main city, lies near the mouth of the Garonne River. The fertile river valley produces grapes and corn.

and Montpellier, lie at the corners of the **Massif Central.** This mountainous plateau in south-central France has poor soils that make the region useful only for grazing livestock.

Toulouse is the fourth largest French city. It is an important transportation center on the **Garonne River,** which flows into the Atlantic. The Garonne is important because of the Canal du Midi, which completes a link between the Atlantic Ocean and the Mediterranean Sea. By sailing up this canal and the Garonne, French vessels can bypass the long trip around the Spanish peninsula.

The **Pyrenees Mountains** rise south of Toulouse and form the border with Spain. The region boasts many deep caves including the Cave of Pierre-St. Martin. These caves descend three times deeper than the deepest caves in North America. The Basques also live in the area. Having one of France's five minority languages, the Basques are working hard to keep their language alive.

Aquitanian Lowlands of the Southwest

The two provinces of southwest France are mostly lowlands. The region is called the **Aquitanian Lowlands.** The Lascaux Cave is famous for its pre-

A group of French boys stumbled on Lascaux Cave in 1940 while hunting for a lost dog. The lifelike animals in the "Hall of Bulls" include bulls, wolves, boars, deer, bison, horses, rhinoceros, and reindeer.

SECTION REVIEW

What are France's . . .

14–1

1. five largest cities?
2. five main rivers?
3. five main agricultural products?
4. five minority languages?
5. three great caves?

💡 Where might a French family choose to vacation in Europe and still speak French? in the Western Hemisphere? Give at least one example in each region.

THE LOW COUNTRIES

The Low Countries are so named because they lie entirely on coastal lowlands and low plateaus. Because these countries are small in area and lie on desirable plains, they include the most densely populated countries in Continental Europe.

The Low Countries lie at the crossroads of Western Europe, between the Franks and the Germans. The empire of the Franks reached its greatest extent under **Charlemagne.** His capital at Aix-la-Chapelle (modern Aachen) was in the center of Western Europe. He failed to reconquer all of the western Roman Empire, however, and it broke up under his three grandsons. The remnants of his empire have borders close to modern France, Germany, and the disputed countries in the center. The central countries have been repeatedly overrun by foreign invaders. Today they are the focus of a movement to unite all the countries on the continent into a United States of Europe.

The Netherlands's Battle with the Sea

After Charlemagne's empire broke up, French dukes from Burgundy began to consolidate lands near the coast. Protestantism spread quickly here. When Catholic Charles V of Spain inherited these lands, however, he persecuted

Charlemagne's Empire

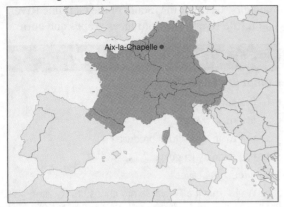

Aix-la-Chapelle ●

the Protestants. The Netherlands revolted in 1568. The national hero, William of Orange, also called **William the Silent,** bravely led the Dutch armies to independence in 1581.

The Golden Age for the Dutch came in the following century. Its navy defeated Spain and became a leader in world trade and colonization. The Dutch East India Company drove out other powers from Cape Town, Ceylon, and Indonesia. They were the only Western nations allowed to trade with Japan. The Dutch purchased Manhattan from Indians in 1626 and founded New Amsterdam, which later became New York City. A reflection of Dutch influence on seamanship are the Dutch words that have passed into common English, such as *skipper* and *yacht.* The Dutch Empire was weakened by a century of periodic wars with England, the other naval power in the North Sea.

Today the Netherlands's greatest enemy is the sea. Sand dunes twenty feet high protect the inland regions from the North Sea. Much of the land farther inland is below sea level. The Dutch have built strong walls of stone and earth, called **dikes,** to hold back the seawater. Big electric generators pump out the water to keep the land inside dry. At one time, windmills were used to generate power, but only a few windmills still operate.

Parcels of land reclaimed from the sea are **polders.** The polder region of the Netherlands covers a wide strip of territory behind the dunes and dikes. Polders have good fertile soil, and tulips and daffodils are important cash crops, but living on polders presents many dangers. The Dutch must wage a ceaseless battle against the sea, constantly pumping out rainwater and maintaining the dikes.

Holland Two of the Netherlands's twelve provinces form the region of **Holland,** which contains 40 percent of the population and all three of the nation's largest cities. **Amsterdam,** the capital and second largest city, is on a polder in the province of North Holland. The same tolerance that made the Netherlands a refuge for Protestants in Catholic Europe has secularized the nation today. The World Council of Churches (WCC) is among the international organizations headquartered in Amsterdam. The WCC has become the leading voice for undermining true Christianity and for breaking down barriers between religions, a movement called *ecumenism.*

Though there is no official religion, the monarch traditionally belongs to the Dutch Reformed Church.

Continental Europe Statistics

COUNTRY	CAPITAL	AREA (SQ. MI.)	POPULATION	NATURAL INCREASE	LIFE EXPECTANCY	LITERACY RATE	PER CAPITA GDP	POP. DENSITY
Austria	Vienna	32,378	8,023,000	0.1%	77	100%	$17,500	248
Belgium	Brussels	11,787	10,170,000	0.2%	78	100%	$18,040	863
France	Paris	210,026	58,040,000	0.2%	79	99%	$18,670	276
Germany	Berlin	137,828	83,536,000	−0.1%	76	100%	$16,580	.606
Liechtenstein	Vaduz	62	31,000	0.5%	79	100%	$22,300	502
Luxembourg	Luxembourg	999	416,000	0.5%	79	100%	$24,840	416
Netherlands	Amsterdam & The Hague	16,033	15,568,000	0.3%	78	100%	$17,940	971
Switzerland	Bern	15,940	7,207,000	0.2%	78	100%	$22,080	452

Let's Go Exploring

1. List all of the major cities of Western Europe that are tied together with the Netherlands by a continuous megalopolis of the highest population density (over 250).

2. Which countries in Western Europe lack any area with a population density over sixty?

3. Where is the lowest population density in France and Germany?

💡 Why is central France less populous than northern and southern France?

Population Density of Europe

Per sq. km		Per sq. mi.
Under 1		Under 2
1-10		2-25
10-25		25-60
25-50		60-125
50-100		125-250
Over 100		Over 250

● Metropolitan area with 2-5 million people

○ Metropolitan area with over 5 million people

About one-third of the people are Dutch Reformed, another one-third are Catholic, and most of the rest do not attend any church.

The province of South Holland includes both the Netherlands's largest city, Rotterdam, and The Hague. Amsterdam has been called the capital since Napoleon moved it there, but the national government of the constitutional monarchy meets in **The Hague.** Rotterdam is the New Orleans of Europe. One of Europe's busiest ports, **Rotterdam** lies in the delta of the busiest river on the continent. The Rhine River flows on the border of seven countries. Rotterdam is also a major industrial town with oil refineries and steel manufacturing.

Ten Outlying Provinces The two northern provinces, Friesland and Groningen lie in the polder region. The dunes rise as a chain of offshore islands. The Netherlands controls the West Frisian Islands, but Germany owns the East Frisian Islands. Frisian is the language of Friesland. Like Dutch, Frisian is a Germanic language. Large deposits make the Netherlands the world's fourth largest producer of natural gas.

The Netherlands or Holland?

The name Holland is sometimes used for the entire country of the Netherlands, but it is only part of the country. The terms to describe the people can be very confusing also. The people of the Netherlands call themselves Nederlanders or Hollanders, but the English call them the Dutch. Their language is also called Dutch. Adding to the confusion, the Kingdom of the Netherlands once included all three Low Countries.

The new name for the modern economic union of the Low Countries, Benelux, is not so confusing. Can you guess where they got this name?

Dutch windmill

High-Tech Dutch Dikes

The Dutch and dikes go together. The Dutch have been building them for centuries. However, two daring projects in the twentieth century have far surpassed any previous attempt to capture land from the sea.

The first challenge was to control the floods along the *Zuider Zee* (Southern Sea), an arm of the North Sea that reaches into the heart of the country. Storm surges in the North Sea would sometimes fill this inlet and flood the coast. In 1931 the Dutch completed a nineteen-mile-long dam called the *Afsluitdijk* (Enclosing Dike), which crossed the Southern Sea. Rivers slowly turned the enclosed portion of the sea into a freshwater lake called *IJsselmeer* (Inner Lake). The portion beyond the dam became known as the *Waddenzee* (Outer Sea).

The next challenge was to drain parts of the IJsselmeer to obtain more land for housing and farming. Building the dikes, draining the water, and preparing the land for settlement took many years. Now, four large polders exist that a few years ago were covered by the salt waters of the Zuider Zee. The Flevoland Polder, the largest, covers over one hundred thousand acres.

Another great project was to protect Zeeland, farther south, from sea storms that might break dikes and

Land Reclaimed from the Sea

flood homes. As much as the Dutch liked their new freshwater lake farther north, they did not want another one. If they did that to all of their estuaries, they would lose the shrimp, mussels, and eels used for food and bird migrations as well. Conservationists thus persuaded the Dutch to undertake an even greater engineering feat. The Oosterschelde Barrier allows 80 percent of the normal tides to flow through the barrier, but the gates can be shut during storms to keep out the squalls.

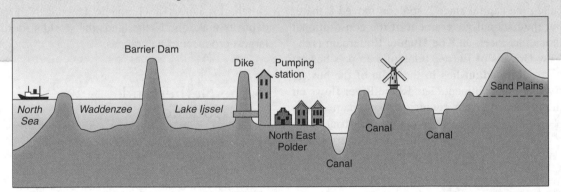

Three other polder provinces lie immediately east and south of Holland. The most important is Zeeland to the south. This region is a series of islands and peninsulas in the delta of the Rhine River. The great Oosterschelde Barrier has enabled the Dutch to convert some of this marshy area into productive ground.

The five provinces along the eastern border are slightly above sea level and do not have polders. However, these sand plains do not have fertile soil either. Fertilizers are used to make them productive. The eastern provinces have some salt deposits, and there are some coal mines in the Ardennes.

Belgium, the Capital of Europe

The Belgae tribes inhabited the area of Belgium when Julius Caesar conquered the region about 50 B.C. It was divided up among various rulers over the next eighteen hundred years. In 1815 Belgium was given to the Netherlands, but the predominantly Catholic people declared independence in 1830.

Belgium has one of the most developed free market economies. Perhaps the country's best-known product is Belgian chocolate, and several of its products are named for the capital: Brussels lace, Brussels carpet, and Brussels sprouts. **Brussels** is the largest city in the country. Many international organizations are headquartered in Brussels, including the Parliament of the European Union and NATO, the defensive alliance for Western Europe.

The nation is divided into two regions, and two official languages—Dutch and French. **Flanders** in the north, much like the Netherlands, is a region of polders and sand plains where people speak Dutch. The people are called Flemings; Belgian Dutch was once known as Flemish. Antwerp, the largest city in Flanders, is one of the busiest ports in the world and a major center for the cutting and setting of diamonds. The Flemish school of painting is also world famous.

The northern lowlands of Flanders give way to a low plateau in central Belgium. In the far south is a series of rolling hills called the **Ardennes.** The forest of the Ardennes covers southern Belgium and much of Luxembourg, extending into France.

Belgium's southern district is called **Wallonia.** The Ardennes is dotted by many villages and hiking trails; most of the cities are on the Meuse River system, which begins in France and flows through central Belgium. The people, called Walloons, speak French. The Flemings and Walloons have had difficulty creating a united country, and a split is sometimes debated. Steel was once the chief industry in the south, but crude steel is now imported and the steel plants have moved to the northern ports in Flanders. Liège (lee AYZH), the largest city of Wallonia, continues to produce guns and glassware.

Luxembourg

Luxembourg is one of Europe's oldest countries. Luxembourg is one of the few remaining duchies and dates back to 963. A **duchy** is a country ruled by a duke, and the Grand Duke is Luxembourg's hereditary monarch. The official title of the constitutional monarchy is the Grand Duchy of Luxembourg. The capital is also called Luxembourg.

All but 3 percent of the people are Catholic, and most people speak all three official languages. Letzeburgesch is the local dialect of German used commonly. German is used in elementary school, while French is used in high school. Although villages still huddle around medieval castles, Luxembourg is now one of the world's most industrialized countries.

Luxembourg plays a leading role in Europe today. Its small size and central location make it a prime neutral location for international endeavors. It is an international financial and banking center. It hosts both the secretariat (administrative staff) of the European Parliament and the European Court of Justice.

Folk musicians play traditional instruments at a promenade in Ostend, Belgium.

SECTION REVIEW

1. What kind of climate does most of Continental Europe enjoy?
2. What low plateau rises from the coastal plains in the Low Countries?
3. What does the Netherlands do to reclaim land?
4. Who are the Flemish people?
5. What city in the Low Countries has the headquarters of the European Union?
- Which Low Countries are likely to develop civil strife? Why?

GERMANY, BIRTHPLACE OF THE REFORMATION

Germany is the birthplace of the Reformation. Martin Luther was born in northern Germany, studied in its schools, was converted, and spent the rest of his life preaching to and teaching the German people. Protestant leaders used the printing press, invented by another German, Johann Gutenberg, to spread the ideas of the Reformation around the world. Today, almost one-half of the German people are Lutherans. They constitute the largest population of non-Catholics in Continental Europe.

Most Lutherans live in the northern plains, while Germans in the southern uplands are Roman Catholics. This division reflects ancient divisions among the German tribes who settled the two regions. They even speak different dialects of German: Low German and High German. At the start of the Reformation, some leaders in the north adopted Protestantism as an easy way to break the power of Rome in their lands.

The Search for National Unity

Germany has a violent history. Warlike German tribes invaded the western Roman Empire and then fought among themselves. While France and Great Britain each united under strong kings, nearly three hundred weak princes and dukes competed for territory in Germany. Wars among the rival German princes culminated in the **Thirty Years War** (1618-48), which killed one-third of the German population. Most of Germany's history focuses on a search for national unity.

The territory of Prussia finally united all of the German territories in 1871, and Berlin became the new capital of the German Empire, or *Reich*. A greedy emperor lost everything in World War I, however. The defeated Germans adopted a republic, but it proved short-lived as strikes, food shortages, and riots shook the country. Adolf Hitler took advantage of this chaos to take power in 1933, promising to revenge Germany's enemies and to restore Germany's greatness.

The **Nazi Empire,** which Hitler said would last for one thousand years, peaked at the end of 1941. Unable to take Britain by air or Russia by land, Hitler's empire crumbled around him, and he committed suicide in Berlin in 1945. The nation still struggles under the guilt of the Nazi nightmare. Not only did Hitler plunge Europe into the most horrific war of its history, he ruthlessly murdered an estimated six million Jews in the **Holocaust,** along with several million Poles, Gypsies, and other races.

As a result of the war, Germany was again divided, not between north and south, but between east and west. The Russian armies had swept two hundred miles past Berlin before meeting American soldiers in western Germany. While the Allied armies in the West wanted to restore Germany's republic, Russia wanted to turn it into a new Communist state. The Soviets broke their promises to allow the whole nation to hold free elections. With Allied assistance, West Germany became a prosperous free republic; while East Germany became a Communist dictatorship.

The Berlin Wall

Berlin is the heart of Germany, both ancient and modern. With 3.5 million people, it is by far the largest city in Continental Europe. The city was founded on the Spree River, a tributary of the Elbe River, in the thirteenth century. Berlin prospered after King Frederick I made it the capital of Prussia in 1701. After World War II, Berlin lay in ruins—isolated in the midst of Soviet occupied territory.

Religions of Europe

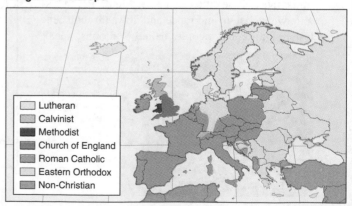

- Lutheran
- Calvinist
- Methodist
- Church of England
- Roman Catholic
- Eastern Orthodox
- Non-Christian

The peace agreement allowed the Allies in the West—the United States, Great Britain, and France—to occupy the western part of Berlin. Refugees escaping the Communists flooded into West Berlin, prompting the Soviets to build a wall around it in 1961. The **Berlin Wall** became a hated symbol of the division caused by the Cold War.

The first chancellor of West Germany, Konrad Adenauer (1949-63), used many free-market ideas to create the *Wirtschaftswunder,* meaning "economic miracle." He rebuilt German industry and revived the German economy. By 1955 the nation was producing more goods than it had before the war, despite the loss of East Germany.

Meanwhile, East Germany fell further and further behind. As the 1980s drew to a close, protests started all across Eastern Europe and could not be stopped. In October 1989 East Germany's Communist leader resigned and was later placed under house arrest. Protesters, joined by the wall's guards, tore down the Berlin Wall in November. The two Germanies united into one nation on October 3, 1990.

It will take decades for the two Germanies to integrate. The cost of linking the wealthy economy of the West with the bankrupt East has proved to be astronomical. **Reunification** also has revealed the inherent weaknesses in the socialist elements of the German "miracle." The government must now provide work and benefits for people in the former Communist lands, who are used to earning much less. In the 1990s production declined in Germany and unemployment grew to its worst levels since the 1930s. To raise more money, the government sharply increased taxes, adding to the people's burdens.

Northern Plains

Germany's northern plains are part of the Great European Plain that stretches from France to Russia. The deciduous forests of France and the Low Countries give way to a mixture of broadleaf trees and evergreens in Germany, especially as you move east and south into the interior of the continent.

The people of the plains, whether east or west, produce the same products. The western plains in particular have some of the best soil in Europe, formed by a thick layer of **loess,** a fine-grained soil deposited by the wind. Germany ranks as the world's third largest producer of rye and leads Europe in hog production. It is also the world's largest producer of both oats and sugar beets. Germany's northern plains have the largest concentration of cities and industry in the nation. Germany is now the most populous country in all of Europe. Diverse industries and great wealth make Germany potentially the most powerful and influential country on the continent.

Germans tore down the Berlin Wall in November 1989.

In the News

European Union

After World War II, various leaders of Western Europe dreamed of forming a federation called the United States of Europe. Under the shadow of Communism in Eastern Europe, the nations in Western Europe laid aside many differences for the common good. A series of treaties have tightened their economic ties, but recent crises have raised new questions about the future of Europe's political order.

Most Europeans have liked the idea of an economic union. Belgium was instrumental in getting six nations to sign a treaty in 1951 establishing the European Coal and Steel Community (ECSC). They agreed to drop import duties and to regulate their coal and steel industries jointly to reduce waste and inefficiency. These six nations followed with the Common Market in 1957 and later the European Community (EC) in 1967. The EC achieved full economic union in 1992, when it dropped all restrictions on the movement of products within its borders.

While some nations were content with a loose union of their economies, others dreamed of a strong political union of their governments. This road was much bumpier. The EC states negotiated a new treaty at Maastricht (MAHS trikt).

Approved in 1993, the Maastricht Treaty converted the European Community into the ambitious new **European Union** (EU). The treaty created a common "citizenship of the union." It had three pillars.

1. Economic and monetary union, "ultimately including a single currency"

2. Common foreign and security policy, "which might in time lead to a common defense"

3. "Close cooperation on justice and home affairs"

The most concrete pillar of the Maastricht Treaty was the monetary union. The goal was to create a single currency, called a *euro,* scheduled to hit the streets by 2002. But joining several currencies into one is extremely complicated. To be eligible, each nation's economy had to meet difficult standards, including low debts. Only one nation—tiny Luxembourg—easily met all the standards.

Economic crises set back the monetary union. After the Cold War, the number of Europeans out of work had risen above 10 percent, a level not seen since Adolf Hitler rose to power in the 1930s. Another crisis came when the German government had to borrow money to pay the cost of converting East Germany to a Western economy. Since

Eastern Germany Germany has a federal government with sixteen states, called *Landers.* Five of them once belonged to East Germany, not including Berlin, which is a city-state. Only recently freed from Communism, the eastern region is struggling to rebuild its economy. Its great potential is not yet fully realized, and it lags behind its counterpart in the west. Under the Communists, East Germany built the boxy Trabant automobile, but the noisy little "Trabi" could not compete in a free market. The plants closed soon after reunification, and one million workers lost their jobs.

The Communists left a legacy of crime, irresponsibility, and waste. The factories were outdated and hazardous. The rivers and air were severely polluted by years of untreated industrial waste. Yet East Germans (or *Ossis,* as they are often called) resent their treatment as "second-class" citizens because of their association with the Communist

regime. They have no experience with democracy and enjoy little political power compared to the West Germans (or *Wessis*). The former Communist Party still has a following in eastern Germany. Unemployed youths have turned to violence and gangs to vent their frustrations. Many of them, called neo-Nazis, wear the Nazi swastika and support racist attacks on Turks and other immigrant workers.

Leipzig, Dresden, and Chemnitz are the largest cities in eastern Germany, after Berlin. All three cities are in the historic state of Saxony. Saxony was a medieval duchy, named for the Saxons who settled all across Germany.

The **Elbe River** and its tributaries flow through the heart of eastern Germany. Upriver from Magdeburg is the town of Wittenberg, where Martin Luther nailed his ninety-five theses to the church door, and where he later wrote "A Mighty

other countries could not pay the same high interest rate to borrowers, they began withdrawing from the monetary union. Great Britain withdrew its *sterling,* Italy pulled its *lira,* and France would have followed suit if Germany had not stepped in and encouraged it to stay.

Joining several independent governments into one superstate is even more complex than joining currencies. The modern debate in Europe has striking parallels to the constitutional debate in 1787 among the original thirteen states in America. The Constitutional Convention labored four months in discussion and compromise, followed by three years of debates to win popular approval within each state. Small states wanted one vote for each state, while the large states wanted votes based on population. Once the big states joined the Union, the remaining states joined, fearing the consequences of being left out.

The main problem is that the EU system was originally designed for only six countries. Every time a new nation joins the club, it rattles the delicate balance of power. A new horde of countries in Eastern Europe is now clamoring to join the EU. The EU wants to help these nations to get on their feet, but the current members do not want to lose their voice in the Union. The civil wars in Eastern Europe, which followed the fall of Communism, have reawakened old rivalries and tested the ability of Western European nations to work together.

Perhaps the greatest weakness in the proposed federal government is the lack of support among the common people. How will a stronger European Union benefit the average worker? Even in Germany, the most vocal advocate of the union, only a third of the people believe it is a good thing. Germany's leader Helmut Kohl made union his own personal crusade, hoping to make a place for himself in history. Without popular support, the union could tear apart at the first sign of trouble.

💡 Christians are watching events in Europe closely, and they are concerned. At the Tower of Babel, God divided the world into distinct nationalities. Efforts to erase the distinctions usually have ungodly motivations. The socialist "one-world government" bureaucrats of Europe are trying to take away the sovereignty of their countries. Is the EU tied to prophesy about a confederation under the rule of the Beast (see Dan. 7:24-26; Rev. 13:1-10; 17:12-13)?

Fortress Is Our God" and a German translation of the Bible. By using the northern dialect, Low German, Luther's Bible helped to establish the standard for the German language.

Western Germany

The northern plains in western Germany cover five states. Two of them are city-states—Bremen and Hamburg. Hamburg, located downstream from Berlin on the Elbe River, is the main seaport and the second largest city in Germany.

Another important harbor lies on the north coast at Kiel. The important **Kiel Canal** directly links the North Sea with the Baltic Sea. This gives German vessels a shortcut that avoids going around Denmark's Jutland Peninsula.

Farthest west is Germany's most important river, the Rhine River, which flows through several important regions of Germany before it winds west into the Netherlands. At the lower end of the river, where the Ruhr River flows into the Rhine, is an industrial megalopolis called the **Ruhr,** the largest industrial region in Europe and perhaps in the whole world. Its ten million people centered around the city of Essen make it one of the most crowded regions in Europe. The coal mines in this "smoke-stack region" make Germany the world's third largest coal producer.

Farther up the Rhine River are the major river ports of Cologne and Bonn. Bonn served as the capital of West Germany while Germany was divided; but after the fall of Communism, the government decided to move the capital back to Berlin. Cologne is by far the largest city in this industrial district, even larger than Bonn, with about one million people.

Germany has made up for its lack of important minerals by importing or synthesizing manmade

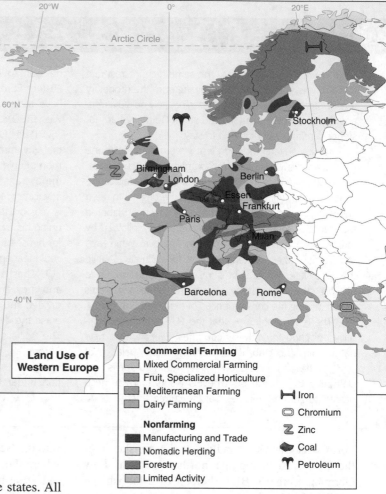

Land Use of Western Europe

Commercial Farming
- Mixed Commercial Farming
- Fruit, Specialized Horticulture
- Mediterranean Farming
- Dairy Farming

Nonfarming
- Manufacturing and Trade
- Nomadic Herding
- Forestry
- Limited Activity

⊢⊣ Iron
⊙ Chromium
Z Zinc
◆ Coal
⊤ Petroleum

materials. By importing iron from Sweden, Germany has become the top-ranking producer of crude steel in Western Europe. Germany also leads Europe in refined copper, smelted lead, smelted zinc, and various synthetic materials, including rubber, rayon, nylons, and polyesters.

Central Uplands

Southern Germany consists of five states. All of them lie on hilly plateaus. Germany's plateaus are part of a wider system of plateaus that begins with the Massif Central of France and stretches through the low Jura Mountains and Ardennes eastward through Germany into the Czech Republic. The whole system is sometimes called the **Central Uplands.**

The Upper Rhine The rivers in Germany's Central Uplands flow into two major rivers: the Rhine in the west and the Danube in the east. Four of the south's five states lie mostly in the drainage basin of the Rhine. The main tributary of the Rhine in southern Germany is the Main. The Main flows past Frankfurt, the banking center of Germany and home of Germany's stock exchange.

Roman Catholic sentiments run deep in southern Germany. In fact, Luther was tried and sentenced to death in the south at Worms, near Mannheim; but he found refuge in a prince's castle at Wartburg. At his trial in Worms, Luther said these famous words,

Unless I am convinced by Scripture and plain reason—I do not accept the authority of the popes and councils, for they have contradicted each other—my conscience is captive to the Word of God. I cannot and I will not recant anything, for to go against conscience is neither right nor safe. Here I stand. I cannot do otherwise. God help me. Amen.

The Black Forest, Germany

The **Black Forest** along the French border is the best-known feature in the southwest. Mountains rise east of the Rhine. Dark forests of spruce and fir clothe the mountains, which contain the headwaters of the Danube River. Lumber mills and granite quarries provide work. Tourists come to health resorts at mineral springs near Baden-Baden or to obtain the handcrafted toys and cuckoo clocks.

Stuttgart is the capital of the southwestern state of Baden-Württemberg. An inventor named Gottlieb Daimler invented the gasoline engine in Stuttgart in the 1880s. He joined with another inventor, Karl Benz, to design an even better car, the Mercedes. Germany is the largest producer of automobiles in Europe and third-largest in the world (after Japan and the United States). Famous brand names include Mercedes Benz, Volkswagen ("people's car"), BMW, Audi, and Porsche.

Missions

Church Planting

The most common missionary work is church planting. Following the example of the apostle Paul, who started churches all over Asia Minor and Europe, missionaries plant the seed of the gospel, others water, but God gives the increase.

I have planted, Apollos watered; but God gave the increase. So then neither is he that planteth anything, neither he that watereth; but God that giveth the increase. (I Cor. 3:6-7)

Your knowledge of common subjects, such as literature, history, math, and science, will come in handy in Europe. These subjects are helpful, not only because they add to your understanding of the Bible but also because

The Independent Christian Church at Stuttgart, Germany

they give you more tools for witnessing about the Lord. Well-educated Europeans enjoy wit and good conversation on difficult topics.

Church planters are sometimes surprised by the pace of life in different German towns. Cities with fast-paced lifestyles and changing conditions, as well as cities with large populations of immigrants and social unrest, are more likely to be open to the gospel. Stable towns in the countryside, however, honor tradition and resist change.

No matter what knowledge you have or how much you understand the people, missionary work is primarily God's work, not yours. Yes, you sweat and toil and battle many difficulties, but only God can perform the miracle of salvation. This fact gives great comfort to missionaries, who realize that God has a greater passion for missions than any mortal man. The church planter can cast all his worries on the Lord and trust Him to produce fruit from his labors.

A choir sings at a small missionary church in Germany. The membership is small in most gospel-preaching churches.

Bavaria The largest state in Germany, **Bavaria** lies in the southeast. Bavaria was a duchy throughout the Middle Ages, but Napoleon made it a kingdom in 1805. After the unification of Germany in 1871, Bavaria became a state. Bavaria contains Grosser Arber (4,780 ft.), the highest peak in the **Bohemian Forest** (known locally as the Bavarian Forest) along the Czech border.

Dairy cattle roam the hills of Bavaria. Hops, used in beer making, are a major cash crop. Munich is the center of the beer industry, celebrated at the annual festival called Oktoberfest. With over 1.2 million people, **Munich** is the third largest city in Germany. Its great collection of baroque, rococo, and neo-classical architecture makes it one of the finest cities in Europe.

The **Bavarian Alps** stretch along Germany's entire southern border with Austria, not far south of Munich. The range reaches 9,721 feet on the Zugspitze, a popular skiing area. Several famous castles adorn the area.

Neuschwanstein Castle

One of Europe's most-photographed medieval castles rises beneath the snowy peaks of the Bavarian Alps. Neuschwanstein Castle has such a fairy-tale appearance that Walt Disney modeled the castle at Disney World after it.

Neuschwanstein Castle is actually not a medieval castle at all, but a nineteenth-century palace made to look like an enchanted castle of old, when gallant knights charged across Europe and saved fair maidens in distress. The castle is one of three built by the Mad King of Bavaria, Ludwig II.

Obsessed with German mythology, the king ordered lavish paintings for every room to depict his favorite scenes from Wagnerian operas, Arthurian legend, and ancient history. Every room is splendidly furnished and decorated. The king's bed is so ornate that fifteen men spent over four years carving it. The Mad King moved into the palace in 1886, only to drown himself a few months later.

Visiting Neuschwanstein Castle requires a one-mile walk into the Bavarian Alps, near Fussen, Germany.

SECTION REVIEW

1. What is the major religion in Germany?
2. What industrial complex lies on Germany's northern plains?
3. What conqueror divided Germany after World War II?
4. What are the two key rivers of southern Germany?
5. What are the highest mountains in Germany?
💡 Was the cost of Germany's reunification justified?

THE ALPS, EUROPE'S BACKBONE

The *Alpine Mountain system* forms a great snowy barrier severing the southern peninsulas of Europe from the rest of the continent. The system runs from Spain all the way to Greece. It forms the third greatest mountain system in the world (after the Himalayan system of Asia and the Western Cordillera of the Americas).

The primary range in the system is the **Alps,** up to 160 miles deep and 660 miles long, which curves across Italy's northern border. These mountains display the splendor of God's creation in many ways. They are home to golden eagles, marmots, and exotic mountain goats, such as chamois and ibex.

The Alps are grouped into three main divisions: the Western Alps, Central Alps, and Eastern Alps. The Western Alps lie in France and Italy, while Switzerland contains the Central Alps. The

Eastern Alps spread south from Germany across Austria and into Eastern Europe.

The Alps have greatly influenced the climate and history of Europe. Few passes cross this barrier, and they can be dangerous, especially in winter. *St. Bernard Pass,* between Mont Blanc and the Matterhorn, links France and Italy. Armies and merchants have crossed this pass for hundreds of years. We know its name from the monastery at the pass, which bred the St. Bernard dogs to rescue travelers lost in the snow.

Neutral Switzerland

Switzerland is divided into **cantons.** The cantons were once Catholic Church districts, like parishes, but they became self-governing districts. The Swiss cantons resented the growing power of the Austrian Hapsburgs in the east during the thirteenth century. Three cantons on Lake Lucerne—Schwyz, Uri, and Unterwalden—took the opportunity in 1291 to declare independence. The nation of Switzerland was born when these cantons signed the Perpetual Covenant. The rugged terrain enabled them to beat off armies ten times their size. Over the years, more cantons joined the league.

In 1515 Switzerland adopted a policy of neutrality in Europe's wars. But in 1798 France invaded the country. After Napoleon's defeat in 1815, the victorious countries guaranteed Switzerland's neutrality. Ever since, the Swiss have avoided joining organizations that could jeopardize their neutrality.

The cities in Switzerland have a strong, independent spirit. When Luther challenged Rome in 1517, several cantons in Switzerland adopted Protestant ideas and threw out the trappings of the Catholic Church. In fact, two of the greatest leaders in the Protestant movement, John Calvin and Ulrich Zwingli, found relative safety in Switzerland. But the Catholic cantons would not tolerate "heresy." The Protestant and Catholic cantons fought four wars, beginning in 1529, but neither side ever gained the edge. Today, out of the twenty-six cantons and half-cantons, fifteen have a Catholic majority and eleven a Protestant majority.

The Jura in the North The rugged Jura Mountains of France and Germany cross over into the northern border of Switzerland. Rhine Falls in this area is the most powerful falls in Europe.

The second largest city in Switzerland, Basel, is located in the Rhine River valley. Basel contains part of the vital canal system that links Germany's Rhine River and France's Rhone River. Basel is where **John Calvin** fled during France's early persecution of Protestants. Here he wrote one of the most influential theology books ever written, *The Institutes of the Christian Religion,* a systematic outline of Protestant doctrine.

Great Cities of the Central Swiss Plateau

The Swiss Plateau, or Mittelland, lies between the Jura Mountains in the north and the Swiss Alps in the south. The average altitude is about thirteen hundred feet. The Jura Mountains protect the plateau from cold northern winds, while a warm, dry wind, called a **foehn** (FUHRN), blows from the Alps in the south. While the winds keep the climate mild, they can cause sudden avalanches.

Glaciers apparently gouged out several long, narrow lake basins on the plateau. The two largest are Lakes Constance and Geneva, at each end of the plateau. The country's two most important rivers—the Rhine and the Rhone—flow from these lakes, respectively. Other large lakes include Lake Neuchâtel, Lake Lucerne, and Lake Zurich.

Geneva Lake Geneva borders France, and the Rhone River flows west from the lake into France. One of Switzerland's five largest cities, **Geneva,** lies on the lake. As you might expect, the people speak French. The Red Cross is one of several international organizations that have made their headquarters in Geneva.

John Calvin (1509-64), a native of France, was asked to reorganize the government of the city of Geneva in an attempt to create a Christian city-state. His influential ministry attracted Protestant leaders from around the world, including John Knox of Scotland. Geneva later was the home of one of the most influential humanistic philosophers in history, **Jean-Jacques Rousseau** (1712-78), who rejected the Protestant faith of his parents and became the Father of Romanticism. He believed in the goodness of man in his natural state. His book *The Social Contract* inspired the leaders in the French Revolution.

The Capital, Bern

All of the Mittleland except Lake Geneva drains into Germany's Rhine River. German, spoken by about 70 percent of the people, is one of four official languages. The people speak Schwyzerdütsch, or Swiss German, at home and in public. But standard German is used in the schools, churches, and the media.

Bern, the capital of Switzerland, is on the Aare River, a tributary of the Rhine. Swiss cheese originated here. Many of its villages manufacture the precision watches for which Switzerland is famous.

The Swiss government is one of the most democratic in the world. The cantons are united as a federal republic, but the people can demand a popular vote on any issue by submitting a petition with sufficient signatures. At one time, people in each canton met in an open-air assembly, called a *Landsgemeinde,* to conduct government by a show of hands. Today five cantons still elect their magistrates in this way.

Zurich

The largest city in Switzerland is **Zurich,** located at the northern tip of Lake Zurich. Unlike French Geneva, the citizens of Zurich speak German. Ulrich Zwingli ministered in this city of the east at the same time that Calvin ministered in Geneva. Zwingli was a Catholic priest who later repudiated everything related to Catholicism, and his view that communion is just a symbol caused him to break from Luther. Zwingli died at the battle of Kappel, near Zurich, in 1531. The Catholic army quartered his body, burned it, and cast his ashes to the wind.

Zurich is the hub of international investment and gold trade. Its banks are considered the safest banks in the world, and laws ensure utmost secrecy. This secrecy has sometimes created controversy, such as that created over the discovery that Nazis had stolen gold and hidden it in Swiss banks.

The triple-cirque Matterhorn pierces the sky. Two of its cirques are clearly visible.

Cultural Diversity of the Swiss Alps

The Alps cover over one-half of Switzerland but less than one-tenth of the population lives there. The **Swiss Alps,** or Central Alps, stretch across southern Switzerland. It has four principal ranges.

The Bernese Alps lie between the Swiss capital, Bern, and the upper Rhone River. Visitors to the resort of Interlaken enjoy the highest waterfall in the Alps, the Giessbach, which spills 1,982 feet down the mountainside.

Three of the four major ranges in the Swiss Alps lie farther south along the Italian border. The Pennine Alps is in the west. It includes both Monte Rosa (15,203 ft.) and the **Matterhorn** (14,692 ft.). Monte Rosa is the highest mountain in Switzerland, but the Matterhorn is more famous because of its rare triple cirque peak. The peak forms a three-sided pyramid with steep bowl-shaped basins (or *cirques*) on each side.

East of the Matterhorn are the Lepontine Alps. Italy is easy to reach from this canton of Ticino, but the Alps separate the people from the rest of Switzerland. People here speak Italian. Italians constitute about 10 percent of the Swiss population. Engineers have bored through the Alps here to make some of the longest highway tunnels in the world. The St. Gotthard highway tunnel is over ten miles long, and the Simplon railway tunnel is over twelve miles long.

The Rhaetian Alps cover southeast Switzerland. In addition to pockets of Italians, Romansch-speaking people live in the small communities of this canton. About 1 percent of the Swiss people speak this quaint language, similar to ancient Latin. Romansch is an official language, along with German, French, and Italian.

Liechtenstein

Between Switzerland and Austria is the tiny principality of Liechtenstein, located on the east side of the Rhine. A prince from Vienna first bought land in the area in 1699, and his descendants—the von Liechtensteins—have ruled ever since. The prince now serves under a constitutional monarchy.

Liechtenstein uses Swiss currency and lets the Swiss represent them internationally. Like Switzerland, it has remained neutral in wars, and has not even had an army since 1868. The official language is German, but most people speak a dialect called Alemannic. About 87 percent of the people are Catholic.

Before 1950, Liechtenstein was primarily a farming country. Today, only 10 percent of the people farm. Now highly industrialized, it has one of the highest standards of living in the world. Over five thousand businesses have headquarters in Liechtenstein because of its reasonable tax rates. The government earns a large portion of its money from the sale of beautiful postage stamps.

The Austrian Empire

Austria has a colorful history. Until A.D. 1000, it had been invaded by several German tribes and had no separate identity. The variety of peoples and German dialects in modern Austria reflect this ancient diversity. The first duchy of Austria was limited to Vienna and the neighboring area. In 1282 the **Hapsburg** family gained control of Austria and by the fifteenth century they controlled an impressive empire. Austria lost its empire, however, after it joined the German emperor during World War I. Hitler, a native of Austria, took over the remnant of Austria in 1938, claiming it as part of historic Germany. After World War II, Austria won its independence, but it adopted a strict policy of neutrality in the Cold War because of its precarious position between the East and the West. Austria still has close cultural and economic ties to Eastern Europe.

The Blue Danube Austrians speak German, and 90 percent of them are Catholic. Most people live in the north, where the **Danube River** winds through the foothills of the Alps.

With 1.5 million people, Austria's capital, **Vienna,** is the largest city in the country. Vienna is known for baroque architecture and its outstanding musicians, including Franz Haydn, Wolfgang Mozart, Franz Schubert, and Johann Strauss. Strauss even named a waltz "The Blue Danube." Concerts, festivals, and operas are performed regularly all over Austria, enjoyed by tourists and natives alike.

Many Alpine Ranges The Alps dominate southern Austria. Austria's forested mountains and valleys make it the leading exporter of wood in continental Europe. Austria's mines make it the world's third largest producer of tungsten.

Most southern people live in the mountain valleys. The main city in the western panhandle is Innsbruck. It stands on the Inn River, a tributary of the Danube that forms most of Austria's northwestern border with Germany. Innsbruck is the capital of the historic province of Tyrol. Italy took South Tyrol from Austria after World War I, a cause of continuing friction between the two countries.

The Danube River is the pride of Vienna.

Lipizzaner Horses

One of the highlights of tours in Vienna is a stop at a majestic hall, decorated with ivory and gold and lighted with chandeliers. But tourists don't come to see the architecture. All eyes are turned to events on the dirt floor. The hall has been the home of the Spanish Riding School for over 250 years. The world-famous performers are a troupe of Lipizzaner horses, "dancing horses," whose performances are unmatched for their combination of grace and strength.

The Spanish Riding School has been training the Lipizzaners for over four hundred years. It usually takes six or seven years before a horse and rider are ready to perform. They move as one, while the orchestra plays the great music of Vienna. The horses perform several ballet movements, such as a *capriole*, in which they

Lipizzaner horses parade around the ring while on tour in Montreal.

take a flying leap in the air. They stand on their hind legs in a pose called the *levade*. Only the very strongest horses can complete a *courbette*. The horse hops into the air and completes three or more leaps without touching its forelegs to the ground.

The highest and most famous mountain in Austria is Grossglockner (12,457 ft.), located southeast of Innsbruck. It lies in a central Alpine range called the Hohe Tauern, the hub of the many other ranges in Austria.

The primary mountain pass that German invaders and merchants have used to reach Italy is Brenner Pass, south of Innsbruck. It is the lowest major pass through the Central Alps, and warm foehns keep it open all year long. Several roads, railroads, bridges, and tunnels now cross Brenner Pass, linking Innsbruck and northern Italy (South Tyrol).

SECTION REVIEW

1. Where are the Bernese Alps? the Hohe Tauern?
2. What river and its tributaries contain most of Austria's population?
3. On what river does Liechtenstein lie?
4. Six of the ten largest glacial lakes in the Alps are in Switzerland. Name two.
5. Name two of the three famous Swiss industries.
6. What political policy do all three Alpine nations share? Why?

REVIEW

Can You Define These Terms?

dike	duchy	loess	canton
polder	reunification	European Union	foehn

Can You Locate These Natural Features?

Seine River	Rhone River	Ardennes	Bavarian Alps
Loire River	Corsica	Elbe River	Alps
Rhine River	Massif Central	Central Uplands	Swiss Alps
Jura Mountains	Garonne River	Black Forest	Matterhorn
Mont Blanc	Pyrenees Mountains	Bohemian Forest	Danube River

Can You Explain the Significance of These People, Places, and Events?

Protestant Reformation	French Riviera	Flanders	Bavaria
French Revolution	Aquitanian Lowlands	Wallonia	Munich
Paris	Charlemagne	Thirty Years War	John Calvin
Louis XIV	William the Silent	Nazi Empire	Geneva
Napoleon Bonaparte	Holland	Holocaust	Jean-Jacques Rousseau
Joan of Arc	Amsterdam	Berlin	Zurich
Brittany	The Hague	Berlin Wall	Hapsburg
Normandy	Rotterdam	Kiel Canal	Vienna
Alsace-Lorraine	Brussels	Ruhr	

How Much Do You Remember?

1. Which countries of Continental Europe are almost entirely Catholic? Which have a large proportion of Protestants?
2. Which countries share these geographic features?
   a. Alps
   b. Jura
   c. Ardennes
   d. Great Northern Plains
   e. Rhine River valley
3. Compare and contrast Paris and Berlin.
4. Compare and contrast Napoleon and Hitler.
5. What ethnic minorities live in each of these nations? Give the province or region where they live.
   a. France
   b. Belgium
   c. Switzerland
6. Why did the Reformation prosper in Germany but not in France?
7. What problems is Germany experiencing as a result of reunification?

What Do You Think?

1. Do you see any evidence that God has blessed nations who have protected Protestants?
2. Continental Europe is often divided between the north and the south. What characteristics are most common within each of these two regions, both their culture and their geography? Where do the small countries belong? Where do you draw the line through France and Germany?
3. Why do you think the Low Countries have been at the center of efforts to unite Europe, while the Alpine countries have traditionally stayed out of European politics?
4. Why did Germany never achieve a world empire, like France and Britain?

CHAPTER 15

MEDITERRANEAN EUROPE

Mediterranean Europe consists of three large peninsulas jutting into the Mediterranean Sea. The **Mediterranean Sea,** the world's greatest "inland waterway," dominates the area. It rarely lies more than 50 miles away and never over 250. The sea offers food, provides harbors, and moderates the climate.

Mediterranean Europe has a subtropical location and a mild climate. The climate is similar to that of Southern California—mild, rainy winters with hot, dry summers. Farms must adapt to winter rains and summer drought. The olive tree and grapevine survive the dry summers due in part to their extensive root systems. Mediterranean Europe supplies three-fourths of the world's olives. Spain produces about one-third, Italy one-fourth, and Greece, most of the rest.

Because of the easy access to trade, this region was the home of three great world empires controlled by Greece, Italy, and Spain. They form the cradle of Western civilization, which eventually spread across the globe. These empires have faded dramatically since the peak of their glory days. God used the ambitions of these empire-builders to accomplish His purposes in history. Today, the ruins serve as reminders of the limits of human ambition.

The king's heart is in the hand of the Lord, as the rivers of water: he turneth it whithersoever he will. (Prov. 21:1)

IBERIAN PENINSULA

The Iberian Peninsula contains the modern countries of Portugal and Spain. The waters of the Atlantic Ocean and Mediterranean Sea surround almost 90 percent of the peninsula. The short land border on the north runs through the rugged Pyrenees Mountains.

Mediterranean Europe Statistics

COUNTRY	CAPITAL	AREA (SQ. MI.)	POPULATION	NATURAL INCREASE	LIFE EXPECTANCY	LITERACY RATE	PER CAPITA GDP	POP. DENSITY
Andorra	Andorra la Vella	181	74,839	0.7%	91	100%	$16,200	413
Greece	Athens	50,949	10,583,126	0%	78	95%	$9,500	208
Italy	Rome	116,366	57,534,088	0%	78	97%	$18,700	494
Malta	Valetta	122	379,365	0.8%	79	91%	$12,000	3,109
Monaco	Monaco	0.75	31,892	−0.1%	78	99%	$25,000	42,522
Portugal	Lisbon	35,574	9,867,654	0.0%	76	90%	$11,000	277
San Marino	San Marino	24	24,741	0.3%	81	98%	$15,800	1,029
Spain	Madrid	194,898	39,244,195	0.1%	79	97%	$14,300	200
Vatican City	Vatican City	0.17	840	1.2%	78	100%	NA	4,829

Spain

Over 80 percent of the Iberian Peninsula lies in Spain. The Romans were the first to control the entire peninsula, although Phoenicians, Greeks, and Carthaginians had earlier trading colonies along the coast. The Romans built many schools for teaching the Latin language, roads for travel, and great aqueducts for channeling water, some of which can still be seen today.

Centuries of war began in 711 when the Moors invaded and conquered most of the peninsula in a seven-year campaign. These Muslims ruled for almost eight hundred years. They introduced the cultivation of figs and oranges and brought a degree of cultural advancement unsurpassed in all of Europe. From their small northern refuge, Christians fought to reconquer Spain. Castile and Aragon were the two principal kingdoms that emerged as they drove out the Moors. El Cid (or "The Cid"), a Castilian and a distinguished leader of the **Reconquista,** has become a national hero.

Spain's main provinces were united in 1469 when Isabella I, queen of Castile, married Ferdinand II of Aragon. During their reign, Christopher Columbus claimed the New World for Spain, and Spain grew rich from its gold and silver. Isabella and Ferdinand also began the **Spanish**

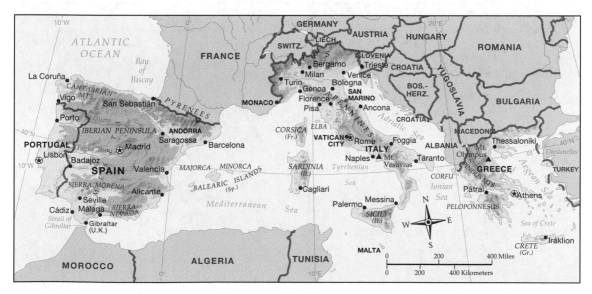

Inquisition, designed to make Spain a nation of Catholics. For over three hundred years, the courts of the Inquisition imprisoned or killed anyone they suspected of not following the doctrine of the Roman Catholic Church. Spain lost many of its writers, physicians, and most of its merchants with the expulsion of the Jews from the country. Most Spaniards are still Roman Catholic, and Castilian Spanish eventually became the primary language of business and government. **Castilian** continues to be the official language of Spain.

Madrid, Capital of Philip II

The capital city of Spain, **Madrid,** perched on top of a two thousand foot plateau, is the highest capital in Europe and the most populous among Europe's mediterranean nations. Madrid is uncomfortably hot in summer and freezing cold in winter. During August, the Spanish government actually relocates to a cooler location on the north coast. Madrid pulses with energy. Its residents, called Madrilenos, are known for their seeming ability to defy the need for sleep. As is the Spanish custom, most of Madrid does not eat dinner until at least ten o'clock. Madrid is the center for Spain's two favorite sports. It is the bullfighting capital of the world and has

one of the world's largest soccer stadiums, seating over one hundred thousand fans. Three splendid museums, including the Prado, make up Madrid's "golden triangle of art."

King Philip II declared Madrid to be the capital of the Spanish Empire in 1562 at the height of Spain's colonial power. At the time, Madrid was a hamlet in the forest. Philip chose Madrid because of its location near the geographic center of Spain. In an effort to protect Spain's fleet from English pirates, King Philip ordered 130 ships assembled in a great Spanish Armada that attacked Protestant England in 1588. However, the English navy defeated the "Invincible Armada" in the English Channel, and a fierce storm claimed most of the remaining ships on their return voyage.

Riches certainly make themselves wings; they fly away as an eagle toward heaven. (Prov. 23:5)

After the defeat of the Armada, wars and revolts caused Spain's empire to decline. Napoleon invaded in 1808 and put his brother on the throne. With the aid of the English, Spain cast off the French rule, but revolts in the New World spelled the end of its world empire. Spain's defeat in the Spanish-American War caused the additional loss

Reconquista in the Iberian Peninsula

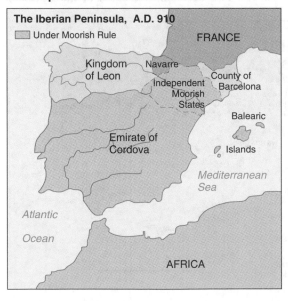

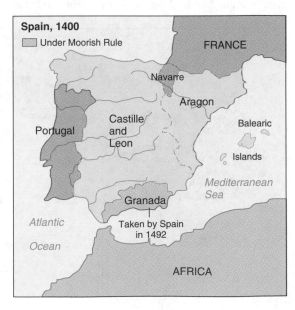

Sports

The Bullfight

The Spanish people enjoy many sports, especially soccer, but bullfighting is their passion. More than four hundred special stadiums, called *plazas de toros,* are scattered across the Spanish countryside. Bullfights highlight many of Spain's festivals from March to October.

Bullfights begin with pageantry. After a parade of matadors, the bull finally charges into the arena. Two horsemen, called *picadors,* provoke the bull with long lances. Next, footmen stab the excited bull in the neck with a pair of long and sharp sticks called *banderillas.* The footmen, called *banderilleros,* take turns until six pairs of banderillas are placed.

The matador enters the ring to face the bull after the picadors and banderillas have driven him into a rage. The matador skillfully waves his red *muleta* (cape) before the bull. The bull charges, but the matador gracefully steps aside—at least he is supposed to. The bull's sharp horns barely miss the matador, whose bravery delights the crowd. The more graceful and daring the matador, the more the crowd enjoys the fight. This contest between man and bull continues until, in a final charge, the matador plunges his sword into the bull's neck. Each matador fights two bulls.

Bullfight in Barcelona

Bullfighting began in Spain in the eighteenth century and spread to Portugal, southern France, and Latin America. Critics have condemned the cruel treatment of the animals. In fact, matadors in Portugal and France do not kill the bull. But fans consider bullfighting an art. The best matadors use graceful, well-timed moves to build the suspense to a peak. The greatest bullfighters have become national heroes. Everyone in Mexico knows the great Carlos Arruza; and in Spain, they still debate who was the greatest—Juan Belmonte, El Cordobés, or Manolete.

---

of Cuba, Puerto Rico, the Philippines, and Guam. In 1936 the country was engulfed in a bloody civil war. Spain's military revolted against the country's newly formed Republican government. The fascist victor, Francisco Franco, ruled as a dictator from 1939 to 1975.

After Franco's death, the disgruntled people restored the monarchy, and Juan Carlos became king of Spain. He pushed democratic reforms, and in 1978 Spain adopted a constitution. The government began to increase local control by allowing the election of regional parliaments. In an attempt to bolster the country's economy, Spain joined the European Economic Community in 1986.

Meseta, Spain's Heartland A high plateau radiates from Madrid across most of interior Spain.

The plateau is called the ***Meseta,*** meaning "Tableland." The Meseta, sprinkled with rocky hills and mountains, is the heartland of Spain. Although the higher elevations are forested, most of the plateau supports only small shrubs and flowering plants. The hot, dry summers, bitterly cold winters, and poor soils make farming difficult. The medieval ruins and small villages of the Meseta are celebrated in Spain's greatest novel, Cervantes's humorous *Don Quixote de la Mancha.*

Spain's largest river, the **Tagus,** cuts the Meseta in half as it flows west to the Atlantic through Portugal. Madrid lies on a tributary of the Tagus upstream from the historic city of Toledo. North of the Tagus, the Meseta stretches to the Pyrenees Mountains. To the south, the Meseta reaches the Sierra Morena. Near Portugal, this mountain range contains Spain's primary mineral resources. Spain ranks among the world's ten leading producers of pyrites, zinc, and silver.

The mountains of the Sierra Nevada rise in the far south. This part of Spain is separated from North Africa by the narrow eight-mile-wide **Strait of Gibraltar.** This makes Spain a land bridge between Africa and Europe. The Moors, for instance, came from North Africa to conquer Spain. Granada, located at the foot of these mountains, was the last Moorish stronghold. The Moors left a lasting cultural legacy and contributed to literature, philosophy, medicine, and mathematics. Moorish architecture can still be seen at the Alhambra at Granada. Spain recaptured Granada in 1492.

Olives in the River Basins

Two rivers, the Ebro and Guadalquivir, flow from the Meseta into fertile lowland basins. Most of Spain's olives come from these basins.

In the north, the Ebro River drains east to the Mediterranean. The broad plain of the Ebro Basin includes the province of Aragon. The river delta is well suited for growing rice, a Spanish staple. Saragossa, Spain's fifth largest city, is the hub of the region's paper and steel industries.

In the south, the Guadalquivir River flows west to the Atlantic just beyond Gibraltar. Seville, Spain's fourth largest city, is a port and its whitewashed houses and narrow shaded streets make it the epitome of what foreigners think Spain is like. Cádiz is

Viewed from space, the narrow Strait of Gibraltar is a striking feature of the earth's surface.

Escorial

Escorial was the royal residence of Spanish kings, located twenty-five miles north of Madrid in the foothills of the Sierra de Guadarrama. In addition to the walled palace, the grounds include a monastery, a domed church, and a college.

Philip II ordered the complex of buildings built after a battle against the French in 1557 destroyed the local church. Completed in 1584, the building had an austere design that reflected Philip's own self-denial. Constructed of granite from a nearby quarry, the exterior of the church is largely unadorned. Escorial is a massive structure, with 1,250 doors and 2,500 windows. However, its interior is highly decorated by Spanish and Italian artists. The royal residence became a symbol of national unity in the difficult times Spain was facing.

Escorial continued to serve as the royal residence until the nineteenth century. Philip II and many other Spanish kings are buried there. Today, the complex includes a museum with valuable collections of books and artwork.

an Atlantic port sixty miles downstream from Seville. Founded by Phoenician traders in 1100 B.C., the city claims to be the oldest continuously inhabited city in Europe. Columbus sailed from Cádiz in 1493 on his second voyage to America.

Ancient Ports on the Mediterranean

Several ancient ports were established on the narrow coastal plain along Spain's Mediterranean coast. In these fertile lowlands, farmers diverted rivers to irrigate their crops. Spain's coastal plain is the world's fourth largest producer of citrus fruits.

Málaga is the largest city in the south. The seaport and resort city of Alicante, known for its bright skies, was built on the site of the Roman city of Lucentum, or "City of Light." Valencia is located about midway up the coast. Located on the Turia River about three miles from the Mediterranean, it is the third largest city in Spain. Valencia's rows of white houses reflect its long period of Moorish occupation.

Located in the northeast corner of Spain, **Barcelona** has been an important seaport since it was founded in 230 B.C. According to legend, Christopher Columbus announced his discovery of the New World in this city. Today it is Spain's most important manufacturing and trading center.

During the Spanish Civil War, Barcelona was a stronghold of opposition to Franco's Nationalists. The people of this region speak Catalan, similar to Provençal, used across the border in France. When Franco forbade the speaking of Catalan, the fiercely independent people continued to use it during soccer matches to cheer for their local team. Today Catalonia is one of three regions of Spain in which there is a second official language. The people here, who think of themselves as Catalonians first and Spaniards second, would like independence.

Green Northern Mountains The mountainous north is the only part of Spain that receives adequate rainfall. Its marine-west-coast climate benefits from the moist winds that blow off the Atlantic. The poor quality soil does not support crops; however, the rain provides adequate pastureland. The pastures and woodlands in this region support thriving dairy and paper industries.

In the summer, Spaniards flock to the cool mountains and the northern beaches. The forested mountain slopes are broken by short, swift rivers that flow into the Atlantic. Although these rivers are not navigable, they are harnessed to generate electricity. The river mouths provide harbors for fishing fleets.

The **Cantabrian Mountains** rise from the northern and northwestern edge of the Meseta and

Alhambra

Alhambra may be the most beautiful and elaborate Islamic architecture in the Western world. Begun by the Moors in the mid-thirteenth century, it took over one century to complete. The complex, which grew to include an entire royal city, occupies thirty-five acres. Originally built as a defensive fortress, situated on a plateau overlooking Granada, it was surrounded by a reddish brick wall with twenty-three towers. The name of *Alhambra* comes from an Arabic word meaning "red," an appropriate name for the Red Castle.

Two Moorish kings, Yusuf I and Mohammed V, are responsible for most of Alhambra's construction. The Alhambra served as their royal palace and displays elaborate decorations fit for royalty. Courtyards contain gardens, fountains, tiles, and calligraphy. In the most famous courtyard, the Court of the Lions, a fountain with twelve white marble lions supports the round central basin. An arched roof is supported by 124 slender white marble pillars, and ceramic tiles cover the floor.

The Alhambra was the last stronghold of the Moors in Spain. In 1492, the same year that Ferdinand and Isabella sent Columbus to the New World, Spanish forces took Granada. The palace suffered from neglect and an earthquake in 1812, but it has now been restored.

Court of the Lions in the Alhambra

Basques

The **Basques** are an ancient people who live in northern Spain. Not much is known about their origins, and their language is unrelated to any known language. The arrival of the Gauls and Iberians forced them to retreat into the defenses of the Pyrenees Mountains. More than two million Basques live in Spain, and about one-half million live across the border in France.

The fiercely independent Basques have clung to their way of life despite foreign invaders. The small beret, or *boina,* is the national headgear of the Basque. The true Basque wears his beret even at meals, removing it only in church and when he goes to bed. Rope-soled shoes called *alpargatas* are also typical of Basque dress.

The dance of the Zamalsain is the oldest Basque dance. In the dance, one group of performers represents good, and another group represents evil. Both groups perform intricate steps around a wine glass until the climax of the dance, when the leader of each group jumps on the wine glass and then springs away. If the leader of the evil dancers spills the wine, tradition has it that good luck will reign in the coming year.

Many Basques make their living from the sea. The adventurous Basques were the first Europeans to hunt whales in the Bay of Biscay during the sixteenth century. Two centuries ago the whales disappeared, so now the Basques fish for tuna and cod instead. Basque sailors accompanied Magellan on his voyage around the globe. In fact, a Basque took over after Magellan was killed in the Philippines in 1521, and he became the first man to circumnavigate the earth. A statue in honor of del Cano still stands in the plaza of the Spanish port of Guetaria.

There are three small Spanish provinces in "Basque Country": Alava, Vixcaya, and Guipuzcoa. But the heart of their ancient land was Navarre, on the border with France. The highlight of the year is the feast of San Fermin at Pamplona, the capital of Navarre. Basques from all provinces spend an entire week in boisterous singing and dancing throughout the town. Each morning of the festival, the bulls are released from their pens to run through narrow streets to the bullring. Many people test their own courage by running with the bulls.

The Basque language, which they call Euskara, is very difficult. It has several dialects. The first "unified Basque" Bible was not translated until 1995. The dictator Franco banned the language and tried to re-educate the young people in Spanish schools. As a result, most Basques speak Spanish and only a minority speak Basque. But the Basque speakers are a vocal minority, and many want independence from Spain. A terrorist group, called ETA, began a terrorist campaign of bombings and political assassinations in 1968. They have killed over eight hundred people.

Montserrat (4,054 ft.), meaning "serrated mountain," is an apt name for this fantastic peak in the foothills of the Pyrenees. On its slope is a popular shrine to Our Lady of Montserrat, the patron saint of Catalonia.

run parallel to the Atlantic Ocean. In the far west, the people speak Galician, a dialect of Portuguese. The Basques live in the eastern Cantabrian Mountains near the port of Bilbao. This area provided iron during the early Industrial Revolution. Today Bilbao is densely populated as a result of industrial development. To the east, the towering Pyrenees rise to over eleven thousand feet and form the formidable barrier between Spain and France.

Andorra

Nestled high in the Pyrenees Mountains, Andorra lies between Spain and France. Its name may have come from an old Moorish word meaning "thickly wooded place," but it is indeed a mixture of Spain and France. The official language is Catalan, and both French francs and Spanish pesetas are legal tender.

Isolated by steep mountains in their fertile valleys, the Andorrans lived as farmers and shepherds when Charlemagne, according to tradition, granted them independence in exchange for help in fighting the Moors. When roads to Spain and France opened in the 1950s, tourism developed. Today, tourists come to view historic sites and to buy Andorra's rare postage stamps. The low tax rate also lures bargain hunters for Swiss watches or Japanese cameras.

Portugal

The country of Portugal lies on the west coast of the Iberian Peninsula. This small country once ruled one-half of the known world. During the sixteenth century, Portugal's empire included Brazil, much of India, and colonies in Africa, the East Indies, and China. Today only three small territories remain from the once great Portuguese empire.

Portugal's empire grew because of its mastery of the sea. **Prince Henry the Navigator,** the third son of the king, started a school of navigation in southern Portugal. He financed voyages to Africa, and his school of top navigators, mapmakers, and astronomers improved the compass and redesigned the caravel, a speedy ship, so that it could sail into the wind. Later, Vasco da Gama rounded the Cape of Good Hope and reached India, and Pedro Cabral landed in Brazil. These men expanded the Portuguese Empire. Spice trade in Asia, slave trade in Africa, and the discovery of gold and diamonds in Brazil brought incredible wealth to Portugal.

Lisbon With a metropolitan population of 2.5 million, **Lisbon** is Portugal's capital and largest city. Lisbon's harbor, at the mouth of the Tagus River, is one of the finest natural harbors in the world. The official language is Portuguese, and most people are Roman Catholic.

The government at Lisbon has not always been stable. From 1928 to 1968, a dictator denied the people basic civil rights. In 1974, a military group seized control of the government and vowed to restore democracy. Two years later Portugal held its first free elections in more than fifty years. The standard of living improved as some state-owned industries were privatized. The country's future growth is now tied to the growth of the European Union, which it joined in 1986.

The Coast Porto is Portugal's second largest city, and it stands at the mouth of the second most important river, the Duero River. Like Lisbon, it is a canning center for sardines, but it is also famous for port wine. The beautiful beaches from Porto south to Lisbon have earned this coast the name Silver Coast. Men from Porto and the fishing villages along the coastal plain fish for tuna, sardines, and cod. Dried cod, called *bacalhau,* is one of the nation's favorite foods. The Portuguese claim that a good cook can prepare it 365 different ways, one for each day of the year.

Interior The Spanish Meseta extends into Portugal almost to the coast. North of the Tagus, the climate is cool and rainy. This populous region supports many small farms that produce grapes, olives, and grains. Deposits of tin and tungsten in this area enable Portugal to rank among the top eight producers worldwide of these minerals.

South of the Tagus River, the climate is warmer and the terrain less rugged. Forests of cork oak trees in this region produce large quantities of cork for export. Portugal is the fifth largest producer of wood pulp in the world. Wealthy landowners have large farms in the area. Because of the forests and large farms, the population is small.

The great port at Lisbon is prone to floods and other disasters. Its greatest tragedy was an earthquake in 1755 that leveled the city and killed sixty thousand inhabitants.

The Colosseum once stood 180 feet high. For its grand opening in A.D. 80, Emperor Titus brought in five thousand wild beasts to battle prisoners and each other. Elevators moved beasts from underground cages to the ring.

THE GRANDEUR THAT WAS ROME

Italy occupies a long and narrow boot-shaped peninsula. The Alps form the top of the boot, while its toe stretches almost to Africa. While Italy usually has a sunny and mild climate, its extremes are exceptional. Winter is cold in the north, while the *sirocco* (winds) may bring to the south the intense heat of the Sahara. The name *Italy* comes from the ancient Romans who referred to the southern part of the peninsula as Italia, meaning "grazing land."

Rome, the First Republic

Rome, the capital, stands along the Tiber River, surrounded by seven steep hills. For the early Romans, the Tiber River provided ready access to the sea, while the hills offered protection in case of attack. Rome was founded by the Latins who lived in small settlements among the seven hills.

Rome blends the ancient and the modern. Each year thousands of tourists flock to the "Eternal City." Many come to view the antiquities which testify of Rome's past greatness. The Colosseum, constructed about two thousand years ago, still stands near the heart of the ancient city. The city also boasts the remains of luxurious Roman baths and the foundations of opulent palaces built for Roman emperors. Today these antiquities exist in the midst of modern office buildings and dawn-to-dusk traffic jams.

The Latins established the Roman Republic in 509 B.C. At that time, Roman society had three classes of people: the patricians or landowners, the plebeian class of common people, and the slaves. The plebeians, who shared in the duties of war, demanded and finally received a share in the government. In 454 B.C. a written code of law, called the Law of Twelve Tables, applied the law equally to all citizens. This written code had a significant influence on future democracies.

Julius Caesar, a military genius who expanded the Roman Empire to include all of Gaul (modern France), brought an end to the republic in 45 B.C. He was assassinated by senators the following year, but a series of emperors controlled the Roman Empire for the remainder of its history. The Roman Empire expanded throughout the Mediterranean Sea region and beyond. However, the empire grew too far and by the end of the fifth century A.D., barbarians had divided up the peninsula.

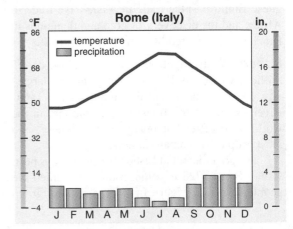

Roman Empire

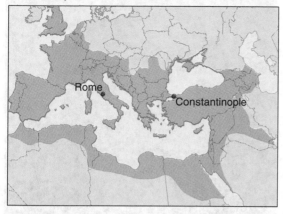

Reunification of the Italian Peninsula

Italy's coastline stretches for some five thousand miles and is known more for its beautiful beaches and resorts than its natural harbors. Nearly three-fourths of the country's land is either hilly or mountainous. Areas isolated by the mountains have their own unique customs, dialects, and cuisine. The main lowland areas lie along the west coast and on the boot heel.

After the fall of Rome, the dream of reuniting the Roman people stayed alive, but none had the power to subdue the many warring city-states. Napoleon Bonaparte invaded Italy and ruled portions of the Italian peninsula. Although his rule was harsh and short-lived, Napoleon reformed the legal system, rebuilt roads, and retrained the Italian army. As the people experienced limited self-rule, feelings of nationalism and a desire for unity began to surface.

During the 1860s **Guisseppe Garibaldi,** Italy's most popular hero, led his volunteer army of "Red Shirts," to unify the country. The goal was realized by 1870, but the different regions continued to show marked cultural differences. Still poor and illiterate, Italians sought a leader to revitalize the economy after World War I. Benito Mussolini and his Fascist Party rose to power on the pledge to lower taxes, prevent labor strikes, and maintain law and order. Instead, he dragged the country into World War II on Hitler's side, and the fighting devastated the country.

Since a parliamentary republic was established in 1946, competing interests in the country have prevented the government from forming a lasting coalition. Over fifty governments rose and fell in the first fifty years after Mussolini. Recently, leaders in the rich north have even called for independence from the poorer south, which wants the government to increase socialist programs that would redistribute the nation's wealth.

Apennine Mountains The **Apennine Mountains** stretch the length of the Italian peninsula. Italy ranks sixth worldwide for the production of pyrites which are mined in the Apennines. The highest peak, Corno Grande, reaches only 9,554 feet, and its once-thick forests have been indiscriminately cleared for crops, resulting in serious erosion. Though lower and less picturesque than the Alps, the Apennines form the backbone of Italy.

Small towns and villages dot the range where people raise sheep and goats. Though sparsely populated overall, the most populous parts lie at the extremes. Calabria, the toe region in the far south,

Unification of Italy

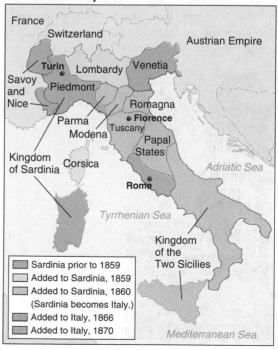

has ports facing the island of Sicily. Genoa and Bologna (buh LOWN yuh), at the north end, are Italy's fifth and seventh largest cities. Genoa is the center of Italy's shipbuilding industry and the hub of the Italian Riviera, an extension of the French Riviera. The Italian Riviera is called **Liguria** because it lies along the coast of the Ligurian Sea.

Renaissance Cities on the Coast

A wide coastal plain lies along the west coast of the Italian Peninsula. The coastal plains rise into foothills as they move inland toward the mountains. The southern regions are the most populous with the cities of Rome and Naples. The northern region, Tuscany, contains the cities of Pisa and Florence.

Florence was the birthplace of the Italian Renaissance. The **Renaissance** marked a "rebirth" of the cultures of ancient Greece and Rome. The study of perspective and anatomy gave rise to magnificent paintings, sculpture, and architecture. Wealthy families, like the Medicis of Florence, promoted the arts by supporting the best artists. The ideal Renaissance person was one who was skilled in many areas. From 1400 to 1550, many of the great Renaissance painters, sculptors, and writers lived in Florence, including Michelangelo. Today about one million tourists visit Florence annually to see the art galleries, museums, and churches.

Head of Young Christ *by Jacopo de Empoli is typical of Renaissance painting. (The Bob Jones University Collection)*

The port city of **Naples** is the country's third largest city. Once a resort for wealthy Romans, visitors still flock to southern Italy's beautiful coastline and ideal climate. Neapolitans, as residents of Naples are called, have a reputation for being carefree and living each moment to the fullest. With minimal industry, residents in southern Italy are poorer than their countrymen in the north. Their cuisine features many different dishes made from pasta. Pizza was first created in Naples by a royal baker during the eighteenth century.

Mount Vesuvius (4,190 ft.), mainland Europe's only active volcano, is about seven miles southwest of Naples. Tourists hike thirty minutes to the volcano's top. It has erupted eighty times since its most famous eruption in A.D. 79. The famous eruption buried the ancient Roman cities of Pompeii and Herculaneum. Volcanic ash and mud preserved the ruins of these cities.

The Boot Heel

The heel of the boot is called **Apulia.** This region is cut off from the rest of Italy by the Apennines. Most of Apulia is a plateau which ends in steep cliffs that drop into the Adriatic

The Leaning Tower of Pisa

The Gondoliers of Venice

Unlike most cities, Venice is built on over one hundred low islands in a swampy lagoon of the Adriatic Sea. The people do not ride in cars and busses over paved streets. Instead, they ride in motorboats or in *gondolas* (long black boats). Gondoliers wearing blue and white shirts and flat black hats guide their gondolas through Venice's canals. Every year thousands of tourists come to ride in a gondola on the Grand Canal, the main waterway through the city.

The seaside buildings are built on piles of mud and supported by debris, logs, and rocks. Many foundations were built during the Renaissance. Saint Mark's Cathedral and the Doges' Palace are two of the most beautiful buildings of the city. Some four hundred footbridges cross the 150 canals, and a major road links the city to the mainland.

The city was known as the "queen of the Adriatic" during the Middle Ages because of its large fleet. Venetian fleets returned from distant ports laden with silk, spices, and gold. Wealthy traders built the opulent palaces that line the Grand Canal in the heart of the city. Venice's navy won battles all over the Mediterranean and carried some of the Crusader's armies to the East.

The unusual shape of the gondola enables a single oar to guide the ship through the canals of Venice.

The sea, which once contributed to Venice's greatness, now poses a threat to its existence. Experts are working on ways to save the foundations of Venice's buildings, which are slowly eroding under the constant washing of seawater and the vibrations from motorboats. During the 1970s, authorities noticed that the entire city was sinking about one inch every five years. They forbade drawing water from Venice's underground wells, and the sinking temporarily stopped.

Sea. Italy produces one-fourth of the world's olives, mostly on large estates in Apulia and Sicily. Bari and Taranto are the main ports and support a large fishing industry.

Mt. Vesuvius is changing elevation with each major eruption—a low of 3,668 feet in 1906 compared to its current elevation at 4,202 feet.

Northern Italy

Northern Italy is cut off from the Italian peninsula by the Apennines. Since the Alps form the northern border, most people live in the lowlands between these ranges.

Italian Alps The Alps form the northern border of Italy. Lake Garda and Lake Como are two of the large alpine lakes that attract many tourists. People from South Tirol who live along the Austrian border speak German rather than Italian.

The Rich Po Valley The **Po River** is the longest river in Italy. From its origin in Italy's northwest corner, the Po flows east until it empties into the Adriatic. The broad plain of the Po is the largest in Mediterranean Europe. The Alps and the Apennines on either side of the valley provoke rains, which wash soil and minerals into the drainage basin. The resulting good soils and adequate rains make this valley the most heavily cultivated part of Italy. Vegetables, grapes, and grains including wheat, corn, and barley are grown here.

Large ships navigate inland on the Po as far as Turin. The region from Turin to Milan is the industrial center of Italy. Large power plants on the upper reaches of the Po provide electricity for factories producing cars, chemicals, and candy. **Milan,** Italy's second largest city, is also a banking center and contains the world famous opera house La Scala. Another city, Turin, is the base of the Fiat automobile empire, founded in 1899.

Adriatic Coastal Plain North of the Po River Delta, the Adriatic Coastal Plain extends to the eastern border. Venice is the most famous city in this area. Trieste is a key port. Austria ruled Trieste for several centuries and later ceded it to Italy in 1918. Yugoslavia held Trieste in World War II but restored it to Italy in 1954.

Italian Islands

Italy controls several islands in the Mediterranean Sea. The large islands of Sicily and Sardinia are very important.

Sicily The island of **Sicily** is situated just two miles from mainland Italy's toe. Mount Etna, Europe's highest volcano, rises to a height of 11,122 feet on the east coast of Sicily. The fertile volcanic soils surrounding Mount Etna encourage farming, but the rough terrain covering 80 percent of the island provides only limited arable land. Where the terrain is too rugged to irrigate almonds, grapes, lemons, oranges, or wheat, sheep and goats graze the hillsides. Sicily is the most populated island in the Mediterranean Sea. Palermo, on the north coast, is Italy's sixth largest city.

Tourist attractions include many historic sites. Syracuse in the south is a biblical site where Paul spent three days on his way to Rome (Acts 28:12). Visitors can also follow the imaginative journey of Homer's *Odyssey,* much of which was set around Sicily.

Sicily is also known for the **Mafia,** an organized crime ring that profits from illegal operations such as gambling, drugs, and providing protection for legitimate businesses. The Mafia began when Sicilians grew disgruntled with the harsh foreign rulers (Greeks, Romans, Arabs, and Normans), who had taken Sicily for its strategic position between Italy and Africa. In exchange for votes, the government has often "overlooked" the Mafia's criminal activities. A strict code of silence, called the *omerta,* has made it difficult for authorities to fight the ruthless and violent Mafia.

Sardinia The island of Sardinia is located about one hundred miles off Italy's west coast and nine miles south of the French island of Corsica. Its mountainous terrain makes for a strikingly beautiful and sparsely populated island. Some consider Sardinia's beaches the finest in the Mediterranean, especially the exclusive Costa Smeralda (Emerald Coast). Cagliari, the main city and port, predates the ancient city of Rome. Prehistoric stone dwellings, called *nuraghi,* are scattered across the island. Not much is known about the origin of the builders of these unique structures.

⊚ SECTION REVIEW

1. What mountain range forms the backbone of the Italian Peninsula?
2. What are Italy's three largest cities?
3. What plateau region covers southeast Italy?
4. What is the main river in Italy?
5. What is the Mafia?
   ○ Name three areas with important ruins. Why are they all in the southern half of Italy?

MINISTATES NEAR ITALY

Four small countries lie in or near Italy. These countries share Italy's mediterranean climate and are popular tourist destinations. All include historic sites, medieval buildings, and museums. Their economies depend on tourism and their rare and valuable postage stamps. Some of these ministates also have limited agriculture similar to adjacent regions of Italy.

Collectors prize stamps from Monaco, San Marino, Liechtenstein, Malta, and other ministates.

Monaco

famous resort area

Monaco is a tiny principality on the French Riviera about ten miles from the Italian border. Italians from Genoa first ruled the area in the twelfth century and built a fort in 1215. Since 1308, the Italian prince has descended from the Grimaldi family. In the mid 1950s, American actress Grace Kelly married Prince Ranier III and became Princess Grace. Her tomb is the most visited site in Monaco.

Although the prince of Monaco has an Italian ancestry, he speaks French. The official language is French, most of the citizens are French, and France is their main trade partner. In 1918, the prince signed a treaty permitting France to annex Monaco if Monaco ever lacks a male heir to the throne. The mixed French and Italian peoples of Monaco are known as Monégasques.

Much of tiny Monaco is built on cliffs overlooking the sea. The palace and fortress is called Monaco-Ville. To the west lies the industrial area of Fontvieille, while to the east lies the secluded harbor and port area of La Condamine. Beyond the port lies Monte Carlo, an area famous for its luxury hotels, shops, beaches, and gambling casinos.

San Marino

San Marino is located in the central Apennines. Like surrounding Italy, the people speak Italian and are Roman Catholic, while grapes, leather, and cheese are the main products. According to tradition, a Christian stonecutter named Marinus and his followers used this mountain refuge to escape religious persecution by Emperor Diocletian in A.D. 301. San Marino remained independent during the unification of Italy, and it now claims to be the world's oldest republic.

Vatican City

The pope leads the Roman Catholic Church from Vatican City. The tiny country, completely surrounded by the city of Rome, obtained independence by the Treaty of Lateran in 1929. With less than one thousand people and an area of only one-sixth of a square mile, it is the smallest country in the world. In spite of its small size, it contains two of the most famous buildings in the world: the Vatican Palace and St. Peter's Basilica.

Vatican City also has its own bank, post office, newspaper, and even a rarely used jail. The Vatican's radio station broadcasts in thirty different languages. Its unique police force consists of Swiss guards whose sole duty is to protect the pope. These brightly costumed guards patrol with swords and halberds.

The pope's involvement in politics helps to explain Italy's inability to reunite. Throughout the

Michelangelo's Last Judgment *in the Sistine Chapel is sixty feet high. Michelangelo's lifelike sculpture* Pietà *depicts Mary sorrowing over Jesus' body.*

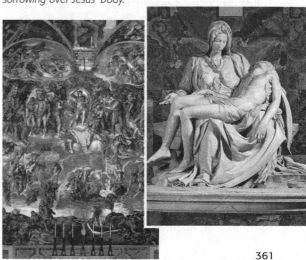

St. Peter's Basilica, the mother church of Roman Catholicism, is almost the same height as the Great Pyramid at Giza.

Middle Ages, the popes owned vast lands in central Italy, called the Papal States. They meddled in European politics as much as in religion. The pope once claimed the right to crown Europe's kings. The modern Catholic Church has a "spiritual empire" of followers around the world, who send money through local churches back to the Vatican. More people are members of the Catholic Church than of any other religious body in the world.

 The creed of the Roman Catholic Church contradicts almost every central teaching of Protestantism. Until the twentieth century, the popes openly supported the persecution of Protestants, whom they considered heretics, in Catholic countries. The Council of Trent (1545-63) defined the differences between the two faiths. The most recent *Catechism of the Catholic Church* (1994) reaffirms the early teachings of the Council of Trent.

Every good Catholic is expected to support Pope Pius's Tridentine Profession of Faith (1564). Its eleven main points specifically include the acceptance of tradition equal to Scripture; the Church's sole ability to interpret Scripture; the seven sacraments; justification by faith and works; the mass; indulgences; and the veneration of saints, relics, and images. It declares *anathema* (a solemn curse) on any teaching contrary to the Council of Trent. Catholics affirm the following: "I acknowledge the Holy, Catholic, Apostolic, Roman Church for the Mother and Mistress of all Churches; and I promise true obedience to the Bishop of Rome,

successor to St. Peter, Prince of the Apostles, and Vicar of Jesus Christ."

Malta

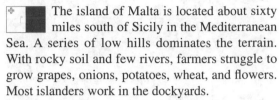 The island of Malta is located about sixty miles south of Sicily in the Mediterranean Sea. A series of low hills dominates the terrain. With rocky soil and few rivers, farmers struggle to grow grapes, onions, potatoes, wheat, and flowers. Most islanders work in the dockyards.

Around A.D. 60 the apostle Paul was shipwrecked on Malta (Acts 27:27–28:11) in the bay which now bears his name. Legend has it that Paul converted the entire population to Christianity during his stay on the island. Today most Maltese are Roman Catholic, and Catholic doctrine is required teaching in the public schools.

With its strategic location in the Mediterranean, Malta was long held by the British as a naval base. The British colony gained its independence in 1964. Though the British navy has departed, English remains an official language together with Maltese.

SECTION REVIEW

1. What small country is a famous resort ruled by an Italian prince?
2. What country lies in the Apennines and is surrounded by Italy?
3. What is the smallest country in the world?
4. What island country lies south of Sicily?
5. What product provides income for all four of these small countries?

💡 Should the United States treat Vatican City as a country, sending an ambassador and negotiating with the pope?

THE GLORY THAT WAS GREECE

Greece occupies the southern tip of the Balkan Peninsula that juts out of Europe at the eastern end of the Mediterranean. Greece's

Alexander the Great's Empire

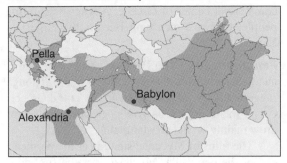

terrain is rough and the soil infertile. Farmers must work hard to get anything to grow in the rocky soil. In the country's many mountainous regions, the population is sparse, with most people residing in small villages. The largest and most productive farms are located either along the coast or on interior plains where irrigation is common.

In ancient times, fiercely independent city-states developed all over Greece and competed for supremacy. Athens enjoyed a brief golden age, but was conquered by Sparta. Then Thebes conquered Sparta, and the fighting continued. Finally, **Alexander the Great** united the country by force and built the largest empire in the ancient world, which stretched to India. But after his death in 323 B.C., Alexander's empire broke up into four kingdoms.

The Romans later conquered the cities of Greece. But the Greek cities prospered under Roman rule, as the ruling class of Romans adopted the Greek language and culture. The Roman Senate actually spoke Greek, not "vulgar" Latin.

The Roman emperor Constantine later built a new capital in the East on the Balkan peninsula. After the fall of Rome, the eastern empire survived another one thousand years. The Byzantine emperors spoke Greek, and the Greek monks preserved the Scriptures while barbarian hordes ravaged the rest of Christendom.

The Greek churches in the East followed a different path from the Roman Catholic churches in the West. The Eastern churches finally broke from Rome in 1054, when the pope demanded that they acknowledge his supreme authority. The Byzantine churches became known as the **Eastern Orthodox churches.** The religious leader in Constantinople and the Roman pope declared a mutual anathema against each other, which remained in effect until the two branches agreed to restore friendly relations in 1965.

Although Eastern Orthodox churches share much in common with Roman Catholicism, they take their differences seriously. The main differences include the authority of the pope, dates for celebrating Easter, the ability of priests to marry, and the use of **icons,** or painted images of Christ, Mary, and the saints. Many Catholics believe the use of icons is idolatry condemned by the Second Commandment, but Eastern Orthodox churches believe that adoring these images aids in worship.

Throughout the challenges of the last thousand years, especially when the Ottoman Turks overran the Balkans, the Greeks have rallied to the Orthodox Church. Nearly 100 percent of the Greek people belong to the Greek Orthodox Church. Like the other nations of Eastern Europe, Greece has its own independent church leader, called a primate, who lives in Athens.

Central Greece

The ancient Roman province of Achaia occupied the heart of Greece around the city of Athens. The mainland portion is *Central Greece.* Achaia also included a large peninsula in the south, called the Peloponnesus.

Today, small villages are scattered across Central Greece. Farmers grow cotton or raise sheep and goats on the hillsides. Lamb is a central feature in many Greek dishes, such as *gyros.* Goat's milk is used to make a cheese called *feta.*

Athens, Birthplace of Democracy   The city of **Athens** sits on a plain in southeastern Greece. Named for Athena, the Greek goddess of wisdom, this city was the cultural center of the ancient Greek world. Many gifted writers, poets, sculptors, and philosophers lived here during Athens's "golden age," from 477 to 431 B.C. The philosophy and art of Athens played a central role in the development of Western civilization.

The Parthenon crowns the Acropolis at Athens. Even in ruins, it has moved generations of Western poets.

Magnificent ruins testify to Athens's past glory. The **Acropolis** is the high flat-topped hill that was the defensive citadel in ancient Athens. The Parthenon, a marble temple dedicated to the goddess Athena, crowns the Acropolis. A thirty-nine-foot-tall statue of Athena, containing more than a ton of gold, once graced its sanctuary.

Athens reached the height of its power and cultural achievement under Pericles. He built the Parthenon and the Long Walls that stretched some five miles from Athens to its harbor, Piraeus. During sieges, the entire population took refuge inside the citadel. Pericles championed democracy.

Athens's glory eventually faded, and it fell to Rome. Later the Muslim Turks captured the whole Balkan Peninsula and oppressed the Greek people. They forced the Greeks to pay high taxes and to send one of every five males to serve in the army. The Greeks revolted in 1821, and after ten valiant years won the War of Independence. Since then, Greece has expanded its territory at the expense of Turkey. War between these two nations is only an incident away.

When Athens became the capital of Greece in 1835, the city's population had declined to just six thousand people. Today, a third of the country resides in this hastily built city, which sprawls over 165 square miles. One-half of the nation's industry takes place in the city, and the pollution is very harmful, both to the people and to the ancient ruins.

With its nearby port, Piraeus, Athens is the commercial center of Greece. Always a seafaring people, Greece's merchant fleet is the largest in Europe.

Peloponnesus The **Peloponnesus** is the large, hand-shaped peninsula in southern Greece. Though rugged, it is less mountainous than Central Greece. Crops including citrus fruits, grapes, and olives grow mainly on the coastal plains.

The ruins of Mycenae stand near the northeast end of the peninsula. Mycenae was the first civilization on mainland Europe—the center of culture recounted in Homer's epic Greek poem the *Illiad*. Northern invaders overthrew Mycenae and other early Greek cities, which suffered through a Dark Age before the rise of Athens, Sparta, and other city-states.

Sparta, in the south of the Peloponnesus, was Athen's chief rival during the fifth century B.C. In sharp contrast with the democracy of Athens, Sparta was ruled by kings and aristocrats who lived for war. The Spartans defeated Athens in the Peloponnesian War in 404 B.C. after twenty-eight years of bitter fighting.

The village of Olympia, home of the Olympic games, is near the west coast of the peninsula. These athletic competitions helped to unite the city-states by gathering the people every four years for the Olympic festival. The Olympics began in 776 B.C. and were dedicated to Zeus, the king of the Greek gods. A magnificent statue of Zeus, constructed of gold and ivory, once stood in Olympia's temple. It was among the Seven Wonders of the Ancient World.

Wheat in the Valley of Thessaly

On the mainland north of Central Greece is Thessaly, a valley coveted by cities in Achaia and people farther north. Its importance arises from the fertile farmland, which produces most of the wheat grown in Greece. The valley is ringed by mountains. The highest and most famous is Mount Olympus (9,570 ft.) at the north end of the valley. The **Pindus Mountains** border the valley on the west and rise to over eight thousand feet. Modern Greece took Thessaly from the Ottoman Turks in 1881.

Macedonia

North of Thessaly is a region of Greece known as **Macedonia.** It is one part of a larger historical region where Alexander the Great rose to power. It is now divided between Greece, Bulgaria, and the modern nation of Macedonia. The Macedonian region of Greece stretches along Greece's northern border east to a three-fingered peninsula on the Aegean coast, called Khalkidhiki Peninsula. The coastal plain of Macedonia is Greece's most productive agricultural area. Major crops include corn, cotton, oats, rice, and wheat. Another major crop, tobacco, is sold in Europe.

Macedonia's excellent seaport, **Thessaloníki,** is the second largest city in Greece. It was named after a sister of Alexander the Great. The apostle Paul preached in three cities of Macedonia, including Thessaloníki (Acts 16:9–17:13).

Throughout its history, Greece has had trouble with the territories that lie on its outer edges. The ancient kingdom of *Epirus* lay west of Macedonia in the Pindus Mountains, and *Thrace* lay east on the coastal plain that touches the Black Sea. Greece took Epirus and much of Macedonia from Turkey during the Balkan War of 1912. It received part of Thrace from Turkey in 1919 after World War I. The eastern half of Thrace remains in Turkish hands. A small minority of Albanians still live in Epirus, Slavs live in Macedonia, and about one hundred thousand Turks live in Thrace. The nations of Albania, Macedonia, Bulgaria, and Turkey still covet these lands.

The Greek Isles

About one-fifth of Greece's territory consists of over 500 islands—166 of which are inhabited. From May to November, the mild climate attracts flocks of tourists to the islands. Foreigners enjoy the clear air and distinctive culture. Local divers collect sponges from the sea floor of the Aegean.

Ever since Greece obtained independence, it has fought to regain control of all the islands off Turkey. Much like America's "Manifest Destiny," Greeks have a name for their goal—the Megali Idea, meaning "Great Idea." Only a couple of islands in the northeast are still held by Turkey, and the eastern island of Cyprus is an independent country divided between Greeks and a Turkish minority.

Crete   The island of **Crete** lies southeast of mainland Greece at the south end of the Aegean Sea. The largest of the Greek isles, it is known as the "Great Island." Mountains rise sharply from the sea along the south shore and provide a scenic backdrop to the cities and beautiful beaches in the north. The most interesting tourist stop is the ruins of the ancient Minoan capital, Knossos, apparently destroyed by a volcano.

Ionian Islands   The **Ionian Islands** lie off the west coast of Greece in the Ionian Sea. These fertile islands, obtained from Britain in 1864, receive more rainfall than the rest of Greece. The main crops include figs, citrus fruits, olives, and grapes. Ithaca, the island home of Ulysses in Homer's *Odyssey,* is a popular destination. The island of Corfu is strategically located at the north end of the chain near Italy and Albania. It has changed hands many times. This beautiful island, the second largest in the chain, is known for its wildflowers.

Aegean Islands   The majority of Greece's islands are **Aegean Islands** in the sparkling Aegean Sea. These rocky and sparsely inhabited islands are

Scholars scoffed at the ancient Greek legends, such as King Minos, minotaurs, and the labyrinth of Daedalus, until Sir Arthur Evans excavated Kephala Mound in 1900 and found a twelve-acre palace with passages connecting fifteen hundred rooms. The excavations uncovered frescoes and ivory figurines of young boys being sacrificed to bulls.

Geographer's Corner

Foreign Exchange Rates

Foreign travel and trade is complicated by the need to exchange American dollars for other currencies. To buy and sell, American businesses must change their dollars into the foreign currencies. This can be a complex, costly procedure because the value of currencies changes daily. Adding to the hardship is the European Union's recent creation of a common currency, called the *euro*.

Rapid swings in *exchange rates* can have a terrible effect on businesses. If the value of the dollar drops, then Americans cannot afford as many foreign goods; if the value rises, then foreigners cannot afford American goods. A drop in the value of the dollar is especially harmful to missionaries, whose income in dollars does not increase to make up for the loss.

After World War II, the United States dollar became the international standard against which many other currencies are exchanged. Merchants in unstable countries, such as Russia, often prefer American dollars without asking for an exchange. Answer the following questions about exchange rates for leading currencies.

1. In 1970, the exchange rate with Canada was 1.01. In other words, one American dollar could be exchanged for $1.01 in Canadian dollars. In 1995 the exchange rate was 1.37. How many Canadian dollars and cents would you receive for one American dollar?

2. In 1994, 3.38 Mexican pesos were worth one dollar. The exchange rate was 6.4 the next year, after a financial crisis. Did this help or hurt Mexican businesses trying to sell goods to America?

3. The exchange rate for Greek drachmas was 30.0 in 1970 and 231.7 in 1995. Which year was probably cheaper for American tourists travelling to Greece?

4. Between 1970 and 1995 the exchange rate for Japan fell from 357.6 yen per dollar to 94.0 yen per dollar. Has this been good for missionaries?

💡 Greece was among the European countries that did not qualify to convert their money into the *euro*. What problems do you foresee in the future for European businesses? for American businesses?

---

subdivided into three groups. The *Cyclades,* a group of 220 islands owned by Greece since its independence, form a circle in the Aegean Sea. The group includes the island Thíra (or Santorin). Its huge volcanic crater indicates that the island once exploded in the largest eruption in history, perhaps accounting for the demise of Minoan civilization.

The *Sporades* stretch across the center of the Aegean to the Turkish coast. Throughout the Aegean, islanders fish for mackerel and harvest sponges. Greece obtained the last of these islands in 1913 as a result of the Balkan Wars.

The *Dodecanese* ("twelve islands") lie southeast of the Cyclades off the coast of Turkey. The largest Dodecanese island is **Rhodes.** (See map of Turkey on page 509.) It is blessed with streams and natural harbors, where ancient ships could spend the night (Acts 21:1). Rhodes made a massive

bronze statue of the sun god, Helios, in the fifth century B.C. that was as tall as the Statue of Liberty. This statue, called the Colossus of Rhodes, was one of the Seven Wonders of the Ancient World.

◎ SECTION REVIEW

1. What city-state was the main rival of ancient Athens?

2. What peninsula contains such famous sites as Mycenae and Olympia?

3. What is the second largest city in Greece?

4. What are the two main divisions of Greek isles? What is the largest Greek island?

💡 Compare and contrast the Greek and Roman Empires.

REVIEW

Can You Define These Terms?

Mafia   Eastern Orthodox churches   icons

Can You Locate These Natural Features?

Mediterranean Sea	Cantabrian Mountains	Sicily	Ionian Islands
Meseta	Apennine Mountains	Peloponnesus	Aegean Islands
Tagus River	Mount Vesuvius	Pindus Mountains	Rhodes
Strait of Gibraltar	Po River	Crete	

Can You Explain the Significance of These People, Places, and Events?

Reconquista	Prince Henry the Navigator	Renaissance	Acropolis
Spanish Inquisition	Lisbon	Naples	Macedonia
Castilian	Rome	Apulia	Thessaloníki
Madrid	Julius Caesar	Milan	
Barcelona	Guisseppe Garibaldi	Alexander the Great	
Basques	Liguria	Athens	

How Much Do You Remember?

1. List five characteristics shared by the major nations of Mediterranean Europe.
2. For each of these four countries—Spain, Portugal, Italy, and Greece—give the following information:
   a. central mountains or plateau
   b. most productive region
   c. main product or industry
   d. biggest city
   e. time period of empire
   f. most famous ruler
3. Compare and contrast Roman Catholic and Eastern Orthodox churches.
4. In which country could you find the following?
   a. Basques
   b. Tower of Pisa
   c. St. Peter's Basilica
   d. Parthenon
   e. Colosseum
   f. Escorial
5. Explain why modern Italy had so much difficulty reuniting as an independent nation. What reunification difficulties did Spain and Greece experience?
6. Name three famous volcanoes in Mediterranean Europe, and give a memorable fact about each.

What Do You Think?

1. Why do you think God lifted up each of the empires mentioned in this chapter? What spiritual reason might explain their downfall?
2. Why do you think the Mediterranean has so many ministates? What is the most likely *new* ministate?
3. Should the ministates be given a seat in the United Nations?
4. Compare and contrast Mediterranean Europe and Continental Europe.

Cumulative Review

1. Name the seven continents and four oceans. Through what narrow strait does the Mediterranean Sea flow into the Atlantic Ocean?
2. Define primary, secondary, and tertiary industries. Which industry is most prominent in Europe?
3. List the eight culture regions of the world. Which regions border the Mediterranean Sea?
4. There are three main regions of Western Europe: Northern, Continental, and Mediterranean. List three characteristics that they all share, and three that are unique to each one. For each region, give the most populous country and the largest country in size.

UNIT VI

Central Eurasia

Chapter 16
Eastern Europe

Chapter 17
Russia

Chapter 18
Caucasus and Central Asia

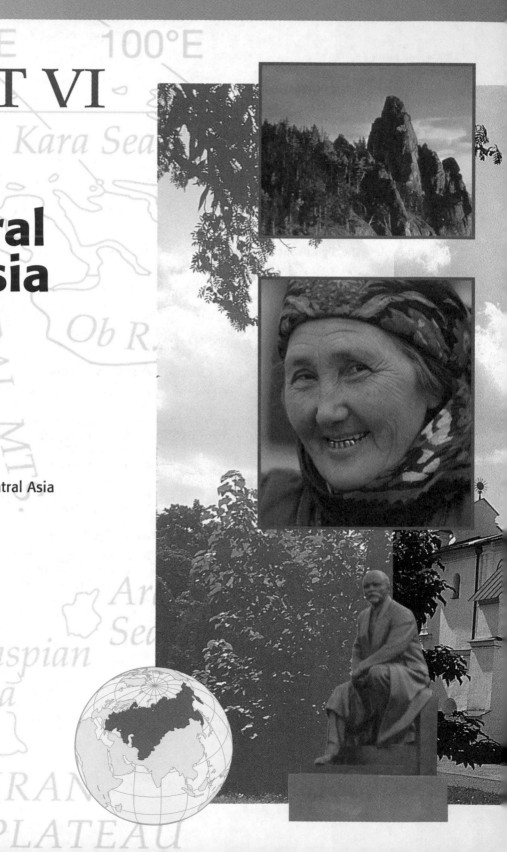

Russia

Carpathian
Divide

Baltic Rim

Eastern
Europe

Balkans

Eastern
Plain

European
Russia

Asian
Russia

Caucasus

Central
Asia

EASTERN EUROPE

After our study of Western Europe's pleasant climate, rich soils, and bustling cities, we turn to another important region on the great Eurasian landmass, called Northern or **Central Eurasia.** It lies in the middle of the continent between Western Europe and Asia. Hunger, mass migrations, and wars have troubled these lands for thousands of years.

Eastern Europe is the subject of this particular chapter. Slightly larger in area than Mexico, it has a colorful profusion of physical features, cultures, climates, and countries.

Eastern Europe is appropriately called a **shatter belt.** The size, shape, and number of countries is constantly changing. The borders have shifted back and forth, reflecting the fortunes of its powerful neighbors. Each time a nation has revolted against its conquerors and set up a new country, it has been conquered again and divided among the victors. Eastern Europe is struggling to rise out of the ashes left by its most recent conqueror—the Soviet Union.

The map on the next page shows the different borders that have existed in the past century alone. After World War II, Soviet Russia drew an **Iron Curtain** around all of Eastern Europe. Communists imposed their harsh economic and political ideas on nearly one hundred million captive people. Since the collapse of Communism in 1989, however, these newly freed peoples have enjoyed a rare opportunity to rebuild. Unfortunately, the newly freed peoples continue to look to government for security rather than to the Lord.

It is better to trust in the Lord than to put confidence in princes. (Ps. 118:9)

BALTIC RIM

Four nations in Eastern Europe—Poland, Lithuania, Latvia, and Estonia—have ports on the Baltic Sea. The dominant land feature is the Northern European Plain, which rolls across northern Europe from France to Russia. Numerous rivers drain this agricultural belt.

The warm, wet climate of Western Europe gradually gives way to a colder climate in the heart of the Eurasian continent. The term for this type of cold, wet climate is a *humid continental climate.* Precipitation averages around thirty inches a year, and temperatures rise and fall with the heating and cooling of the huge landmass. Summer temperatures often reach the eighties, and freezing temperatures endure through much of the winter. The same climate prevails in New England and southern Canada.

Poland, the First to Taste Freedom

Farmers, such as this couple near Lublin, Poland, have tilled the land of the Great European Plain for centuries.

Poland lies almost entirely within the Northern European Plain. In fact the name Poland is derived from the Latin word *Polonia,* meaning "people of the plain." Unfortunately the Polish people have suffered from a lack of natural barriers.

Poles are descendants of the **Slavs,** who migrated into Europe from Asia over two thousand years ago. The Slavic language evolved into a dozen languages. The Poles, who account for 98 percent of Poland's people, belong to the branch called the Western Slavs.

The Poles were among the first Slavic tribes to convert to Christianity. In the great division of 1054 between the Eastern Orthodox and Roman Catholic (western) Churches, Poland sided with Rome. They have since remained staunch Roman Catholics, fiercely clinging to the Catholic Church as a rallying point throughout their turbulent history.

In the eighteenth century Poland was caught between three growing empires—Prussia, Austria,

A Century of Border Changes in Europe

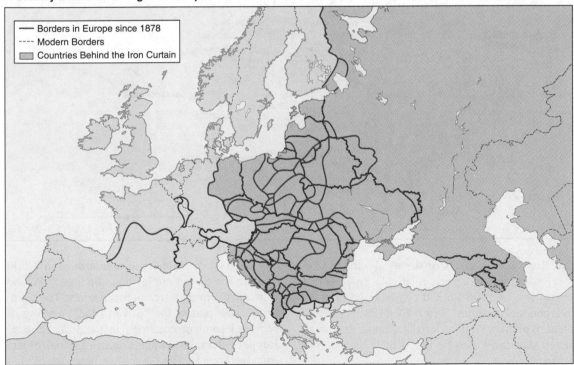

Borders in Europe since 1878
---- Modern Borders
Countries Behind the Iron Curtain

and Russia. In a series of three agreements, the foreign emperors agreed to divide up Poland's territories. In 1795 Poland ceased to exist as an independent country. After World War I, President Woodrow Wilson of the United States insisted that the Poles be given their own nation again.

Then came Hitler's German armies in World War II. The Soviet armies that "liberated" Poland from the Germans were not much better. The country became part of the **"Soviet bloc,"** a string of semi-independent countries in the Iron Curtain. **Puppet rulers,** like puppets on strings, took orders from the Soviets. The "year of surprises"—1989—

showed the world just how unpopular the Soviet system was among the people. In a few remarkable months, all the countries within the Soviet bloc cast off Communism and threw open their borders to the West. Poland started the movement on April 18, 1989, when it legalized a labor union called *Solidarity* and a few months later held the first free elections in Eastern Europe in forty years.

Many Changes in Warsaw A monument in Castle Square honors Sigismund III Vasa, the king who first moved the capital to **Warsaw** in 1596. With a population near two million, Warsaw is by far the largest city on the Baltic Rim.

This historic city has seen many conquerors. The last invaders, the Nazis, levelled the city in 1944 during the sixty-two-day Warsaw Uprising, killing over one-quarter million of the city's inhabitants. In an unusual gesture of kindness, the Soviets restored the quaint buildings of Old Warsaw after the war, using old photographs and written accounts. Ironically, thousands of Poles remained homeless while they worked. The rest of the city now has a modern appearance, with plain rectangular apartments and high-rise buildings. The city remains the focus of a struggle to create a stable, new republican government to replace the old Communist system.

Productive Plains and Coastal Ports Larger than either Italy or the United Kingdom, Poland has played a central role in the history of Europe. The best farmland and most of the nation's major cities lie on the Central Plains. Warsaw lies on the **Vistula River,** the major artery of shipping through the Central Plains. Poland's farms rank second worldwide in rye, third in potatoes, fifth in oats, and sixth in hogs. Poland's sausages are world renowned.

However, few people live on the plains near the coast, where glaciers have left many lakes and rocky moraines. The Masurian Lakes lie east of the Vistula on the coastal plains, and the Pomeranian Lakes lie in the west.

373

Eastern Europe Statistics

COUNTRY	CAPITAL	AREA (SQ. MI.)	POPULATION	NATURAL INCREASE	LIFE EXPECTANCY	LITERACY RATE	PER CAPITA GDP	POP. DENSITY
The Baltic Rim								
Estonia	Tallinn	17,462	1,444,721	−0.3%	68	100%	$7,600	83
Latvia	Riga	24,946	2,437,649	−0.4%	67	100%	$5,300	97
Lithuania	Vilnius	25,213	3,635,932	0.1%	69	98%	$3,400	144
Poland	Warsaw	120,728	38,700,291	0.2%	72	99%	$5,800	320
The Carpathians								
Czech Republic	Prague	30,450	10,318,958	−2.1%	74	99%	$10,200	339
Hungary	Budapest	35,919	9,935,774	−0.4%	69	99%	$7,000	277
Slovakia	Bratislava	18,933	5,393,016	0.3%	73	100%	$7,200	284
The Balkans								
Albania	Tiranë	11,100	3,293,252	1.4%	68	100%	$1,210	293
Bosnia-Herzegovina	Sarajevo	19,741	2,607,734	−0.8%	60	86%	$300	132
Bulgaria	Sofia	42,855	8,652,745	−0.5%	71	98%	$4,920	202
Croatia	Zagreb	21,899	5,026,995	−0.2%	73	97%	$4,300	235
Macedonia	Skopje	9,928	2,113,866	0.5%	72	89%	$880	216
Romania	Bucharest	91,699	21,399,114	−0.3%	70	97%	$4,600	233
Slovenia	Ljubljana	7,821	1,945,998	−0.1%	75	99%	$11,000	248
Yugoslavia	Belgrade	39,449	10,655,317	0.4%	72	98%	$2,000	269
The Eastern Plain								
Belarus	Minsk	80,153	10,439,916	−0.1%	70	98%	$4,700	130
Moldova	Chişinau	13,012	4,475,232	0.5%	65	96%	$2,310	343
Ukraine	Kiev	233,100	50,684,635	−0.3%	67	98%	$3,370	217

These lakes, nestled among low hills, are popular among campers.

Near the mouth of the Vistula is Gdańsk (formerly Danzig), Poland's largest port and once its most populous city. The hard-working ship-builders of Gdańsk formed *Solidarity,* the first trade union in the Iron Curtain. **Lech Walesa,** the head of the union, demanded changes in the 1980s that helped to bring about the end of Communism in Eastern Europe. He later became the first president of free Poland, introducing many reforms to the economy.

Minerals in the Southern Uplands The Polish plains rise into a series of hills and scattered mountains in southern Poland. Mines produce zinc and tin; Poland ranks eighth worldwide in both copper and silver production. A coal field, which crosses the border with the Czech Republic, is the largest source of coal in Europe outside the German Ruhr.

Galicia Southeastern Poland consists of hills and low mountains, rising into the Carpathian Mountains on the border. Farms cover the uplands, although they are not as productive as farms on the Central Plains.

This region, drained by the upper Vistula River, is known as Western Galicia. (The Soviet Union took Eastern Galicia away from Poland during World War II.) **Kraków,** the third largest city in Poland, is located on the upper Vistula River. Kraków was the first capital of Poland. Here King Casimir the Great (1333-70) built the magnificent Wawel Castle on a rocky hill above the Vistula River. Kraków was the only major city in Poland that escaped destruction during World War II. UNESCO lists it as one of the twelve most historic

Gdańsk, formerly called Danzig, has been an important trade center on the Baltic Sea for one thousand years. For centuries this was a German city, a fact reflected in the town's early architecture.

sites in the world because of its fine castles and medieval architecture.

Today many foreigners visit a rail center thirty-three miles west of Kraków, called **Auschwitz** (*Oświecim* in Polish). Auschwitz was the largest of several Nazi "death camps" where the Nazis killed over 2.5 million Jews and Poles, whom Hitler considered "inferior races." Many Jews have lived in Poland, a haven for oppressed peoples who were

forced to flee other countries in Europe. The Jewish population of Poland was about 750,000 in 1772—the largest concentration of Jews in Europe.

Silesia The Sudetic Mountains lie on the southwest border of Poland. Waters from the Sudetic Mountains flow into the **Oder River,** which flows west and then north along the German border into the Baltic Sea. The industrial city of Wroclaw, located on the upper Oder, processes minerals from the mountains.

The region drained by the Oder River is known as **Silesia.** Many emperors have fought over this valuable piece of property. Frederick the Great's invasion in 1740 sparked a major war fought on three continents. (Americans called it the French and Indian War.) Until World War II, most of the Silesian people were Germans. When the Soviets gave land to Poland in return for land it took from eastern Poland, over three million Germans left their homes in Silesia, and many Poles resettled there.

Geographer's Corner

City Models

Few cities in the world were planned. Instead, their layout reflects the events of their history, as businesses grew and as people moved into the city. Today, city planners in every country are attempting to foresee future growth and decline so that they can avoid problems of congested roads, pollution, or abandoned neighborhoods.

Like scientists, city planners use models to help them summarize and analyze complex information. Most city models break down the city into at least five components.

The *central business district* (CBD) refers to the original office buildings and skyscrapers, where property value is a premium. Soviet planners had a chance to use "science" to rebuild cities in Eastern Europe after World War II. But their layouts proved bad because their goal was wrong—to make everyone equal. In the process, they reduced everything to the lowest level of quality.

Cities have changed rapidly with the rise of suburbs and high-tech industries that allow people to work on computers at home. Examine these three early models of cities typical in the early twentieth century and answer the questions.

1. What type of buildings are near the CBD in every model?

2. What type of housing is near industry in every model?

3. Which city appears the least planned?

4. Which model appears to show development along roads?

💡 Which model is most similar to a city near you? How is your city different from any of these models?

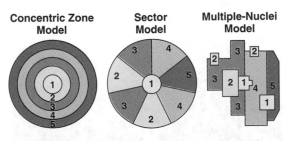

Concentric Zone Model

Sector Model

Multiple-Nuclei Model

1 = Business
2 = Industrial
3 = Low-income residential
4 = Middle-income residential
5 = High-income residential

Kaliningrad: Russia's Last Outpost in Europe

In 1255, some Germans known as the Teutonic Knights founded a fortress at Königsberg. It soon became a prosperous port on the Baltic. The German state of East Prussia later made it their capital, and two Prussian kings were crowned in the city. Its most famous citizen was the German philosopher Immanuel Kant, born in 1724 and buried in a local cathedral.

Russia, which coveted an ice-free port on the Baltic Sea, captured Königsberg in 1758 during the Seven Years War but gave it back. Russians again entered the city in World War II, this time to stay. Stalin renamed the city Kaliningrad after Mikhail Kalinin, whom he placed over the local government. The Soviets deported 139,000 Germans and replaced them with Russian colonists. Stalin flaunted his victory by building a twenty-two-story-high House of Soviets on the ruins of the Prussian Royal Castle. However, because the Soviets did not know about the tunnels and secret compartments underground, the foundation sagged, and they never could use the building.

Nearly a million Russians now live in Kaliningrad, separated from the rest of Russia by two hundred miles. With comfortable temperatures and beautiful beaches, most Russians want to stay. But no one knows what the future holds for this isolated region.

Baltic States of the Former Soviet Union

Three small countries on the Baltic Sea are known as the **Baltic States.** All three have large commercial fishing fleets. Located on the Northern European Plain, the Baltic States have low rolling hills with many shallow lakes and swamps. Besides rye, farmers grow potatoes or raise dairy cattle.

All three Baltic states have a rich heritage, which they celebrate with annual festivals that display traditional dress and recall the glorious deeds of the past. After centuries of occupation by foreigners, they received independence after World War I. But the Baltic States were incorporated into the Soviet Union. Recalling their independent spirit, they were the first of the fifteen republics in the Soviet Union to declare independence. Their bravery helped to hasten the breakup of the Soviet Union.

The Former Kingdom of Lithuania

Of all the Baltic States, Lithuania is the farthest from Russia's capital. It is populated almost entirely by ethnic Lithuanians. Like their neighbor Poland, over 90 percent of the people are Roman Catholic.

Lithuania has the oldest documented history among the Baltic States. Tacitus in the second century A.D. mentioned that this Baltic region sold amber to the Romans. Lithuania united with Poland in the twelfth century when its king converted to Catholicism and married the heir to the Polish throne. Russia later ruled Lithuania after the partitioning of the kingdom of Poland, except for the brief respite between World Wars I and II. Today it is struggling to establish a free republic.

Russians in Latvia

Latvian, the official language, is related to Sanskrit, making it one of the oldest languages on the European continent. Latvia suffered raids by Vikings, Russians, and then the German crusaders called **Teutonic Knights.** Lithuania and Sweden later ruled Latvia until Russia took over.

About one-half the people are ethnic Latvians, similar to Lithuanians, and another one-third are Russians who came during the Soviet

Vilnius on the Vilnia. The Lithuanian capital was founded by the ancient Balts and has been host to numerous conquerors, from the Crusaders to the Soviets.

Latvia's Statue of Freedom, a monument raised during its brief independence of the 1920s and 1930s, symbolizes Eastern Europe's longing for freedom.

era. Most Latvians are Lutherans, while the Russians are Russian Orthodox. This ethnic division has made it very difficult for Latvia to establish its independence.

The Finnic People of Estonia

Estonia is the smallest Baltic State. It has much in common with Scandinavia. The people speak Estonian, a Finnic language, and about 80 percent are Lutheran. Though controlled successively by Germany, Denmark, Sweden, Poland, and Russia, Estonia has kept a separate identity.

At 59° N Tallinn, the capital, is as far north as Juneau, Alaska. The Baltic Sea, however, moderates the climate of the port, which averages 24°F in the winter and 62°F in the summer.

SECTION REVIEW

1. Distinguish the terms *Iron Curtain, Soviet bloc,* and *shatter belt.*

2. To what people do the Poles trace their ancestry?

3. What are Poland's two most important rivers?

4. What two regions of Poland lie in the hills along southern mountains?

5. Name the Baltic States. Which state is not primarily Lutheran?

💡 In what ways has God blessed Poland because of its treatment of Jews (Gen. 12:3)?

PROSPEROUS NATIONS OF THE CARPATHIAN DIVIDE

The Alps are the dominant mountain system in Western Europe, cutting the region in half. But they die out in Austria. The **Carpathian Mountains** (kar PAY thee uhn) pick up on the east side of the Danube River, becoming the dominant system in Eastern Europe. They divide the northern plains from the south.

There are many subranges within the Carpathian system. The Tatras rise in the far north along the border of Poland and Slovakia. The Tatra range is the continental divide, separating the rivers that flow north into the Baltic Sea and the rivers that flow south and east into the Black Sea. Most people on the Carpathian Divide live in the river valleys, not in the mountains.

Three landlocked nations share parts of the Carpathians—the Czech Republic, Slovakia, and Hungary. Most of the people are Roman Catholics, but Protestants form a substantial minority. Czech Protestants are mostly Brethren, while Hungarian Protestants are mostly Reformed or Lutheran.

The Czech Republic's Velvet Revolution

The Czech Republic was formerly part of Czechoslovakia, a union of Czech and Slovak peoples. These two peoples, like the Poles, are Western Slavs. The Allies created Czechoslovakia after World War I when they broke up the Austria-Hungary Empire. The Allies hoped this union would give the Slavic people enough strength to defend themselves against future threats by their stronger neighbors. But Czechoslovakia fell to Hitler's armies in 1939 and then to the Soviet armies in 1945.

Czechoslovakia's Communist leaders introduced new freedoms, such as travel, in 1968. The "Prague Spring" lasted eight months, until one-half million troops from the Warsaw Pact quashed the movement. The Soviets imposed harsh measures, which lasted until the Soviet Empire crumbled in 1989. The overthrow of the Communist Party in

Climates of Central Eurasia

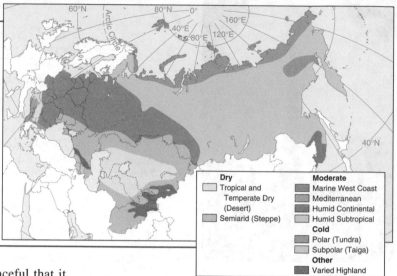

Let's Go Exploring

1. What climate occurs east of Europe's marine-west-coast climate?

2. What is the only nation in Central Eurasia with a subpolar climate?

3. What are the only nations in this chapter with a semiarid climate?

4. For which countries is the climate entirely marine west coast? humid continental?

💡 Which culture region of the world has a climate most similar to Central Eurasia?

Dry
- ☐ Tropical and Temperate Dry (Desert)
- ☐ Semiarid (Steppe)

Cold
- Polar (Tundra)
- Subpolar (Taiga)

Other
- Varied Highland

Moderate
- Marine West Coast
- Mediterranean
- Humid Continental
- Humid Subtropical

Czechoslovakia was so swift and peaceful that it was called the Velvet Revolution.

Since then, the Czechs have introduced the most radical, pro-Western reforms in all of Central Europe. To get property back in the hands of the people, leaders handed out vouchers to private citizens in an experiment called **mass privatization.** Each adult became a shareholder in the nation's various industries. After a brief period of economic hardships, the country swiftly regained its vigor.

The Bohemian Spirit

The western half of the Czech Republic, called **Bohemia,** is a large basin ringed by highlands. Its waters drain north into Germany's Elbe River. Farmers raise cattle as well as barley, corn, wheat, and potatoes. The entire country enjoys a marine-west-coast climate, similar to Western Europe.

Protected by the mountains, an independent spirit has thrived in Bohemia over the centuries. Prague Castle reminds visitors that Bohemia was an independent kingdom during the Middle Ages. A huge statue of "good king" Wenceslas (921-29), the patron saint of the Czechs, dominates Wenceslas Square in the center of Prague. He is credited with uniting the Slavic peoples of Bohemia and with spreading Christianity.

Prague, the Historic Capital

The capital of the Czech Republic, **Prague,** has over one million people. The City of a Hundred Spires, Prague has many churches, bridges, and historical landmarks, which were spared from bomb attacks during World War II.

A prominent statue in Prague's city square reminds visitors that the nation was once a leader in the Protestant movement. It depicts the famed Czech preacher **John Huss,** who stood for the truth of God's Word against the false teachings of Roman Catholicism—a century before Martin Luther challenged Rome. Huss was burned at the stake in 1415, but his martyrdom stirred Bohemia. Today visitors can see a restoration of Huss's pulpit at Bethlehem Chapel.

Prague Castle, which stands on a hill overlooking the Vltava River, was the home of the kings of Bohemia. Today the president of the Czech Republic lives in a portion of the castle.

Huss's followers held sway over Bohemia and threw back five armies that the pope sent against them. In 1458 Bohemia crowned a Protestant king, the first in all of Europe. But Austria's Hapsburg rulers later stamped out Protestantism in Eastern Europe, with the help of zealous Jesuits, during the Counter Reformation. Most modern Czechs are now Catholic.

Disputed Mines in the Sudetenland The Bohemian Basin is ringed by the Sudetic Mountains on the northern border with Poland, and the Bohemian Mountains on the western boundary with Germany. The Bohemian range includes the famed Bohemian Forest in the west and the Erzgebirge (EHRTS guh BIER guh), meaning "Ore Mountains," in the northwest, which produce uranium and coal. The coal mines make the Czech Republic the tenth largest producer of coal in the world.

Many Germans live in this valuable mountain region, called the Sudetenland. The Allies gave it to the Czechs after World War I to guarantee them a defensible border against Germany. But Hitler invaded in 1938, claiming a right to recover German lands. The Nazis killed and displaced many Czechs; then in retribution after World War II the Czechs forced three million Germans out of their homes. Relations between the two countries have been sour ever since.

Moravia The eastern part of the Czech Republic is **Moravia.** About 15 percent of the Czech population is still Moravian. Moravia takes its name from the Morava River, which drains south into the Danube. This fertile basin is similar to Bohemia except that it lies on the opposite side of the continental divide.

Slovakia's Velvet Divorce

When Czechoslovakia turned out its Communist leaders in 1989, the Czechs and Slovaks disagreed about the pace of economic reform. The Slovak economy, based on weapons manufacturing, was suffering from unemployment. The socialist leaders feared the effects of radical changes. So members of parliament negotiated a peaceful breakup in 1993, known as the Velvet Divorce. While the Czech Republic has prospered under its radical reforms, the Slovaks have languished under authoritarian rule.

Slovakia is in the heart of the Carpathian Mountains. The White Carpathians divide Slovakia from the Czech Republic. A spruce-fir forest carpets the mountains. Bratislava, the capital, lies on the Danube River, just downstream from Vienna. Farmers in this lowland area raise wheat, cattle, and hogs.

The Former Hungarian Empire

Hungary is part of a basin within a sweeping curve in the Carpathian Mountain system. The basin is near the geographic center of Europe.

Conquering Magyars The Hungarians are not like their neighbors. They are descendants of **Magyar** tribes from the East, who invaded Central Europe in A.D. 896, enslaving the Slavic and Germanic peoples. They speak a Uralic language associated with the Ural Mountains in Asia. The Magyars turned to Roman Catholicism under King Stephen, the patron saint of Hungary, whom the pope crowned in the year 1000.

The kingdom lasted over five centuries until it fell to the Turks and then to the Austrian Hapsburgs. But in 1867 it regained a measure of independence in the joint monarchy of Austria-Hungary. After the crushing defeat of World War I, however, the Allies took away 70 percent of Hungary's empire and gave it to its new neighbors. The welfare of the people in these neighboring lands concerns the government of Hungary.

Cities in the Hungarian Basin Eight countries include parts of the **Hungarian Basin,** the most valuable piece of property between Greece and the Baltic Sea. The waters of the Danube, Europe's second longest river, make the fertile Hungarian Basin one of Europe's major population centers. The capitals of eight nations lie on Eastern Europe's "great artery" or on one of its tributaries.

The capital of Hungary, **Budapest,** lies on a lovely stretch of the Danube River at the foot of the mountains. Buda was founded on one side of the river by Romans in the second century. It became the capital of Hungary in the fifteenth century. In 1872 Buda merged with the town of Pest across the Danube. Its two million people make it the third largest city in all of Eastern Europe.

Hills roll across the Hungarian Basin west of the Danube to the foothills of the Austrian Alps. Lake Balaton, the "Hungarian Sea," is the largest lake in the basin and a favorite vacation resort. Major products from the foothills include timber and uranium. Hungary's mines are the tenth largest producers of bauxite in the world.

Grasslands rise east of the Danube. They provide the best farmland in all of Eastern Europe, sufficient to meet Hungary's food demands. The chief crops are corn, potatoes, grapes, beets, and wheat. After Communism collapsed, Hungary privatized its farms.

SECTION REVIEW

1. What mountain system extends from the Alps across Eastern Europe?
2. What three nations were settled by Western Slavs?
3. Compare and contrast the two regions of the Czech Republic.
4. What important basin lies in the mountains of Eastern Europe?
5. How is Hungary different from all its neighbors?
   💡 What geographic features aided Hungary's rise to power and hindered Slovakia?

THE BALKAN POWDER KEG

The **Balkan Peninsula** is a mountainous region that sticks down from Europe into the eastern end of the Mediterranean. Eight countries of Eastern Europe, called the Balkans, lie on the peninsula. They share the peninsula with Greece and Turkey.

The Balkans' rugged ranges once isolated numerous tribes that migrated into the region, causing them to develop separate cultural identities.

The terrain encouraged disunity and conflict between these peoples. About one-half the size of Texas, the Balkans are a complex knot of two dozen separate nationalities in eight countries. The tendency of such diverse territories to break up into small, hostile nations is called **Balkanization.**

Civil War in the Dinaric Alps

The **Dinaric Alps** run down from the border of Italy along the western edge of four Balkan countries—Slovenia, Croatia, Bosnia-Herzegovina, and Yugoslavia. The Dinaric Alps divide the waters that flow into the Adriatic Sea from the waters that flow east into the Hungarian Basin. Few good ports are available on the rugged coast of the Adriatic.

Most of the people in these four Balkan countries belong to the language group of the Southern Slavs—including Slovenes, Croats, and Serbs. But they are divided by religion and culture. The Slovenes and Croats once belonged to the Austrian Empire, and they share its Western culture, Roman alphabet, and Catholic religion. But the Serbs belonged to the Byzantine Empire and share its Eastern culture, Cyrillic alphabet, and Orthodox religion. The uniting factor between these peoples was their common enemy in the south—the Ottoman Turks, who at one time conquered all their lands.

At the end of World War I, the Allies helped the Southern Slavs to form the Kingdom of the Serbs, Croats, and Slovenes. The kingdom had a rocky start, however, because the former Austrian territories wanted a weak federal government and a high degree of independence, while Serbs wanted a strong central government under the Serb king. Facing constant opposition, King Alexander I abolished the constitution in 1929 and created a dictatorship he called the Kingdom of Yugoslavia (meaning "land of Southern Slavs"). In response, Croats formed a radical nationalist group called the Ustashi, which apparently ordered Alexander's assassination in 1934.

After World War II, the difficult task of rebuilding the nation fell on the shoulders of a Croat named Josip Broz, better known as **Marshal**

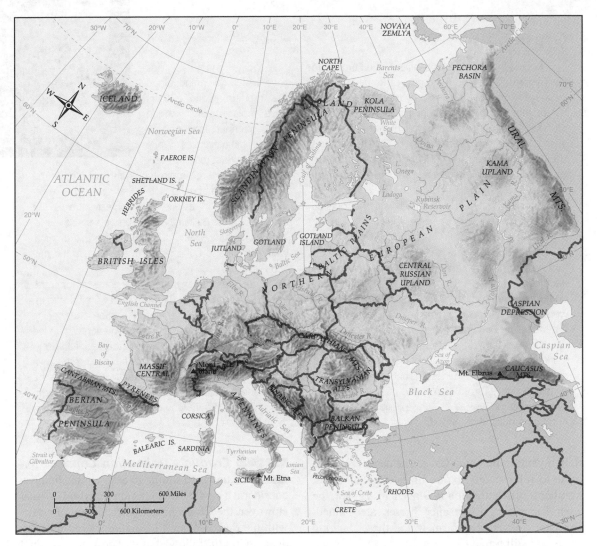

Tito. He was the leader of the local Communists who overthrew the Nazis. Tito ruled as a dictator and left the Soviet bloc in 1948 to set his own course. To weaken the Serbs, he divided the land into six republics. Together they led the country, choosing one of their members to be the official president of the whole country on a rotating basis. After the fall of Communism in the Soviet bloc, civil war erupted in Yugoslavia.

Slovenia, the First to Break Away

The Alps extend down from Austria and Italy into most of Slovenia. The highest peak in Slovenia is Triglav (9,393 ft.) in the Julian Alps at the northwest corner. From here the Sava River flows southeast across the country and later enters the Danube. South of the river rise the Dinaric Alps. Koper is the only commercial seaport on Slovenia's tiny Adriatic coastline.

The **Karst** (or Kras) region, famous for its sinkholes and limestone caves, lies in the west central section of the country. Postojna, located east of the Italian city of Trìeste, boasts the largest caverns in Europe. Toscanini once conducted in the Concert

381

Gypsies

One of the largest ethnic minorities in Europe are the **Gypsies.** Gypsies call themselves Roma and their language Romany. This swarthy people arrived in Europe at the time of the Ottoman invasion. They were mistakenly thought to be Egyptians, thus the term *gypsy.* Although the precise origin of Gypsies remains shrouded in mystery, they evidently came from northwest India a thousand years ago and have been moving ever since.

Gypsies limited their contact with the outside world and consequently preserved their own tribal language, laws, and customs. Their work reflected the life of wanderers. Some took seasonal jobs as circus performers, musicians, and acrobats. Others worked as peddlers, smiths, tinkers, woodcarvers, hangmen, undertakers, dogcatchers, or horse traders. Gypsy women, who had fewer alternatives, begged or took up fortune telling with crystal balls and palm reading.

Gypsies earned a bad reputation because of their work. The few who were tricksters or fortunetellers made it harder for the honest majority. Even today, the verb *gyp* derives from *Gypsy* and means "to cheat." Hitler targeted Gypsies as "undesireables," and four hundred thousand of them died in Nazi death camps.

A Gypsy girl in Warsaw, Poland

Today, many Gypsies have settled down and joined the modern world. Others have replaced their wagon with a camper and now follow traveling circuses. While Gypsies have spread to every continent, the three main tribes are in Europe. The Gitanos in Spain and the Sinti in France number fewer than one million apiece. The largest tribe is the Kalderash of the Balkans, which numbers over five million. More than two-thirds of them live in Romania, while Bosnia and Bulgaria each have almost one million Gypsies.

One great trophy of God's grace among the Gypsies was a teenager named Rodney Smith. Fifteen-year-old Rodney came under conviction after seeing the change in his father's life after a mission worker led him to Christ. Soon he too came to the Savior. Eager to tell others, Rodney started preaching in rescue missions, tent meetings, and from street corners. It was the beginning of seventy years of evangelistic ministry in which "Gipsy" Smith would travel the world and win thousands to Christ.

Hall, a vault in Postojna Cave. The name *karst* has come to refer to any exotic limestone landscape. Another tourist attraction in Slovenia is Lipica, the town for which Lipizzaner horses are named. Tourists can visit the farm where these dancing horses are still trained.

Ljubljana (LOO blee-AH nuh), the capital, has a one-house National Assembly that elects the prime minister. Slovenia was the first Yugoslavian republic to demand independence. After brief fighting in 1991, the European Union negotiated a *cease-fire* (temporary end of fighting until a permanent agreement is reached). Yugoslavia let Slovenia go because Slovenia has no common borders with Yugoslavia and has few minority Serbs. Because of its ancient ties with the western nation of Austria, Slovenia is by far the richest and most industrialized nation in the Balkans.

Croatia's Dalmatian Coast Croatian is so similar to Serbian that linguists consider it a single language called Serbo-Croatian. However, the Croats have a long history of rivalry with the Serbs. When Slovenia declared independence, Croatia followed suit. The war was much worse in Croatia. The large Serb minority in Croatia declared independence from Croatia and looked to the Yugoslav army for help. Over ten thousand people died in the fighting, until the European Union negotiated a cease-fire and sent in thirteen thousand soldiers to keep the peace.

Croatia is shaped like a pair of angel wings. The southern wing of Croatia includes most of **Dalmatia.** Dalmatia is familiar as the source of the dog breed in *101 Dalmatians*. The Dalmatian Coast has large beach resorts on the mainland as well as on hundreds of islands. The mild mediterranean

A dry mediterranean climate is evident on the Dalmatian Coast of Croatia.

climate and the scenic backdrop of the Dinaric Alps draw many tourists.

The eastern wing of Croatia lies on the Pannonian Plains, part of the Hungarian Basin. Low mountains roll across most of the plain. Zagreb, the capital and largest city, lies on the Sava River. The most fertile plain is a contested region in the east, called **Slavonia,** along the border with Yugoslavia. Croatia secretly built a well-disciplined army, which overran Serb lands in 1995, forcing hundreds of thousands of Serbs to flee their homes.

Rump Yugoslavia

The Serbs are the most dominant Slavic people in the Balkans. At the peak of their power in the fourteenth century, **Serbia** ruled Albania, Bulgaria, and even Greece. At the famed **Battle of Kosovo** in 1389, the Serbs made a valiant stand against the expanding Turkish Empire. But they lost, and the Turks ruled Serbia until it gained complete independence in 1878.

The Serbs bitterly opposed the imperialistic goals of the Austrian Empire, especially in Bosnia. A Serb nationalist's assassination of the Austrian Archduke Ferdinand sparked World War I in 1914. Russia mobilized her army to defend her weak "brother Slavs" in Serbia against the Austrians. Since the breakup of Tito's old Yugoslavia in 1991, two of the six regions, Serbia and Montenegro, have united to form a *Rump Yugoslavia.*

Much poorer than Slovenia and Croatia, Yugoslavia followed an authoritarian path under the leadership of Slobodan Milósevic. He won popular support by calling for a "Greater Serbia" that includes all the bordering lands where Serbs live. He played a game with the Western powers, promising to stay out of the surrounding civil wars while secretly supplying the Serb minorities.

Serbia's Northern Heartland

The agricultural heart of Serbia is the northern plains or Pannonian Plains. This fertile farmland is part of the Hungarian Basin. The region of Vojvodina covers most of the Pannonian Plains in Serbia. Although one-half of the people are ethnic Serbs, one-fifth are Hungarian and there are several other minorities of Romanians, Croats, Slovaks, Germans, Ruthenians, and Montenegrins. Serbia received this province after the breakup of the Hungarian Empire.

Belgrade, the capital since 1404, lies near the edge of the Pannonian Plains where the Sava River joins the Danube. The centrally located city has been conquered and destroyed more than thirty times. With 1.5 million people, it is the second largest city in the Balkans.

Mountains of Southern Serbia

The rest of Serbia is mountainous. The Dinaric Alps cross into the southwest. The Balkan Mountains rise in the southeast before crossing into Bulgaria. Between the Dinaric Alps and the Balkan Mountains lies a complex maze of minor mountain ranges. The central ranges contain the largest lead deposits in Europe.

Serbia has a large province in the south, called Kosovo, next to the border of Albania. Ninety percent of the people are Albanians. Like Vojvodina, this ethnic region enjoyed self-rule under Tito, but Serbia has removed its special rights. Kosovo declared independence in 1991, but the rest of the world did not recognize it (except for Albania).

Montenegro's Access to the Sea

Montenegro, meaning "Black Mountain," is the coastal region of Yugoslavia. Montenegro was founded when Serbs fled into the Dinaric Alps to escape the Turks after the Battle of Kosovo. Russia recognized its independence in 1799, after the local army helped them in their war against Turkey. It now has equal legal status with Serbia. Though small in population and size, Montenegro has Yugoslavia's only coastline.

Bosnia-Herzegovina, No Man's Land

During the five-hundred-year-long Muslim occupation of the Balkans, many Slavs adopted the Muslim faith. Most of them were located in Bosnia, a no man's land between Croatia and Serbia. Most of the people are either Croats or Serbs, but followers of Islam are sometimes listed as a separate ethnic group.

A bitter civil war erupted in 1991 after Bosnia declared independence, and the Serb minority refused to join the new nation. The bitter fighting between Serbs, Muslims, and Croats dragged on until 1995, when the president of the United States invited the leaders of Serbia, Croatia, and Bosnia's Muslims to sit down at a military base in Dayton, Ohio, and hammer out the **Dayton Peace Accords.** The United States agreed to send in twenty thousand troops to keep the peace while the nation set up a new government. The accords failed to work out the biggest sticking point—the powers of the local Serbs and Croats, each of whom kept their own armies and parliaments and desired to join a "Greater Croatia" and a "Greater Serbia."

Most of the Serbs live near the Sava River that flows through northern Bosnia. The river valley, part of the Pannonian Plains of the Hungarian Basin, provides the country's best farmland. Most of the Croats live west in the Dinaric Alps near the border with Croatia. Pockets of Muslims live elsewhere and in Bosnia's capital, Sarajevo, in the mountainous south.

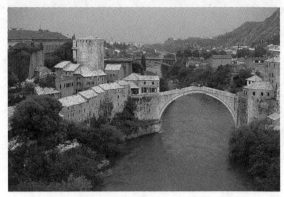

Mostar is divided between Croats and Muslims. This bridge over the Neretva River, which once linked the two sides, was destroyed during the civil war in Bosnia.

crossed by one of the three mountain ranges from the north. Difficulties with their southern neighbors have complicated their history.

Albania, the First Atheist Nation

Albania lies in the west facing the Adriatic Sea. The Dinaric Alps extend into northern Albania, where they are called the North Albanian Alps. The Pindus Mountains extend from southern Albania into Greece.

Unlike the city dwellers crammed into the capital, Tiranë, most Albanians live on small farms raising livestock, wheat, and grapes. Like Dalmatia, Albania's west coast lies on the Adriatic and has mild, dry summers typical of mediterranean nations. Albania's chief mineral is chromite, ranking fifth in production worldwide. Albanians are not Slavs but speak a unique Indo-European language. Albanians are divided between the Ghegs in the north and the Tosks in the south, who speak different dialects. The

The Shkodër is one of the few well-watered valleys in mountainous Albania.

SECTION REVIEW

1. Name the mountain range that runs along the Adriatic coast in the Balkans.
2. What advantages help to explain why Slovenia is the most prosperous country in Eastern Europe?
3. Compare and constrast the Croats and the Serbs.
4. What two provinces of Serbia have a large non-Slavic minority?
5. Why is Bosnia a no man's land?
   💡 Why is the United States concerned about peace in the Balkans?

The Southern Balkans

Three countries on the southern Balkan Peninsula border Greece and Turkey. Each is

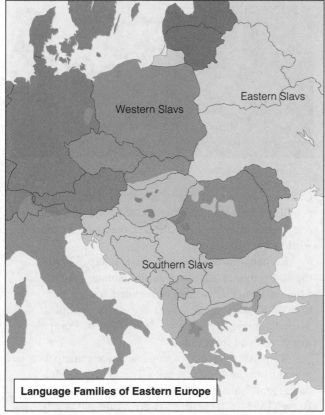

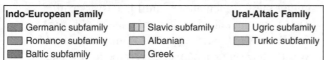

Language Families of Eastern Europe

Indo-European Family
- Germanic subfamily
- Romance subfamily
- Baltic subfamily
- Slavic subfamily
- Albanian
- Greek

Ural-Altaic Family
- Ugric subfamily
- Turkic subfamily

brought little change. The Communists were finally ousted in 1992, and Albania opened its doors to the world. Within the next three years, Albania had more foreign missionaries per capita than any other place in the world. But Albania has a long way to go before it catches up with the developed nations of Europe.

The fool hath said in his heart, There is no God. They are corrupt, they have done abominable works, there is none that doeth good. (Ps. 14:1)

Macedonia, Nation in Limbo The historic region of Macedonia was the home of Alexander the Great. After the decline of the Ottoman Empire, the Balkan countries fought for control of this region. In the **Balkan Wars** of 1912 and 1913, Greece, Serbia, and Bulgaria joined together to defeat the Turks, but then they fought among themselves.

The northern part went to Yugoslavia and became one of the six republics under Tito. Macedonia declared independence after the breakup of Yugoslavia, but Greece refused to let the European Union formally recognize its independence. Greece feared a movement to reunite the old lands of "Greater Macedonia." From 1946 to 1949 Macedonian guerrillas fought a bloody war against Greece. When the UN first admitted the nation, it did not get immediate approval for its new name. The Greeks call it Skopje, after its capital.

Landlocked Macedonia is one of the poorest countries in Europe. Resources include cotton, wheat, and fruit, which grow in the valley of the Vardar River. Limited mining and grazing is possible in the mountains. The official language is Macedonian, a Southern Slavic language with its own alphabet. Most people attend Orthodox churches.

Bulgars on the Black Sea Cyril and Methodius were brothers from Thessaloniki, Greece. In the mid-ninth century they went as missionaries to Bulgaria and then to Moravia. They wanted to translate the Bible into the Slavic languages, but the pagan tribes had no written language. The brothers modified the Greek alphabet to create an alphabet suitable for Slavic

long influence of the Ottoman Empire resulted in a population that is 70 percent Muslim, the only Muslim majority in any European nation.

Albania won independence from the Turks in 1912, but Mussolini's Italian armies invaded during World War II. The Communist partisans who overthrew the Fascists introduced a severe form of Communism in Albania. Their leader, Enver Hoxha, broke away from the Soviet Union in 1960 because he thought it was becoming too soft! He turned to Mao Zedong of Communist China for aid, but this alliance also broke down when Mao died. Hoxha then isolated his country from the rest of the world and prohibited all religions. He boasted of having the first truly atheistic country in the world.

Hoxha's harsh regime created food shortages and widespread discontent. His death in 1985

languages, called **Cyrillic.** Today, 90 percent of Bulgarians are Eastern Orthodox.

The Bulgars probably rode in with the Huns, but unlike Attila and his Asian hordes, the Bulgars settled down on the western shore of the Black Sea. The Bulgars mixed with the Slavs, who had arrived from Poland a little earlier. Bulgars account for 85 percent of the people, and Turks account for another 10 percent.

Bulgaria was an independent kingdom from 681 to 1330, except for 150 years under Byzantine kings. The kingdom was a powerful force in the Balkans until it fell to the Serbs and later to the Ottoman Turks. After four attempts at independence, they finally won freedom in the late nineteenth century with Russian help.

Danube Valley   Northern Bulgaria is a fertile valley along the Danube River. The river forms most of Bulgaria's northern border, but it winds up into Romania just before it enters the Black Sea. Ruse is Bulgaria's only port on the Danube. Its main port, Varna, lies on the Black Sea. Farm products from the valley include barley, millet, swine, sheep, corn, wheat, and grapes.

Mountains of Southern Bulgaria   Mountain ranges rise south of the plain. The **Balkan Mountains** cut across the country to the Black Sea. Sofia, the capital, lies on a mountain tributary that flows into the Danube River.

South of the Balkan Mountains, the **Rhodope Mountains** cut another swath across the country. The Rhodope Mountains reach 9,596 feet at Mount Musala, the highest peak in Eastern Europe. Several cities lie in the river valley between the Balkan and Rhodope ranges.

Romania, Last Outpost of the Romans

Romania is a large country caught in the crossroads of Eastern Europe. It shares mountain features with the Carpathian Divide, a long border on the Danube River, and cities near the Black Sea. Although it does not share any of the Dinaric Alps or a border with Greece, Romania is still an outpost on the Balkan Peninsula. Unlike the

A Christian family gathers around their Bible in Romania.

Catholic nations of the Carpathian Divide, its people are Eastern Orthodox. In fact, it has the second largest number of Orthodox members in the world (after Russia).

Romania means "land of the Romans." It was the last province captured by the Roman Empire. Modern Romanians have descended from a mixture of Roman soldiers and the native peoples. Their language is the only one in Eastern Europe that developed from Latin.

Romania consisted of three separate principalities during the Middle Ages—Transylvania, Moldavia, and Walachia. Romania's hero Michael the Brave (1593-1601) resisted Turkish rule and briefly united these principalities, until his assassination. They were not united again until after World War I.

When the Soviets captured Romania in World War II, they set up a puppet government. A wicked tyrant named **Nicolae Ceausescu** (NIH-KOH-lay chou-CHES-kew) rose to power in 1967. In the name of Communism, he lived in high luxury while his people suffered from grinding poverty.

The city of Arad lies in a narrow, fertile plain of western Romania, called Banat, on the edge of the Hungarian Basin. Arad was a center of revolt against the Communist government of Nicolae Ceausescu.

His foolish building programs, intended to increase his fame, left Romania with a huge debt and dangerous food shortages. As other Communist governments began to topple in 1989, Ceausescu's secret police and army tried to stamp out all protest. Finally, the army refused to shoot any more Romanians. Ceausescu was captured, hastily tried, and executed on Christmas Day. Modern Romania is struggling to overcome the bitter legacy of so many years under Communist tyranny.

Transylvania in the North Nearly half of Romania is a section of the Carpathian Mountain system called **Transylvania.** The range extends from Slovakia into northern Romania and then curves west across the center of the country, where it is known as the **Transylvanian Alps.**

The heart of Transylvania is a hilly plateau in the west encircled by the Carpathian ranges.

Hungary ruled the principality of Transylvania for much of its history. Romania received Transylvania after World War I. Hungarians are Romania's largest minority. The forested hills and gloomy castles of this region have long intrigued Western Europeans, who view Transylvania as a place of mystery and danger.

Walachia, the Populous Plain in the South The Danube flows east from the Hungarian Basin through a break in the Carpathian Mountains called the **Iron Gate.** Steep rock walls, only 150 feet apart, guard both sides of this gorge. The Danube then flows east through a broad fertile plain, shared by Romania and Bulgaria.

The populous plain below the Iron Gate is called **Walachia.** Farms produce flax, corn, wheat, and livestock. Romania's capital, **Bucharest,** is located on a tributary of the Danube. It is the second largest city in Eastern Europe.

Count Dracula

According to legend, vampires are spirits of the dead which leave their coffins at night and suck the blood of sleeping victims, who in turn become vampires. A garlic necklace or the sign of the cross supposedly wards off vampires, but killing one requires driving a stake through its heart. Today, tourists from all over the world come to Transylvania to see the castle of the most famous vampire of all, Count Dracula.

But the story is all wrong. Dracula was not a count, and he did not live in Transylvania. Vlad Tepes, a prince of Walachia in the fifteenth century, became a hero among the local Romanians because he defied the Turks. As a reward for his bravery, Tepes was knighted into the order of Dracul. When the Turks invaded in 1462, he attacked them at night and, according to the popular accounts, impaled some twenty thousand captive Turks in a massive field of stakes.

The modern story comes from the pen of English author Bram Stoker, who never even visited Transylvania. Stoker read the story of Vlad the Impaler in a book and took a little poetic license. Even Vlad's supporters would admit that he was a cruel ruler, impaling criminals to instill fear among his own people. But Stoker's famous novel *Dracula,* published in 1897, changed Vlad's reputation forever.

Movies about vampires have created a tourism boom for Romania. But Dracula's true castle lies in ruins at Aref, Walachia. So the government built a castle farther north at Borgo Pass, where Stoker described it, in the Carpathian Mountains of Transylvania.

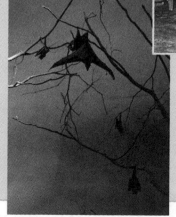

(above) *Bela Lugosi plays* Dracula *in the 1931 film that made him famous.* (left) *Are these bats hanging in wait for the full moon?*

In the east, the slow-moving Danube loops northward along the coast and becomes a broad swamp land before entering the Black Sea. During the dictatorship of Ceausescu, workers were forced to build a huge canal that bypassed the swampy loop and connected the Danube directly with the seaport of Constanta. Over one hundred thousand men died constructing the Canal of Death (*Canalul Morti*).

Moldavia in the East Walachia was the historic center of the Romanian people. But many rural people also lived on the Moldavian Plateau. If you look at the relief map on page 372, you will see the Moldavian Plateau and its many valleys. The plateau continues east into the country of Moldova, which Romania owned until the Soviets snatched it away in World War II.

◉ SECTION REVIEW

1. Name the three main mountain ranges of the southern Balkans. What two main ranges are farther north, in Romania?
2. What two countries in the Balkans are not related to the Slavic peoples?
3. What is the poorest Eastern European country? Why?
4. What alphabet was developed for the Slavic languages? Who developed it?
5. What are the three main regions of Romania?

💡 Why are two landlocked nations—the Czech Republic and Hungary—so much richer than Romania, which has a Black Sea port?

FORMER SOVIET REPUBLICS ON THE EASTERN PLAINS

A huge plain extends east from the Carpathian Mountains and connects with the Northern European Plain. Together, these plains form the **Great European Plain,** which continues over one thousand miles east into Russia. The Great European Plain provides much of the world's swine, potatoes, and rye.

Three countries lie on the eastern plains: Belarus, Ukraine, and Moldova. Like the three Baltic States, these young countries were once among the fifteen republics, or soviets, in the Soviet Union. Most of the people who settled the eastern plains are Eastern Slavs, including Belarusians, Ukrainians, and Russians.

After the breakup of the Soviet Union, the former republics created the **Commonwealth of Independent States (CIS),** begun on December 21, 1991. All of the republics eventually joined, except the Baltic States. The original emphasis of the agreement was an alliance of *independent* states. But Russian leaders became worried because the leaders of the new states started resisting Russia's wishes. Many of them showed little interest in continuing to trade with Russia, and they wanted Russia's troops to leave. Russia was most angered by the failure of some countries to pass human rights provisions to protect Russian minorities living there.

Russia has been tightening its control over the CIS republics. The first elected president of Russia, Boris Yeltsin, even asked the United Nations "to grant Russia special powers as a guarantor of peace and stability in the former countries of the USSR." Russia refers to these nations as the **"near abroad."** It would like to transform the weak CIS into a common market similar to the European Union.

Belarus and Ukraine are the least prepared to resist Russia's demands. They still rely on trade with their next-door neighbor. Russia supplies almost all the oil and gas needed by their industries, and Russia buys most of their agricultural products. Political debates about their future have slowed their efforts to improve their economy and to establish new governments.

Belarus, Capital of the CIS

Belarus, or "White Russia," has old ties with Russia. **Minsk,** the capital and the largest city, is the headquarters of the CIS.

Although they are closely related to Russians, Belarusians have their own distinctive culture and language. For many centuries they belonged to the Lithuanian Empire and its successor, the Polish-Lithuanian Empire. During the partition of Poland

Rye

The countries of the Great European Plain produce over 90 percent of the world's rye. All five top rye producers lie on the plain: Germany, Poland, Belarus, Ukraine, and Russia. **Rye,** a grain similar to wheat, grows well in cool climates. Two thousand years ago, Europeans learned how to grind rye into flour for bread. Rye bread is dark brown and much heavier than the wheat bread that is popular in the West. Eastern Europeans still eat a great deal of rye bread, while most rye grown in America is used to feed livestock.

in the eighteenth century, Belarus fell into Russian hands. The Russian czars and later the Soviets tried to replace Belorussian with the Russian language. Today, most people in the cities speak Russian.

Most farms and cities are in the center of the country on the Northern European Plain. Only China and Russia produce more flax than the plains of Belarus. The far north has large forests, made of mixed deciduous and coniferous trees. The Belovezha Forest, a large natural preserve on the western border, is noted for the only surviving herd of wisent, or European bison.

Few people live south in the **Pinsk Marshes.** This is the largest marshland in Europe, extending about three hundred miles on the drainage basin of the Pripyat (or Pripet) River, a tributary of the Dnieper River. The swamps and marshes yield potash for fertilizers; Belarus is second only to Canada in potash production. Landlocked Belarus has few other valuable resources and little hope of becoming a strong, independent nation.

Ukraine, Breadbasket of Eastern Europe

After Russia, Ukraine is the most important industrial and agricultural center in the CIS. Indeed, it is the largest nation on the continent of Europe. Western Europeans are concerned about Ukraine's future role in East European politics. Ukraine is almost twice the size and population of Poland, the next largest nation in the region.

Except for two small strips of mountains, the entire country lies in the eastern plain. Low plateaus cross the center but give way to lowlands in the north and south.

Capital in the Northern Lowlands   Ukraine's northern lowlands include swamps and marshes along the border with Belarus. These waters flow into the **Dnieper River,** the third longest river in Europe, which continues south through the heart of Ukraine.

Kiev, the most populous city in all of Eastern Europe, lies at the junction between the Dnieper and its main tributary, the Pripyat River. It is the cultural center and capital of the Ukraine. Kiev arose in the ninth century on an important link in the trade route between the Baltic Sea and the Black Sea. The Vikings conquered the local Slavs and organized the first Russian state, **Kievan Rus,** with their capital at Kiev. The Mongols later conquered Kiev, and the Slavs farther east built a new Russian state, called Muscovy, around Moscow. A series of Lithuanians, Poles, and then Muscovites captured Kiev.

Farms and Factories of the Central Uplands
The Central Uplands, which cut across central Ukraine, are the "Breadbasket of Europe." With adequate rainfall and rich soils, these vast uplands produce many agricultural products, including cattle, corn, and sunflowers. Ukraine ranks in the world's top ten in the production of four grains: barley, rye, wheat, and oats.

The Dnieper River flows through Kiev, Ukraine.

Chernobyl: Winds of Death

The rusted jungle gym sits quietly in a tangle of weeds. Beyond is the schoolhouse, a shell of concrete and broken glass. The abandoned apartment buildings and empty streets are silent. Welcome to Pripyat, Ukraine, a once thriving city of forty-five thousand. Two miles away is V. I. Lenin Atomic Electric Generating Station in **Chernobyl.**

The disaster struck on a Saturday morning, April 26, 1986. Technicians, who were testing Reactor Number 4's efficiency at low power, had turned off the automatic safety precautions. It took only four seconds for the unstable uranium to explode, blowing off the top of the reactor and spewing tons of radiation into the atmosphere. The fallout blanketed fifty thousand square miles in Ukraine, Russia, and Belarus (an area the size of New York State). Winds carried radiation all over Europe, affecting everything from vegetables in France to reindeer in Lapland. Airborne radiation even set off sensors at the Three-Mile Island nuclear station in Pennsylvania.

Back in Pripyat, folks knew something was very wrong—burning skin, irritated throats, dead phone lines. Soviet officials foolishly imagined they could keep a lid on news of the catastrophe. Consequently, evacuation efforts were terribly slow. Thousands waited for days before getting out, while families of officials somehow made it out. As a result, there was another kind of fallout from Chernobyl. Chernobyl awakened nationalism among the once-loyal Slavs in Ukraine, who condemned the coverup and gross incompetence of their Communist masters. They eventually joined the other republics in rejecting the Soviet government.

Thirty-one people died the day of the meltdown, mostly firefighters. But at least five thousand more victims died in the years that followed, and another thirty thousand were disabled due to radiation poisoning. Most of these were troops and workers responsible for evacuation and cleanup.

Today Reactor Number 4 is entombed in concrete; and a forty-mile circle of barbed wire, called the Zone of Estrangement, attempts to contain the catastrophe. Yet with contaminated water, soil, and forests, the thousands of people who live in and around this restricted zone face a bleak future. Among the greatest tragedies of Chernobyl are children suffering from thyroid cancer, the result of exposure to radioactive iodine.

East of the Dnieper River lies the valuable **Donets Basin,** or Donbas. On a tributary of the Donets River is Kharkov, Ukraine's second largest city. Two other cities—Dnepropetrovsk and Donetsk—have over one million people each. Donetsk is a major coal-mining center, and iron ore comes from the adjoining Krivoi Rog. Ukraine leads Europe in production of pig iron, steel, and synthetic nitrogen. It also ranks eighth in the world as a producer of coal, fifth in iron ore, and first in manganese. The Communists, who built many of the region's industries, created a pollution disaster that will take years for Ukraine to clean up.

Southern Coasts Almost all of Ukraine's southern coast is a low plain. Because of the arid climate, farms must divert water from the Dnieper River. Odessa, Ukraine's largest port, lies on the coast of the Black Sea.

The most valuable southern region is the Crimean Peninsula, which juts out into the Black Sea. **Crimea** is barely attached to Europe by a narrow 2.5-mile-wide isthmus. A long series of conquerors have held the peninsula. Russia took Crimea from the Turks in the late eighteenth century and converted it into the "jewel in the crown" of the Russian Empire.

What makes Crimea unique is the Crimean Mountains, which rise from the sea along the southern tip. The mountains block the cold northern air and permit a pleasant mediterranean climate on the southern shore. Wealthy Russians flock to this coast, known as the "Russian Riviera." The czars even had a palace at Yalta, the best seaside resort in

Winston Churchill and Franklin D. Roosevelt met with Joseph Stalin at Yalta in 1945. "The ghost of Yalta" still lingers in Eastern Europe, which felt betrayed by the decision to let Stalin take the East.

Crimea. Russia's main naval base in the Black Sea is Sevastopol, just west of Yalta.

The Crimea has been a sore spot between Russia and Ukraine. As a gesture of friendship, the Soviet Union gave Crimea to the Ukrainian soviet in 1954, and it passed to the independent country in 1991. But most of the natives are Russians, who

Mountains rise from the Black Sea along the south coast of the Crimean Peninsula.

would like independence. Russia and Ukraine have had difficulty reaching an agreement on the future of the strategic port at Sevastapol and of the Black Sea Fleet anchored there.

Divided Moldova

Moldova is a hilly, land-locked country between Romania and Ukraine. It is the most densely populated country in Eastern Europe. Moldova is the eastern part of Romania's historic principality of Moldavia. Two-thirds of the people speak Romanian. The Soviets took control of the region during World War II, but it gained independence along with the other Soviet republics. A minority wants to rejoin Romania.

A third of the population consists of Slavs, both Ukrainians and Russians, who live on a sliver of land east of the Dniester River. This valuable **Trans-Dniester** region, which has 40 percent of the nation's industry, once belonged to Ukraine. In 1990 the Slavs declared themselves a semi-independent republic. Fighting erupted in 1992, and Russia sent its army to restore peace. Russia has allowed Moldova to keep the region, in return for an agreement to let Russia keep a military base there.

SECTION REVIEW

1. What do Belarus and Ukraine have in common geographically? historically? ethnically?
2. What is the main river of Ukraine?
3. Why is central Ukraine so valuable to the country?
4. What two mountain ranges are in Ukraine?
5. To what country does Moldova have the closest cultural ties?

💡 What disputed region lies in Ukraine? Why has a final solution been so difficult to reach?

REVIEW 16

Can You Define These Terms?

shatter belt	puppet ruler	karst	"near abroad"
Iron Curtain	mass privatization	Cyrillic	rye
Soviet bloc	Balkanization		

Can You Locate These Natural Features?

Vistula River	Balkan Peninsula	Transylvanian Alps	Dnieper River
Oder River	Dinaric Alps	Iron Gate	Donets Basin
Carpathian Mountains	Balkan Mountains	Great European Plain	Crimea
Hungarian Basin	Rhodope Mountains	Pinsk Marshes	

Can You Explain the Significance of These People, Places, and Events?

Central Eurasia	Bohemia	Slavonia	Walachia
Slavs	Prague	Serbia	Bucharest
Warsaw	John Huss	Battle of Kosovo	CIS
Lech Walesa	Moravia	Belgrade	Minsk
Krakow	Magyars	Dayton Peace Accords	Kiev
Auschwitz	Budapest	Balkan Wars	Kievan Rus
Silesia	Marshal Tito	Cyril and Methodius	Chernobyl
Baltic States	Gypsies	Nicolae Ceausescu	Trans-Dniester
Teutonic Knights	Dalmatia	Transylvania	

How Much Do You Remember?

1. What two Christian religions are most common in Eastern Europe? Which of the two is associated with Western Europe?
2. List all the countries whose ethnic majority belongs under each language group.
   a. Western Slavic
   b. Southern Slavic
   c. Eastern Slavic
   d. Baltic
   e. Finnic
   f. Albanian
   g. Latin (or Romance)
3. Write what each pair of words has in common.
   a. Wenceslas, King Stephen
   b. Marshal Tito, Nicolae Ceausescu
   c. Bohemia, Moravia
   d. Serbia, Montenegro
   e. Belgrade, Budapest

4. Which Eastern European countries fit each description?
   a. coast on the Baltic Sea
   b. coast on the Adriatic Sea
   c. coast on the Black Sea
   d. landlocked

What Do You Think?

1. Contrast the fall of Communism in Czechoslovakia and Romania. Can you explain why events turned out so differently?
2. Where do you think the next big war will take place in Eastern Europe? Will the United States be involved?
3. Was it wise for the United States to extend NATO's alliance to include Poland, the Czech Republic, and Hungary?

CHAPTER

RUSSIA

Russia is the only country in the world that spans two continents—Europe and Asia. Five thousand miles separate its Atlantic shores from the Pacific Ocean, and about two thousand miles separate its northern shores on the Arctic Ocean from the Chinese border. With over one-tenth of the world's land area, Russia is easily the largest country on earth.

Russia's huge size and northern location help to explain many features of Russian culture and history. Like the shatter belt in Eastern Europe, it is "lost" in a vast expanse of lowlands without clear natural borders, except the frigid ocean in the north. Russia's search for safe borders and a united people has been pursued for over one thousand years of history. Like America's "manifest destiny" to stretch from ocean to ocean, Russia believed its destiny was to control port cities stretching from the west to the east and from the north to the south.

Although the United States and Russia have much in common, their histories are worlds apart. America was founded by free men who elected

their leaders and plowed their own farms. In contrast, Russia was oppressed by powerful rulers and a few wealthy landholders, while the Russian peasants lived in poverty. Revolts were common. The rulers kept the people under control with the help of secret police, torture, and periodic **pogroms** (massacres of local minorities, especially Jews).

Revolutionaries cast off Russia's cruel rulers in 1917, only to replace them with much worse tyrants—Communists. These atheists employed guns, lies, terror, and any other means necessary to spread their radical ideas to all corners of the globe. Throughout the Cold War, Russia was America's greatest rival and biggest threat. The end of the Soviet Union in 1991 brought new hope of reform.

But the first elected president, Boris Yeltsin, fired tanks at his own legislature and bombed one of his own rebellious territories. At the same time, Russia began bullying its neighbors to make them accept Russian terms for trade and Russian troops within their borders. Such authoritarian rule is a regular feature of Russian history and does not give

ARCTIC OCEAN

FRANZ JOSEF
LAND

UNITED
KINGDOM

North
Sea

NORWAY

Barents
Sea

NOVAYA ZEMLYA

DENMARK

SWEDEN

Gulf of
Ob

Kara
Sea

Murmansk

GERMANY

Baltic Sea

FINLAND

White
Sea

Archangel

WESTERN
SIBERIAN
LOWLAND

CZECH
REPUBLIC

LITHUANIA

Kaliningrad

ESTONIA

St. Petersburg

RUSSIA

LATVIA

POLAND

NORTHERN

Lake
Ladoga

Lake
Onega

Ob R.

Yenisey R.

SLOVAKIA

Minsk

EUROPEAN PLAIN

BELARUS

Pinsk
Marshes

UKRAINE

20°E

Moscow

Nizhniy Novgorod

MOLDOVA

Chernobyl

Kiev

RUSSIA

Ob R.

Yekaterinburg

KUZNETSK
BASIN

Chişinău

Kharkov

MOUNTAINS

DONETS
BASIN
(DONBAS)

Crimea

Volga R.

Samara

Trans-Siberian Railroad

40°N

Black
Sea

Sea of
Azov

Rostov

Volgograd

Ural R.

URAL

Don R.

Dnieper R.

Novosibirsk

CASPIAN
DEPRESSION

Astrakhan

S T E P P E S

Irtysh R.

CAUCASUS MTS.

Mt.
Elbrus

Aqmola

GEORGIA

TURKEY

KAZAKHSTAN

ALTAY MTS.

ARMENIA

Tbilisi

Yerevan

Caspian Sea

Aral
Sea

Syr Darya

Lake
Balkash

Lake
Zaysan

SYRIA

Baku

40°E

AZERBAIJAN

TURKMENISTAN

UZBEKISTAN

TIEN SHAN

IRAQ

KOPET
MTS.

Amu Darya

Tashkent

Bishkek

KYRGYZSTAN

Ashkhabad

Dushanbe

SAUDI
ARABIA

KUWAIT

IRAN

TAJIKISTAN

PAMIRS

60°E

80°E

ARCTIC OCEAN

WRANGEL ISLAND

Bering Strait

Chukchi Sea

Bering Sea

East Siberian Sea

NEW SIBERIAN ISLANDS

NORTH LAND

Laptev Sea

TAYMYR PENINSULA

VERKHOYANSKI MTS.

Lena R.

KOLYMA MTS.

Kolyma R.

Indigirka R.

Anadyr R.

CHERSKOGO MTS.

KAMCHATKA PENINSULA

Petropavlovsk

S I B E R I A

Yakutsk

Sea of Okhotsk

160°E

CENTRAL SIBERIAN

Lower Tunguska R.

PLATEAU

R U S S I A

SAKHALIN ISLAND

KURIL ISLANDS

Angara R.

Lena R.

STANOVOY RANGE

Amur R.

Trans-Siberian Railroad

YABLONOVY MTS.

Lake Baikal

Shilka R.

Ussuri R.

40°N

SAYAN MTS.

Irkutsk

Yenisey R.

Vladivostok

MONGOLIA

N
W   E
S

NORTH KOREA

Sea of Japan

JAPAN

140°E

SOUTH KOREA

C H I N A

0   300   600 Miles
0   300   600 Kilometers

100°E

120°E

Russia

Capital	Moscow
Area (sq. mi.)	6,592,800
Population	147,987,101
Natural Increase	−0.5%
Life Expectancy	64
Literacy Rate	99%
Per Capita GDP	$5,300
Population Density	22

the nation much hope of becoming a prosperous democracy. The people would be wise to stop seeking temporal peace and comfort, and turn instead to Christ. God's servants have a completely different perspective on the hardships of this world.

For our light affliction, which is but for a moment, worketh for us a far more exceeding and eternal weight of glory; while we look not at the things which are seen, but at the things which are not seen: for the things which are seen are temporal; but the things which are not seen are eternal. (II Cor. 4:17-18)

EUROPEAN RUSSIA

Russia looks both east and west. Its culture has borrowed elements from both—the authoritarianism of Asia and the longing for individual rights in Europe. The Great European Plain, which has played such a major role in European history, extends into Russia and has played a decisive role there as well. The plain covers only one-fifth of Russia, but over four-fifths of the population live on this plain.

Like the countries of Eastern Europe, Russia has suffered under the heel of many Asian tribes, including Scythians, Huns, and Slavs. The modern Russians are descendants of the Slavs and speak a Slavic language. Over one hundred different nationalities have settled in Russia over the centuries, but 83 percent of the people are ethnic Russians.

The Slavs were once pagans, like other tribes in the East. But in 988 their ruler, Vladimir I, adopted Eastern Orthodoxy as the official state religion. The church experienced dark days after the

"Golden Horde" of fierce Mongolian Tatars destroyed Russia's capital at Kiev in 1237. During the foreign occupation, the people clung to the Orthodox Church as the center of national identity. Two centuries later, Moscow overthrew its conqueror and slowly recaptured the surrounding lands. After the Slavic countries of Eastern Europe fell to the Muslims, Russia considered itself the last heir to historic Christianity. Russians even began referring to their capital as the "Third Rome."

Moscow's Turbulent Past

With about nine million people, **Moscow** is the largest city in all of Europe. Its architecture, landmarks, galleries, and theaters display the great achievements of Russian culture.

Moscow is colder than most capitals of Europe. Its climate is determined by its location in the interior of the continent, far from the moderating influence of the oceans. The humid continental climate is similar to that of Quebec. During the summers, temperatures average in the sixties. Winters are harsh and snowy, with an average January temperature of less than 20°F. In most summers, adequate rainfall reaches this far inland, but rains are unpredictable and crops often fail. Deciduous forests lie south of Moscow, with aspen, oak, and linden; but much of this has been cleared for agriculture, settlement, and industry. Evergreen trees grow in increasing numbers as you travel north of Moscow.

Growth of the Russian Empire, 1462-1917

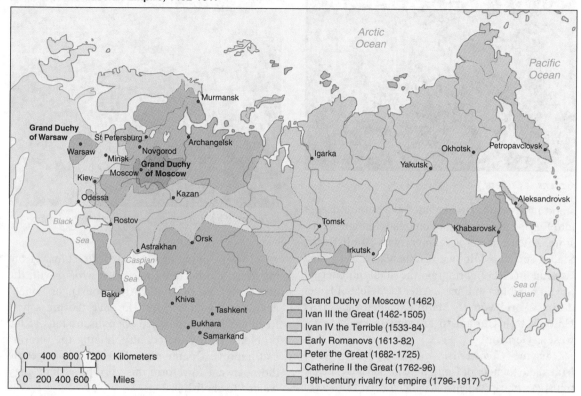

Legend:
- Grand Duchy of Moscow (1462)
- Ivan III the Great (1462-1505)
- Ivan IV the Terrible (1533-84)
- Early Romanovs (1613-82)
- Peter the Great (1682-1725)
- Catherine II the Great (1762-96)
- 19th-century rivalry for empire (1796-1917)

Rise of the Grand Duchy of Moscow Moscow was only a small town in the twelfth century, but it rose to prominence under a series of wise princes, or *boyars,* who stayed on friendly terms with the Tatars. Ivan the Great (Ivan III), who became head of the Grand Duchy of Moscow in 1462, decided to break from the Tatars by refusing to pay tribute money.

Ivan's grandson, **Ivan the Terrible,** formally crowned himself **czar** in 1547. The word *czar* comes from the old Latin word *caesar* and was used by rulers of the eastern Roman Empire, or the Byzantine Empire, which had never fallen to barbarians from western Europe. The Byzantine Empire lasted until it was sacked by the Muslims in 1453. Ivan considered himself the new heir to the eastern Roman Empire and the defender of the Orthodox faith. He conquered Tatar lands around Moscow and far to the east and south, but resistance from the Poles checked his westward expansion.

A total of twenty-four czars ruled Russia throughout its long and checkered history prior to Soviet rule. The czars never improved conditions for the people. Instead, the peasants became **serfs,** virtual slaves eking out a living on farms owned by a few wealthy landholders. During World War I under the last czar, Nicholas II, Russia experienced humiliating defeats. In the resulting confusion, Vladimir Ilich Lenin led the Bolshevik Revolution in 1917 and executed the last czar the following year.

Soviet Rule In 1922, Lenin created the **Union of Soviet Socialist Republics (USSR).** This union gave limited power to several "republics." Communists claimed Russia was no longer an empire but a land of equals. In reality, the rulers were mostly Russians. Joseph Stalin, Lenin's brutal successor, killed or shipped to Siberia anyone who

Kitayenko's Orchestra in Moscow

Even after the fall of Communism, people waited in long lines to see Lenin's tomb in Red Square, Moscow.

stood in his path. He extended the empire deeper into Europe than any czar could have dreamed possible. After a secret agreement with Adolf Hitler, Stalin seized Moldova, Lithuania, Latvia, and Estonia in 1939, bringing the total number of Soviet republics to fifteen. After the defeat of Hitler during World War II, Stalin extended the Soviet Union's Iron Curtain to encompass lands as far west as Germany.

In the *Communist Manifesto* (1848) **Karl Marx,** the founder of Communism, had attacked the injustices of capitalism and called on the workers of the world to revolt. The workers, or proletariat, would then usher in a perfect society—all people would share their wealth in peace, brotherhood, and equality. Lenin came to power promising "peace, land, and bread." But his rigid system of centralized socialism was never able to deliver. Soviet leaders forced their people to produce weapons instead of houses, food, and other essentials.

Soviet Collapse   By the 1980s the West had left the Soviets far behind in consumer goods and technology. The hypocrisy of the Soviet system could no longer be covered up. **Dissidents** (those who openly disagreed with the government) gained more and more hearers among the Soviet people. A young Communist leader named Mikhail Gorbachev (GAWR buh CHAWF) finally agreed to *perestroika* (PEHR ih STROY kuh), or "restructuring," of the stagnant Communist economy, shifting to more free-market policies and some private ownership of property.

To win public support and to attract loans from the West, Gorbachev linked *perestroika* with the concept of *glasnost* (GLAHS nohst), or "openness," in Soviet society. He gave the press new freedoms and encouraged open discussions of the problems facing the country, hoping to "reform" and improve Communism. But the Soviet people did not want to reform this corrupt system; they wanted to abolish it.

The whole system collapsed in 1991, as the leaders of the various republics declared independence. Boris Yeltsin, the president of the largest republic—Russia—joined the others. By December 25, Gorbachev was a ruler without a country,

St. Basil's Cathedral was built in the 1550s to commemorate Ivan IV's victory over the Mongols. Russians have rallied to the Orthodox Church for over one thousand years.

Kremlin

The **Kremlin,** a massive fortress at the heart of Moscow, has served as the center of Russian government since it was built in 1475. Red brick walls sixty feet high enclose sixty-five acres of buildings. Surrounded by a moat, the Muscovite Kremlin became the greatest citadel in Europe.

After conquering Novgorod, the main competitor in Moscow's early rise to power, Ivan the Great built the Kremlin to showcase his new wealth and influence. The highest building in the Kremlin, the onion-domed Bell Tower of Ivan the Great, towers 267 feet above the many royal palaces. Ivan recruited Italian architects from the West, who built the original Palace of the Czars. The Terem Palace and the Palace of the Patriarchs were both built in the seventeenth century, and the Great Kremlin Palace was completed in 1849.

Besides palaces, the architects also built cathedrals. Ivan the Great built the Cathedral of the Assumption, where the czars were crowned. The carved walnut throne of Ivan the Terrible, made in 1551, can still be viewed in the cathedral. Ivan the Great built the Cathedral of the Annunciation, whose domes are made of gold, and the Cathedral of St. Michael the Archangel, where some of the czars are buried. All three cathedrals display valuable frescoes and icons. These Russian Orthodox Cathedrals formed the heart of the Kremlin, the place of royal weddings, coronations, and burials.

Outside the Kremlin is a large open area called Red Square. Once a marketplace, it now hosts parades and public entertainment. Lenin's tomb stands outside the Kremlin wall in Red Square. Also on the square is St. Basil's Cathedral, now a museum, with its eight colorful, onion-shaped domes. Ivan the Terrible built this Russian Orthodox church and then blinded the architect so that he could never design a more beautiful building. Ivan was infamous for his brutality, killing his own son in a fit of rage.

Arsenal Tower

Nikolskaya Tower

Troitskaya Tower

Arsenal Building

Council of Ministers Building

Lenin Mausoleum

Spasskaya Tower

Palace of Congresses

Cathedral of the Assumption

Great Kremlin Palace

Archangel Cathedral

Bell Tower of Ivan III the Great

Water Tower

and he quietly resigned. In the place of the Soviet Union, Yeltsin formed the Commonwealth of Independent States to retain economic ties among the former Soviet states. All fifteen republics are experiencing a difficult time of transition in their economy and politics.

A Nation in Transition Russia faces problems quite different from those of the United States. America borders two countries, and only one is unstable—Mexico. Russia borders fourteen countries—more than any

Communists built smoking industries all across Russia, such as this timber plant on the Siberian frontier.

other on earth—and many of these are unstable and dangerous. The Russians must now adjust to new freedoms of speech and religion that they have never experienced before. The government-owned land must pass into private hands by some fair system.

The Communists left the country in ruins, with deteriorating buildings, antiquated machinery, and polluted lakes and rivers. Even in Russia, the wealthiest of the CIS states, living conditions are horrendous. Four million people live in regions contaminated by nuclear waste. Air pollution in industrial cities far exceeds that of any city in the United States. Health care in government facilities is extremely outdated.

The greatest concern among Russians is the dramatic rise of organized crime. The murder rate in Russia is now double the rate in the United States. The war against crime is the new government's number one priority. But drastic measures have violated the nation's own constitution. For instance, police can now search without a warrant. Boris Yeltsin even resurrected the old Communist "secret police," which can make arrests without making charges.

Greater Moscow, Russia's Industrial Heartland Moscow lies in the center of Moscow oblast. An **oblast** is a large region or administrative

Missions

Ambassadors for Christ

Russian believers suffered severe persecution under the Soviets, who imprisoned, tortured, and even killed some pastors. Of the many changes in Russia after the fall of the Soviet Union, religious freedom was the most important. Unfortunately, the Orthodox leaders pressured Moscow to pass new restrictions on religious groups in 1997. Some of the ethnic republics have also begun imposing their own severe restrictions too.

A major reason for the new restrictions was the flood of cults and rich Western missionaries, who appeared to be winning converts by simple virtue of the money they could spend. Orthodox churches argued that the national church needed a breathing space to reestablish its rightful role as the unifying force in the nation.

In truth, some Western evangelists were too pushy or boastful. To avoid political controversy, Christians need to remember their heavenly *citizenship* (translated "conversation," in Phil. 3:20). We are all ambassadors for Christ, bringing good news from the King of kings, who sits on His throne in heaven and sends messengers abroad. We are not ambassadors of the United States, and we must never let our Western ideas interfere with mission work. It is tempting to criticize governments that make life difficult for missionaries by delaying visas, changing laws, and passing arbitrary restrictions. But missionaries must resist the temptation.

Now then we are ambassadors for Christ, as though God did beseech you by us: we pray you in Christ's stead, be ye reconciled to God. (II Cor. 5:20)

The Lord is like an Emperor, directing the activities of all kings and lords under His power (Dan. 5:21). Instead of seeing the Russian government as an enemy, it is helpful to see it as just another one of God's instruments. Instead of becoming bitter against God or against local officials, missionaries can rejoice knowing that our Lord is in control of circumstances (Rom. 8:28). All of us need to learn that we are merely His messengers, who may be spit upon or even killed while we do His will.

Let's Go Exploring

1. What is the northernmost major city in Central Eurasia?

2. Does Russia have any densely populated regions with over 250 people per square mile?

3. Where is Russia's largest concentration of people on the Pacific Coast?

4. Find the ribbon of population that ties European Russia to the Pacific. At what latitude does it lie?

What natural features explain Russia's unusual pattern of settlement in Asia above 60° N?

Population Density of Central Eurasia

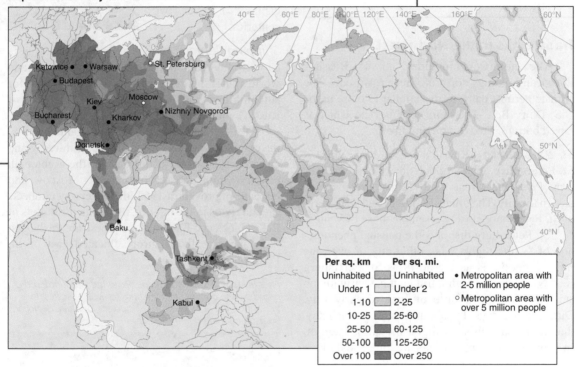

district similar to a state or province. Russia has over fifty oblasts.

Moscow and ten nearby oblasts comprise the Greater Moscow region of fifty million people, one-third of the country's population. It is Russia's most important industrial area and is appropriately called Central Russia. Central Russia developed around the headwaters of three important river systems: the Dnieper, Don, and Volga. These allowed easy access to trade, both north and south.

The Communists forced cities to specialize to avoid "wasteful" competition, so many cities produced a single commodity. Yaroslavl produced tires, Ryazan assembled agricultural machinery, and Tula built armaments. Now these cities are struggling to diversify and develop other industries. Russia produces few quality products, except weapons, that outside countries want to buy, and Eastern Europe can no longer be forced to buy Russian manufactured goods.

SECTION REVIEW

1. What religion is most common among ethnic Russians?
2. List three culture traits that Russia shares with Eastern Europe.
3. What title did Ivan the Terrible take for himself as ruler?
4. What kind of government did Lenin initiate?
5. What is an oblast?
6. Is Russia still a potential threat to the United States?

Sea. He marched west and defeated Sweden in the **Great Northern War** (1700-1721). On the marshy shores of the Baltic he founded a new Russian capital, St. Petersburg, which remained the Russian capital for over two centuries.

Trade Links in the Northwest

The northwest includes all of Russia's European holdings north of Greater Moscow. The climate permits dairy farms, similar to those in the U.S. Dairy Belt. The main crop is flax, which is raised both for flaxseed oil and fiber.

St. Petersburg   Russia's second largest city is **St. Petersburg,** with a population of over five million. Peter the Great hired Italian architects to design the city. The ornate buildings and waterways of St. Petersburg closely resemble those of Venice.

St. Petersburg displays the unusual phenomenon of "white nights." No other city of over one million people is as far north as St. Petersburg (60° N). At such a high latitude, it has virtually no sunsets from the middle of June to early July. During those days, for about five hours each day, the city has a whitish twilight instead of a sunset. In contrast, the winter nights are long and dark.

Russia's Second Capital   The energetic czar **Peter the Great** towers above all other czars in Russian history. From his youth he was fascinated by the West and its bustle. In 1697 he became the first czar ever to tour western Europe, learning all he could about modern shipbuilding, warfare, and industry. Upon his return he reorganized the army and embarked on a program of *Westernization,* which included forcing the noblemen to pay a tax if they refused to shave their beards. His plan included new lands and a new port on the Baltic

Shipping Center   In spite of its great size, Russia has very few good ports with access to oceans and world trade. St. Petersburg is a major center for shipbuilding, and it accounts for 10 percent of Russia's manufactured products.

St. Petersburg's importance was enhanced by the completion of the **Volga-Baltic Waterway** and an interior network of railroads in the eighteenth century. Ships can reach inland to Moscow and beyond. Improved in 1964, the waterway connects several rivers in the interior, including the outlets of Lake Onega and Lake Ladoga. These are the largest two lakes in all of Europe, located east of St. Petersburg.

After his tour of Western Europe, Peter the Great ordered a grand palace built at St. Petersburg to rival Versailles. In front of his Great Palace is a spectacular fountain, depicting Samson opening a lion's mouth.

Geographer's Corner

Comparing Maps

At this point in the textbook, you have studied over fifty maps of all different kinds. By now it should be obvious that the many maps of each region—physical geography, climate, land use, population, languages, religion, and history—are all closely related.

Some of the relationships between maps of Russia give us helpful clues into its history and culture. Compare the six maps in this chapter to answer the questions below.

1. What economic activity is most widespread in the polar climate? (Compare climate and land use.)

2. Look on the population map and find the population ribbon that runs across Siberia, from Europe to the Pacific Ocean. What are the three most common ways that land is used? How is this area different from the less populous areas north and south of the ribbon? (Compare population and land use.)

3. Do the Caucusus Mountains have any significant effect on Russia's land use? population density? history? (Compare the relief map with each of these other maps.)

4. Answer the questions in Number 3, but this time look at the *Ural* Mountains.

5. Which ethnic minorities in modern Russia were the first to fall to Russia? which minorities were the last? (Compare the ethnic republics to the history map.)

♀ Explain why some republics became separate soviets in the USSR and won independence in 1991 but others remained part of Russia. Give as many reasons as you can based on the maps in this chapter.

Novgorod, the First Russian City Older even than Moscow, Novgorod was a key link at the north end of the ancient fur trade route between the Baltic Sea and the Black Sea. According to tradition, a Viking raider named Rurik gained control of Novgorod in 862, establishing the first ruling dynasty of Russia. This little nation, far from the centers of life in Europe, repulsed later attacks by Tatars from the east, Swedes from the north, and Teutonic Knights from the west. The Grand Duke of Moscow, Ivan the Great, finally conquered Novgorod in 1471.

Timber in Karelia Karelia is a flat glaciated plain north of St. Petersburg. Karelians are much like the neighboring Finns in language and culture. However, with the coming of the Russians, ethnic Karelians now comprise only 11 percent of the population. For a brief six years (1940-46), Karelia enjoyed a status equal to Ukraine or Russia itself as a sixteenth Soviet republic.

With the completion of the **White Sea–Baltic Canal** in 1939, Russia successfully linked Karelia's Arctic coast to St. Petersburg. The 141-mile canal links the White Sea to the Volga-Baltic Waterway. Ships carry timber from Karelia through the canal to St. Petersburg. Russia is the second leading producer of cut wood in the world. The canal saves twenty-five hundred miles as compared to a journey around Scandinavia.

Minerals on the Kola Peninsula The **Kola Peninsula** lies north of Karelia. Murmansk is the key arctic port because the currents of the Barents Sea keep the port free of ice most of the year, and icebreakers break through even when there is ice. Murmansk is north of the Arctic Circle and is the world's northernmost large city. The Barents Sea provides herring, the world's most important commercial fish, as well as cod and haddock.

The Kola Peninsula is sparsely inhabited by Lapps as in Finland, but it has important mineral resources. Miners dig phosphates, cobalt, and nickel. Russia provides more than one-fourth of the world's nickel. Russia also ranks second in producing uranium, the most important resource of the peninsula.

Vast forests and tundra stretch from Archangel east across northern Russia. Among the ethnic minorities who herd reindeer in these wastelands are the Komi, a Finnic people, and the Samoyeds, whose breed of furry dogs, bred to herd reindeer, is popular in the United States.

Icebreakers Arctica *and* Lotta *in port at Murmansk*

SECTION REVIEW

1. What is Russia's main port?
2. What two canal systems link the northern ports with Moscow?
3. What principality once controlled much of northwestern Russia before it was conquered by Moscow?
4. Compare and contrast Karelia and the Kola Peninsula.

💡 St. Petersburg was called Leningrad during the Communist era. Why has the name been changed back?

Non-Slavic Peoples on the Volga

The **Volga River** is the longest river in Europe, 2,290 miles long. Canals make it the hub of Russia's shipping system. Central Russia lies along the Upper Volga River. Russia's second great industrial area, the Greater Volga, includes most of the rest of the Volga and its major tributary, the Kama River.

The Russian Federation The Greater Volga, like the rest of Russia, is experiencing problems of **devolution,** a passing down or "de-evolution" of power. Under the Soviet Union, Moscow regulated everything. Even the train schedules in Siberia used Moscow time. With the breakup, Moscow has shifted some responsibilities to local governments. This transition, though necessary, threatens to tear Russia apart because some local areas enjoy their new powers and want more—even independence.

Countries like the United States have always had different levels of government—national, state, county, and city—each with its own clearly defined responsibilities and taxing powers. But under the czars and Communists, Moscow collected all the taxes and made all the rules. Finally, in 1996, each of the fifty-plus *oblasts,* or states, began electing their own governors. Russia also has six *krais,* or territories, governed by Moscow.

However, over thirty ethnic minorities have their own districts and have signed treaties with the government that give them a measure of self-rule. The twenty-one **autonomous republics** (*autonomous* means "self-rule") have the most population, power, and status. Since the autonomous republics were formed around ethnic groups within Russia, they are also called ethnic republics, internal republics, or Russian republics. These terms contrast them with the republics of the USSR, which were external republics or Soviet republics. There are also eleven large, sparsely populated areas, mostly in the north, that are called **okrugs** (areas).

The czars and Soviets never divided power into three branches, as the United States did. Instead, the same leaders passed the laws, interpreted the laws, and enforced the laws. In 1993 the people voted for a new constitution, which attempted to separate powers among three branches of government. The new country is called the **Russian Federation.**

The Russian legislature is divided into two houses. The *Federation Council,* elected by the oblasts and ethnic republics, defends local concerns.

Autonomous Republics and Okrugs of Russia

The powerful **Duma,** elected by the total population, is responsible for the budget and national concerns. Like many European political systems, the government is run by a prime minister and cabinet. Unlike most other parliamentary governments, however, Russia's president has broad powers. He nominates the prime minister and the cabinet. Russia's third branch of government is the Constitutional Court, which tests the constitutionality of all laws and decrees.

Middle Volga The Middle Volga extends from Nizhniy Novgorod to Samara. **Nizhniy Novgorod** (formerly Gorki) is the third largest city in Russia with 1.5 million people, while Samara ranks sixth. This industrial region makes Russia the world's leading producer of synthetic rubber as well as cellulosic fibers. It is also the "Detroit of Russia," manufacturing automobiles.

Though Ivan the Terrible conquered the Tatars and tried to destroy their culture, Tatars remain the most numerous ethnic minority in Russia. Tatars compose about one-half of the population of Tatarstan, one of six **Greater Volga republics.** Their capital, Kazan, near the confluence of the Kama and Volga Rivers, is the ninth largest city in all of Russia.

Bashkortostan, like Tatarstan, is a key ethnic republic with a large population. Ethnic Bashkorts comprise one-quarter of the population, and Tatars account for another one-quarter, resulting in a majority. The republic has the most accessible oil fields in Russia, the greatest producer of petroleum in the world.

Lower Volga The Lower Volga begins below Samara and flows to the Caspian Sea. **Volgograd,** called Stalingrad during the Soviet era until 1961, has about one million people. Although one dozen Russian cities are larger, Volgograd ranks after Moscow and St. Petersburg in importance because it is Russia's southern shipping hub. It is also the "Pittsburgh of Russia," producing much of its steel. Downriver from Volgograd is the port of Astrakhan in the Volga River delta, which allows Russia to trade with other countries on the Caspian Sea.

Motherland

The tallest statue in the world stands on a hill outside Volgograd, Russia. The concrete statue was designed in 1967 to commemorate the Battle of Stalingrad (August 24, 1942–February 2, 1943). Hundreds of thousands of soldiers died in the bitter street-to-street fighting between the Nazi and the Russian armies. Stalin called upon the Russians' ancient love of "Mother Russia" to inspire them to victory. In spite of their hatred of Communism, the soldiers rallied to this call against a foreign invader, as they had done against Napoleon and so many other invaders.

The statue depicts a woman with sword raised high. Rising 270 feet, the woman's figure is taller than the woman depicted in the Statue of Liberty.

The Don River Basin

The 1,224-mile-long **Don River** flows south through a fertile region of Russia very similar to neighboring Ukraine. It loops east and then west before emptying into the Sea of Azov. This important region includes part of the Donbas, Ukraine's mineral-rich eastern territory.

Russia's Agricultural Heartland The Don drainage basin consists of rolling grasslands called **steppes** (STEPS), similar to the Great Plains of North America. Instead of prairie dogs, ground squirrels and gerbils scurry over the black soil of the steppes. Rich in humus and nutrients, this productive land is called the **Black Earth** region of Russia.

As in the Great Plains, the semiarid climate of the steppes provides less than twenty inches of rain. Farm production soars in rainy years, but only irrigation can prevent disaster in drier years. The Black Earth region helps to make Russia the world's fourth largest producer of wheat, sheep, and swine, and the fifth largest producer of beet sugar and cattle. Russia leads the world in the production of potatoes, rye, oats, and barley. The abundant grains make this area the "Breadbasket of Russia." Nevertheless, it cannot meet the huge demands of Russia's population. Russia must sometimes import grain from the United States.

Shipping The Don River is second only to the Volga in importance. The vital port at the mouth of the Don is **Rostov** (or Rostov-on-Don). Much of the Don is shallow, but large ships sailing on the

Let's Go Exploring

1. What economic activity occurs north of the Arctic Circle?
2. What economic activity is most common among the nations south of Russia?
3. What is the most common economic activity along the Baltic Sea?
4. How is the economy different along the Black Sea than anywhere else in Russia?
💡 Compare and contrast the patterns of economic development in Russia and in the United States (p. 211).

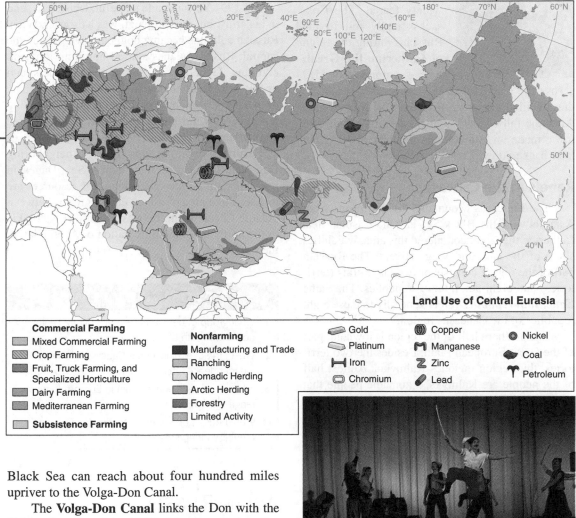

Land Use of Central Eurasia

Commercial Farming
- Mixed Commercial Farming
- Crop Farming
- Fruit, Truck Farming, and Specialized Horticulture
- Dairy Farming
- Mediterranean Farming
- **Subsistence Farming**

Nonfarming
- Manufacturing and Trade
- Ranching
- Nomadic Herding
- Arctic Herding
- Forestry
- Limited Activity

- Gold
- Platinum
- Iron
- Chromium
- Copper
- Manganese
- Zinc
- Lead
- Nickel
- Coal
- Petroleum

Black Sea can reach about four hundred miles upriver to the Volga-Don Canal.

The **Volga-Don Canal** links the Don with the Volga. Completed in 1952, this sixty-three-mile-long canal with thirteen locks is Russia's final link in its European shipping system. Ships from Moscow can now reach any Russian port in Europe.

Cossacks Territory The steppes are famous for the **Cossacks,** fiercely independent nomads whose place in Russian lore is very similar to the Plains

Don Cossack singers and dancers perform in Moscow.

Indians in America. Novocherkassk near Rostov was the capital of the Cossacks.

The name *Cossack* comes from the Turkic word *Kazakh,* or "adventurer." Tracing their Slavic

Catherine the Great (1729-96)

and Tatar origins is impossible, but their communities were independent and their elite cavalry units widely feared. The Cossacks finally fell to the Russians during the reign of **Catherine the Great,** whose empire extended across the Caucasus. Later czars often turned to these skilled horsemen to defend the Motherland. After the fall of Communism, the Cossacks asked to be made an autonomous republic in 1993 but later backed down.

Rebels in the Caucasus

The Caucasus Mountains divide Europe from Asia between the Black Sea and the Caspian Sea. Catherine the Great conquered this area, which lies south of the Don and Volga Rivers. The Russian part of the region consists of two large krais (territories) and eight autonomous republics. The name *Caucasian republics* refers generally to these eight republics of the Caucasus region.

The northern half of the region is lowland, part of the Great European Plain. Besides the two territories, this region includes Kalmykia. Almost half of the people are Kalmyks, a nomadic people that keep livestock and speak a Mongol language. Their religion is Tibetan Buddhism, but some have converted to Islam.

The mountains along the southern border are the highest in all of Europe. The highest of these is **Mount Elbrus** (18,510 ft.). This mountainous region is a haven for ethnic minorities and consists of seven of the eight Caucasian republics. (See map of Russian Republics.)

The greatest challenge to the Russian Federation came from a small republic of one million people called **Chechnya.** When the Soviet Union broke apart in 1991, the Chechens took the opportunity to secede from the Russian Federation. The czars had spent thirty years trying to subdue these

people, who had never willingly bowed to Moscow. Russian parents would scare their children, saying a Chechen might come and get them in the night. While Yeltsin was distracted with politics in Moscow, lawless gangsters flocked to this "refuge" in Chechnya.

In 1994 Yeltsin made a fateful decision to send in his army, but the campaign was a disaster. When Russian columns became bogged down outside the capital, Russian planes started bombing innocent civilians. Generals refused to obey orders and openly criticized the attack. The Chechens became desperate, occupying Russian hospitals and taking hostages. Several peace agreements were signed and broken. Chechnya's future is still in doubt.

Thirty people groups live in neighboring Dagestan. Located on the Caspian Sea, Dagestan has important oil resources, but these resources are in a sensitive area of mixed ethnic groups between volatile Chechnya in the west, Buddhist Kalmykia in the north, and the Shiite nation of Azerbaijan in the south.

SECTION REVIEW

1. What group of people have their cultural center near the mouth of the Don River?
2. What ethnic republic in the Caucasus declared independence after the fall of the Soviet Union?
3. What is the highest mountain in Europe? In what range is it found?
- Would Russia be better off to give the Caucasian republics independence?

ASIAN RUSSIA

Alexis de Tocqueville, a French writer who visited the United States during the early nineteenth century, predicted that Russia and the United States would one day become the dominant nations of the world. At that time, both countries shared vast frontiers that held great promise. American frontiersmen were expanding west, while Russians moved east. Russia's east coast is nothing like California's coast, however. It has more in common with Alaska. Most Russians have preferred to stay in Europe, though a few have been lured by minerals, furs, and stretches of fertile farmland. The czars and Communist dictators shipped many dissidents to Asian Russia. Not surprisingly, an independent spirit flows through the blood of many peoples on the frontier.

Russia's supply of mineral and fuel resources is the greatest in the world. Deposits of almost every industrial mineral from aluminum (bauxite) to zinc lie in Russia. It has the world's largest reserves of iron ore, magnesium, manganese, chromium, coal, and natural gas, and it has a large supply of oil as well. Many of these resources, however, lie in remote parts of its vast Asian landmass.

Ural Mountains

The **Ural Mountains** form a geographic border between the continents of Europe and Asia. Much as the Appalachians marked the early American West, the Urals once marked Russia's eastern frontier.

Northern Urals The Ural Mountains reach elevations similar to the Appalachians. The highest peak, Mount Narodnaya in the north, reaches 6,217 feet. While mineral resources lie in this part of the range, they are less developed than those farther south. The range continues north into the Arctic Ocean to form the two large islands of Novaya Zemlya. These two islands are the largest islands in the Eurasian Arctic.

Southern Urals The Ural Mountains share several other traits with the Appalachian Mountains. Both ranges are low with several passes that enable people to cross freely. Both ranges are more populous in the south, and both have unique cultures.

The most important mineral deposits in the Urals are iron ore and copper. With one-tenth of the world's copper reserves and one-third of the iron reserves, Russia ranks fifth in copper mining and fourth in iron ore production. Mining in the Urals also enables Russia to rank among the top ten producers of pyrites, potash, bauxite, vanadium, magnesium, and silver.

A final similarity to the Appalachians is that important industrial cities have grown up near the mineral resources. **Yekaterinburg** and Chelyabinsk each have over one million people and rank as Russia's fifth and eighth largest cities, respectively. Yekaterinburg is a major chemical manufacturer, named after Catherine the Great. The Yekaterinburg oblast has declared itself the Urals Autonomous Republic but has not been recognized by Russia.

Siberia, "The Sleeping Land"

All of Asian Russia east of the Urals is broadly termed **Siberia,** or "the Sleeping Land." Just as the Urals can be compared to the Appalachians, Siberia has similarities to the American West, with its plains, plateaus, and high mountains. However, Siberia's vegetation and climate is similar to that of Canada, especially in the north. Russia's interior has no east-west mountain ranges to block cold fronts that push down from the Arctic.

Walrus and seals feed along the Arctic coast, while reindeer browse the mosses and lichens of the tundra. The polar climate keeps water and soil in a state of permafrost, that is, frozen most of the year. South of the tundra, the climate warms slightly. Wolves prowl the coniferous forests that blanket most of Siberia. The subpolar climate has freezing temperatures half the year, which drop to –60°F on occasion, and summer highs as hot as 100°F. The taiga—great coniferous forests of spruce, pine, fir, and larch—is an important source of wood products.

Southwest and southeast Siberia, where most Siberians live, has a more hospitable climate similar

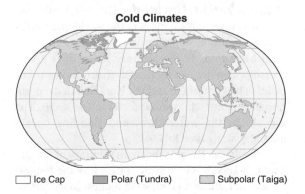

Cold Climates

☐ Ice Cap   ■ Polar (Tundra)   ☐ Subpolar (Taiga)

Trans-Siberian Railway

The Trans-Siberian Railway, which runs 4,608 miles from Moscow to the Pacific Ocean, is the longest line in the world that has regular service. The route crosses eight time zones and requires seven days to travel. It was built to exploit Siberia's mineral resources, which are so inaccessible and costly to bring to market.

When construction began in 1891, a rail system already joined Moscow to Chelyabinsk and Yekaterinburg. By 1898 the line extended across the Irtysh, Ob, and Yenisey Rivers, and ended at Irkutsk. At this point

The Trans-Siberian Railway stops at Severobaykalsk, near the north end of Lake Baykal.

COUNTRY	PASSENGER-MILES (MILLION)	FREIGHT NET TON-MILES (MILLION)	LENGTH OF TRACK, MILES
United States	14,000	1,183,000	149,040
Russia	141,000	17,244	95,634
Canada	852	166,057	43,579
India	195,926	171,213	38,789
China	225,590	853,576	36,266
Germany	35,567	46,254	27,303
Poland	19,179	44,082	15,628
South Africa	556	62,605	13,309
Romania	12,057	819	7,063
Czech Republic	5,311	17,250	5,846

a British-built icebreaker ferried passengers across Lake Baykal. Meanwhile, a separate line was being built from the east. The final connection was made in 1905, including a section around the southern end of Lake Baykal. The czar ordered a 2,250-mile extension, completed in 1916, that would enable Russia to rush troops to its disputed border with China. Only the United States has more miles of track.

to Moscow. These populous regions are separated by Asian mountains that cross the border. The **Trans-Siberian Railway** links these regions, resulting in a ribbon development similar to Canada. Farmers grow crops on the scattered prairies, and loggers cut trees from nearby forests.

West Siberian Lowland

The West Siberian Lowland is the largest plain in the world and covers over one million square miles. Extending from the Ural Mountains to the Yenisey River, it is a vast marshy plain drained by the Ob River and its tributaries. The Gulf of Ob and the Kara Sea in the north remain frozen, while snow melts in the south. The ice blocks the water flow, and flooding occurs annually along the Ob.

The Irtysh River is the main tributary of the Ob. The **Ob-Irtysh** River system ranks as the longest system in Eurasia and the sixth longest in the world.

Novosibirsk (New Siberia), with about 1.5 million people, is the largest city in Siberia. Situated on the Ob River, it has experienced phenomenal growth due to natural resources available nearby. Petroleum and natural gas deposits lie north. To the southeast lie deposits of lead, zinc, and iron ore. The region contributes to Russia's status as the fourth leading producer of coal worldwide.

An elderly Russian who lives near the Volga River

Lake Baykal

Lake Baykal (or Baikal) is the deepest lake in the world. Over one mile deep, 395 miles long, and up to forty miles wide, it contains more water than all the Great Lakes combined.

The Baykal seal, a freshwater seal, sunbathes on the shore. Over twelve hundred animal species in the lake are found nowhere else in the world. These include many unusual fish that swim near the lake's surface. The black and frigid depths are virtually lifeless and little-explored.

Over 330 rivers feed the lake, but only the Angara River drains it toward the north. The Angara provides hydroelectric power to the city of Irkutsk, an ancient trading post located on a vital pass through the mountains near the lake. The large haul of fish from the lake is loaded on trains at Irkutsk.

Lake Baykal has beautiful blue waters, like the Great Lakes, but it lacks many other advantages. It has no navigable outlet to the ocean. The climate is typical of cold Siberia, and taiga surrounds the shores. The lake surface remains frozen from December to May.

Chuvorkusky Bay is one of the many beautiful bays on Lake Baykal.

Central Siberian Plateau The Central Siberian Plateau covers one-third of Siberia and stretches between the Yenisey and Lena Rivers. It averages about two thousand feet in elevation. The lower north coast, or **Taymyr Peninsula,** is the northernmost mainland area in the world. Near the mouth of the Yenisey, miners dig nickel, cobalt, and platinum. Russia provides over 40 percent of the world's platinum; only South Africa produces more (50 percent). Diamonds come from the remote central part of the plateau.

The Trans-Siberian Railroad enters the central plateau at Krasnoyarsk, the largest city of the plateau with almost one million people. The city lies on the **Yenisey River,** the eleventh longest river in the world.

Without railroad connections, two ethnic republics of southern Siberia—Altaya and Tuva—retain their ethnic majority. Remote Altaya is especially interesting because it is at the sensitive border between four large nations: Russia, China, Mongolia, and Kazakhstan. Altaya contains Mt. Belukha (14,783 ft.), the highest peak of the **Altai Mountains.** The mountainous republic also contains the headwaters of the Ob. There are four **Altaic republics** in this region of Siberia.

East Siberian Upland The East Siberian Upland is a mountain wilderness between the Lena River and the Pacific Ocean. The **Lena River** is the seventh longest river in the world.

Interior The largest Russian republic is **Sakha** (formerly Yakutia); it has the world's harshest climate of any inhabited area. It contains much of the Lena and Kolyma River basins as well as the New Siberian Islands in the Arctic. Covering almost 1.2 million square miles, it would be the eighth largest country in the world if it obtained independence.

Ethnic Yakuts speak a Turkic language and constitute over one-third of the population, while Russians constitute over one-half. Yakutsk, the main city, was founded in 1632 but has grown to become the largest city of northern Siberia. The growth has come from mining in the **Yakutsk Basin** along the Lena and in the mountains. The Sakha gold fields make Russia the fifth largest producer of gold in the world.

The Far East Russia has more Pacific coastline than any other country. The Pacific coast has a more moderate climate and includes some farmland, but the ports still freeze in winter. Russian

Igor Epiyen tends reindeer in Koryakia.

leaders are hopeful that its Far East will share in the booming trade of the Pacific Rim.

Russia's Far East has land within a few miles of all the great Pacific powers. Its land borders China and North Korea, while Japan is across a narrow channel from Russia's **Sakhalin Island** (SAK uh LEEN). The island has both coal and petroleum resources. Russia's **Kuril Islands** also extend in a chain from the Kamchatka (kam CHAT kuh) Peninsula to Japan. The United States is just across the Bering Strait (Alaska).

The Siberian Railway links **Vladivostok,** Russia's main Pacific port, with Russia's European ports. The large fishing fleet catches enough salmon for Russia to rank third worldwide, and it leads the world in its Pacific cod catch. Vladivostok is the center of the Maritime Republic, a self-declared autonomous republic unrecognized by Russia.

Two peninsulas dominate the far north coast. The Chukchi Peninsula reaches toward Alaska and divides the Bering Sea from the Chukchi Sea. The **Kamchatka Peninsula** extends south into the Pacific. Kamchatka contains some twenty-five active volcanoes, including Siberia's highest peak, snow-capped Mt. Klyuchevskaya (15,584 ft.). Its southern end has the Russian port city of Petropavlovsk.

The Russian Empire once crossed the Pacific, including Alaska and trading centers as far south as California. The first permanent settlement in Alaska was founded in 1784. Russia did not have the means to protect these distant lands, however, and sold them to the United States in 1867. Instead, it concentrated its energies on expanding its empire in Central Asia, closer to home.

SECTION REVIEW

1. What mountain range divides Europe and Asia?
2. What are the three major geographic regions of Siberia?
3. Name the three major rivers of Siberia.
4. What is the largest city in Siberia? the main seaport?
5. Name a key mineral for each of the four regions in Asian Russia.

💡 Compare and contrast the Ural and Appalachian Mountains.

REVIEW

Can You Define These Terms?

pogrom	dissident	devolution	okrug
czar	oblast	autonomous republic	steppes
serf			

Can You Locate These Natural Features?

Kola Peninsula	Ural Mountains	Taymyr Peninsula	Yakutsk Basin
Volga River	Siberia	Yenisey River	Sakhalin Island
Don River	Ob-Irtysh	Altai Mountains	Kuril Islands
Mount Elbrus	Lake Baykal	Lena River	Kamchatka Peninsula

Can You Explain the Significance of These People, Places, and Events?

Moscow	Volga-Baltic Waterway	Volgograd	Chechnya
Ivan the Terrible	Karelia	Black Earth	Yekaterinburg
USSR	White Sea–Baltic Canal	Rostov	Trans-Siberian Railway
Karl Marx	Russian Federation	Volga-Don Canal	Novosibirsk
Kremlin	Duma	Cossacks	Altaic republics
St. Petersburg	Nizhniy Novgorod	Catherine the Great	Sakha
Peter the Great	Tatarstan	Caucasian republics	Vladivostok
Great Northern War	Greater Volga republics		

How Much Do You Remember?

1. What major event occurred at each of these dates in Russian history: 862, 988, 1237, 1462, 1547, 1917, 1991?
2. How does the history of the Russians explain their love of country, in spite of so many hardships?
3. Why are Russia's European lands more populous than its Asian lands?
4. Why does Russia's development have a ribbon pattern in Asia?
5. Give Russia's key port on each body of water.
   a. Arctic Ocean
   b. Baltic Sea
   c. Lower Volga
   d. Sea of Azov (Don River)
   e. Sea of Japan (Pacific Ocean)
6. How many ethnic republics are in each region and what languages do they speak?
   a. Greater Volga republics
   b. Caucasian republics
   c. Altaic republics

7. List two ethnic republics that have land above the Arctic Circle. What characteristics do they have in common?
8. Why is devolution dangerous in Russia? Why is it important?
9. Give the main river, product, and city in each of the three main geographic regions of Siberia.

What Do You Think?

1. For each event given in Question 1 above, find the most similar event that is significant in America's heritage.
2. How would you compare the life of Russian peasants under the czars to that of Russians today?
3. Give five major similarities and five major differences between the United States and Russia.
4. Why do you think the Communist Party is still strong in Russia?
5. What is the greatest threat to freedom in Russia today?

CHAPTER 18

CAUCASUS AND CENTRAL ASIA

The nine nations of the Caucasus and Central Asia were once part of the Soviet Empire. Eight were republics in the Soviet Union, ruled by Communist Russia for seventy years. Russia had coveted the ninth nation, Afghanistan, for nearly a century. The Soviets backed a military coup in Afghanistan in 1978, but armed resistance forced them to send Soviet tanks the next year to prop up their puppet ruler. In spite of an international outcry, the Soviets occupied Afghanistan for ten years. The bitter fighting cost many Russian lives and precious resources, helping to bring down the whole Soviet system.

Nevertheless, Russian influence has remained even after these nations gained their freedom. All of them except Afghanistan now belong to the Commonwealth of Independent States (CIS). Russia's promise of assistance has come with deadly strings attached. Every nation should be wary of alliances with powerful neighbors. Ancient Israel learned this lesson when it turned to Egypt for help instead of to the Lord.

Lo, thou trustest in the staff of this broken reed, on Egypt; whereon if a man lean, it will go into his hand, and pierce it: so is Pharaoh king of Egypt to all that trust in him. (Isa. 36:6)

CAUCASUS, "MOUNTAINS OF A THOUSAND LANGUAGES"

The **Caucasus Mountains** lie at the crossroads between Europe, Asia, and the Middle East. The western border of the mountains runs along the Black Sea. The eastern border touches the coast of the Caspian Sea, which was settled by Asian nomads and by Muslim conquerors from the Middle East.

A complex diversity of peoples has arisen in the isolated valleys of the Caucasus Mountains.

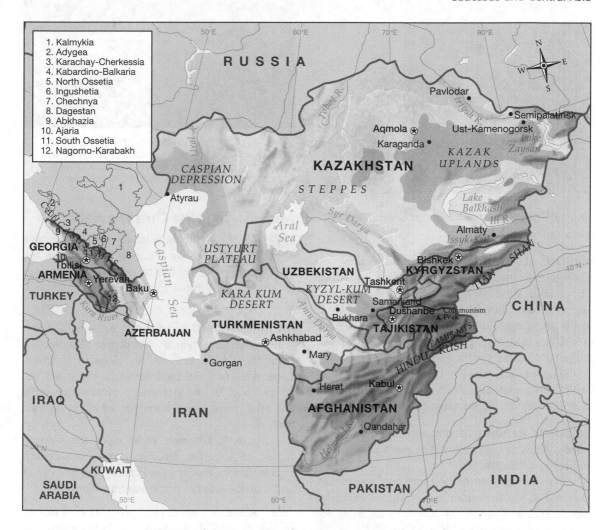

1. Kalmykia
2. Adygea
3. Karachay-Cherkessia
4. Kabardino-Balkaria
5. North Ossetia
6. Ingushetia
7. Chechnya
8. Dagestan
9. Abkhazia
10. Ajaria
11. South Ossetia
12. Nagorno-Karabakh

These peoples are fiercely independent and are constantly fighting each other. The Arabs call the Caucasus the "mountains of a thousand languages."

Many foreign empires have tried to subdue the region, at their own peril. The latest was that of the Soviets. Modern nations want access to the vast oil deposits in the Caspian Sea. Three small nations in the Caucasus—Georgia, Armenia, and Azerbaijan—gained independence from the Soviet Union in 1991. The Soviets intentionally drew borders across ethnic lines to weaken nationalism, but lumping enemies together left a recipe for trouble.

Georgia

From about A.D. 1000 to 1212, Georgia enjoyed an age of independence and prosperity. This glorious period carried its people through the dark intervening years of domination by Mongols, Turks, Persians, and Russians. With the weakening of the Soviet Union in 1990, Georgia became the second Soviet republic to declare independence.

Georgia's language is unrelated to other known languages. It also uses its own unique alphabet. Seventy percent of the people are Georgians and

Vineyards have been common in Georgia since ancient times.

Small villages are common in Georgia. This one lies near the base of Mount Kazbek, the second highest mountain in Georgia (16,512 ft.). The highest mountain in the Caucasus is Mount Elbrus, located across the border in Russia.

worship in the Georgian Orthodox Church, a type of Eastern Orthodoxy.

Central Lowlands The central valley of Georgia is formed from two river basins. The Rioni River drains west into the Black Sea. The surrounding area has a humid subtropical climate. Citrus fruits and grape products come from this region. The Black Sea ports permit trade with Russia and Ukraine, Georgia's main trade partners.

The capital, Tbilisi, is on the Kura River, which flows southeast into Azerbaijan. Irrigation in this drier region supports tobacco and wheat.

Highland Rebels Mountains lie both north and south of this central valley. The south is rich with copper and manganese.

Two regions on the northern borders contain dissatisfied Muslim minorities: Abkhazia, along the Black Sea, and South Ossetia, across the border from Russia's republic of North Ossetia.

Armenia, the First Christian Nation

The **Armenians** have a unique language with its own alphabet, invented in the fifth century. In the fourth century their nation became the first in the world to adopt Christianity officially.

An Independent Kingdom Armenia's mountain stronghold provided some degree of protection from the Greek, Persian, and Roman Empires. Later the Arabs defeated Armenia, but it did not adopt Islam. In 884, Armenia overcame the Arabs and established a new kingdom, which lasted two centuries.

By 1639, Ottoman Turks ruled the western region of Armenia, and Persia ruled the eastern region. Russia annexed the Persian portion in 1828 and took the western portion during World War I.

Life Armenia's dry climate provides only twenty inches of rainfall annually and is conducive to

Caucasus and Central Asia Statistics

COUNTRY	CAPITAL	AREA (SQ. MI.)	POPULATION	NATURAL INCREASE	LIFE EXPECTANCY	LITERACY RATE	PER CAPITA GDP	POP. DENSITY
Afghanistan	Kabul	251,825	23,738,085	2.5%	46	32%	$600	90
Armenia	Yerevan	11,500	3,465,611	0.9%	69	99%	$2,560	301
Azerbaijan	Baku	33,400	7,735,918	1.3%	65	97%	$1,480	232
Georgia	Tbilisi	26,831	5,174,642	0.2%	68	99%	$1,080	193
Kazakhstan	Aqmola	1,049,200	16,898,572	0.9%	64	98%	$2,700	16
Kyrgyzstan	Bishkek	76,600	4,540,185	1.7%	64	97%	$1,140	59
Tajikistan	Dushanbe	55,300	6,013,855	2.6%	64	100%	$1,040	108
Turkmenistan	Ashkhabad	188,500	4,225,351	2.0%	62	100%	$2,820	22
Uzbekistan	Tashkent	172,700	23,860,452	2.2%	65	97%	$2,370	138

What Is a Caucasian?

The word *Caucasian* has come to refer to light-skinned peoples because of the work of anthropologist Johann Friedrich Blummenbach. Studying skulls in the 1770s, he grouped all people into one of five races. He chose the skulls of women from Georgia, in the Caucasus Mountains, as the most typical skull of the white race. However, modern theories no longer recognize the term or limit the list of races to five.

Ships on the Caspian Sea near the port of Baku, Azerbaijan

farming barley, wheat, and potatoes. Copper and bauxite are the major mineral resources.

Armenia is the most densely populated nation in the Caucasus and Central Asia. A **1988 earthquake** killed twenty-five thousand people and left one-half million people homeless; lack of supplies has prevented Armenia from rebuilding.

Armenia's most serious problem is its Muslim neighbor, Azerbaijan. Azerbaijanis attacked Armenian minorities in their country before the breakup of the Soviet Union. In response Armenia invaded Azerbaijan to protect its ethnic brothers. These poverty-stricken nations could ill afford this war.

Muslims in Azerbaijan

Iran (formerly Persia) has had the greatest influence over Azerbaijan. Persians controlled this region from 700 B.C. to A.D. 600

An earthquake devastated Spitak, Armenia, in 1988.

(except for the brief interruption of the Greek Empire) and from the sixteenth century to 1813 (except for a brief period under the Ottoman Turks).

The people of Azerbaijan speak the Persian language and follow the Arab religion, but they are descended from Turkic peoples. Their industry and military makeup come from Russia, which controlled the region from the nineteenth century until Azerbaijan won independence. Russian people compose a 5 percent minority.

Populous Lowlands A long plain runs southeast across the nation. The Kura River flows through this lowland valley of the Caucasus, where farmers grow cotton, grain, and tea. Some raise silkworms in the semiarid temperate climate. The Kura River provides water for textile and chemical plants.

The Kura River empties into the **Caspian Sea,** the largest lake in the world. It provides key resources, such as fishing and salt. Azerbaijan's capital, Baku, is the leading port. Unfortunately, rising waters have threatened the lowland city with floods.

Petroleum is by far the most important resource of the Caspian. Oil companies believe the reserves may be larger than those in the Middle East. Russia has promised to help Azerbaijan fight Armenia in return for rights to this oil. The region could become a major battleground in the twenty-first century, as nations compete for the Caspian's oil wealth.

Highland Minorities Azerbaijan's highland regions have cooler climates than the lowlands.

The most important highland region lies between the Kura Valley and Armenia. The major part of this region is **Nagorno-Karabakh,** a territory where a large Armenian minority lives. Armenian soldiers have fought Azerbaijan for control of this territory.

CENTRAL ASIA, HEART OF THE SILK ROAD

Central Asia is a broad term that encompasses all the dry steppes between the Caspian Sea and western China. Deserts and high mountains separate this region from the rest of the world. In times past, fierce nomads launched raids into neighboring lands in Asia, Europe, and the Middle East. The *Huns* threatened ancient Rome in the fourth and fifth centuries after Christ. The **Turkic peoples,** who later settled most of Central Asia, conquered Turkey; and the *Mongols,* who briefly conquered Central Asia, terrorized all of Eurasia between the thirteenth and fourteenth centuries.

Central Asia was once a major trade route between the East and the West. The **Silk Road** linked the two great ancient empires: Rome and China. Europeans gladly traded gold, silver, wool, jewels, and anything else of value to the Chinese in return for silk.

Eventually, European traders discovered a new water route to China that avoided Central Asia. Little is left on the dusty Silk Road except struggling cities and memories of past greatness.

In the twentieth century, the Soviets dramatically changed life in Central Asia. They forced the nomads to settle down on collective farms and to grow cotton, even though this lifestyle did not fit the dry steppes.

The new nations of Central Asia are struggling to find their place in the modern world. They suffer from a devastating shortage of water and land-locked borders that isolate them from international trade. To make matters worse, former Communist rulers continue to exercise power in Central Asia.

Kazakhstan on Russia's Frontier

Kazakhstan is the only Central Asian nation that borders Russia. The histories of the two nations are closely linked. For years, Russian farmers have settled in Kazakhstan.

Europeans on the Northern Steppes

Kazakhstan's northern steppes are good for grazing sheep and cattle. Russian and Ukrainian farmers began arriving on the northern borders in the 1730s, and Russian armies had conquered the region by the 1850s.

The modern population is composed of native Kazakhs (42 percent), Russians (37 percent), Ukrainians (5 percent), and Germans (5 percent). The Slavic immigrants follow the Eastern Orthodox religion, but the Kazakhs are mostly Muslim. The Soviet capital was in the south at Almaty, but the new government decided to move the capital north to Aqmola nearer the Russians. This move will take years to complete.

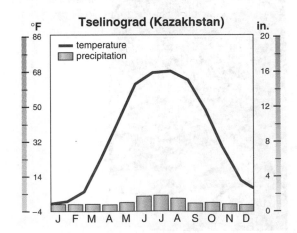

Tselinograd (Kazakhstan)

The mosque at Panfilov, near Kazakhstan's eastern border with China, has a mixture of architectural styles—Islamic minarets and Oriental pagodas.

In the middle of these deserts, the Syr Darya flows into the **Aral Sea.** Like the Caspian Sea to the west, the Aral Sea is a salt lake with no outlet to the ocean.

Western Kazakhstan consists of lowlands on the Caspian Sea. Unlike Azerbaijan, Kazakhstan has no major cities on this salt sea. There are no Caucasus Mountains to create orographic rainfall. Instead, it is a barren wasteland. The lowland forms a deep bowl, or *depression,* in the earth. At its lowest spot, the **Caspian Depression** is 433 feet below sea level—lower than any location in the Western Hemisphere.

Two Desert Nations of Central Asia

Uzbekistan and Turkmenistan lie south of Kazakhstan. Like Kazakhstan, these two desert nations were settled by Turkic peoples, speak Turkic languages, and follow the Turkish branch of Islam, called Sunni Islam.

Turkmenistan on Iran's Frontier
The Turkmens account for about 70 percent of the people of modern Turkmenistan. Russians compose another 10 percent, and there are

Mines in the far northwestern steppes produce over one-quarter of the world's chromite. Kazakhstan ranks second worldwide in chromite production.

Eastern Kazakh Uplands The Kazakh Uplands cover the eastern lake regions around Lake Balkhash and Lake Zaysan. The climate is similar to the northern steppes. Karaganda and Ekibastuz are important industrial centers. Large lead mines have made Kazakhstan the second leading smelter of lead, behind the United States.

The major industrial city at the south end of the uplands is **Almaty** (Alma Ata). With 1.2 million people, it is Kazakhstan's largest city and its cultural center. Dense orchards provide one of its main products—fruit.

Southern and Western Deserts Most of the south is a desert that contains great wealth. Copper comes from Betpak-Dala, the desert north of the country's main river, Syr Darya. Uranium is mined south of the river.

Ethnic Groups of Central Asia and the Caucasus

Russian
Caucasian
Armenian
Turkic
Azerbaijani
Kazakh
Kyrgyz
Turkish
Uzbek
Other Turkic
Iranian
Pushtun
Tajik
Other

China

Iran

Drying of the Aral Sea

The Aral Sea once had the sixth largest area of any lake in the world. However, the saltwater is not very deep, and the area is shrinking at an alarming rate. Since 1960 the sea has lost 40 percent of its surface area, or over eleven thousand square miles. The remaining water is so salty that all twenty-four species of fish that used to be found in the lake have died.

The shrinkage has caused an economic disaster. Before 1960 Muynak was a bustling fishing village of ten thousand people, which supplied 3 percent of the world's annual catch of pike, perch, and bream. Now the village of two hundred people sits in a desert surrounded by beached ships, twenty miles from the lake.

What happened? In 1918 the Soviet government decided to raise cotton in the desert. They built the world's longest canal, the Kara Kum Canal, in 1956 to divert water from the two rivers that feed the lake:

Ships are stranded in the desert where the Aral Sea once roared.

Syr Darya and Amu Darya. As the lake dried, salt storms blew out from the dry lake bed onto the cotton farms. As a result, the salty soil needed more and more water to stay productive. From 1977 to 1987, water never even reached the lake.

---

smaller minorities of Kazakhs, Uzbeks, Tatars, Ukrainians, and Armenians.

Turkmenistan lies south of Kazakhstan and east of the Caspian Sea. Turkmenistan's most important border is on the south with Iran. It is the only former Soviet republic bordering Iran.

The Turkmens displaced the Persians about A.D. 900. But in the fourteenth century, they converted to Islam under the influence of Sufis from Persia. Mary became the central city. In 1924 the Soviets moved the capital west to Ashkhabad.

The **Kara Kum** is a desert that covers 80 percent of Turkmenistan. Summer temperatures can exceed 122°F. The five-hundred-mile-long Kara Kum Canal diverts water from the Amu Darya on the country's northern border south to Ashkhabad, where cotton crops grow.

The desert's most important resources, petroleum and natural gas, make Turkmenistan the richest Central Asian nation. As in Kazakhstan, the petroleum lies along the Caspian Sea. Natural gas is found throughout the desert.

Uzbekistan, the Heart of Turkistan

Uzbekistan's population is made up of Uzbeks (70 percent), Russians (10 percent), and small minorities of Tatars, Kazakhs, Tajiks, and Karakalpaks. Uzbekistan is the most populous nation in Central Asia.

Uzbekistan is in the heart of Central Asia, completely surrounded by other Central Asian nations. When Central Asia broke from the Soviet Union, Uzbekistan hoped that the Turkic peoples of

An Uzbek woman sells melons at Tashkent, Uzbekistan.

The citadel at Bukhara, Uzbekistan. This oasis town was once a necessary stop on the Silk Road.

Mongol Empire and the Silk Route

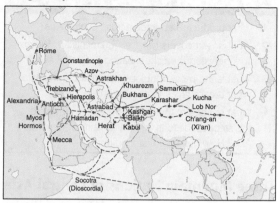

Central Asia would unite into a single nation called **Turkistan.** Uzbekistan, with its large population, had much to gain from union because it lacks wealth and trade opportunities. Not surprisingly, no other nation shared Uzbekistan's enthusiasm.

Desert Oases The **Kyzyl-Kum** is a vast desert that covers 80 percent of Uzbekistan, except for a few mountains on the eastern edge. The main crop, cotton, requires irrigation. The diversion of the two rivers for irrigation has hurt Uzbekistan just as it has hurt Kazakhstan. Uzbekistan's cotton industry, the fifth largest in the world, is in deep trouble.

Most of the Kyzyl-Kum is wilderness, but it does have a few oases and mining towns. The greatest oasis lies at **Bukhara,** north of the Amu Darya. Bukhara served as a crucial juncture of the Silk Road as caravans crossed eight hundred miles through the deserts.

In the tenth century Bukhara was the capital of a Muslim dynasty, the Samanids, and was second only to Mecca as an Islamic holy place. It still boasts Ulugh Beg madrasah, the oldest madrasah (Islamic seminary) in Central Asia, dating from 1418. It also has the largest madrasah in Central Asia, Kukelbash, dating from 1509. This Islamic center of learning was the home of the famed Muslim philosopher **Avicenna,** who wrote commentaries on the ancient Greek philosopher Aristotle. Today, Bukhara is a center of Tajik culture in the middle of an Uzbek nation.

The Crowded Foothills Most of Uzbekistan's population lives in the foothills of the great Asian mountain system. Both of the largest cities are here.

The capital, **Tashkent,** has over two million people and is the largest city in all of the Caucasus and Central Asia. The region around Tashkent contains some of the world's greatest uranium mines.

Samarkand lies near the eastern border of Uzbekistan, where the Kyzyl-Kum Desert reaches the first spur of the mountains. Alexander the Great defeated the local tribes and destroyed the city in 329 B.C. But it was rebuilt and became a leading city on the Silk Road between Rome and China. The Mongol conqueror Tamerlane, the last ruler to unite Turkistan, made Samarkand his capital in the fourteenth century.

Tamerlane's tomb (Gur Emir) is at Samarkand, Uzbekistan.

Three Mountain Nations of Central Asia

Of all the continents, only Asia has mountains that reach twenty-three thousand feet (seven thousand meters). Three of Asia's highest mountain ranges lie in Central Asia.

◉ Kyrgyzstan on China's Frontier

Kyrgyzstan is dominated by the **Tien Shan,** or the "Celestial Mountains." This northern range runs eighteen hundred miles from Tashkent to Urumqi in China and divides Kyrgyzstan from China.

One-half of Kyrgyzstan's people are of the Kyrgyz ethnic group. Another one-fifth are Russians, who hold most of the technical jobs. Uzbeks, Ukrainians, and Germans constitute smaller minorities. While the Kyrgyzs and Uzbeks are Muslims, the other groups are Orthodox.

Osh, on the edge of the Fergana Valley, is the center of Kyrgyzstan's Uzbek minority. Historically, it was where Silk Road caravans began the arduous crossing of the Pamirs into China's city of Kashgar.

Tajikistan, the Southern Knot

Tajikistan is the mountain hub of Central Asia. It shares borders with China and Afghanistan and is only a few miles north of Pakistan. Russia has kept its soldiers stationed on the borders of this volatile region.

Pamirs   The **Pamirs** cover the eastern half of Tajikistan. This range is sometimes called the Pamir Knot because it ties together the great

ranges: the Tien Shan, the Hindu Kush, the Himalaya (and Karakoram), and the Kunlun.

The Pamirs have three seven-thousand-meter peaks, all of which lie on or near the northern border of Tajikistan. Communism Peak, the highest, rises to 24,457 feet (7,495 m). The other two are Lenin Peak and Korzhenevskoi Peak.

Divided People   Tajiks comprise 62 percent of Tajikistan's people. Uzbeks form the largest minority (23 percent), but others include Russians, Kazakhs, Turkmens, Kyrgyzs, and Tatars.

Tajikistan is unusual in Central Asia. Its language is more Iranian than Turkic. This similarity to Iran would appear to make Tajikistan a natural inroad for Iran in the struggle to influence Central Asia. Ironically, the two nations do not even share a border.

Tajikistan has few resources except its rivers. Nurek Dam, the highest in the world, harnesses waterpower for industries at the capital. When completed, Rogun Dam will be even taller.

Afghanistan, a Buffer State

The mountains of Afghanistan harbor more than twenty ethnic groups, including Turkic, Mongol, Arab, Aryan, and Persian peoples. The two largest, the Pushtuns and Tajiks, constitute about three-quarters of the population.

The warring tribes of this region united for the first time in 1747 under a monarchy, but rivalry among chieftains kept the country weak. In the

The Pamir Mountains are the hub of the world's seven highest ranges.

Relative Humidity and Wind Chill

Statistics for temperatures in a city are not always what they may seem. Feeling hot or cold depends on more than the temperature on a thermometer. On a hot day, the body needs to cool off by releasing water through the skin into the air; and on a cold day, the body needs to bundle up to keep the skin from releasing body heat into the air.

Conditions in the air can make it more difficult to cool off or to stay warm. In the harsh interior of Central Asia, conditions make the summers unbearably hot and the winters bitterly cold. The two main factors that change the body's ability to cope with weather is relative humidity and wind chill. A high *relative humidity* means that the air already has as much water as it can hold. High winds create a *wind chill* that increases the speed at which the body loses heat. Examine these tables and answer the questions about "apparent temperature" and the temperature on the thermometer.

Wind Chill

Wind Speed (mph)	Temperature on a Thermometer (°F)													
	−30	−25	−20	−15	−10	−5	0	5	10	15	20	25	30	35
5	−36	−31	−26	−21	−15	−10	−5	0	7	12	16	21	27	33
10	−58	−52	−46	−40	−34	−27	−15	−15	−9	−3	3	10	16	22
15	−72	−65	−58	−51	−45	−38	−25	−25	−18	−11	−5	2	9	16
20	−81	−74	−67	−60	−53	−46	−31	−31	−24	−17	−10	−3	4	12
25	−88	−81	−74	−66	−59	−51	−36	−36	−29	−22	−15	−7	1	8
30	−93	−86	−79	−71	−64	−56	−41	−41	−33	−25	−18	−10	−2	6
35	−97	−89	−82	−74	−67	−58	−43	−43	−35	−27	−20	−12	−4	4
40	−100	−92	−84	−76	−69	−60	−45	−45	−37	−29	−21	−13	−5	3
45	−102	−93	−85	−78	−70	−62	−46	−46	−38	−30	−22	−14	−6	2

Heat Index

Relative Humidity	Temperature on a Thermometer (°F)										
	70	75	80	85	90	95	100	105	110	115	120
0%	64	69	73	78	83	87	91	95	99	103	107
10%	65	70	75	80	85	90	95	100	105	111	116
20%	66	72	77	82	87	93	99	105	112	120	130
30%	67	73	78	84	90	96	104	113	123	135	148
40%	68	74	79	86	93	101	110	123	137	151	
50%	69	75	81	88	96	107	120	135	150		
60%	70	76	82	90	100	114	132	149			
70%	70	77	85	93	106	124	144				
80%	71	78	86	97	113	136					
90%	71	79	88	102	122						
100%	72	80	91	108							

1. If the thermometer says 80°F, what is the apparent temperature on a morning with 10% humidity? 70% humidity?

2. If the thermometer says 100°F, what is the apparent temperature at noon with 10% humidity? 70% humidity?

3. If the thermometer says 35°F, what is the apparent temperature at night if a light wind blows at 5 mph? a strong wind at 35 mph?

4. If the thermometer says 0°F, what is the apparent temperature if a light wind blows at 5 mph? a strong wind at 35 mph?

💡 Find (a) the most dramatic single increase in temperature due to humidity and (b) the most dramatic single drop in temperature due to wind. Now find the *least* dramatic changes and explain the pattern.

nineteenth century, the growing Russian empire began to push south into Afghanistan and threatened Britain's empire in India, which at that time included Pakistan. The British invaded Afghanistan in 1839 to install a friendly king. But three years of bloody revolt forced the British to withdraw.

Afghanistan became a **buffer state,** a neutral state between two rivals who agree to keep their armies out. But worries about Russia led the British into another futile war (1878-80). Eventually, the British stayed out for good, and the world recognized Afghanistan as a sovereign nation.

Afghanistan was independent but remained weak. From 1978 to 1989, Russia waged a costly and ultimately unsuccessful campaign to set up a Communist dictatorship in Afghanistan. Since then the nation has broken up into warring factions.

A Pass Through Hindu Kush The **Hindu Kush,** Persian for "Hindu Death," is a mountain barrier extending southwest from the Pamirs and across central Afghanistan. It has thirty-four seven-thousand-meter-high peaks. All of them lie in the eastern **Wakhan Corridor,** a narrow panhandle that Russia and Great Britain created to stretch the buffer zone to China.

Most Afghan people live in these central and eastern mountain regions. The **Pushtun** people are predominate. Their domain includes the nation's largest city and capital, **Kabul.** Kabul lies in one of the many mountain valleys of the Hindu Kush. Its small industries include afghans, rugs, and jewelry made from gems mined locally. Afghanistan mines more lapis lazuli than any other nation in the world.

Kabul became important because of the **Khyber Pass,** one hundred miles southeast of the city, which allows easy passage through the Hindu Kush. Great conquerors have passed through this pass, including Genghis Khan and possibly Alexander the Great. A southern extension of the old Silk Road brought goods from India to Samarkand.

Border Regions A semicircle of less rugged land rings the Hindu Kush borders on the north, west, and south. The northern plains support crops and livestock. In the valleys, farmers grow wheat, barley, corn, and cotton. Between the valleys, herders graze sheep and goats for milk, mutton, and wool. Many Tajiks, the other major ethnic group, live in this northern region, which borders

The blue mosque at Mazar-i-Sharif has the tomb of Ali, Muhammad's son-in-law.

Tajikistan. In the southwest lies the Rigestan Desert, Afghanistan's least populous region.

The country's second biggest city, Qandahar, lies at the southern edge of the Hindu Kush, near the border with Pakistan. In 1993, Pushtun students restored law to the city by amputating hands of thieves and by insisting on traditional Islamic morality, including veils for women. The **Taliban** ("seekers") movement moved north toward Kabul and captured the city. Iran accused Pakistan of secretly supporting the rebel group whose goal is to reunite the country into one rigid Islamic state.

SECTION REVIEW

1. What mountains cross into Kyrgyzstan? Tajikistan? Afghanistan?

2. Through what modern nation did the Silk Road pass into China?

3. Which nation speaks a language closer to Iranian than to Turkish?

4. What famous pass links Central Asia with India?

💡 Why has Afghanistan had so much difficulty building a strong nation? Does it have a better chance than Tajikistan or Kyrgyzstan?

REVIEW

Can You Define These Terms?

Turkistan   buffer state

Can You Locate These Natural Features?

Caucasus Mountains	Caspian Depression	Tien Shan	Hindu Kush
Caspian Sea	Kara Kum	Pamirs	Khyber Pass
Aral Sea	Kyzyl-Kum		

Can You Explain the Significance of These People, Places, and Events?

Armenians	Turkic peoples	Avicenna	Pushtun
1988 earthquake	Silk Road	Tashkent	Kabul
Nagorno-Karabakh	Almaty	Samarkand	Taliban
Central Asia	Bukhara	Wakhan Corridor	

How Much Do You Remember?

1. Choose three nations in this chapter and explain how the Russians have influenced their cultures.
2. List all of the nations in Central Asia and the Caucasus that fits each description.
   a. Muslim
   b. Eastern Orthodox Christianity
   c. member of CIS
   d. Russian minority over 25 percent
3. Which term in each list has the least similarity with the other terms?
   a. Kazakhstan, Uzbekistan, Turkmenistan, Turkestan
   b. Kazakhs, Uzbeks, Turkmens, Tajiks
   c. Mary, Bukhara, Aqmola, Samarkand
   d. Pamirs, Tien Shan, Caspian Depression, Hindu Kush
   e. Nagorno-Karabakh, Kyzyl-Kum, Kara Kum, Betpak-Dala
4. Why is the Caspian region likely to become a battleground in the future?
5. What two great challenges hinder economic development in Central Asia?
6. Which group left the longest-lasting impact on Central Asia: Huns, Turkic peoples, Mongols?
7. Why is the cotton industry bad for Central Asia?
8. What countries in this chapter lack major mountains? In what other ways are these countries different from the ones with mountains?
9. Which nations in this chapter have no ethnic groups that represent over 50 percent of the population?

What Do You Think?

1. In what ways has Russian influence been beneficial in the Caucasus and Central Asia?
2. Compare and contrast the cultures of the Caucasus with the cultures of Central Asia.
3. Give reasons that the Caucasus region should be included in each region below.
   a. Europe
   b. Asia
4. What political and economic problems do you foresee in Kazakhstan's future?
5. Why is the Caspian Sea flooding while the Aral Sea is drying up? Is human activity the only culprit?

Cumulative Review

1. Name the seven continents and four oceans. What is the only country that spans two continents?
2. Define primary, secondary, and tertiary industries. What country in Central Eurasia has the most tertiary industries?
3. List the eight culture regions of the world. What culture regions border Central Eurasia?
4. Describe how Russia is typical of countries in Central Eurasia: land features, climate, people, history, economy, and government.
5. Which nations in Central Eurasia once belonged to the Soviet Union? were in the Soviet bloc? never had a Soviet-backed government?

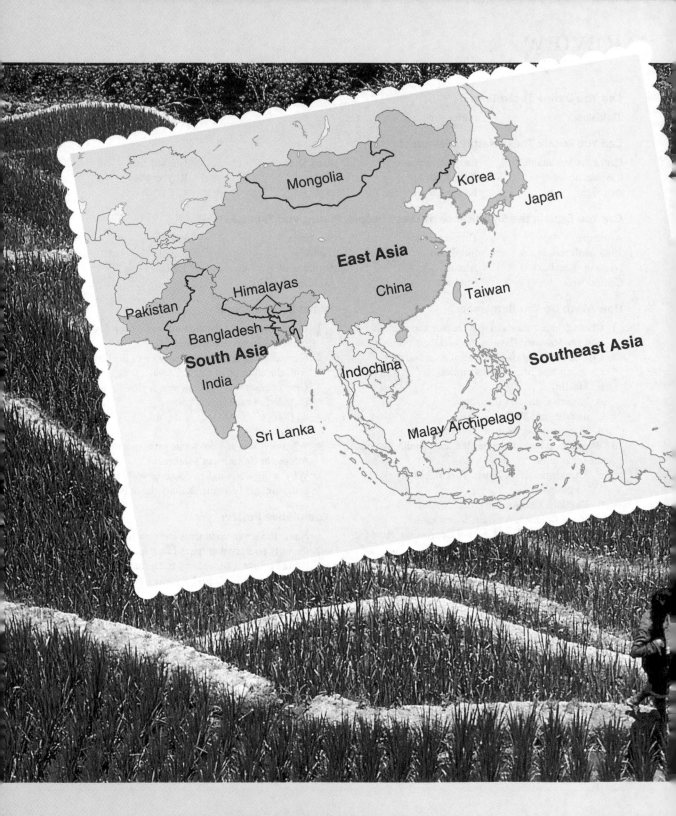

UNIT VII

Asia

CHAPTER 19

SOUTH ASIA

Asia is an exotic region of contrasts between wealth and poverty, high culture and demonic paganism, insurmountable peaks and broad river plains. Mountains and deserts have long isolated Asia from the West, creating distinct differences in culture and history. Because South Asia is severed from the rest of Asia by the mighty wall of the Himalayas on the north and by the Indian Ocean on the south, it is sometimes called a **subcontinent.** It is bigger than a peninsula and smaller than a continent.

The Himalayas dominate the weather system of the subcontinent. They block the cold temperatures to the north because the cold cannot rise over the mountains to spill into South Asia. As the summer heat rises in the south, the resulting low pressure system draws warm, wet air from the Indian Ocean. The winds are called **monsoons;** South Asia has the strongest monsoon winds in the world. The Himalayas cause the airborne water to fall as rain. A reverse monsoon pushes cool dry winds

across the mountains into South Asia to cause a dry season. Some islands escape the dry season because the ocean provides moisture regardless of wind direction.

The monsoon rains begin in June or July and supply the rain needed for agriculture, on which all South Asian countries depend. If the monsoons come late or with too little rain, the plants wither and die. If the rains are early or cause floods, the rice rots. Either way the subcontinent experiences famine since it is largely a subsistence economy.

Since India covers three-fourths of the region, South Asia is also called the Indian subcontinent. The name is appropriate since India's influence is felt throughout the region, and several of the countries were once part of India. Political and religious strife characterize the crowded Indian subcontinent. William Carey (1761-1834) was the first modern missionary to seek to reach these exotic cultures. Carey translated the Bible into many of

South Asia Statistics

COUNTRY	CAPITAL	AREA (SQ. MI.)	POPULATION	NATURAL INCREASE	LIFE EXPECTANCY	LITERACY RATE	PER CAPITA GDP	POP. DENSITY
Bangladesh	Dhaka (Dacca)	55,598	125,340,261	1.9%	56	38%	$1,130	2,200
Bhutan	Thimphu	18,147	1,865,191	2.3%	52	42%	$730	103
India	New Delhi	1,266,595	967,612,804	1.6%	60	52%	$1,500	792
The Maldives	Male	115	280,391	3.5%	67	93%	$1,560	2,438
Nepal	Katmandu	54,362	22,641,061	2.4%	54	28%	$1,200	398
Pakistan	Islamabad	310,403	132,185,299	2.4%	59	38%	$2,100	389
Sri Lanka	Colombo	25,332	18,762,075	1.2%	73	90%	$3,600	740

the region's languages. God motivated Carey to enlarge God's kingdom among the Gentiles from the following Scripture:

Enlarge the place of thy tent, and let them stretch forth the curtains of thine habitations: spare not, lengthen thy cords, and strengthen thy stakes; for thou shalt break forth on the right hand and on the left; and thy seed shall inherit the Gentiles, and make the desolate cities to be inhabited. (Isa. 54:2-3)

INDIA

India is the seventh largest country in the world, and it has the second largest population. The population increases by 1.5 million people every month and is expected to exceed China's population in the twenty-first century. India is often described as the world's largest democracy. India is a federal republic with twenty-five states and six territories. Each state represents at least one of the major languages in India.

Ganges

The **Ganges River** (GAN JEEZ) begins in an ice cave in the Himalayas. It flows southeast more than fifteen hundred miles across north central India before emptying into the Bay of Bengal. The plain along the river covers five states and two territories. The Ganges Plain also extends east up its largest tributary, the Brahmaputra.

The Ganges is very muddy and deposits an estimated nine hundred thousand tons of sediment daily. The wide river supplies much water needed to irrigate India's farms. The Ganges is one of the largest rivers in the world and the most important river in India.

Hinduism   **Hindu** religious traditions direct life in India, which is over 80 percent Hindu. Two of the most sacred things according to Hindu traditions are cattle and the Ganges. India has more cattle than any other nation in the world.

Hindu tradition assigns privileges and responsibilities for different classes of people. Each class, called a **caste,** strictly determines one's social status. A Hindu must fulfill the role of his caste. Brahmins (priests) and warriors occupy the highest castes. Farmers belong to lower castes, and despised occupations are considered so low that they

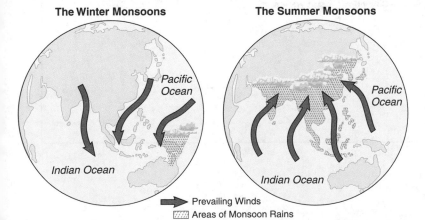

The Winter Monsoons

Pacific Ocean

Indian Ocean

The Summer Monsoons

Pacific Ocean

Indian Ocean

➡ Prevailing Winds
▨ Areas of Monsoon Rains

429

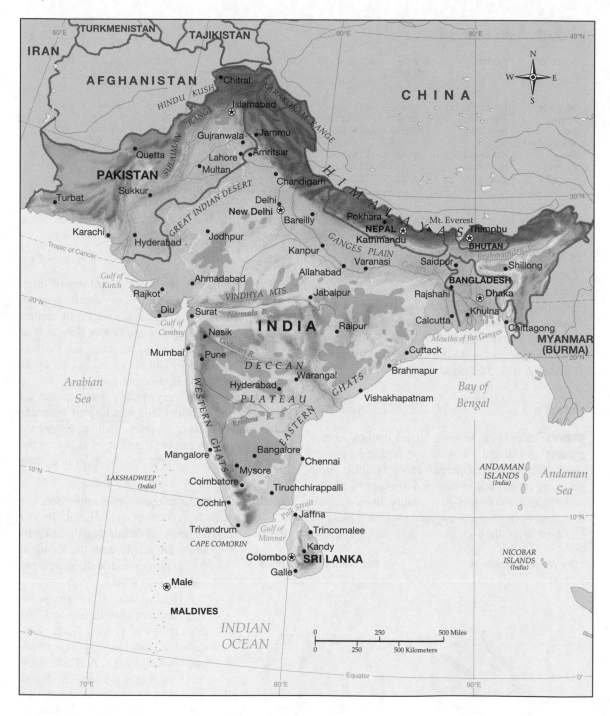

Bathing in the Sacred Ganges

According to Hindu legend, the Ganges River is the goddess Ganga, who took physical form. Hindu temples line the banks of this sacred river, and stairs lead down to the water. Pilgrims believe the holy water cleanses their souls. Many pilgrims also come for healing, and others come to die, hoping to enter paradise immediately. The smoke from cremated bodies rises above the riverbanks of the Ganges. In spite of the filth from this activity and from industry, Hindus use the river water for drinking, cooking, and washing. As a result, diseases such as cholera are common.

The Ganges is one of many rivers that people have worshiped as "the giver of life." The ancient Egyptians worshiped the Nile. Naaman the leper told Elisha that he could wash in the rivers at home rather than the dirty Jordan (II Kings 5:1-15). But the prophet

Ghats *permit bathers to descend into the Ganges River at Varanasi, a city in the province of Uttar Pradesh, India.*

showed him who brings healing—the Lord Almighty, not the waters of any river. Christ later revealed to the Samaritan woman that He is the living water, who alone offers everlasting life (John 4:14).

---

are beneath caste. They are called "untouchables." Today castes are divided into hundreds of subcastes, called *jatis*. A Hindu is born into the *jati* of his parents, and he must marry someone from that *jati*. He must also hold an appropriate occupation and can never change his caste.

Hindu beliefs include **reincarnation,** the idea that every person follows an endless cycle of birth, death, and rebirth. Hindus believe that when they die, they will be reborn into another life. A Hindu accepts the caste into which he is born as the reward or punishment for his works in his past lives, and he tries to do good works so that his future lives will be better. The works determine whether his merits are good or bad. This merit is called **karma.** If a Hindu behaves well in this life, he thinks that he may be reborn as a Brahmin or a rich man because of his good karma. If he does not live as he should in this life, his bad karma will cause him to be reborn into a lower caste, as an untouchable, or even as an animal.

Ultimately the Hindu hopes to be so good that he will escape reincarnation and instead become a part of Brahman, the world spirit. This world spirit is not personal but rather the force energizing the entire physical world. The view that God is nothing more than the life force throughout the world is called *pantheism.* The Bible proves that God existed before He created the universe. He is not limited to it. God transcends creation, yet He has revealed Himself as a personal God who loves man.

Other Hindu beliefs vary greatly because there are many holy books and no single great founder or teacher. Some Hindus believe in one god, some in many. Many **gurus** (holy men) attract followers to their own teachings. Hindus try to escape reincarnation by prayers, by seeking spiritual wisdom from gurus, by helping others, or by enduring strict discipline and self-denial (asceticism). These are the good works that Hindus hope will save them.

God's Word clearly teaches that man has only one life on earth but that after death he will live eternally in heaven or in hell. If we reject the salvation offered through Jesus Christ, we will suffer eternally in hell. If we accept Christ, we will live forever with Him in heaven. We are not trapped in an endless cycle of reincarnation. Regardless of caste, no matter how rich or poor, we all have the opportunity to find salvation in Jesus Christ.

And as it is appointed unto men once to die, but after this the judgment: so Christ was once offered to bear the sins of many; and unto them that look for him shall he appear the second time without sin unto salvation. (Heb. 9:27-28)

Life on the Plains   The Ganges Plain is the most populous region of India. With over 110 million people, Uttar Pradesh is the most populous state in India and contains about one-half of the course of the Ganges, including its headwaters in the Himalayas. The state's major crop is sugar cane; India is the world's leading producer of sugar cane. India also leads the world in cashews, pulses, and sesame seeds.

Three-fourths of India's vast population live in small towns or rural villages. Uttar Pradesh is no exception. The largest city, Kanpur, has only 1.5 million people—not many people for such a populous state. Many make their living by subsistence agriculture or in cottage industries, making simple products in their homes. During the Green Revolution, India's government provided fertilizers, pesticides, and better seed to small farms in order to improve the harvest. India now produces enough rice to feed itself, except in years that monsoon variations cause crop failures.

Hindi is the leading language of Uttar Pradesh. Since it is the most used language along the Ganges (the largest population center), it became the national language. However, fewer than one-half of the people know Hindi; fourteen other major languages and hundreds of minor languages are spoken. Urdu is another common language of the area and is similar to Hindi.

Two states downstream from Uttar Pradesh contain the rest of the Ganges. The more important state is West Bengal, where Bengali is the major language. Its main city near the mouth of the Ganges, **Calcutta,** houses eleven million people, making it the second largest city in India. West Bengal produces rice and jute. India produces almost one-half of the world's jute (fibrous plant used for rope and burlap cloth), making it by far the leading producer. More importantly, India produces about one-fifth of the world's rice, making it the second largest producer of that staple crop.

The **Brahmaputra River** (BRAH muh POO truh) provides water and irrigation for the state of Assam in northeastern India. Assamese is the main language in this state. The main product of the region is tea. India is the world's leading producer of tea.

The Jumna River is another important tributary of the Ganges in the plains. This river begins west of the Ganges in the Himalayas of Uttar Pradesh but then forms the boundary between Uttar Pradesh

Sacred Cows

Cattle roam freely through India's villages and city streets, eating whatever they wish. Hindus allow the animals complete freedom because they are believed to be the reincarnation of past lives. Hindus refuse to eat beef to avoid accidentally eating a grandfather in his present incarnation.

Hindus consider cattle especially sacred, the symbol of all life. They pull plows, transport carts, and supply milk and butter. Manure serves as fuel for cooking and as building material for village homes. To show thanks, Indians occasionally leave small offerings of food for the cows. Cattle in India have multiplied to over 250 million (twice the number in the United States). Most are too scrawny too serve as beef cattle, even if the Hindus did eat meat.

A sacred cow wanders at will in the streets of Jaipur, a city in the province of Rajasthan, India.

Rupees and Rajas

Kaisa hae aap. If you lived in India, your money would be in *rupees.* What would you buy with your rupees? Western items are readily available in the cities. You could even go to the McDonald's that recently opened in New Delhi. One thing would be different about this restaurant, though. It is the first McDonald's franchise with no beef on the menu. The Maharaja Mac has two "all-mutton" patties!

While Western clothes are popular, every wardrobe includes some traditional Indian garments as well. Indian clothing tends to be brightly colored and lightweight. Indians frequently wrap lengths of cloth between their legs to make *dhotis,* or loincloths. Loose-fitting trousers are called *pajamas* and have become popular in English-speaking lands as bedtime garments. Indians also wrap cloth into hats called *turbans.*

Ladies drape lengths of cloth around them to form a long dress called a *sari.* The loose end hangs over the shoulder. Expensive saris are made of silk with borders of pure gold thread. In some regions women wear veils, bracelets, and earrings. Women also adorn themselves with a *kumkum,* a red or black powder dot in the middle of the forehead.

Several generations usually eat and sleep under one roof, especially in the villages. As a sign of respect to an elder, you would perform a *namaskar,* touching the elder's feet

Indian women wear traditional saris, kumkums, and jewelry.

Indian children from Rajasthan province

with your fingers. Elders usually arrange the marriages of children, and wives are expected to run the household and to serve their husbands. At one time, young girls were forced to become brides, and widows were burned on the funeral pyres of their husbands in a practice known as *suttee.* These barbaric practices have been outlawed and are not practiced openly today.

Meals are an important daily ritual. The head woman serves the food and eats only after everyone else is done. Most Indians eat meals with their fingers. The typical meal includes either rice or wheat breads, depending on where you are from. No meal would be complete without *dhal,* a porridge made from pulse (vegetables that come from seed pods such as peas, beans, and lentils). You may not be excited about such a meal, but Daniel preferred it to the king's meat (Dan. 1:12). Hindus do not eat beef, but many eat chicken and lamb. *Curries* are spicy sauces made with powdered curry leaves. India's sauces can be even hotter than Mexican dishes. Other dishes include mangoes, yogurts, and other cool or sweet desserts.

Indians enjoy good poetry and music. In fact, they have about five hundred musical instruments. The oldest instruments are gongs and drums. Western audiences are familiar with the twenty-stringed *sitar,* once used by court poets and today played at concerts across Europe and the United States.

Most Indian villagers would consider the average American visitor to be as rich as a *raja* (prince). But you must be careful how you spend your money in the marketplace. You might be buying one of the millions of Indian gods. For instance, a carving of a man riding a white elephant is likely to be the god Indra. *Phir Daekna.*

Vishnu, the preserver, and many-armed Shiva, the destroyer, are the two principal idols in Hinduism. The third member of this trinity is Brahma, the creator, who is not usually depicted.

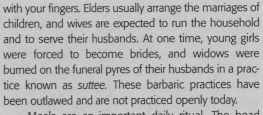

Taj Mahal

Shah Jahan became emperor of India in 1628 at the age of thirty-six. Tragedy struck the next year. His favorite wife, who had been devoted to him through eighteen years of marriage, died in childbirth. He grieved for two years after her sudden death and spent twenty-two years building a tomb in her honor. The wife's name was Mumtaz Mahal, "Chosen of the Palace." Her monument is known by the simple abbreviation Taj Mahal. Visitors to the city of Agra, in the state of Uttar Pradesh, still marvel at the Taj Mahal's beautiful lines and curves.

Twenty thousand laborers were required to quarry the marble from two hundred miles away and to raise the monument. The tomb extends 186 feet on each side, and archways rise as high as 109 feet. A great onion-shaped dome in the center adds another 120 feet. The white marble is inlaid with forty-three kinds of precious stones, including sapphires, jade, crystal, and diamonds. Quotations from the Koran, carved in black

Many would call the Taj Mahal the most beautiful building in the world.

marble, decorate the tomb. The tomb rests on an even larger red sandstone platform. Prayer towers, called minarets, stand at each corner of the platform. The garden setting and large pools add to the beauty and serenity of the Taj Mahal.

The shah was later overthrown by his son and buried beside his wife. After the collapse of the Moghul Empire, robbers ransacked the Taj Mahal's treasures, but it remains a symbol of undying love.

and the central state of Haryana. **Delhi,** India's third largest city with nine million people, stands on the Jumna River between Uttar Pradesh and Haryana. The city is a major manufacturing center. Its suburb, New Delhi, is the national capital. These two cities are not part of any state but lie in the separate capital territory of Delhi.

SECTION REVIEW

1. What is the major religion of India?
2. What is reincarnation?
3. Name two major products of the Ganges Plain.
4. What is the largest city on the plain?
5. What river flows through the plain to the northeast?
- Refute at least three key Hindu doctrines with Scripture.

Deccan

India's triangular-shaped peninsula extends southward toward the Indian Ocean. The peninsula consists of a high plateau called the **Deccan.** The

Deccan includes eight states, parts of two others, and three territories.

West Side The Deccan is bounded on the west by the Arabian Sea. The coast has a very narrow coastal strip. The southern half of this coast is called the Malabar Coast. Beyond, the highland barrier called the Western Ghats rises to the Deccan.

Bombay (now called Mumbai) is located on the northern half of the coast. With 12.5 million people, Bombay is the largest city in India and is the capital and major manufacturing center of the state of Maharashtra. Cotton is the major crop in this state; India is the world's third largest producer of cotton. Marathi is the state's primary language. About two hundred thousand *Parsees* (followers of Persian Zoroastrianism) live around Bombay as well.

Jainism is another religion of the region with even more rigorous practices than Hinduism. For instance, Jains cannot kill any living creature and must not eat meat. Some Jains wear cloths over

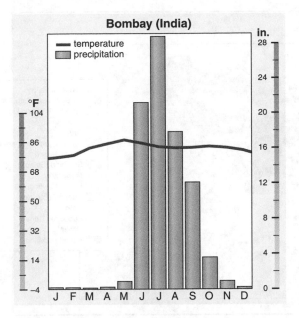

Bombay (India)

temperature
precipitation

°F
104
86
68
50
32
14
-4

J F M A M J J A S O N D

in.
28
24
20
16
12
8
4
0

Inland, the rain forest changes abruptly to a dry climate. From over 120 inches annually at Mangalore on the Malabar Coast, the rainfall diminishes to less than 40 inches at Bangalore, a manufacturing city of over four million and the only inland capital of the four west Deccan states. Much of the Deccan has a dry climate. Scattered trees punctuate the tall grasses of these savannas. Though semiarid, the plateau's altitudes keep the temperatures cooler than those in the tropical lowlands.

East Side The east half of the Deccan Plateau also rises in a highland barrier, called the Eastern Ghats. The coastal plain is somewhat wider than the west, and its coast on the Bay of Bengal is called the Coromandel Coast. All the major rivers of the plateau flow to this coast. Three states cover the coast, and India's largest state covers most of the northern plateau. Jabalpur and Raipur are two major towns in the huge state of Madhya Pradesh.

The Deccan has most of India's mineral resources. The largest of several deposits of iron ore and coal are in the northeast portion of the plateau. Some iron ore is exported, but India does produce

their mouths to avoid accidentally inhaling and killing an insect. Today there are about 2.5 million Jains in India. The religion started about 500 B.C. near the Ganges east of Varanasi, but today most Jains live on the west coast.

The Malabar Coast has an interesting heritage. The unique Christian sect called the St. Thomas Christians live here. Prawns are the major seafood catch, and the tropical coast makes India the world's leading producer of mangoes and bananas.

Street market in Bombay, India

Meenakshi Temple

The Meenakshi Temple is one of the most popular destinations of Hindu pilgrims. It is dedicated to the Hindu god Shiva, Lord Sundareshwara, and a fabled princess named Meenakshi. The original temple was founded in the twelfth century, but many additions were made later, including the Hall of a Thousand Pillars. In all, the temple has seven grand gateways, three of them inside the later additions. The elaborate gateways rise up to two hundred feet. A jumble of humans, gods, and goddesses are sculpted on the gateways and on the thousand pillars.

Meenakshi Temple is located in the southern Indian city of Madurai. Hindu pilgrims flock to the city in January or February for the Teppam Festival, when the images of Lord Sundareshwara and Princess Meenakshi are taken from the temple and displayed on floats on a nearby manmade lake.

Let's Go Exploring

1. Find the mountainous region in the center of Asia. What climate is common just south of these mountains? What climate is common just north of these mountains?

2. How many climate regions does India have? What is most common in the northeast? the west? the south?

3. What climate is most common on the islands of Southeast Asia?

4. What country has the largest area with a moderate climate? What country is second largest?

Compare and contrast the climate of China and the United States.

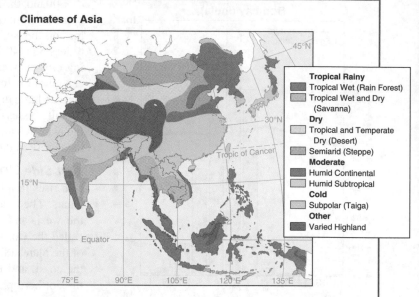

Climates of Asia

Tropical Rainy
Tropical Wet (Rain Forest)
Tropical Wet and Dry (Savanna)
Dry
Tropical and Temperate Dry (Desert)
Semiarid (Steppe)
Moderate
Humid Continental
Humid Subtropical
Cold
Subpolar (Taiga)
Other
Varied Highland

its own iron and steel using the coal resources to fuel the steel mills. India also mines large deposits of bauxite, manganese, and mica from this part of the plateau. India imports much of its petroleum.

Madras, India's fourth largest city, has over five million people. It is a famous source of spices such as turmeric and cardamon. Together with Bombay and Calcutta, it was a center of the British East India Company from its inception in 1600. Expanding from these centers, the company gained control of most of India by 1763 and turned over its rule to the British government in 1858.

Britain increased Indian representation in the government as compensation for India's help in World War I. The minor changes caused unrest. The most famous leader in these protests was **Mahatma Gandhi,** the Father of the Nation. He led the people in a policy of nonviolent protests, or **satyagraha,** encouraging the people to destroy British power simply by making their own goods rather than trading for them. One of his most famous marches was a march to the sea in 1930 to protest a salt tax. The protest resulted in over sixty thousand imprisonments. Gandhi was imprisoned many times. India joined the British in World War II as the Japanese conquered

Burma and then invaded eastern India. Britain granted full independence in 1947. The long British occupation spread English among the educated, and English is still used for administrative purposes.

Pondicherry, south of Madras, is the capital of a territory consisting of four small coastal settlements that belonged to France during the British occupation. India did not obtain the territory from France until 1954.

The short dark-skinned people of southern India are believed to have arrived before 1500 B.C. This group is called **Dravidians.** The taller and

India's British heritage is obvious in the distinctive dress of Indian soldiers.

lighter-skinned Aryans moved into northern India during the following century and introduced the caste system to reinforce their superiority.

Disputed Border Regions

India's border regions lie at the extreme edges adjacent to other nations. Some of these regions are remote wilderness areas. The cultures of these areas show influence from India's neighbor nations, especially in religious worship.

Uniting such a mixed bag of religions and peoples into one nation has not been easy, and religious violence has racked the nation from its birth. A Hindu assassinated Mahatma Gandhi in 1948 because Gandhi wanted to make peace with the Muslims in India. Hoping to stop the killing, the first prime minister, Jawaharlal Nehru, a close associate of Gandhi, established a "secular" federal republic in 1949. But religious fighting has only increased. Since 1984, a radical Hindu party

has been trying to replace the secular state with a pure Hindu kingdom, or *Hinduvita*. This political party, the Bhratiya Janata Party (BJP), won more seats than any other in 1996. For the first time since India's independence, the Congress Party of Nehru failed to win the most votes.

Western Border   Three distinctive states lie along the western border. People in the coastal border state of Gujarat speak Gujarati. The state capital, Ahmadabad, is a manufacturing center with two million people. To the south, the Kathiawar Peninsula sticks into the ocean. The peninsula produces one-third of the world's peanuts, making India the leading producer of peanuts worldwide. West of the peninsula is a great salt marsh called the Rann of Kutch.

The **Thar** or Great Indian Desert covers the next state to the north. Other than palm trees near springs, only small desert plants will grow without irrigation here. Rajasthan, like many Indian states,

Geographer's Corner

Using Outside Resources

A few facts about the world never change. Mount Everest will probably be standing when Christ returns. But dams change the flow of rivers, wars erase cities, and even mountains "change" heights with each new topographical survey.

Yet some regions experience more changes than others. By now you have learned some likely places for the next new island or new volcano. You should also have learned some likely places for the next changes in governments and national boundaries. While any government can change overnight, some countries are more unstable than others. The United States, for example, will probably remain a constitutional republic during your lifetime. But other places, such as the Indian subcontinent, may experience changes this year. An assassination, civil war, or even nuclear war could strike at any moment. Your goal this year in geography class is to gather information that will help you to understand such changes.

You are a citizen of one of the most influential countries in the world, which stations soldiers and diplomats around the world. As a citizen, you have a responsibility to understand changing world events. Here are four projects that should help you to see the value of studying geography.

1. Find any newspaper article on a country discussed in this chapter. Underline every geographic location mentioned in the article.

2. Find any magazine article on India. Explain what has changed since this textbook was written.

3. Listen to news reports until you hear a story about the Indian subcontinent. Give a brief summary of the report: the media you listened to, the time you heard it, and the topic.

☿ Find a report about U.S. activity in the Indian subcontinent. Summarize the issues at stake, the official U.S. position, and your position as a Christian.

is also organized around its principal language, Rajasthani.

The state of **Punjab,** north of the Thar, contains the Punjab Plains. These plains cross into India from Northeast Pakistan, and extend to meet the Ganges Plain. The Sutlej River, a tributary of the Indus River in Pakistan, drains the plains. Most people speak Punjabi and worship as Sikhs. Sikhs are followers of Guru Nanak (1469-1539), who sought to reconcile Islam with Hinduism. Sikhs now number over ten million (about 2 percent of India's population). The most sacred site of **Sikhism** is the Golden Temple in Amritsar.

Some Sikhs have rebelled against India hoping to restore their own independent nation called Khalistan. In 1984, they assassinated India's prime minister, Indira Gandhi. Their terrorism has cost twenty-five thousand lives and caused a decade of fear. The Muslims conquered and ruled India from about 1200 to 1700. The Muslims brought their religion, Islam, with them. Today, over 10 percent of India's people are Muslim, mostly in Kashmir.

Eastern Hills South of the Brahmaputra lie five of the seven smallest states in all of India. These states are small in both area and population.

The Golden Temple in Amritsar, India

This is the only region in India with a Christian majority. Unlike the St. Thomas Christians, these Christians converted after the days of William Carey, a missionary to Calcutta who translated the Bible into Hindi, Assamese, and many other languages of India. India has over ten million Christians (about 2 percent of the total population).

The wet and dry monsoons create a humid subtropical climate. Instead of rain forests, maple, walnut, birch, and other deciduous trees grow in the hills along with some tropical fruit trees and palms.

St. Thomas Christians

According to tradition, the apostle Thomas came to India in A.D. 50 and established several churches on India's west coast before being martyred. European explorers of the fifteenth century were surprised to find groups of Christians, called the St. Thomas Christians, in India. Over the years, however, these churches had become bound by ritual and tradition with no real understanding of the gospel. Most of the St. Thomas Christians joined the Roman Catholic Church, but some remained independent. In the nineteenth century, one group of St. Thomas Christians came under the influence of Protestant missionaries. They broke with their ritualistic church and formed the Mar Thoma Church, a more Protestant group. All combined, the members in the St. Thomas churches number about two million.

Religions of Asia

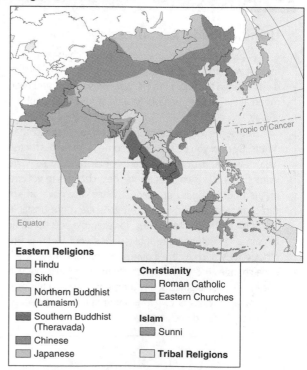

Eastern Religions
- Hindu
- Sikh
- Northern Buddhist (Lamaism)
- Southern Buddhist (Theravada)
- Chinese
- Japanese

Christianity
- Roman Catholic
- Eastern Churches

Islam
- Sunni

Tribal Religions

However, many of the trees of the region have been cut for fuel and other needs.

Northern Himalayas The Himalayas follow the border of China from Pakistan to Burma. Many of India's Himalayan peoples practice the Lamaistic form of Buddhism common in neighboring Nepal and Tibet. This is India's only region with a Buddhist majority, which is somewhat surprising since Buddhism began near the Ganges. Besides the disputed region of Kashmir, the Himalayas cover three widely separated states of India.

In north India, between Kashmir and Nepal, the Himalayas cover an entire state and part of another. Uttar Pradesh contains some fifteen seven-thousand-meter peaks, including Kamet and Nanda Devi. **Sikkim,** India's second smallest state, between Nepal and Bhutan, contains about one dozen seven-thousand-meter peaks. Kanchenjunga (28,208 ft.), the third highest mountain in the world, forms part of Sikkim's border with Nepal.

◎ SECTION REVIEW

1. What is the largest city in India?
2. What European country controlled India for nearly two hundred years?
3. What are the most important products from the Deccan?
4. What desert region is at the border with Pakistan?
5. Name two religious groups in border states and tell where they live.

💡 What natural barriers make India a distinct and separate subcontinent?

SEPARATED FROM INDIA

The histories of Pakistan and Bangladesh are very closely tied to that of India because these lands were a part of India until 1947. Britain offered independence to India if it could decide on a system of government. Since Hindu and Muslim conflicts prohibited agreement, Britain separated the main Muslim regions from Hindu India to form the nation of Pakistan. One-half million people died in the conflict that followed, as Muslims and Hindus fled to their respective countries.

Pakistan consisted of two parts. Both parts were Muslim, but they lay one thousand miles apart. The capital and government resided in West Pakistan, but the majority of the people lived in East Pakistan. Communications were difficult, and the people felt little unity with those in the other part of the land. The awkward situation finally prompted East Pakistan to seek independence. With help from India, East Pakistan became the independent country of Bangladesh in 1971. Since that time West Pakistan has become simply Pakistan.

Pakistan

Pakistan is sometimes included as a part of the Middle East because of its dry climate and Muslim culture. Indeed, about 98 percent of all Pakistanis are Muslims. Its relations with Hindu India remain tense. A prime minister governs Pakistan's four provinces and the Pakistani portion of Kashmir territory. The national language is Urdu, but only 10 percent of the people speak this language.

Indus Valley The **Indus River** valley forms the major part of Pakistan. Flowing from the mountainous north, the river waters a very dry region. Only those areas that can be watered from the river are suitable for agriculture. The remaining land east of the river is part of the Thar Desert along the border with India. Most Pakistanis live in the two provinces along the river and its tributaries.

The province of Punjab contains Pakistan's portion of the Punjab Plains. The province includes Islamabad, Lahore, Multan, and surrounding regions. People of this area speak Punjabi, and they control the government, economy, and military. Pakistan built a new capital, Islamabad, which has about one-third of a million people. The region supports wheat and cotton crops. Lahore, the provincial capital, is the second largest city in the nation with 3.5 million people.

To the south, the river flows through the province of Sind. The delta at the mouth of the Indus

A Pakistani man harvests wheat by hand in an irrigated field southeast of Islamabad.

supports large rice crops. Karachi, west of the delta, is the provincial capital and the nation's leading port. With over seven million people, it is also the largest city. Most of the people speak Sindhi. The province extends north beyond Hyderabad and Sukkur. These areas have major natural gas deposits.

About fifty miles downstream from Sukkur lies a ruined city now known as **Mohenjo-Daro.** The ancient civilization that flourished here from 2500 to 1700 B.C. was one of the earliest on earth.

Remote Regions In some nations, the remote areas offer important natural resources. Unfortunately for Pakistan, even these regions have only small deposits of coal and petroleum. Most of the people herd sheep or goats.

The largest province, **Baluchistan,** is also the least populated. Elevations on this large plateau reach over eight thousand feet and give some relief

Ruins of Mohenjo-Daro, Pakistan

from tropical heat. However, it is so arid that there is little plant life. Many of the people are nomads and speak Baluchi. They lead their sheep or goats from one oasis to the next. The large province includes all of the coast west of Karachi and north to the capital, Quetta, and beyond.

The last province is the North-West Frontier Province. The people of the area are called Pushtuns. They speak Pashto and live in the mountain valleys where precipitation is adequate. The capital, Peshawar, is south of Chitral, and is just east of Khyber Pass. This pass is the famous route from Afghanistan, traveled by many Afghan refugees who fled after Russia invaded Afghanistan in the 1980s.

Bangladesh

The prospects for the little country of Bangladesh seem even more bleak than for Pakistan. Over one hundred million people live in this land that is about the size of Alabama. **Bengali** is the official language of this crowded country. The population density for the country is over two thousand people per square mile. Bangladesh is usually considered the most densely populated nation in the world, even though some microstates have a greater density.

The Bay of Bengal dominates the nation. Both the country itself and the language take their name from this bay. As the bay narrows, it funnels the winds and waves onto the lowlands of the Ganges delta. Besides the monsoons, the weather includes frequent cyclones called **typhoons** and destructive tidal waves called **tsunamis.**

Living conditions are terrible. Since two-thirds of the people rely on agriculture for their livelihood, the limited farmland and destructive weather patterns cripple the country. Rice and jute are the main crops, but production is minimal. They cannot afford to import food, so they depend on millions of tons of food donated by other nations to avert famines. With little hope for agricultural improvement and few industries, Bangladesh appears to be trapped in poverty.

THE HIMALAYAS

Asia contains the greatest mountains on the earth. The highest mountain outside of Asia is only a six-thousand-meter peak—Aconcagua (22,834 ft. or 6,960 m) in the Andes of South America. Asia has so many mountains between six-thousand and seven-thousand-meters high that a simple list would take up a whole book. The two most famous six-thousand-meter peaks are Ama Dablam (22,350 ft.), a fang-shaped peak in Nepal, and Mt. Kailas (22,027 ft.), the source of the Brahmaputra and Indus Rivers in Tibet. Asia has all 314 of the world's seven-thousand-meter peaks.

The *Himalayan Mountain System* forms the great mountain barrier that runs fifteen hundred miles along the south border of China. It is the only mountain barrier in the world with peaks exceeding eight thousand meters. There are fourteen of these extremely high peaks. These facts make the Himalayas the highest and most rugged mountain barrier in the world. Many of its seven-thousand-meter peaks have never been climbed.

The Indus and Brahmaputra River valleys divide the Himalayan system into three distinct ranges. North of the Brahmaputra in China is the Trans-Himalaya, which contains three seven-thousand-meter peaks. West of the Indus River is the **Karakoram,** which extends three hundred miles across Kashmir to the Pamir Knot. With 113 seven-thousand-meter peaks and 4 eight-thousand-meter peaks in this small area, it is the most rugged range in the world. Its ruggedness is aptly displayed at K2 (28,250 ft.), the second highest mountain in the world and perhaps the most dangerous for climbers.

The **Himalayas** proper extend twelve hundred miles from the Indus River to the great eastern curve of the Brahmaputra River. The Karakoram and Trans-Himalaya are not technically part of the range. The name *Himalaya* is Sanskrit for "House of Snow." The name is appropriate for the greatest mountain range on earth. It includes **Mt. Everest** (29,028 ft.), the highest mountain in the world. An equivalent height could be obtained by stacking the Appalachian Mountains on top of the Andes.

The Himalayas also boast most of the world's highest mountains. The 150 seven-thousand-meter peaks and 10 eight-thousand-meter peaks far exceed the totals for any other range including the Karakoram. On Nanga Parbat (26,660 ft.), in the western Himalaya of Kashmir, one side rises 14,700 feet from its base. This side, called the Rupal Face, is the highest rock wall in the world.

Nepal, the World's Highest Nation

Nepal is a monarchy with its capital at Kathmandu. The king is the head of state and commander in chief of the army. At one time he was an absolute monarch, but he gave in to popular demands for multiparty elections in 1991.

The national language is Nepali, but one-half of the people speak it as a second language. Fifty other languages are used in various parts of the nation. Less than one-third of the population can read. Like surrounding nations, life expectancy is in the fifties, and the people are poor. Many suffer from cholera, leprosy, and tuberculosis.

Highlands Nepal has most of the eight-thousand-meter peaks of the Himalayas. Kanchenjunga, the most easterly of these fourteen peaks, is on the eastern border with India. Four others stand on the border with China, including Mt. Everest. Three others are

441

completely within Nepal, including the first one ever climbed, Annapurna.

Since the timber line is at about twelve thousand feet, even the lower peaks rise into the alpine zone, while the highest enter the permanent ice zone. The few people that live in the mountains raise sheep and yaks, which graze on the mosses and grasses.

The **Sherpas** have earned worldwide fame for their strength and endurance in these mountains. Climbing parties from all nations hire the men as porters to carry heavy loads up to the higher camps. Nepal has about 150,000 tourists every year that come to see the Himalayas, many of whom try to climb one of the high peaks.

On May 29, 1953, Edmund Hillary and Tenzing Norgay did what no other human had ever done—they stood on the summit of the world's highest mountain, Mount Everest, at 29,028 feet. Mount Everest is the peak in the background.

Habitable Lands South of the Himalayas is a strip of hills and valleys that are high enough to remain cool, but low enough to be forested. Along the border with India is the Tarai, a region of tropical

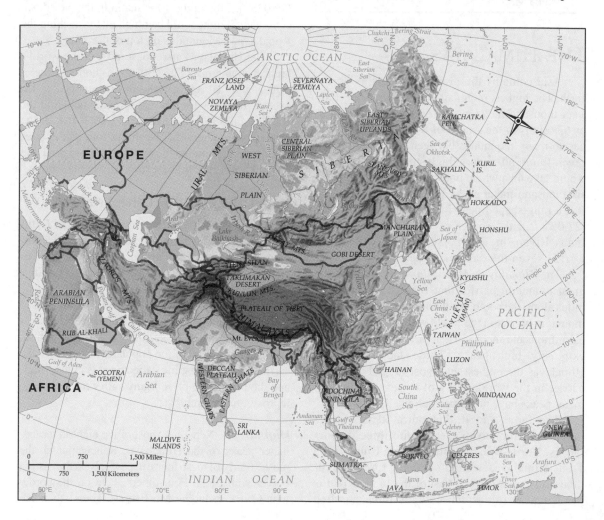

Population Density of Asia

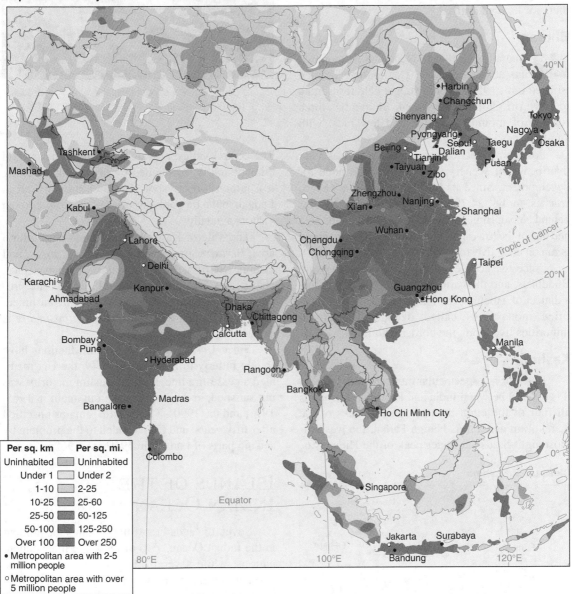

Per sq. km		Per sq. mi.
Uninhabited		Uninhabited
Under 1		Under 2
1-10		2-25
10-25		25-60
25-50		60-125
50-100		125-250
Over 100		Over 250

• Metropolitan area with 2-5 million people

○ Metropolitan area with over 5 million people

lowlands (only 150 feet in elevation). Crocodiles, elephants, and tigers roam the Tarai. Farmers raise wheat in the hills and sugar cane and tobacco in the Tarai. Corn and rice grow in both regions. Ninety percent of Nepalese people are farmers.

Nepal's peoples are a mixture of Tibetans and Indians. Nepal's official religion is Hinduism, but it is mixed with many Buddhist elements. Buddhism is as strong as Hindu teaching, but the distinctions become blurred. Some Indians practice polygamy, while some Tibetans practice *polyandry,* in which a woman marries multiple husbands.

The **Gurkhas** are another unique people group that are famed for strength. Impressed by their

443

fighting abilities, Great Britain hires Gurkha soldiers for its own army.

Bhutan

Bhutan is similar to Nepal but its monarch has absolute power. The nation remained isolated until 1959, when it sought help from India to stave off China. Like Nepal, Bhutan has three regions of mountains, hills, and lowlands, with similar crops and living conditions.

Possessing practically no natural resources other than beautiful scenery, Bhutan has little hope for development. Since its highest peak, Kula Kangri, reaches "only" 24,783 feet, even tourism lags far behind Nepal. Bhutan has the lowest GDP in the area and one of the lowest in the world. The little economy is run on coal, livestock, and postage stamps.

Since the people are mostly Tibetan, they are Buddhists, and the national language is Dzongkha, a dialect of Tibetan. The lamas (monks) live in fortified monasteries called **dzongs.** The Hindu minorities live along the border with India.

Kashmir

Kashmir is a spectacular mountain territory, but it is divided between India and Pakistan. It contains all four of the eight-thousand-meter peaks of the Karakoram as well as Nanga Parbat, the westernmost eight-thousand-meter peak of the Himalayas.

Close-up of Kashmir

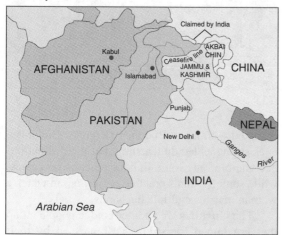

Tongsa Dzong is the dominant feature on the Tongsa River valley, a central valley in Bhutan. Like other dzongs, the fortified monastery is a local cultural center.

The central valley, or Vale of Kashmir, has a mild climate and is surrounded by high peaks, making it a famous scenic spot. The area around Leh in Ladakh in the far north permits only a dozen foreign visitors annually.

The Vale of Kashmir is the main agricultural area. Farmers grow corn, rice, grapes, roses, and jasmine. Saffron, the world's most expensive spice, also comes from the area. Wool and silk are produced here, some of which is woven into cashmere shawls, rugs, and carpets. The name *cashmere* is derived from the region, Kashmir.

Since 1947, Hindu and Muslim factions have fought bitterly in Kashmir. In 1949, the UN mediated a cease-fire line, but the Muslim majority was not satisfied, and fighting broke out again in 1965, 1971, and the 1990s. The dispute remains unsettled after fifty years, and China added to the problem by seizing parts of Ladakh in 1959 and 1962.

ISLANDS OF THE INDIAN OCEAN

Several islands lie off the Indian subcontinent in the Indian Ocean. Two of these are independent nations, while several others are territories. The two nations are the only South Asian nations with normal life expectancy and high literacy rates.

Bengal tigers roam the forests from Pakistan to Bangladesh, but only India has established sanctuaries for this endangered animal.

Sri Lanka, the "Resplendent Isle"

 The island country of Sri Lanka (SREE LAHNG-kuh) lies twenty miles off the southeast coast of India. Mountains rise over eight thousand feet in the southern portion of the large island, and plains cover the rest of the island. The climate is tropical, and the natural vegetation is rain forest. Rice and coconuts are the two major food crops of Sri Lanka. Plantations in the south produce the main exports of tea and rubber. Sri Lanka's tea is world famous, and its mines produce rubies and sapphires.

Sinhalese people from northern India settled on the northern plains of Sri Lanka about 400 B.C. and spread their Buddhism across the island. Today they make up about three-fourths of the population. Tamils from southern India began arriving three hundred years later. These Hindus finally won the northern Jaffna peninsula from the Buddhists and comprise almost one-fifth of the island's population. Both Sinhala and Tamil are official languages, but strife continues over political, economic, and religious issues. The government has failed to stop the Tamil terrorists, who demand independence. At least fifty thousand people died in the recent civil war.

Other groups have also influenced the island's history. Arabs came in the eighth century, trading for cinnamon, and left descendants called Moors (now 7 percent of the population). The Portuguese arrived in 1505, but the Dutch took over these coastal claims in the next century. The few remaining **Burghers** descended from Dutchmen who married Sri Lankans. The British came in the 1790s and made Sri Lanka (then called Ceylon) a crown colony in 1802. In 1815, Britain conquered the Sinhalese mountain kingdom of Kandy, thus uniting the island for the first time. Britain granted independence to Ceylon in 1948. The new nation changed its name to Sri Lanka in 1972.

A Buddhist temple in Sri Lanka

Walking Trees?

The banyan is a very large and interesting tree found in South Asia. The trees grow from the top down. Branches send out roots through the air until they reach the ground. Each root thickens into a new trunk and sends out more branches, which in turn grow roots. Each root becomes a new leg as the tree grows and expands across the countryside. Roots that grow down through the air are called *aerial roots*.

As the tree grows, it begins to look like a whole forest. The largest banyan tree has 350 large trunks and three thousand smaller ones. This record tree is in Sri Lanka.

Maldives

The Maldives is the smallest nation in Asia. Its twelve hundred coral islands sprinkle the sea southwest of India over a region 475 miles long and 80 miles wide. About 210 islands are inhabited. The government-controlled fishing industry dominates the economy. It trades its bonito and tuna harvests with India and Sri Lanka.

Almost all the people are Muslims. Most are descendants of Sinhalese people from Sri Lanka, and the national language is Divehi, which is related to Sinhalese. Minorities are from India or descended from Arab traders. The tropical islands obtained their independence from Britain in 1965 and became a republic three years later.

◎ SECTION REVIEW

1. Where are the majority of the eight-thousand-meter Himalayan peaks?
2. What is the last absolute monarchy in South Asia?
3. What island nation was first united by Great Britain?
4. What two groups are fighting in Sri Lanka?
5. What fishing nation occupies a group of coral islands near India?
   - Compare and contrast the Himalayas and the Karakoram.

445

REVIEW

Can You Define These Terms?

subcontinent	reincarnation	Jainism	typhoon
monsoon	karma	Satyagraha	tsunami
Hindu	guru	Sikhism	dzong
caste	Hindi	Bengali	

Can You Locate These Natural Features?

Ganges River	Deccan	Indus River	Himalayas
Brahmaputra River	Thar	Karakoram	Mt. Everest

Can You Explain the Significance of These People, Places, and Events?

Calcutta	Mahatma Gandhi	Sikkim	Sherpas
Delhi	Dravidians	Mohenjo-Daro	Gurkhas
Bombay	Punjab	Baluchistan	Burghers

How Much Do You Remember?

1. How do the mountains along the northern borders affect the climate of South Asia?
2. Why is India called the world's largest democracy?
3. What do we call the social classes of Hindus in India? What race imposed this system on the people it conquered?
4. What is the major religion of Pakistan?
5. What country split from Pakistan in 1971? Why?
6. What two nations lie in the Himalayas?
7. What two island countries lie near India in the Indian Ocean?
8. What is the poorest nation in South Asia?
9. What mountain range contains 250 of the highest mountains in the world?

What Do You Think?

1. In what major ways does the religion of Hinduism differ from true Christianity? What do you think would be the best approach in witnessing to a Hindu?
2. Make a list of the problems common to the countries of South Asia. What is the root cause of these problems and the best hope for improvement?

CHAPTER 20

SOUTHEAST ASIA

Southeast Asia covers a region as large as the forty-eight contiguous United States. Bordering both India and China, these lands have great contrasts, from primitive tribes to skyscraper office complexes. Like the other Asian regions, life is regulated by the seasonal changes of the monsoons.

Asia's monsoon climate is ideal for rice farming, which produces large crops in a small plot and feeds many mouths. More people of the world rely on rice than any other staple. Without their abundant rice crop, many Asians would face starvation. Rice is common throughout Asia, but the countries of Southeast Asia depend on it even more than their larger neighbors. They eat rice at every meal, and some eat as much rice in a week as most Americans eat in a year.

The first modern missionary to Southeast Asia was Adoniram Judson (1788-1850). Judson was America's first missionary. God burdened his heart for the whole world to hear the gospel, including the large population of Southeast Asia. Two verses challenged Judson to go.

O earth, earth, earth, hear the word of the Lord. (Jer. 22:29)

Go ye therefore, and teach all nations, baptizing them in the name of the Father, and of the Son, and of the Holy Ghost. (Matt. 28:19)

INDOCHINA

The mainland portion of Southeast Asia is a peninsula called **Indochina.** Indochina is so named because of its dominant neighbors India and China. These large neighbors influence the culture, politics, and economy of the entire region. Even in physical features, many Indochinese people resemble either Indian or Chinese peoples.

Myanmar (Formerly Burma)

 Myanmar, formerly known as Burma, is about the size of Texas. It has been inhabited since ancient times by the Mon people. Burmese, Karen, and other peoples arrived in

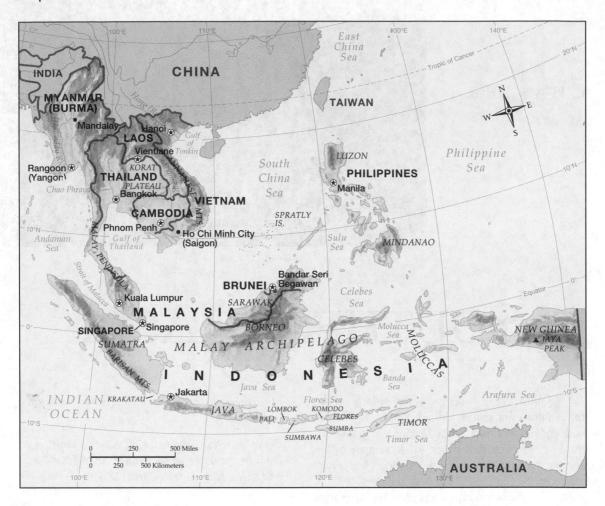

Myanmar about A.D. 800. The Burmese king Anawratha united these groups under his rule in 1044. In the nineteenth century Britain conquered and incorporated Burma into India. Burma gained independence from Britain in 1948.

Once the richest country in Southeast Asia, Burma adopted socialism after independence and began a downward spiral. The president drove out the Indians and Chinese and began a policy of isolation. By 1988 conditions were so bad that major riots erupted. The military took over and renamed the country Myanmar. Multiparty elections were held in 1990, but the military junta refused to surrender control to the elected leaders.

Irrawaddy River Basin Most of the population lives on Myanmar's coastal lowlands where the rain forest offers sufficient water for rice paddies. Myanmar ranks seventh in rice production worldwide. Some rubber plantations also operate along the coast.

The capital, Yangon (formerly Rangoon), a city of almost four million people, lies in the lowlands on the delta of the **Irrawaddy River.** The lowland cities tend to offer better education and a more modern lifestyle, but poverty exists throughout the land. Burmese is the official language, although two hundred other languages are spoken. The Baptist missionary Adoniram Judson

Shwe Dagon Pagoda, one of the highest pagodas ever built, rises 326 feet in Yangon, Myanmar. It is covered with gold.

translated the Bible into Burmese and wrote a dictionary that is still a standard resource. A number of Christian groups have been started in Myanmar as a result of his efforts and the efforts of later missionaries.

 Buddhists, however, make up 85 percent of the population. **Buddhism** is a religion that promotes the teachings of Buddha. Siddhartha Gautama lived about five hundred years before Christ. Visions prompted him to search for enlightenment and release from the sickness and sorrow of the physical world. One day, after several hours of meditation, he felt enlightened and relieved. Others gave him the name *Buddha,* meaning "Enlightened One."

Buddha began teaching others how to become enlightened. He traveled across India teaching what he called *dharma,* or saving truth. Dharma is the

Middle Way of moderation between self-indulgence and self-torture. This Middle Way requires following an eightfold path of moral principles, such as self-control, respect for life, and resisting evil. Buddha stressed the need to free oneself from desires and worldly things. He claimed that this is the way to find release from suffering. Those who succeed reach a state of complete happiness and rest called **nirvana.**

Christians know that the Bible also promotes moderation (Phil. 4:5). God denounces both extremes of carnal living (I John 2:15-17) and self-inflicted pain (Col. 2:20-23). However, none of the Buddhist practices can bring salvation or peace. Salvation comes only by trusting Jesus Christ (Acts 4:12). Saving truth comes from the Bible, not Buddha's dharma. Jesus said,

If ye continue in my word, then are ye my disciples indeed; and ye shall know the truth, and the truth shall make you free. (John 8:31-32)

Today, there are several schools of Buddhism. Theravada dominates life in Burma, the rest of Indochina, and Sri Lanka. **Theravada,** which means "Way of the Elders," stresses the simple teachings of the historical man Buddha. The oldest type of Buddhism still practiced, Theravada stresses philosophy—not worship of a man. It is sometimes called Hinayana (meaning "Lesser Way") by Mahayana Buddhists of East Asia, who think they have the "Great Way."

Southeast Asia Statistics

COUNTRY	CAPITAL	AREA (SQ. MI.)	POPULATION	NATURAL INCREASE	LIFE EXPECTANCY	LITERACY RATE	PER CAPITA GDP	POP. DENSITY
Myanmar	Yangon	261,789	46,821,943	1.8%	57	83%	$1,000	179
Thailand	Bangkok	198,456	59,450,818	1.0%	69	94%	$6,900	300
Laos	Vientiane	91,429	5,116,959	2.8%	53	57%	$1,100	55
Cambodia	Phnom Penh	69,898	11,163,861	2.7%	50	74%	$660	159
Vietnam	Hanoi	128,401	75,123,880	1.6%	67	94%	$1,300	587
Malaysia	Kuala Lumpur	127,316	20,376,235	2.0%	70	84%	$9,800	159
Indonesia	Jakarta	735,268	209,774,138	1.5%	62	84%	$3,500	283
Philippines	Manila	115,830	76,103,564	2.2%	66	95%	$2,530	656
Singapore	Singapore	247	3,461,929	1.2%	79	91%	$22,900	13,847
Brunei	Bandar Seri Begawan	2,226	307,616	2.0%	72	88%	$15,800	138

Geographer's Corner

Interpreting Satellite Images

The earth's upper atmosphere is filled with more than four thousand satellites, which relay all sorts of information back to the earth. The United States government has put Landsat satellites in orbit to take infrared and color images of the earth's surface. From these images, scientists can gain a wealth of knowledge about the effects of seasonal change and of human activity.

This is a *mosaic* image of Myanmar, made from a combination of satellite images. Part of Bangladesh and India appear in the upper left. Lush vegetation is red, water is dark blue or black, and bare ground is light blue. See what you can learn from the image.

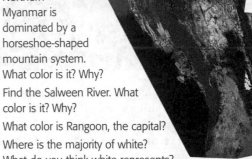

1. Which part of Myanmar has the lushest vegetation?

2. Northern Myanmar is dominated by a horseshoe-shaped mountain system. What color is it? Why?

3. Find the Salween River. What color is it? Why?

4. What color is Rangoon, the capital?

💡 Where is the majority of white? What do you think white represents?

Mountainous Borders Mountain ranges lie along the east and west borders of Myanmar and outline the drainage basin for the Irrawaddy River. The mountain at the northern tip is Hkakabo Razi (19,296 ft.), which rises almost as high as the Himalayas to the west. The Shan Plateau covers the eastern part of the country. The eastern mountains provide some of the best jade and rubies in the world.

The interior region has a tropical wet-dry climate. The northerly winter monsoon winds cause a dry season that prevents the growth of rain forest. This climate supports grasslands on the Shan Plateau and eastern mountains and deciduous trees in the Irrawaddy Basin.

The tribal peoples of the highlands are subsistence farmers who grow yams and other vegetables. In the distant interior, tribal people grow opium poppies as a cash crop. In spite of government efforts to stamp it out, Burma is responsible for at least 60 percent of the world's trade in illegal heroin. The poppy fields are centered in the remote **Golden Triangle,** where the borders of Myanmar, Laos, and Thailand meet.

The Salween River flows through the rugged eastern mountains to its delta in the south, near the border with Thailand. The Karen people who live here are the largest minority in Burma. They are among many minorities that have been fighting for independence since Great Britain gave Burma independence in 1948. Recently government troops have been trying to force villagers in the Karen Baptist Church to renounce their faith and to follow Buddhism.

SECTION REVIEW

1. What is Southeast Asia's most important crop?
2. What is the mainland portion of Southeast Asia called?
3. What fertile river crosses Myanmar?
4. What kind of Buddhism is practiced in Myanmar?
5. What is the older name of Myanmar?
💡 Refute Buddhist doctrine from the Scripture.

French Indochina

In the past two thousand years, several countries have fought over eastern Indochina. China ruled the north for over one thousand years, until the Vietnamese defeated China in 938. France took

A typical Vietnamese village

control in the late nineteenth century and dominated the region until 1954, when the Communist
leader **Ho Chi Minh** led Vietnamese rebels to victory at the decisive battle of Dien Bien Phu. Soon
Communism spread throughout former **French
Indochina.**

Communists in Vietnam Though
somewhat corrupt, South Vietnam's republican government encouraged trade and industry and
made the country fairly prosperous. Communists in
North Vietnam, being poor, coveted the southern
region and began a guerrilla war. Discontent grew in
South Vietnam, and despite American help during
the Vietnam War, Communist power grew. After
American troops withdrew in 1973, the South collapsed, and Vietnam was reunited in 1975 as a
Communist state. It remains one of the last outposts
of Communism in the world today.

Vietnam stretches over one thousand miles
from north to south. The entire country has tropical

rain forests similar to coastal Myanmar, and rice is
the principal crop. All of the coasts are populous,
but the centers of population lie along two river
deltas. The Hong (Red) River Delta lies just south
of China. The capital, Hanoi, is on this delta. The
other delta is south near Cambodia, at the swampy
mouth of the Mekong River.

Ho Chi Minh City, the former capital of South
Vietnam (then called Saigon), is located north of
the Mekong Delta. It once knew prosperity, but
Communism has erased that and brought poverty to
all Vietnamese except the party leaders. The Soviet
Union, facing imminent collapse in the 1980s,
stopped giving aid to Vietnam in 1986. Vietnamese
leaders introduced free market reforms in order to
avert famine. Such changes encouraged the United
States to reopen trade in 1994 and to send a new
ambassador in 1996.

Vietnam's highest peaks rise in the northwest
along the border with China. Another major range,
the **Annamese Mountains,** extends along the western border with Laos and Cambodia. The Vietnamese people stay in the lowlands, where their rice
culture thrives. Several highland tribes live in the
interior jungles, living by slash-and-burn agriculture. Missionaries have reached many of these tribes
with the gospel, while other tribes still worship spirits. Throughout their history, these
tribal peoples have resisted the Vietnamese. They aided the French, who
called them Montagnards, and later
they aided the United States in their

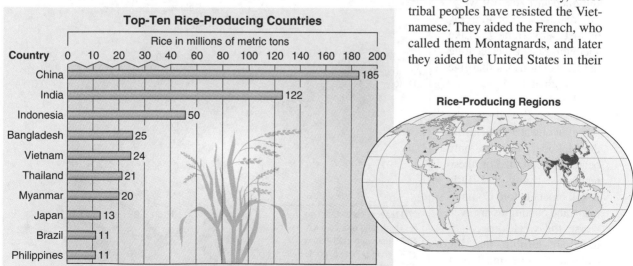

Top-Ten Rice-Producing Countries

Rice in millions of metric tons

Country	Rice (millions of metric tons)
China	185
India	122
Indonesia	50
Bangladesh	25
Vietnam	24
Thailand	21
Myanmar	20
Japan	13
Brazil	11
Philippines	11

Rice-Producing Regions

Who Owns the Spratly Islands?

The **Spratly Islands** are in the South China Sea between Vietnam and the Philippines. Six nations claim all or part of the islands—China, Vietnam, the Philippines, Taiwan, Malaysia, and Indonesia. The islands were seized by Japan in 1940 for a submarine base, but Japan gave up its rights in 1951.

Why are these islands so important? Oil. Any nation controlling the islands has a strong claim to the undersea oil reserves. The **South China Sea** is believed to hold a wealth of oil, and all neighboring countries want it.

war against Ho Chi Minh. Since the fall of the South, the Communists have persecuted these tribes, particularly the remote Hmong.

Laos Laos (LAH ohs) lies between the Annamese Mountains and the **Mekong** (MAY KONG) **River,** one of Asia's great rivers. The country gained independence along with Vietnam in 1954, but civil war began in 1960. The Vietnamese backed the Communists, and the king finally resigned in 1975. The Vietnamese troops stationed in Laos still wield the real power behind the puppet government. Like Vietnam, Laos is persecuting the Christian tribes that live in the highlands.

Laos has rich mineral resources as well as the potential of water power from the Mekong, but it has only begun to capitalize on these resources. Laos had little development before Communism, and conditions are even worse today. Health conditions are terrible, and life expectancy is not much over

fifty years. Educational opportunities are rare. Fewer than one-half of the people read, giving Laos the lowest literacy rate in Southeast Asia. General poverty prevails—the per capita GDP is lower than that of Bangladesh.

Killing Fields of Cambodia The Funan Empire occupied what is now Cambodia in the first centuries after Christ. The Chenla Empire succeeded the Funan, followed by the great **Khmer Empire,** which built the wondrous religious complex at Angkor Wat. French control lasted from 1863 to 1953. A monarchy ruled Cambodia until the 1970s.

Communist influence began during the Vietnam War. Vietnamese-backed Communists, who called themselves the Khmer Rouge, devastated the land. Though South Vietnam and the United States tried to prevent it, the Khmer Rouge took control in 1975. Their leader, Pol Pot, believed that the solution to the nation's problems was to erase all memory of colonial life, to empty the cities and return the people to the primitive life of farmers. The cruel Khmer Rouge executed minorities, religious leaders, missionaries, and any Western-educated professionals and businessmen

Early Asian Empires

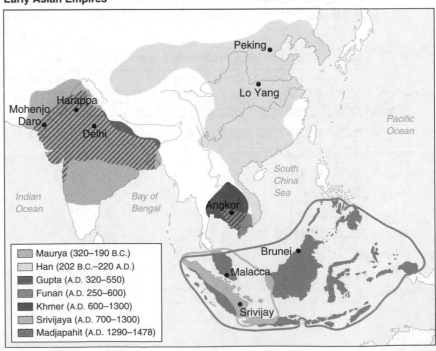

Maurya (320–190 B.C.)
Han (202 B.C.–220 A.D.)
Gupta (A.D. 320–550)
Funan (A.D. 250–600)
Khmer (A.D. 600–1300)
Srivijaya (A.D. 700–1300)
Madjapahit (A.D. 1290–1478)

Angkor Wat

Hindu temple [handwritten note]

Angkor Wat is the pinnacle of Hindu architecture. The ruins of this temple, or *wat,* occupy almost a square mile within the ancient city of Angkor, Cambodia. Angkor Wat is the largest known temple ever built for any religion.

The central building had five pagodas, or towers, representing Mount Meru, which Hindus believe is the center of the world. The central pagoda soars over two hundred feet into the air. In the heart of the temple is an idol of the Hindu god Vishnu, to whom Angkor Wat was dedicated. Hundreds of thousands of carved figures line the passages of the *wat* and depict the history of the world according to Hindu mythology. Carvings include elephant combat, kings, gods, dancers, and seven-headed cobras. An alligator-infested moat once surrounded the temple, symbolizing the ocean at the end of the world. A wide causeway led to the entrance.

A French missionary discovered the ruins of the city of Angkor in 1850. The city had two hundred *wats,* including Angkor Wat, within its complex. Covering one hundred square miles, it is the largest ruined city in the world. At its height, under the reign of Suryavarman II (1113-50), this capital of the Khmer Empire housed one million people, making it the largest city in the

Dozens of other ruins surround the main temple at Angkor Wat, the world's largest Hindu temple.

world at that time. Suryavarman ordered the construction of the fabulous Angkor Wat.

The Chinese historian Chou Ta-kuan, who visited Angkor in 1296, left a written description of its wonders. He marveled at the gold statues of lions that flanked a gold bridge. The Khmer king wore a golden crown and anklets, golden rings inlaid with gems, bracelets loaded with pearls, and garlands of jasmine. All this finery vanished when the Thai king plundered the city in 1431.

Today, the reservoirs, canals, and moats that controlled the flooding of the Mekong River have dried up. Many statues have been destroyed, and the jungle has reclaimed some of the site. Nevertheless, tourists can still visit many of the temples.

who might oppose them. Over one million Cambodians—one-fifth of the nation's population—died in the "killing fields," most by starvation, but at least one hundred thousand by execution.

In 1979, Vietnamese Communists overthrew the Khmer Rouge and took direct control. They withdrew ten years later when the Soviet Union ended its support of Vietnam. Since then, the United Nations has tried to mediate between the Khmer Rouge, the former puppet government, and two other rebel groups. To oversee free elections, the United Nations sent an unprecedented twenty-two thousand peacekeepers in 1993. But violence continues, and Cambodia suffers from the lowest life expectancy and the lowest per capita GDP in Southeast Asia.

Cambodia's coast supports rain forest. The monsoons produce a tropical wet climate. Kompong

Son is a deep water port, and roads link the port to the capital, Phnom Penh. The major products are rice and rubber. The northern parts of Cambodia are hilly, have a tropical wet-dry climate supporting deciduous forests, and are sparsely populated.

Thailand, "Land of the Free"

Thailand (TYE land), the oldest country in Southeast Asia, is an ancient kingdom with a proud heritage. Its name means "Land of the Free." Thailand is the only country in Southeast Asia never controlled by a European country.

Central Valley Like Myanmar, Thailand has a major river flowing from the northern highlands. The Chao Phraya (CHOU prah-YAH) empties into the Gulf of Thailand near Bangkok, Thailand's capital. The river lies in a valley between two mountain ranges. This valley is the most populous area in Thailand and was the hub of its ancient civilization.

Rice farming dominates the Central Valley, but **Bangkok** is a modern city. Bangkok is Indochina's largest city, with a population of about six million. It is famous for the canals *(klongs)* that tie the city together. Bangkok's industries are growing and include refineries, textile industries, and international companies that assemble cars and electronic equipment.

In 1782 the current dynasty came to power. The king moved the capital to Bangkok and named the kingdom Siam. This dynasty has made many changes. Slavery was abolished about 1900, the absolute monarchy was changed to a constitutional monarchy in 1932, and the name was changed from Siam to Thailand seven years later.

The Communist threat from Vietnam and the many refugees on its borders have strained the economy, but Thailand has creatively overcome these obstacles. For instance, Thailand has begun new industries, such as flower growing and crocodile farming. Though Thailand no longer has wild crocodiles, seventy thousand crocodiles are raised on farms. The Thais sell the crocodiles for meat, handbags and shoes. Some are even sold to farmers to be used as garbage disposals.

Thailand has become the most developed country in Indochina. It was the only country in Indochina to join in founding the Association of Southeast Asian Nations, or **ASEAN.** This is an economic and social alliance originally designed to strengthen the members against Communist and Chinese influence. Since the decline of the Communist threat, all the nations of Southeast Asia have now joined ASEAN.

Buddhist monks serve at the Temple of the Emerald Buddha in Bangkok, Thailand.

Thailand is more powerful than most of the other members, however, because of its large population and booming economy. It is one of four **"Little Dragons"** in Southeast Asia. *Dragon* refers to economically powerful countries in the Orient, and *Little* describes their power compared to China.

One of Thailand's advantages is that nearly all its people speak the same language—Thai. Also, Thailand avoids religious conflict because almost all of its people have the same religion—Buddhism.

Imperialism in the Far East, 1914

Sports

Elephant "Rodeo"

Many of the work elephants of Thailand meet once a year in a big roundup. This gathering is something like a Western rodeo—with elephants. People from far and near come to watch the huge animals display their skills.

Special events fill the day. To open the activities, over one hundred elephants parade before the crowds. Their trainers, called *mahouts* (muh HOUTZ), sit proudly on the shoulders of the beasts. The mahouts give commands by using their feet to nudge the elephants behind the ears.

A small group of elephants demonstrate the way in which wild elephants are caught and tamed. A few of the animals pretend to be wild. The others chase them until men riding the backs of the trained elephants can rope the wild beasts by their hind legs.

In other events the elephants show off their speed, skill, and agility. Imagine lying on the ground, as some of the spectators do, and having four or five eight-thousand-pound animals step over you! One misstep, and you could be squashed. Between races and log-lifting demonstrations, Thai dancers in colorful costumes perform traditional Thai dances.

In the most exciting elephant race, elephants race to a line several yards away; then they stop and pick up a banana or other small article with their trunks. They return to the starting point and place the article in a small circle. They gallop back and forth picking up articles until the last article, a red flag, is returned. The first elephant to return with his red flag wins.

Border Regions The Korat Plateau covers eastern Thailand. The plateau lies between Cambodia on the south and the Mekong River on the north and east. Like the Central Valley, this region

An interesting Buddha sits in Wat Trimitr, Thailand. When the statue was accidentally dropped in 1953, the plaster cracked and revealed a solid-gold statue inside. Monks in the thirteenth century had concealed the priceless treasure, which weighs 5.5 tons, in plaster.

has a tropical wet-dry climate. The vegetation on the plateau is deciduous rather than rain forest. This fertile region has helped to make Thailand the leading exporter of rice in the world.

The **Malay Peninsula** is almost one thousand miles long. The northern section is shared by Thailand and Myanmar. The middle section belongs entirely to Thailand, but the southern section belongs to Malaysia. This sparsely inhabited region has tin mines and rubber plantations. The forests produce teak, bamboo, and other woods.

20-2

SECTION REVIEW

1. What was the first Communist country in Southeast Asia?
2. What European country colonized Vietnam, Laos, and Cambodia?
3. What is the largest city in Indochina?
4. What is the long, narrow peninsula attached to mainland Southeast Asia?
5. What is the oldest country in Indochina?
💡 Why has Thailand become so prosperous?

Food vendor along the streets of Bangkok, Thailand

MALAY ARCHIPELAGO

Southeast Asia includes Indochina on the mainland and the Malay Archipelago off the coast. The **Malay Archipelago** is the largest group of islands in the world. It includes two major groups of islands: the East Indies and the Philippines. The region also includes much of the Malay Peninsula, which juts into the archipelago. Five countries lie in this region.

Most of these islands are volcanic, and several active volcanoes stand in this part of the Pacific Ring of Fire. Mountains dominate many of the islands. Apart from these highland areas, all of the islands have a tropical wet climate. A few areas receive as much as two hundred inches of rain annually, and most receive at least one hundred inches. The surrounding ocean provides moisture even during the dry season, which means that the archipelago has few interior areas that support savanna or deciduous forests.

Malaysia

The states of the southern Malay Peninsula united to form the Federation of Malaya in 1948 and became an independent country in 1957. Six years later, this country united with several states on islands to become Malaysia (muh LAY zhuh). The entire region has a tropical wet climate and is covered by tropical rain forest.

Peninsular Malaysia

The southern one-third of the Malay Peninsula belongs to Malaysia. Four-fifths of Malaysia's people live on the peninsula. The modern skyline of the capital, Kuala Lumpur, boasts Petronas Towers, the tallest buildings in the world. The peninsula also has ports on the west coast along the important shipping lane through the Strait of Malacca.

Like Thailand, Malaysia is one of the four "Little Dragons" with developing industries. The great Kinta Valley tin deposits near the northwest coast and other deposits to the south make Malaysia the world's fourth largest producer of tin. Malaysia also produces rubber, palm oil, rice, coconuts, cacao, and valuable timbers such as ebony, mahogany, and sandalwood.

Just over one-half of the people are Malays, most of whom are Muslim. The official language is also a dialect of Malay. One-third of the people, however, are Chinese. Their ancestors moved to the area during British rule to find work. Many of these Chinese have attained high positions in banking and business. The Malays resent the Chinese wealth and have kept control of the government away from the Chinese. Racial tensions have arisen from this situation and continually threaten the country.

Insular Malaysia

Malaysia has two states on the north coast of the island of Borneo: Sarawak and Sabah. This region is slightly larger in area than the portion on the peninsula; however, it has less than one-fourth of the population. Many of the people of this region descended from groups native to Borneo. Although Sabah and Sarawak remain largely undeveloped, offshore oil wells have begun operating along the coast.

The most amazing feature of Sarawak is its cave system. Sarawak Cave covers the largest surface area of any cave system in the world. One

The world-record Petronas Twin Towers building, completed in 1997, rises 1,476 feet above the capital of Malaysia. The base is in the shape of an eight-pointed Islamic star. This skyscraper is only the first stage of a massive new government program to modernize the country.

room has a surface area of over 1.7 million square feet. This is five times the surface area of the Big Room in Carlsbad Caverns (the largest room in the United States and ninth largest in the world).

Malaysia's Small Neighbors

Malaysia has two small neighbors that are very rich. Both share Malaysia's climate and rain forest vegetation. Singapore is an island off the tip of the peninsula. Brunei is a small country on the island of Borneo.

 Singapore Singapore is the name of a city, an island, and a country. Inhabited since A.D. 100, the town was once called Temasek, meaning "sea town." In the thirteenth century, it took the Sanskrit name _Singapore,_ meaning "lion city." It continued as a shipping center until 1377 when Java invaded and made it a pirate base. After being a British colony for over 140 years, Singapore became an independent country in 1965. Singapore is one of the world's busiest ports because all shipping between Japan and the Middle East must round the Malay Peninsula to enter the Strait of Malacca. The term **entrepot** (AHN truh poh) describes such intermediate ports.

The island of Singapore covers over 220 square miles at the southern tip of the Malay Peninsula. The city of Singapore lies on the south coast and serves as the capital. Ninety percent of Singapore's population lives in the capital. Over 3.4 million people live on the island, three-fourths of whom are Chinese in ancestry. Major minorities include Malays and Indians. The rain forest vegetation has been mostly cleared for urbanization except in the mangrove swamps along the northern coast.

Singapore includes the entire island and about fifty other small nearby islands totaling less than twenty square miles. The large population and small area give Singapore the highest population density in the world. This "Little Dragon" has four official languages, each reflecting part of its history: Chinese, Tamil (from India), Malay, and English.

Trade and industries have made Singapore the richest country in Southeast Asia. While lacking

Countries with the Highest Population Density

COUNTRY	POPULATION DENSITY
1. Singapore	13,847
2. Malta	3,109
3. Maldives	2,438
4. Bahrain	2,251
5. Bangladesh	2,200
6. Barbados	1,553
7. Taiwan	1,550
8. Mauritius	1,464
9. South Korea	1,197
10. San Marino	1,029

resources, it relies on its key shipping location to obtain raw materials for its industries. Singapore manufactures electronic equipment, machinery, paper, rubber, ships, textiles, and many other items. Other industries process foods and refine oil. Investors thrive among Singapore's stock exchange and its many banks.

Brunei The small Muslim country of Brunei (BROO nie) has been an important center of trade with China since the seventh century. Sultans have dominated the government since the thirteenth century and most people are Muslims. Britain took Brunei in the nineteenth century to protect British shipping from local piracy. It remained a British colony until 1984. Most people are Malays, but Chinese and English minorities reflect historical ties with those nations.

Sunset at the Great Mosque in Brunei's capital

Oil and natural gas, discovered off the coast in 1929, have greatly improved the standard of living. The large oil income and small population give Brunei one of the highest per capita GDPs in Southeast Asia. Since the reserves are not expected to last another decade, the comparative luxury is fleeting. Brunei must invest wisely as a good steward of God-given resources or suffer economic decline for wasting them (Luke 16:1-2).

SECTION REVIEW

1. The nation of Malaysia is divided into what two regions?
2. What makes the Strait of Malacca important?
3. What products have helped Malaysia and Singapore become "Little Dragons"?
4. What distinguishes the nation of Singapore from the island of Singapore?
5. What products make Brunei rich?
- Why did Singapore and Brunei remain separate from Malaysia?

Indonesia, the Largest Muslim Nation

Indonesia is a very large country. Even without the rest of the Malay Archipelago, its seventeen hundred islands would make it the largest island group in the world. It stretches over three thousand miles from west to east, a distance equal to that between New York and Seattle.

There are over 250 languages in use across this vast, fragmented country. But the schools teach only the official language, Bahasa Indonesia. This is the most widely spoken artificial language in the world, developed in the 1920s by Dutch linguists. Between sixty and one hundred million people speak Bahasa Indonesia. Indonesia, the fourth and last "Little Dragon" of Southeast Asia, is developing its many resources.

Java The island of **Java** has been the hub of Indonesian civilization. Two kingdoms were founded about A.D. 600: the Hindu kingdom of Mataram in Java and the Buddhist kingdom of Srivijaya in Sumatra. By the ninth century, the Buddhists controlled most of Java and continued to expand until the **Madjapahit Kingdom** arose in 1290. The Madjapahits were the first to build an economy on both rice production and sea trade. During this period Indonesia enjoyed its Golden Age of art and music.

In the fifteenth century Arab traders took control of Melaka (in the country of Malaysia) and converted the city to Islam. Now in control of sea trade, Muslims spread Islam throughout the islands of Indonesia. The Muslims took over the Mataram Kingdom in the sixteenth century, and the Hindu leadership fled to the small island of Bali. Indonesia is now the largest Islamic country in the world.

By the end of the eighteenth century the Netherlands had control of what was called the Dutch East Indies. After World War II, nationalists began demanding independence. The Dutch finally acknowledged the country of Indonesia in 1949. Communist rebels threatened the country until General Suharto took power in 1965 and ruled by an iron hand. He was "elected" in 1968 and every five years afterward for the next three decades.

Java has over one hundred million people, more than one-half of Indonesia's entire population. Modern **Jakarta,** the capital and largest city, has over eight million people. It is the largest city in Southeast Asia and the only one larger than Bangkok. The many villages around Jakarta are called *kampongs,* but the poverty of the villages has made the term synonymous with slums. Surabaya, with over two million people, and Jakarta are the major ports. Java's people are similar to Malaysia's. The people are Malays with Chinese and Indian minorities. Islam remains the predominant religion.

The climate and products of Java are also similar to Malaysia's. The wet climate supports tropical rain forest across the rugged mountains. Rice and rubber are grown throughout the island. Indonesia is the third largest producer of rice in the world and the largest producer of natural rubber. Petroleum comes from wells along the northern coast. Java is also the third largest producer of coffee; Java coffee is world famous.

Borobudur

A Buddhist temple on the island of Java is the largest Buddhist monument in the world. It depicts Mount Meru, the golden mountain in Indian mythology that holds up the universe. The five lower terraces are squares, representing the earthly world; the three circular terraces on top represent the spiritual world. Around the edge of each upper terrace are bell-shaped shrines, called *stupas,* each containing a separate

Bell-shaped stupas encircle the upper tiers of Borobudur.

Buddha. According to superstition, reaching through the shrine to touch a Buddha brings good fortune.

Pilgrims climb the 1,310-foot-high pyramid through the material world to the spiritual world. At each level the pilgrim walks all the way around the terrace before ascending to the next level. This three-mile walk takes him past fifteen hundred carved reliefs. They depict the life of Buddha, his doctrines, and daily life in ninth-century Java. At the top, the pilgrim reaches the largest stupa, fifty feet in diameter, representing nirvana.

The Sailendra dynasty built the temple over a period of seventy-five years, beginning about A.D. 700. This dynasty was absorbed by the Srivijaya Kingdom, which eventually abandoned the great temple. It was buried by jungle weeds and volcanic ash until a British officer rediscovered it during the Napoleonic Wars. The temple was partially restored by Dutch archeologists and then completely redone by the United Nations in the 1960s. It has since become a major center of Buddhist ceremonies.

The Largest Islands Indonesia contains all or part of four of the world's eleven largest islands. While large Java ranks thirteenth worldwide, four others are even larger. New Guinea is the largest of these. The other three, together with Java, are collectively called the **Greater Sunda Islands.** Like Java, all four of the larger islands boast mountains over ten thousand feet high.

Sumatra is the world's sixth largest island. The Barisan Mountains line the western coast. Sumatra is the second most populous island in Indonesia, with about one-third the population of Java. Most of the people live in the eastern lowlands, and the two port cities of Medan and Palembang each exceed one million people.

Borneo is the third largest island in the world. Various mountain ranges divide Kalimantan (Indonesia's portion of the island) from Sarawak and Sabah (Malaysia's portion). Most of the ten

million people live in the coastal lowlands and on the rivers. The Dayak tribes on Borneo are spirit-worshipers, and the warriors were headhunters until recently.

Celebes, also called Sulawesi, is the eleventh largest island in the world. Celebes has a strange shape. Its four peninsulas form three gulfs. Six different ethnic groups live on these mountainous lands. One of these groups is nomadic and tribal. Several groups are Muslim. Two groups profess Christianity, including the Minahasa.

New Guinea is the second largest island in the world. It is connected to Australia's continental plate, rather than to Asia. Its people share the same culture and physique as the people of the nearby Pacific Islands. Only the western half of the island, the province of **Irian Jaya,** belongs to Indonesia. Mass conversions to Christianity occurred among the remote mountain tribes early in the twentieth century. Jaya Peak (16,500 ft., also called Carstensz Pyramid) is Indonesia's highest peak. It also ranks as the highest peak in Australasia (Australia and its surrounding islands in the Pacific).

Island Chains The remainder of Indonesia consists of two island groups. People live on about one thousand of these islands, many of which are as mountainous as the Greater Sunda Islands. Unlike overcrowded Java, however, these islands are less populous.

The **Lesser Sunda Islands** lie east of Java, stretching from Bali to Timor. These savannah-covered islands have a tropical wet climate. **Timor,** the largest island of the group, was annexed by Indonesia in 1975. The Timorese resent Indonesia's ownership, and some are fighting for independence.

Bali is the most famous island in this chain. It is the center of Balinese Hinduism. Unlike surrounding Muslim islands, Bali has clung to its older heritage. When Hinduism came to Indonesia in the Middle Ages, the Balinese combined it with many of their ancient traditions. Bali's sacred dances and colorful costumes reflect this mixed culture.

The **Moluccas,** also called the Spice Islands, is an archipelago between Celebes, New Guinea, Timor, and the Philippines. These islands have a complex mixture of wildlife, vegetation, and climate that manifests characteristics of both Southeast Asia and Australasia. The Dutch captured the spice trade from the British in the 1620s and made Ambon the commercial center. The Christian influence from Europe remains.

Philippines

The Philippine Islands stretch north to south for over one thousand miles. The Spanish explorer Ferdinand Magellan discovered the Philippines in 1521 and claimed them for Spain. They remained under Spain's control for almost five hundred years, and the Spanish influence is still evident today.

The United States defeated the declining Spanish Empire in 1898, during the brief Spanish-American War. The United States then ruled the Philippines, hoping to prepare it for independence. Japanese occupation during World War II delayed the move toward independence, but the islands were granted independence in 1946. About

The Komodo dragon is the largest living lizard found anywhere in the world. Adult males grow to a length of ten feet and weigh over three hundred pounds.

83 percent of the people remain Catholic, a reflection of their Spanish heritage.

The Philippines established a republican government based on the American model of checks and balances. But violence and government corruption afflicted the land. Poverty caused many Filipinos, particularly in the southern islands, to embrace Communism. Guerrilla warfare raged.

After several decades of conflict, recent reforms have brought new hope to the Philippines. The economic growth rate has improved and the Philippines now seems poised to compete with the growing economies of Asia's "Little Dragons." The future of reform will depend on new elections.

The Philippines has great potential. Because of the U.S. emphasis on schooling, it has one of the highest literacy rates in all of Southeast Asia. Most people speak English as well as Filipino, the two official languages. Filipino is one of seventy languages in use. Knowledge of English is a valuable asset in the modern economy.

Luzon **Luzon** at the north end is the largest and most populous island. The capital, **Manila,** has about two million people. The metropolitan area has over six million people because it includes other major cities like Quezon City. The impressive volcano Mount Mayon rises near the southern tip of the island.

A Filipino drives a heavily laden cart.

Bible Translation

Two-thirds of the world's sixty-six hundred language groups do not have a single verse of Scripture in their own language. According to Wycliffe Bible Translators, only 341 languages have a complete Bible, and only another 2,092 have even one book of the Bible in their language. Asia is one of the most neglected regions. With two thousand language groups in this region, only fifty-two have so much as a complete New Testament.

Did you ever try to speak to someone who could not speak English? It can be very frustrating. When learning a language, it is easy to confuse words, turning a compliment into an insult. Even a mistake in word stress may turn a serious request into a joke. Most missionaries make many embarrassing mistakes as they learn the new language. Yet it is important not to get discouraged.

Preparation for Bible translation is challenging. Most translators must learn five languages before translating Scripture (English, Greek, Hebrew, the national trade language, and the tribal language). If you are interested in translation, the many island tribes of the Philippines remain a wide-open field. The missionary translator must learn English grammar in school and then Greek and Hebrew to understand what the Bible says. Once in the Philippines, he must learn Tagalog, the national trade language. Only then is he prepared to learn the language of the tribe that God has called him to.

Understanding the local language is especially critical for Bible translators, who will be conveying the Word of God. It is important for the translator to work closely with nationals to be sure the meaning is the intended one. When working with locals, it is natural for conflicts to arise. Disagreements with Christian coworkers are just as common as disagreements with nonbelievers. The missionary can meet such challenges, however, with God's help. You can too.

I can do all things through Christ which strengtheneth me. (Phil. 4:13)

Luzon produces the most important products, pineapples, copper, and gold, as well as most of the country's rice and tobacco. Rice is often grown on terraces in this mountainous region. Neighboring Mindoro, the seventh largest island of the Philippines, produces rice, sugar cane, and Philippine mahogany. The Philippines is the leading producer of coconuts and coconut oil in the world and ranks fourth in banana production.

Mindanao Mindanao (MIN duh NAH oh) is the second largest island. The largest city is the port of Davao. It is the southernmost major island, but the four hundred islands of the Sulu Archipelago lie between Mindanao and Borneo. Mindanao is a leading producer of abaca, which is a strong fiber used to make rope.

Visayan Islands About seven thousand islands lie between Luzon and Mindanao, but only nine hundred are inhabited. The seven largest produce rice, corn, and coconuts. The largest city is the port of Cebu, to which fishermen can bring their tuna catch.

Rice farmers find relief from the sun under a shed.

20-4

◎ SECTION REVIEW

1. What island in Indonesia is the most densely populated?
2. What important products come from Indonesia?
3. Name the three island chains of Indonesia.
4. What is the largest island in the Philippines?
5. What are the major products of the Philippines?
   - ⚲ Has the Philippines benefited from its association with the United States?

REVIEW

20

Can You Define These Terms?

Buddhism	Theravada	"Little Dragon"
nirvana	ASEAN	entrepot

Can You Locate These Natural Features?

Indochina	Mekong River	Sumatra	Bali
Irrawaddy River	Malay Peninsula	Borneo	Moluccas
Annamese Mountains	Malay Archipelago	Celebes	Luzon
Spratly Islands	Java	Lesser Sunda Islands	Mindanao
South China Sea	Greater Sunda Islands	Timor	

Can You Explain the Significance of These People, Places, and Events?

Golden Triangle	Khmer Empire	Madjapahit Kingdom	Irian Jaya
Ho Chi Minh	Bangkok	Jakarta	Manila
French Indochina			

How Much Do You Remember?

1. Why are the monsoons important to Southeast Asia?
2. What crop is critical to all Southeast Asian countries?
3. What river forms the central valley of Myanmar?
4. Which countries were ruled by the French?
5. What is the major river of French Indochina?
6. Why are most of the countries of Indochina so poor?
7. What are the four "Little Dragons"?
8. What two island groups constitute the Malay Archipelago?
9. What three island groups are in Indonesia?
10. What European country colonized the Indonesian islands?
11. What three countries controlled the Philippines before its independence?
12. Name the country that best fits each description.
    a. largest Muslim nation
    b. Spanish heritage
    c. never colonized by Europe
    d. Communist rule
    e. oil riches

What Do You Think?

1. In what ways does Buddhism differ from true Christianity?
2. Make a list of the problems common to the countries of Southeast Asia. What is the greatest hope for these countries?

CHAPTER 21

EAST ASIA

Until the last few centuries, the West knew very little about the exotic lands of the Far East. The customs, religion, and even the appearance of the East Asian people differ from the people of the West. Towering mountains, harsh deserts, and treacherous seas isolated the nations of East Asia from the rest of the world. Left alone, these nations built advanced civilizations that endured the test of time.

During the nineteenth century, the ancient societies of the East came face to face with the industrialized West. The twentieth century brought revolutionary changes to every area of life in the Far East. Each nation responded in vastly different ways to the threat of the West, and they are still reaping the consequences of their choices. Two nations—China and Korea—split in two, between communist and republican governments.

While the Far East has adopted many Western ideas about industry and government, their love of tradition has kept them closed to the promise of the gospel. Nestorians reached China at least as early as A.D. 735, and Jesuits came in the thirteenth century,

but with little impact. The most influential missionary in the region has been Hudson Taylor (1832-1905), who organized the China Inland Mission. God used the verse below, from the Gospel of John, to burden Taylor to reach people beyond the coastal cities, who had never heard the name of Jesus. According to some estimates, China now has as many as eighty million Christians.

And this is life eternal, that they might know thee the only true God, and Jesus Christ whom thou hast sent. (John 17:3)

CHINA

China is slightly larger in size than the United States. Only Russia and Canada surpass its immensity. Like America, it has some of Asia's richest farmlands and driest deserts. Like those in the United States, China's most populous cities are in the east. However, China has four times the population of the United States. Indeed, one out of five people in the world lives in China.

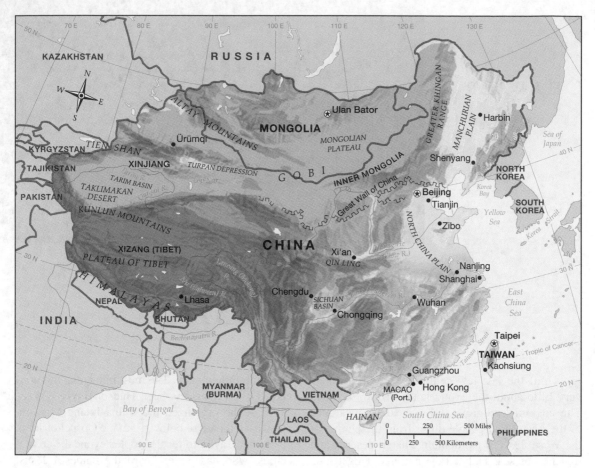

About 92 percent of the people in China are called **Han.** Their language is one of the oldest in the world. Although it has many spoken dialects, the written language is the same throughout China and helps to unite the nation. To improve communication, the government has made the Mandarin dialect the official language, which is now taught in all schools.

Because of its size and numbers, China has always dominated the Far East. The ancient Chinese viewed their land as the "Middle Kingdom"—the geographical and cultural center of the universe, surrounded by barbarians. China's recorded history of over four thousand years is longer than that of any other nation. Although China has been conquered at times, the conquerors have adopted Chinese ways and not vice versa. The Chinese have made a number of important contributions, including gunpowder, paper, printing, and the magnetic compass, although it was the West that saw the full potential of these discoveries.

The bustling cities of Asia attract people from many countries with different dress and lifestyles.

East Asia Statistics

COUNTRY	CAPITAL	AREA (SQ. MI.)	POPULATION	NATURAL INCREASE	LIFE EXPECTANCY	LITERACY RATE	PER CAPITA GDP	POP. DENSITY
China	Beijing	3,696,100	1,210,004,956	1%	70	82%	$2,500	327
Japan	Tokyo	145,850	125,716,637	0.2%	80	100%	$21,300	861
Mongolia	Ulan Bator	604,800	2,538,211	1.6%	61	83%	$1,970	4
North Korea	Pyongyang	47,399	24,317,004	1.7%	71	95%	$920	513
South Korea	Seoul	38,375	45,948,811	1.1%	74	98%	$13,000	1,197
Taiwan	Taipei	13,969	21,655,515	0.9%	76	94%	$13,510	1,550

The Productive North China Plain

The **North China Plain** is the heart of the People's Republic of China and is sometimes called the "real" China. The plain now supports countless villages and one-half of the thirty-five Chinese cities that exceed one million people. The plain also offers petroleum and coal. China is the world's leading coal producer, and it ranks fifth in petroleum.

Chinese farmers practice **intensive farming,** a form of subsistence farming in fertile areas that allows many individuals to raise crops on a small plot of land. The crops differ, however, depending on the climate. A major climate barrier is the **Qin Ling Mountains,** which run east to west across the middle of the plain, rising to 13,474 feet. The two main rivers of China flow on each side of the range.

The dry north is good for growing wheat, corn, soybeans, and sorghum. China is among the top five producers of all of these crops, and it is the leading producer of wheat. Because of the monsoons, the climate south of the Qin Ling Mountains is much wetter than the climate to the north. Here the people grow rice and tobacco and raise swine. China is the world's top producer of each of these, producing more than one-third of the world total. China also ranks among the top three in the production of peanuts and citrus fruits, and it leads in cotton.

First Dynasty on the Huang He   The northern river on the plain is the **Huang He** (or Yellow River), which flows through seven of China's twenty-two provinces. According to legend, Chinese civilization began in this river valley about 2200 B.C. Several small, warring states appeared. Finally in 221 B.C., one of the local rulers defeated the other states and united all of China for the first time. Emperor Shih Huang Ti, or the "first emperor," founded the Qin dynasty (pronounced Chin, from which is taken the name China). A **dynasty** is a series of rulers who come from the same family. Shih Huang Ti ruled with an iron fist and burned books that he feared might cause rebellion. The emperor introduced currency, standardized weights and measures, and standardized the Chinese system of

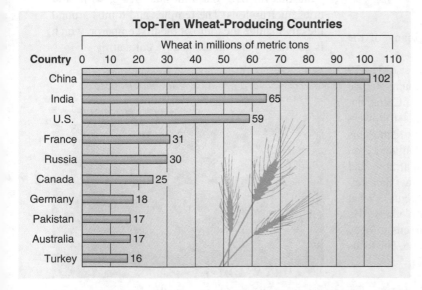

Top-Ten Wheat-Producing Countries

Wheat in millions of metric tons

Country	
China	102
India	65
U.S.	59
France	31
Russia	30
Canada	25
Germany	18
Pakistan	17
Australia	17
Turkey	16

China's Sorrow

The river along which Chinese civilization began, the Huang He, is called China's Sorrow. Snaking three thousand miles from the Tibetan Highlands, the river deposits precious silt along a fertile plain. Although the river's valley provides the agricultural land for the Chinese, its water threatens them with devastating floods. Floods in the Huang He Valley have claimed millions of lives.

Huang He (meaning Yellow River) is named for the fine, yellow sand it picks up as it loops through the northern deserts. The silt-laden river then passes through a series of breathtaking gorges before it widens into the North China Plain. Here the river, the muddiest in the world, deposits much of its silt. When the buildup becomes too great, China's Sorrow suddenly overflows its banks and severely floods the plains. By the time the waters subside, the river has often cut a new channel.

Over fifteen hundred times the Huang He has breached man-made dikes. Since records were first kept, its course has changed twenty-six times. For example, a flood in 1852 shifted its five-century-old course northward from the Yellow Sea to the Chingling Gulf. In 1938 the Chinese diverted the course back to the Yellow Sea, hoping to stop advancing Japanese armies. But in 1947 the Huang He returned to its former channel, where it has remained.

writing. These policies established many of the basic traits of Chinese civilization.

The great philosopher Confucius (ca. 551-479 B.C.) grew up near the mouth of the Huang He. He lived long before the Qin dynasty united China, but it was under the Han dynasty that his followers molded a philosophy called **Confucianism.** This philosophy became the single greatest influence on Chinese society. Confucius taught that harmony and order would exist when men began to treat their fellow men properly. According to Confucius, "What you do not wish for yourself, do not do to others." He taught children to respect parents, citizens to obey rulers, and rulers to seek moral excellence. The focus

on respect of parents fit right in with the **ancestor worship** that the Chinese had always practiced.

China became a "scholar's world" where the educated were the most admired. In fact, complex ancient games, such as "elephant chess" and go (or *weiqi*), remain favorite board games today. Although expensive and competitive, schools prepared citizens for rigorous civil service examinations. Those who scored highest obtained the best positions as government officials. This stabilized Chinese society and slowed government corruption.

Lao Zi (formerly spelled Lao-tzu, meaning "Old Master") lived during the fifth century B.C. Though he lived before Confucius, his teachings were not developed as a complete philosophy until much later—about 100 B.C. This religion is called **Taoism** (TOW IS um). Taoism presents the world as a competition between two equally matched forces, called *yin* and *yang*. Yin represents the female, darkness, cold, and water, whereas yang is the male, light, heat, and fire. The main book is the *Tao Te Ching.* Taoists use charms, meditation, and diet to keep spiritual forces balanced. Some also use spells and the *I-Ching,* a fortunetelling book. Taoism's emphasis on the supernatural and magic is quite different from Confucianism, which stresses practical service to others.

The city that is now **Xi'an,** on a tributary of the Huang He, served as the capital of the Chinese dynasties for over one thousand years, with only brief interruptions. The temples and tombs around the city include the tomb of the first emperor, which is guarded by the fabulous terra cotta army.

Farmers discovered the first emperor's terra cotta army while digging for a well in 1974. The vault included over six thousand warriors in full uniform.

Three Gorges Dam

Both the Huang He and the Chang Rivers begin high on the Plateau of Tibet in Qinghai, the largest and least populated of China's provinces. As the Chang River drops down into the North China Plain, it passes through a series of three gorges, known as the Ichang Gorges. Scenic limestone cliffs rise up to two thousand feet above the rushing water.

Recently, Communist China began a controversial project to dam the river and to drown the gorges. After it is completed around the year 2009, the Three Gorges Dam will generate electricity equivalent to eighteen nuclear power plants. Measuring 1.3 miles long and 607 feet high, it will be the most powerful dam in the world, even more powerful than Itaipu (Brazil) and almost three times as powerful as America's most powerful dam, Grand Coulee. This project will be China's greatest project since the Great Wall.

The controversy involves the displacement of 1.9 million people, whose homes will be submerged by the reservoir. Several historical sites will be lost too. Some environmentalists have condemned the destruction of the beautiful scenery and the loss of habitat for the river dolphin. Outsiders have expressed concern about sewage from former factory sites that may pollute the reservoir. Upstream, Chongqing is concerned about buildup of sediment at its harbor. Authorities expect the dam to cost $17 billion, but some estimates place the actual cost at $75 billion.

Many foreign goods and ideas followed the Silk Road to its final stop at the capital, Xi'an. Buddhism arrived from India in the sixth century B.C., Nestorian Christianity came from Syria in A.D. 735, and Islam came from Arabia in the mid-eighth century. Marco Polo, arriving at Xi'an in 1275, brought Catholicism from Italy. Of these religions, only Buddhism made a significant impact. Modern Chinese folk religions consist of a combination of ancestor worship, legends, and teachings from Confucianism, Taoism, and Buddhism.

The Populous Chang River The southern river of the North China Plain is the **Chang** (or Yangtze), which flows through four provinces. Its enormous drainage basin encompasses an area nearly the size of Mexico. The world's third largest river and the most important river in China, the Chang is known as China's "main street." Ocean liners can travel seven hundred miles inland to Wuhan, and smaller vessels are able to navigate as far as one thousand miles inland. The Chang is one of the busiest waterways on earth and is also the deepest river in the world with depths of six hundred feet.

The upper Chang follows the western boundary of Sichuan Province, the most populous of all China's provinces. The Chang flows through the large **Sichuan Basin** before it leaves the mountains. The basin contains two of China's ten largest cities, Chengdu and Chongqing, each with over two million people. The Sichuan Basin is one of the richest agricultural regions in China. Besides rice, crops of fruit, cotton, and tea grow on terraces cut from the hillsides.

MAJOR DYNASTIES	DATES	HIGHLIGHTS
Shang	1766-1122 B.C.	Oldest Chinese writing, pottery, and bronze objects
Zhou (Chou)	1122-221 B.C.	Confucius
Qin (Chin)	221-206 B.C.	First emperor unites China and builds Great Wall.
Han	206 B.C.–A.D. 220	Invention of paper; Silk Road
Tang	618-907	Invention of printing; empire from Korea to Aral Sea; Golden Age
Song (Sung)	960-1279	Scenic paintings and fine porcelain
Yuan (Mongol)	1279-1368	Marco Polo
Ming	1368-1644	Chinese rule restored; European trade
Qing (Manchu)	1644-1912	Braided pigtails symbolize submission to Manchus.

The mountain-ringed basin made Chongqing a defensible capital for China's republic from 1937 to the end of World War II.

Nanjing, with over two million people, lies downstream on the Chang River, only about 150 miles from the coast. When the Ming dynasty came to power in 1368, the emperor moved the capital to Nanjing, where it stayed until 1421. In 1928 the capital once again moved to Nanjing when Nationalists under **Chiang Kai-shek** reunited China after years of civil war.

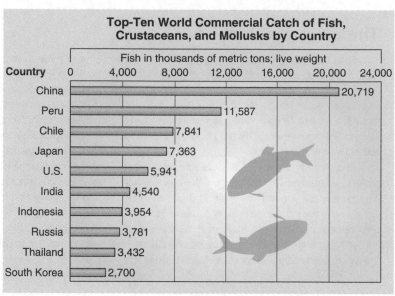

Top-Ten World Commercial Catch of Fish, Crustaceans, and Mollusks by Country

Fish in thousands of metric tons; live weight

Country	Fish
China	20,719
Peru	11,587
Chile	7,841
Japan	7,363
U.S.	5,941
India	4,540
Indonesia	3,954
Russia	3,781
Thailand	3,432
South Korea	2,700

Chiang attempted to institute a republican form of government, but Communists opposed the Nationalists and began terrorist activities. Such terrorists murdered John Stam (1907-34) and his wife, Betty, missionaries with the China Inland Mission, west of Nanjing. The Japanese invasion during World War II forced the opposing Chinese armies to work together. After the victory over the common enemy, the Communists fought Nationalists for control of Nanjing. The Communists won in 1949 and then moved the capital north to Beijing, where it remains today.

The Open Port of Shanghai

China's largest city, **Shanghai,** lies on the Huang P'u River near the mouth of the Chang. Its textile mills make cloth from the cotton of the plain, and nearby iron mines provide raw materials for heavy manufacturing. Shanghai is now a center of world trade and banking.

The port at Shanghai handles one-half of China's international trade. Its growth began in 1842, when the British forced China to open it to foreigners. Shanghai took on a Western appearance as foreigners built homes, churches, and office buildings. Hudson Taylor made his base of operations in Shanghai. Today most of Shanghai's residents are factory workers who dress and eat well by Chinese standards. Communist China has opened several other cities to trade. These **open cities** are in a special economic zone within Communist China.

As a major fishing center, Shanghai contributes to China's world-leading fish catch. China nets one-third of its catch through **aquaculture,** or fish farming. Farmers raise fish and shellfish in tanks, ponds, reservoirs, estuaries, and shallow bays. China's coasts offer shrimp, salmon, eel, mackerel, and sardines.

A Chinese junk *in the harbor near Shanghai*

Communists in the Forbidden City

Beijing (formerly Peking) is China's second largest city and the eighth largest in the world. Located on the North China Plain, it is only about thirty-five miles south of the Great Wall. It has served as China's capital since 1267, except for several brief periods totaling fifty-six years. For centuries, Beijing has been the country's center for culture. Its thirty colleges, universities, and technical schools make it an educational center as well. After the Communists rose to power in 1949, the city became industrialized and now produces iron, tools, and textiles.

Most of the city walls have been torn down to make way for roads. The city streets are thronged with bicycles as the population of seven million people cycle to and from work. The heart of the city is the Forbidden City, where the Chinese emperors once lived. To the north is the Gate of Heavenly Peace (Tiananmen) which overlooks **Tiananmen Square.** Leaders review parades displaying the country's military might on the thirty-four-acre grounds, the largest square in the world.

Communist Politics **Mao Zedong,** the Communist leader who defeated the Nationalists, proclaimed the birth of the People's Republic of China (also called Communist China or Red China) on October 1, 1949, in Tiananmen Square. Since only 13 percent of China's land is arable, Mao immediately faced the challenge of feeding the world's largest population. He also wanted to "catch up" with the economic and military strength of other world powers.

The Forbidden City

The Imperial City, a parklike area in the center of Beijing, contains the Forbidden City. Separated from the outside world by a broad moat and a wall, only the emperor and his household could enter the beautiful Forbidden City. Today, however, the buildings are museums open to the public.

Emperor Yong-le of the Ming dynasty built the Forbidden City and moved his capital to it from Nanjing in 1421. Its Dragon Throne remained the seat of the Ming emperors until 1644, when the Manchus pillaged the city. The Manchus restored it to its glory and ruled there until 1912, when rebels took over and imprisoned the last emperor in the palace, where he stayed for twelve years.

The Forbidden City has exactly 9,999 rooms. Beyond the Dragon Throne in the Hall of Supreme Harmony, two other great halls served as ceremonial

chambers: the Hall of Perfect Harmony and the Hall of Preserving Harmony. The Forbidden City's palace also contained the living quarters of the Chinese emperor. In the Temple of Heaven, the emperor led religious rituals. From the main gate of the Forbidden City, Tiananmen, the emperor reviewed his troops.

Bikes of all sorts crowd the streets of Chinese cities.

Mao began programs he thought would strengthen the economy. First, he executed over fifty thousand rich landlords and redistributed the land to make **collective farms,** in which the peasant workers and managers ran the farm under government supervision. In the **Great Leap Forward** of 1958, Mao combined collectives into huge government farms called **communes.** However, bad weather and discontented workers resulted in poor crops and widespread famine.

To stop angry protests, Mao launched the **Cultural Revolution** in 1966, sending young people called Red Guards to remove his opponents

Mao Zedong (1893-1976)

throughout China. Millions of educated citizens died or were forcibly moved from the "corrupting" influence of the cities to be "purified" in rural communes. Mao called out the army to stop the Cultural Revolution only a year later, but the schools did not reopen until 1970. All of his programs had been disastrous failures.

After Mao's death in 1976, China changed direction. Mao's successor, Deng Xiaoping, vigorously pursued economic modernization. Deng sent students to Western universities to learn how to improve industry and economy. He also permitted some citizens to own private gardens and businesses. As Communism teetered on the brink of collapse in Europe, Chinese students took the opportunity to protest in Tiananmen Square, erecting a thirty-foot replica of the Statue of Liberty. They sought freedom, but on June 4, 1989, Communist tanks rolled into the square, killing perhaps five thousand people. Communism had not changed.

Shipping   Tianjin, the port for Beijing, lies at the mouth of the Hai River. With 5.8 million people, Tianjin is China's third largest city. Tianjin is at the north end of the Grand Canal, which permits inland shipping to Shanghai. When it opened in 486 B.C., the canal was the longest artificial waterway in the world. Over one thousand miles long, it linked China's two largest rivers. Kublai Khan finished the northern extension to Tianjin by A.D. 1292. The canal has fallen into disrepair, although one-third of it is still open to barges.

Tanks rolled into Tiananmen Square to quash the freedom movement in 1989.

The three great cities—Shanghai, Beijing, and Tianjin—are China's leading industrial centers. Each is a distinct political unit called a **special municipality** and is not part of any province.

Rise and Fall of Manchuria

Because the three provinces of **Manchuria** are located northeast of the Great Wall, the Chinese commonly refer to them as the Northeast. The broad Manchurian Plain is an extension of the North China Plain. Crops such as soybeans, millet, corn, apples, and spring wheat grow well in the relatively short growing season with its severe winters and summer droughts. The forested mountains to the north and east contain much valuable timber. Manchuria boasts eight cities with over one million people. Shenyang, with over 4.1 million people, is the fourth largest city in the country and the industrial center of Manchuria.

The **Manchus,** the last foreign power to control China, came from Manchuria. During the early part of Manchu rule, the empire expanded its influence over the lands in the north, south, and west. However, the leadership declined in the early nineteenth century, just as European vessels were swarming along China's east coast and as Russia

Chinese Empire, Nineteenth Century

was gaining strength in the north. By the end of the century, the Manchu dynasty had lost northern tracts of land to Russia, Burma to Great Britain, and Annam (French Indochina) to France. Another threat—imperialist Japan—took Korea and Taiwan. The China Inland Mission sent Jonathan Goforth (1859-1936) to evangelize Manchuria during these turbulent times.

The Chinese people, however, resented the Western and Christian influences in China. Their strong feelings and national unity prompted secret societies opposing Western influences. In 1900, the Boxers, a society named for its ceremonial practice of shadowboxing, attacked Westerners and Chinese Christians in the foreign quarter of Beijing. The Boxer Rebellion lasted fifty days before eight foreign nations, including the United States, combined to crush it. Although the Manchus implemented reforms after the rebellion, the dynasty collapsed in 1912.

Southern Uplands

Eight populous provinces lie south of the Chang River basin in southeast China. Nine cities in this region exceed one million people. The Southern Uplands harbors more ethnic groups and languages than anywhere else in China. Many of these groups speak Thai languages. The five million Miao form one of the larger groups. The China Inland Mission sent missionaries to the many peoples. One such missionary, Isobel Kuhn (1901-54) went to the Lisu, a remote people who speak a Tibeto-Burmese language and live along the Salween River in China.

Green hills and mountains characterize the Southern Uplands. Rice grows throughout the region, but this region also contributes other important resources for China. China grows three-fourths of all the sweet potatoes in the world and almost one-quarter of the world's tea. Sugar cane also is produced in these uplands. The hills and mountains produce over one-half of the world's tungsten and enough phosphates, zinc, iron ore, lead, vanadium, and manganese to boost China into the top ten list for the production of each. China is also the world's

Kweilin Karst

Kweilin (or Guilin) is a city northwest of Guangzhou. A center of the silk trade, the city is most famous for the nearby karst region, which stretches into North Vietnam. Water has eroded the limestone to form caves and sinkholes. The most unusual feature of the Kweilin Karst is the hundreds of domes that rise like camel humps up to 325 feet. It has the world's best examples of this formation, called *tower karst*.

The karst has inspired Chinese artists for centuries. Slow-moving rivers reflect the rows of towers. Vines, orchids, and a few trees cling to the sheer slopes, adding a special charm to the fantastic setting.

Freer Gallery of Art, Smithsonian Institution, Washington, D.C.: Gift of Charles Lang Freer, F1916.538.
This Chinese painting from the Song Dynasty shows a landscape from the Kweilin Karst.

leading producer of tin, producing about one-fifth of the world total.

China's Southern Uplands is also one of the few places in the world that produces silk. Silkworms spin a cocoon consisting of one long thread. The Chinese weave these light, strong threads into silk, but they kept the production technique secret for many centuries. The silkworms require both a warm climate and a diet of leaves from mulberry trees.

The Southern Uplands also includes China's southernmost province, Hainan. Hainan is the largest island in China. It is also the source of China's natural rubber; China is the world's fifth largest producer of natural rubber. The island also produces bananas and pepper.

Cantonese on the Xi River

The **Xi River** (West River) is the transportation hub of the Southern Uplands. Its volume of flow is nearly three times that of the Yellow River as a result of heavy monsoon rains.

The delta of the Xi River is the largest arable plain in the Southern Uplands. The deep, rich soil and the warm, moist climate make the delta extremely productive. With a year-round growing season, rice fields are **double cropped** (two crops a year). Tea, fruits, and sugar cane are also grown where the terrain permits.

Located on the delta of the Xi is **Guangzhou** (or Canton). With 3.2 million people, Guangzhou is the region's largest and China's sixth largest city. The people speak the **Cantonese** dialect of Chinese. Westerners are familiar with Cantonese cooking, which offers a variety of steamed fresh vegetables. Sun Yat-sen, the first Nationalist Party leader, was from Guangzhou. It was he who ended the Manchu dynasty in 1912 and became the first president of the Republic of China.

Guangzhou is an important industrial and transportation center. The Xi River, railroads to the interior, and the deep water port at nearby Whampoa make it a center for international trade. Guangzhou is a bustling, lively city—quite different from orderly Beijing.

Colonial Ports

Two foreign colonies arose on China's southern coast during nineteenth-century European colonialism. **Hong Kong** is about ninety miles southeast of Guangzhou. During the nineteenth century, Britain forced China to cede Hong Kong Island and the tip of Kowloon Peninsula. Hong Kong's deep harbor made it an ideal trading center for the heavy sea traffic in the South China Sea. Business blossomed under its low taxes and political freedom. The colony grew rapidly and soon needed more farmland and water supplies. In 1898 Great Britain leased nearby islands and the rest of the Kowloon Peninsula, known as the New Territories. The entire area became part of China again in 1997.

Hong Kong's economy was one of the strongest and most varied in all of Asia. Though only four hundred square miles in area, its fifteen thousand people per square mile make it a bustling center for trade, finance, manufacturing, and tourism. Hong Kong's people hope that China will keep its promise to protect Hong Kong's way of life for fifty years ("one country, two systems"). Christians in particular wonder if Communist China will soon restrict church activities.

Portugal settled Macao (muh KOW), the oldest European colony in Asia, in 1557. It lies across an estuary from Hong Kong. Its six square miles consist of a small peninsula and two small islands. Macao is a tourist trap, famous for gold smuggling and gambling (prohibited in China). Like Hong Kong, the population is about 95 percent Chinese. Portugal agreed to give the colony back to China in 1999.

SECTION REVIEW

1. What disastrous reforms did Mao Zedong implement?
2. Name China's three special municipalities.
3. What is northeast China called?
4. Name the major river in China's Southern Uplands.
- Which region of China is an ethnic melting pot? Why?

China's Autonomous Regions

China has five autonomous (self-governing) regions in addition to its twenty-two provinces and three special municipalities. Three of the autonomous regions rank as the largest of China's thirty political divisions. As in Russia, each autonomous region offers self-rule to a minority, but each group has very limited powers. China has fifty-five ethnic minorities, but only five have been given autonomous regions.

Guangxi   The autonomous region of Guangxi is on the coast at the border with Vietnam. China's largest minority, the **Zhuang,** live in Guangxi and number over thirteen million. The Zhuang are ethnic Thai people that speak a northern Thai dialect. Many also speak Cantonese since they are somewhat outnumbered by Chinese in Guangxi.

Tibet, the Roof of the World   You were introduced to some of the seven greatest ranges of the world in Central Asia. The Pamirs, at Tajikistan's border with China, form the hub. The Tien Shan and Kunlun stretch into China to the northeast and east respectively. The Karakoram and Himalayas extend southeast to form China's southern border. Four of these ranges, the Kunlun, Pamirs, Karakoram, and Himalayas, lie on the border of a great plateau called the Plateau of Tibet, or simply **Tibet.**

Plateau   The Plateau of Tibet rises west of China's Southern Uplands. Many high peaks are in Tibet. Tibet shares Mount Everest with Nepal. Shisha Pangma, another of the eight-thousand-meter Himalayan peaks is in Tibet. The **Kunlun,** the mountain range on the northern edge of the plateau, contains six seven-thousand-meter peaks, the highest of which is Kongur (25,325 ft.).

The Brahmaputra River flows through a valley that separates the Himalayas in the south from the **Trans-Himalaya** just north of the Himalayas. The Trans-Himalaya includes three seven-thousand-meter peaks, the highest of which is Nyenchentanglha (23,497 ft.). "The Roof of the World," Tibet has an average elevation that exceeds sixteen thousand feet.

The Plateau of Tibet is quite rugged and is one of the world's most isolated regions. Many of Asia's great rivers begin on the plateau. Besides the Indus, Brahmaputra, and Huang He, four other major rivers cut through parallel gorges within a space of one hundred miles: the Irrawaddy, Nu (Salween), Lancang (Mekong), and Chang (Yangtze).

Tibetans   Because of its ruggedness, Tibet is the least populated of all of China's political divisions. In fact, there are about five times more people in Beijing than in all of Tibet. Only a few scattered valleys are habitable, where the climate is milder and the soil is suitable for cultivation. The capital, **Lhasa,** lies in one such valley, the Tsangpo Valley.

Defended by mountains, the indigenous Tibetans enjoyed independence for most of their history. However, in 1950, Communist troops

Let's Go Exploring

1. Does any commercial farming take place in East Asia? If so, what kind?
2. Which two countries have the majority of the land used for subsistence farming?
3. What country is almost entirely devoted to nomadic herding?
4. What region has most of the shifting agriculture—South Asia, Southeast Asia, or East Asia?

💡 Why is commercial farming so uncommon in Asia?

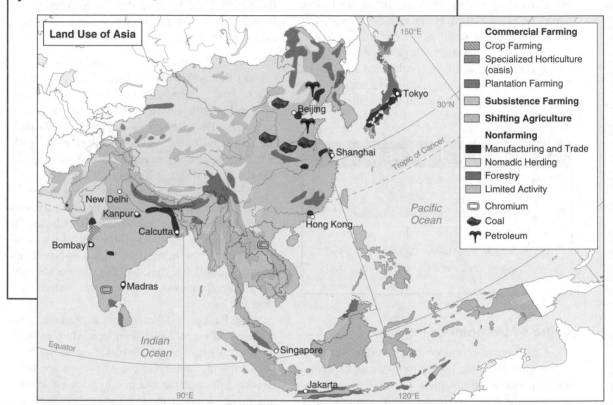

Land Use of Asia

Commercial Farming
- Crop Farming
- Specialized Horticulture (oasis)
- Plantation Farming
- **Subsistence Farming**
- **Shifting Agriculture**

Nonfarming
- Manufacturing and Trade
- Nomadic Herding
- Forestry
- Limited Activity
- Chromium
- Coal
- Petroleum

invaded Tibet and seized control. The Chinese army squelched a Tibetan rebellion in 1959, destroyed Tibetan religious shrines, and looted the temples. In 1965 much of the plateau became the autonomous region of Xizang, usually called Tibet. In 1987 and 1993 Tibetans staged violent protests against Communist rule.

Intensely religious, Tibetans follow a branch of Buddhism called Lamaism. Tibetans worship each **Dalai Lama** as a reincarnation of Buddha. He is considered both the political and spiritual leader. Before Communism, the Dalai Lama ruled from

Potala Palace in Lhasa as a **theocrat,** one who rules by religious or divine authority. When the Chinese took over, he escaped to India.

Xinjiang Xinjiang (SHIN JYANG) covers an area the size of Alaska in northwest China, making it by far the largest of China's political divisions. Like Tibet, this large autonomous region has high mountains. The Kunlun forms its southern border with Tibet, and the Tien Shan, or Heavenly Mountains, cross the middle of the region and contain two seven-thousand-meter peaks.

Bactrian camels graze on the steppe in Xinjiang.

Unlike Tibet, however, most of Xinjiang consists of desert basins. The Tien Shan divides the two large basins: the Tarim Basin in the south and the Junggar Basin in the north. Both basins are extremely dry because the high mountains almost completely block off any rain-bearing winds. The people of the area, both Uygurs and Kazakhs, are Muslims and speak Turkic languages. China fears a growing independence movement among the people of Xinjiang, especially after the independence of the former Soviet republics in Central Asia.

The **Taklimakan Desert** occupies the Tarim Basin. It may be the driest area in Asia. The Turpan Depression in this desert is 505 feet below sea level, the lowest elevation in the world after the Great Rift Valley in Israel and Africa. A string of oases along the edges of the desert once served as stations on the Silk Road. Today the region remains sparsely populated because of its harsh climate and remoteness.

The Junggar Basin lies between the Tien Shan and the Altai Mountains on the Mongolian border. This basin still offers a key trade route and railroad link with Central Asia. Ürümqi is the main city on the route and the capital of Xinjiang. The basin is an extension of the Gobi Desert. Mildred Cable (1879-1952) crossed the Gobi on this route several times as a missionary for the China Inland Mission, extending the mission's outreach to the most remote sections of interior China.

Inner Mongolia   The term *Mongolia* can refer to the region beyond the Great Wall of China. **Inner Mongolia** is the part controlled by China,

Potala Palace

The Dalai Lama, similar to the pope in Vatican City, is the religious and political leader of Tibet. The title means "Ocean of Wisdom." The ruler of Mongolia, the khan, conferred this title on the leader of the Tibetan Buddhists after the khan's own conversion in the sixth century. In 1951 Communist China occupied Tibet, which was then ruled by the fourteenth Dalai Lama. He escaped to India eight years later.

A Buddhist king of Tibet from the seventh century built the original royal residence at the city of Lhasa. His palace sits on the Potala, or Buddha's Mountain, overlooking the city. The fifth Dalai Lama began rebuilding Potala Palace in 1645. The new palace far exceeded the old ruins and rose thirteen stories. When the Dalai Lama died in 1682, the monks kept his death secret until the building was finished in 1694.

The massive palace has one thousand rooms, ten thousand shrines, and twenty thousand statues. The

top floor served as a secluded place for the Dalai Lama to meditate. Other floors provided living quarters, meditation halls, libraries, storerooms, and a school for monks. The palace also contains armories, the tombs of eight Dalai Lamas, torture chambers, and the Cave of Scorpions dungeon. The palace is now a museum.

between the Great Wall and the country of Mongolia. Slightly smaller than Tibet, it stretches along two-thirds of the Mongolian border and southward to the Great Wall. The Gobi Desert covers most of the region, but steppes (dry grasslands) mark its edges. The Chinese government has tried to increase the production of spring wheat, millet, and oats in this region. During the Middle Ages, the Mongol armies of Genghis Khan roamed throughout the Gobi. Mongols still inhabit this autonomous region. They speak a Mongol language and are traditionally Tibetan Buddhists.

Ningxia The last of China's five autonomous regions is Ningxia. This small region lies just inside the Great Wall where the Huang He flows into Inner Mongolia. The Hui people who live in this region have the same physical features as the Han, but they follow Islam. Numbering over seven million, they form one of China's largest minorities—the only minority recognized for religious rather than ethnic reasons.

Modern yurts use canvas rather than animal skins and protect their inhabitants from extreme temperatures ranging from −57 to 96°F.

SECTION REVIEW

1. What is the largest minority in China?
2. What region is "The Roof of the World"?
3. Who leads the Tibetan Buddhists?
4. What is Tibet's capital?
5. What desert in the Far East contains the lowest elevation?
- Which four autonomous regions border a foreign country? Identify each opposing country.

MONGOLIA

Mongolia is the ancestral home of a nomadic people called the **Mongols.** These hardy and independent people wandered over the grassy plateaus grazing their herds. They dwelt in collapsible round tents called *yurts.* These dwellings, made of layers of felt and covered with hides, protected them from extreme temperatures.

During the thirteenth century the Mongols conquered the largest land area in history. **Genghis**

Khan and his grandson Kublai Khan ruled from East Asia to Eastern Europe. The Mongols were among the most savage conquerors of all time. Skilled horsemen, they developed a system similar to the pony express, which linked the great khan in China with the outer reaches of his realm. Though they spread their Mongolic language afar, the khan's heirs and his Mongol tribes never fully united, and the empire soon disintegrated.

The Manchus next controlled this region, called Outer Mongolia, until the civil war of the early twentieth century. While China was distracted, Russia stepped in to guarantee a measure of "independence" for Mongolia. The Communist Party came to power in 1924 and imposed harsh rule on the people. The party collapsed in 1990 as the rest of the Soviet bloc dissolved, but freedoms were short-lived. As in other Central Asian countries, Mongolia soon clamped down on Christian missionaries.

Mongolia's main urban center is the capital, Ulan Bator. A railroad has joined the caravan route across the six hundred miles between Ulan Bator and the Great Wall of China near Beijing. The capital lies in the best grazing lands of north central and northeast Mongolia. Though few nomads remain, one-half of the people still raise livestock. The large farms raise mostly sheep, but also camels, horses, cattle, and goats. Cattle and wool are the main exports.

The **Gobi,** which covers over five hundred thousand square miles in Mongolia and China, is larger than any other desert in the world except the Sahara. The desert averages four thousand feet above sea level and extends twelve hundred miles from west to east. The Gobi is the world's coldest and most northerly desert. The soils are sandy but rarely result in sand dunes. In the 1920s protoceratop eggs were discovered here, preserved by the dry soil. They were the first dinosaur eggs found.

CHINESE NATIONALISTS IN TAIWAN

Taiwan is an island in the South China Sea about one hundred miles off the coast of China. A mountain range reaching 13,113 feet forms the backbone of the island. The gentle western slopes descend to plains, which support most of the island's population. Summer monsoons bring heavy rains and strong winds. Farmers have terraced many hills to make more land for growing rice. Chemical fertilizers and insecticides enable farmers to grow at least two crops of rice per year on the same field. Other crops include soybeans, sweet potatoes, bananas, and sugar.

In 1949, the Chinese Nationalists led by Chiang Kai-shek fled to Taiwan and reestablished

A man works in a terraced field in Taiwan.

Wei Chuan Foods is an example of modern industry in Taiwan.

their government at Taipei. Taipei, on the north end of the island, is a busy industrial center of over two million people. Taipei's history reaches back less than three hundred years, but the city museums hold many priceless treasures of China's past, brought by Chiang Kai-shek from the mainland. The chains of Communism do not shackle this modern city, which enjoys freedom and prosperity.

The Nationalists inherited the roads, factories, and irrigation projects that the Japanese developed during their rule from 1895 to 1945. The Nationalists then combined cheap Taiwanese labor with money from American investors to build one of Asia's first industrialized countries. Taiwan's manufacturing includes high tech industries, such as computers and electronics. The United Nations expelled Taiwan in 1971 so that Communist China could be admitted. In 1978, the United States broke off diplomatic relations with Taiwan. Nevertheless, U.S. warships continue to prowl the Taiwan Strait, guarding its old ally. Though the United States does not officially recognize its status as a country, Taiwan is America's sixth largest trading partner.

Though mainland China claims Taiwan, Taiwan believes that the legitimate government is in Taipei, not Beijing. Taiwan stops short of formally declaring independence for fear that China might use that as an excuse to invade. With the end of martial law in 1987, Taiwan became a democracy and lifted the ban on new political parties. Lee Teng-hui became Taiwan's first democratically elected president in 1996. But the potential for war with mainland China remains.

DIVIDED KOREA

Korea, "the Land of the Morning Calm," lies on a peninsula that extends south from northeastern China. Mountain ranges cover most of the **Korean Peninsula.** The mountains provide mineral resources, and the two countries on the peninsula rank among the world's top ten producers of tungsten and smelted zinc. Both also produce coal, graphite, iron, and lead. Two rivers, the Yalu and Tumen, form the border between Korea and its northern neighbors, China and Russia. These rivers flow down from Korea's highest mountain, Mount Paektu, at the north end of the Hamgyong Mountains. This volcanic mountain has a famous crater lake. The peninsula's most beautiful range runs down the center of the peninsula—the Taebaek Mountains.

A minor coastal plain lies on the east coast in North Korea, but mountains are dominant in the east. The most important coastal plain stretches along the western and southern coasts. This plain has most of the arable land on the peninsula, and the climate is generally humid continental. Two-thirds of all Koreans live on this plain. All five of the peninsula's major cities lie in this plain, including the capitals of North and South Korea.

The turbulent history of the peninsula is due in part to its unfortunate geographic position. The Korean Peninsula serves as a bridge between the larger, more powerful countries on every side. China conquered Korea in 108 B.C., the Mongols in A.D. 1259, Japan in the 1590s, and the Manchus in the 1630s. These invaders wanted not only to expand their borders but also to protect their respective countries from attack. Within a few centuries, the Koreans drove out each wave of invaders.

In 1910, Japan took complete control of Korea and began to govern it as a colony. The Japanese initiated an extensive modernization program, building railroads and developing industries. However, this was done solely for Japan's self-interest. The Korean people resented Japan's repressive government, which took away their freedoms. The Japanese drafted Korean men to work in factories and mines, and even to fight in their military. After Japan's defeat in World War II, Korea was divided into two states, North Korea and South Korea.

North Korea

The United States and the Soviet Union agreed that Soviet forces would occupy northern Korea to oversee the Japanese surrender, and the United States would do the same in the south. Much to the dismay of the United Nations, the Soviet Union refused to give up its territory. Instead, the Soviets established a Communist satellite called the Democratic People's Republic of Korea.

Hoping to unify the peninsula under Communism, the superior North Korean army invaded South Korea in 1950. Troops from the United States and the United Nations were rushed to the peninsula just in time to avert certain defeat. Eventually China joined the fray on North Korea's side. After three years of death and untold destruction, a truce was declared and the fighting stopped. The boundary between North and South Korea is a **demilitarized zone,** a strip of land in which no troops or weapons are allowed. However, a peace treaty was never signed, so technically the two nations are still at war. Ever since then, America has kept tens of thousands of soldiers on patrol in South Korea.

North Korea's Communist ruler "Great Leader" Kim Il Sung, isolated his country from the rest of the world. He taught self-reliance *(chuch'e).* The government owns all industries and farms and discourages religion. Everything is centralized. The capital, Pyongyang, has the only university. The capital is also the manufacturing center, and all the minerals are brought to factories there. Recent food and fuel shortages have forced the Communists to seek aid to avert famine.

South Korea

South Korea, also known as the Republic of Korea, occupies an area slightly larger than Indiana. Cheju is the largest of its three thousand islands. The favorable climate and irrigation

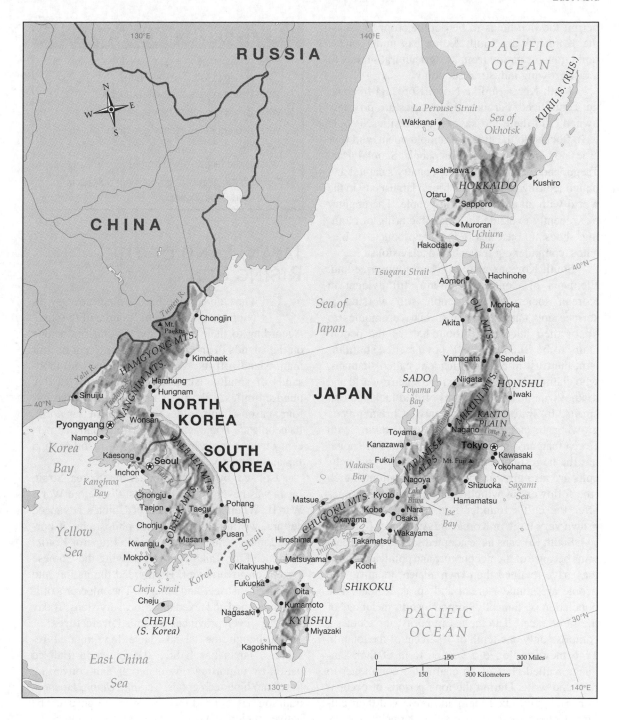

permit the rice fields to be double cropped. Since the Korean War, South Korea has undergone a rapid transformation from an agricultural society to a fast-growing industrial economy.

South Korea, unlike North Korea, is free and not centralized. Farms and industries are privately owned, and there are several universities. People have flocked to the cities for employment, and four cities now exceed two million people: Seoul, Pusan, Taegu, and Inchon. **Seoul,** the country's capital and manufacturing center, is the fourth largest city in the world with about ten million people. The country has recently expanded its manufacturing of clothing, shoes, and textiles to include products such as autos, computer equipment, and televisions.

South Koreans also enjoy religious freedom. Elements of Confucianism are still evident in Korean society. Many people still worship at shrines and participate in special ceremonies to honor their ancestors. About half of the people claim to be Buddhists, but they practice **shamanism,** the trust in religious leaders, called shamans, who claim to have contact with the spirit world and to know magic spells to ward off bad luck and evil spirits. In spite of this darkness, Christianity is growing. In fact, there are more converts in South Korea than anywhere else in East Asia. The capital has the largest church in the world. Unfortunately, cults are also growing, and the Unification Church (the followers of which are often called Moonies after the cult's founder Sun Myung Moon) has grown very large in Korea and America.

South Koreans have adopted some Western customs because of their economic and political ties, but they have retained their own ancient identity. The people are ethnic Korean and speak Korean. The population is ethnically **homogeneous,** meaning "of the same race." The largest minority, the Chinese, comprise only one-tenth of 1 percent of the total. In 1446 they developed a written form of their language, called Hangul, to enable the commoner to read and write. During the long periods of occupation, Hangul unified them and preserved their culture. Korean food is very spicy. Kimchi, a spicy pickled cabbage dish, is served at most meals.

SECTION REVIEW

1. What nomadic people dominated the Far East and Central Asia under Genghis Khan?

2. What desert covers southern Mongolia?

3. What island is run by Chinese nationalists?

4. What two countries occupy a peninsula in Far East Asia?

5. What is the largest city in Korea?

- Contrast the effects of government policies in North and South Korea.

JAPAN, LAND OF THE RISING SUN

The Japanese refer to their country as Nippon, which means "source of the sun." According to their mythology, the sun first shone on the islands of Japan. Japan is a crescent of four main islands off the Asian coast, along with thousands of smaller islands that stretch for twelve hundred miles. Like the United States, Japan has four seasons, with colder winters in the far north. Its people are homogeneous; only one-half of 1 percent of the people have ethnic origins other than Japanese (mostly Korean).

Isolated by the 120-mile-wide Korea Strait, Japan was never invaded successfully before World War II. When Japan learned of China's advanced culture, writing, literature, and philosophy, it borrowed many Chinese ideas. In 645 Emperor Kotoki introduced the Taika Reform, copying the Chinese system of government. He divided the nation into provinces, districts, and villages. The emperor's officials governed and taxed these local divisions. Today the forty-seven provinces are called **prefectures.**

Although the islands have few mineral resources, Japan has built a thriving industrialized nation by importing raw materials and converting them into high tech goods. Yet, like China, Japanese tradition has blinded the people to the gospel. The native religion of Japan, called **Shinto,** promotes the worship of many gods, called *kami*. Japanese believe

The bronze statue Daibutsu, or Great Buddha, rises forty-two feet in the air. It sits at Kamakura, Japan, ten miles southwest of Yokohama.

these gods indwell mountains, rivers, trees, and other parts of nature. Nearly all Japanese practice some Shinto ceremonies. Offering flowers and cakes to appease the kami is one of the most common practices. Over time, the Japanese people have learned to follow elements of Buddhism and Confucianism too.

Buddhism came in A.D. 552. Almost two-thirds of the Japanese accept some Buddhist teaching, so Japan is a difficult mission field. About 3 percent of the Japanese are Christians, yet conversions are rare because a new convert must break strong ties with family traditions and culture.

A man's foes shall be they of his own household. He that loveth father or mother more than me is not worthy of me. (Matt. 10:36-37)

The Emperors of Honshu

Japan's population is about one-half of that of the United States, but all of its people are concentrated in an area the size of California. Narrow coastal plains

Fujikyu Highlands amusement park in Japan

lie around the mountains and support most of the population. The precious arable land is intensely cultivated to produce some of the world's highest yields. **Honshu,** Japan's largest island, is home to over 80 percent of the Japanese people. It contains thirty-four of the forty-seven prefectures, including Tokyo.

Many Changes in Tokyo Tokyo has over eight million people. It is now the largest city in Japan and part of the largest metropolitan area in the world. Yokohama, Japan's second largest city and main port, is close to Tokyo. Another major city, Kawasaki, lies between them. Over twenty-six million people live in the combined cities of the Tokyo-Yokohama metropolitan area. This populous area constitutes the Keihin Industrial Region, which produces ships, petroleum, steel, and electronic equipment. The entire industrial region is on Japan's largest lowland, the **Kanto Plain,** a major agricultural region that produces silk, wheat, and rice.

Tokyo is a state-of-the-art financial center. It has one of the world's leading stock exchanges. Its banks and industries make Japan one of the richest nations in the world. Japanese students flock to Tokyo after graduation from school, hoping to find work. With rapid growth, land is scarce and expensive. Traffic and pollution are problematic, but Tokyo's crime rate is significantly lower than that in most Western cities.

Tokyo, meaning "eastern capital," became the name for the city of Edo in 1868. Soon after a visit by the American admiral Perry, who showed off

Samurai warriors in traditional dress

Tokyo at night

America's ironclad fleet, Emperor Mutsuhito introduced one of the most amazing decisions in the modern world. He attempted to transform a feudal society into an industrial giant in one generation. Mutsuhito adopted the title *Meiji,* or "enlightened rule," and set out to modernize Japan by seeking Western ideas and technology. During the **Meiji Restoration,** counselors went abroad to study government, education, and industry. The emperor established modern schools, modern industry, a parliament, and a modern army and navy.

But the ancient military traditions did not die. The government tried to remove Buddhist and other foreign influences in the nineteenth century. "State Shinto" stressed patriotism, the divine origin of the emperor, and the rightful world rule by the Japanese emperor. State Shinto spurred the Japanese to seek an empire in World War II. Following Japan's defeat, the leaders abolished State Shinto and the emperor renounced all claims to divinity.

Japan made another miraculous change after the war. The Allied occupation forces, particularly the United States, established a new republican constitution in 1947. It transferred the emperor's power to the people. The **Diet,** Japan's parliament, has two houses and selects a prime minister. The constitution forbids waging war; however, Japan maintains armed forces for defense. The emperor is still a symbol of Japan, but he has ceremonial duties only.

Shoguns of Kyoto Mountains cover about 85 percent of Japan. The loftiest peaks are found in the center of Honshu, at the Japanese Alps. Several peaks exceed ten thousand feet. The highest, **Mount Fuji,** reaches 12,389 feet. Earthquakes are common. In 1995 a quake killed more than five thousand people in Kobe. The Japanese Alps provide zinc and lead. Tin deposits lie in the Chugoku Mountains to the west.

Japan's third largest city is **Osaka.** Osaka belongs to the metropolitan area, called the Hanshin Industrial Region. This is the second largest metropolitan area in Japan, which includes both Kobe and Kyoto, both cities of over one million people. These cities produce pharmaceuticals, textiles, and steel.

Kyoto served as Japan's capital for over one thousand years, beginning in 794. During this time, warriors *(samurai)* protected estates of feudal lords *(daimyo),* whose rivalries escalated into civil war. When the Yoritomo clan established itself as the country's strongest clan in 1192, the emperor granted Yoritomo the title of *shogun,* meaning "great general" of the people. Shoguns ruled Japan in the emperor's name until 1867.

Other Industrial Centers Honshu still has three other major industrial regions besides scattered industrial cities. Nagoya is Japan's fourth largest city, and the Chukyo Industrial Region around it produces many Japanese cars, synthetic fibers, ceramics, and aircraft. Only the United States has a greater ratio of car owners than Japan. The

Japanese Colonial Empire

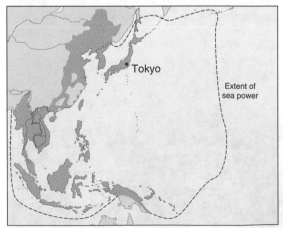

Tokyo

Extent of sea power

Sushi and Sumo

Ohio. Japan has had the greatest influence on America of any country in the Far East. Japan has become a world leader in business and marketing. The Japanese *yen* always compares favorably to the American dollar.

Japanese traditionally eat rice and seafoods at every meal, usually with chopsticks. Many dishes include *tofu,*

Japanese family

pickled vegetables, or soy sauce. *Sukiyaki* is made with beef strips, vegetables, bean curd, and noodles. Favorite seafoods include fish, lobster, shrimp, squid, octopus, and eel. Fish are dried, cooked, or eaten raw. Raw fish is called *sashimi.* It is often served in cold, bite-sized rice cakes wrapped in seaweed. These cakes are called *sushi.*

A typical arrangement of sushi *and* sashimi

Traditional Japanese houses have large rooms divided by wood-and-paper sliding doors. Thick straw mats called *tatami* cover the floors, and people sit on cushions on the floor. Traditionally, men and women wore a *kimono,* a robe with long wide sleeves and a sash. These practices are changing as a result of Western influences.

The Japanese no longer have *samurai* warriors, with their own elaborate garb and sword. Nor do the Japanese often commit ritual *seppuku,* or suicide. But their lives continue to revolve around the concept of "saving face." They hold dearly to their ancient duties to their group, to their elders, and to their juniors. Everyone is expected to keep his place, and there are rules governing every social situation. To avoid bringing shame on themselves or others, the Japanese avoid the blunt statements common among Americans.

Japanese students attend school six days a week with short vacations in spring and fall. Because they have no school buses, students come on foot, bike, or public buses. Schools also do not have janitors, so students help with cleanup. Clubs after school include swimming, gymnastics, flower arranging, and English. Students are very competitive among their peers during final exams.

Although Japan borrowed its painting and pagoda architecture from China, Japan also has its own art forms. *Haiku* poetry, with three short lines, is popular in America. Because good land is scarce, Japanese gardeners honor efficient use of space, such as *bonsai.* The Japanese have also perfected the art of paper folding, or *origami.* Another specialty is the art of flower arrangement, or *ikebana.*

Japanese have borrowed much Western entertainment, especially baseball. But they have their own traditions too. *Geisha* means artist, and geisha girls are artists of social graces who wear traditional kimonos as they entertain patrons in restaurants with formal tea ceremonies. *Kabuki* is a theatrical performance dating from the seventeenth century, involving lavish costumes and melodramatic scenes. *Kendo* is a type of fencing with bamboo sticks. Japanese martial arts include *aikido, judo,* and *karate.* The huge and powerful *sumo* wrestlers are national heroes. *Sayonara.*

Masked actor in the kabuki *theater*

Bonsai

Gardens

Japanese gardens are so famous that most public gardens in America have a section in the Japanese style. Japanese gardens often include arched footbridges, small pagodas, flowers, conifers, and ponds. Such gardens may include an outdoor café where tea is served. These gardens are always carefully laid out and never look cluttered. Tokyo has many popular Japanese gardens. Two old and famous Japanese gardens are Korakuen Garden and Rikugien Garden.

Japanese garden

One unique aspect of Japanese gardening is *bonsai*. Bonsai is the practice of growing miniature trees. By growing the trees in flowerpots or trays with carefully selected soil and fertilizer, the trees remain healthy but are stunted. Pruning develops branches in the desired places. Shaping by tying, bracing, or using copper wires makes the full-grown tree look exactly like a normal tree, though it stands only two or three feet high. The gardener must continually care for his potted tree by watering, fertilizing, pruning, and shaping it.

Hokuriku Region on the west coast extends from Niigata to Kanazawa and produces machinery and chemicals, typical of all five industrial areas. The final industrial area is the Inland Sea Region. It lines both sides of the **Inland Sea** and produces rubber, trucks, and agricultural machinery. Hiroshima, a city of over one million and the site of the first atomic bombing, is part of this industrial area.

Rural Shikoku

Shikoku, the smallest of Japan's four main islands, lies south of Honshu. With only 3 percent of the Japanese people, this mountainous and heavily forested island has only four prefectures. It has remained somewhat separate from the rest of Japan. Rice farms and villages nestle in the valleys and appear as they have for over a century. Japanese Buddhists still take pilgrimages to the island's eighty-eight sacred temples, hoping to be released from the cycle of rebirth.

Until recently, religious and medical travelers had to take a ferry across the Inland Sea to reach the island. With the opening of the 7.5-mile-long bridge, which is high enough for ships to pass under, life is changing. Most people live on the north shore along the beautiful Inland Sea, where cities and factories are growing as part of the Inland Sea Industrial Region. Copper from Shikoku's mines can be transported to Honshu.

Shikoku was the last of Japan's main islands linked to Honshu. The great Seto Ohashi Bridge, completed in 1988, crosses five small islands on its 7.5-mile journey. The system includes three suspension bridges, two cable-stayed bridges, and a truss bridge. The cable-stayed spans are the longest of their type in the world.

Kyushu, the Birthplace of Japan

Kyushu is the southernmost and second most populous of Japan's main islands. Because it is nearest to the Korean Peninsula, the early settlers built Japan's first cities here. The mild climate and lush green countryside support 10 percent of Japan's population in seven prefectures. Two cities exceed one million people on its north coast. The chief agricultural region in the northwest grows rice and tea. Northern coal fields produce about one-half of the coal mined in Japan.

Because of its proximity to Korea and China, this island has faced the brunt of foreign attacks. In 1281 Kyushu natives repelled Kublai Khan's Mongol warriors. The natives were aided by a *kamikaze,* meaning "divine wind," which blew the Mongol ships out to sea. When Japan opened its doors to foreigners in 1859, the port city of Nagasaki became the most important trading center in the country. Nagasaki is often referred to as the San Francisco of Japan. The United States chose to drop its second atomic bomb on this city in 1945, hoping to end World War II.

Japan has many small islands. The United States captured the more important ones in World War II to use as bases for bombers. The Ryuku Islands form a chain of one hundred islands from Kyushu to Taiwan. These include **Okinawa,** Japan's fifth most populous island and the only prefecture not on one of the four main islands. The ninety-seven Bonin Islands are southeast of Japan. Iwo Jima is one of the three Volcano Islands further south.

Hokkaido, the Cold Northern Frontier

The northernmost of the four main Japanese islands is **Hokkaido.** The population is concentrated in Sapporo, a city of over one million people. Hokkaido's winters are long and severe, and its summers are cool due to the influence of the cold Oyashio (or Kuril) Current. Surrounding waters provide a rich source of pollack and mackerel. Japan has the world's largest fish processing industry and the second largest annual catch. Of Japan's many seafoods, it leads the world in its tuna catch and ranks second to the United States in its salmon catch.

Hokkaido compares to the American West as Japan's last frontier. As the second largest island and the largest prefecture, it is a big area but with a small population (only 5 percent of Japan's population) and is developed in pockets. Like the American frontier, Hokkaido has several natural resources. Lumber comes from the island's heavily

Itsukushima Shrine

The Itsukushima Shrine near Hiroshima has Japan's largest *torii,* or gateway, marking a sacred Shinto site. The buildings of the shrine sit on an island in the Inland Sea, while the gateway stands offshore in the shallow waters of the bay. The two main supporting beams of the gateway rise fifty-three feet. The shrine dates from the twelfth century, and the magnificent gateway was added in 1875.

The sacred shrine is dedicated to three Japanese gods: Susano, Okinonushi, and Tenjin. No cemeteries defile the island, and dogs are prohibited so as not to disturb the deer. The wooded island has two pagodas, a treasury building, and the Hall of One Thousand Mats. But most of the white and red buildings stand on wooden platforms in the bay. The platforms make the

The torii welcomes guests to the Itsukushima Shrine on Miyajima Island, off the coast of Honshu.

shrine seem to float above the water. Bridges and covered walks link the buildings to one another and to the island. The shrine's beauty is unsurpassed at dusk, when the sunset reflects on the water and the lanterns glow.

Geographer's Corner

Balance of Trade

For most of its history, the United States sent most of its goods to Europe. But in recent years the Pacific Rim has become its primary focus of trade. This new trade has created new concerns because the Asian countries are selling more than they are buying.

Balance of trade is the value of exports minus imports. A negative balance means that the country is buying more goods than it is selling. The two countries that have the largest impact on U.S. balance of trade are China and Japan. The news media often report these statistics as a threat to the safety of the U.S. economy.

Yet it is the *volume* of trade that is more important than the *balance* of trade. In 1955 the United States exported $14 billion and imported $12 billion worth of goods (+$2 billion balance). In 1996 it exported $625 billion and imported $795 billion (-$170 billion balance). America's exports had increased almost fifty times. Which is better for the United States, a +$2 billion balance of trade or a +$611 billion increase in volume of trade?

1. Which country buys the most U.S. exports?

Top U.S. Trade Partners

COUNTRY	U.S. EXPORTS TO (BILLIONS)	U.S. IMPORTS FROM (BILLIONS)	U.S. TRADE BALANCE (BILLIONS)
1. Canada	$127.2	$145.3	–$18.1
2. Japan	$64.3	$123.5	–$59.1
3. Mexico	$46.3	$61.7	–$15.4
4. United Kingdom	$28.9	$26.9	$2.0
5. South Korea	$25.4	$24.2	$1.2
6. Germany	$22.4	$36.8	–$14.4
7. Taiwan	$19.3	$29.0	–$9.7
8. Netherlands	$16.6	$6.4	$10.2
9. Singapore	$15.3	$18.5	–$3.2
10. China	$11.7	$45.5	–$33.8

2. How many Asian countries sell more goods to the United States than they buy?

3. How many of the countries buy more goods from the United States than they sell? What regions of the world are they from?

💡 What is China's trade balance? In what way is this worse than any other country on the chart?

---

forested mountains, and manganese comes from its southern peninsula. It is also a haven for recreation, including summer hiking and winter skiing. The Seikan Tunnel, the world's longest railway tunnel, transports these resources under the sea to Honshu.

Hokkaido also has its version of Indians, the **Ainu** people, Japan's original inhabitants. The Japanese have always considered the Ainu an inferior people. Over time, the Ainu retreated north to Hokkaido. They survived by hunting, fishing, and planting small gardens. Intermarriage with Japanese has since made full-blooded Ainu rare. Their most unusual trait is white skin. After World War II, social reforms assimilated the Ainu into the Japanese culture. As a consequence, their culture and their language—which were never fully studied—declined. Recently the Japanese government has begun to compensate the Ainu for the years of mistreatment and discrimination.

Having studied South, Southeast, and Far East Asia, you can see that few Asian countries are open to the gospel. God has withheld final judgment, in part, to give the multitudes a chance to choose the Lord's salvation before the day of judgment. Pray for Asia.

Multitudes, multitudes in the valley of decision: for the day of the Lord is near in the valley of decision. (Joel 3:14)

SECTION REVIEW

1. What is the religion that influences all Japanese people?
2. What is the world's largest metropolitan area?
3. Who are shoguns? samurai? Ainu?
4. What is the highest mountain in the Japanese Alps?
5. Name the four main Japanese islands.
💡 How many Japanese cities exceed one million people? How many of these are on Honshu? Are they evenly spread across Honshu?

REVIEW

Can You Define These Terms?

intensive farming	open city	double cropped	shamanism
dynasty	aquaculture	Cantonese	homogeneous
Confucianism	collective farm	theocrat	prefecture
ancestor worship	commune	yurt	Shinto
Taoism	special municipality	demilitarized zone	Diet

Can You Locate These Natural Features?

North China Plain	Tibet	Taiwan	Inland Sea
Qin Ling Mountains	Kunlun	Korean Peninsula	Shikoku
Huang He	Trans-Himalaya	Honshu	Kyushu
Chang River	Taklimakan Desert	Kanto Plain	Okinawa
Sichuan Basin	Gobi	Mount Fuji	Hokkaido
Xi River			

Can You Explain the Significance of These People, Places, and Events?

Han	Great Leap Forward	Zhuang	Genghis Khan
Xi'an	Cultural Revolution	Lhasa	Seoul
Chiang Kai-shek	Manchuria	Dalai Lama	Tokyo
Shanghai	Manchus	Xinjiang	Meiji Restoration
Beijing	Guangzhou	Inner Mongolia	Osaka
Tiananmen Square	Hong Kong	Mongols	Ainu
Mao Zedong			

How Much Do You Remember?

1. What are the two main rivers of China?
2. What three influences shaped the Chinese folk religions?
3. Why is the Qin Ling important?
4. Why did the Chinese select Chongqing as a capital in World War II?
5. Name the three special municipalities in China.
6. What key products come from the Southern Uplands of China?
7. Which two of the seven great ranges of Asia are completely within China?
8. What is China's largest autonomous region?
9. What desert dominates Mongolia?
10. Where did Chiang Kai-shek flee from Mao Zedong?
11. What is the largest city of the Korean Peninsula?
12. What are the two largest cities in Japan?
13. Which Japanese island . . .
    a. has the largest population?
    b. is the most northerly and wild?
    c. has the highest peaks?
    d. was a place for religious pilgrims?
    e. is home to the Ainu people?

What Do You Think?

1. Explain what is wrong with Communism. Use countries in this chapter as positive and negative examples.
2. Identify the five most important differences between China and Japan.
3. Why has God allowed Communism to become so powerful in China?

Cumulative Review

1. Name the seven continents and four oceans. What two oceans touch the culture region of Asia?
2. Name the seven high ranges of the Asian Mountain System.
3. Define primary, secondary, and tertiary industries. Which industry is most prominent in India? in Japan? in China?
4. List the three cultural subregions of Asia. For each subregion, give the most populous nation, the largest country in size, and the biggest city.
5. Pick the most interesting Asian country that you have studied. Give the most important land features, one famous person, a famous man-made structure, and at least one major event.

Turkey

Syria

Eastern Mediterranean

Palestine

Iraq

Iran

Egypt

Persian Gulf

Arabia

UNIT VIII

The Middle East

Chapter 22
The Persian Gulf

Chapter 23
The Eastern Mediterranean

CHAPTER 22

THE PERSIAN GULF

The **Middle East,** located at the crossroads of three continents, has been the focus of world history. The descendants of Noah founded the first civilization here. The three major monotheistic religions—Judaism, Christianity, and Islam—began here. Conquering armies have swept back and forth across the ancient trade routes, bathing the land in blood. The Middle East is at once a region of wealth and poverty, of beauty and terror, of ancient ways and modern industry.

The next chapter will cover the western half of the Middle East, on the rim of the Mediterranean Sea. This chapter will look at the eastern half, where the **Persian Gulf** is the center of population and trade. The gulf has been a hub of activity since ancient times, as ships have sailed through the Arabian Sea to ports in Asia and Africa. Islam was founded in this region during the Middle Ages, and it has come to dominate every aspect of life.

Although Muslims believe Jesus was a prophet, they have the only major world religion whose founder directly attacked the deity of Jesus Christ: "Allah could not take to himself any son!" By rejecting the Son of God, the leaders of Islam have made themselves the enemies of the Father.

The kings of the earth set themselves, and the rulers take counsel together, against the Lord, and against his anointed. . . . He that sitteth in the heavens shall laugh: the Lord shall have them in derision. Then shall he speak unto them in his wrath, and vex them in his sore displeasure. (Ps. 2:2, 4-5)

The great Islamic empires fell into decay long ago. The discovery of oil in the twentieth century put the Persian Gulf back at the center of world politics, and money from oil has revolutionized life in the region. But most of the money benefits Western businesses and rulers, while the common people continue to struggle in poverty under their harsh rulers. They envy the wealth of the West and look to their ancient cities and archeological sites as reminders of fallen glory, which they long to regain.

SAUDI ARABIA, BIRTHPLACE OF ISLAM

Saudi Arabia is the most influential country in the Middle East. Besides being the largest Middle Eastern nation, it is the greatest oil

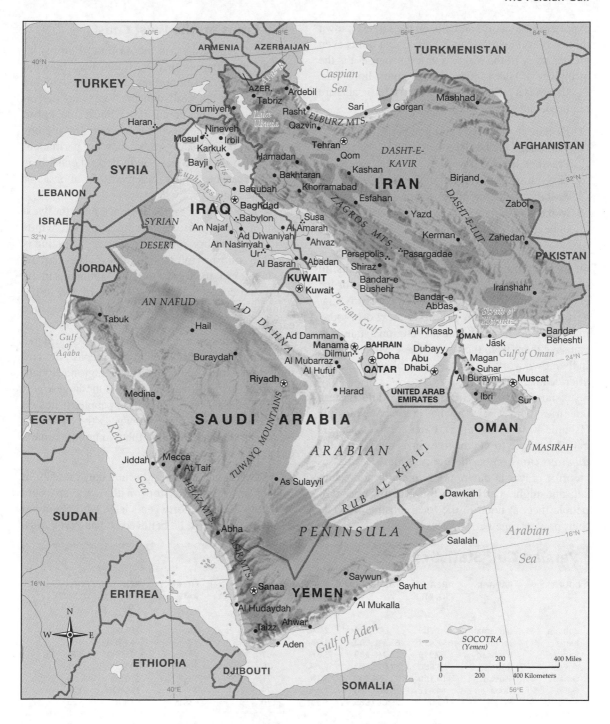

exporter in the world and sits on the largest known oil reserves on earth. But Saudi Arabia holds even greater sway in the Muslim world because it is the birthplace of Islam and home to its most holy sites.

Islam is a religion of works. Five basic acts are required, called the Pillars of Islam.

1. Declare that "There is no god but Allah, and Muhammad is His Messenger."
2. Pray five times a day.
3. Give alms (or the *zakat*) to the poor.
4. Fast during the month of **Ramadan.**
5. Make a pilgrimage (or *hajj*) to Mecca at least once in a lifetime.

Repeating the declaration of the first pillar is all that is required for one to become a **Muslim** (follower of Islam). Therefore, it was easy for the early Muslims to force conquered people to "convert." Over one billion people in the world today make this declaration, but no religious statement can save them from their sins. These Muslims trust in their own works to get them to a blissful paradise after death.

Islam permeates life in most Middle Eastern countries today. Every city has at least one **mosque** (Islamic worship building). Criers or loudspeakers call the people to prayer five times daily from the *minarets* (towers) beside the mosques. Businesses stop for prayer at dawn, noon, midafternoon, sunset, and night. On Friday, the Muslim holy day, people meet at noon in the local mosque to recite their prayers together.

Holy Cities on the West Coast

Saudi Arabia lies on the **Arabian Peninsula,** which juts down from the Middle East into the Arabian Sea. Two important arms of the Arabian Sea—the Persian Gulf and the Red Sea—lie on either side of the peninsula. Almost the entire peninsula is desert, except for two semiarid regions near the coast. Saudi Arabia has no permanent rivers and no lakes. Since Saudis depend on springs or wells for water, most settlements are at oases or along the coasts.

A rare strip of highlands rises near the west coast of the peninsula, forcing monsoon winds periodically to drop precious moisture. Terracing is possible on the mountain slopes. The narrow coastal plain at the foot of the Asir Mountains in the southwest corner is the most fertile region in the country. This vital region has been inhabited since early history.

The primary highlands in the west are the Hejaz Mountains, which run parallel to the coast. Several important cities lie in the Hejaz region. Jiddah, meaning "Bride of the Red Sea," is the largest port on the Red Sea, with 1.5 million people. It lies on the narrow coastal plain known as the *Tihamah*. Nearby in the highlands are the two holiest centers of Islam: Mecca and Medina.

Mecca Muhammad was born about A.D. 570 in **Mecca,** an important stop on the caravan route along the Red Sea. Forty years later, while living in a cave in the desert, he believed he had revelations

Saudi Arabia, Yemen / Qatar all share

Persian Gulf Statistics

COUNTRY	CAPITAL	AREA (SQ. MI.)	POPULATION	NATURAL INCREASE	LIFE EXPECTANCY	LITERACY RATE	PER CAPITA GDP	POP. DENSITY
Bahrain	Manamah	268	603,318	2.0%	75	85%	$12,000	2,251
Iran	Tehran	632,457	67,540,002	2.6%	68	72%	$4,700	107
Iraq	Baghdad	167,975	22,219,289	3.6%	67	58%	$2,000	132
Kuwait	Kuwait	6,880	2,076,805	1.7%	76	79%	$17,000	301
Oman	Muscat	118,150	2,264,590	3.3%	71	59%	$10,800	19
Qatar	Doha	4,412	665,485	1.7%	74	79%	$20,820	150
Saudi Arabia	Riyadh	865,000	20,087,965	3.3%	70	63%	$10,100	23
United Arab Emirates	Abu Dhabi	32,278	2,262,309	1.5%	75	79%	$24,000	70
Yemen	Sanaa	205,356	13,972,477	3.6%	60	43%	$2,520	67

Let's Go Exploring

1. What is the most obvious contrast between the north and the south?

2. What is the predominant climate along the eastern edge of the Mediterranean Sea?

3. How many countries appear to be made up entirely of desert?

4. What climate does Iran have on the southern end of the Caspian Sea?

💡 From what you have learned about monsoon winds, why does the entire coast of the Arabian Sea have a dry climate?

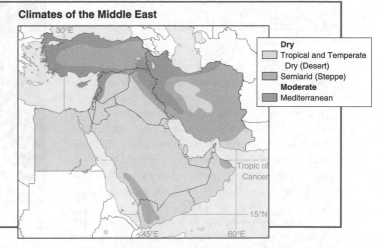

Climates of the Middle East

Dry
Tropical and Temperate
Dry (Desert)
Semiarid (Steppe)
Moderate
Mediterranean

from Allah (the Arab word for "God"). Muhammad became the prophet of Allah and founded Islam.

The **Koran,** the Muslim holy book that records Muhammad's revelations, requires every Muslim to make at least one pilgrimage to Mecca, although exceptions are made for the ill or poor. The pilgrimage is called a *hajj.* Every year during Ramadan two million *hajis* (pilgrims) from around the Muslim world converge on Mecca. They buy the Koran, prayer beads, and other mementos of their visit. Assembled in the Great Mosque, they recite prayers and march around the *Kaaba,* Islam's most holy shrine. On the walls of many houses in the Middle East, paintings commemorate the resident's *hajj.*

Medina Muhammad was run out of Mecca, and he fled to Medina. It was July 16, 622, according to the Western calendar. Islam's calendar begins on this date, called the Hegira. This date on the Muslim calendar is 1 A.H. (Anno Hegirae, meaning

"the year of the Hegira"). Unlike the West's calendar, based on the 365-day solar calendar, the Muslim world uses a 354-day lunar calendar. The year A.D. 2000 is 1420 A.H. to Muslims.

During Muhammad's eight years in Medina, he had to drive back several attacks from Mecca. In A.D. 630 his army entered Mecca in triumph. Most people accepted him as the Prophet of Allah. From here, he led the Arab people on a march to conquer the world in the name of Allah. By 750 Arab armies had spread their faith as far east as the Indus River and as far west as Spain.

Muhammad died in 632 and was buried at **Medina.** The Prophet's Mosque over his tomb is the second most holy place for Muslims. Most pilgrims visit the mosque at Medina after they visit Mecca.

Deserts and Oases of Inland Arabia

The interior of the peninsula is even drier than the coast. Most of the land receives less than four inches of precipitation annually. About one-half of Saudi Arabia is tropical, and the rest is temperate, but freezing temperatures are rare. The heating and cooling of the rock and sand tend to make the climate uncomfortably hot, and temperatures over 100°F are common in the summer months. Hot, dry winds add to the discomfort.

The most desolate parts of Saudi Arabia are in the far north and the south. At least seven parts of

Spread of the Arab Empire

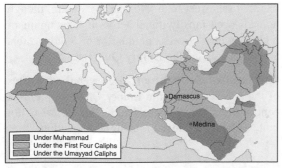

Damascus

Medina

Under Muhammad
Under the First Four Caliphs
Under the Umayyad Caliphs

493

Of Veils and Pilgrims

Assalamu 'aleikum. ("Peace be unto you.") Muslim women must wear a veil in public. Only their families are allowed to see their faces. In Saudi Arabia, they are also expected to wear a black cloak, called a *abaaya.* Even in cities, where these practices are not always observed, few jobs are open to women because they are not permitted to socialize with men outside their relatives. Islamic women hold the family honor in the highest regard, and they follow these traditions to ensure that they avoid any improper actions that might dishonor the family.

Men wear a turban or a *kaffiyeh* (head scarf). Among their friends they are open and expressive, but with strangers they tend to be reserved and formal. Men often hold hands when they walk together in public as an innocent expression of friendship. But couples are forbidden to hold hands and will be arrested by the religious police, or *mutawa.*

Muslims often pray and fast. They wash their face, hands, and feet and also remove their shoes before praying. Most men kneel on a prayer rug with their forehead to the ground as they recite the same prayers day after day. When they hear the call to prayer, they stop whatever they are doing, even if they are on the street. During the month of *Ramadan,* Muslims fast in daylight hours, but they eat at night.

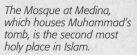

This Saudi woman displays her Najdi tulle dress, complete with sequined cuffs.

Shoppers inspect goods at the bazaar in Abu Dhabi, the capital of the United Arab Emirates.

Alms and pilgrimages are also among the Muslim Five Pillars. The government collects a voluntary tax, called *zakat,* and distributes it to the poor. The amount ranges from 2.5 percent to 10 percent. All Muslims are familiar with the currency in Saudi Arabia, the *riyal,* because they need it for their *hajj* (pilgrimage) to Mecca. Men who have completed the *hajj* earn the formal title *Hajji,* similar to Sir. If you meet Hajji Ali, you know that Ali has been to Mecca. *Ma' ssalama.*

The Mosque at Medina, which houses Muhammad's tomb, is the second most holy place in Islam.

the Arabian Desert have their own names. The most important one in the north is the An Nafud. The sands of the An Nafud eventually give way to the rocky Syrian Desert in the far north.

Rub al Khali

The key southern desert, the **Rub al Khali** (ROOB ahl KAH-lee), covers an area larger than California. It is the third largest desert in the world, surpassed only by the Sahara and the Gobi. The Rub al Khali is also the largest sand desert in the world. Shifting winds whip sand into dunes up to one thousand feet high. No one lives there, though nomads occasionally travel across it. This uninhabited wasteland covers one-quarter of Saudi Arabia and is aptly called the **Empty Quarter.**

The Capital Boomtown

Between these wastes of the An Nafud and the Empty Quarter is a large central plateau called the Nejd. This desert is not quite as harsh because of its higher elevation.

Missions

Tent Making

What kind of work can you do well? Many missionaries have developed skills in trades such as carpentry or mechanics. Others have studied English and can teach it for high school or college courses. These missionaries sometimes have the option of going directly to the mission field without raising support. In this position, they have a great opportunity to assist full-time missionaries. This type of missions work is called *tent making,* after the apostle Paul's practice of earning his own way by sewing tents (Acts 18:1-3).

Tent making has the disadvantage of taking time away from spreading the gospel and reducing prayer support from churches. But for Christians who want to spread the gospel in Muslim countries, they have no option. Few Muslim countries allow missionaries, but teachers and skilled technicians are welcome. Such missionaries can take comfort from Paul's example. Paul seldom received financial support from churches (Phil. 4:15).

Even if the missionary is honorably employed in his new country, he must be prepared to face serious opposition. In this case, missionaries remember the reminder in Scripture that "all that will live godly in Christ Jesus shall suffer persecution" (II Tim. 3:12). Are you willing to suffer for Jesus' sake?

Several oases dot the plateau. Riyadh, the capital, was built around one such oasis. In the early twentieth century, Riyadh was just a mud village. Since it became the capital of a united kingdom, it has become the largest city in the country, with about two million people.

Ibn-Saud conquered the desert tribes of Arabia and formed the kingdom of Saudi Arabia in the early twentieth century. To confirm his alliances, he married at least 282 women, divorcing them in turn so that he kept the Islamic requirement of no more than four wives at one time. His many descendants continue to rule Saudi Arabia with full authority. There is no constitution. The king is bound only by Islamic law and tradition. This religious influence is great, however. Non-Muslim peoples are almost outcasts in such a society, and Christian evangelism is strictly forbidden.

Black Gold on the East Coast

The eastern lowlands along the Persian Gulf are mostly sand and gravel, but there are several fertile oases. The Al-Hasa Oasis, at the base of the Nejd, is fed by over fifty springs and covers seventy square miles. The town of Al Hufuf lies in this oasis. The people grow such diverse crops as citrus fruits, rice, and wheat. Ad Dammam is the largest city on the coast, and Ras Tanura is the major port from which Saudi Arabia exports most of its oil.

The discovery of oil in 1936 created a new economy for Saudi Arabia. It has no other major resources, so the oil boom enabled the country to advance rapidly in industry, education, and health care. Now it must prepare new industries for the time when its oil supplies run out.

On the other hand, the oil supply should last a long time. The onshore and offshore oil wells tap the world's largest petroleum reserve. Only Russia exceeds Saudi Arabia in oil production worldwide. The West relies on a steady supply of inexpensive oil and is concerned about the succession of the next king. The lavish lifestyle of the Sauds has

(left) *His Majesty King Fahd ibn 'Abd al-'Aziz Al Sa'ud;* (below) *Oil workers*

Bedouins

The nomads of the Arabian Desert are called **Bedouins.** Traditionally, Bedouins have lived in tents, "houses of hair" carefully woven by the women. Bedouins in Saudi Arabia make the outside of their tents from black goats hair, but the inside is very colorful. Hand-woven curtains divide the interior, and carpets are cast on the dirt floor. The Bedouins wander between oases, seeking water for their livestock. Most Bedouins keep camels, sheep, and goats. They enjoy dates and dairy products and trade in village markets for pots, tools, and other household items.

Today there are about one million Bedouins, but very few of them wander all year. Many prefer the steady jobs and easier life that the oil-rich government has made available for them.

A Bedouin mother in Iraq attends to her child.

fueled a radical antigovernment movement. A civil war or an anti-West leader could cut the West off from eight million barrels of oil per day. The resulting energy crisis could dwarf any previous economic disaster.

◉ SECTION REVIEW

1. Who founded Islam?
2. What are the two most holy cities of Islam?
3. Who are Bedouins?
4. Who founded the Kingdom of Saudi Arabia?
5. What is another name for the Rub al Khali?
   ♀ Which Islamic pillars are unscriptural? Explain.

MINOR STATES ON THE ARABIAN PENINSULA

In the West, the Muslim world is sometimes called the "Arab world." The Muslim religion began on the Arabian Peninsula, and it was first spread by tribes of Arabic-speaking people, called **Arabs.** The Arabs spread their language and writing as well as their religion. No matter what language they speak in daily life, all Muslims in every nation study and memorize the Koran in the original Arabic language. Translations are not permitted.

Early in the history of Islam, the center of power shifted to the populous cities far north, leaving the Arabian Peninsula forgotten in the dust. Only a few towns thrived on the coast of the peninsula, visited by rare caravans and adventurous merchant ships. Separated by harsh deserts from the rest of the Middle East, these distant towns developed an independent spirit, resisting the later invasions of other Arabic tribes, Turks, and Europeans.

Farmers on the Arabian Sea

Six small coastal countries border Saudi Arabia on the east and south. Most of these lie on the Persian Gulf, but two lie farther out on the Arabian Sea. The two nations on the Arabian Sea—Yemen and Oman—do not share the wealth from the Persian Gulf oil reserves. Though they have some oil, their economies revolve around farming and trade.

Muslims worship at the most holy place in Islam, the Kaaba at Mecca.

Yemen, the First Arab Democracy

The Arabian Peninsula rises sharply in the southwest corner. From these highlands, the rest of the peninsula slopes downward. Yemen occupies this corner. Most people are poor. Their meager subsistence involves farming or herding. They trade their goods at *bazaars* (markets). Yemen has the lowest literacy rate and life expectancy in the Middle East.

Yemen has many other difficulties. Saudi Arabia still claims some of the northern border, which lies in the desert wastes of the Rub al Khali. At times, armies from the two nations have clashed.

Another problem is a history of civil war. Until 1990, Yemen was divided into two countries, North and South Yemen. South Yemen had the only Communist government in the Arab world during the Cold War, and it fought several battles with North Yemen. After the collapse of Communism in Europe, South Yemen agreed to unite with North Yemen. The northern capital became the capital of the now-united country. Like Germany, reunified Yemen faces many challenges, as it must improve South Yemen's economy, shattered by Communist rule. In 1993 Yemen became the first Arab nation to hold a multiparty general election, but the country's future is still uncertain.

The World of Islam

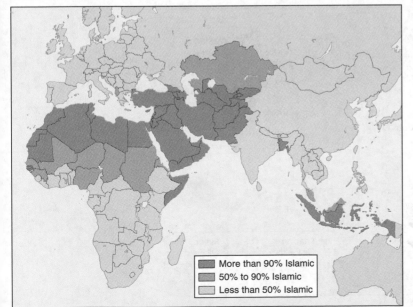

More than 90% Islamic
50% to 90% Islamic
Less than 50% Islamic

Northern Yemen on the Red Sea   Yemen has the highest peaks of the Arabian Peninsula. Rainfall in these highlands give Yemen the only permanent river on the entire peninsula. Sanaa, the capital, lies in these highlands in the major agricultural area. The main cash crops are coffee and **khat** (a shrub whose leaves are chewed in East Africa as a narcotic). Yemen is famous for mocha coffee, which is shipped from the coastal town of Mocha, west of Taizz.

This land on the Red Sea, once known as Sheba, was occupied long ago. The Queen of Sheba journeyed from here to visit Solomon (1 Kings 10:1-13). Sheba once contained gold and other minerals, but they have long since been exhausted.

Southern Yemen on the Gulf of Aden   The Red Sea is the westernmost arm of the Arabian Sea. But before its waters enter the Arabian Sea, they pass through a narrow spot called Bab el Mandeb and then pass into the **Gulf of Aden.** The vital port at Aden is Yemen's main city and the former capital of South Yemen. Aden was under British control for many years.

Yemen has several islands off the eastern horn of Africa. Socotra, the most important, was a major stop on the early Arab shipping routes across the Arabian Sea. Today, most islanders live by spearfishing from single-sail boats called *dhows*.

Sultanate of Oman

Oman is among the hottest countries in the world, with temperatures often reaching 130°F. Most of the country is part of the Rub al Khali desert. The people wear long white robes and turbans to protect themselves against the heat, wind, and blowing sand.

Although the Portuguese captured several ports in 1507, they could not take all of Oman. Arab tribes forced the Portuguese completely out by 1650. Oman even took part of East Africa. The present

The narrow Strait of Hormuz flows by Cape Musandam on Oman.

line of *sultans* (Muslim monarchs) came to power in 1740. The government is called a **sultanate.** Because Oman's ships could not compete with modern iron vessels, however, its trade declined in the nineteenth century, and it lost its African territory in 1861. Since 1970 it has begun a major push to modernize.

Dhofar Southwestern Oman, around the cities of Salalah and Dawkah, is a plateau called Dhofar. It is known for its many frankincense trees. The plateau gets slightly more rain than the surrounding desert.

Strategic Cities on the Gulf of Oman The main population center is a stretch of highlands that rises at the southeast corner of the Arabian Peninsula. This is the heart of Oman. It is one of only two places on the peninsula where mountains cause some regular rain to fall. A fertile coastal strip with date palms lies at the base of the mountains. The capital, Muscat, is on this coast.

The coast is important today because of its strategic location at the entrance to the Persian Gulf. Before the Arabian Sea enters the Persian Gulf, it passes through the **Gulf of Oman.** In addition to the main territory along this gulf, Oman controls Cape Musandam, at the narrowest junction of the Gulf of Oman and the Persian Gulf. The Omani town of Al Khasab on the cape guards the strategic Strait of Hormuz, which all oil tankers pass through from the Persian Gulf.

Emirates on the Persian Gulf

In the nineteenth century various rulers on the coast of the Persian Gulf asked Great Britain to protect them from their powerful neighbors. In return, they gave Britain control of foreign affairs. When Britain withdrew from the Persian Gulf in 1971, these tiny British protectorates became independent. Since oil was discovered in the 1930s, all four minicountries on the Persian Gulf have greatly profited.

Petroleum Reserves of the World

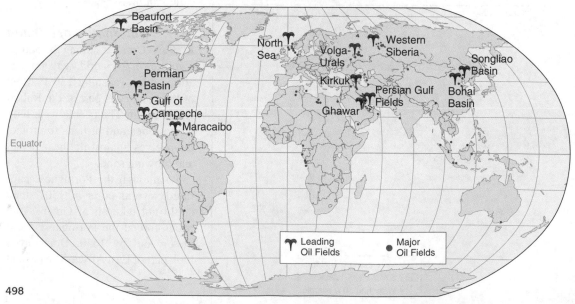

United Arab Emirates The United Arab Emirates is the richest country in the Persian Gulf. It ranks as the eighth largest producer of oil in the world. The oil has brought riches (per capita GDP over $20,000), but the prosperity has drawn waves of immigrants from Saudi Arabia.

Seven small states, each with its own traditions, lie along the shore of the Persian Gulf. Each is ruled by a prince, or *emir*, and its government is therefore called an **emirate.** During the nineteenth century, when Britain dominated the area, it enforced truces between the states to keep the naval lanes open. The area was called the Trucial States because of these truces. These states have retained sovereignty over local affairs but are now united into a single country called the United Arab Emirates. The seven emirs form the Supreme Council and appoint a president as head of state.

Qatar Like the United Arab Emirates, Qatar is an emirate that has grown rich from oil. The prosperity has drawn so many immigrants that over two-thirds of the people are foreign born. Qatar's dynasty of emirs has ruled since the nineteenth century. Before the discovery of oil, the Arab peoples supported themselves by raising camels, diving for pearls, and fishing.

Qatar is on a peninsula that extends into the Persian Gulf. Most of the peninsula is stony desert, but the southern region consists of salt flats. Since there is little water, the people distill seawater to drink. The process of **desalination** (removal of salt from saltwater) is too expensive for most countries. However, it is cheaper than importing water from hostile neighbors.

The Islands of Bahrain Bahrain consists of a large island and a number of small ones just north of Qatar. Bahrain is an emirate led by a *sheik,* the male leader of an extended Arab family.

Mounds mark the burial sites at the ruins of ancient Dilmun. It is the largest known necropolis in the world.

The many springs of Bahrain provide water for this date plantation.

Many international companies have headquarters in Bahrain, which operates an oil refinery on Sitra Island. Pipelines bring crude oil from the island of Bahrain as well as from Saudi Arabia. The business has enabled the country to become the leading banking and financial center in the Persian Gulf region. It is also a major port of call for U.S. warships traveling in the gulf.

Many natural springs provide the islands of Bahrain with a resource that is rare in the Middle East. The fresh water made the ancient port of Dilmun an important stop on the trade route between Sumer and India. The four-thousand-year-old ruins of Dilmun include tombs and a ziggurat, like those in Sumer. Copper from Magan and African ivory have been found here as well as flint weights and soapstone seals from Mohenjo-Daro (in modern Pakistan). The ancient Sumerians said that this was where Noah (whom they called Ziusudra) settled after the Flood.

War in Kuwait The barren land of Kuwait, at the north end of the Persian Gulf, was uninhabited until 1710, when Arab settlers found a water source at what is now the capital of Kuwait. Kuwait Bay, with its excellent harbor, soon became an important port. But its existence has been threatened by its two large neighbors, Saudi Arabia in the south and Iraq in the north.

Kuwait prospered immediately after the discovery of oil. Soon hundreds of oil wells dotted the east. In 1960 it joined Saudi Arabia and other oil-producing countries in the Organization of Petroleum Exporting Countries **(OPEC).** OPEC members agree to limit their production of oil in an attempt to increase prices. This proved most effective in 1973,

Types of Graphs

Graphs are a useful tool to display complex information in a simple format. The three basic types are *line graphs,* which show changes over time; *pie graphs,* which compare individual quantities to the total; and *bar graphs,* which compare similar quantities to each other. Sometimes bar graphs are shown as *pictographs,* which use pictures instead of bars to show the quantities.

The governments of the Western world watch closely the statistics related to the world supply of petroleum, which they need to run their modern industries. Most Western countries consume more energy than they produce, so they rely on a steady supply of imports from oil-producing countries. Conflicts in these countries threaten the flow of oil and drive up prices, creating havoc in Western economies. Study these graphs and answer the questions that follow.

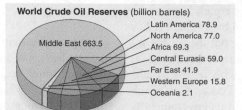

World Crude Oil Reserves (billion barrels)

Middle East 663.5
Latin America 78.9
North America 77.0
Africa 69.3
Central Eurasia 59.0
Far East 41.9
Western Europe 15.8
Oceania 2.1

Middle East Crude Oil Reserves (billion barrels)

Middle East 663.5

Country	
Saudi Arabia	261.2
Iraq	100.0
United Arab Emirates	98.1
Kuwait	96.5
Iran	88.2
Oman	5.1
Yemen	4.0
Egypt	3.9
Qatar	3.7
Syria	2.5
Bahrain	0.2

1. What country consumes the most energy? What percentage does it consume of the world total (365 quadrillion btu)?

2. How many of the top ten consumers of energy are developing countries? Are any in the Middle East?

3. Which region has the largest oil reserves? What percentage of the world total does it hold?

4. How many countries on the Persian Gulf have more oil reserves than any other region in the world outside the Middle East?

5. In what year did U.S. oil imports from the Persian Gulf reach their highest level?

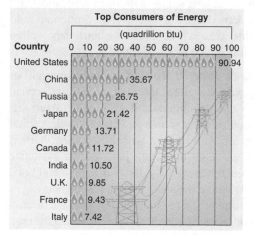

Top Consumers of Energy

Country	(quadrillion btu)
United States	90.94
China	35.67
Russia	26.75
Japan	21.42
Germany	13.71
Canada	11.72
India	10.50
U.K.	9.85
France	9.43
Italy	7.42

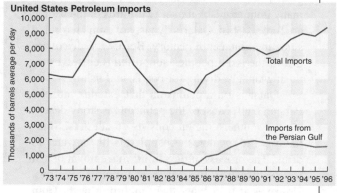

United States Petroleum Imports

Thousands of barrels average per day

Total Imports

Imports from the Persian Gulf

'73 '74 '75 '76 '77 '78 '79 '80 '81 '82 '83 '84 '85 '86 '87 '88 '89 '90 '91 '92 '93 '94 '95 '96

6. What was the lowest level of U.S. imports during the energy crisis of the 1970s? What was the lowest level during the Iran-Iraq War (1980-88)?

💡 Find the difference between the highest and lowest level of U.S. imports from the Persian Gulf. Would a sudden drop of this oil today have the same impact on the U.S. economy that it had in 1973?

when the availability of oil dwindled as a result of the Arab-Israeli War. Since then, however, OPEC nations have generally fought among themselves because of the glut of oil.

In August 1990 Iraq invaded Kuwait, claiming that it had exceeded OPEC production limits. This sparked the **Persian Gulf War,** the most significant war ever fought on the Arabian Peninsula since

U.S. armored vehicles were the key to success in the encirclement of Iraq's forces in Kuwait during the Gulf War.

World War I. Iraq not only seized control of the huge oil reserves of Kuwait but also threatened the safety of Saudi Arabia. The Arab nations dropped their typical opposition to Western powers and joined a grand alliance, led by the United States and Great Britain, to protect the flow of oil. The UN authorized "all necessary means" to liberate Kuwait if Iraq did not withdraw by January 15, 1991. When Iraq ignored the demand, the United States made its first official declaration of war since World War II. On January 16, UN Allies began five weeks of massive, around-the-clock air strikes, followed by a lightning ground attack that lasted just one hundred hours before Iraq agreed to a cease-fire. Since the war, radical Muslims have been growing stronger in the Middle East.

22-2

SECTION REVIEW

1. What poverty-stricken Arab country once had Communist leaders?
2. Which small country on the Arabian Peninsula was never controlled by Britain?
3. What is a sultan? emir? sheik?
4. What advantages does Bahrain have over the other countries of the Arabian Peninsula?
5. What factors caused the Persian Gulf War?
- Should the United States stay in the Persian Gulf?

THE RIVERS OF IRAQ

The **Tigris** and **Euphrates Rivers** are the most important rivers in the Middle East. They begin in the mountains of Turkey before entering Iraq. Rain and melting snow in the mountains provide a constant flow of water in spite of the low rainfall downstream—only ten inches annually. The lifeblood of Iraq, these rivers provide water for irrigation and hydroelectric projects. Also navigable, rivers are as important to Iraq as the Mississippi River is to the United States.

The rivers flow almost parallel in Iraq for five hundred miles. Since ancient times, the land between them has been called **Mesopotamia,** which means "land between the rivers." This well-watered plain was the home of several of the world's early civilizations: Sumer, Babylonia, and Assyria.

Today, Iraq is one of many Arab nations that have attempted to lead the Muslim world. A ruthless dictator named **Saddam Hussein** took over the country in 1979. His efforts to win glory for himself and power for his nation have led the country into chaos.

Shiite Rebels in Southern Iraq

Most Iraqis live in Lower Mesopotamia, or southern Iraq. It extends from the Tigris just above the capital south to the Persian Gulf. Though most of the people are Arabs, their religious views are sharply divided.

All Muslims accept the five Pillars of Islam, but they disagree over particular teachings and authority. Many wars in the Middle East can be traced to rival Muslim groups. About 80 percent of all Muslims are **Sunnis** (SOON ees). The name means "well-trodden path," showing their orthodoxy and conservative, pragmatic position. They follow the *caliphs,* the appointed successors to Muhammad. Most Arabs in Saudi Arabia are Sunnis.

Shiites (SHEE ITE) compose most of the remaining Muslim factions. Shiahs honor the *imam,* the hereditary successor of Muhammad. The imam claims to be a divine manifestation and qualified to interpret the holy writings. Shiites are outspoken, but they argue over who is the rightful heir of Muhammad. Only four countries have Shiite majorities: Iran, Iraq, Bahrain, and Azerbaijan.

Marshes Near the Ruins of Ancient Sumer and Babylon
The two great rivers of Iraq join in the far south to form the **Shatt al Arab,** which continues about one hundred miles through marshy lowlands before it empties into the Persian Gulf. Many Shiites live in the marshes and cities of the Shatt al Arab. After the Persian Gulf War, the

Shiites rebelled against Hussein and his Sunni government. The UN cease-fire kept Hussein from flying planes south of the 32nd parallel. But Hussein moved his ground troops in and began massacring the rebels. In 1992 he completed a 351-mile canal to drain the marshes, hoping to destroy the Shiite way of life and to remove this hideout.

Ruins remind us that this is an ancient region. Iraq is very familiar with the stories of ancient civilizations, and it considers itself the heir of these empires. The Bible recounts the founding of the first cities after the Flood in this location. This civilization in the plains of Shinar is now called **Sumer** (Gen 10:9-10). North of Shinar near modern Baghdad are the ruins of an even greater civilization—the Babylonian empire. Under Nebuchadnezzar, Babylon reached the pinnacle of ancient glory (Dan. 2:31-45). The walls of the city, which stretched about twenty-eight miles, were the thickest city walls ever made. Nebuchadnezzar also made the Hanging Gardens, one of the seven wonders of the ancient world.

Baghdad As one of the few Middle Eastern areas with enough water for a large population, Lower Mesopotamia has always been very populous. Today, about three-fourths of all Iraqis live in Lower Mesopotamia. Small mud-brick houses and bazaars line many of the narrow streets throughout Lower Mesopotamia.

Baghdad, with a population of four million people, is the capital and largest city in Iraq. It is more than twice as large as any city on the Arabian Peninsula. Baghdad is most famous in the West as the setting of *The Thousand and One Nights,* a collection of such popular tales as "Sinbad the Sailor," "Ali Baba and the Forty Thieves," and "Aladdin and His Magic Lamp." It became the capital of a mighty Muslim empire, called the Abbasside Caliphate (750–ca. 1000), which overthrew the early Arab empire that had fallen into decline. Al-Abbas was a descendant of Muhammad's uncle.

Deserts The Syrian Desert covers western Iraq, and the Arabian Desert sprawls across southern Iraq to the Euphrates River. Without adequate rain

The imposing Ishtar Gate of Babylon has been reconstructed at a museum in Berlin. The blue-glazed bricks show regal beasts such as lions and dragons. The entourages of Nebuchadnezzar, Darius, and Alexander rode through this gate.

or rivers, a warm and dry desert climate prevails. The desert has only a few settlements at oases. Some of these oases produce dates from palm trees.

Conflict in Northern Iraq

Upper Mesopotamia is rich with oil wells. As in most of the Middle East, oil is the primary resource in Iraq. Like the rest of the Middle East, Iraq also has a history of conflict.

Out of that land [Shinar] went forth Asshur, and builded Nineveh, and the city Rehoboth, and Calah. (Gen. 10:11)

A great ancient empire arose in the mountains of northern Iraq. Asshur went north from Sumer and founded Nineveh, which became the capital of the **Assyrian Empire** in Upper Mesopotamia. It struggled with Babylon for many years over control of the western trade routes to the Mediterranean Sea.

The northeast corner of Iraq is mountainous. The high mountains are part of the same range

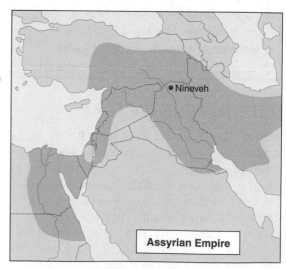

Nineveh

Assyrian Empire

Sargon II, the greatest king of Assyria, built a capital in 707 B.C. and named it after himself. Two great winged bulls with Sargon's head flanked the entry gates to his palace. Excavated in the 1840s, one bull is on display at the University of Chicago's Oriental Institute.

called the Zagros Mountains in Iran and the Taurus Mountains in Turkey. The **Kurds** have lived in this mountain region for at least four thousand years, lost in the midst of ancient and modern conquerors. Kurds have been fighting for an independent homeland, called Kurdistan, for a long time. The Kurds have suffered in all four countries where they live, but especially in Iraq. The world was shocked during the Iran-Iraq War when reports surfaced that Hussein had used chemical and biological weapons to wipe out Kurdish villages.

After the Persian Gulf War, Hussein began a campaign of slaughter against the Kurds that forced the United States and its allies to close off

Language Families of the Middle East

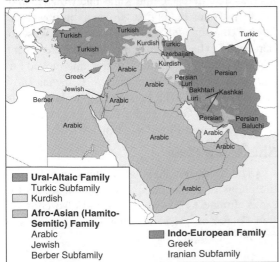

Iraqi flights north of the 36th parallel. Under the guard of the "no-fly zone," Iraq's Kurds built a semi-independent state with its own police, courts, and elected parliament. In some schools the forbidden Kurdish language was again being taught. Foreign aid helped many villages to rebuild.

Yet the fragile Kurdish government suffered greatly from a "double embargo," unable to trade across Iraq's borders and unable to trade with the rest of Iraq. The neighboring Muslims feared that Kurdish independence in Iraq would encourage revolts of Kurds in their own countries. Kurdish factions began fighting among themselves.

22-3

SECTION REVIEW

1. What are the two major rivers that drain into the Persian Gulf?
2. What is the fertile region between these rivers called?
3. What was the first civilization after the Flood?
4. Name the two ancient empires that arose in Iraq and the greatest leader of each.
5. What is Iraq's capital?
   ♀ Why would God have left out Assyria when he summarized world history in Daniel 2:31-45?

REVOLUTIONARY IRAN

Because of its oil resources, Iran became a relatively successful industrial nation in the mid-twentieth century. At this time Iran was headed by a hereditary leader, or **shah.** But radical Muslim sects began stirring up strife and violence in the 1970s. Fanatical Shiite Muslims opposed the shah's attempts to modernize the country and to impose a Western-style government. They also denounced the cruelty of his regime. In 1979 Iranian revolutionaries led by the religious leader Ayatollah Ruholla Khomeini overthrew the shah. **Ayatollah** is the highest title of honor that a Shiite Muslim can hold. The Iranian Shiites instituted an "Islamic Republic" in which ancient religious law, or **sharia,** was to guide the state.

The Iranians viewed their revolution as a first step in worldwide change. Khomeini said, "We will export our revolution to the four corners of the world because our revolution is Islamic; and the struggle will continue until the cry of 'There's no god but Allah, and Muhammad is the messenger of Allah' prevails throughout the world." Iran's extremism is the most visible expression of a movement that has affected many other Muslim nations. Other groups have begun to echo the Iranian call for "pure" Islamic states untainted by contacts with the "corrupt" ways of the West. Other Muslim states have adopted some measure of sharia, including Saudi Arabia and Pakistan.

The West sometimes gets the false impression that all Islamic nations are Arabic and that they all think alike. Two main contestants for the "voice of Islam" are Iran and Iraq. They have had a long history of dispute, dating back to troubles between ancient Persia and Babylon. After the revolution in Iran in 1979, Saddam Hussein feared the spread of radical Shiites in his country, and he saw an opportunity to seize some of the disputed, oil-rich territories on his border. In 1980 he launched a massive attack, expecting to win in three weeks. Instead, the **Iran-Iraq War** lasted eight years. Hussein resorted to chemical weapons and bombing of cities to break Iran, but he gained nothing. Over three hundred thousand people died in the fighting, but neither country received any important gains from the war.

Iran remained silent while the Western allies crushed Iraq during the Persian Gulf War. After the war, Iran began to reassert itself. With its oil-based economy booming, Iran continued stockpiling billions of dollars worth of modern tanks, planes, submarines, and missiles. It also began secretly acquiring the technology to produce its own chemical and nuclear weapons. In 1992 its troops occupied three islands in the Persian Gulf that it had been sharing with the United Arab Emirates.

Zagros Mountains, First Home of the Persians

Iran is an ancient kingdom. Its people are not Arabs, but Persians. The ancient Persian Empire included all of modern Iran, and Iran was called

Posters and murals of Ayatollah Khomeini are a common sight in Tehran.

Persia until 1935. The name Persia originally designated a small region in the southern **Zagros Mountains.** The Zagros Mountains cover most of the southwestern third of Iran. These rugged mountains offer a cooler climate than the plains of Iraq.

Persian Empire

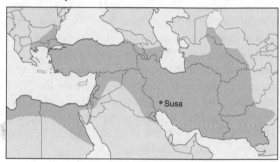

Cyrus the Great began the **Persian Empire** in 550 B.C., when he usurped the throne in the city of Ecbatana. Another Persian ruler, Darius (duh-RYE-us) the Great defeated nine kings and won a total of nineteen battles in his first two years in power. He moved the capital twenty-five miles west to Persepolis. The Persian kings stayed here during the spring and fall. In summer, the king moved farther north to the cooler climate at Ecbatana (now called Hamadan). The Persian Empire later fell to Alexander the Great at the Battle of Gaugamela (now in Iraq near Mosul and Irbil).

Khuzestan Plain

The Khuzestan Plain is an extension of the fertile plains of Mesopotamia. This plain shares the same climate as Mesopotamia and also contains Iran's major oil-producing area. It was the focus of fighting during the Iran-Iraq War.

Persepolis

Located in Iran (handwritten)

Persepolis was the largest and greatest Persian capital. About twenty-five miles east of modern Shiraz, the ruins still dwarf visitors. The Audience Hall of Darius held ten thousand people, and Xerxes built the even larger Hall of a Hundred Columns. The gold, silver, ivory, and marble have long since been removed, but many fine relief sculptures remain. Naqsh-i Rustam, a cliff near Persepolis, contains four royal tombs cut into the rock, including that of Darius.

These are only a few of the thousands of pillars and walls that have been excavated at Persepolis.

In the winter, the Persian kings moved to these plains in the southwestern corner of Iran. The winter capital, Susa or Shushan, appears in Nehemiah 1:1 and Daniel 8:2. It is also the setting for the book of Esther. To help the movement of soldiers and messengers, the Persians constructed a Royal Road from Susa all the way to the Aegean Sea.

Behistun Rock

Along the caravan road between Ecbatana and Babylon is a high cliff that displays one of the greatest treasures from the ancient world. Behistun Rock is five hundred feet high. Darius ordered an account written there in stone for all to read of how he took the throne and organized the realm into *satrapies* (provinces). The inscription is important because it held the key to reading the undeciphered letters of the ancient Babylonian language. Darius had given the account of his accomplishments in three languages: Babylonian, Old Persian, and Elamite. Unlocking the words on the Behistun Rock ranks with the Rosetta stone, which was used to unlock the mysteries of ancient Egyptian hieroglyphics.

Eastern Deserts

Eastern Iran is desert. The Dasht-E-Kavir and the Dasht-E-Lut together cover thirty-eight thousand square miles of the barren Plateau of Iran. The plateau averages three thousand feet in elevation and consists of barren rocky hills and large salt flats. Most cities stand on the western edge. The border city of Zabol lies beyond the plateau in the Rigestan Desert of Afghanistan.

Zarathustra (Zoroaster in Greek) founded the ancient religion of the Persian Empire, **Zoroastrianism.** The Arabs defeated the last Zoroastrian forces in A.D. 635 near Baghdad. However, the religion is still practiced by a persecuted minority in the plateau cities of Kerman and Yazd (and in India, where they are called Parsees). Their sacred book is the *Avesta* and they worship the god Ahura Mazda.

As with many false religions, Zoroastrians destroy the dead. They do not want reminders of death and the grave. To such religions, cemeteries are grim reminders of the consequences of Adam's sin. While some religions promote cremation, Zoroastrians put the naked corpses on Towers of Silence, where vultures strip off the flesh within a few hours. As much as false religions try to hide it, even death glorifies the true God.

And as it is appointed unto men once to die, but after this the judgment: so Christ was once offered to bear the sins of many. (Heb. 9:27-28)

Elburz Mountains in the North

The **Elburz Mountains** run along the northern border of Iran. These mountains connect the Caucasus Mountains on the west with the Hindu Kush to the east in Afghanistan. Like these neighboring ranges, the Elburz Mountains are high, rising to 18,376 feet at Mount Demavend near Tehran.

Tehran With at least ten million people, **Tehran** is easily the largest city among the Persian Gulf nations. The population has grown rapidly. Until the rise of a caravan route in the thirteenth century, it was a small town. It did not become the capital until 1788. Most sections of the city have been built since 1910, and many have a distinctly European flavor.

As the capital, Tehran sets national policies. The official language is Farsi (Persian), an Indo-European language. The official religion is the Shiite branch of Islam, which is followed by about 90 percent of all Iranians. The Sunni minority has a difficult time in the country.

Iran has been stepping up its persecution of Christians in recent years. It has forbidden the sale of Bibles in bookstores and barred Muslims from attending church services. Only two Christian churches can hold services and the services must be in Farsi, the common language of Iran. In 1993 the Iranian parliament required all citizens to make public their religious affiliation. The government has used this information to remove Christians from government jobs, such as teaching and civil service. Converts from Islam are threatened with torture unless they deny their new faith in Christ. Since the 1979 revolution the number of Christians in Iran has dropped from 310,000 to under 100,000.

The Baha'i Renegades
Baha'i is a religion based on the writings of two renegade Shiites: the Bab and Bahaullah. In 1844, the Bab predicted the imminent coming of an imam who would bring truth and justice. The government executed the Bab in Tabriz in 1850 and imprisoned his disciple Bahaullah in the Black Pit in Tehran, where Bahaullah came to view himself as the predicted imam. He was later exiled first to Baghdad (Iraq), then to Istanbul (Turkey), and then to Acre (Israel).

In spite of bitter persecution, about 350,000 Baha'is remain in Iran. Baha'is have spread to

The Elburz Mountains offer a snowy backdrop to the skyline of Tehran, Iran.

Africa, India, and the United States and have international headquarters in Haifa, Israel. Baha'is promote the unity of all religions. They offer no salvation from sin, and in contrast to the one true God of biblical Christianity, the Baha'i's god is unknowable.

And we know that the Son of God is come, and hath given us an understanding, that we may know him that is true, and we are in him that is true, even in his Son Jesus Christ. This is the true God, and eternal life. (I John 5:20)

Another Muslim minority that started in Persia is the **Sufis,** the mystics of Islam. Sufism teaches that nothing exists except God. Though they are not orthodox Muslims, Sufis are at least peaceful. No countries are predominantly Sufi, though Sufi influence is felt throughout Islam (much as the New Age cult has spread throughout "Christian" lands).

Caspian Coast
Iran has some lowlands at the base of the Elburz Mountains, bordering the Caspian Sea. This region enjoys a mediterranean climate and is the most heavily populated in all of Iran. Farmers here grow cotton and rice.

Iranians are renowned for their handmade Persian rugs.

⊚ SECTION REVIEW

1. Which mountain range contains two ancient capitals of Persia?

2. During what season did the Persian kings go to the palace in Susa on the Khuzestan Plain? Why?

3. What ancient religion is still practiced in small pockets on the Plateau of Iran?

4. What mountains cross Iran in the north?

5. Iran is the only country of the Persian Gulf that has an official language other than Arabic. What is the language?

💡 Why was Persepolis a good location for the capital of an empire?

REVIEW

Can You Define These Terms?

Ramadan	khat	Sunnis	sharia
Muslim	sultanate	Shiites	Zoroastrianism
mosque	emirate	shah	Baha'i
Koran	desalination	Ayatollah	Sufi
Bedouin	OPEC		

Can You Locate These Natural Features?

Persian Gulf	Empty Quarter	Tigris River	Shatt al Arab
Arabian Peninsula	Gulf of Aden	Euphrates River	Zagros Mountains
Rub al Khali	Gulf of Oman	Mesopotamia	Elburz Mountains

Can You Explain the Significance of These People, Places, and Events?

Middle East	Arabs	Baghdad	Persian Empire
Mecca	Persian Gulf War	Assyrian Empire	Persepolis
Medina	Saddam Hussein	Kurds	Tehran
Ibn-Saud	Sumer	Iran-Iraq War	

How Much Do You Remember?

1. The Middle East lies at the crossroads of what three continents?
2. What language is spoken throughout most of the Persian Gulf region?
3. What are the two holiest cities of Islam?
4. What are the two main arms of the Arabian Sea? What other body of water lies between them and the Arabian Sea?
5. Which of the six minor states on the Arabian Peninsula best fits each description?
   a. highest per capita GDP
   b. Persian Gulf War
   c. sultanate
   d. first Arab democracy
   e. frankincense of Dhofar
   f. Dilmun
6. What advantages does Bahrain have over the other Gulf States?
7. Distinguish sultan, sheik, shah, and emir.
8. Distinguish ayatollah, imam, and sufi.
9. The Tigris and Euphrates Rivers empty into what body of water?
10. Why is the Muslim world divided against itself?
11. What is the holy book of Islam? of Zoroastrianism?
12. For each empire, give the main leader and the primary capital. Also give the modern location of the capital's ruins.
    a. Babylon
    b. Assyria
    c. Persia

What Do You Think?

1. Do you believe God has shown His wrath on the countries of the Middle East that have mistreated Christians?
2. Compare and contrast what you know of the religion of Islam with true Christianity.
3. The countries that surround the Persian Gulf now profit greatly from their petroleum resources. What problems has the new wealth brought? Are these countries better off?
4. What are the three most powerful countries on the Persian Gulf? What advantages do each of them have in their struggle to become the leader of the Muslim world?
5. Is the Middle East more similar to Asia or to Europe?

CHAPTER 23

THE EASTERN MEDITERRANEAN

The jagged peninsulas of southern Europe have plentiful harbors and a mild mediterranean climate. But the coasts along the eastern Mediterranean Sea have few good ports, scarce water, and almost no natural resources. Yet the strategic location of this region has placed it at the center of the world stage.

The countries at the eastern edge of the Mediterranean touch three continents. Turkey is anchored in Europe, Egypt is anchored in Africa, and several nations in between lie in Asia. Ancient cultures from all three continents have mixed together here over thousands of years.

While oil is the primary source of controversy in the Persian Gulf, religion has been the primary cause of trouble in the eastern Mediterranean. Muslims overran the area long ago, but in 1948 the Jews established an independent state in the heart of Muslim territory. Modern history shows that God still judges nations based on their treatment of God's chosen people.

And I will bless them that bless thee, and curse him that curseth thee: and in thee shall all families of the earth be blessed. (Gen. 12:3)

TURKEY'S SECULAR GOVERNMENT

 Although predominantly Muslim, Turkey has close ties to Europe. Turkey allied with Europe and the United States when it joined NATO in 1952. Turkey has sought to become a secular (nonreligious) state, like its European neighbors. The man who introduced this policy was **Kemal Atatürk,** the "Father of the Turks," who won control of Turkey in 1923. He is considered the father of modern Turkey.

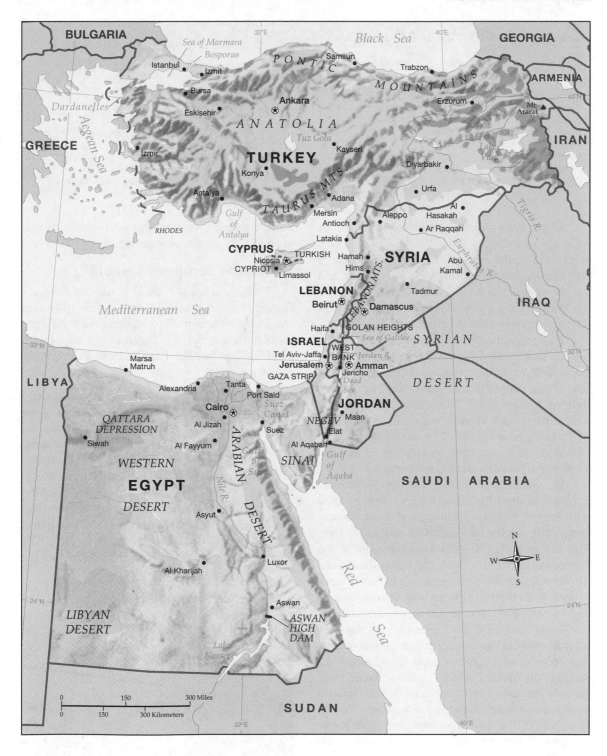

Eastern Mediterranean Statistics

COUNTRY	CAPITAL	AREA (SQ. MI.)	POPULATION	NATURAL INCREASE	LIFE EXPECTANCY	LITERACY RATE	PER CAPITA GDP	POP. DENSITY
Cyprus	Nicosia	3,572	752,808	0.7%	77	95%	$13,000	211
Egypt	Cairo	385,229	64,791,891	1.9%	62	51%	$2,760	168
Israel	Jerusalem	7,876	5,534,672	1.4%	78	95%	$15,500	702
Jordan	Amman	34,342	4,324,638	3.2%	73	87%	$4,700	125
Lebanon	Beirut	3,950	3,858,736	2.2%	71	92%	$4,900	976
Syria	Damascus	71,498	16,135,899	3.3%	67	71%	$5,900	225
Turkey	Ankara	300,948	63,528,225	1.6%	72	82%	$5,500	208

As president, Atatürk introduced a long list of reforms, including a new non-Arabic alphabet, Western laws, the right of women to vote, a ban on polygamy, a ban on wearing veils and turbans, and the adoption of the West's solar calendar to replace the Muslim lunar calendar. These Western reforms have remained in effect to this day.

Turkey has the second largest population in the Middle East (behind Egypt) and the second largest population in Europe (behind Germany). About half of the people live in rural areas. In spite of reforms, rural people have limited health care, and a large percentage of them remain illiterate. Much of Turkey's economy revolves around the primary industries of agriculture and mining. Even so, Turkey is slowly developing its resources.

The great hope of Turkey's secular government is its proximity to Europe. Turkey wants to trade with the rich nations of Europe and avoid the religious strife that has hurt the rest of the Middle East. The key to Turkey's hopes is membership in the European Union (EU). But so far Europe has forced Turkey to wait for three reasons: Turkey's weak economy, its historic conflict with Greece, and its history of human rights abuses against the Kurds.

To the Turks, the EU's rejection is evidence of prejudice. The common people have grown increasingly bitter, and religious leaders are pushing for a return to the Muslim world. A radical Islamic Party came to power in 1996, hoping to replace Turkey's civil laws with the sharia and to withdraw Turkey from NATO. But the army intervened—as it has in the past, threatening to seize power unless the

Muslim leaders promised to uphold democracy and to protect the secular constitution.

Thrace, the European Toehold

Turkey includes a small corner of Europe's Balkan Peninsula, called **Thrace.** This hilly area has a mediterranean climate and is good for agriculture. Thrace includes **Istanbul,** the largest city in all of the Middle East and the heartbeat of Turkey.

Strategic Straits The water passage that separates Europe from Asia is the only route out of the Black Sea. To sail from the Black Sea to the Mediterranean, ships first enter the narrow strait called the **Bosporus.** Istanbul is on the European side of this strait. Next, ships enter the small Sea of Marmara. Finally, they must pass through a second strait, called the **Dardanelles,** which empties into the Aegean and the Mediterranean. The Greeks referred to the Dardanelles as the Hellespont. The armies of both Xerxes of Persia and Alexander the Great crossed here.

A suspension bridge spans the Bosporus in Turkey.

Rise and Fall of the Byzantine Empire For most of its history, Thrace belonged to Greeks, not Turks. The two peoples have fought each other for centuries, and the Greeks have never forgotten their claims. Modern Turkey has come to blows with Greece several times. Indeed, Atatürk won his reputation after World War I by defending Turkey against an invading Greek army.

Thrace was the center of the last Greek Empire, which lasted over one thousand years. It began when emperor Constantine moved the capital of the Roman Empire to Byzantium in the year 330, renaming the town Constantinople. When the Roman Empire split in 395, the eastern capital remained at Constantinople. After the collapse of the western Roman Empire, the empire in the east became known as the **Byzantine Empire** (after Byzantium).

The Byzantine Empire reached its height under Emperor Justinian (527-65). After his death, however, the empire began to decline. Western Europe later sent Crusaders to defend the Byzantines against Arabs and Turks, but the empire

Byzantine Empire

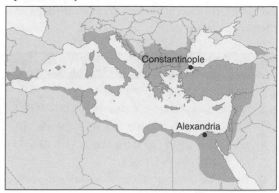

continued to shrink. The final blow came in 1453, when the Turks overran the capital and renamed it Istanbul.

The Byzantine Empire kept Greek civilization alive while the rest of Europe fell to barbarians. It preserved Greek literature and philosophy, as well as Roman government and legal order. Until its fall, Constantinople was the center of the Eastern Orthodox Church. Even today, after centuries of

The Wonders of Istanbul

Among the many wonders in the ancient city of Istanbul are the Hagia Sophia, Topkapi Palace, and the Blue Mosque. The Hagia Sophia was the mother church of the Byzantine Empire, commissioned by Emperor Justinian in 532. The interior moldings are covered with gold leaf, and the crucifix and altar are of pure gold. But the Turks turned the Hagia Sophia into a mosque. They added four minarets, and they covered up the mosaics of Christ and the archangels because images are a form of idolatry according to the Koran. But Atatürk had the

The Blue Mosque in Istanbul

old church restored as a museum, and the mosaics have since been uncovered for visitors.

Topkapi Palace was the seat of the Ottoman Empire. Mehmet II, who conquered Constantinople, first built the palace. It includes three hundred rooms, fountains, and even secret passages. Adding to the splendor are a wealth of diamonds, rubies, and emeralds. At first only government officials lived in the palace, but Suleiman the Magnificent made it his home in the 1540s. The palace included rooms for a harem of as many as four thousand women. It is now a museum.

In 1609 Sultan Ahmed I commissioned a mosque to be built across from the Hagia Sophia. It became known as the Blue Mosque because of the twenty thousand blue ceramic tiles decorating the interior. The unusual design includes a series of half-domes leading up to the central dome. The mosque also has six minarets, rather than the traditional four.

Muslim rule, the patriarch of the city is the most honored Orthodox leader, reverently called the *ecumenical patriarch*.

Ancient Cities of Anatolia

The Asian section of Turkey is called **Anatolia.** The Mediterranean Sea, the Black Sea, and the Aegean Sea surround Anatolia on three sides. In the east it is connected to the mainland of Asia.

Many historic cities lie on this crossing between Asia and Europe. The ancient city of Troy once stood on the Asian side of the Dardanelles, near the Aegean. German archeologist Heinrich Schliemann discovered the ruins of Troy in 1871, thereby proving that Homer's epic poem the *Iliad* was not a complete myth. Another ancient city is Troas, where Paul boarded ship on his first missionary journey to Europe.

The peninsula, small compared to the continent of Asia, is sometimes called **Asia Minor.** Several empires have arisen here. The first was the Hittite Empire (1700-1200 B.C.), whose expertise at ironworking allowed them to build war chariots and to win many battles.

The Seven Churches in the Western Valleys

Most of Asia Minor consists of mountains and a high central plateau. But in the west, long fertile valleys drop from the plateau to the Aegean coast. This is the most productive land in all of Turkey. Known as Asia in ancient times, the west coast has long been inhabited. Tourists can visit many sites described in the New Testament, including the seven key churches of Revelation (1:11–3:22).

Ephesus, the first of the seven, is now a ruin located on a large peninsula near the modern city of Izmir. Smyrna, the second of the churches, became the dominant port when the harbor at Ephesus silted up. Today, it is named Izmir and has about two million people. Greek forces invaded Turkey at Izmir at the end of World War I. Izmir is Turkey's chief Aegean port, as Ephesus once was.

Rise of the Ottoman Empire in the Pontic Mountains

The **Pontic Mountains** stretch across northern Turkey from the Dardanelles to the eastern border. The Pontic Mountains rise along the Black Sea and leave only a narrow coastal strip. The coast has no harbors for large, modern ships; though Trabzon was once a port stop on the Silk Road. Many of the modern coastal villagers are fishermen. The coastal lowlands also have a mild mediterranean climate that enables farmers to grow corn.

Turkish tribes called Seljuks began settling in Anatolia about one thousand years after Christ. But the Crusaders weakened the power of these Seljuk Turks, and in their wake the Ottoman Turks rose to power. In 1326, the sultan of the **Ottoman Empire** captured Bursa in the Pontic Mountains and made it his capital. The Ottomans expanded their control of Byzantine lands until they held all of Asia Minor in 1390. With the final conquest of Constantinople in 1453, the Byzantine Empire came to an end. The Turks then moved their capital to Constantinople.

Ottoman Empire

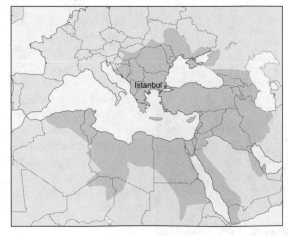

The Ottoman Empire was the last of the great Muslim Empires that ruled the eastern Mediterranean. It reached its pinnacle under Suleiman the Magnificent (1520-66). He captured Budapest, the capital of Hungary, and in 1529 he reached the walls of Vienna but was defeated. Over time, the Ottoman Empire declined, and several of its lands broke away. Nevertheless, the remnants of the empire survived until its final defeat in World War I. The Allied nations divided the remaining lands, intending to prepare them for eventual independence.

Capital on the Central Plateau

The high Central Plateau is the most dominant feature of Asia Minor. Because the mountains block most moisture, the plateau gets less than ten inches of rain annually. Irrigated portions are very productive, and Turkey is by far the largest producer of wheat and barley in the Middle East. It also produces sugar beets.

The plateau is much like the steppes of Central Asia. Even today, a few nomadic herders roam with their flocks over the dry grasslands. The Seljuk Turks, who originally came from Central Asia, settled here in the eleventh century. Their victory at the battle of Manzikert (1071) broke the power of the Byzantine Empire. They brought with them the Turkish language and Islam. Turkish, a Ural-Altaic language, remains the official language and is spoken by 90 percent of the people.

When Turkey became a nation in 1923, Atatürk moved the capital from Istanbul to the town of Ankara. It quickly became the most important city in the Central Plateau, with about three million people.

Taurus Mountains in the South

The rugged **Taurus Mountains** cross southern Turkey. The Taurus Mountains continue east until they meet the Pontic Mountains near Mount Ararat, the highest mountain in Turkey (17,011 ft.). The Taurus Mountains form a barrier to travel between the south and the rest of Turkey. The only historic pass between the Central Plateau and the coast was the Cilician Gates, north of modern Adana. The Crusaders and other conquering armies had to pass this way.

The Turquoise Coast

Narrow coastal plains lie at the foot of the Taurus Mountains. These coasts, along with the western valleys, have a mediterranean climate with twenty-five inches of precipitation annually. Farmers grow grapes, citrus fruits, olives, tobacco, and cotton. The beautiful scenery has earned the south the title "the Turquoise Coast."

Kurds on the Southeastern Borders

The headwaters of the Tigris and Euphrates Rivers are in the eastern Taurus Mountains. These rivers wind their way through the plateau, then drop into the upper Mesopotamian Plain. Most of the region is dry, except for the fertile riverbanks, which allow farmers to grow grains and fruit. Abraham once stayed in the city of Haran, near Urfa. The main modern cities are Urfa and Diyarbakir.

Turkey's largest minority group, the Kurds, live here in southeastern Turkey, near the border with Iraq and Iran. The Kurds form 10 percent of Turkey's population. Some Kurds have moved to cities, dropping the Kurdish language and customs; however, over one-half still herd sheep in the mountains. The recent Persian Gulf War has hindered the vital trade in this region.

Many Kurds want independence. A faction of communist Kurds started a rebellion in 1984, which has claimed the lives of over twenty thousand people. In 1995 Turkey launched its largest military attack since World War I, driving deep within northern Iraq to wipe out rebel Kurdish bases. Europeans have heard reports of terrible human rights abuses, committed by both sides.

Civil War in Cyprus

The island of Cyprus is almost twice the size of Delaware. Two mountain ranges cross Cyprus from east to west and rise as high as 6,406 feet. The plain between these forested mountains is called Mesaoria. The valley and coasts have a typical mediterranean climate—rainy, mild winters and hot, dry summers. Only the mountains get snow in winter. The climate supports grapefruit, lemons, oranges, grapes, and olives.

Cyprus has a rich history. Greeks, Persians, Romans, Byzantines, Franks, and Venetians have occupied it. The Ottoman Turks ruled it from 1571 until the British gained administrative control in 1878. As a result of Byzantine and Turkish rule, modern Cyprus is a divided island. Over 500,000 of its people are Orthodox Greeks; but the remaining 150,000 are Muslim Turks.

After gaining independence in 1960, Cyprus attempted to balance the interests of the Greek and Turkish communities. Most wanted to stay together, though a few Greek Cypriots wanted to reunite with Greece, while a few Turkish Cypriots wanted to **partition** (split up) the country. Fighting broke out in 1963, but the UN stepped in to restore peace. In 1974 Greece backed a coup that overthrew the president. In response, Turkey invaded the island and captured one-third of the land for the Turkish Cypriots.

United Nations peacekeepers have remained in Cyprus since 1964. The UN's goal is one sovereign Cyprus, but recent events have not been promising. The European Union has hinted that the southern, Greek part of Cyprus might become a member of the EU. Turkey resents the implication that the division is permanent, and it fears that the south will join Greece in voting down Turkey's request for EU membership. Disagreements could lead to another war.

SECTION REVIEW

1. Give two names for the part of Turkey in Asia.
2. When did the Ottoman Empire end?
3. Name two biblical cities in Anatolia.
4. What two mountain ranges border the Central Plateau? What climate is typical of the plateau?
5. What two rival ethnic groups live on Cyprus?

💡 Should Cyprus be partitioned?

THE MANDATE OF SYRIA

The land south of Turkey along the eastern Mediterranean is often called the **Levant.** The lowlands and mountain ranges of the Levant have a mediterranean climate. These fertile lands contrast with the wastes of the Syrian Desert in the interior. The Levant, together with the river valleys of Mesopotamia, form a crescent-shaped area called the **Fertile Crescent.** The Fertile Crescent has been

Let's Go Exploring

1. Which countries have some mediterranean agriculture?
2. Which two countries on the Arabian Peninsula have large areas of subsistence agriculture?
3. Find a continuous path of agriculture from Israel to Iran. Which countries share parts of this agricultural region, known as the Fertile Crescent?

💡 Which country in the Middle East appears to have the largest area of productive land?

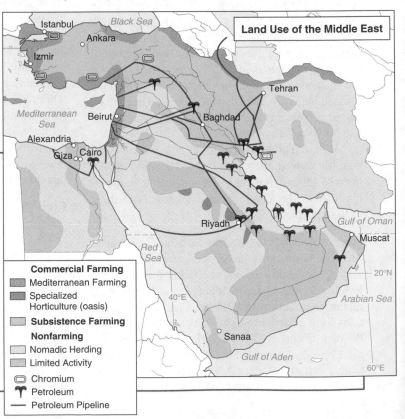

Land Use of the Middle East

Commercial Farming
- Mediterranean Farming
- Specialized Horticulture (oasis)

Subsistence Farming

Nonfarming
- Nomadic Herding
- Limited Activity
- ⬭ Chromium
- ⍦ Petroleum
- — Petroleum Pipeline

heavily populated since Bible times. For thousands of years, merchants and marching armies have passed through this fertile land route.

The Levant belonged to Turkey until Turkey's defeat in World War I. France and Britain took over these territories, called **mandates,** which they governed in the name of the League of Nations. Their goal was to prepare the people for self-government and independence. The French mandate was called Syria, and the British mandate was called Palestine. Two nations were born out of France's mandate: Syria and Lebanon.

Syria

Syria has arable lowlands along the Mediterranean coast, which rise to the An Nusayriyah Range. Many farming towns lie in this region, where forty inches of rain fall each year. Arvad was the most important port in Bible times (Ezek. 27:8-9), but today the major port is Latakia.

The **Syrian Desert** covers most of Syria east of the mountains. Almost uninhabited, the rocky desert plateau slopes downward and eastward from the mountains to the Euphrates River valley. The desert provides phosphates, but the most important resource is oil. Syria also gets most of its precious water from the Euphrates.

Syria's second largest city, Aleppo, lies in the north on the dry side of the mountains, near the border with Turkey. Aleppo has been a major hub of transportation since ancient times. Many railroads in the Middle East meet here. Aleppo is known for its textile industry, and it ships most of its goods through the port at Latakia.

Syria's capital and largest city, **Damascus,** is also on the arid side of the mountains—but in the south. The Barada River, which flows off the mountains, made Damascus a virtual oasis. In

ancient times, the city was a convenient stop for caravans traveling through the desert to and from the Euphrates. Indeed, Damascus claims to be the oldest continuously inhabited city in the world. It was already a city by Abraham's time (Gen. 14:15). Later, Paul became a Christian on the road to Damascus (Acts 9). Today, shoppers at the old marketplaces *(suqs)* can still buy beautiful samples of old-fashioned textiles and metalwork.

Northeast of Damascus are the ruins of Palmyra, another major stop on the caravan route between the Mediterranean Sea and the Persian Gulf. This ancient town arose at an oasis in the Syrian Desert. Solomon first fortified "Tadmor in the wilderness" (I Kings 9:18, II Chron. 8:4). The name *Tadmor* means "palm." The Greeks later called the town by the Greek word for palm, *Palmyra.* The city was destroyed after it revolted against Roman rule in 273. The ruins have been excavated near the modern town of Tadmur.

Today, 90 percent of all Syrians are Muslim, and Arabic is the official language. Syria claims to be a republic, but a military leader, Hafez al Assad, took power in a 1970 coup. The government strictly controls the economy and limits personal freedoms. The U.S. government believes that Syria, like Iran, has been supporting terrorists around the world.

Lebanon

Southwest of Syria is the country of Lebanon. Two parallel mountain ranges, called the Lebanon and Anti-Lebanon Mountains, run down the length of the country. Their highest peaks are Qurnet as Sauda (10,115 ft.) and Mt. Hermon (9,232 ft.), respectively. Between the two parallel ranges lies the Bekáa Valley.

France received Lebanon as part of its mandate after World War I. In 1920 France separated Lebanon from Syria, and both remained under French control until 1946.

Ruins of Ancient Tyre The major city of ancient Lebanon was Tyre. Built on an island, it was the capital of Phoenicia until 583 B.C. Tyre was a great trading center in the ancient world. King Hiram of Tyre exported cedars to Solomon (I Kings 5), and a

Mount Hermon rises on the border between Lebanon and Syria. It is the only snowcapped peak in Palestine.

Ruins of Tyre

Photo of war-torn Beirut in 1977

park preserves the last major grove of the Cedars of Lebanon near the mountain Qurnet as Sauda. As prophesied, God brought Nebuchadnezzar against Tyre in a destructive siege (Ezek. 26). Later Alexander the Great built a causeway to take the island in 332 B.C.

Ruins of Modern Beirut   The present capital is **Beirut.** With over one million people, it is the largest city in the country. Beirut once had a thriving economy based on its resorts and its fruit crop (apples, cherries, grapes, lemons, oranges, and peaches). Until the recent civil war, it was known as the "Paris of the Middle East."

Lebanon has the largest proportion of Christians in the Middle East. About 1.2 million people, or 30 percent of the total population, claim to be Christians. These Christians are called **Maronites,** descendants of a Syrian hermit named St. Maron. In 684 one of their leaders, St. John Maron, led them to victory and independence against the Byzantine armies. For centuries, the Maronites lived in the mountains and resisted both Arabs and Turks. The Maronites later united with the Roman Catholic Church as a separate religious community, acknowledging the pope but following its own format for religious services.

Lebanon also has several competing Muslim groups. Sunni Muslims are the largest minority, consisting of over one million followers. Next are over one-half million Shiites. There are also about two hundred thousand **Druze** (or Druse). The Druze broke from the Shiites and followed an eleventh-century Egyptian ruler named Al-Hakim,

who claimed to be God. Like the Maronites, they moved to the mountains and resisted foreign domination. In 1860 the Druze massacred many Maronites, and the two groups have been bitter enemies ever since.

Warfare between Maronites, Sunnis, Shiites, and the Druze erupted in 1975. Street fighting, bombings, and the taking of European hostages became commonplace. Terrorists assassinated the Sunni prime minister and Maronite president. The war became more complex when the Israelis moved into the Bekáa Valley in the south to reduce terrorist bases. Israel eventually carved out a "security zone" in southern Lebanon. The Syrians also

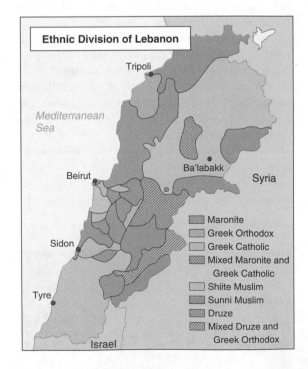

Ethnic Division of Lebanon

Tripoli

Mediterranean Sea

Beirut

Ba'labakk

Syria

Sidon

Tyre

Israel

- Maronite
- Greek Orthodox
- Greek Catholic
- Mixed Maronite and Greek Catholic
- Shiite Muslim
- Sunni Muslim
- Druze
- Mixed Druze and Greek Orthodox

moved in to extend their own authority. Once beautiful, Beirut became a pile of rubble.

In 1983 four nations (the United States, France, Italy, and Britain) sent peacekeepers to Beirut, but they could not stop the fighting. The United States withdrew after a suicide bomber drove a truck into the marine base and killed 241 men. When Saddam Hussein invaded Kuwait in 1990 and diverted the West's attention to the Persian Gulf, Syria took the opportunity to destroy the last Christian army and to end the civil war. Although the peace agreements granted all four religions proportional representation in the government, many Christians refused to participate. The people have begun rebuilding their country, but peace is by no means assured.

SECTION REVIEW

1. What is the Fertile Crescent?
2. What desert forms the southern edge of the Fertile Crescent?
3. What is Syria's main resource?
4. What two parallel mountain ranges run down the length of Lebanon?
5. What were mandates? Give two examples in the Middle East.

Why does Lebanon have a larger coastal population than Syria?

THE MANDATE OF PALESTINE

Palestine was the British mandate formed out of the Ottoman Empire. The British kept the mandate until 1948, when the territory became the two nations of Israel and Jordan. In modern usage, the term Palestine refers only to Israel. In ancient times it included all of what is now Israel, as well as the part of Jordan called Gilead.

Jews and Christians call Palestine the **Holy Land** because most of the events recorded in Scripture took place there. Abraham, Joshua, David, and Elijah walked its dirt roads. Most importantly, Christ came to this corner of the earth two thousand years ago. And here He will return at His Second Coming.

Modern Israel's Struggle for Existence

Thou mayest go in unto the land which the Lord thy God giveth thee, a land that floweth with milk and honey; as the Lord God of thy fathers hath promised thee. (Deut. 27:3)

Israel is the **Promised Land,** the place God gave His chosen people to live forever. The Israelites conquered the Promised Land under Joshua and built a great nation that lasted about fifteen hundred years. But the Romans destroyed Jerusalem in A.D. 70, and the Israelites spent the next two thousand years dispersed in foreign lands and persecuted by all peoples. The modern state of Israel is the result of the Jews' undying dream of returning to their homeland.

This dream became a burning passion at the end of the nineteenth century with the rise of the **Zionist Movement.** Hardy pioneers began moving to Zion to build farms on the rough Palestinian frontier. At first, their numbers were few, and the Turks would not give them legal recognition of owning land. But after Palestine became a British mandate, Jewish immigrants began to pour into the area, especially during the Nazi persecution of the 1930s. Against overwhelming odds, the Jews won independence in 1948.

The Eternal Flame at the Holocaust Museum in Jerusalem

Since its independence, Israel's leaders have welcomed Jews from all over the world. They revived the dead Hebrew language and created words for modern items. Though all immigrants claim to be Jews, they come from at least one hundred nations and speak nearly as many languages. As part of the process of adapting to the new country, immigrants can take a five-month course on the nation's culture. In addition, the first job of every immigrant is to serve in the military. Every adult citizen serves in the military: women serve two years, and men serve three.

In spite of efforts at unity, Israel is divided between two distinct Jewish ethnic groups. The **Ashkenazim** were the early Zionists who came from northern and eastern Europe. The Ashkenazim were steeped in the Western way of life. The **Sephardim** came later from Asia and from North Africa. Their lifestyle and attitudes are more similar to Arabs than to Europeans, and they do not have the same social status as the Ashkenazim.

Ancient Religion of Judaism

The Jews are not like any other people in the Middle East. After the death of David's son King Solomon, the ten northern tribes broke away; but the two southern tribes remained faithful to God. Their land became known as the Kingdom of Judah, after the larger tribe. Their religion became known as **Judaism,** and the people as Jews. Oral traditions became increasingly important to religious life.

The Romans destroyed the Jewish capital in A.D. 70, forcing the Jews to find homes in other lands. A group of refugees in Galilee collected the oral traditions of Judaism into sixty-three books, called the *Talmud.* Just as Muslims have a basic creed, "There is no god but Allah, and Muhammad is His Messenger," Jews have a basic creed, which they have rallied around: "Hear, O Israel, the Lord Our God, the Lord is One."

Today, Judaism has many different branches differing by the level of their devotion to tradition. Orthodox Jews believe that the Pentateuch, or *Torah,* is God's Word given to Moses, and they strictly follow the *Talmud.* A new branch formed in the early nineteenth century as a result of Enlightenment thinking. This branch, called Reform Jews, rejects many of the old traditions but believes the Old Testament is still useful as a moral code. A newer branch, known as Conservative Jews, broke off from the Reform Jews in the nineteenth century because they believed in keeping more of the old traditions. A liberal branch, called Reconstructionists, formed in the 1930s. They see Judaism not as a religion, but as a source of social identity.

Two Warring Peoples

Jews are not the only people who claim Palestine. The Arabs are the descendants of Abraham, through his son Ishmael. God promised to make of Ishmael a great nation (Gen. 17:15-20). The Arabs conquered Palestine in the seventh century and have lived there ever since. But Palestine fell to the Ottoman Turks in 1517, and the Turks ruled the Arabs. Ironically, both the Arabs and the Zionist farmers joined the British to overthrow the Turks during World War I. In gratitude, the British government promised to safeguard the rights of the Arabs and to "view with favour the establishment in Palestine of a national home for the Jewish people."

From the beginning, however, the Arabs and Jews have quarreled over their respective rights, especially in the Holy City Jerusalem. After World War II, Britain turned to the United Nations to resolve the conflict. The UN proposed a plan to divide Palestine into two parts and to make Jerusalem an international city. The Jews reluctantly accepted the plan in 1948, and modern Israel was born.

The Arabs, however, rejected the plan and refused to give up claims to any portion of Palestine. The day after Israel became independent, Arab nations began the first of four wars to drive out the Jews. In the first war, Israel conquered West Jerusalem and annexed it to their country. Thousands of Arab Palestinians were forced into exile. These refugees became an added source of bitterness between the two sides. Another full-fledged war against Egypt in 1956 proved inconclusive.

In 1967 three Arab nations—Egypt, Syria, and Jordan—began planning a new attack on Israel. But Israel decided to strike first. In the **Six-Day War,**

Jews in a World of Goyim

Boker Tov. The Jews worship on Saturday because the Old Testament commanded rest, a sabbath, on the seventh day of the week (Exod. 20:8-10). Today Jews worship in *synagogues,* meeting places developed for instruction in Hebrew and the Old Testament. The *rabbi* leads services consisting of readings from Scripture and chants from the *siddur* (prayer book). The Scripture readings are selected from the *Torah* (the Pentateuch or first five books of Moses) so that the entire Torah is read each year.

Jewish boys are circumcised after birth, in accordance with Leviticus 12:3. On the Saturday after his thirteenth birthday, the boy celebrates his *Bar miztvah,* when he becomes a "son of the commandment." At this ceremony, he reads from the Torah and may give a speech to show his knowledge of Scripture and Jewish traditions. Afterward, the boy receives presents at a special feast. He has now entered manhood. He is fully responsible for keeping the commandments and can participate fully with the other men at worship services. Ten men are needed to form a synagogue.

The Hebrew calendar has twelve lunar months totaling 354 days. The calendar is reconciled with the solar year by adding 28 days in 7 out of every 19 years. The western dates for Jewish holidays therefore change from year to year. *Rosh Hashanah* is the Jewish New Year and occurs in the autumn. The main time of fasting is the Ninth of *Av* (second to last month) in our autumn. This fast commemorates the two destructions of the temple (in 586 B.C. by the Babylonians and in A.D. 70 by the Romans).

Ten days after the New Year is *Yom Kippur,* the Day of Atonement (Lev. 23:27-28). *Sukkot* (Tabernacles) is the harvest festival, which begins five days later (Lev. 23:34). In early winter, *Hanukkah* (Feast of Lights) celebrates the victory over the Syrians in 165 B.C. In late winter, *Purim* celebrates the deliverance through Queen Esther (Esther 9:28). In the spring, during the week of *Pesah* or Passover (Exod. 12:24-27), Jews eat only *matzah* (unleavened bread). At the end of the week, each family eats the *Seder* (Passover meal). Fifty days later is *Shavuot* (First Fruits or Pentecost, Lev. 23:15-21).

Orthodox Jews carefully follow the laws of Judaism. They eat only *kosher* foods made according to Old Testament dietary laws. They do not eat pork and other unclean meats (Lev. 11). In prayer, Orthodox Jews wear prayer shawls and *phylacteries* (tefellin) strapped to their foreheads or arms (Deut. 6:8). The *tefillin* are small boxes containing Scripture verses.

Many Jews in Israel pray at the Wailing Wall. This wall is the last remaining part of the foundation of the temple that was destroyed in A.D. 70 by the Romans. Today, two Islamic mosques stand on top of the temple ruins. Muslims and all other non-Jews are called *goyim* (gentiles) by the Jews. Trodden down by these gentile nations, Jews look forward to reclaiming the site and offering sacrifices to God as described in the Old Testament. *Shalom.*

Jew at the Wailing Wall

the Israelis easily routed the unprepared Arabs. Israel captured much land on its borders: Egypt's Sinai Peninsula, Syria's Golan Heights, and three Palestinian regions (the West Bank of the Jordan River, the Gaza Strip along the Mediterranean coast, and East Jerusalem). Almost one-quarter million Arabs fled from these "occupied territories." Egypt and Syria attacked Israel again in the Yom Kippur War (1973), but the Israelis narrowly won at great cost.

Ever since the Six-Day War, Israel's politics have focused on the disposal of the occupied territories. Two views prevail: one group believes that Israel should trade land for peace; the other group believes that the land should remain Israel's forever. Heavily armed Jewish settlers have built

communities in the occupied territories and have vowed to die before they give up one inch of their "God-given" soil.

The Coastal Lowlands

At its widest point, Israel reaches only about seventy miles from east to west. The total land area is about the size of Massachusetts. Israel shares the coastal lowlands and the mountain system of Lebanon. Lowlands lie along the Mediterranean Sea and then rise into low hills called the Shephelah. The Lebanese mountains rise east of the Shephelah. In the south lies the arid Negev. We will look at each of these regions in turn.

Jewish Cities on the North Coastal Plain

The coastal plain along the Mediterranean Sea has Israel's best farmland. North of Mount Carmel, the coastal plain is called Acre (or Acco), named for the ancient city. However, the modern city of Haifa has far surpassed Acco and is now the third largest city in Israel.

The Plain of Sharon stretches south from Mount Carmel to Tel Aviv, Israel's largest port and second-largest city. Tel Aviv is short for Tel Aviv-Jaffa, which includes the ancient port of Joppa (Jaffa) in its city limits. Sharon is renowned for its fertility and flowers, especially the Rose of Sharon (Song of Sol. 2:1).

Independent Palestinian Cities in the Gaza Strip

The Plain of Philistia extends from Tel Aviv south to Egypt. The land is not as productive as the other coasts. In the Six-Day War Israel won the coastal strip that is called the **Gaza Strip.**

The Philistines of the Bible converted to Islam during the Muslim conquests. These Arabs are now known as **Palestinians.** Although they represent only 15 percent of Israel's population, they form a majority in the Gaza Strip. Many other Palestinians live as refugees in neighboring Arab states. Two opposing Arab groups arose among these Palestinians. The Palestine Liberation Organization (PLO) was created in 1964 by the Arab nations to represent all the Palestinian Arabs. The PLO refused to recognize Israel's right to exist, and in the 1970s, Palestinian terrorists hijacked airplanes and ships, bombed school buildings, murdered innocent people, and took hostages.

The PLO leader, **Yasir Arafat,** supported terrorism at first, but he claimed to change course in order to win support from the United Nations for the PLO. He even called for an end to terrorism. He envisioned a secular Palestinian state where Jews, Muslims, and Christians could live in peace. Israel refused to give in to PLO demands. In 1987 a violent uprising, called the *intifada,* began in the occupied territories. The Israeli army was forced to take extreme measures, such as curfews and street battles, to keep order. With no end in sight to the fighting, the Israeli people became disillusioned with the costly military occupation.

Yitzhak Rabin, who became prime minister in 1992, decided to open negotiations with Arafat

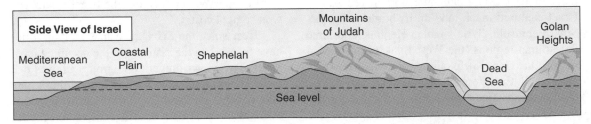

Yasir Arafat

over the future of the occupied territories. Without the knowledge of their own governments or any other nation, Rabin and Arafat secretly began negotiations in Oslo, Norway. Both men received the Nobel Peace Prize in 1994. The Oslo Accord gave guidelines for a series of compromises. Both sides hoped that early successes would encourage support for a final settlement in 1999. The first land returned to Palestinian authority was the Gaza Strip and the city of Jericho. But violence threatened the peace process at every stage. A radical young Jew assassinated Rabin—the first Israeli leader ever to die by an assassin's bullet.

Arafat's "moderate" views are not popular among Muslim radicals, who wish to unite the Arab nations into one Islamic "fundamentalist" state. The most feared of these terrorist groups are the Hamas and the Islamic Jihad, who wish to destroy Israel by any means.

Wadis in the Shephelah
The **Shephelah** (Shuh FAY luh) is a region of low hills between the coastal plain and the mountains. Its average elevation is one thousand feet.

Wadis descend from the mountains and cross the Shephelah on their way to the coast. **Wadis** are dry stream beds that fill up with water after rainstorms. The parched ground soaks up little moisture from these infrequent torrents. In the ancient struggle between the Philistines and Judah, the main routes from the plain into the mountains of Judah followed the wadis.

Mountain System
The Lebanon and Anti-Lebanon Mountains continue south from Lebanon.

They rise less than four thousand feet in this area, but between them is the northern end of the Great Rift Valley, which falls below sea level. The **Jordan River** flows through this valley from its headwaters on Mount Hermon south to the Dead Sea. South of the Dead Sea, the Great Rift Valley continues to the Red Sea and into East Africa.

The mountains of Judah (or Judea) lie west of the Jordan River. The main mountain in this range is the Mount of Olives (2,737 ft.). The main cities of ancient Judah, including Jerusalem, lie along the top of the mountain range. Many Palestinians live in these cities today.

Israel also occupies a small part of the Anti-Lebanon Mountains northeast of the Sea of Galilee. It is called the **Golan Heights** after Golan, one of the old cities of refuge (Josh. 21:27). Israel took this region from Syria during the Six-Day War, but Syria wants it back. In Bible times it was called Bashan, famous for its pastures and bulls (Ps. 22:12).

Mountains of Galilee
Galilee refers to the northernmost mountains of Israel. The main peaks are Mount Tabor (1,929 ft.) and Mount Meron (3,963 ft.), the highest mountain in Israel. Jesus lived most of his life in Galilee and preached in its synagogues (Mark 1:39). His childhood home, Nazareth, overlooked the Valley of Esdraelon, where the battle of Armageddon will take place.

The Brook Elah in the Shephelah, where David found the five smooth stones and used one to kill Goliath, is actually a wadi that flows seasonally.

Geographer's Corner

Bible Geography

A knowledge of geography is an invaluable tool in understanding events in the Bible. Maps help a person understand why some cities were so important, why Bible characters picked the routes they did, and why battles were fought in the manner they were.

Perhaps the single most important factor in Israel's history was the trade routes that crossed the country. Armies and merchants generally follow well-watered lowlands. Ever since ancient times, the main route from Egypt to Mesopotamia followed the coast until it reached Mount Carmel (1,789 ft.). But because the slopes of Mount Carmel descend directly into the sea, the mountain created a barrier to travel along the coastal plain. There, the ancient trade route veered inland to the Iron Pass, at the fortress of **Megiddo.** Traders traveled east to the Jordan River before continuing north to Damascus.

The valley from Megiddo to the Jordan is the only valley through the mountains. The valley has two parts, divided by the narrowest spot in the valley near the town of Jezreel. The western part of the valley, from Megiddo to Jezreel, is called the **Plain of Esdraelon** (or Valley of Megiddo). This plain will become the greatest battlefield in history, where Jesus Christ defeats the forces of Antichrist.

Megiddo was a strategic city guarding the west entrance to the plains of Armageddon. Steps ascend the city's circular altar among these ruins.

The eastern part of the valley, from Jezreel to the Jordan River, is the Valley of Jezreel. The ancient fortress of Beth-shan (later Scythopolis) guarded this vital entrance to Jordan's side of the valley.

Beth-shan and Megiddo, guarding each end of the valley, were the most strategic cities in ancient Palestine. These two cities, together with Jezreel in the center of the valley, controlled trade between Egypt and the Persian Gulf. Israel's enemies from the east gathered in the valley of Jezreel, where Gideon defeated them. Josiah died at Megiddo, attempting to prevent an Egyptian army from using the pass on its way to Assyria (II Kings 23:29). The Philistines later controlled Beth-shan and displayed the body of King Saul on the city walls (I Sam. 31:10).

These places will become important again, according to prophecy. *Armageddon* comes from *Har Megiddo* or Mount of Megiddo. Revelation 16:12-16 tells about vast armies that will come from the Orient to a battle at Armageddon. Revelation 19:11-21 tells how Christ will be the conqueror at this battle. His clothes will be blood-stained because of a slaughter compared to the trampling of grapes. All nations will be gathered to this slaughter.

Read the following passages about this same time period, and answer the questions. Use the map for place names.

1. According to Zechariah 14:4, where will Jesus first arrive on earth when He returns for this battle?

2. According to Zechariah 14:1-9, what will happen when His feet touch the ground?

3. According to Luke 21:20-28, what city will be surrounded by these armies from all nations?

4. According to Isaiah 63:1-6, how far south will they be ranked? Find the city on the map.

◍ According to Revelation 14:20, how deep will the blood be from all of these troops? For what distance will this blood run (in modern units)? How far is it between the northern and southern extent of these armies, according to the map?

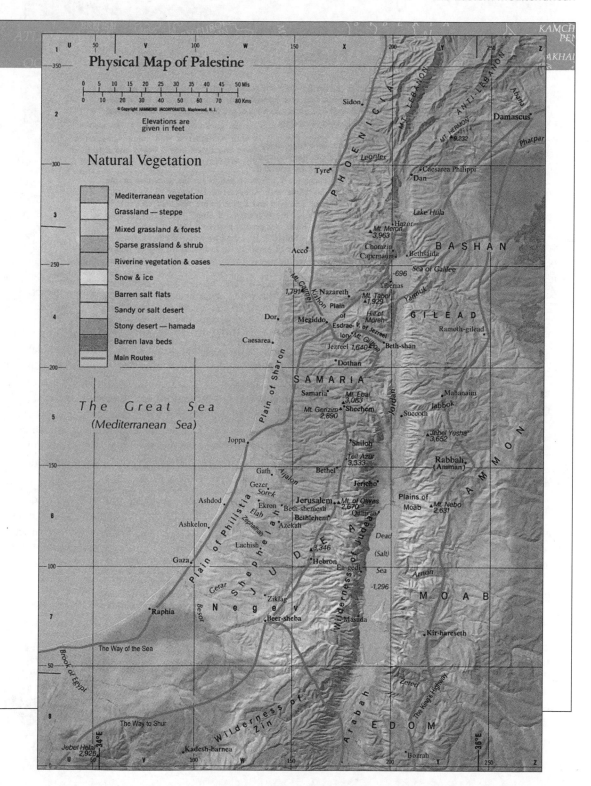

Physical Map of Palestine

© Copyright HAMMOND INCORPORATED, Maplewood, N.J.

Elevations are
given in feet

Natural Vegetation

Mediterranean vegetation
Grassland — steppe
Mixed grassland & forest
Sparse grassland & shrub
Riverine vegetation & oases
Snow & ice
Barren salt flats
Sandy or salt desert
Stony desert — hamada
Barren lava beds
Main Routes

The Great Sea
(Mediterranean Sea)

PHOENICIA

Sidon

MT. LEBANON

ANTI-LEBANON

Abana

Damascus

Leontes

MT. HERMON
9,232

Pharpar

Tyre

Caesarea Philippi

Dan

Lake Hula

Mt. Meron
3,963

Hazor

BASHAN

Acco

Chorazin
Capernaum

Bethsaida

Sea of Galilee
-696

Mt. Carmel
1,791

Nazareth

Tiberias

Mt. Tabor
1,929

Yarmuk

GILEAD

Dor

Megiddo

Plain
of
Esdrae-
lon

Hill of
Moreh

V. of Jezreel

Mt. Gilboa

Ramoth-gilead

Caesarea

Jezreel 1,640

Beth-shan

Dothan

Plain of Sharon

SAMARIA

Samaria

Mt. Ebal
3,083

Mahanaim

Jabbok

Mt. Gerizim
2,890

Shechem

Succoth

Jebel Yusha
3,652

AMMON

Joppa

Shiloh

Tell Azur
3,333

Jordan

Rabbah
(Amman)

Gath

Aijalon

Bethel

Jericho

Gezer

Sorek

Ekron

Jerusalem

Mt. of Olives
2,670

Plains of
Moab

Mt. Nebo
2,631

Ashdod

Elah

Beth-shemesh

Bethlehem

Qumran

Zephathah

Azekah

Ashkelon

Lachish
3,346

Hebron

Shephelah

JUDEA

En-gedi

Dead
(Salt)
Sea
-1,296

Arnon

Gaza

Gerar

Besor

Ziklag

Negev

Beer-sheba

Masada

MOAB

Raphia

Kir-hareseth

Wilderness of Judea

The Way of the Sea

Brook of Egypt

Zered

The King's Highway

Arabah

The Way to Shur

Wilderness of Zin

EDOM

Jebel Helal
2,925

Kadesh-barnea

Bozrah

Masada

Near the Dead Sea is a flat-topped mountain with steep sides, called Masada. *Masada* means "fortress or stronghold." This is the setting for the stirring story of the Jewish Zealots' last stand for freedom in their revolt against Rome. Masada has become a symbol for Israel, much as the Alamo is a symbol for Texas.

King Herod built a major citadel on the summit about 35 B.C. A Roman garrison took over the fort in 4 B.C., but the Zealots seized control in A.D. 66 in the revolt against Rome. After the Romans took Jerusalem in A.D. 70, Masada became the last holdout of the Jewish revolt. Two years later, the fifteen thousand men of the Tenth Legion, led by Silva, arrived to quell the resistance. He surrounded the mountain with eight camps and built a siege ramp on the west side. After

Old storehouses have been excavated on the top of Masada. The Dead Sea is in the background.

nearly two years, Silva's men breached the walls—only to find dead bodies. Rather than be tortured by the Romans, the 960 men, women, and children had committed suicide the night before.

Visitors can reach the twenty-acre plateau on the summit by cable cars or by climbing the siege ramp. One other path, the Snake Path, climbs the steep eastern face on a winding route that few visitors attempt.

The remains of Tabgha Harbor, a natural amphitheater on the Sea of Galilee near Capernaum where Jesus preached to five thousand

This region includes the **Sea of Galilee** in the Great Rift Valley. The Jordan River pauses in this lake on its way to the Dead Sea. The lake is subject to strong winds, which swoop down from the north into the Rift Valley. Today the main town is Tiberias on the west coast. During Jesus' life on earth, Capernaum at the north end was more important.

Archeologists have excavated ruins all over Israel. The largest tell in all of Israel is Hazor. A **tell** is a huge mound formed as cities are destroyed and then rebuilt on top of the old ruins. Archeologists dig layer by layer, investigating the history of each time period. Hazor was strategic because it guarded the entrance to the Jordan Valley from the northern trade route to Damascus.

West Bank The **West Bank** is the mountain region west of the Jordan River and south of Galilee, which Jordan owned until Israel captured it during the Six-Day War. This region includes much of the famous biblical regions of Judah and Samaria.

The ten northern tribes established a new capital at Samaria. Their land included the strategic passes at Megiddo and the Valley of Jezreel, and so they were often invaded by advancing empires.

The Divided Capital **Jerusalem,** the most populous city in Israel, sits in the mountains of Judah at the western edge of the West Bank. It has again become the heart of Israel. The Hebrew parliament, or **Knesset,** is located in the city. Israel established

Hazor commanded a view over swampy Lake Huleh in the Great Rift Valley.

the first true democracy in the Middle East. The government guarantees all three great religions access to their holy sites in Jerusalem. Jewish industries have excelled. Israel's per capita GDP exceeds all its neighbors' and even exceeds that of many oil-producing nations in the Middle East. Israel's health care and educational opportunities are excellent.

Jerusalem has two parts: the Old City and the New City. Israel took East Jerusalem, or the Old City, during the Six-Day War. It has small, winding streets and many ancient buildings. A wall built by Suleiman the Magnificent surrounds the Old City. The Knesset is located in West Jerusalem, the more modern part of the city. The streets are wider and the atmosphere pulses with new life. Other buildings in the New City include the Holocaust Museum and the Shrine of the Book, where the Dead Sea scrolls are housed. The United Nations has not recognized Jerusalem as Israel's rightful capital, however, and most foreign embassies are based in Tel Aviv.

Modern Negev

The Hebrew word *negev* (or negeb) simply means "south." Today, the **Negev** refers to the southern part of Israel. It has three parts: historical Negev, the wilderness of Zin, and Arabah.

Historical Negev

In the Bible, the Negev always refers to a small arid region around the towns of Beersheba and Ziklag. Because it supports marginal agriculture, it was sharply distinguished from the uninhabited wastes of the southern wilderness. In the best years this region gets just enough moisture for some agriculture. Abraham and Isaac settled in Beersheba (Gen. 26:33), and David lived in Ziklag

Inside the Shrine of the Book, visitors can study the Isaiah scroll, dated to the second century before Christ.

before he became king (I Sam. 30:1-2). Beersheba's position as the southernmost habitable city in Israel made it proverbial in the phrase "from Dan to Beersheba" (I Sam. 3:20).

Wilderness of Zin

The Wilderness of Zin lies south of the biblical Negev. Steep wadis cut through its rugged mountains, and several craters gouge the landscape. The largest crater, Maktesh Ramon, is called the Grand Canyon of Israel.

Arabah

East of the wilderness and south of the Great Rift Valley is a wide barren valley called the **Arabah.** The Wadi Arabah descends through the valley northward into the Dead Sea. Elat (Eloth in I Kings 9:26), at the south end of the valley on the Gulf of Aqaba, is Israel's only port on the Red Sea. Solomon built a fleet at Ezion-geber, next to Eloth.

Though the modern Negev is an apparent wasteland, the ingenious people have devised a method using small amounts of salt water to grow hardy plants, such as tomatoes, peanuts, and cotton. This specialized farming, called brackish water agriculture, has allowed Israel to become a major supplier of these products to Europe.

Kibbutz

A **kibbutz** is a Jewish community in which the people share everything in common. No one in the community owns private property, and all members of the kibbutz have an equal say about how the kibbutz is run. The first kibbutz began in 1909 and originally all the communities grew crops. Since then some have expanded into manufacturing or resorts. Kibbutz En Gev operates a popular resort on the southeast shore of the Sea of Galilee and is quite prosperous.

The plural of kibbutz is kibbutzim (typical of Hebrew—cherubim, seraphim, Elohim). There are over eight hundred kibbutzim in Israel with an average of 275 members each. Each member works hard to help his community succeed. To join a kibbutz, a prospective member works on a trial basis. After a year, the community votes on whether to accept him.

SCENES FROM THE HOLY CITY AND ITS FIVE FAMOUS MOUNTS

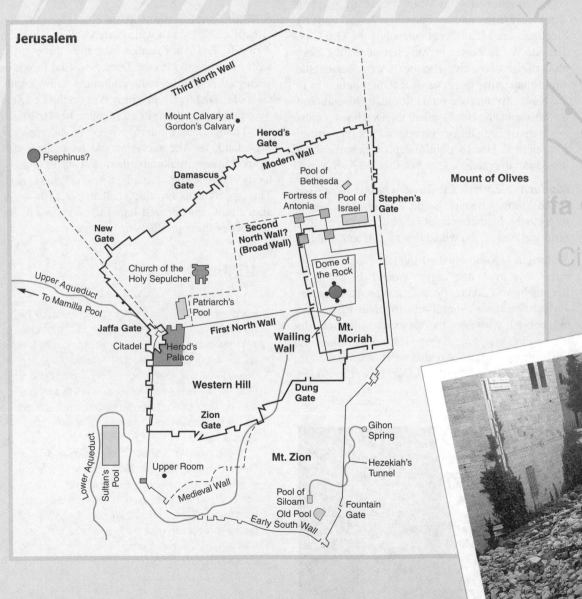

Jerusalem

Third North Wall

Mount Calvary at Gordon's Calvary

Herod's Gate

Psephinus?

Modern Wall

Damascus Gate

Pool of Bethesda

Mount of Olives

Fortress of Antonia

Pool of Israel

Stephen's Gate

New Gate

Second North Wall? (Broad Wall)

Dome of the Rock

Church of the Holy Sepulcher

Upper Aqueduct

To Mamilla Pool

Patriarch's Pool

First North Wall

Jaffa Gate

Mt. Moriah

Citadel

Herod's Palace

Wailing Wall

Western Hill

Dung Gate

Zion Gate

Gihon Spring

Lower Aqueduct

Sultan's Pool

Upper Room

Mt. Zion

Hezekiah's Tunnel

Medieval Wall

Pool of Siloam

Old Pool

Fountain Gate

Early South Wall

The Dome of the Rock, an Islamic mosque, now occupies the site of Solomon's Temple (II Chron. 3:1).

The Wailing Wall is the last remnant of the foundation of God's temple (Mark 13:1-3).

Nehemiah built the "broad wall" (Neh. 3:8).

Mount Moriah   Abraham offered Isaac on Mount Moriah (2,430 ft.). This fact is recognized by the world's three great monotheistic religions: Christianity, Judaism, and Islam. The Dome of the Rock now stands on this mountain. According to Islamic legend, Muhammad departed from Mount Moriah on horseback. A beautiful mosque commemorates that event rather than Abraham's act of obedience.

Mount Zion   When Joshua conquered the Jebusites, the city stood on Mount Zion (2,200 ft.). Even during David's thirty-three year reign, the walls enclosed only Mount Zion. Solomon built the spectacular temple just north on Mount Moriah and extended the city walls to include it. Both Christians and Jews know that Jerusalem is the only city that God called His own and in which God dwelt.

Mount Calvary   The name Jerusalem means "City of Peace." Here on Mount Calvary (2,500 ft.) mankind found hope of peace with God. The most important event in the history of the universe occurred here in Jerusalem when Jesus Christ, God's Son, was crucified for our sins. Three days after His burial, He rose from the grave. By this act He proved that He is God and that He is able to forgive sins and give eternal life.

Western Hill   By the time of Christ, the city walls of Jerusalem included the Western Hill (2,550 ft.). Many of the walls and gates around the Old City still reflect the layout during that time. These sights remind today's visitors that Jerusalem is the Holy City. From the last vestige of the temple to the garden tomb of Christ, the photos in this essay are reminders of Jerusalem's holy heritage.

Mount of Olives   Jerusalem is the City of David. God promised David a descendant to sit upon his throne forever. The Romans destroyed the temple in A.D. 70, but David's heir, the King of kings, is coming again. When He returns in glory to the Mount of Olives (2,737 ft.), He will end all strife and set up an everlasting kingdom.

St. Stephen's Gate is the traditional gate through which Stephen was dragged out of Jerusalem to be stoned, thus becoming the first martyr for Christ (Acts 7:54-60).

Visitors can wade through Hezekiah's Tunnel, which diverted the water of the Gihon Spring into the city walls (II Chron. 32:30).

The Chapel of the Ascension, built at the top of the Mount of Olives, is the traditional site from which Christ ascended (Acts 1:9).

The Pool of Siloam is where Hezekiah's Tunnel emerges. (John 9:1-11).

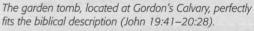

The garden tomb, located at Gordon's Calvary, perfectly fits the biblical description (John 19:41–20:28).

At the Garden of Gethsemane on the Mount of Olives, Jesus prayed and was arrested (Matt. 26:30, 36-46).

The Golden Gate, now walled up, will not deter the glorified Christ when He returns to His temple (Ezek. 43:4).

At the Pool of Bethesda, Jesus healed a crippled man who awaited the stirring of the waters (John 5:2-9).

According to Roman Catholics, the Church of the Holy Sepulchre is built over the tomb where Jesus was buried (Luke 24:46-53).

The summit rock of Mount Moriah, where Abraham and David sacrificed, is now enclosed by the Dome of the Rock (Gen. 22:2).

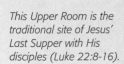

Golgotha, "the place of the skull," is located at Gordon's Calvary. It marks the site where Jesus was crucified (Mark 15:22-28).

This Upper Room is the traditional site of Jesus' Last Supper with His disciples (Luke 22:8-16).

The Pavement, where Jesus was arrested (John 19:13), was probably in the Fortress of Antonia, built by Herod.

The Kingdom of Jordan

Jordan is about the size of Indiana, and most of its land is uninhabited desert. Unlike some Middle Eastern desert areas, Jordan lacks petroleum. Furthermore, only 3 percent of Jordan can be farmed. Many Jordanians work abroad and send money home to their families. Adding to the difficulties are the large number of Palestinian refugees who fled to Jordan as a result of the Arab-Israeli wars. More Palestinians now live in Jordan than native Jordanians! In spite of these problems, Jordan has been one of the more stable and peaceful countries in the region. Its government is a constitutional monarchy.

The primary resources come from the Great Rift Valley. The **Dead Sea** contains deposits of potash, bromine, and salt. The Jordan River valley produces citrus fruits, cabbage, melons, eggplants, and cucumbers. At the south end of the Arabah lies Jordan's only port and its only major town in the Great Rift Valley, Al Aqabah (for which the gulf is named). The Syrian Desert, which covers the eastern half of Jordan, offers few if any resources.

Between the Great Rift Valley and the Syrian Desert is the **Transjordanian Plateau,** where most people live. The northern border of this plateau is the Yarmuk River, which runs through a wadi dividing Jordan from Syria on the north.

The Moabites and Ammonites, descendants of Lot, lived on the plateau (Gen. 19:36-38). The wadi called Arnon runs west to the middle of the Dead Sea. This wadi divided Moab in the south from Ammon in the north. **Amman** has always been the capital of the Ammonites. In ancient times, it was called Rabbah (I Chron. 20:1) or Rabbath Ammon. Today, it has some industries, and nearby farms produce wheat, barley, grapes, olives, and nuts.

Salt-encrusted rocks on the Dead Sea

The Dead Sea

The Dead Sea, fifty miles long and ten miles wide, lies at the bottom of the Great Rift Valley between Israel and Jordan. The Dead Sea boasts the lowest shoreline in the world as well as the saltiest water. Its shore lies 1,310 ft. below sea level—a lower elevation than any other point of land on the earth. Its waters are up to eight times saltier than ocean water, and they are about 25 percent more salty than the nearest rival, the Great Salt Lake. The Jordan River supplies most of the water, but desert wadis bring additional salts.

The Dead Sea is a lake with no outlet. Since the water evaporates quickly in the dry climate, salt deposits collect around the edges. Every ton of water from the Dead Sea contains about 125 pounds of common salt, potash, bromine, and other minerals. A peninsula called Al Lisan (The Tongue) divides the Dead Sea into two parts. The larger northern section reaches a depth of 1,312 feet. The southern portion averages only twenty feet deep and is shrinking due to mineral mining.

The salty sea and surrounding desert make for harsh environments, but life persists. Brine shrimp and a few plants and bacteria live in the water. Springs in the rugged desert hills surrounding the lake create desert oases. One such spring, En-gedi, or Spring of the Goat, creates a large waterfall. The spring takes its name from the ibex, a wild goat living in the canyons.

People have lived in the area since ancient times. Masada, a fortress, overlooks the west shore. Bedouins found the oldest known manuscripts of the Old Testament, called the Dead Sea Scrolls, in caves at Qumran on the northeast shore. The ancient cities of Sodom and Gomorrah also stood near the Dead Sea (or Salt Sea, Gen. 14:3). Many people believe that the ruins of these cities lie under the southern part of the sea. Today, people visit health resorts on the Dead Sea to float in the salty mineral water.

EGYPT'S SEARCH FOR PEACE

Like Turkey, Egypt has an unusual place in the Middle East. Its history goes far back before the Arab armies spread Islam across the region. Most people still associate Egypt with ancient pyramids and temples, which stand along the Nile Valley. Modern Egypt is proud of its ancient heritage and displays its treasures to millions of tourists each year.

Egypt has the second largest population in the Middle East, and it is struggling to find its place in the modern world. During the Middle Ages, Egypt fell to the Arabs and to other foreign conquerors. The Ottoman Turks won control in 1517. In the early nineteenth century, however, a Turkish officer named Mohammed Ali took power. He helped to modernize the country and open it to the West. His most significant decision was to allow France to build the Suez Canal. But wasteful spending by the king of Egypt forced him to sell his shares to Great Britain. The people despised the presence of British troops. After an uprising, Britain took control in 1882. It granted Egypt a form of independence in 1922, but it kept troops there. A military coup in 1952 replaced the monarchy with a republic. Only one man's name now appears on the ballot for president: he is first elected by Egypt's legislature and then his name is presented to the people for approval.

Egypt joined the other Arab nations in their wars with Israel. But after the Six-Day War, it lost the Sinai Peninsula and became weary of war. Egypt was the first to break ranks with the other Arab nations. In 1976 President Anwar Sadat made a surprise peace overture to Israel. With the help of the U.S. president, Sadat and Israel's prime minister Menachem Begin came to an agreement known as the Camp David Accords (1977). Egypt agreed to recognize Israel's right to exist; Israel agreed to return the Sinai Peninsula and to remove its settlers. However, another decade passed without any other Arab nation accepting the existence of Israel.

A large minority of radical Muslims is threatening to overthrow the government in Egypt. The government's harsh response to these groups has raised fears that Egypt is following the path of the shah of Iran, whose unpopular government was toppled by the revolution of 1979 that put Ayatollah Khomeini in power.

The Gift of the Nile

The **Nile River** is the lifeblood of Egypt. Palm trees shade the houses and villages in the valley. The climate is hot and dry, with temperatures generally ranging from 50° to 100°F. Only one inch or less of rain falls in the valley each year, but the delta region near the Mediterranean Sea may receive up to ten inches.

Sailboats on the Nile in Egypt

Until this century, the Nile flooded every year, bringing with it precious silt. The farmers channeled the floodwaters into their fields to sustain their crops of grain and cotton. The population was restricted to about ten miles on either side of the Nile, where the floodwaters could be channeled.

Aswan High Dam   Beginning in 1902, new dams ended the flood patterns. The largest, **Aswan High Dam,** was finished in 1971. Lake Nasser, the reservoir behind the high dam, stretches southward about three hundred miles. About two million acres of land receive the waters automatically throughout the year. The dam and lake have stopped the destructive flooding and allow year-round irrigation. Now two or three crops can be raised in one year. However, the dam also traps the rich sediments in Lake Nasser, rather than replenishing the soil downstream. Egyptian farmers must now rely on fertilizers.

The rural farmers are called **fellahin** (FEL uh HEEN). They live in houses made of sun-dried brick and plow their fields with wooden plows pulled by buffalo. While they now have radios and other modern conveniences, they lack adequate health care. Sanitation is poor, and disease is rampant. Small worms called bilharzia live in the murky Nile and spread an intestinal disease.

Upper Egypt   The area between the Nile Delta and Aswan High Dam is called **Upper Egypt.** Temples and tombs stand along the Nile in this region. The greatest ruins are at Thebes, which served as Egypt's capital during some dynasties.

The three pyramids at Giza

Lower Egypt   About one hundred miles from the Mediterranean, the Nile River splits and fans out to a width of about two hundred miles. Early geographers noted that this region was triangular in shape like the Greek letter delta. They called it the Nile Delta, and the term *delta* became the term for alluvial deposits at the mouth of any river. The Nile Delta is also called **Lower Egypt** because it has the lowest elevation of the river.

Alexander the Great established the city of **Alexandria** near the mouth of the delta. It was the site of the huge lighthouse called the Pharos, one of the seven ancient wonders of the world. In Alexandria was the largest library ever compiled in the ancient world. Today, Alexandria is the second largest city in Egypt, with 3.4 million people.

Muslim conquerors moved the capital from Alexandria to **Cairo** (KYE roh), near the start of the delta. With seven million people, Cairo is the largest city in Africa and the second largest in the Middle East. Cairo has become a major tourist center because of the pyramids located across the river at Giza. Like most cities, Cairo mixes prosperity and poverty. Shantytowns stand across from modern business and industrial centers.

A fellahin peasant leads a camel in Upper Egypt.

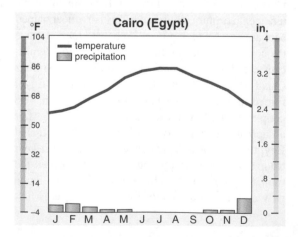

Valley of the Kings

Thebes was the great capital of Egyptian kings for fifteen hundred years, but almost nothing is left. The modern city of Luxor stands in its place. One reminder of the kings' ancient glory is the ruins of the Temple of Karnak. Sphinxes once lined the avenue leading to the front gateway, flanked by towers 143 feet high. Inside, a colonnade enclosed the Great Court, and the 140 pillars of the Great Hall of Pillars supported an eighty-foot-high ceiling. Huge pylons, or gateways, led into the central court and then into the inner sanctuary, where the golden statue of Amun, god of the wind and air, stood in his sacred boat. The temple complex also has temples for Amun's consort Mut and their son Khons.

Across the Nile on the west bank is a desolate valley circled by mountains. Two giant statues depict

The giant Temple of Karnak stands in the Valley of the Dead near Luxor, Egypt. The ancient city of Karnak, which once stood by the temple, was known as Thebes in the Bible.

Pharaoh Amenhotep III on his throne. The seated figures, called the Colossi of Memnon, rise fifty feet. The nearby tombs of sixty pharaohs explain the name Valley of the Kings. Most of the tombs were robbed long before archeologists explored them, but in 1922 an English archeologist chanced upon fabulous riches in the previously untouched tomb of eighteen-year-old Tutankhamen, or King Tut.

Deserts East and West

Deserts cover the rest of Egypt. While most Egyptians are Muslims, a large minority of Christians live in the country, many of them in the deserts. The Coptic Church boasts around five million members. Christianity spread throughout Egypt soon after the time of Christ, and it survived after the Arab conquest. The religion of the **Copts** is one of ritual and tradition, similar to Roman Catholicism and Eastern Orthodoxy. But they follow the heretical belief that Jesus has only a divine nature, not a human nature.

Sinai Although most of Egypt lies in Africa, the **Sinai Peninsula** is part of Asia. Israel captured the peninsula in the Six-Day War but restored it to Egypt in 1982. The main resource of the area is manganese, mined on the west coast.

Mount Sinai rises on the Sinai Peninsula.

The Wilderness of Sinai The mountainous Wilderness of Sinai lies at the south of the peninsula and takes its name from Mount Sinai. On this mountain Moses received the Ten Commandments (Exod. 31:18). Jewish, Christian, and Islamic traditions all identify Mount Sinai with Jebel Musa (meaning Mount of Moses, 7,497 ft.). At the foot of Mount Sinai, Orthodox monks live in the Monastery of St. Catherine. It is the oldest Christian monastery in the world (built A.D. 530).

Besides attracting religious pilgrims, the Wilderness of Sinai attracts divers to Ras Muhammad (Cape Muhammad). The Ras Muhammad Reef off the southern tip of the peninsula is one of the four greatest coral reefs in the world.

The Isthmus of Suez The **Gulf of Suez** is the western arm of the Red Sea. It separates Asia from Africa. At the north end of the gulf is Egypt's largest port on the Red Sea, Suez. The Isthmus of Suez is the bridge of land between the Gulf of Suez and the Mediterranean Sea. The **Suez Canal** cuts through this isthmus to join these two bodies of water. Canal tolls have boosted Egypt's economy.

Sahara The Sahara Desert hems in the Nile Valley on both sides. However, the two sides are quite different. The Eastern Desert is rugged and covered by barren mountains reaching over seven

Population Density of the Middle East

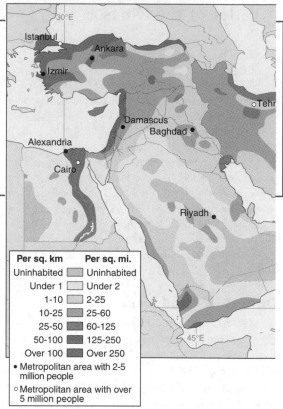

thousand feet high. It is sometimes called the Arabian Desert, but it should not be confused with the larger Arabian Desert that covers the Arabian Peninsula. The nation's largest petroleum deposit lies near the villages on the Red Sea coast.

The Western Desert or Libyan Desert is a low plateau. A few hills, salt flats, and depressions interrupt the flat sand horizons. Oases dot the vast wasteland, the largest of which is Al Kharijah. The

Per sq. km		Per sq. mi.
Uninhabited		Uninhabited
Under 1		Under 2
1-10		2-25
10-25		25-60
25-50		60-125
50-100		125-250
Over 100		Over 250

• Metropolitan area with 2-5 million people

○ Metropolitan area with over 5 million people

Qattara Depression in the northwest drops to 436 feet below sea level. It covers an area almost as large as New Jersey. Egypt has considered digging a fifty-mile canal northward to the Mediterranean to flood the basin and create a new lake.

Suez Canal

The Suez Canal was the longest canal in the world when it was completed in 1869. It stretches 118 miles from the Red Sea at Suez to the Mediterranean Sea, where a new commercial center, Port Said, was built. The canal cut six thousand miles off the trip from Europe to Asia, and it has become the busiest waterway in the world.

The canal is 64 feet deep and 450 feet wide, with wider spots every six miles for ships to pass. Around twenty-five thousand workers took ten years to complete the job. Many workers died in the arduous work of building the canal. Their sacrifice put Egypt back in the forefront of world affairs.

Interestingly, the French engineer Ferdinand de Lesseps was not the first to dig a canal here. Pharaoh Necho lost 120,000 slaves in his attempt to build the canal in the seventh century B.C. King Darius of Persia conquered Egypt and completed the job in 522 B.C. The Romans made improvements to the canal, but it eventually filled with silt.

◎ SECTION REVIEW

1. What is the most populous region in Egypt?

2. Which is farther north: Upper Egypt or Lower Egypt?

3. Name three desert areas in Egypt.

4. What are Egypt's peasant farmers called?

💡 Why does Egypt have so much influence in the Arab world?

REVIEW

Can You Define These Terms?

partition	Druze	Sephardim	tell
Fertile Crescent	Promised Land	Judaism	kibbutz
mandate	Zionist Movement	wadis	fellahin
Maronite	Ashkenazim		

Can You Locate These Natural Features?

Bosporus	Syrian Desert	Plain of Esdraelon	Transjordanian Plateau
Dardanelles	Palestine	Sea of Galilee	Nile River
Asia Minor	Shephelah	Negev	Sinai Peninsula
Pontic Mountains	Jordan River	Arabah	Gulf of Suez
Taurus Mountains	Golan Heights	Dead Sea	

Can You Explain the Significance of These People, Places, and Events?

Kemal Atatürk	Damascus	Megiddo	Upper Egypt
Thrace	Beirut	West Bank	Lower Egypt
Istanbul	Holy Land	Jerusalem	Alexandria
Byzantine Empire	Six-Day War	Knesset	Cairo
Anatolia	Gaza Strip	Amman	Copt
Ottoman Empire	Palestinian	Aswan High Dam	Suez Canal
Levant	Yasir Arafat		

How Much Do You Remember?

1. The Middle East lies at the crossroads of what three continents?
2. Name the European and Asian sections of Turkey.
3. What are the two factions that divide Cyprus?
4. What language is spoken in Syria, Lebanon, Jordan, and Egypt?
5. What desert surrounds Damascus?
6. Which of the four main factions in Lebanon claims to be Christian?
7. Put the following events in chronological order:
   a. King David ruled the Israelites.
   b. Muhammad founded the religion of Islam.
   c. Abram journeyed through the Fertile Crescent.
   d. The Ottoman Turks built a vast empire.
   e. Jesus Christ was born.
   f. Palestine became a British mandate.
8. What plain contains the Gaza Strip? What people live here?
9. Name the two cities that once guarded the entrance to the Plain of Esdraelon.
10. Name two lakes and a river in the Great Rift Valley.
11. In what part of Israel are the Arabah and the Wilderness of Zin?
12. What river is the lifeblood of Egypt?
13. What Christian sect survives in Egypt?
14. What part of Egypt lies in Asia?

What Do You Think?

1. Compare and contrast Judaism with Christianity.
2. How is Turkey different from the rest of the Muslim world? How is Egypt different?
3. Should the United States continue to send billions of dollars in free aid to Israel and Egypt to promote "peace in the Middle East"?
4. Why is the United States allied with Turkey? What problems does this alliance create?

Cumulative Review

1. Name the seven continents and four oceans. List five seas that touch Middle Eastern shores.
2. Define primary, secondary, and tertiary industries. Which industry is most prominent in the Middle East? What is the most developed country in the Middle East?
3. From what you have studied about the Middle East, give the most populous country, the largest country in size, the biggest city, the most-spoken language family, and the most common religion.
4. Pick the country you think is most typical of the Middle East. Give five characteristics that it shares with most other Middle Eastern countries. Then name three features unique to that country.

535

North Africa

Sahara

Sahel

West Africa

East Africa

Central
Africa

South
Africa

UNIT IX

Africa

Chapter 24
North Africa

Chapter 25
West and Central Africa

Chapter 26
East and South Africa

CHAPTER 24

NORTH AFRICA

In many ways North Africa has more in common with the Middle East than with the rest of Africa. Like the Middle East, water is the central concern of life. North Africa has few natural resources, but it was a major trade route for most of history, caught between warring armies that marched back and forth across its borders.

The life and history of the region is dominated by the **Sahara,** the world's largest desert. It is the only desert in the world that spans an entire continent from shore to shore. The desert-hardened Arabs looked at this vast, barren expanse and simply called it "the desert," or *Sahara.* About the same size as the United States, the Sahara is like no other place on earth. The parched soil receives less than five inches of rain annually, and portions are dry all year long. Average temperatures hover around 90°F but frequently exceed 120°F.

Ever since Muslim armies sprang out of Arabia in the seventh century, Islamic influence has sunk deep into the life of North Africa. Islam is the dominant religion, especially on the coast, where Arab armies faced little resistance. But Islam has not

brought prosperity. North Africa is struggling with poverty worse than any in the Middle East or in Europe. Muslim nations have closed their borders to Christian missionaries, who have the only solution for their thirsty land.

But whosoever drinketh of the water that I shall give him shall never thirst; but the water that I shall give him shall be in him a well of water springing up into everlasting life. (John 4:14)

BARBARY COAST

Most of North Africa's people live along the Mediterranean Sea. The reason is obvious. Rains on the coastal hills provide the only dependable water supply to support crops, livestock, and cities.

Over three thousand years ago, a group of people called the **Berbers** moved into the coastal lands west of Egypt. Little is known of their early history, except that they traded with the Phoenicians, Greeks, and Romans. This **Barbary Coast** was named after the Berbers. Major settlements arose at the few good ports on Africa's coast: Tripoli, Tunis, Algiers, and Tangier. These became the foundations of the Barbary States of Tripoli, Tunisia, Algeria, and Morocco.

As the Arabs spread across North Africa, they intermixed with the Berbers. The Arab-Berber ethnic group now accounts for over 97 percent of the population in all four nations of the Barbary Coast. Arabic is the official language, and Islam (Sunni Muslim) is their religion. A small minority still speaks the Berber language and continues traditional Berber farming practices, folk dances, and marriage customs.

Pirates flourished along the Barbary Coast between the sixteenth and nineteenth centuries. Muslim raiders captured European ships and held sailors for ransom. Most nations, including the newly independent United States, paid tribute in return for protection. When the pasha of Tripoli demanded an increase in payments, the daring U.S. Navy sailed "to the shores of Tripoli" and won international respect with its victory in the Tripolitan War (1801-5). France ended piracy in these waters once and for all when it captured Algiers in 1830. This European domination lasted until the Barbary States gained independence in the mid-twentieth century.

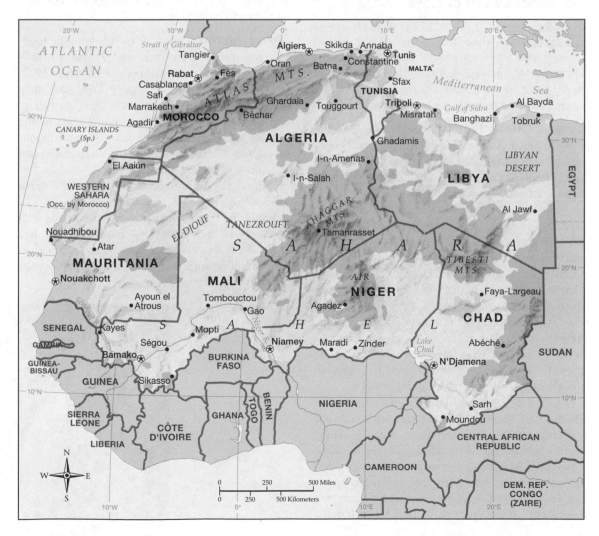

North Africa Statistics

COUNTRY	CAPITAL	AREA (SQ. MI.)	POPULATION	NATURAL INCREASE	LIFE EXPECTANCY	LITERACY RATE	PER CAPITA GDP	POP. DENSITY
Algeria	Algiers	919,591	29,830,370	2.2%	69	62%	$3,800	32
Chad	N'Djamena	495,753	7,166,023	2.7%	48	48%	$600	14
Libya	Tripoli	679,359	5,648,359	3.6%	65	76%	$6,510	8
Mali	Bamako	478,764	9,945,383	3.2%	47	31%	$600	20
Mauritania	Nouakchott	397,954	2,411,317	3.2%	50	38%	$1,200	6
Morocco	Rabat	173,413	30,391,423	2.1%	70	44%	$3,000	171
Niger	Niamey	489,189	9,388,859	3.0%	41	14%	$600	18
Tunisia	Tunis	63,170	9,183,097	1.9%	73	67%	$4,250	144

The Sandy Desert of Libya

Desert covers over 95 percent of Libya's land. Most people live on the coastal plain, where a mediterranean climate allows them to grow grain, olives, dates, and citrus fruits. About one-quarter of the people are rural, surviving by raising crops or herding livestock, such as sheep.

Coastal Cities   The Gulf of Sidra extends south into the center of Libya. Here the desert comes right up to the coast because there are no hills to bring rain. This desert divides the pleasant Mediterranean coasts east and west, where the people live.

Since the time of the Roman Empire, the hump on Libya's eastern coast has been called Cyrenaica, after the early capital of Cyrene. In New Testament times it was the home of Simon, who carried Christ's cross (Mark 15:21), and of Lucius, a church member at Antioch (Acts 13:1). Banghazi is the main eastern city today.

The western coast is known as Tripolitania. **Tripoli,** the capital, is the largest city in Libya. A series of foreign Islamic empires dominated the coast for over one millennium, until Italy crossed the Mediterranean and took control in 1911.

Libya became an independent kingdom in 1951, but Colonel Muammar Qaddafi overthrew the king in 1969. He removed all signs of Italian culture and instituted socialism. His rogue nation has supported Islamic terrorists for three decades. At one time he hoped to create a mighty new empire, attacking neighbors in Chad, Sudan, and Niger. The United States put a check on his terrorist activities in 1986, when U.S. bombers struck several cities in retaliation.

Desert Interior   Libya's desert is hot. The highest temperature ever measured in the world—136°F—was recorded just south of Tripoli in 1922.

When most people hear the word *Sahara,* they think of sand deserts. These wide areas of drifting, blowing sand are called **ergs.** While most of the Libyan desert has ergs, *hammadas* rise in the mountains along the southern borders. A **hammada** is a solid mass of barren, windswept rock.

Little vegetation grows in the desert. Coarse grasses, woody shrubs, and palm trees survive only at wadis and oases. Many oases are small and support only enough trees for a family or two. But about ninety oases in the Sahara are large enough to support entire towns and cities. Date palms are the main product of such oases.

Muammar Qaddafi (1942-)

Caravan routes, which have crossed the vast Sahara since ancient times, stopped at these oases to resupply. Libya's large oases, which lie in the west, became centers of trade. Various empires of Black peoples in the south sold gold, ivory, and slaves in return for salt, cloth, and dates from the Mediterranean region. Arabs used camels to transport goods across the dry terrain, where horses or other draft animals would perish. The sweet fruit of the date palm, which does not spoil as quickly as other fruits, provided convenient food for desert travel.

The eastern half of Libya has some of the most barren desert of the Sahara, where not even desert nomads wander. This area, called the Libyan Desert, extends east into Egypt and south into Sudan. Opinions about this wasteland changed in 1959 with the discovery of petroleum just south of the Gulf of Sidra.

All the Barbary States have some oil in their desert regions, but Libya has the most. With one of the three lowest population densities in Africa, Libya's oil wealth gives it the largest per capita GDP in North Africa. Libya has used its oil profits to develop educational and health facilities and to build industries and transportation. Unfortunately, some of the money goes to support radical Islamic causes.

SECTION REVIEW

1. What is the largest desert in the world?
2. What is the difference between ergs and hammadas?
3. What major group of people lived in North Africa before the Arabs invaded?
4. What is Libya's language? religion? climate?
   💡 Why must American political leaders keep abreast of Libya's foreign policy?

Nations along the Atlas Mountains

Africa differs from other continents in that no mountain range crosses the entire continent of Africa. Where ranges do occur, they have a major impact on the weather and culture. The fifteen-hundred-mile chain of **Atlas Mountains** lies along the

Snow covers a high peak of the Atlas Mountains. Below is the Ourika Valley in Morocco.

northwest coast of Africa. The mountains rise to a maximum elevation of 13,661 feet at Jebel Toubkal in Morocco.

The Arabs call the mountains the *Deizira el-Maghreb,* meaning "Island of the West," because they are a haven of life in the bleak desert. The mountain barrier blocks winds blowing off the sea, causing orographic rainfall. The water flows down to the sea, bringing moisture to the valleys and coastal plains. Although precipitation is less than twenty inches annually, it far exceeds the rainfall on the desert rain shadow.

The coast enjoys a pleasant mediterranean climate and scenery comparable to southern Europe. Summers are dry but mild. Rains come in winter, with snow falling in the high mountains. Scattered trees include olives and palms. Grapes are an important crop, and phosphate is mined on the mountain slopes.

The Arabs refer to the three nations of northwest Africa—Tunisia, Algeria, and Morocco—as the **Maghreb,** meaning the "West." The Berbers first settled the region. Some farmed the coastal plains and valleys, while others kept livestock on the mountainsides or at the edge of the desert. France gained control of Maghreb during the era of European colonialism, and close cultural ties to France remain, even though Maghreb gained independence in the mid-twentieth century.

Tiny Tunisia Tunisia has several geographic advantages over its desert

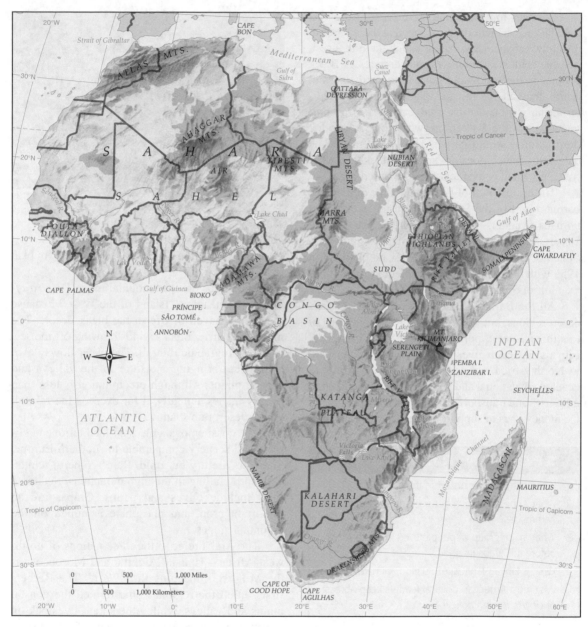

neighbors. Though only one-tenth as large as Libya, it supports twice the population because of a pleasant climate, consistent water supply, and productive land. Tunisia's life expectancy is the highest in Africa.

Most of the cities and farms are in the north, at the edge of the Atlas Mountains. These highlands rarely exceed two thousand feet, but it is enough to cool the region and bring moisture. The average temperature in the north varies from 52°F in winter to 79°F in summer. Little rain falls in the southern desert, and temperatures are much hotter.

Part of Tunisia is a prominent peninsula that juts into the Mediterranean, almost cutting the sea in half. **Tunis,** the capital, is ideally located for trade as it is only a short distance from Sicily and the Italian peninsula. Armies have used it as a launch pad to invade Europe and vice versa. More than two thousand years ago, the ancient city of Carthage on this peninsula controlled trade passing through the western Mediterranean.

Troubles in Algeria Algeria is the second largest nation in Africa (after Sudan), but most of it is desert. Algeria's 750 miles of Mediterranean coast rises into a hilly region, called the Tell, where oaks, cedars, olive trees, and maquis grow. A species of tailless apes, known as the Barbary apes, live here. The Barbary sheep, the only wild sheep in Africa, roam the dry mountains.

Ninety percent of Algeria's population lives in this coastal area. The capital, **Algiers,** is the biggest city on the Barbary Coast. American naval hero Stephen Decatur led the United States in winning the second Barbary War (1815) by capturing Algiers's main warship, sailing into the port, and threatening to destroy the city. Algiers had temporarily resumed piracy on U.S. ships while the navy was distracted by the War of 1812.

Revolution Algeria has many historic ties with Europe. Saint Augustine, the most noted Christian theologian of the ancient world, was born at Tagaste (south of the modern port of Annaba) and later became bishop of nearby Hippo. The Arabs later conquered the region. France took the north in 1830 and subdued the whole region by 1914. But the native Muslims resented French rule and the Catholic colonists, known as the *colons,* who ran the country.

A violent revolution broke out in 1954, and the French soldiers responded brutally—torturing rebel leaders and forcing millions into concentration camps. More than one-quarter million people died before Algeria was granted independence in 1962. Around one million *colons* fled in fear. The new Muslim rulers established a socialist government and kept power under one party.

Money from natural gas and petroleum helped the nation to industrialize, but demands for political freedom grew. The rulers allowed free elections in 1991, but they canceled the results when a radical Islamic party won the most votes. In response, radical Muslims started a campaign of terror, slaughtering over fifty thousand people by 1997.

Geographer's Corner

Making Inferences

At this point, you have studied many kinds of maps. You should now be able to pick up maps of completely new areas and draw *inferences,* or reasonable conclusions, from what you see. Look again at the map of North Africa at the beginning of this chapter. Answer each question and make the inference.

1. What African capitals lie on the Mediterranean coast? Why these three?

2. What Spanish islands lie off the coast of Morocco? Why are they Spanish?

3. How many nations touch Lake Chad? Why were so many borders drawn to include this lake?

4. Where are the geometric boundaries in North Africa? Why here and not the other places?

Now look more closely at the map of Africa, which shows places you will not read about until the next two chapters. What do you expect to see discussed? Begin by considering these questions.

1. What mountain ranges or highlands are labeled outside North Africa? What impact do you expect each to have on climate?

2. List all the labeled rivers. Which are most likely to support big cities?

3. Where is the largest number of small countries? Why there?

4. What is the most prominent natural border that divides nations in the east from the west? What impact does this natural feature appear to have on the physical geography?

The Varied Desert   South of the Atlas Mountains are the varied features of the Sahara Desert. The Grand Erg cuts a swath across central Algeria. Its sands cover thousands of square miles, with only a few large oases to break the monotony. The discovery of oil and natural gas reserves in the Eastern Grand Erg has provided the socialist government with capital for industries, such as chemicals, machinery, textiles, and cement. Algeria has the largest proportion of factory workers in the Arab world.

Date palms grow at Algeria's oasis of El Oued, near the border of Tunisia. The oasis lies in the Grand Erg Oriental.

Ergs, or desert sands, cover less than 20 percent of the Sahara. Much more common are **regs,** flat desert areas covered with pebbles. The Tanezrouft Reg, on Algeria's southern border, is a monotonous gravel plain that stretches hundreds of miles. Algeria has hammadas too. The bare rock of the **Ahaggar Mountains** seems to rise out of nowhere in the middle of the Sahara Desert.

The central land between the Atlas and Ahaggar Mountains has no drainage to the sea and no permanent streams. Wadis lead to shallow salt lakes called **chotts.** The chotts usually contain little or no water—just mineral deposits left behind after the water evaporates. The lowest such basin is Chott Melrhir, 102 feet below sea level.

Morocco   Morocco has coasts on both the Mediterranean and the Atlantic. A narrow peninsula juts out between these coasts, almost

Cave Art in the Sahara

Herodotus, a Greek historian who lived more than four centuries before Christ, described horse-drawn chariots that crossed the Sahara. Scholars scoffed at how naive Herodotus was. How could horses survive in the waterless wastes of the Sahara?

In the twentieth century, however, several caves were discovered in the desert of Algeria that gave credibility to his story. Some four thousand paintings, now protected in an Algerian national park, adorn the walls of the many shelter caves at Tassili-n-Ajjer, just north of the Ahaggar Mountains. The drawings include chariots drawn by four horses. Dating from 1200 to 100 B.C., these drawings prove contact with the Mediterranean world. After 100 B.C., the paintings show camels, which are more suited to an arid climate.

The cave paintings also show scenes of cattle, wild sheep, giraffes, and even hippos. Bones of hippos have been found as well, indicating that hippos may once have lived in this region. Obviously, hippos require standing water and do not live in the Sahara today. Apparently oases were once larger and more numerous in the Sahara, at least along some viable trade routes.

The Flood would explain the source of this lost water. The land probably dried slowly after the Flood. Initially, the Sahara would have been filled with standing ponds and lakes in its basins. Herodotus was not so naive after all.

touching Europe. It is only eight miles across the **Strait of Gibraltar** to Europe. Many conquerors have crisscrossed this strait to invade either Africa or Europe. The border town of **Tangier** has been occupied at various times by Berber, Roman, Vandal, Byzantine, Arab, Fatimid, Moor, Portuguese, Spanish, British, and French troops.

Morocco's two other major ports—Casablanca and Rabat—lie on the Atlantic coast. **Casablanca,** with over 2.5 million people, is the largest North African city outside Egypt. Casablanca is a popular tourist resort with a unique mixture of Spanish and French heritage. Troops from the United States

This fort at Laayoune was the capital of Spain's former province, Spanish Sahara (modern western Sahara). Morocco now occupies the fort, which it calls El Aaiun.

landed in Casablanca in their campaign to free North Africa from Axis forces in World War II.

Rabat is the capital of Morocco. After gaining independence, the young Islamic nation created a constitutional monarchy. The king assumed broad powers, including the command of the army. Morocco's royal family claims direct descent from the prophet Muhammad.

Coastal lowlands provide rich farmland across northwestern Morocco. Beyond the coastal lowlands, the Atlas Mountains cover most of the rest of Morocco. The mountains provide water for hydroelectric plants as well as lead and phosphates. Morocco is the world's leading exporter of phosphates.

Morocco claims a phosphate-rich area in the southwest known as the **Western Sahara.** When Spain gave up this territory in 1976, Mauritania and Morocco moved in. But Algeria opposed this illegal land grab and supported an effort by the native population to gain independence. In the bitter fighting, Mauritania withdrew its claim, but Morocco then claimed the entire region. While Morocco's troops captured the coastal cities, they could not defeat the nomads in the interior.

THE SAHEL, A TRANSITION ZONE

South of the Sahara lies the **Sahel,** a transitional region between the northern deserts and the central jungles of Africa. This band of grass-covered plains is about three hundred miles wide. The northern parts near the Sahara are the driest. Their short grasses support scattered populations of Berber and Arabic nomads, who herd cattle and sheep. To the south, the grasses become more plentiful. This region receives up to forty inches of rain annually, enough for crops of wheat and millet. Most of the farmers are Blacks, who settled the region long before the Muslim nomads intruded from the north.

Four nations are dominated by the Sahel—Mauritania, Mali, Niger, and Chad. The Sahara covers the northern half of these nations, and grazing lands cover much of the rest. Only a southern sliver of land supports crops, but it also supports most of the population. Unfortunately, the rain comes all at once, during the summer. Droughts often devastate the subsistence farmers, who do not have irrigation equipment. The people are so poor that they rarely let their children attend schools. As a result, the Sahel nations have the lowest literacy rates in all of Africa.

The Sahel is a **transitional zone** in more ways than just climate and agriculture. The four nations of the Sahel display a complex mix of peoples and lifestyles. Islam is the leading religion in all four

◎ SECTION REVIEW

1. What mountain range provides water for much of the Barbary Coast?
2. What famous ruin in Tunisia once controlled trade in the western Mediterranean?
3. What high mountains form *hammadas* in southern Algeria?
4. What is the largest city in North Africa outside of Egypt?
💡 What European nation lies due north of the capital of each Barbary Coast nation?

Dry Climates

☐ Tropical and Temperate Dry (Desert)　　　▨ Semiarid (Steppe)

In the News

Desertification of the Sahel

Once, scattered acacia, mahogany, and baobab trees made the Sahel a true savanna. But recent droughts and famines have raised fears that the Sahara Desert is spreading southward. This process is called **desertification,** or desiccation. Some estimates claim that the desert is moving at a rate of four to five miles per year. If this is true, the Sahara claims an average of fifteen million acres annually.

Two conditions may contribute to desertification. One is human abuse of the land. In the past thirty years, the number of people has more than doubled in the Sahel. With this increase has come an increased demand for more pasture, firewood, and cropland. Poor farming techniques can compound the loss of soil through erosion. The loss of trees and soil may open the way for the desert to invade.

Another possible factor in desertification, often ignored, is natural cycles. Droughts are a fact of life, depleting soil and vegetation wherever they strike. A few years of bad weather does not necessarily mean the climate has changed. On the other hand, perhaps climate is changing. Evidence supports the view that the earth goes through cycles of warming and cooling, perhaps related to solar flares. If this is the case, then no amount of human effort can stop the climate changes.

Scrawny cows search for food as the desert sands creep across the Sahel in Mauritania.

Whatever the cause of climate change, people must recognize that God is in control of the weather. Our responsibility, as always, is to follow biblical mandates about hard work and good stewardship of resources. Some measures are being taken to reduce desertification in the Sahel, such as planting trees in rows to slow down wind erosion. But no one should ignore the fact that God sometimes uses drought for judgment. Poor nations have relied on politicians to solve their problems, and they support violence if their ends are not met. In this case, the solution is repentance and a turn to righteous living, not more aid and government programs.

💡 Should the United States send money to help poor nations in Africa? If so, what is the best way to ensure that the money is used effectively? Can desertification be stopped without considering God and the opportunity for missionaries to preach the gospel?

---

countries, but its influence weakens as one progresses south and east into Black Africa. Mauritania is almost 100 percent Muslim, and Mali and Niger are over 80 percent Muslim, but Chad is only about one-half Muslim. Christianity and tribal religions make up the other half.

The mix of languages in the Sahel is complex. Arabic is an official language in the westernmost nation, Mauritania, along with the most common Black language (Wolof). Arabic is also an official language in the easternmost country, Chad, but over one hundred Black languages are spoken there. The Arabs had less impact on the two central nations, Mali and Niger, where several native Black languages are common. French became the official language in Mali and Niger and an official

language in Chad. While all four nations were once part of French West Africa, Mauritanians never adopted French.

Drought in Mauritania

Mauritania is the only country of the Sahel that has a seacoast. But rainfall is rare because the land is fairly flat and the ocean currents are cold. The only advantage Mauritania gets from its coast is shipping.

Desert North The Sahara covers most of Mauritania. The mining of iron ore is the only major industry in the nation. The nomadic people who live in this region are Moors, of mixed Arab and Berber ancestry. Moors account for over two-thirds of all the people in Mauritania. The Moors once enslaved Blacks, but France outlawed the practice. Yet slavery continued, and Mauritania officially outlawed it in 1980. Foreigners suspect that some thirty thousand "servants" in Mauritania remain virtual slaves.

Poverty in the South   The southern border is more hospitable. One-third of the population consists of Black tribes, which farm the country's only fertile plain along the Sénégal River. Because of drought, rural people have swelled the capital, located on the coast. Most people live in makeshift camps and rely on foreign aid for survival.

The Sahel region was not always so poor. It once supported great empires. The first great empire—Ghana—was centered in a city at the southeast corner of Mauritania. It arose in the third century and lasted one thousand years. The **Ghana Empire** controlled all the western trade routes across the Sahel, keeping all the gold nuggets and allowing the gold dust to continue north. Kumbi Saleh, the ancient capital, now lies in ruins.

Mali

Mali is the hub of the Sahel. Three great African empires vied for control of the region. Most of the people are Black, and they converted to Islam long ago.

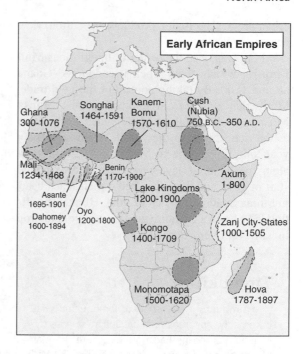

Early African Empires

Ghana 300-1076
Songhai 1464-1591
Kanem-Bornu 1570-1610
Cush (Nubia) 750 B.C.–350 A.D.
Mali 1234-1468
Benin 1170-1900
Axum 1-800
Asante 1695-1901
Lake Kingdoms 1200-1900
Dahomey 1600-1894
Oyo 1200-1800
Kongo 1400-1709
Zanj City-States 1000-1505
Monomotapa 1500-1620
Hova 1787-1897

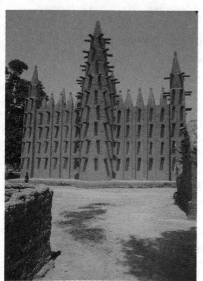

Mosques are made of mud in Mali. Wooden beams support the mud construction.

Salt in the Desert   The Sahara covers the northern half of Mali. The sparse population of Berbers and Moors accounts for only 10 percent of the total population.

Most early caravan routes in the western Sahara stopped at a desolate basin in the northern tip of Mali, where salts were plentiful. The salt mines of Taghaza provided traders with a valuable commodity, prized among the people of the southern rain forests, who gladly traded gold for salt. In Taghaza, on the other hand, salt was so plentiful that the workers lived in houses made of salt blocks.

Empires on the Niger River   Two major rivers, the Sénégal and the Niger, flow through the Sahel in southern Mali. Local wildlife includes elephants, wart hogs, baboons, panthers, leopards, giraffes, crocodiles, and hippopotamuses. The **Niger River,** the third largest river in Africa, is the most important river in the Sahel. The upper Niger is navigable for one thousand miles. Most ancient and modern cities of Mali lie on this river. The capital, Bamako, is the largest city in the entire Sahel. However, less than one-quarter of the people live in urban areas. The major products are cotton, rice, peanuts, and sorghum.

Mali was once the center of the glorious **Mali Empire,** which arose when it conquered Ghana around 1200. By taking control of the gold trade, Mali's riches grew to mythic proportions. **Mansa Musa,** a leading king of Mali, gained a reputation as the richest man in the world. When he made a year-long pilgrimage to Mecca in 1324, he took along five hundred slaves, each bearing a six-pound staff of gold, and three hundred camels, each bearing three hundred pounds of gold. His lavish gifts flooded Mecca's economy and caused gold to drop in value for over a decade.

A woman plows a peanut field near Kita, Mali.

Timbuktu

Timbuktu (now spelled Tombouctou) has become the epitome of remote and mysterious civilization. Europeans had no idea where the Mali Kingdom existed or where it got its riches. The Mali people guarded all the trade routes in the north, and water routes were impossible in the disease-ridden swamps and rapids to the south at the mouth of the Niger.

After his trip to Mecca, Mansa Musa brought back Muslim scholars to teach Arabic and the Koran at new seminaries in his empire. He chose Timbuktu as the site of a new capital, and he built a large central mosque. The city soon became the key university city in all of North Africa, known worldwide for its learning.

No European laid eyes on Timbuktu until 1826, though many tried. The Scottish explorer Alexander Laing finally reached Timbuktu after a two-year-long odyssey. Tragically, Laing was murdered before he could return. Hoping to sneak into the city, a Frenchman named René Caillié learned Arabic as a convert to Islam. In 1827 he posed as an Arab from Egypt and joined a caravan from Senegal. He reached Timbuktu a year later and returned to Paris to report his findings, earning him a prize of ten thousand francs offered by the Paris Geographical Society. All he found, however, was a town of mud houses and huts, long ago fallen into decline.

Niger

The Sahara covers two-thirds of Niger. The low **Aïr Mountains** in the north interrupt the vast ergs of the Sahara. The mountains are an extension of Algeria's Ahaggar Mountains. This "Switzerland of the desert" supplies lush vegetation in some valleys and oases. The Aïr Mountains in Africa are the biggest source of uranium. Niger has almost no other valuable industry. Over three-fourths of the people are subsistence farmers.

Tall, white desert nomads, called **Tuaregs,** came from the north about A.D. 1000 and took control of Niger's trade routes through the mountains. The largest oasis and market town, Agadez, was their capital. Today less than 2 percent of all Nigerians are Tuareg. They speak a Berber language and have the only written language among the Berber peoples.

A wide savanna spans the southern border of Niger. In spite of average daily summer temperatures of up to 100°F, the Niger River in the southwest is the country's most attractive and populous region. The modern capital, Niamey, is on this river.

The largest of all African empires, Songhai, was born along this river. **Songhai** began at Kukiya in the eighth century in what is now Niger. This Black African kingdom grew slowly at first. Its first great ruler, Sunni Ali, took over the declining empire of Mali in 1464. He divided the empire into provinces and moved the capital to Gao in what is now Mali.

Songhai conquered the Tuaregs to the north in the early sixteenth century. However, Morocco blamed the Songhai for economic decline and invaded in 1591. Morocco won easily because they were the first to use firearms in a battle on African soil. Although this ended the last empire of the Sahel, a reduced Songhai kingdom remained until France came in the nineteenth century.

Impoverished Chad

Chad's problems are worse than those of any other Sahel nation. It has one of the lowest per capita GDP and the lowest life expectancy. Chad does not have a single railroad, and even bicycles are scarce. There are hardly any paved roads, and less than 1 percent of the people have a car. Most people walk for transportation, and 70 percent of the population is rural. Most are subsistence farmers.

Arab Rebels in the Northern Desert The northern two-thirds of Chad is one of the driest regions of the Sahara. The Arabs of the region are nomads. The far north also has the highest elevations in the Sahara. Like the Ahaggar Mountains, the **Tibesti Mountains** rise up in the middle of the desert. The highest Tibesti peak is Emi Koussi (11,204 ft.).

Chad has reserves of uranium and petroleum, but disputes between the Arab people of the north and the Black people of the south have kept the country from developing. France has supported the southern government, while Libya has aided the northern rebels. Libya once invaded, hoping to annex Chad, but the rebels broke with Libya and

helped the south force them out. The UN finally forced Qaddafi out of the Aozou strip in the far north in 1994. The rebels have continued to fight the southern regime.

Farms in the Southern Savanna The Chari River and its tributaries provide a fertile region for agriculture in the south. Cotton is the only main crop. The river flows into **Lake Chad** on the western border. This lake harbors a wealth of fish. The capital, N'Djamena, lies near Lake Chad at the confluence of the Chari River and its largest tributary.

The empire of **Kanem-Bornu** on Lake Chad was never conquered by the African empires located further west. Begun as Kanem about 800, it conquered Bornu, another empire, in the fourteenth century. Its merchants traded across the Sahara with Tripoli. Although it declined later, the empire still existed when Europeans arrived.

Chad suffered during the colonial days. Many of its people died working on the Belgian railroad to the south in the Belgian Congo. The northern Arabs captured and enslaved thousands of Sara tribesmen. Meanwhile, however, missionaries introduced Christianity and opened Bible schools. The Sara people are the most educated in the nation and have gained most of the leadership positions in government and business. Their language dominates the more than one hundred language groups in the nation.

A man teaches a rural class east of Bamako, Mali.

SECTION REVIEW

1. What savanna region lies along the southern edge of the Sahara?
2. What European country controlled the four nations of the Sahel until 1960?
3. What nation in the Sahel has been influenced the most by Islam? What nation in the Sahel is about one-quarter Christian?
4. Through which nations of the Sahel does the Niger River flow?
   💡 What was the largest empire in Africa? Explain the geographic advantages that made a large empire possible.

REVIEW

Can You Define These Terms?

erg   reg   transitional zone   desertification
hammada   chott

Can You Locate These Natural Features?

Sahara Desert   Ahaggar Mountains   Niger River   Tibesti Mountains
Barbary Coast   Strait of Gibraltar   Aïr Mountains   Lake Chad
Atlas Mountains   Sahel

Can You Explain the Significance of These People, Places, and Events?

Berbers   Algiers   Ghana Empire   Tuaregs
Tripoli   Tangier   Mali Empire   Songhai Empire
Maghreb   Casablanca   Mansa Musa   Kanem-Bornu Empire
Tunis   Western Sahara   Timbuktu

How Much Do You Remember?

1. What climate is common on the north coast of Africa in addition to desert? Why?
2. Name the country and specific location of a large sample of each desert feature.
   a. erg
   b. hammada
   c. reg
3. What were the Barbary States?
4. Name the three major European nations that lie north of the Barbary Coast. For each European nation, give its counterpart on the African coast where the European nation has had the most recent influence.
5. Why is Mauritania's climate so dry?
6. Give the modern nation where each ancient empire began.
   a. Ghana Empire
   b. Kanem-Bornu Empire
   c. Mali Empire
   d. Songhai Empire
7. List the major goods that were carried on caravans traveling north to the Mediterranean through the ancient empires of the Sahel. What goods were brought back south? Why has this trade stopped?

8. List three characteristics that the nations of the Sahel share with the nations of the Barbary Coast. List three other characteristics that they share with Black Africa.
9. For each Sahel nation name one distinctive feature that is different from the other three nations. Then list four characteristics that all of them share in common.

What Do You Think?

1. Why are missionary activities extremely limited in North Africa? How could the peoples of North Africa be reached?
2. Compare and contrast Tunisia and Libya. Why do you think Tunisians say they are glad *not* to have great oil wealth?
3. Why are there tensions in the Sahel countries between the peoples of the north and south? What should be done?
4. Should the nations of the Barbary Coast be listed in the Middle Eastern culture region rather than the African region? Why or why not?

WEST AND CENTRAL AFRICA

Just as North Africa suffers from too little rain, the nations farther south suffer from too much rain or unpredictable rains. All of the lands below the Sahara are called **sub-Saharan Africa.** The environment and cultures differ radically from the north. One of the most obvious differences is the prevalence of Black races. But there are many other differences, discussed in the next two chapters.

FROM VILLAGE LIFE TO MODERN LIFE

Except for a strip of the Sahel in the north, jungles and savannas dominate the landscape and lifestyles of the twenty nations in West and Central Africa. The equator runs through the center of this region. Regular winds off the Atlantic continually dump rain along the equator, just as they do in the Amazon River Basin. A few degrees north and south of the equator, the winds shift, creating a rainy and dry season. A savanna rises here.

Unlike mediterranean climates and river valleys in the Sahel, tropical rain forests and dry savannas cannot generally support intensive agriculture. Typically the people are hunters and gatherers, sometimes practicing slash-and-burn agriculture to supplement their meager existence. Their simple agriculture permits small villages, but there is not enough food to support large groups in one place.

The **village** is an important concept in understanding life in Africa. In the traditional African village, each person plays a vital role in the survival of the whole community. Having more than one wife is a sign of wealth, so polygamy is common. Young children pull weeds or sort vegetables, while older children herd livestock or do household chores. At age sixteen, young men and women go through *initiation rites,* including hunts, dances, and ceremonies with masks, to mark their transition into

West and Central Africa Statistics

COUNTRY	CAPITAL	AREA (SQ. MI.)	POPULATION	NATURAL INCREASE	LIFE EXPECTANCY	LITERACY RATE	PER CAPITA GDP	POP. DENSITY
West Africa								
Benin	Porto-Novo	43,483	5,902,178	3.3%	53	37%	$1,380	136
Burkina Faso	Ouagadougou	105,869	10,891,159	2.6%	42	19%	$700	103
Cape Verde Islands	Praia	1,557	393,843	2.8%	70	72%	$1,040	253
Côte d'Ivoire	Yamoussoukro	124,503	14,986,218	2.5%	45	40%	$1,500	120
Gambia	Banjul	4,361	1,248,085	2.4%	54	39%	$1,100	302
Ghana	Accra	92,099	18,100,703	2.3%	57	64%	$1,400	197
Guinea	Conakry	94,964	7,405,375	2.4%	46	36%	$1,020	78
Guinea-Bissau	Bissau	13,948	1,178,584	2.3%	49	55%	$900	84
Liberia	Monrovia	43,000	2,602,068	3.1%	59	38%	$770	68
Nigeria	Abuja	356,667	107,129,469	3.0%	55	57%	$1,300	300
Senegal	Dakar	75,750	9,403,546	3.4%	57	33%	$1,600	123
Sierra Leone	Freetown	27,699	4,891,546	2.9%	48	31%	$960	176
Togo	Lomé	21,622	4,735,610	3.6%	58	52%	$900	215
Central Africa								
Cameroon	Yaoundé	183,568	14,677,510	2.9%	52	63%	$1,200	80
Central African Republic	Bangui	240,534	3,342,051	2.2%	45	60%	$800	14
Congo	Brazzaville	132,046	2,583,198	2.1%	46	75%	$3,100	20
Democratic Republic of Congo	Kinshasa	905,563	47,440,362	3.1%	47	77%	$400	52
Equatorial Guinea	Malabo	10,831	442,516	2.6%	54	78%	$800	41
Gabon	Libreville	103,346	1,190,159	1.5%	56	63%	$5,200	12
São Tomé and Príncipe	São Tomé	386	147,865	2.5%	64	73%	$1,000	383

adulthood. The men under age thirty-five traditionally protect the village, while older men govern.

This loyalty to the village extends to larger social units. Several villages that trace their descent back to a common ancestor form a clan. Two clans or more, in turn, form a tribe. A headman wields the highest authority in the village, while a strong tribal **chief** unites several villages, using headmen as his administrators.

Whenever people are isolated in small groups, their speech patterns diverge quickly. Dialects arise and then turn into new languages. Africa has one-third of the world's languages even though it has only one-tenth of the people. The strong identification with a tribe that speaks the same language or dialect is called **tribalism.** In spite of European influence, tribalism continues to be a central feature of sub-Saharan Africa. Individuals

Masks are used in West Africa for tribal rituals.

feel more allegiance to their tribe than to their nation-state.

Fear of demonic spirits dominates tribal religions, and Africans have developed many rituals to appease these spirits. The tribal religions of Africa follow **animism,** the worship of the "souls" (Latin *anima*) of animals, rivers, trees, and other objects. Superstitious and demonic practices are still common. The shamans in Africa, called witch doctors, communicate with spirits, offer healing, and use sorcery. Sub-Saharan Africa has the largest remaining area of tribal religions in the world today. (See the map of world religions on page 94.)

A teacher helps students in a high school history class in Banjul, the capital of Gambia.

European *colonialism* brought radical changes to life in sub-Saharan Africa. The people now have a mixture of traditional ways and modern Western ways. People in the cities wear clothing reflecting both African and Western styles, and they shop in both department stores and street markets. Cities have modern hospitals, schools, industries, homes, and entertainment. In contrast, villages lack electricity and plumbing, and villagers prefer witch doctors to medical clinics.

While the people in the twenty nations of West and Central Africa still speak their various tribal languages, the *official* language of each nation is the language of the most recent European ruler. Two of these African countries speak Portuguese, the language of the first colonial power in the region. One nation speaks Spanish. But the majority speak French and English.

Europeans introduced modern economic and political ideas. Lumbering and plantations have stripped much of the rain forest. Plantations are now common in the rain forests near the coast. Colonialism ended in the 1960s and 1970s after World War II, but then sub-Saharan Africa became a battleground between Marxists and capitalists. **Autocrats** ruled their governments with an iron hand, sometimes allowing elections but not allowing competitive political parties. Civil wars and coups were common.

The end of the Cold War in 1989 has brought new hope to this troubled land. Autocrats can no longer count on aid from Communists or free nations, who were once willing to overlook the leaders' shortcomings in their quest for allies. In 1991 Benin became the first nation on mainland Africa ever to vote a president and his political party out of office in free elections.

The greatest benefit of European contact has been the recent spread of the gospel. Christ offers a miraculous peace that no government can give or take away, a peace that is not disturbed by wars or economic disasters.

Peace I leave with you, my peace I give unto you: not as the world giveth, give I unto you. Let not your heart be troubled, neither let it be afraid. (John 14:27)

WEST AFRICA

Today, thirteen countries cover the great western bulge of Africa. The largest, Nigeria, is bigger than Texas. But the others are quite small. Gambia, about the size of Connecticut, is the smallest country on the continent. All thirteen would fit into India. Although there are many Muslims in the north, animists and Christians make up the majority farther south.

West Atlantic Coast

Black Africans populate the four mainland nations of the west Atlantic coast. Lying above the equator, the region has both a wet and a dry season.

Senegal, Anchor of French West Africa Most of Senegal lies in the dry Sahel. It has suffered greatly from droughts and from an influx of refugees fleeing Mauritania in the north. Its advantage over Mauritania is the prominence of the **Sénégal River** and its tributaries. Over 90 percent of the Senegalese are Muslims. Many are nomadic herders, tending cattle, sheep, and goats in the north. Farmers grow peanuts in the south.

France wrested final control of the region from Muslim rulers in 1893. Two years later, French colonies in North Africa and West Africa were combined into **French West Africa,** with the capital at **Dakar.** In 1958 all the territories voted for self-government. Guinea became independent that year, and Senegal and the others followed two years later. With independence, Senegal became a stable socialist republic.

The national capital, Dakar, is the largest city in the four nations on the west Atlantic coast. Tourists from America are often moved at the sight of the infamous slavehold of Maison des Esclaves off Dakar.

Great Britain in Gambia, Africa's Smallest State

Gambia has an odd shape and location. Surrounded by Senegal, it stretches two hundred miles up the Gambia River but is only twenty miles wide. Mangrove swamps line the river. As in Senegal, peanuts are the main cash crop and Islam the main religion. Banjul is the only city and serves as both port and capital. Gambia was Britain's first African possession. After independence in 1965, Gambia joined Senegal in a confederation for a while.

Guinea

Guinea is a Muslim nation. Conakry, the capital, is the only major port other than Dakar on the west Atlantic coast. A Marxist government took over Guinea after it gained independence from France in 1958.

While mangrove swamps cover the coast, as they do in Senegal and Gambia, a plateau rises near the Atlantic and continues into the interior. Forests cover the hills and low mountains in the eastern half of the country. The headwaters of two great rivers—the Sénégal and Gambia—lie in Guinea's mountainous north, called **Fouta Djallon.**

With a third of the world's reserves of bauxite, Guinea is second only to Australia in bauxite mining. Most of the bauxite

Women fish with triangular nets on the Niger River near Conakry, Guinea.

comes from the north. Guinea also has deposits of iron ore, gold, and diamonds.

The Portuguese in Guinea-Bissau

Guinea-Bissau (GIN ee-bih SOU) lies on the coast between Guinea and Senegal. Subsistence agriculture dominates the economy, while large

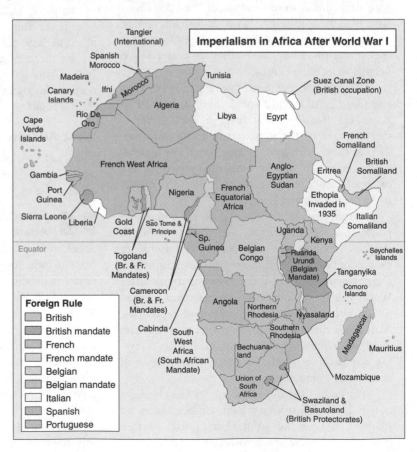

Imperialism in Africa After World War I

Tangier (International)
Spanish Morocco
Madeira
Canary Islands
Ifni
Morocco
Rio De Oro
Cape Verde Islands
Gambia
Port Guinea
Sierra Leone
Liberia
Gold Coast
São Tomé & Principe
Togoland (Br. & Fr. Mandates)
French West Africa
Tunisia
Algeria
Libya
Egypt
Suez Canal Zone (British occupation)
French Somaliland
Eritrea
British Somaliland
Ethiopia Invaded in 1935
Italian Somaliland
Anglo-Egyptian Sudan
French Equatorial Africa
Nigeria
Sp. Guinea
Cameroon (Br. & Fr. Mandates)
Cabinda
South West Africa (South African Mandate)
Angola
Belgian Congo
Ruanda Urundi (Belgian Mandate)
Uganda
Kenya
Northern Rhodesia
Southern Rhodesia
Nyasaland
Bechuana-land
Union of South Africa
Swaziland & Basutoland (British Protectorates)
Mozambique
Tanganyika
Seychelles Islands
Comoro Islands
Madagascar
Mauritius

Equator

Foreign Rule
- British
- British mandate
- French
- French mandate
- Belgian
- Belgian mandate
- Italian
- Spanish
- Portuguese

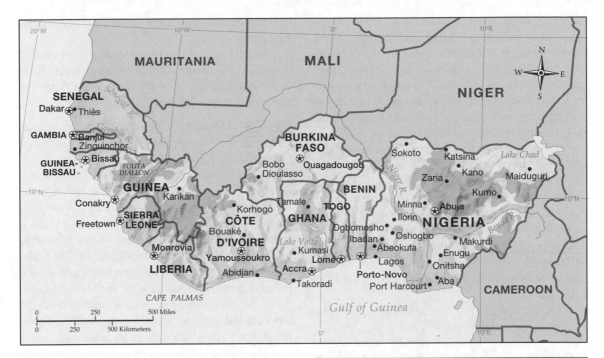

deposits of bauxite lie untouched. Two-thirds of the people practice animism, and most of the rest are Muslim.

Portuguese exploration began in the fifteenth century. They hoped to find a route to India that bypassed the Ottoman Empire. By 1430 the Portuguese traded regularly along the coast of West Africa. Guinea-Bissau was one of the few regions that remained in Portuguese hands throughout Europe's competition for global empire. Portugal did not give up the colony until 1974, after years of bitter fighting. Marxist leaders then kept a grip on the nation until the end of the Cold War.

The Cape Verde Islands The Cape Verde Islands, consisting of ten main islands and five islets, lie four hundred miles west of the coast of Senegal. One island has a volcano that is still active. The Portuguese discovered the uninhabited islands in 1460 and settled them with slaves, who were eventually converted to Roman Catholicism. Almost three-fourths of the people are mulatto, and the rest are Black Africans. In 1975, Cape Verde became one of the last nations in Africa to gain independence.

SECTION REVIEW

1. List four culture traits that distinguish sub-Saharan Africa from North Africa.

2. What is the primary religion of Senegal, Gambia, and Guinea?

3. In the west coast region of Africa, where is animism dominant?

💡 Where was Marxism common on the west coast? Which country developed a stable, Western government? Why was there a difference?

Two Colonies on the "Free" Coast

Slavery was practiced on every continent since ancient times. Europeans enslaved Europeans, Asians enslaved Asians, and Africans enslaved Africans. God even permitted the Jews to have slaves, but they had to treat them fairly. The evils of the African slave trade remain an ugly blotch in world history, and its bitter legacy still plagues Africa.

The slave trade flourished in West Africa in the seventeenth and eighteenth centuries. Muslim

555

nations controlled much of the slave trade on the west coast and in the Sahel, but Europe found slaves along the southern coast of the African bulge. At first, the more powerful African tribes captured enemies and sold them to European traders at ports. Later, Europeans went hunting in Africa's interior for slaves. The traders shipped the slaves to the Americas to labor on plantations.

Great Britain shared in the blame for the worldwide trade in slaves. But later it became the world's first empire to successfully abolish slavery. As a result of Christians in England, particularly the Quakers, the British Empire abolished the slave trade in 1807. The British later banned slave ownership in 1833. (The United States Constitution outlawed the slave trade in 1807 as well, but the federal government did not abolish slavery until the Civil War.)

The antislavery movement left an interesting legacy in two countries of West Africa. While slavery continued up and down the coast and in the interior, two spots became havens for freed slaves. Reformers in Great Britain and the United States thought they could best help freed slaves by resettling, or *repatriating,* them in their African homeland.

The Guinea Highlands isolated the coastal settlements from the turmoil in the interior. Mangrove swamps line the coasts, but just inland lie many coffee, cacao, palm oil, and rubber plantations. Away from the coast, forested highlands stretch northward into Guinea. Subsistence farmers grow rice and cassava, a root first used in the Amazon.

Sierra Leone

The Englishman Granville Sharp established Sierra Leone in 1787 as a settlement for freed slaves, and the capital was appropriately called Freetown. The British colony gained independence from Britain in 1961. Only 2 percent of the people, however, are descended from freed slaves. They live near Freetown, the capital. They follow Christianity and speak a form of English called Krio. The mostly Muslim, indigenous tribal peoples resent the prosperity, education, and influence of this small minority. Sierra Leone's independence has been marred by a bloody civil war that began in 1991 and wasted the country.

Sierra Leone is one of the leading producers of diamonds. The diamonds are found in gravel beds in the swampy rivers of the southeast. Control of this wealth is one reason for the fighting.

Liberia

Liberia is the only African nation never colonized by Europeans. Furthermore, it was the first Black republic in Africa and the second in world history (after Haiti).

In 1822 a charitable society in the United States sent a boat with freed American slaves to the coast, naming the city Monrovia after James Monroe, U.S. president and one of the sponsors. Monrovia is the capital of Liberia. In 1847, the Black leaders declared independence and established a republic modeled after the United States. As in Sierra Leone, descendants of freed slaves form a small minority (only 5 percent of the population) but have wielded the most influence.

The sixteen native tribes each have their own language. Missionary efforts have reached some of the indigenous peoples, but about half of the population are animists and the rest Muslim. The natives, led by a sergeant in the army, overthrew the coast's old True Whig Party in 1980 and killed the president. The sergeant, in turn, was overthrown and killed in 1990, sparking one of the most horrifying civil wars in history.

The hills of Liberia rise into mountains along the border with Guinea. However, Liberia has no important resources other than its flag. Liberia collects a fee from ship owners who wish to register their ships in Liberia and fly the Liberian flag. By this means, the ship owners avoid the many regulations of industrialized nations. Liberia and Panama each generate a large income from this source. Because of this policy, Liberia has the largest commercial fleet in the entire world—one-fifth of the world's tankers and one-seventh of all merchant ships.

A French Colony on the Ivory Coast

The curved coast of Africa from Côte d'Ivoire to Gabon bounds the **Gulf of Guinea.** Côte d'Ivoire, Ghana, Togo, Benin, and

Nigeria lie in a row along the north shore of this gulf. Each part of this coast has a separate name based on early trade: the Ivory Coast, the Gold Coast, and the Slave Coast.

French sailors arrived in 1483 and began trading with the interior for ivory. This prompted the French name for the country Côte d'Ivoire, meaning "Ivory Coast." Formerly part of French West Africa, the nation gained independence in 1960 and made **Abidjan** the capital. With almost three million people, this major port city is by far the largest city in all of West Africa. In contrast to Liberia and Sierre Leone, Côte d'Ivoire has become a relatively prosperous and fairly stable nation.

Côte d'Ivoire produces almost one-third of the world's cacao beans. It ranks fifth in coffee

Gimme your Guineas

A *guinea* is a gold coin that was used in England from 1663 to 1813. It was named after the gold-rich Guinea Coast of Africa. Other kinds of "guineas" have remained in circulation.

While merchants sought gold guineas, nations sought land "Guineas." France, Portugal, and Spain each got one in Africa. But they couldn't have the same name, especially after independence. The first independent colony was lucky: French Guinea became plain old *Guinea.* Portuguese Guinea added the name of its capital, becoming *Guinea-Bissau.* The former Spanish colony took a different tack. It became *Equatorial Guinea* because it lies on the equator.

In Southeast Asia the Dutch got a guinea. They colonized the island of *New Guinea,* which they thought looked like the "old" Guinea. To complicate matters, however, the island was later split between Indonesia and the independent nation of *Papua New Guinea.* Do you know the name of Indonesia's portion of the island?

Guinea fowl were named for the Guinea Coast of Africa; however, *guinea pigs* were not. . . . But that's a different story.

production and exports cotton, pineapples, bananas, and lumber. Unlike many African countries that reject ties with former colonial powers, it welcomes French businessmen, teachers, and other skilled workers. Though the foreigners seem to be the richest inhabitants, the entire nation benefits from growing businesses and industries. The standard of living ranks in the top ten for all of Africa.

The first autocratic leader, Félix Houphouët-Boigny, developed a stable government. In 1983 he moved the capital to the interior. The capital city of Yamoussoukro boasts a presidential palace with its own crocodile lake. However, Houphouët-Boigny's opposition to democracy created many enemies. While his nation struggled against poverty, he lavished tax money on a huge cathedral, Our Lady of Peace. Finished in 1989, it is the largest church in the world, but the pope made sure it was not taller than St. Peter's.

The Volta

The Volta River is a major river that empties into the Gulf of Guinea. The three main headwater streams are the Red Volta, the White Volta, and the Black Volta. Some of the headwaters flow through the interior country of Burkina Faso and then into the coastal nation of Ghana.

Ghana, the Gold Coast The Portuguese first visited Ghana in 1471. The abundant gold prompted them to call it the **Gold Coast.** Initially, the Portuguese paid rent to the Ashanti Empire for their coastal base. Later, the British took over and made it a colony. Britain granted independence in 1957, and the new nation took the name Ghana after the ancient African empire based in the Sahel. Mines still produce some gold, and the Ashanti people display gold treasures on festive occasions.

Today, however, Ghana's chief export is cacao. Ghana is the world's third largest producer of cacao beans. Bauxite, manganese, and diamond mines provide additional income. A dam provides hydroelectric power for aluminum smelting, although debts claim most of the profits. One of the best museums in sub-Saharan Africa is Ghana's Cape Coast Castle, where Black Americans tour blood-stained Portuguese dungeons that once held some of their ancestors.

Landlocked Burkina Faso Burkina Faso lies in the Sahel but shares the Volta River with Ghana. Like the rest of the Sahel, savannas cover the land and droughts are frequent. Low life expectancies, literacy rates, and per capita GDPs are typical of the Sahel nations. Burkina Faso has the lowest statistics in all three categories in West Africa. Most of its people are poor cattle herders and subsistence farmers, raising millet or peanuts.

The independent nation of Upper Volta was born in 1960 from French West Africa. In 1984, after suffering four military coups, the leader changed the name from Upper Volta to Burkina Faso, which means "Land of the Dignified People." He hoped to rally the people but succeeded only in provoking a fifth coup.

The Slave Coast

A **bight** is a large bay formed by a long curving coast. If you look at the map, you can see the **Bight of Benin,** an extension of the Gulf of Guinea that pushes north into the coast of three nations—Togo,

This farmer practices slash-and-burn agriculture.

Benin, and Nigeria—between the Volta and Niger Rivers. This coast was called the Slave Coast because so many slave ships operated from its ports.

Togo Togo was a German colony until World War I, when France was given control by the peace settlement. Togo gained independence in 1960 along with the other French territories. Lomé, on the coast, is the capital of Togo. Few people live in the northern savanna.

Voodooism in Benin Neighboring Benin, formerly Dahomey, was also once part of French West Africa. Porto-Novo is the capital. While there are sixty ethnic groups, the southern Fon tribe is in the majority. The Bariba are the main group in the sparsely populated northern savanna.

About two-thirds of the people of Benin practice a form of animism called voodoo. The rest of the people are Christians or Muslims. Voodoo was declared an official state religion in 1996 with a paid holiday. The people of Benin feel a close tie to

This woman from Togo carries a large load on her head with perfect balance.

Sources of Slaves

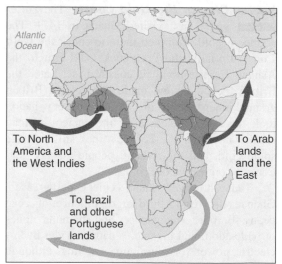

Atlantic Ocean

To North America and the West Indies

To Arab lands and the East

To Brazil and other Portuguese lands

descendants of slaves transported to the Caribbean and to Brazil's northeast coast.

Nigeria, Africa's Population Center

With over one hundred million people, Nigeria is the most populous nation in Africa. Unlike most other West African nations, Nigeria was an English colony, and English remains the official language. Nigeria received independence from Britain in 1960, but it has epitomized Africa's struggles to rise above its troubled past.

The Niger River is the lifeline of Nigeria. If you look at the relief map, you will see how rivers divide the nation into three distinct geographic regions: the Niger flows in from the west and then south to the Gulf of Guinea; Niger's main tributary, the **Benue River** (BAYN way), enters from the east to complete the division. A different tribe has dominated the history and culture of each region.

In 1991 Nigeria moved its capital from the southwest city of Lagos to the central city of Abuja, which is between the three major tribes. It hopes to

A typical dugout canoe on the Niger River in Nigeria

boost regional development and to build a new national identity.

Hausaland's Muslims in the North   North of the Niger and Benue Rivers rise the plateaus of the Sahel. The dominant **Hausa** tribe is the largest ethnic group in Nigeria. About 21 percent of all Nigerians are Hausa. Unlike most other tribes, they

The Year Europe Stole Africa

European colonization of Africa proceeded slowly between the fifteenth and nineteenth centuries. But modern technology suddenly opened the interior of the continent to exploration and rapid conquest. This conquest reached a feverish pace when Germany united for the first time in 1871, and the German Empire turned its eyes abroad to find national glory in world empire. German soldiers and pioneers suddenly appeared in unclaimed regions of Africa. A major war seemed imminent.

To avoid war, the chancellor of Germany, Otto von Bismarck, invited the United States and fourteen European nations to the **Berlin Conference** in November 1884. The goal was to carve up remaining territories around the world, particularly in Africa. After three months of negotiations, borders between unclaimed and unexplored regions were settled. The Europeans even agreed to help one another subdue the native tribes. Then the race was on. Within thirty years, all but Liberia and Ethiopia fell to Europe.

The cunning Bismarck played on the rivalry between France and England to Germany's advantage. He gained strategic lands between the rivals. In West Africa, Germany got Togoland, between Britain's colonies in Ghana and Nigeria. In Central Africa, Germany got Kamerun (modern Cameroon) between Nigeria and French lands. After the defeat of the German Empire in World War I, France and Great Britain divided these two territories. British Togoland eventually joined Ghana, and French Togoland became modern Togo. Part of British Cameroon merged with Nigeria, and the rest joined French Cameroon. The modern nation of Cameroon has both English and French for official languages.

Almost nothing remains of the German meddling in Africa, except the legacy of the Berlin Conference. National lines split native tribes in half, closed ancient migration routes, and lumped historic enemies together. Perhaps the greatest challenge of modern African governments is to develop a sense of national unity that supersedes thousands of years of tribalism.

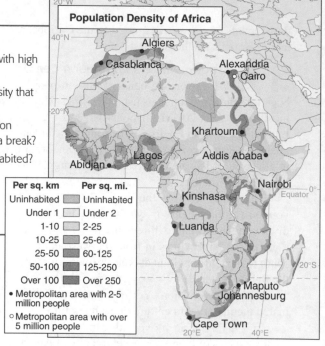

Population Density of Africa

Per sq. km		Per sq. mi.
Uninhabited		Uninhabited
Under 1		Under 2
1-10		2-25
10-25		25-60
25-50		60-125
50-100		125-250
Over 100		Over 250

• Metropolitan area with 2-5 million people

○ Metropolitan area with over 5 million people

are Muslims, and their language belongs to the Afro-Asiatic family—the same family as Arabic.

The Hausa built many city-states before the arrival of the Europeans. Three are still important cities: Katsina, Zaria, and Kano. Kano is the largest city in the north and the fourth largest in Nigeria. The Fulani tribe took control in the nineteenth century and intermixed with the Hausa. The Fulani account for another 9 percent of the population.

Today, most of these northern people are rural. They live in traditional ways on the savanna, grazing cattle or growing crops. Two of these crops are especially important. Nigeria is the fourth leading producer worldwide of both peanuts and millet. Conflict is common between Hausa Muslims and Ibo Christians in the region. Religious wars in 1995 led to hundreds of deaths and to the destruction of numerous Christian and Muslim villages.

Yorubaland's Christians in the Southwest

The **Yoruba** dominate the lands south and west of the Niger. The Yoruba make up about one-fifth of the entire population of Nigeria as well as a leading portion of Benin. The entire Slave Coast was once Yoruba territory. Unlike the Hausa, the Yoruba have adopted many Western ways, and many have converted to Christianity. Half of Nigeria's population is nominally Christian.

Most of Nigeria's people live in the southwest. This region rises slowly through dense rain forests to the grassy Plateau of Yorubaland (2,000 ft.). The two largest cities in this region are Lagos and Ibadan, each with about 1.5 million people. **Lagos** was an important slave market. Once the capital of Nigeria, it is now the most important industrial center in all of West and Central Africa.

To the east of Lagos lies Benin City, the former capital of the **Benin Kingdom,** one of the greatest kingdoms of West Africa, which flourished between the thirteenth and eighteenth centuries. Its bronze and brass statues won international esteem, but the king's wealth depended on the slave trade, which declined after Europeans banned slavery.

Development of Nigeria's many resources has helped industries keep growing. Southwest Nigeria has the most resources of any region in the country.

The leafless baobab tree is a common sight in the Sahel. This one grows north of Kano, Nigeria.

A street market at Ibadan, the second largest city in Nigeria

◎ SECTION REVIEW

1. Which two nations were settled by freed slaves?
2. What was the main product of Côte d'Ivoire in colonial days? What is the main product today?
3. Through what two nations does the Volta River flow?
4. What are the three largest tribal groups in Nigeria?
5. ♀ Why is the future of West Africa dependent on Nigeria's politics and economy?

Near the Gulf of Guinea, cacao and palm trees produce major exports. Nigeria ranks third in palm oil production and cassava production, sixth in cacao production, and tenth in petroleum production worldwide. Nigeria leads Africa in production of both hardwoods and petroleum.

Petroleum is the most important resource. Most of it comes from the Niger Delta. Unfortunately, a corrupt military dictatorship has allowed the profits to vanish into the pockets of government officials. A poll of international businessmen indicated that Nigeria is the most corrupt country in the world. To do business in Nigeria, foreigners are almost forced to join in the bribery and fraud. West Africa will continue to languish until Nigeria improves its government.

The Biafran War The southeast part of Nigeria is called Biafra, named for the **Bight of Biafra,** which lies east of the Niger Delta and continues south into Central Africa. Most of the region is lowland, but mountains rise over six thousand feet along the southeastern border with Cameroon. The region provides palm oil, hardwood, and rubber.

In 1967 the **Biafran War** erupted as the **Ibo** people fought for an independent nation. Like the Yoruba, the Ibo have adopted Western ways and Christianity. Both tribes have a similar language in the Kwa language family—common across the southern coast from Liberia to Nigeria. But the Ibo still wanted to be dominant. A terrible famine compounded the suffering of war. After a million Ibo had died, they finally surrendered in 1970. Instead of punishing the Ibo, however, the Nigerian government tried to bring reconciliation.

DISEASE-RIDDEN CENTRAL AFRICA

The equator crosses the heart of Central Africa. Most of Central Africa has a tropical wet climate, with average temperatures of 80°F and one hundred inches of rainfall each year. Mangrove swamps, with their tangled vegetation and stagnant waters, barricade the coastal lands. Where rivers or clearings break through this barrier, dense jungles line the path inland. Forest elephants, gorillas, and panthers roam these jungles, and pythons grow up to thirty-two feet long. Unlike the Amazon River, which flows through a low coastal plain and is navigable for one thousand miles, the rivers of Africa drop down from high plateaus to the coast. The frequent rapids and waterfalls prevent easy travel to the interior.

Dense jungles, wild beasts, rough waters, and, worst of all, diseases plague Africa. Snails carry the disease bilharzia, which afflicts the Nile Valley as well as tropical Africa. More serious are the diseases spread by insects, such as *Aëdes aegypti* mosquitoes, which spread jungle **yellow fever.** Though treatments and preventative vaccines are available, epidemics still occur.

As it feeds on the blood of animals and humans, the **tsetse fly** spreads African sleeping sickness. Over twenty thousand Africans contract African sleeping sickness each year. The disease progresses from fever to seizures and finally to delirium and coma. Death results unless the victim seeks medical help in time. Sleeping sickness killed many explorers and left others stranded by killing

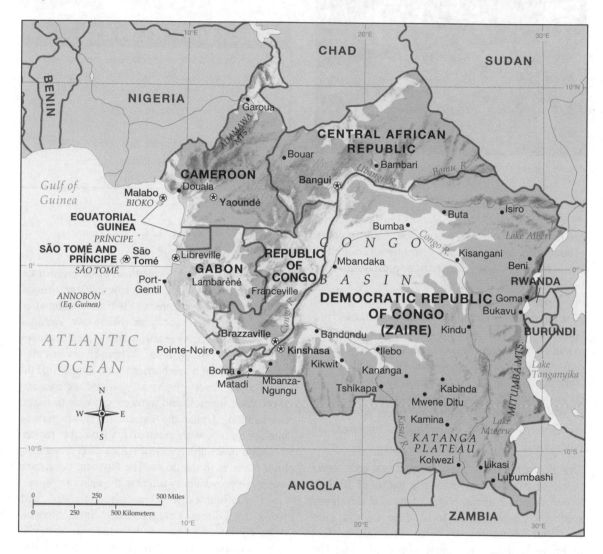

their packhorses or oxen. Even today, farmers cannot raise cattle or horses in the regions infested by tsetse flies.

The anopheles (uh NOFF uh LEEZ) mosquito infests many of the world's tropical areas, including most of the African continent. It spreads the dreaded killer **malaria,** for which there is no known remedy. The World Health Organization estimated in 1997 that malaria infected 270 million people a year and killed 2.1 million of its victims.

A new epidemic spread across sub-Saharan Africa in the 1970s. The Acquired Immune Deficiency Syndrome, or AIDS, destroys the body's immune system. It is most often spread by sexual immorality and sometimes by drug users who share needles. Over nineteen million Africans have been infected with the HIV virus, which is thought to cause AIDS. Scientists have not yet found a cure.

Lower Guinea Coast

The Bight of Biafra turns south after Nigeria along a region called the Lower Guinea Coast. In addition to three nations on the mainland, an island nation lies off this coast.

Range of Diseases in Africa

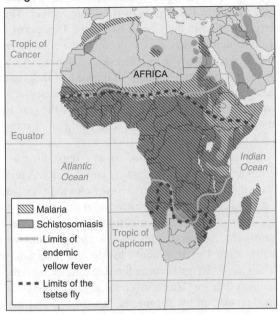

- ▨ Malaria
- ▦ Schistosomiasis
- Limits of endemic yellow fever
- ■ ■ ■ Limits of the tsetse fly

Divided Cameroon Germany lost its colony of Cameroon to France and Britain after World War I. Each of these two European countries ruled part of Cameroon until 1960. Since then, Cameroon's stable, autocratic government has made steady progress. It built manufacturing plants and mines. The most important product is petroleum, drilled in the Gulf of Guinea. One-half of the people are animists, one-third Christian, and the remainder Muslim.

Cameroon has an odd shape. A sliver of land extends seven hundred miles north of the Bight of Biafra to reach the swampy shores of Lake Chad, which Cameroon shares with Nigeria and two other nations. The Adamawa Mountains lie in central Cameroon along the border with Nigeria. The highest mountain in West and Central Africa is farther south near the coast. Mount Cameroon rises dramatically to 13,353 feet just west of Douala, but most of the region is a rugged plateau.

Southern Cameroon, the most populous region of the country, consists almost entirely of lowlands clothed with rain forest. The village of Debundscha is one of the wettest places in the world, receiving as much as four hundred inches of rainfall annually. Several rivers flow southwest to the Gulf of Guinea. Both the capital, Yaoundé, and the largest city, Douala, lie on these rivers.

The tribes in Cameroon speak a number of Bantu languages. Bantu is a subgroup of the **Niger-Congo family** of languages. Most Africans south of 5° N speak a language in this group. Bantu was first spoken somewhere in the mountains of Cameroon, and it later spread as the conquering Bantu moved south. About three hundred tribal groups in Africa see themselves as Bantu, each with its own name, history, and language or dialect. The size of these tribes ranges from a few hundred people to millions.

Gabon on the Equator A country the size of Colorado, Gabon gained its independence from France in 1960. It had been part of **French Equatorial Africa,** which included the Congo, Central African Republic, and Chad. The Ogooué River, which drains the country, supports a vast, wild rain forest.

Timber from Gabon's jungles, including ebony and mahogany, is an important product. Gabon has the second highest per capita GDP in mainland Africa. Manganese, uranium, and petroleum supplement the lumber profits. These funds are slowly helping to improve living conditions, education, and health care. Most of the people are Christians.

This cableway carries buckets of manganese from mines in Gabon, which supply more than one-tenth of the world's supply. Gabon is the world's third largest supplier of manganese.

Equatorial Guinea Equatorial Guinea consists of several islands and a small mainland region, often called Rio Muni, sandwiched between the coast of Cameroon and Gabon. The capital, Malabo, is on the island of Bioko. Portugal first claimed the region in 1471. Spain gained control in the mid-nineteenth century, forming the only Spanish colony in sub-Saharan Africa. Roman Catholicism is the main religion. After independence in 1968, Equatorial Guinea became the only African nation with Spanish as its official language.

São Tomé and Príncipe The islands of São Tomé (SOUN too-MEH) and Príncipe (PREEN see-puh) are similar to the Cape Verde Islands. The islands were uninhabited until the Portuguese came in 1470. The nation gained independence from Portugal in 1975. Today, 70 percent of the people are Creoles, and most are Roman Catholic. The two main islands and the half-dozen islets are volcanic and have good soil. Major crops include cacao, copra (dried coconut), and coffee.

SECTION REVIEW

1. Which insect spreads African sleeping sickness? malaria?
2. What is the highest mountain in Central Africa?
3. Which nation of Central Africa uses Spanish, not French?
4. What is the only nation on the mainland of Africa with an island capital?
- 💡 Why did Malabo become more important than the mainland?

The Congo Basin

The **Congo River** is the great river of Central Africa. The fifth longest river worldwide, the Congo is second only to the Amazon in volume. It pours more than one million cubic feet of water into the Atlantic every second. Like the Amazon, it drains a vast basin, the **Congo Basin,** which covers all or part of five nations. Tropical rains caused by evaporation continually replenish the river.

The Belgian Giant Three nations share the waters of the Congo River. The largest nation in the Congo Basin, the **Democratic Republic of Congo,** is the third largest country on the continent and the largest in sub-Saharan Africa. It was the personal property of the king of Belgium, Leopold II, from 1885 until 1908. The Blacks were treated so badly that the king had to give the land to the Belgian government. The Belgian Congo received independence in 1960.

With over two hundred tribal groups, the government has struggled for unity and stability. A military leader named **Mobutu Sese Seko** took control during a civil war that occurred after independence. He later renamed all the nation's geographic features with African names, and he changed his own name from Desiré Mobutu to Mobutu Sese Seko. The Congo River became the Zaire River, and the country became Zaire. Mobutu also took over all businesses run by Europeans, but the national language remained French. A rebel leader from the eastern forests later overthrew the aging Mobutu in 1997 and restored the nation's name to Congo, but the old problems remain.

Rain Forest Throughout the jungle regions of the Congo Basin, cassava is a staple crop. Congo is the fourth largest producer of cassava worldwide. Congo has very little Atlantic coastline but enough to obtain a valuable resource—offshore oil wells.

Near the mouth of the Congo River are several rapids. The ocean port of Matadi lies just below the lower rapids. Above the rapids is **Kinshasa,** the capital. With 4.7 million people, it is by far the largest city in sub-Saharan Africa. Navigation is possible from Kinshasa upstream for over a thousand miles northeast to the city of Kisangani.

A thick rain forest lies in the northeast. Stanley (now Boyoma) Falls marks the end of navigation on the Congo River just upstream from Kisangani. This region is famous for isolated Pygmy villages. The quiet okapi, a short-necked giraffe with striped legs, also roams these dark forests.

The Congo River has a major tributary in the south, the Kasai River. The city of Ilebo lies at the

Geographer's Corner

Health Statistics

Sub-Saharan Africa and the Sahel have some of the poorest, least-developed nations in the world. You have already studied several statistics that indicate poor development, including low per capita GDP. But why does poverty lead to high infant mortality and low life expectancy? People need money to buy proper food and health care.

Everyone needs a certain amount of dietary energy for the body to fight off disease. People whose energy intakes are significantly reduced are considered malnourished. *Per capita calorie intake* indicates the amount of dietary energy the average person receives in each country.

Another important ingredient in a healthy nation is medical care. Developed countries provide some kind of clinic within every small town, or at least within a short driving distance. But in poor countries, most health facilities are in the cities. Even when free care is available, rural people have difficulty reaching the facilities. Two statistics indicate the ease of getting medical care: *population per physician* and *population per hospital bed.*

Use the statistics on the chart on the left to answer these questions.

1. The people of which African country have the highest energy intakes?

2. Which countries have a per capita calorie intake below 2,000?

3. Which country has the greatest need for doctors? for hospital beds?

4. What African country has the best ratio of people per physician? per hospital bed?

💡 Find the four Sahel nations. How do their statistics compare to nations of West and Central Africa? Can you find a pattern among the landlocked nations?

NATION	PER CAPITA CALORIE INTAKE	POPULATION PER PHYSICIAN	POPULATION PER HOSPITAL BED
Benin	2,383	13,879	4,280
Burkina Faso	2,218	27,158	1,837
Cameroon	2,208	11,848	370
Cape Verde	2,780	2,931	667
Central African Republic	1,847	18,660	672
Chad	1,733	27,765	1,429
Congo-Brazzaville	2,295	15,584	303
Cote d'Ivoire	2,565	11,745	1,698
Equatorial Guinea	2,243	3,532	350
Gabon	2,442	2,504	196
Liberia	2,264	24,600	NA
Mali	2,259	18,046	2,500
Mauritania	2,447	11,085	1,429
Niger	2,240	54,444	2,000
Nigeria	2,199	4,496	1,070
São Tomé and Príncipe	2,153	1,881	209
Senegal	2,323	14,825	1,041
Sierra Leone	1,899	10,832	1,000
United States	3,642	381	232

farthest navigable point on this tributary. Kananga, the third largest city in Congo, lies on a branch of the Kasai.

Mineral Riches in the Highland Borders

Highlands mark the end of the Congo Basin along the eastern border: the Virunga Mountains in the north and the Mitumba Mountains farther south along Lake Tanganyika. The mountains produce tin but are better known as a haven for chimpanzees and the endangered mountain gorillas in Virunga National Park.

Great mineral wealth lies in the southern lip of the nation, at the **Katanga Plateau.** Lubumbashi, Congo's second largest city, is the capital of the important province of Katanga. Copper is the nation's primary export. The mining city of Kolwezi is the hub of Africa's largest copper deposits. This copper belt has the third largest copper reserves worldwide. Other mines make Congo the world's

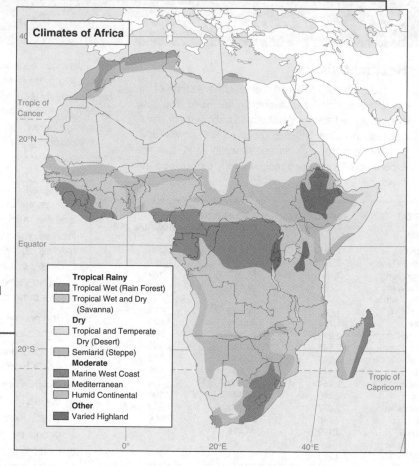

Let's Go Exploring

1. What are the only three climates found in North Africa?

2. What *two* climates appear in southern Africa and nowhere else?

3. At 20° N, what is the climate on the west coast? on the east coast?

4. At the equator, what is the climate on the west coast? on the east coast?

5. At the tropic of Capricorn, what is the climate on the west coast? on the east coast?

Do you see a pattern in Africa's climate as you proceed north and south of the equator?

Climates of Africa

Tropic of Cancer

20°N

Equator

20°S

Tropical Rainy
Tropical Wet (Rain Forest)
Tropical Wet and Dry (Savanna)
Dry
Tropical and Temperate Dry (Desert)
Semiarid (Steppe)
Moderate
Marine West Coast
Mediterranean
Humid Continental
Other
Varied Highland

Tropic of Capricorn

0°   20°E   40°E

leading producer of cobalt. Additional products include diamonds, uranium, and zinc.

Congo's potential wealth and market make it the main hub of Central Africa. Unfortunately, poor leadership has hindered its development. Mobutu used the wealth of the mines to line his own pockets, while the rest of the nation suffered from extreme poverty.

The Other Congo Africa has two Congos. The other, on the west side of the Congo River, belonged to France. The capital of French Equatorial Guinea was here at **Brazzaville,** across the river from Kinshasa. It is the largest city in all of the former French colonies. Like French West Africa, this territory ended in 1960 when all of its nations became independent. This "other" Congo is simply called the Republic of the Congo, or Congo-Brazzaville.

The Congo River and its northern tributary, the **Ubangi River,** form the eastern border. The northeastern state of Likouala, west of the Ubangi, includes a remote swampy jungle, the largest and least explored jungle wilderness in the world.

Most of the people live in the hills and low plateaus along the southern border. The population is almost evenly split among animists and Christians. Subsistence agriculture is common throughout the country, but plantations export cacao, coffee, and peanuts. Although not as rich as Gabon, Congo-Brazzaville produces a little petroleum.

Pygmies

The Pygmies are one of the most unusual peoples of Africa. Their average height is only four feet six inches, and they continue to live in the jungle by hunting and gathering food. Pygmies travel in small groups of about ten or twenty families, building villages of sticks and leaves, where they live for a few months before moving on. They have no chiefs but make decisions by group discussion.

Survival depends on their intimate knowledge of the jungle. Pygmies know the life cycles of more than one thousand species of plants: they know when to gather the food and what is edible or medicinal. They also know the habits of over three hundred animals. Women dig wild yams and gather edible leaves, nuts, berries, and mushrooms. In the rainy season, men may help the women gather caterpillars.

The men prefer to gather honey and to hunt. To shoot monkeys, some tribes use crossbows, while others use small bows and poison-tipped arrows. A group of two or three men can hunt porcupines and four-pound Gambian rats, but large groups are needed to track elephants, red hogs, and gorillas, bringing them down with iron-tipped spears. Men, women, and children may form lines to drive duikers (the smallest antelope) into nets or into groups of waiting spearmen.

Pygmy tribes live in the various countries of the Congo Basin and its borders. Each tribe speaks the Bantu languages of the settled tribe in their area. The Pygmies' ability to survive in the jungle gives them a mystique even among Africans. The settled farmers attribute supernatural powers to Pygmies, especially as diviners and healers. Welcomed in farming areas, Pygmies often help clear fields and harvest crops. In return, they receive the right to gather bananas and manioc from the fields. They also trade meat to the settled tribes for iron knives and rice.

Central African Republic The Central African Republic is the only landlocked country in Central Africa. Half of the people are rural farmers raising grains, beans, and yams. Seventy percent of the people practice animism. Plateaus averaging three thousand feet in height split the nation into two drainage basins. Savannas cover the northern plateau, where water flows into the Chari River and empties into Lake Chad.

The southern regions are equatorial rain forests and part of the Congo Basin. The Ubangi River forms the southern border. This populous region includes all the main cities, including the capital, Bangui.

Goods for sale in a small forest town in the Central African Republic

SECTION REVIEW

1. What is the name of the country formed from the Belgian Congo?
2. What are the only two African capitals that face each other across a river?
3. What is the main river of the Central African Republic?
   - Why would the Democratic Republic of Congo keep French as the national language?

REVIEW

Can You Define These Terms?

village   animism   yellow fever   malaria
chief   autocrat   tsetse fly   Niger-Congo family
tribalism   bight

Can You Locate These Natural Features?

sub-Saharan Africa   Gulf of Guinea   Bight of Biafra   Katanga Plateau
Sénégal River   Bight of Benin   Congo River   Ubangi River
Fouta Djallon   Benue River   Congo Basin

Can You Explain the Significance of These People, Places, and Events?

French West Africa   Hausa   Benin Kingdom   Democratic Republic of Congo
Dakar   Berlin Conference Biafran War   Mobutu Sese Seko
Abidjan   Yoruba   Ibo   Kinshasa
Gold Coast   Lagos   French Equatorial Africa   Brazzaville

How Much Do You Remember?

1. List all the nations in each coastal region. Then give a major modern product from each region.
   a. West Atlantic Coast
   b. Ivory Coast
   c. Gold Coast
   d. Slave Coast
   e. Lower Guinea Coast
2. What four European languages are national languages in West and Central Africa?
3. Which two cities served as capitals of French colonies in sub-Saharan Africa? Name the two main territories and all the modern nations that were once in each one.
4. What is the main river among the nations of West Africa? of Central Africa?
5. Name four tropical diseases that plague Africa.
6. Why was the exploration of sub-Saharan Africa difficult?
7. Why is Côte d'Ivoire one of the most developed countries in sub-Saharan Africa?
8. Which nation has the most people? the largest area? the highest mountain?

9. What is the largest city in all of West Africa and Central Africa?
10. What nations in West Africa are landlocked? in Central Africa?
11. What nation contains most of the Likouala, the largest jungle wilderness remaining in Africa?
12. What three tribal groups dominate Nigeria?
13. Which nations have islands?
14. Which nation uses Spanish as the national language? Which two use Portuguese?

What Do You Think?

1. Explain the benefits and problems that village life has created in Africa's history.
2. What characteristics are common to prosperous countries in sub-Saharan Africa?
3. Have the national governments improved life compared to the colonial governments?
4. Based on your knowledge of South America, what climate do you expect in the nations south of Central Africa?

CHAPTER 26

EAST AND SOUTH AFRICA

The nations of eastern and southern Africa generally lie on higher ground and have drier climates than those in the west. In fact, the tableland rises over five thousand feet above sea level. Africa's rivers plunge over the edge of this plateau, preventing ocean vessels from sailing very far upriver. Arab and European traders lacked easy access to the interior, and trade remains a problem today. The difficulties of the east are much the same as those of the rest of sub-Saharan Africa.

In contrast to West Africa, where France gained a large empire, Great Britain dominated the east. Among the great British explorers and missionaries was **David Livingstone** (1813-73), who gave his life exploring the interior and striving to win lost souls to Christ. In the late nineteenth century, East Africa was caught in the middle of Europe's scramble for empire. **Cecil Rhodes** (1853-1902), in particular, drove the British government to acquire a continuous path of land from Cape Town to Cairo. The European empires crumbled, however, in the wake of World War II.

In the last half of the twentieth century, Africa found itself caught in the middle of another contest, between communists and the Free World. Most African colonies won independence, but civil wars and the meddling of outsiders hindered their development. The collapse of communism has changed everything. The West no longer needs allies, and the Soviet Union has ceased to exist. Several autocratic rulers have found themselves out of a job, and the poor find reason for hope.

For the needy shall not always be forgotten: the expectation of the poor shall not perish for ever. Arise, O Lord; let not man prevail: let the heathen be judged in thy sight. (Ps. 9:18-19)

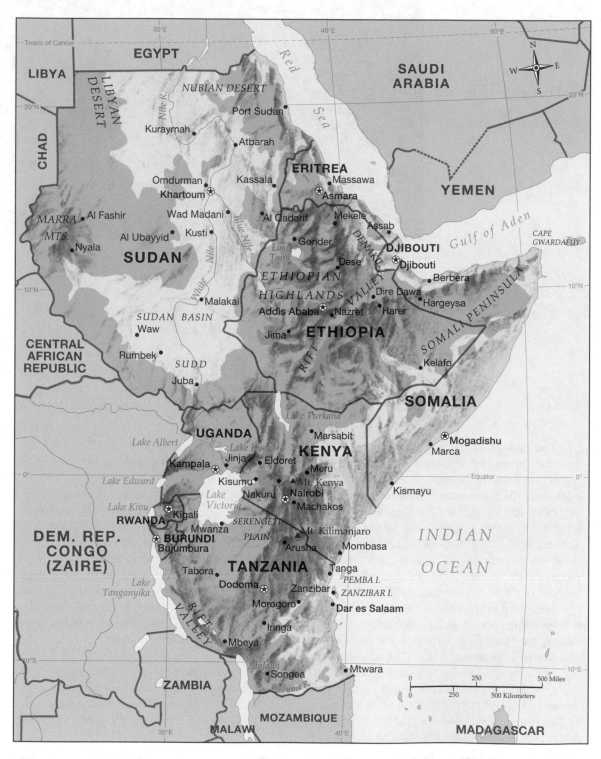

THE GREAT RIFT OF EAST AFRICA

Africa's highest mountains and some of its most important ranges speckle the plateau in East Africa. The most impressive feature, however, is the **Great Rift Valley.** You have already studied about a section of this deep valley in the Middle East, which runs through the Sea of Galilee, the Jordan River, the Dead Sea, and the Arabah. This gash in the earth continues southward through East Africa. The valleys and lakes in the Great Rift Valley have been important since ancient times. East Africa shares many other features with the Middle East, located just across the Red Sea.

Another significant feature in the region is the Nile River and its tributaries, which flow west of the Great Rift Valley. The Nile is the longest river in the world. The source of this mighty river was long a mystery to Europeans. Two rivers join to form the Nile: the Blue Nile and the White Nile. In 1770 the daring Scottish explorer Robert Bruce found the source of the **Blue Nile** at the Geesh Springs in the mountains of Ethiopia. Bruce's book about his adventures sparked the modern exploration of Africa. The source of the **White Nile,** the longer of the two tributaries, lay hidden until 1862 when John Speke, a British officer, pushing ever deeper into the interior, found that Lake Victoria is the source of the Nile. We now know that the Nile begins in Burundi on the Ruvubu River, which empties into Lake Victoria. From Lake Victoria, the water makes its way to Sudan, where it becomes the White Nile.

East and South Africa Statistics

COUNTRY	CAPITAL	AREA (SQ. MI.)	POPULATION	NATURAL INCREASE	LIFE EXPECTANCY	LITERACY RATE	PER CAPITA GDP	POP. DENSITY
East Africa								
Burundi	Bujumbura	10,740	6,052,614	2.7%	49	35%	$600	564
Djibouti	Djibouti	8,950	434,116	2.7%	51	46%	$1,200	49
Eritrea	Asmara	45,300	3,589,687	2.9%	51	20%	$570	79
Ethiopia	Addis Ababa	471,776	58,732,577	2.8%	47	36%	$400	134
Kenya	Nairobi	224,960	28,803,085	2.2%	54	78%	$1,300	128
Rwanda	Kigali	10,169	7,737,537	1.8%	39	61%	$400	760
Somalia	Mogadishu	246,200	9,940,232	3.1%	56	24%	$500	40
Sudan	Khartoum	966,757	32,594,128	2.9%	56	46%	$800	33
Tanzania	Dar es Salaam	346,898	29,460,753	2.1%	42	68%	$800	80
Uganda	Kampala	91,134	20,604,874	2.4%	38	62%	$900	221
South Africa								
Angola	Luanda	481,351	10,623,994	2.7%	47	40%	$700	22
Botswana	Gaborone	231,804	1,500,765	1.5%	45	70%	$3,200	7
Comoros	Moroni	719	589,797	3.5%	59	57%	$820	820
Lesotho	Maseru	11,720	2,007,814	1.8%	52	71%	$4,900	171
Madagascar	Antananarivo	226,657	14,061,627	2.8%	53	46%	$820	62
Malawi	Lilongwe	45,747	9,609,081	1.6%	35	56%	$700	210
Mauritius	Port Louis	788	1,154,272	1.2%	71	83%	$9,600	1,464
Mozambique	Maputo	309,494	18,165,476	2.6%	45	40%	$700	57
Namibia	Windhoek	318,580	1,727,183	2.9%	65	76%	$3,600	5
Seychelles	Victoria	176	78,142	1.3%	70	84%	$6,000	443
South Africa	Pretoria & Cape Town	471,443	42,327,458	1.5%	56	82%	$4,800	89
Swaziland	Mbabane	6,704	1,031,600	3.2%	58	77%	$3,700	153
Zambia	Lusaka	290,584	9,349,975	2.0%	36	78%	$900	32
Zimbabwe	Harare	150,803	11,423,175	1.3%	41	85%	$1,620	75

Islamic Law in Sudan

Sudan shares many similarities with Egypt, its northern neighbor. Egypt controlled Sudan in ancient times. During the Middle Ages, Arabs conquered Egypt and pushed south into Sudan, bringing their religion and language with them. Most Sudanese today speak Arabic, the official language. About one-half of the population is Black, and Arabs constitute nearly 40 percent.

Egypt regained control of Sudan in the early nineteenth century. The Sudanese threw off Egyptian rule briefly, but British and Egyptian forces combined in 1898 to subdue the rebels, who were led by a local hero known as the Mahdi, or messiah. Sudan gained independence in 1956, but military coups and civil war between the Muslims in the north and animists and Christians in the south have hindered development.

Khartoum

Khartoum, the capital, sits in the heart of Sudan, where the White Nile and Blue Nile branches join to form the main Nile River. The city has two main parts. North Khartoum lies across the Blue Nile, and Omdurman is located across the White Nile. Over three million people live in this metropolitan area. Khartoum has most of Sudan's few industries, consisting of cement and textiles.

Northern Desert

Sudan is the largest country in Africa, but large areas are desert or swamp. From Khartoum, the Nile flows north toward Egypt into the Sahara. The Libyan Desert lies to the west and the Nubian Desert to the east. Port Sudan is the only major port on the Red Sea in the northeast. The people are subsistence farmers, most of whom live along the Nile.

The Nile flows over six falls or rapids, called **cataracts.** The First Cataract is at Egypt's Aswan Dam, but the rest are in Sudan. The cataracts prevent ships from sailing up the river, isolating Sudan from the civilization in Egypt. Around 2000 B.C., a kingdom called **Nubia** united the peoples from Khartoum to Aswan. The Nubians traded gold and slaves with Egypt. Egyptian pharaohs often took control, and their influence is evident in many of the pyramid ruins. From 1000 B.C. to A.D. 350, the

This bas relief, found in the ancient Nubian city of Ombos, shows Egypt's influence on Nubia. Sebek is the crocodile-headed god with two plumes and a solar disk between his horns. The god of death, Sebek holds the ankh of eternity. Beside him is the goddess Nekhbet, who wears the mitre of Upper Egypt.

kingdom of Cush (or Kush) arose in Nubia. In the Bible, Cush is often called Ethiopia. Around A.D. 500, the Nubians converted to Christianity but fell to Islamic invaders by 1300.

Central Savannas

Sudan gets its name from the Sahel, which rises in the center of the country, south of the deserts. The term *Sudan* originally referred to the entire Sahel. (Mali was called French Sudan in colonial times.) Herders raise sheep, goats, and cattle on the savannas of the Sahel. Camels provide transportation as well as milk and meat.

The El Gezira Plain lies in the central savannas between the Blue Nile and the White Nile. The Blue Nile flows from the highlands on the eastern border of Sudan, where heavy summer rains cause floods and carry silt downstream to Khartoum. The silt makes the plain the most fertile area in the country. Cotton is the country's chief agricultural product and major export. The seasonal floods of the Blue Nile still affect Sudan.

Southern Sudan

The White Nile flows to the west of the Blue Nile across southern Sudan and is called the Mountain Nile between Juba and Malakal. The White Nile does not flood because its waters spread out over a large marsh called the **Sudd.** These shallow wetlands cover an area the size of Maine, and much water is lost through evaporation. Egypt is helping Sudan build a canal so that the Nile will bypass the Sudd. By reducing evaporation, both countries will obtain more water for irrigation.

Rain forests lie along Sudan's southern border. One-quarter of Sudan's population is animist and lives in the rain forests. The Muslims in northern Sudan are attempting to impose Islamic law, or sharia, in the southern highlands where Christians also live.

◎ SECTION REVIEW

1. What is the largest country in Africa?
2. What two geographic features cross most of East Africa?
3. What kingdom controlled Sudan in ancient times?
4. What are the two main branches of the Nile?
5. What did *Sudan* originally mean?
 ♀ Compare and contrast Sudan and the Sahel.

The Horn of Africa

On the east side of Africa, the wide Somali Peninsula jabs toward the Middle East. Because the peninsula is shaped like an animal horn, the region is often called the **Horn of Africa.** The four nations in this area are closely linked. All three coastal nations have mountain peaks higher than the Appalachians, and the large interior nation of Ethiopia has peaks twice that height. The region is one of the poorest in the world because each nation has been devastated by war and famine.

The waters of the Red Sea actually lie in part of the Great Rift Valley. It continues down into the north coast of the Horn of Africa. Many places in the Great Rift Valley are far below sea level. The hot, dry lowlands near the coast are part of the **Denakil Desert.** One spot on the coast of Eritrea plummets to 360 feet below sea level. Another spot in Ethiopia is 381 feet below sea level. But the valley falls to its lowest point down the coast in the tiny country of Djibouti. Here beside Lake Assal, the Denakil Desert sinks 509 feet below sea level. It is the lowest spot in Africa.

Landlocked Ethiopia In Africa, only Nigeria and Egypt have more people than Ethiopia. In addition to Ethiopia's large population, its unique history and geography have given it a special place in Black Africa's growing sense of pride. The first athlete from Black Africa ever to win a gold medal at the Olympics was fleet-footed Abebe Bikila, who won the marathon in 1964 and again in 1968 with a world-record time. Bikila's win made him a hero across sub-Saharan Africa.

Ethiopia is the only nation in Africa that no foreigner has ever successfully colonized. The rough terrain of the Ethiopian Highlands provided refuge from advancing empires. In 1896 at the battle of Adwa, Ethiopia became the first Black African nation to win a war against a European colonial power when it defeated Italy. In the 1930s under Mussolini, Italy sought revenge and invaded Ethiopia. The temporary conquest ended a few years later when Italy lost World War II.

Haile Selassie, the last emperor of Ethiopia, who ruled from 1930 to 1974, began developing modern industries. Discontent grew, however, because the people did not benefit equally. Several droughts and famines added to the turmoil. Marxist rebels supported by the Soviet Union overthrew Selassie, and Ethiopia endured a military rule from 1974 until rebel groups united and overthrew the junta in 1991. Ethiopia held its first multiparty elections in 1995.

Ethiopian Highlands North and central Ethiopia is a rugged highland plateau. The **Ethiopian Highlands** rise to 15,158 feet at Ras Dashan in the far north. With such towering peaks, the highlands stay cool and receive large amounts of rainfall. The Blue Nile begins in Lake Tana and circles through

Women draw water from a well in this village near Harer, Ethiopia.

the northern highlands before its descent west to the Sudan. Most Ethiopians live in the highlands because of the cooler climate and fertile soil. Farmers produce corn, wheat, cotton, coffee, and sugar cane. Ethiopia is the legendary home of the coffee bean, from the town of Kafa in the southwest. Coffee accounts for almost two-thirds of Ethiopia's exports.

Like other isolated highlands of the world, Ethiopia has a diversity of peoples—at least one hundred ethnic groups and over seventy languages. Amharic, the language of the last emperors, is the official language. Ethiopia's emperors claimed to be descended from Solomon and the queen of Sheba, and they allegedly kept the ark of the covenant after Israel's fall.

Almost 40 percent of Ethiopia's people are Christian, 45 percent are Muslim, and the rest are a mix of tribal religions. Most of the Christians belong to the Ethiopian Orthodox Church. This ancient form of Christianity is similar to that of the Copts in Egypt, who were isolated from the rest of the world after the Arab conquests. The ancient language Ge'ez (or Ethiopic) is used in the church services much as Latin is used in the Catholic church. Manuscripts from the thirteenth century still exist today.

The capital, **Addis Ababa,** stands on the plateau at the center of the nation. With over two million people, this city is the largest in the four nations of the Horn of Africa. The various heads of state in Africa

Languages of Africa

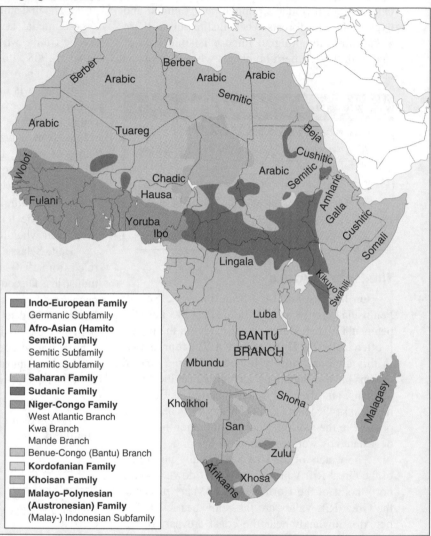

met at Addis Ababa in 1963 and chartered the **Organization of African Unity (OAU),** to promote the common good of the continent. The headquarters of the OAU remains in the capital.

The Great Rift Valley cuts through Ethiopia south of Addis Ababa. Ethiopia has roads connecting it to all of its neighboring countries, but only one vital railroad links Addis Ababa to Djibouti through the Great Rift Valley. The part of the valley that continues southwest from the capital into

These Amhara boys are herders in the Ethiopian Highlands.

Kenya contains over one-half dozen small salt lakes with no outlets.

Ethnic Minorities on the Lowland Borders

The eastern part of Ethiopia is called the **Ogaden.** This section is one of the hot, dry lowlands along the Ethiopian border. The Somalis who live in the city of Kelafo and the surrounding plains of Ogaden are Muslim. Britain allowed Emperor Selassie to annex the region in 1948. But after Somalia gained independence in 1960, Ethiopia had to fight two wars against Somalia to keep Ogaden, in 1962 and again in 1977-78. But the Somalis still want independence.

A lowland similar to Ogaden lies along the west border. Animists, speaking Nilo-Saharan languages, live in this region.

Breakaway Eritrea

Eritrea, which lies north of Ethiopia on the coast, has ancient ties to its large neighbor. Eritrea was once part of the ancient kingdom of **Axum,** which reached its height after conquering the Cush Empire in the west around A.D. 350. The ancient capital was located just across the border in modern Ethiopia, at the city of Axum, but the main port of the empire was in Eritrea at Adule (modern Assab) on the Red Sea. The Tigre people, who founded the Axum Empire, are an influential minority in both Ethiopia and Eritrea today.

Eritrea fell to Italy in 1889. After World War II, the United Nations made Eritrea an autonomous territory under the Ethiopian crown. But when Ethiopia annexed Eritrea outright in 1952, Eritrea

revolted. When the Marxist government collapsed in 1991, Eritrea finally gained its independence. It was the first and only region in postcolonial Africa to break away from its parent.

The Denakil Desert has oil, which is refined at Assab. But most of the people live in desperate poverty as a result of the long war—the longest war for independence ever fought in Africa. The people are evenly divided between Muslim seminomads, who live on the coast, and Christians (mostly Ethiopian Orthodox), who raise crops in the highlands.

Strategic Djibouti

The little country of Djibouti (jih BOO tee), about the size of Massachusetts, lies at a strategic spot on the coast of Africa. It guards the Bab al-Mandeb, the twenty-mile-wide entrance to the Red Sea. Djibouti was once called French Somalia, a strategic colony that France took in 1864. Djibouti received its independence in 1977. Ninety-four percent of the people embrace Islam.

With no natural resources, rural people eke out a living raising camels on the bleak and barren landscape. International transportation is the backbone of the economy. The capital, also called Djibouti, is a convenient stop for ships sailing between the Indian Ocean and the Mediterranean Sea. Ethiopia relies on the railroad from Addis Ababa to ship goods, especially coffee, through this key port.

Divided Somalia

Somalia occupies the east coast of the Horn of Africa. In ancient times, it was called Punt (or Put as in Nahum 3:9). Italy gained control of much of Somaliland in the late nineteenth century, and Somalia still buys food and fuel from Italy today. In 1960 the Italian and British Somaliland territories joined to form the nation of Somalia. Since then, Somalia has alienated all three of its neighbor nations by trying to annex portions where Somalis live. It invaded Ethiopia in 1977, and it refused to sign a peace treaty until 1988.

Northern Somalia consists of dry, grassy plains. Nomads herd livestock in this area. In 1991 northern Somalia—former British Somaliland—declared itself an independent nation, the Somaliland Republic, but no foreign country has recognized it.

Southern Somalia has some arable land watered by two rivers. The rivers join and empty into the Indian Ocean at Kismayu. The capital, Mogadishu, lies near the northern end of the arable region. The people of Somalia share the same ethnic and cultural background. The vast majority are Somalis, a Black African tribe that speaks the Somali language. Somalis are Muslims and keep close ties to Saudi Arabia, which buys Somali fruit and livestock.

In spite of its ethnic unity, the region has suffered from constant internal strife between six main clans and dozens of subclans. In 1991 the government disintegrated, and clan warfare engulfed the south. Two years later, a famine claimed 270,000 lives. In 1993 the United Nations sent twenty-eight thousand troops, including over four thousand American soldiers, into Somalia to restore peace. However, the United States pulled its troops out after fifteen Americans died in a raid to capture one of the clan leaders. After the UN withdrew, anarchy and famine returned to Somalia.

◉ SECTION REVIEW

1. What four nations compose the Horn of Africa?
2. The *Horn of Africa* is the name for what peninsula?
3. What desert extends into all four nations of the Horn of Africa and contains the lowest elevations in Africa?
4. What nation contains a key port?
- 💡 Have ethnic and religious differences been the primary causes of civil war in the Horn of Africa? If not, what has been the main cause?

Lakes Region

Think of wild lions, giraffes, elephants, zebras, and rhinoceroses. You are probably recalling scenes from the large nations of Kenya and Tanzania, which border the Indian Ocean south of the Horn of Africa. Although these two countries do not have a monopoly on wildlife, they are the destination of many big-game safaris, jeep tours, and wildlife documentaries. Grasses and scattered trees cover the savannas of these countries. In the west, Kenya and Tanzania share the lakes of the Great Rift Valley with three other small countries—Uganda, Rwanda, and Burundi—where mountain gorillas roam.

The Great Rift Valley runs through the interior of this region, dividing into two parts at Lake Turkana in Kenya. The Eastern and Western Rifts extend south and rejoin at Lake Malawi in Tanzania. The largest lakes in Africa lie in this rift region. Like the Great Lakes of the United States, this area is a hub of transportation, population, and industry.

The **Eastern Rift** runs from Lake Turkana south through such towns as Nakuru, Tabora, and Mbeya. Many salt lakes lie in the Eastern Rift, but Lake Turkana is the only one included in the seven "Great Lakes."

The **Western Rift** runs along the western edge of East Africa and contains five great lakes. Lake Edward drains north into Lake Albert and then into the Nile River. Lake Kivu drains into Lake Tanganyika and then west into the Congo River. Lake Malawi drains south into the Zambezi River.

The land between these rifts has dropped to create a large basin that contains the Serengeti Plain and Lake Victoria. **Lake Victoria** is the second largest freshwater lake in the world. Waters

Rift Valleys of Africa

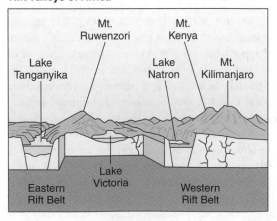

Swahili

The people on the east coast of Africa traded frequently with Arab merchants long before the first Portuguese ships arrived. The common language between the coastal people and Arabs became a hodgepodge of Arabic and Bantu languages called **Swahili.** Later, Swahili incorporated some Portuguese and English words, such as *blanketi.* English has gained some words from the Swahili people too, such as *safari* and *impala.*

This language has since become a *lingua franca* in East Africa. Swahili is one of the two official languages of Tanzania and Kenya and is spoken by at least fifty million people. Yet even Swahili has many dialects. Missionaries who translated the Bible into Swahili developed what is now the East Africa Standard version of Swahili. While dreamers talk about making Swahili the common tongue of Africa, English is more common in colleges and printed media.

from Lake Victoria flow north into the White Nile. The British explorer Speke found the source of the Nile, where the waters first drop from the lake at Ripon Falls in Uganda. Three countries have coastlines on this vital lake.

Kenya Kenya is a little smaller than Texas, but its advanced cities make it the key to East Africa, much like Nigeria is the key to West Africa's future. Its name means "the place where there are ostriches"; the wildlife here draws tourists from all over the world. The equator crosses Kenya, and most of the country experiences hot temperatures. Most people live in the highlands located in the southwest, where the air is a little cooler and more comfortable than it is on the coastal lowlands. Two-thirds of the people are Christians, and most of the rest are animists.

Nairobi **Nairobi** (nye ROH bee), the capital of Kenya, is the largest city in the Lakes region. Situated on a plateau at an elevation of about five thousand feet, Nairobi has a cool climate compared to other cities near the equator. This modern city lies in its own capital district, separate from the seven provinces of Kenya. The government stationed here has been one of the more stable African governments since the country's independence from Britain in 1963.

Lacking mineral resources, Kenya has built small industries. The one-half million tourists every year, however, provide far more money to the economy. The government has set aside over thirty-five parks and game reserves across the nation to protect the wildlife that draws these tourists. Nairobi National Park, on the outskirts of the capital, enables sightseers to photograph wild lions and giraffes with the skyscrapers in the background.

East Kenya Mombassa is the largest port and capital of the Coast Province. The mangrove swamps, lagoons, and rain forests look much like coasts in West Africa, but they are interspersed with fine beaches and groves of coconut palms. The Northeastern Province lies along Kenya's border with Somalia. These hot lowlands are dry except for the Lorian Swamp. Few people live in this province.

The Eastern Province rises from the low Coast and Northeastern Provinces in tiers. The grassy plains have the driest climate in the nation. The Chalbi and Dida Galgalu Deserts lie east of Lake Turkana at the northern border. The main towns of Marsabit, Meru, and Machakos lie on the higher

Many tourists in East Africa take safari vans to the game parks from the modern city of Nairobi, Kenya.

elevations (4,000 ft.) toward the west. The province has eight national game reserves and parts of seven national parks.

West Kenya West Kenya is dominated by high plateaus and mountains. The agricultural lands in the highlands are very fertile. The production of coffee and tea in this area is very important, since it is the only part of the national economy that provides significant foreign income outside tourism.

Kenya's highest peak lies in the Central Province and is just north of Nairobi. Mount Kenya (17,058 ft.) is the second highest mountain in

Over half of the world's flamingoes live in Africa. Flamingoes congregate together all along the soda lakes of Africa's Eastern Rift.

In the Shambas

Jambo. The Swahili word for a small, subsistence garden is *shamba.* Such gardens are common throughout sub-Saharan Africa. The garden is essential to life, since most people earn very little money to buy food. Pastors in Kenya do well to earn sixty *shilingi* (shillings, or about ten dollars) a month. Yet they can support their typical family of six to ten. Only the rich can afford a motor car, or *moto kaa.* Most people ride a city bus or a close-packed *matatu* (a privately owned minibus). Nomadic tribes have even less. They wrap themselves in a single length of cloth. They fence their dirt-floored huts with high brush to keep out wild animals.

In spite of what seem to be difficult circumstances, Africans are happy people. Greetings begin *Habari yako?* (What's the news?) and everyone answers *Habari njema* (good news) or *nzuri sana* (very good). In fact, to Africans, any problem can be resolved easily, and it is common to hear them say *hakuna matata,* which means "no problem."

A Barabaig man dresses in the traditional manner.

Africans love to sing. Most music is rhythmic. One singer leads and the rest echo the words. If an instrument is used, it is a percussion instrument or possibly a guitar. While such rhythmic music can easily become fleshly, as it does when used by witch doctors or rock musicians, rhythm is an essential element of good music too. Christians in Africa also sing. The hymns are sung according to various cultural patterns, as the choir sways from side to side with the beat. Both *Mungu* and *Allah* are acceptable names for God in Swahili, but Christians insist on the use of *Mungu.* Since *Bwana* means "sir," East Africans may call Christ *Bwana,* much as we use the term *Lord. Kwa heri.*

A family of Masai

A choir sings at a church east of Machakos, Kenya.

Missions

Bible Colleges

Many young Christians in other countries want training in the Bible but have little opportunity to receive it in their own language and nation. Your own Christian training is a great privilege and gives you extra responsibility to share it with others. Christians should entrust what they have learned to others, just as Paul did with Timothy.

A missionary professor teaches at Nairobi Bible Institute, Kenya.

And the things that thou hast heard of me among many witnesses, the same commit thou to faithful men, who shall be able to teach others also. (II Tim. 2:2)

One of the greatest blessings that a missionary can have in a foreign field is to train local pastors to be fully equipped to teach the Word of God. Seminary professors now serve in many countries, such as Kenya, where seminaries abound. Teaching in seminaries is not easy, however. Professors face constant challenges with poor communication and discouragement. A good teacher must work daily to improve his ability to share truths by learning the local traditions, manners, customs, and nonverbal signals. The more you learn about an unfamiliar culture the easier it will be to make illustrations that help students understand theological points. Jesus used analogies frequently in His teaching, as did Paul.

Africa. In the west is the Nyanza (or Lake) Province on Lake Victoria. Kisumu, Kenya's third largest city and the chief port on Lake Victoria, is located here.

Of Kenya's many national parks and reserves, two are quite famous. Amboseli National Park, on the southern border, offers spectacular views of Tanzania's snowcapped peak, Mount Kilimanjaro, which rises above the savanna. Masai Mara Game Reserve, Kenya's portion of the Serengeti, is home to the **Masai** tribe. The Masai people are nomads famous for their ritual dances and skills as warriors.

Tanzania Germany established a colony called German East Africa in the late nineteenth century, preventing Great Britain from controlling a continuous string of land along Africa's east coast. It held the colony until the British took over after World War I. The land was known as Tanganyika when it became independent in 1961. The name changed to Tanzania when the island of Zanzibar joined it in 1964. Over 120 ethnic groups live in Tanzania, and Swahili is the common language.

Zanzibar, Pemba, and Mafia are three large tropical islands off the coast. **Zanzibar** was once the Arabs' largest slave-trading port on the East African coast. It was also the largest producer of cloves, supplying 80 percent of the world's needs. Today, it is a resort area, and it guards its autonomy by making visitors from the mainland pass through customs. Unlike the rest of the country, Zanzibaris sometimes clamor for full independence. Most of the people who live in Zanzibar are Muslims.

Tanzania is much like Kenya. Game reserves cover one-fourth of the country. The coastal region has mangrove swamps and beaches. Dar es Salaam is the largest port. In 1996 the capital moved inland

Mount Kilimanjaro dominates the horizon behind these wild water buffalo at Amboseli National Park, Kenya.

Serengeti Plain

The **Serengeti Plain** has more large land animals than any other place on earth. It is also the only place left in the world where vast herds of large mammals still migrate. For these reasons, the Serengeti National Park in Tanzania is the most famous national park in all of Africa.

All five of the famous African big-game animals—lions, elephants, rhinoceroses, water buffalos, and leopards—are now protected in the 5,700-square-mile park. Both elephants and rhinos are endangered due to poachers.

Wildebeest migrate one thousand miles north across the Serengeti every year to spend the dry season around Kenya's Masai-Mara Game Reserve. The wildebeest, or gnu, has a funny appearance, with the mane and tail of a horse, beard of a goat, and horns of an ox; but it can run fifty miles per hour. Zebras often migrate with the 1.5 million wildebeests, which provide safety in numbers. Nevertheless, danger lurks at every turn. Lions attack from the high grasses, cheetahs from rock outcroppings, leopards from trees, and huge crocodiles from the rivers and water holes.

Elephant on the Serengeti

Many other animals live on the Serengeti Plain, such as the impala, topi, eland, and the dik-dik (the smallest antelope in the world). Foxes, jackals, gazelles, giraffes, baboons, and monkeys also roam the park, while vultures, storks, egrets, and flamingoes soar overhead. Hyenas compete with vultures for leftovers from lion kills. Packs of wild dogs are excellent hunters, succeeding even more often than lions. Cheetahs, which reach speeds of seventy miles per hour, are the fastest animals in the world.

from Dar es Salaam to Dodoma, with the hopes of boosting the economy in the interior. From the first inland plateau at Morogoro, the land rises to Iringa and Dodoma. North of Dodoma is the Masai Steppe, where the Masai live and herd their cattle.

Also as in Kenya, highlands cover western Tanzania. **Mount Kilimanjaro** (KIL uh mun JAHR oh) rises to 19,340 feet near the border with Kenya. This massive volcanic peak is the highest mountain in Africa. Snow falls on this mountain even though it is near the equator. West of Arusha is Serengeti National Park and Ngorongoro Crater. More wildlife is concentrated at this crater than in any other area in Africa.

Farther west lies the largest lake in all of Africa, Lake Victoria. Tanzania's main lake port, Mwanza, is located on the southern border of Lake Victoria. The best soils also lie around this lake. As in Kenya, farmers produce coffee and tea as well as tobacco and cotton. Tanzania's main port on Lake

Tanganyika is the small port of Kigoma, near the border with Burundi. Four miles away at the town of Ujiji, the reporter Henry M. Stanley discovered David Livingstone, whose whereabouts had become a mystery. Their encounter on October 28, 1871, began with the now-famous words "Dr. Livingstone, I presume."

Uganda Uganda (yoo GAN duh) has been independent from Britain since 1962, but it has found little peace. A bloody dictator named Idi Amin ruled the land from 1971 to 1979. He killed thousands of his opponents. Since his overthrow the government has been unstable, and conditions have remained poor for the people.

Uganda lies on a plateau about four thousand feet in elevation. Savanna covers the north, while the region around Lake Victoria in the south offers the best farmlands. The capital and main port, Kampala, lies on the northern edge of Lake Victoria. Owen

Falls Dam at Jinja has the largest capacity reservoir in the world.

Highlands cover the southeast. The Ruwenzori Mountains, or Mountains of the Moon, are located on Uganda's western border and stretch from Lake Edward to Lake Albert. These mountains are very rugged, remote, and cloud enshrouded most of the time. Mountain gorillas draw many tourists to the area.

R ***Massacres in Rwanda*** Landlocked Rwanda (roo-AHN duh) is about the size of Maryland. Plateaus cover the nation and rise highest in the west. The western border follows the Great Rift Valley through Lake Kivu and Volcanoes National Park. The park has one-half of Africa's remaining mountain gorillas.

Rwanda has a high population density with over six hundred people per square mile. Most people speak Kinyarwanda (a Bantu language), but French is also an official language. Three-fourths of the people are Catholic, and the rest are animists.

The Hutu constitute 90 percent of all Rwandans, and most are subsistence farmers. One percent of the people belong to the Twa, a Pygmy tribe. The Tutsi (or Watusi), typically over six feet tall, were traditionally cattle herders who ruled as feudal lords over the Hutus. Today they run most businesses and industries, but account for only 9 percent of the population. In a bloody civil war in 1959, the Hutus wrested control from the ruling Tutsis. The nation gained independence from Belgium in 1962, but tribal conflicts continue.

In 1994 a missile destroyed a plane carrying the Rwandan president. Both ethnic groups blamed each other, and hundreds of thousands died in the resulting slaughter. Over two million Rwandans fled the country to escape the massacres. A rebel Tutsi army recaptured the government and attempted to restore order.

Burundi Like Rwanda, Burundi (boo ROON dee) is a small country with a large population. The nation received independence from Belgium in 1962 and has two official languages: French and a Bantu language (Kirundi). It has the same tribal divisions as Rwanda. Unlike Rwanda, however, the Tutsi minority retained rule until it lost multiparty elections in 1993. The Tutsi army officers kept power in the army, however, and restored Tutsi control in 1996.

Lake Tanganyika lies on Burundi's western border, supplying the country with ten thousand tons of fish annually. The capital, Bujumbura, lies at the head of this lake. Swamps along the southern coast breed deadly insects, such as the tsetse fly. Coffee is the major crop in both Rwanda and Burundi, but overseas trade is difficult for both landlocked nations.

SECTION REVIEW

1. How many great lakes lie in East Africa? Which is the largest?
2. What is the largest city in the five nations of the Lake Region?
3. What is Africa's highest mountain? What nation contains it?
4. What important mountain range lies in southwest Uganda?
5. Why are national parks important in the Lake Region?

SOUTH AFRICA

The culture region known as South Africa is also called Southern Africa and includes several countries south of the rain forests of the Congo Basin. The most important nation in the region is South Africa.

South Africa

The Portuguese rounded the **Cape of Good Hope** in 1488. The Cape is an ideal location because it is the only part of sub-Saharan Africa with a mediterranean climate. By 1652 the Dutch East India Company had set up a supply station there. In the early nineteenth century, the British took over the Dutch station and made it the capital of a British colony.

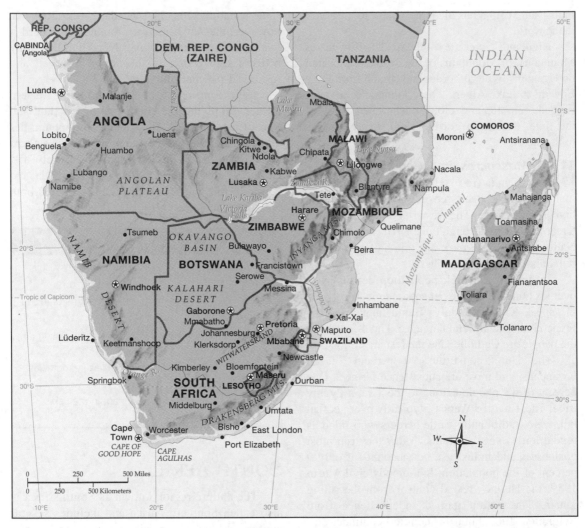

Over 2.4 million people live in **Cape Town** today, making it the largest city in eastern and southern Africa. The Dutch, and later, the British intermarried with the Africans. The people of mixed descent are called coloreds and constitute 9 percent of the population of South Africa. Most of the colored population live around Cape Town. They have joined the National Party, the second largest political party in the country, which opposes the Black majority that won control of the country in 1994 elections.

The Cape After the British took over the Cape Colony in 1814, British settlers began to arrive.

Table Mountain (3,563 ft.) rises above Cape Town in the distance, while the ocean rages offshore.

Britain declared English the only official language in 1828, and it ruled the Cape region until South Africa gained independence in 1910.

In 1871, prospectors discovered diamonds at Kimberley in the interior. These diamond mines are the largest in the world. One man who profited was Cecil Rhodes, who used his wealth from the diamond fields to finance further British expansion in Africa. With the rush of English prospectors to Kimberley, the British extended the jurisdiction of Cape Colony to include most of western South Africa.

Only a small part of the Cape region is coastal lowland. The region's climate varies radically, from desert west of Cape Town to marine west coast in the east. Most of the Cape is a large plateau with a steppe climate. The **Orange River** is the longest river flowing through the steppe to the west coast. It cuts across the middle of the region and forms the northwestern border with neighboring Namibia. Ships on the Atlantic Ocean cannot navigate up the river because the powerful Augrabies Falls drops 480 feet near the coast.

Zululand   Only a few tribes of Bushmen and Hottentots lived in the Cape Colony. But farther east were the **Zulu,** the most famous of the Bantu tribes. A fierce warrior named **Shaka** became chief in 1818 and led the Zulu against all neighboring tribes. Hearing of his conquests, even distant tribes fled rather than risk war. Under Shaka, a great kingdom called Zululand emerged.

Britain annexed the southeast Zulu territory in 1843. The Zulu rebelled and decimated a British regiment in 1879, but later that year the British won the war. The British policy of indirect rule permitted the Zulu to govern themselves in Natal as a British colony. The Zulu continue to defend their unique identity. While the other tribes support a strong central government, the Zulu leaders in the Inkatha Party desire a weak federation.

With a population of one million, Durban is the largest city in Natal. Asians now account for a large local population (about 2 percent of the national

Land Use of Africa

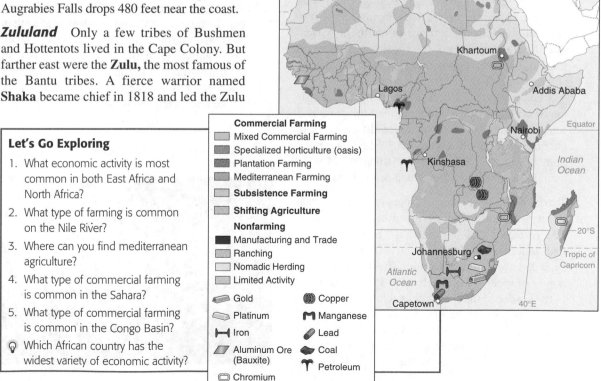

Commercial Farming
- Mixed Commercial Farming
- Specialized Horticulture (oasis)
- Plantation Farming
- Mediterranean Farming
- **Subsistence Farming**
- **Shifting Agriculture**

Nonfarming
- Manufacturing and Trade
- Ranching
- Nomadic Herding
- Limited Activity

- Gold
- Platinum
- Iron
- Aluminum Ore (Bauxite)
- Chromium
- Copper
- Manganese
- Lead
- Coal
- Petroleum

Let's Go Exploring

1. What economic activity is most common in both East Africa and North Africa?

2. What type of farming is common on the Nile River?

3. Where can you find mediterranean agriculture?

4. What type of commercial farming is common in the Sahara?

5. What type of commercial farming is common in the Congo Basin?

💡 Which African country has the widest variety of economic activity?

total). The British originally brought Indian laborers on contract in the 1860s to work on Natal's
sugar plantations.

The **Drakensberg Mountains** rise from the
coastal plain of Natal to 11,072 feet above sea level
on Champagne Castle. The mountains are actually
an **escarpment,** a steep rise from a plain to a
plateau. Winds rising off the ocean give Natal a
humid subtropical climate. The second highest
waterfall in the world, Tugela Falls, takes a 3,110-
foot plunge on Natal's border with the tiny country
of Lesotho.

Orange Free State   The original Dutch farmers, called **Boers,** spread out from Cape Town
across the fertile coastal plain. When the British
took over, many Boers fled inland. In 1836 some
left for the far interior. This Great Trek ended after
they crossed the Orange River. They called their
new nation the Orange Free State.

The Orange Free State eventually stretched
east to the Vaal River, a tributary of the Orange
River. Much of the plateau belongs to a vast
savanna, called the **veldt,** that spreads across several countries in the interior of southern Africa.
The Boers established their capital at Bloemfontein, but faced opposition from both the British
and the Zulu.

Over time, the Boers assimilated Zulu words
into their High Dutch and simplified the grammar.
The resulting language is quite different from
Dutch and is called **Afrikaans.** Today, the Dutch
South Africans call themselves Afrikaners. Most of
them belong to Dutch Reformed denominations.

Transvaal   A number of Boers crossed the Vaal
River to distance themselves further from Britain.
The Transvaal ("across the Vaal") became the second independent Boer country in the veld. It
extended north to the **Limpopo River,** the northern
border of modern South Africa. It also reached east
to the border of the Portuguese colony on the coast
(Mozambique). Some of the eastern border is still
unsettled. Kruger National Park is among the
largest in Africa and claims to have the greatest
variety of animals. As at Tanzania's Serengeti,

Johannesburg, South Africa

visitors can watch elephants, lions, giraffes, leopards, antelope, and cheetahs. Rhinos and hippos are
more common at Kruger than at Serengeti.

In 1886 prospectors struck gold near Johannesburg in the Witwatersrand District. English-speaking
foreigners poured in and staked claims. The influx of
people made **Johannesburg** the second largest city
in southern Africa. It now boasts two million people.

The Boers clashed with Britain over the treatment of British immigrants. After a valiant stand,
the Boers lost the Boer War (1899-1902). Less than
one hundred thousand ill-equipped farmers faced
the largest gathering of British soldiers in British
history, nearly one-half million. Four colonies later
joined in 1910 to form the Union of South Africa.
In 1961 the name changed to the Republic of South
Africa.

*These gold miners drill holes for dynamite at Witwatersrand,
South Africa.*

Former South African Provinces and Homelands

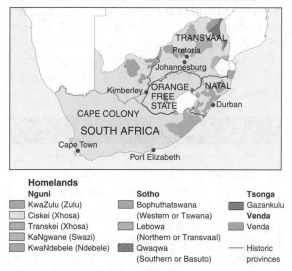

Modern Provinces

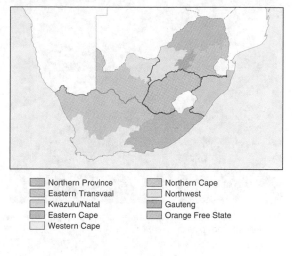

Homelands

Nguni	Sotho	Tsonga
KwaZulu (Zulu)	Bophuthatswana (Western or Tswana)	Gazankulu
Ciskei (Xhosa)		**Venda**
Transkei (Xhosa)	Lebowa (Northern or Transvaal)	Venda
KaNgwane (Swazi)		
KwaNdebele (Ndebele)	Qwaqwa (Southern or Basuto)	— Historic provinces

Modern Provinces legend:
- Northern Province
- Eastern Transvaal
- Kwazulu/Natal
- Eastern Cape
- Western Cape
- Northern Cape
- Northwest
- Gauteng
- Orange Free State

After World War II, the Afrikaners gained control of the government. **Pretoria,** near Johannesburg and the nation's third largest city, became the administrative capital of the nation to balance the legislative capital at Cape Town. These two cities are the major national capitals, while Bloemfontein is the judicial "capital."

Eleven Official Languages Many tribes settled the diverse lands of South Africa. Almost all of them are of the Bantu tribes. The **Bantu** peoples include hundreds of tribes across sub-Saharan Africa. Linguistic studies trace the Bantus to the Benue River in Cameroon during the time of Christ. Whether due to drought, war, or need for more land, the Bantus began their Great Bantu Migration around 1300 and reached South Africa in the seventeenth century. They brought with them iron-working skills that enabled them to conquer any groups who resisted. The Pygmies retreated into the forests, while the San and Khoikhoi fled to the western desert.

The largest group of Bantu in South Africa today is the Nguni, accounting for 60 percent of all the Blacks. The Zulu and Xhosa (KOH suh) speak the main languages of the Nguni, but the Swazi and Ndebele are also included in this group. The other Blacks are divided among three smaller Bantu groups: 33 percent are Sotho, 5 percent are Tsonga, and 2 percent are Venda.

Three-fourths of all South Africans are Blacks. However, in 1948 the Afrikaner minority instituted **apartheid** (uh PART HITE), a policy of racial separation. Apartheid regulated life for Blacks. They could not vote in national elections and could hold public meetings only in churches. Since they could not get certain jobs, many suffered from poverty.

Under apartheid, the Blacks were expected to live on territories called Bantu homelands, modeled after the reservations for American Indians. The government changed the name to Black States and granted four of the states independence by 1981, but every nation in the world refused to recognize their independence.

President F. W. de Klerk responded to foreign criticism and trade embargoes by easing the apartheid restrictions. In 1990, he released the rebel Xhosa leader, **Nelson Mandela.** Two years later, a referendum proved that most Whites wanted reform—two-thirds voted to negotiate a new constitution. The negotiations between de Klerk and Mandela won them both a Nobel Peace Prize in 1993.

The old provinces were broken up into nine provinces. The number of official languages rose from two to eleven, and a new constitution was approved in 1997.

Nelson Mandela and his wife Winnie signal triumph upon his release from prison in 1990.

The rest of sub-Saharan Africa is looking to South Africa for signs of new hope for peace and prosperity on the continent. Yet the new government faces some incredible challenges. After almost a half century of apartheid, Whites enjoy ten times the income of Blacks. Nearly one-half of all Blacks are unemployed, one-third cannot read or write, and one-fourth live in shantytowns without running water. The greatest challenge for the new government is the lawlessness that Mandela's party helped to create. The murder rate is one of the highest in the world—two times the rate in the United States.

Lesotho During the Zulu conquests under Shaka, Moshesh led the Basotho (or Southern Sotho) tribe to refuge in the Drakensberg Mountains. Later, the Basotho also defended the rugged terrain from Boers and British. Under attacks from Boers, they asked for British help and became the protectorate of Basutoland in 1868. The kingdom gained independence in 1966. Lesotho contains the headwaters of the Orange River, which provide water for crops and livestock; but most farmers remain poor. Lesotho is entirely surrounded by South Africa, one of only a few nations in the world that are entirely surrounded by another nation.

Swaziland After being ruled by the Boers and then the British, Swaziland gained independence in 1968. Ninety percent of the people are Blacks, and most of those are Swazi. Mbabane is the administrative capital, but the traditional royal capital is the nearby village of Lobamba. The well-watered mountains and plateaus of Swaziland offer the same good agriculture and mineral wealth of adjacent South Africa.

SECTION REVIEW

1. What four colonies joined to form South Africa?
2. Name two great rivers of South Africa.
3. What tribe conquered most of the other tribes of southern Africa?
4. What peoples settled the Orange Free State and the Transvaal? What language do they speak today?
5. What mountainous escarpment divides the coastlands from the veldt?

💡 How are the Western Cape and KwaZulu-Natal different from the other seven provinces of South Africa?

Southwest Plateau

Three nations lie on the plateau in southwest Africa—Botswana, Namibia, and Angola. The land is hot and dry. The coast and parts of the interior are desert, and the rest is grassland.

Botswana The British protectorate of Bechuanaland became the independent nation of Botswana in 1966. Botswana, a landlocked country, remains part of the British Commonwealth.

Eighty percent of the people live along the Limpopo River and its tributaries in the southeast. The area produces nickel, cobalt, and copper, but little development has occurred. Diamond mines were discovered in Botswana in 1967, and diamonds account for 80 percent of the country's export income. However, a majority of the people work as farmers. Many seek jobs across the border in prosperous South Africa.

Bantus and Europeans drove the **San** (or Bushmen) out of South Africa and into Botswana.

The three prized virtues of the San—trust, peace, and cooperation—have enabled them to survive as hunters and gatherers in the Kalahari Desert.

The **Kalahari Desert** is the fourth largest desert in the world (after the Sahara, Gobi, and Rub al Khali). The Kalahari lies on the tropic of Capricorn, much as the Sahara lies on the tropic of Cancer. The desert spreads across southwest and central Botswana, and into neighboring Namibia and South Africa. This large desert (200,000 sq. mi.) covers over half of Botswana. The largest diamond mine in the world lies in the northeast part of the desert at Orapa.

Northern Botswana consists of several basins with no outlet to the sea. One basin contains the Makgadikgadi Salt Pans, a large region of salt flats. The largest basin is the Okavingo Basin. Rivers draining into this basin create the **Okavingo Swamp.**

Namibia South-West Africa was a German colony until World War I, when South Africa gained the region as a mandate. After decades of negotiations, UN interventions, and communist guerilla warfare, Namibia gained independence in 1990, but the government is not yet stable. Because of South African influence, English is the official language. Eighty percent of the people are Christians, and most of those are Lutherans.

The barren **Namib Desert** stretches eight hundred miles along the Atlantic coast. Just as the San were forced into the Kalahari, Bantu and European expansion in South Africa drove the Khoikhoi (or Hottentots) into the Namib Desert. Mines provide most of the nation's resources: diamonds, zinc, lead, tin, and uranium. A cold ocean current keeps the air very dry and causes temperature inversions and thick fogs. The frequent fogs, resulting in countless shipwrecks, have given the northern shore the nickname **Skeleton Coast.**

In spite of several rivers on its borders, Namibia is a bleak and arid land. Most people live in the arid but cooler hills between the Kalahari and Namib Deserts. Almost three-fourths of the small population raises cattle. The main port is Walvis Bay, west of the capital, Windhoek.

Civil War in Angola Angola, almost twice the size of Texas, lies mainly on a high plateau with altitudes of around six thousand feet. Savanna covers most of the land except for the rain forests in the far north and deserts in the southwest. The capital, **Luanda,** with two million people, is the largest in southwest Africa. Warfare has kept Angola from benefiting from its abundance of diamonds and its arable land, which once enabled the country to export large amounts of coffee.

Angola is an important exception to British rule in southern Africa. Portugal had forts in the area dating to the sixteenth century. The Portuguese influence remains obvious in Angola. Portuguese is still the official language, and one-half of the people have converted from animism to Catholicism. In 1961 Angola revolted against the Portuguese, and most of the White settlers fled the country.

Hillside housing near the coastal town of Lobito, Angola

Gemsbok (or oryx) at Etosha National Park in Namibia

After several years of fighting, Portugal granted Angola independence in 1975.

Angola has continued to suffer since gaining independence. It became the main battleground between Cold War superpowers in sub-Saharan Africa. The civil war claimed over one-half million lives. Despite UN intervention, fighting continued even after the cold war ended.

Angola has an isolated piece of land north of the Congo River, called **Cabinda,** which has valuable petroleum reserves. Cabindans resent the fact that most of their wealth goes south to the capital, and a rebel group is seeking independence.

The Zambezi River Nations

The **Zambezi River** (zam BEE zee) rises in eastern Angola and flows across southern Africa to the Indian Ocean. The Zambezi is the longest of the African rivers that empty into this ocean. It runs through four countries of southern Africa: Zambia, Zimbabwe, Malawi, and Mozambique.

David Livingstone won renown after crossing the continent between 1853 and 1856. He started in Luanda, the capital of the Portuguese colony in Angola and followed the course of the Zambezi to the far coast in Mozambique. Great Britain later claimed the lands between these two coastal colonies.

Civil War in Mozambique

Like Angola on the western coast, Mozambique (MOH zum BEEK) was a large Portuguese colony on the eastern coast. Although rebel armies gained independence in 1975, Portuguese remains the official language. However, less than one-third of the people are Christians, while almost two-thirds are animists. The country suffers from a loss of skilled laborers, who fled during the war for independence.

Marxist rebels won control of Mozambique, but they faced another rebel group called RENAMO (Mozambique National Resistance). As many as one million people died in the struggle between the two factions. After the fall of communism in Europe, the UN brokered a peace agreement. Smarting from its embarrassment in Angola, the UN insisted that both sides lay down their weapons *before* elections. Elections were finally held in 1994.

Mozambique's future appears brighter than Angola's. It has twelve hundred miles of coast on the Indian Ocean. A wide coastal plain covers one-half of the nation and supports many agricultural products, including sugar, cotton, cashews, tea, and copra. Mozambique even has some coal in the southwest.

The long coast also makes Mozambique vital to shipping and transportation. Even in ancient times Sofala served as a port for the interior kingdom of Zimbabwe, and later, the Boers shipped goods through Maputo. Today, Mozambique serves four landlocked neighbors.

White Revolt Against Britain in Zimbabwe

The landlocked country of Zimbabwe borders Mozambique and South Africa. In 1890 Cecil Rhodes founded Fort Victoria and Fort Salisbury, hoping to find gold and to extend British influence north of South Africa. White colonists built prosperous industries and hired Blacks and Asians as workers. In 1895 they named the colony Rhodesia after Rhodes. Whites remained a minority, however, and they refused to accept Black rule. For a time, between 1953 and 1963, Great Britain allowed the colony to form a federation with the other two landlocked British colonies north of the Zambezi River. But the Blacks in the other colonies broke away. When Britain criticized White rule, the White leaders declared independence in 1965. This was the first full-fledged revolution by a British colony since 1776.

Black rebels fought the White rulers until they won in 1979. Britain recognized the country's independence the following year. The country changed its name from Rhodesia to Zimbabwe and the capital's name to Harare. Most Whites fled the Black rule, depleting the colony of skilled workers and businessmen.

Zimbabwe lies on the veldt, the savanna that covers much of southern Africa. Like South Africa, Zimbabwe produces gold, iron, nickel, and asbestos. The Zambezi River crosses the northern border. **Victoria Falls** lies on the river near the northwest corner. Downstream is Lake Kariba, the fourth largest reservoir in the world. Zimbabwe also has Mtarazi Falls, the fifth highest waterfall in the world (2,500 ft.).

Great Zimbabwe

Zimbabwe took its name from an ancient ruin called **Great Zimbabwe.** It is the largest stone monument in Africa outside the pyramids. The ruins show evidence of the only ancient metalworking civilization south of the equator. Among the ruins were found birds carved in soapstone, which have become symbols of the nation. With no written records, the civilization that built Great Zimbabwe remains a mystery.

The ruins of Great Zimbabwe consist of three parts: a Great Enclosure on a fertile plain, a Hill Fortress overlooking the plain, and about sixty acres of lesser ruins. The granite wall of the Great Enclosure is thirty feet high, sixteen feet thick, and eight hundred feet long. It encloses platforms, passages, rooms, and two stone towers. The builders cut and fit the stones together without the benefit of mortar. Other civilizations in sub-Saharan Africa are built from mud or wood, so the stonework is unique.

The Hill Fortress stands two hundred feet above the plain. The ingenious design converts rock outcroppings and caves into rooms and pathways. The pathway to the fortress is steep and narrows to single file. One of the caves has special resonance characteristics, similar to a "whispering chamber." The voice of a person speaking in the cave resounds loud and clear inside the enclosure far below.

The BaLemba tribe in the nation of South Africa claims descent from the builders of Great Zimbabwe. According to their legends, their ancestors migrated south after King Mwali died. Their legends describe Mwali as ruling from a stone fortress and speaking unseen in thunderous tones. The legends make sense in light of these ruins, where a king could rule from the

The Great Enclosure on the plain, as seen from the Hill Fortress at Great Zimbabwe

Hill Fortress and speak unseen to the Great Enclosure below, the cave making the king's voice seem like the voice of a god.

Great Zimbabwe stood in the heart of an early gold-mining region. Other valuable goods from the region included copper and ivory. Porcelain, beads, and other artifacts from Nanking, Persia, Arabia, and Indonesia have been unearthed in the Great Enclosure, showing the extent of the ancient trade.

The civilization died long before 1552, when a Portuguese historian found that the local tribes could no longer read the inscriptions. In 1867 Karl Mauch and Adam Rauch rediscovered the ruins and believed them to be the palace of the queen of Sheba from the time of Solomon. A later view was that Sofala, on the coast of Mozambique, was the biblical city of Ophir, where King Solomon obtained his gold (I Kings 10:10-11). Arab records document Sofala as being rich in gold, which would have come from the region of Great Zimbabwe.

Zambia David Livingstone visited Zambia in 1851, but it was not until the 1890s that Britain obtained the region through treaties that Rhodes negotiated with the natives. It was eventually called Northern Rhodesia, the Zambezi River dividing it from Southern Rhodesia. Great Britain granted Northern Rhodesia independence in 1964, and the country adopted the name Zambia.

Western Zambia lies on the Angolan Plateau but supports forests. Sharing the great copper belt with Congo in the north, Zambia is the fourth largest producer of copper in the world and the largest producer in Africa. Kitwe is the mining center for copper and cobalt, while zinc and lead mines operate near Kabwe. Corn, the most important crop, grows near the capital, Lusaka.

Victoria Falls

Victoria Falls ranks among the four most spectacular waterfalls in the world. The falls drops 355 feet over a crest that spans one mile. The roar is audible twenty-five miles away. Even the twelve-hundred-foot-high mist is visible at that distance. The discoverer of the falls, David Livingstone, learned its native name *Mosioatunya,* "the smoke that thunders."

Livingstone visited the falls on November 16, 1855, while on his great trek down the Zambezi River. He named it in honor of Queen Victoria of England, and the name has stuck. He wrote in his diary that "scenes so lovely must have been gazed on by angels in their flight." He later described the falls as "the most wonderful sight I had witnessed in Africa."

Victoria Falls drops into a chasm on the border of Zambia and Zimbabwe.

The Muchinga Mountains run through eastern Zambia. North of the mountains are two lakes in the Congo River drainage system. Lake Mweru is the deeper of the two large lakes in this area. However, swampy Lake Bangweulu is more famous—David Livingstone died there in 1873 while seeking the "fountains" of the Nile, which were described by the Greek historian Herodotus.

Malawi The size of Pennsylvania, the British colony of Nyasaland was nestled along Lake Nyasa in the Great Rift Valley. Britain granted the country independence in 1964, the same year that it gave independence to Zambia. The people renamed both the nation and the lake Malawi.

Most of Malawi lies about four thousand feet above sea level on plateaus. The high savannas have a pleasant climate. Malawi has been called "the Switzerland of Africa" because of its beautiful mountains and lakes. Yet Malawi is one of the world's poorest nations. It lacks natural resources, and its remote location hinders transportation and tourism. However, many of Lake Malawi's tropical fish find their way to pet shops in America. The lake is famous for its beautiful but feisty cichlids.

Indian Ocean Islands

Several islands lie in the Indian Ocean off the coast of India. France controlled each of these beautiful tropical islands at various times. Some of the people are Creoles, being of French descent mixed with African or Indian. However, there is a very cosmopolitan mixture of Black Africans, Indonesians, Arab and Chinese traders, Indian laborers, and European settlers.

Madagascar Madagascar, an island about the size of Texas, is separated from Africa's southeast coast by the Mozambique Channel. It is the fourth largest island in the world. During the seventeenth and eighteenth centuries, pirates, such as Captain Kidd, hid on Madagascar.

A range of mountains parallels the east coast, leaving only a narrow coastal plain. The range

Geographer's Corner

Transportation Routes

Only one nation in Africa ranks among the ten leading nations in total length of railroad tracks. That country is South Africa. But the limited number of railroads in the whole of Africa says nothing about their importance to the region. In fact, railroads may be more important in Africa than on any other continent. In landlocked nations where roads and cars are rare, keeping railroad lines open to the coast is a vital concern. Railroads make an easy target in the civil wars that trouble Africa.

Examine the map carefully and answer the questions.

1. Can you trace a complete railroad from Cairo to Cape Town?

2. Which nations of eastern and southern Africa appear to have no major railroads?

3. Of Africa's five culture regions, which one appears to have the largest concentration of railroads?

4. How many railroads cross from the Atlantic to the Indian Ocean? What countries do they pass through?

💡 Outside South Africa, what port appears to be the most vital link in Africa's railroad system?

Principal Railroads of Africa

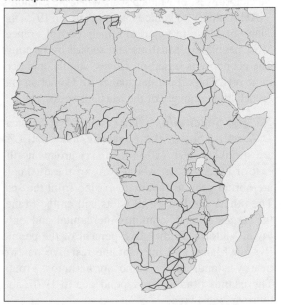

Ring-tailed lemurs in Madagascar

reaches to 9,436 feet at the north end, and reefs block most of the east coast. To the west, the range drops gradually with long fertile valleys. The capital, Antananarivo, lies on the cooler crest of the range.

The southern end of the island is desert, and many of the forested places have been cleared for agriculture. Eighty percent of the people grow rice as subsistence farmers. As the population of the island grows, more wildlife becomes endangered. This is especially unfortunate because lemurs, aye-ayes, and other species live nowhere else in the world.

The people are probably a mixture of Africans and Indonesians whose ancestors arrived about two thousand years ago. The Malagasy language, similar to Malay and Indonesian, spread throughout the island. Madagascar gained independence from France in 1960.

Comoros The Comoro Islands consist of four main volcanic islands and several islets northwest of Madagascar. When the Comoros (KAHM uh ROZE) gained independence in 1975, the island of Mayotte voted to remain part of France. Most people are Muslims and subsist by farming. The economy is based on cloves, vanilla, and perfume oils. The official languages are Comorian and French, though many of the Muslims speak Arabic.

Seychelles The eighty-five tropical islands of the Seychelles (say SHELZ) are sprinkled over 750 miles in six groups northeast of Madagascar. About forty of these islands are abrupt granite mountains rising from the sea. The others are low coral islets and atolls. Mahé, the largest island, contains the capital and only town, Victoria. Eighty-five percent of the people live on Mahé, and most of the rest live on two nearby islands in the same northernmost group. The islands obtained independence in 1976, and tourism is growing.

The people of Seychelles are descendants of French settlers and African slaves that the French brought with them. English and French are the official languages, but most people speak Creole. Almost all the people are Catholic.

Mauritius Mauritius (maw RISH us) is a volcanic island east of Madagascar. Ruled in turn by the Dutch, French, and British, Mauritius opted to remain part of the British Commonwealth when it gained independence in 1968. Over half the population is Hindu, over one-quarter is Christian, and the rest is Muslim. Sugar cane, tea, and tobacco are exported. Both Mauritius and nearby Reunion, which voted to remain part of France, are tropical islands with a booming tourist industry.

SECTION REVIEW

1. What two deserts lie in southern Africa?
2. What nation in southern Africa, like Tanzania, was controlled by the Germans until World War I?
3. What two nations in southern Africa did Portugal rule before their independence?
4. What four nations are drained by the Zambezi River?
5. Of the four island nations, which is the largest? which did not retain the French language?

💡 Why do you think Cecil Rhodes marched north to claim Rhodesia for Britain? Include political, economic, and personal reasons.

Can You Define These Terms?

cataracts   escarpment   Afrikaans   apartheid
Swahili

Can You Locate These Natural Features?

Great Rift Valley   Ethiopian Highlands   Cape of Good Hope   Kalahari Desert
Blue Nile   Eastern Rift   Orange River   Okavingo Swamp
White Nile   Western Rift   Drakensberg Mountains Namib Desert
Sudd   Lake Victoria   veldt   Zambezi River
Horn of Africa   Serengeti Plain   Limpopo River   Victoria Falls
Denakil Desert   Mount Kilimanjaro

Can You Explain the Significance of These People, Places, and Events?

David Livingstone   Ogaden   Zulu   Nelson Mandela
Cecil Rhodes   Axum   Shaka   San
Khartoum   Nairobi   Boers   Skeleton Coast
Nubia   Masai   Johannesburg   Luanda
Addis Ababa   Zanzibar   Pretoria   Cabinda
Organization of African   Cape Town   Bantu   Great Zimbabwe
  Unity (OAU)

How Much Do You Remember?

1. Name four important rivers of eastern and southern Africa.
2. What four deserts cross eastern and southern Africa?
3. In what country would you find each feature? Drakensberg Mountains? Ruwenzori? Serengeti Plain? Okavingo Swamp?
4. What waterfall makes an impressive plunge on the Zambezi River?
5. Match each feature with the country to which it is most closely related.

   1. an unusual island   a. Tanzania
   2. apartheid   b. Somalia
   3. Nile's Cataracts   c. Namibia
   4. Mount Kilimanjaro   d. South Africa
   5. copper   e. Kenya
   6. flamingoes   f. Sudan
   7. Horn of Africa   g. Madagascar
   8. Skeleton Coast   h. Zambia

6. What two countries formed Rhodesia?
7. Who are the Afrikaaners, and where did they come from?
8. What are the similarities among the four nations of the Horn of Africa?
9. Why do eastern and southern African lands have a milder and drier climate than those of West Africa?
10. In which country do the Masai live? Basotho? Somali? Tutsi? San? Zulu? Shona? Amhara? Xhosa? Khoikhoi? Malagasy? Hutu? Swazi?

What Do You Think?

1. What important characteristics can help a country in this region prosper?
2. Why was the exploration of sub-Saharan Africa difficult?
3. Should the UN be involved in peace-keeping attempts in Africa? Why or why not?

Cumulative Review

1. Name the seven continents. Which two continents are crossed by the equator? How are their climates similar?
2. Name the four oceans. Which oceans touch Africa?
3. Define primary, secondary, and tertiary industries. Which industry is most prominent in Africa? What is the most developed country in Africa?
4. List the eight culture regions of the world. What is the only culture region that borders Africa?
5. Give the five culture subregions of Africa. For each subregion, name the most prominent nation, land feature, a famous person, and a major city.

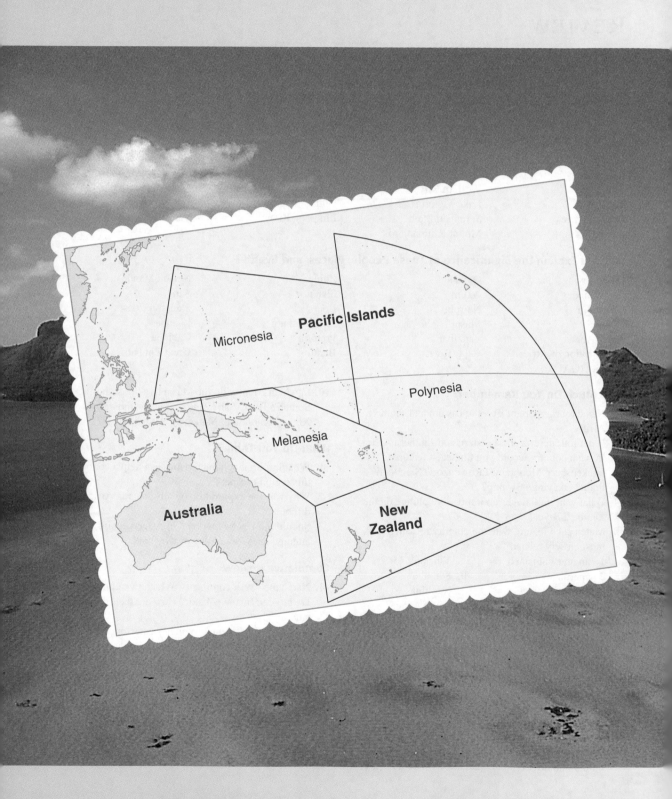

UNIT X

Oceania

CHAPTER 27

AUSTRALIA AND NEW ZEALAND

The remainder of your textbook will explore the most remote region of the earth, known as **Oceania.** Hidden by the broad Pacific Ocean, the many islands of Oceania were among the last lands settled by Noah's descendants. When the Europeans began exploring the islands in the late eighteenth century, they discovered an interesting variety of heathen peoples who had forgotten God. Missionaries rejoiced when these people responded openly to the gospel.

Ask of me, and I shall give thee the heathen for thine inheritance, and the uttermost parts of the earth for thy possession. (Ps. 2:8)

English settlers also discovered rich soil and grassland on the islands of New Zealand and on the continent of Australia. Here they planted a European culture and built a society very similar to their home on the other side of the world.

AUSTRALIA

Australia is often referred to as the Land Down Under because it lies on the opposite side of the earth from Europe and North America. In the Southern Hemisphere, the seasons are opposite those in the Northern Hemisphere. Australian families celebrate Christmas in the middle of the hot summer, with picnics and other outdoor activities.

Australia is unusual in many other ways. It is the smallest and flattest continent. Its highest peak is less than half the height of high peaks on the other continents. Australia is the driest inhabited continent, with an average annual rainfall of only seventeen inches. As an "island" continent, Australia is the only inhabited continent with no land bridge to another continent.

Australia has many exotic animals that are found nowhere else. The best known are the **marsupials,** mammals that raise their young in a pouch on the mother's belly. The most widespread marsupials are the kangaroos, which thrive in forest and plain alike. There are many species of kangaroos, ranging in size from the tiny muskrat kangaroo to the giant red kangaroo, which grows taller than a man and can hop 30 miles per hour.

The continent is also home to some peculiar birds. It has the second and third largest birds in the world—the emu and the cassowary. Like the world's largest bird, the ostrich, these birds cannot fly. The beautiful lyrebird has an amazing ability to mimic as many as forty different calls. Perhaps the most famous Australian bird is the kookaburra, whose fiendish laugh is a familiar sound in the cities.

Australia has many unique plants too. In all, thirteen thousand plant species grow here and nowhere else in the world. Eucalyptus trees are the most common type of tree in Australia. There are six

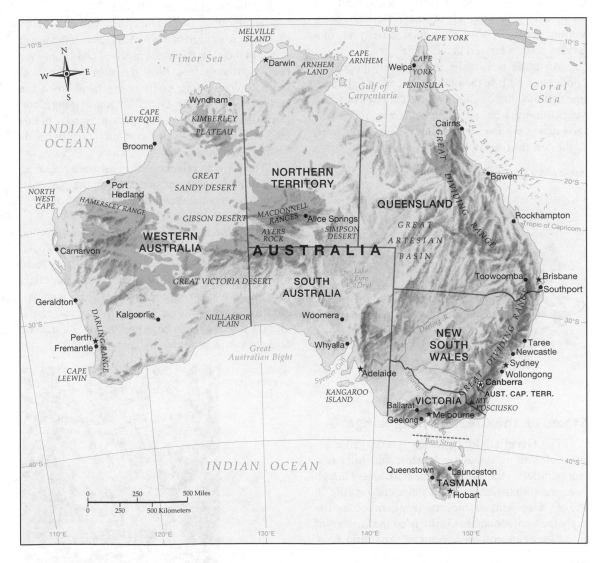

hundred varieties, ranging from dwarfs in the dry interior to three-hundred-foot giants in the northern rain forests—the tallest hardwoods on earth. The only other important tree is the acacia, which is pictured on the national coat of arms beneath an emu and kangaroo. Early settlers called acacia trees **wattles** because they wove, or "wattled," the trees together to build frames for their mud homes.

Australia is unique for another reason. It was the last continent to be settled by Europeans. The first British colonists did not arrive in Australia until nearly two hundred years *after* Jamestown was founded in Virginia. In fact, Americans were voting on the Constitution the same year that British settlers arrived in Australia.

Australia is still the least densely populated continent, and it is the only continent united under one national flag. In slightly more than two hundred years, pioneers have created a thriving, industrialized nation with six proud states, each symbolized in the center of Australia's coat of arms.

Australia's National Coat of Arms

States on the Great Dividing Range

The **Great Dividing Range** is a rugged complex of low mountains, plateaus, and hills that run parallel to the east coast of Australia. Though low, the mountains have played a central role in the development of the continent, much as the Appalachian Mountains influenced the history of the American colonies. Four of Australia's six

Australia and New Zealand Statistics		
	AUSTRALIA	**NEW ZEALAND**
Capital	Canberra	Wellington
Area (sq. mi.)	2,967,894	103,736
Population	18,438,824	3,587,275
Natural Increase	0.7%	0.8%
Life Expectancy	80	77
Literacy Rate	100%	100%
Per Capita GDP	$22,100	$18,300
Population Density	6	34

states—New South Wales, Victoria, Tasmania, and Queensland—are located in eastern Australia, astride the Great Dividing Range.

The mountains influence the weather patterns of the whole continent. As winds blow off the warm ocean in the east, the moist air rises and cools over the mountains, depositing moisture by frequent rains. Several short, swift rivers flow down the eastern slope of the Great Dividing Range and empty into the ocean. The narrow coastal plains receive much more water than the vast, dry lands west of the mountains.

The lakes and rivers on the east coast are home to Australia's most unusual animal, the platypus. Though a furry mammal, the platypus has webbed feet and a duck bill, and it lays eggs.

Large forests of eucalyptus trees grow in the excellent climate on the east coast. The koala, Australia's most-loved marsupial, dwells in these forests. Resembling a furry teddy bear, the koala gets all its water and nourishment from eucalyptus leaves, without ever having to descend to the ground. Once killed in large numbers by fur traders, koalas are now protected by law.

Koalas are a national symbol in Australia.

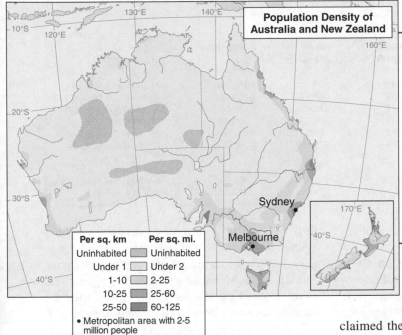

**Population Density of
Australia and New Zealand**

Per sq. km	Per sq. mi.
Uninhabited	Uninhabited
Under 1	Under 2
1-10	2-25
10-25	25-60
25-50	60-125

• Metropolitan area with 2-5 million people

Let's Go Exploring

1. How many city areas have a population density over 60 per sq. mile?
2. Which large city is farthest from any other?
3. What is the average population density of the interior of Australia?
4. Which island of New Zealand has the largest area of low population density (under 2 per sq. mile)?

🔎 Find the names of the four uninhabited regions.

The first British settlements on the continent were founded near the rich alluvial soils of the coastal rivers. Australia's major cities and industrial areas arose on its eastern seaboard, just as America's first industries appeared on its Atlantic seaboard.

New South Wales

Captain James Cook (1728-79), the greatest ocean explorer of all time, was the first European to map the east coast of Australia. He found fertile soil and one of the continent's few deep harbors at a place he named Botany Bay. Later this harbor became the site of the first English settlement on the continent.

First Settlement at Sydney

At first, the king of England had little interest in this far-off land. A revolt by the colonies in America in 1776, however, changed his view. No longer able to send prisoners to a prison colony in Georgia, England needed an alternative destination.

England selected New South Wales for its new prison colony. Captain Arthur Phillip, a retired naval officer, was appointed to lead the eleven ships of the "First Fleet" and to serve as governor of the new colony. After an arduous eight-month journey, the ships anchored in Botany Bay. On January 26, 1788, the captain hoisted the British flag and formally claimed the eastern half of the continent and the island of Tasmania. The territory was called New South Wales. Each year Australians celebrate this date as Australia Day.

Of the one-thousand-plus initial settlers, 759 were convicts sentenced to "transportation." They included men, women, and children convicted of minor offenses, such as petty theft or failure to pay their debts. In the new colony, they were given an opportunity to pay off their debts by farming. The rest of the First Fleet consisted of about 200 British soldiers, approximately 30 wives of soldiers, and a few children.

This small settlement, called **Sydney,** became the base for the exploration and settlement of Australia. Although prison ships stopped coming in 1868, the flow of settlers never stopped. Today Sydney is Australia's largest city, with a population in excess of 3.5 million. It is also Australia's chief manufacturing center and main port.

Mother of States

Like Virginia, the first colony in America, New South Wales became a "Mother of States" in Australia. Over the years, its land was carved up into new states and territories. Although the modern state of New South Wales is only fourth in total area among Australia's six states, it remains first in industry, shipping, and agriculture.

STATE	CAPITAL	DATE OF COLONY	AREA (SQ. MI.)	POPULATION	HIGH POINT, ELEVATION (FT.)
New South Wales	Sydney	1788	309,500	6,190,000	Mount Kosciusko, 7,310
Queensland	Brisbane	1859	666,990	3,355,000	Mount Bartle Frere, 5,287
South Australia	Adelaide	1836	379,900	1,479,000	Mount Woodroffe, 4,724
Tasmania	Hobart	1825	26,200	473,000	Mount Ossa, 5,305
Victoria	Melbourne	1851	87,900	4,541,000	Mount Bogong, 6,508
Western Australia	Perth	1829	975,100	1,763,000	Mount Meharry, 4,104
Territories					
Australian Capital	Canberra	NA	939	308,000	Bimberi Peak, 6,273
North Australia	Darwin	NA	519,800	178,000	Mount Zeil, 5,023

Numerous factories dot the coastal plain, manufacturing products from textiles to tractors.

Unlike their "stuffy" counterparts in Great Britain, where rank and privilege are still important, Australians consider themselves equals. Australia was settled by hard-working families who scratched out a rough existence in the new country. The continent offered plenty of land for everyone. Cities were not built up; they were built out. Tall buildings and apartments are rare. Nearly three out of every four Australian families own a home. The pace of life is relaxed and informal. Bragging about your degrees at Oxford or your aristocratic friends will not impress anyone.

Blue Mountains and the Australian Alps
Within view of the coastal cities is the Great Dividing Range. The mountains west of Sydney are called the Blue Mountains. Though they appear blue to residents of the city forty miles away, they are actually covered with green eucalyptus trees, which secrete a bluish oil into the air. The Blue Mountains are actually a low plateau that has been eroded by water. Here visitors enjoy exploring the Jenolan Caves, the largest cave system on the continent.

South of the Blue Mountains is another part of the Great Dividing Range, called the Australian Alps. These snow-covered mountains are much higher than the Blues. The highest range in the

Sydney Opera House

Many consider Sydney Opera House the most beautiful building in the world. Built on a point that juts out into Sydney Harbor, the opera house looks like a huge ship that is flying into the harbor with open sails. The "sails" are high partial domes.

A Danish architect provided the winning design in a worldwide competition. The original design called for wide sails, but they proved impossible to make. The engineering problems were finally overcome after thousands of hours of computer simulations. Unfortunately, the $7 million budget blossomed to $100 million. Queen Elizabeth presided at the formal opening on October 20, 1973.

One million ceramic tiles, specially made in Sweden to remain bright white and free of fungus, cover the concrete sails. The interior design mixes 67,000 square feet of Gothic tinted glass with space-age steel ribs and concrete fans. There are five performing halls, a theater, and two restaurants. The theater's wool curtains are the largest in the world. In addition, the world's largest mechanical organ—consisting of 10,500 pipes—sits in the concert hall.

Peakhill Station is located near Broken Hill, New South Wales. An expert can shear up to one hundred sheep per day.

Farmers harvest wheat in the wetter regions of the outback.

Australian Alps is the Snowy Mountains. Here **Mount Kosciusko**—Australia's highest point—rises 7,316 feet above sea level. Covered with snow for half the year, it is the area's main attraction for skiers and hikers.

Jumpbucks in the Interior Just west of the mountains are fertile grasslands much like the American prairie. Wheat fields are common. But Australia is most famous for its jumpbucks (sheep). Jumpbucks are everywhere—on the coast, around the mountain slopes, and in the dry interior. There are ten jumpbucks for every Australian. Australia is the world's leading producer of wool. New South Wales produces 40 percent of the nation's wool.

The nation is becoming less dependent on "the sheep's back," however, as manufacturing increases. The mines near Broken Hill on the western border of the state are major producers of silver, zinc, and lead.

SECTION REVIEW

1. List six ways that Australia is an unusual continent.
2. What mountain system runs along Australia's eastern coast?
3. What is the highest peak in Australia?
4. Where did the first European settlers land in Australia? What year did they arrive?
5. What are jumpbucks?
  Why do most Australians live on the east coast?

Victoria Victoria is located on the southeast corner of Australia. In 1851 it split from New South Wales and became a separate state. The two states have been competitors ever since. Although Victoria is Australia's smallest mainland state, it is home to approximately one-fourth of Australia's population.

Melbourne, Australia's Sports Capital Nearly three-fourths of Victoria's population is located in **Melbourne,** the state capital and the nation's second largest city. Originally Melbourne was a prosperous mining port; however, its remote location has hurt its competition with Sydney for trade and commerce. It is too far away from world shipping routes. Nonetheless, its factories still play an important role in the Australian economy.

The city of Melbourne is the most "English" of Australia's cities. Stately buildings and beautiful parks display statues of prominent Australians. The world-renowned Victoria National Gallery is home to the finest collection of art in the nation.

Melbourne is also the sports center of Australia. Melbourne hosts the Davis Cup tennis finals, cricket matches with players from England, and Australia's richest horse race. The nation's passion for sports is world renowned. Aussies (Australians) have a larger proportion of winning sports teams than any other nation. As often occurs in wealthy nations, sports take priority over church attendance.

For bodily exercise profiteth little: but godliness is profitable unto all things, having promise of the life that now is, and of that which is to come. (I Tim. 4:8)

The Ballarat Gold Rush Melbourne is within sight of the Great Dividing Range, which curls around Victoria's coast. The mountains near Melbourne contain great mineral wealth. In 1851 the discovery of gold at Ballarat started a gold rush, which increased the state's population sevenfold. After the rich veins of gold were mined out, the city became a major railroad junction. Ballarat is also the country's most populous inland city.

Victoria is home to Australia's largest oil field and a major natural gas field off the coast. Coal is also mined in the state. The Latrobe Valley holds the world's largest deposit of **lignite,** or brown coal. Lignite is the lowest grade of coal, however, because its high moisture produces little heat and a

Cricket is the most popular spectator sport in Australia.

lot of smoke. Three vast power plants in Latrobe Valley produce nearly 90 percent of Victoria's electricity.

Murray River System On the other side of the Great Dividing Range is the continent's dry interior, where rain is scarce. Runoff water from the Great Dividing Range is vitally important. This low area just west of the mountains is known as the **Central Lowlands.** Waters flowing down the Great Dividing Range form long, leisurely rivers in the flat, inland terrain. The map on page 597 shows the three places where these rivers drain: the Gulf of Carpentaria in the tropical north, Lake Eyre in the center, and the Great Australian Bight in the south.

Land Use of Australia and New Zealand

Let's Go Exploring

1. What type of farming occurs in the Tropics?
2. What is the most widespread type of land use in Australia and New Zealand?
3. What is the main commercial grain grown in Australia?
4. What two types of farming appear to be common in the Murray River basin?

💡 Find the geographic names of the four main primitive hunting grounds (of the Aborigines).

Australian English

Although Australia is thoroughly English in its customs and lifestyle, Australians have developed their own colorful dialect. Speech is slow and relaxed and there are plenty of smiles. The typical greeting is "G'day" (Good day). When meeting a friend, you say, "G'day, mate." Here are a few of the many distinctly Australian words and expressions.

barbie—barbecue grill
billy—pan
billabong—water hole
jumpbuck—sheep
up a gum tree—in trouble
willy-willy—windstorm
humpty do—all mixed up
take a squiz—look over
get all wet—get angry
oscar—money

Most rivers in the Central Lowlands dry up during the dry season. The major exception is the sixteen-hundred-mile-long **Murray River** and its tributaries, the most important water system on the continent. These rivers provide a steady supply of water for farms and pastures in the south. A large wheat crop grows in the wide plains of the Murray drainage basin. Many varieties of fruit also grow in the fertile river valley that forms the border between Victoria and New South Wales.

Canberra, the Capital Over the course of the nineteenth century, arguments over trade and taxes hurt the six independent colonies on the continent.

Old and New Parliament Houses in Canberra

Late in the century, the militaristic emperor of Germany began planting colonies in the Pacific region and threatened the British colonies. The six colonies of Australia agreed to unite as a federation in 1901. As part of the settlement, the two largest states agreed to build a new seat of government midway between Sydney and Melbourne. New South Wales set aside nine hundred square miles for the capital.

The government sponsored an international competition to determine the best possible design for the new city. Of the 137 designs submitted, the design of architect Walter Griffin of Chicago won. He moved to Australia in 1913 to direct the construction of the capital. In 1927, the Australian Parliament met there for the first time. The federal government ran the Australian Capital Territory until 1989, when it was granted self-government. The capital city is named **Canberra** after the Aboriginal word *canburry,* meaning "meeting place."

Like Canada, Australia has a constitutional monarchy with a parliament and claims the British monarch. Like the United States, Australia adopted a written constitution and a federal system of state governments. The British monarch is the head of state and is represented by a governor-general in Parliament. The monarch also approves six governors, one for each state government. The Labor Party, organized in 1891, has established a socialist government that closely controls businesses, wages, and working conditions.

Tasmania, the Apple Isle Off the coast of Victoria is Australia's smallest and least populous state. The beautiful island of **Tasmania** has so many apple orchards that it is sometimes called the Apple Isle. Apple trees, introduced in 1788, now produce Australia's most important fruit crop. The best orchards are located in the Huon Valley about twenty miles southwest of the capital, Hobart. In addition to exporting apples worldwide, the state also produces pears, berries, and potatoes.

The narrow Bass Strait separates Tasmania from Victoria. Like Victoria, Tasmania has low mountains and a pleasant marine-west-coast climate. Blessed with abundant rainfall, Tasmania is

The Great Barrier Reef

Just off the northeast shore of Queensland is the largest coral formation in the world. The **Great Barrier Reef** stretches for 1,250 miles—about the length of the entire western coast of the United States. The "barrier" makes travel hazardous for ships sailing to the coast. Captain Cook ran aground and barely escaped shipwreck when he discovered the reef.

This underwater garden is made up of hundreds of coral islands or islets. **Coral** is formed over thousands of years by tiny animals, called polyps, that take lime from the sea. When the animals die, their skeletons add to the coral reef. There are about four hundred types of coral of all shapes, sizes, and colors. This diverse biome attracts colorful fish, sponges, squids, giant clams, sea turtles, poisonous sea snakes, dolphins, and even humpback whales. In fact, the reef harbors more types of life than any other place in the world.

In the 1960s scientists began warning that the reef was disappearing. The reef came under attack by a poisonous starfish that devoured the polyps by the millions. Also, insecticides on nearby farms were washing

Schools of fish in the Great Barrier Reef

into the sea and destroying the coral. A few fertilizer companies were even mining the reef for limestone. To protect the reef, the government set aside most of it in 1975 as a national park. Hundreds of thousands of visitors come to Queensland each year to see the reef.

home to magnificent rain forests and powerful waterfalls. The fierce Tasmanian devil (a marsupial) lives in the rugged central plateau, which remains sparsely settled. Most Tasmanians inhabit the fertile coastal lowlands. The availability of cheap hydroelectric power has attracted many industries, such as pulp and paper works, a zinc refinery, and aluminum smelting. Because of its isolation, Hobart's population is small. Unlike the busy cities on the mainland, Hobart enjoys a quiet, slow pace of life.

Queensland: The Frontier State

Located on the northeast corner of the continent is Queensland, the youngest state of Australia. It was formed in 1859 when Queenslanders pressed for separation from New South Wales. A frontier spirit still exists in this sparsely populated state, nearly two and one-half times the size of Texas. The majority of Queensland's residents are clustered along the eastern seaboard.

The Wet Coast The capital, **Brisbane,** is located in the southeast corner of the state on the Brisbane River. Originally founded as a prison colony, Brisbane grew rapidly to become Australia's largest river port. Because it is so near the Tropics, the capital of the "Sunshine State" attracts many tourists each winter. Brisbane's numerous parks are filled with subtropical flowers.

South of the capital is the Gold Coast, which extends to New South Wales. Spectacular waves and beautiful beaches make it a surfer's paradise. A fertile plain in the southeast corner, called the Darling Downs, produces pineapples and other fruits and vegetables.

The coast north of Brisbane reaches into the Tropics. Frequent rains from moist trade winds make this Australia's wettest region. Sugar cane and cotton are grown along the narrow coastal plain. The northern tip of the east coast, Cape York Peninsula, is extremely hot and humid. Few people

Artesian Wells

The livestock in Queensland get most of their water from a vast underground reservoir of water, called the Great Artesian Basin. The landscape is dotted with **artesian wells,** where warm water bubbles up to the surface without the need for pumps. Although the water is too salty for crops and people, cattle drink it without any problem.

As water flows west off the Great Dividing Range, some of it seeps underground into the Great Artesian Basin. This water moves through a layer of underground rock called an **aquifer** (meaning "water bearer"). The Great Artesian Basin is the largest reserve of underground water in the world.

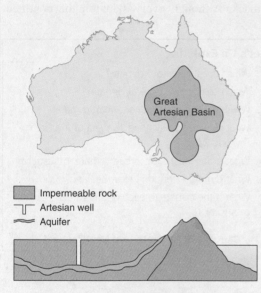

Great Artesian Basin

▨ Impermeable rock
⊓ Artesian well
〰 Aquifer

There are two basic kinds of aquifers. The most common are *unconfined aquifers.* They occur where the layer of rock above the aquifer is permeable, allowing water to seep through. Permeable layers include gravel, sand, clay, and loose rock. If a well is dug to this aquifer, the water must be pumped to the surface.

The Great Artesian Basin, on the other hand, is a *confined aquifer.* It has an impermeable layer of rock above it that traps the water and keeps it from rising to the surface. As the water pressure builds, it pushes out through breaks in the surface. Natural artesian springs result. When a hole is dug into a confined aquifer, water pushes up to the surface, creating an artesian well.

live in this tropical area. Climbing "tree kangaroos" feed on the leaves of the jungle canopy.

The Dry Interior   To the west, beyond the low mountains and hills of the Great Dividing Range, the land becomes increasingly dry and grassy. Cowboys, called stockmen, live on large cattle **stations** (Australia's word for ranches). Some stations are the size of Delaware. More beef is produced in Queensland than in any other state. Australia exports more beef than any other country in the world, shipping it to eager markets in the Far East.

Queensland also has great mineral deposits. During the gold rush of 1867, thousands of men poured into the state in search of instant wealth. Today, bauxite (aluminum ore) is mined on Cape York Peninsula, near Weipa. North of Brisbane are large deposits of bituminous coal. Lead, zinc, silver, and copper are mined near the interior town of Mt. Isa, Queensland's largest industrial complex.

Australia is the world's leading producer of bauxite and lead and the second leading producer of zinc (behind Canada). Australia exports more coal than any other nation.

Ranchers muster cattle at Lawn Hill Station in Queensland.

◎ SECTION REVIEW

1. What are the two most populous cities in Australia? Which states are they in?
2. What is Australia's capital?
3. What is the only island state in Australia?
4. What is a station?
5. What are the leading products of Queensland?
💡 Why was the original colony of New South Wales divided into several states?

States of the Western Plateau

The western two-thirds of Australia is the dry, flat **Western Plateau.** Most of this shield is desert or semiarid grassland. The only relief is a few scattered mountain ranges. Two states, South Australia and Western Australia, were carved out of this plateau.

South Australia, Gateway to the Outback

The south-central state of South Australia, colonized in 1836, was the only state not settled by convicts. It is shaped like a keystone along the waters of the **Great Australian Bight.** The state is divided into two distinct geographic regions: the populous coast and the arid interior.

The Mediterranean Coast The coastal portion of South Australia supports 98 percent of the state's population. Much of the coast enjoys an excellent climate similar to that of the Mediterranean. Cold Antarctic currents in the Great Australian Bight keep the land dry in the summer, but steady rains fall in the winter.

Adelaide, the capital, has an ideal harbor protected by Kangaroo Island from the violent willy-willies (windstorms) that blow on the Great Australian Bight. Laid out with wide streets and many parks, the city boasts a warm climate and relaxed atmosphere.

East of Adelaide is some of the nation's most productive land. The Murray River system drains into this part of the state and empties into the Great Australian Bight. The lush Barossa Valley, thirty miles northeast of Adelaide, is known for its wine.

The valley was originally settled by Lutheran immigrants from Germany seeking religious freedom.

After World War II, South Australia experienced unprecedented industrial expansion. Today the state leads the nation in lumber, shipbuilding, and smelting. Two large plants near Adelaide produce Australia's first native car, the Holden.

The Outback The sparsely populated areas beyond the coastal cities of Australia are collectively known as the **outback.** Life is hard and lonely for the stockmen and miners who live there. They tell many tall tales about the "blowies" (flies), sandstorms, and other common features of the outback. Although every state on the continent

Let's Go Exploring

1. Which coast has a dry climate?
2. Which coast has a tropical climate?
3. Which coast has a mediterranean climate?
4. What climate appears directly west of the Great Dividing Range?
5. What is the most widespread climate in Australia?
6. What climate is found in New Zealand?
💡 What is the climate in each of the six state capitals of Australia?

Climates of Australia and New Zealand

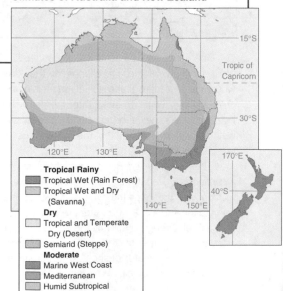

Tropic of Capricorn

Tropical Rainy
Tropical Wet (Rain Forest)
Tropical Wet and Dry (Savanna)
Dry
Tropical and Temperate Dry (Desert)
Semiarid (Steppe)
Moderate
Marine West Coast
Mediterranean
Humid Subtropical

Lake Eyre

Australia's largest lake is located in the northeast corner of South Australia. **Lake Eyre** is the lowest point on the continent, fifty-two feet below sea level. Most rivers of the Central Lowlands, including the Great Artesian Basin, drain into this lake. These rivers—and the lake itself—are dry most of the time. A few times each century, rare heavy rains fill the rivers and lake. Within a period of two years, however, the lake returns to a barren salt bed.

includes part of the outback, South Australia is known as "the gateway to the outback."

The two basic activities of the outback are mining and ranching. South Australia's outback is especially famous for its mineral wealth. The discovery of opals in 1915 attracted thousands to Coober Pedy, which means "hole in the ground." Most of the world's opals come from this region. The first "diggers" not only dug holes in search of riches but also made their homes in the ground to escape the intense heat. Even with the invention of air conditioning, many residents still prefer to live underground.

Western Australia, the Wild Flower State

Western Australia is Australia's largest but most sparsely populated state. Three-fourths of the people reside in the southwest corner, where good land and tall evergreen forests abound. Blessed with a mild mediterranean climate, this region has beautiful wild flowers. In the spring, tourists and residents flock to the countryside to view fields ablaze with color. Many of these flowers are unique to Australia.

A Beautiful, Isolated Capital The capital of **Perth** is home to more than half of the state's population. With its ideal climate, Perth is often compared to cities in Southern California. Residents enjoy swimming at sandy beaches and boating on the Swan River. West of the business section is King's Park, the pride of Perth. It includes one thousand acres of natural bush vegetation. Driving through the park provides a spectacular view of the city, with the Indian Ocean to your back and the Darling Range ahead in the distance.

Perth is over one thousand miles from the nearest large city, Adelaide. Not until 1970 was a transcontinental railroad completed that connected the two coasts. It crosses the treeless Nullarbor Plain, the flattest landform on earth. The name comes from two Latin words, *nulla* and *arbor,* which mean "no tree." Here engineers laid the longest stretch of straight railroad track in the world—297 miles long.

The Inhospitable Interior The dry and inhospitable climate did little to attract early settlers to the treeless interior of Western Australia. The discovery of gold in the late nineteenth century changed everything. Gold mining camps sprang up east of Perth around the town of Kalgoorlie, along the famed "Golden Mile." Veins of rich ore were mined to a depth of four thousand feet. As the gold began running out, nickel became the major source of revenue. Bauxite is also mined in the Darling Range.

One of the richest iron ore reserves in the world was discovered in the **Hamersley Range.** Towns, mining facilities, and railroads were built to exploit these resources. The ore is moved by rail to Port Hedland on the coast. Port Hedland ships more tons of freight than any other port in Australia, except Sydney.

The central part of Western Australia is covered with deserts. The Great Victoria Desert, the Gibson Desert, and the Great Sandy Desert combine to make up the second largest desert area in the world. The deserts gradually give way to grasslands in the northern Tropics and in the south near Perth. Large cattle and sheep stations are common.

Northern Territory, Heart of the Outback

The Northern Territory is located at the heart of the desolate outback. Outside the capital of Darwin, the average population density is only one person for every five square miles of land. This territory, nearly the size of Alaska, is administered by the federal government.

Tropical Coast Most of the Northern Territory is located in the Tropics. Tropical rain forests abound along the northern coast, gradually becoming grasslands and then desert farther inland. Trade winds bring heavy rains to the coast in the summer

Racers jockey for position at the Alice Springs Camel Cup in the Northern Territory.

season, called "The Wet," but dry monsoon winds blow from the interior desert in the winter. Cyclones are common.

Nearly half the territory's population lives in Darwin, located on the coast. Tourists fly to Darwin as the starting point for tours into the interior. Darwin is the only Australian city ever attacked by foreigners. During World War II Japanese bombers based in New Guinea dropped bombs on the city.

Life in the Interior   The primary industry in the outback is mining. Scattered mountain ranges hold considerable mineral wealth, including gold, manganese, and iron ore. The world's greatest deposit of bauxite was discovered on Arnhem Land. Australia also has the largest known reserves of uranium.

The second major industry is cattle ranching. One cattle ranch covers six thousand square miles—an area larger than the state of Connecticut. Families in the outback sometimes live fifty miles from the nearest town and fifteen miles from their nearest neighbor. Regular schools and hospitals are impossible. Instead, doctors make "house calls" by plane, and children attend school over two-way radio. The Royal Flying Doctor's Service and the School of the Air operate out of the central town of Alice Springs, often called "The Alice."

At the heart of the Northern Territory lies the **Simpson Desert,** sometimes called the Red Center of Australia. No one, not even the hardiest stockman, lives here. Red sand is piled into waves that can rise as high as 100 feet and stretch for up to 180 miles. The red color comes from rusted iron in the sand.

The Aborigines   When the first British settlers landed in Australia in 1788, there were about five hundred tribes of dark-skinned people scattered throughout the continent and nearby islands. These Aborigines had migrated from Asia long ago. (The term **aborigine** refers to the earliest known settlers of a region. It comes from the Latin words *ab origine,* meaning "from the beginning.")

Though they spoke over three hundred languages and lived in both rain forests and desert, the

Ayers Rock

The monotony of the outback is broken by the majestic **Ayers Rock,** the world's largest monolith, or freestanding rock. Jokingly referred to as the largest pebble in the world, it rises 1,134 feet above the surrounding desert. The rock forms an oval that is one and a half miles wide and four miles long. The monolith, composed of a kind of rock called a conglomerate, changes color throughout the day. The early morning sun makes it appear orange and deep red; it changes to violet and blue later in the day.

Erosion has cut deep gullies and basins in the rock that run from the top to the bottom. Rare desert rains cause raging falls. The base of the rock is pocked with shallow caves, which contain many aboriginal paintings of scenes from the Dreamtime. Aborigines consider this great rock sacred. They call it Uluru.

Ayers Rock is the world's largest monolith.

Mount Olga, a monolith in the Northern Territory near Ayers Rock, consists of thirty-six huge egg-shaped rocks called olgas.

Aborigines shared the same basic culture. Each tribe was nomadic, constantly moving in search of food. Their only domestic animal was the dingo, a type of dog, and their only weapons were the spear and the boomerang. One of the common foods in the bush was a fat, white grub that was eaten raw.

Like the American Indians, the Aborigines had developed a detailed knowledge of natural cycles, plants, and animals. They believed that spiritual beings created the world in a time they called the Dreamtime. These beings became a part of nature and mankind. The superstitious religion of the Aborigines guided every aspect of their lives, including when they moved and where they camped. Their world-famous bark paintings depict scenes from their myths.

The Aborigines were no match for the Europeans. As the colonists' need for land grew, they drove the Aborigines away from the fertile river valleys and into the barren backcountry. Some were killed, and many others died as a result of diseases introduced by the white settlers. In time, the newcomers considered the Aborigines to be a passing race, to be left alone to die out on reservations. Christian missions, however, were successful in teaching the Aborigines about Christianity and Western ways.

In the 1960s, liberal leaders in Australia decided to follow the new world trend to respect minorities and "ancient cultures." The Aborigines demanded civil rights and a return of their ancestral lands. Although Aborigines account for only 1 percent of the nation's population, they gained control of large tracks of land in northern and central Australia. The government has kept control of all mineral rights, however, even within the aboriginal reservations.

The land-use map on page 602 shows where Aborigines continue to live as hunters and gatherers, like their ancestors. Only a few thousand live this way, however. Most Aborigines work on the large sheep and cattle stations in the outback of Australia's five mainland states. Three-quarters of the Aborigines are part white and have fully adopted Western ways. On occasions called "walkabouts," some Aborigines return for a period of time to the bush life of their ancestors.

◎ SECTION REVIEW

1. Why do so few people live on the Western Plateau?
2. What type of climate is common on the coast of South Australia?
3. What are the two main industries in the outback?
4. What important product is mined in the Hamersley Range?
5. Who were the native people of Australia?
   ♦ List five similarities between the Australian Aborigines and the American Indians.

Aboriginal art near Darwin

Geographer's Corner

Interpreting Photos

Tourists who spend years reading about places are often shocked when they actually visit. Word descriptions and maps give only tantalizing hints about the tastes, sounds, and sights of the real thing. Even photos can be misleading.

Most cameras depict only a small fraction of the 360° landscape you can see in person. Photos are also limited to one instant in time. They cannot show movement. They cannot show changes in lighting and seasons. To keep from misinterpreting a photograph, you need to be aware of "the rest of the picture" not shown. Look up these photos and answer the questions.

1. Where is the photographer located—on the ground or in a helicopter? (p. 605)
2. What is the time of day? (p. 609 top)
3. What season is it? (p. 601 top right)
4. How might the scene look later in the day? (p. 603)
5. Is the scene posed and cleaned up for the photographer, or is it natural and unaffected by the photographer's presence? (p. 598)
6. Compare photos of the Sydney Opera House on pages 596 and 600. What information is shown on one photo but not on the other?

💡 On which side of the photographer was the sun shining when he photographed Ayers Rock? (p.608)

NEW ZEALAND

New Zealand is a beautiful island country isolated from the rest of the world. Its nearest neighbor, Australia, is 1,200 miles to the west, across the stormy Tasman Sea. New Zealand has many similarities to Australia, including a British heritage and a similar history. However, New Zealand lacks the land area and mineral wealth of its continental neighbor. For its economic survival, New Zealand relies almost solely on agricultural exports. Meat, wool, and dairy products account for nearly half of what it sells abroad. New Zealand is the world's largest exporter of butter, cheese, and wool.

New Zealand enjoys a marine-west-coast climate similar to that of Tasmania. Prevailing winds blow off the Tasman Sea, bringing warm, moist air that showers the islands 150 days of the year. Because clouds are so common, the native islanders called their home *Aotearoa* (AH oh tay ah roh ah), or "land of the long white cloud."

Like Australia, New Zealand has unusual flora and fauna. Its variety of trees is especially noteworthy. More than 112 species appear in the broadleaf evergreen forests that cover one-fourth of the country. The unique kauri is New Zealand's largest tree. European shipbuilders once cut them down to make masts for their ships. Unfortunately, kauri take nearly one thousand years to reach their full height.

New Zealand has some unusual native animals too, most of them birds. Several flightless birds once thrived on the island. Monster birds, called moa, sometimes grew to thirteen feet in height. Their kick could kill a man. The smaller kiwi is New Zealand's national bird. About the size of a chicken, the kiwi has no wings, an extremely long beak, and feathers that look like hair. New Zealanders are nicknamed "kiwis."

Kiwis are unique to New Zealand. This species, the giant spotted kiwi, lives only around Nelson on South Island.

Maori Meeting House, Rotorua, North Island

The Maori Wars

The First Inhabitants   The **Maori** (MOW ree), a brown-skinned people from the islands of Polynesia north of New Zealand, were the first humans to discover the islands. They arrived on magnificent warships made of hollowed logs. At first, they lived by hunting and fishing. After the "moa hunters" hunted the moas to extinction, they learned to clear forests and plant crops. They also became brilliant wood carvers using stone tools.

Constant wars and superstitious rituals were central to Maori life. It was not uncommon for them to eat their defeated foes. The Maori proved to be a difficult challenge for Abel Tasman, who

discovered the islands in 1642 while searching for a fabled continent south of Australia. When Tasman attempted to land, the Maori killed several of his men. Tasman did not try to land again. In 1769, Captain James Cook landed and established relations with the Maoris. He succeeded in mapping the coasts of the two main islands.

British Settlers   The first White settlers on the islands were escaped convicts from Australia and deserters from British ships. Whalers and seal hunters also built small stations along the coast to resupply their ships. Christian missionaries soon followed. English traders gave rum and guns to the Maoris in return for flax, a strong fiber used for ropes. The introduction of guns led to bloody fighting among Maori tribes and between the Maori and the Whites. The settlers also introduced diseases to which the Maori had no resistance, greatly reducing the Maori population.

White settlers asked England to annex New Zealand and bring badly needed law and order. On February 6, 1840, a group of Maori chiefs signed the Treaty of Waitangi in which they recognized the British monarch as their sovereign. In return, the Maori received full property rights over their land. They also agreed to sell land only to the British crown. New Zealanders celebrate the signing of the treaty each year in a holiday called National Day.

Tensions remained high on the North Island, where most of the Maori lived. Shiploads of settlers began arriving and made illegal purchases. In 1845 opposition to land sales inspired a Maori uprising. This marked the start of the Land Wars. Much like the out-numbered American Indians, the Maori put up a stiff, though hopeless, resistance. When war ended in 1872, the Maori's power was broken, and the government seized the "rebel" land.

After the Maori Wars, the British colony grew rapidly. England gave it a large loan to attract one hundred thousand new settlers. The loan was also used to improve the transportation and communication systems. In 1872 the development of refrigerator ships enabled New Zealand to begin shipping meat to Europe. New Zealand has become the world's leading exporter of mutton.

611

At New Zealand's request, Great Britain granted the colony dominion status in 1907.

The Government Today The government of New Zealand is similar to those of other independent nations that make up the British Commonwealth. The British crown is represented by a governor-general. The legislative authority is the parliament. New Zealand's parliament consists of one chamber called the House of Representatives. Elections are held every three years. Members are elected to represent ninety-one general districts and four Maori districts.

Like Australia, New Zealand has a long history of government programs. In 1890 the Liberal Party began implementing a big welfare system. In 1893 it became the first country to give women the right to vote. New Zealand's benevolent socialism resembled its counterparts in Europe. But by the 1980s it became obvious that the cost of welfare benefits was stifling initiative and driving businesses out of the country. So in 1985 the government began dismantling the socialist system, giving New Zealand one of the freest economies in the world.

The North Island

New Zealand has two main islands and many smaller islands. **North Island** is slightly smaller than South Island, but it is home to twice as many people.

The Populous Northern Peninsula New Zealand has a reputation for scenic beauty and huge sheep stations. There are over fifteen sheep for every New Zealander. Yet more than 80 percent of the people live in cities. **Auckland,** New Zealand's largest city and chief seaport, has nearly a million people. It is located on a beautiful harbor of the northern peninsula. In addition to shipping much of the region's dairy, sheep, and timber products, this colorful city is also the country's chief industrial center.

In recent years, thousands of Pacific Islanders have come to Auckland seeking a better life. The city now has the largest population of Polynesians in the world. Many of the country's Maori also live in the city and the region around Auckland. Although the Maori population is relatively small (under 15 percent of the population), they have a powerful

Mt. Ngauruhoe (7,516 ft.) is one of the imposing volcanoes on North Island, New Zealand.

voice in the government. These Aborigines claim that their rights, established by the Treaty of Waitangi, have been violated. Some leaders are demanding compensation and a return of all government lands.

The Geothermal Center New Zealand is on the Pacific "ring of fire." The center of North Island is a volcanic plateau with some volcanic peaks that are still active. Near the town of Rotorua are hot springs, boiling mud pools, and spouting geysers. Two geysers, Pohutu and the Prince of Wales Feathers, spray hot water as high as one hundred feet into the air. A large geothermal plant uses underground steam to generate substantial amounts of electricity.

Lake Taupo, New Zealand's largest lake, is located just south of Rotorua, near the very center of the island. It fills the crater of a dormant volcano. In fact, it is the largest volcanic lake in the world. Fishermen from around the world come to fish for the large trout found in this beautiful lake.

Southern Hills A series of low, rugged hills and mountains forms a *V* to the south and east of the island. On the slopes, sheep and beef cattle graze.

New Zealand has sixty million sheep and less than four million people.

New Zealanders eat the greatest amount of red meat per person in the world. (Australia is second.)

Fruit and vegetables are grown on the coastal lowlands in the east. New Zealand is the world's leading producer of kiwi fruit, a brown, fuzzy fruit shaped like an egg with an emerald-green interior.

On the southern tip of the North Island is the city of Wellington, the second largest city in New Zealand. The capital was moved from Auckland to the more centrally located Wellington in 1865. Its main office building, shaped in a series of stacked circles, is appropriately called the Beehive. Ferries and hydrofoils transport people from the capital across the narrow **Cook Strait** to South Island. Wellington has one of the deepest natural harbors in the world. Miles of docks receive oceangoing vessels from around the world.

South Island

South Island is known for its country atmosphere and relaxed pace. Because few Maori ever settled on this island, white settlers established a distinct European lifestyle. The rugged west side of the island contrasts sharply with the plains on the east, where most people live.

Southern Alps The Southern Alps, a three-hundred-mile-long mountain chain, dominates the west coast. The magnificent alpine scenery includes snowfields, crevasses, and glaciers. Near the center of the chain is snowcapped **Mount Cook,** New Zealand's highest mountain, rising 12,349 feet above sea level. The Maoris called it *Aorangi,* which means "cloud piercer." Running westward to the sea are the Fox and Frans Josef Glaciers. On the eastern slope is the great Tasman Glacier. Airplanes drop off skiers at the heads of these glaciers and the skiers can ski uninterrupted for stretches as long as sixteen miles. Farther south, glaciers carved a series of long valleys into the sea. These fjords create a jagged coastline similar to the coast of Norway. A highlight of the region is Sutherland Falls, one of the world's twenty highest waterfalls.

Rainfall is heaviest on the west slope of the mountains, averaging three hundred inches per year. The many swift rivers supply much of the country's

Sailing yachts is a popular sport near Wellington.

energy needs at low cost. An underground sea cable carries surplus electricity from the South Island to the populous and industrial North Island.

Canterbury Plains East of the Southern Alps are the Canterbury Plains. These plains are dry because the prevailing westerly winds drop their moisture on the mountains before they reach the plains. Most of New Zealand's cereal grains, such as barley, wheat, and oats, are raised on these flat, fertile plains. Farther south, livestock graze on the plains and rolling hills.

About seven miles from the coast is Christchurch, the largest city on the South Island. Hydroelectric power has turned Christchurch into a major industrial center. Tourists visiting the Southern Alps first come to this city. Named for a college in Oxford, England, Christchurch is well known for its parks, gardens, and British architecture. It is the most "English" of all New Zealand's cities.

◎ SECTION REVIEW

1. Why is New Zealand called the land of the long white cloud?
2. Who were the first people to live in New Zealand?
3. What are the two main islands of New Zealand?
4. What is New Zealand's largest city?
5. What are the two main geographic regions of South Island?
- 💡 Compare and contrast the economies of New Zealand and Australia.

REVIEW

Can You Define These Terms?

marsupial	coral	aquifer	outback
wattle	artesian well	station	Aborigine
lignite			

Can You Locate These Natural Features?

Oceania	Tasmania	Lake Eyre	North Island
Great Dividing Range	Great Barrier Reef	Hamersley Range	Cook Strait
Mount Kosciusko	Western Plateau	Simpson Desert	South Island
Central Lowlands	Great Australian Bight	Ayers Rock	Mount Cook
Murray River			

Can You Explain the Significance of These People and Places?

Captain James Cook	Canberra	Adelaide	Maori
Sydney	Brisbane	Perth	Auckland
Melbourne			

How Much Do You Remember?

1. Name four outstanding features of Australia that appear on its coat of arms.
2. What is Australia's tallest mountain? In what range is it located?
3. What are the three major geographic features of Australia?
4. What was the First Fleet?
5. What is Australia's largest city?
6. List ten memorable features of the outback.
7. Give the state of Australia that best fits each description.
   a. largest area
   b. largest population
   c. largest city
   d. first settled
   e. last settled
   f. island
   g. lignite
   h. opals
   i. cattle stations
8. Give the island of New Zealand that best fits each description.
   a. most populous
   b. highest peak
   c. geothermal activity
   d. Canterbury Plain
9. Describe the differences between the Aborigines and the Maori.

What Do You Think?

1. Read Psalm 2. Does verse 8 allude to missionary work among Aborigines and Maoris?
2. The land west of the Appalachians is wet, but west of the Great Dividing Range is dry. Why the difference? (Hint: Compare currents and wind patterns.)
3. How has Australia's location as "the Land Down Under" affected its history and economy?
4. List five important similarities and five differences between Australia and New Zealand.
5. Why do you think Australia used to be called "the lucky land"?
6. Compare the histories of the Aborigines of Australia, the Maoris of New Zealand, and the American Indians of the United States.

PACIFIC ISLANDS

Over twenty-five thousand islands are scattered across the vast Pacific Ocean. Although the region is larger than all seven continents combined, the **Pacific Islands** have less land area than the state of Alaska.

The first Europeans to visit the islands sent home vivid descriptions of a paradise on earth, with warm breezes, sandy beaches, friendly natives, and abundant tropical fruits. Because most of the islands lie in the humid Tropics, temperatures average a balmy 80°F.

Early reports of paradise were misleading, however. Islanders face the threat of typhoons, volcanic eruptions, and earthquakes. Disease, superstition, and tribal warfare only make matters worse.

In the past two hundred years, the islanders have been thrust into the difficult process of adopting foreign values and lifestyles, called **acculturation.** Most people still eke out a living in small villages of thatched houses. Most islands lack mineral resources, and the only major export is dried coconut meat, called **copra.** The people are struggling to make a good living in the modern world.

Although the Pacific Islanders are poor in the world's eyes, they have been very open to evangelism. Many have discovered that Jesus Christ is the one real hope of paradise.

He that hath an ear, let him hear what the Spirit saith unto the churches; To him that overcometh will I give to eat of the tree of life, which is in the midst of the paradise of God. (Rev. 2:7)

FROM THE STONE AGE TO THE MODERN AGE

People settled the Pacific Islands long before European explorers arrived. When one island became overcrowded, a group of natives set out for another island. Because of the great distances between islands, the people developed distinct cultures, languages, and physical features.

Magellan was the first European to chart the Pacific during his voyage around the world in 1519-21. After battling the stormy seas on the southern tip of South America, Magellan reached

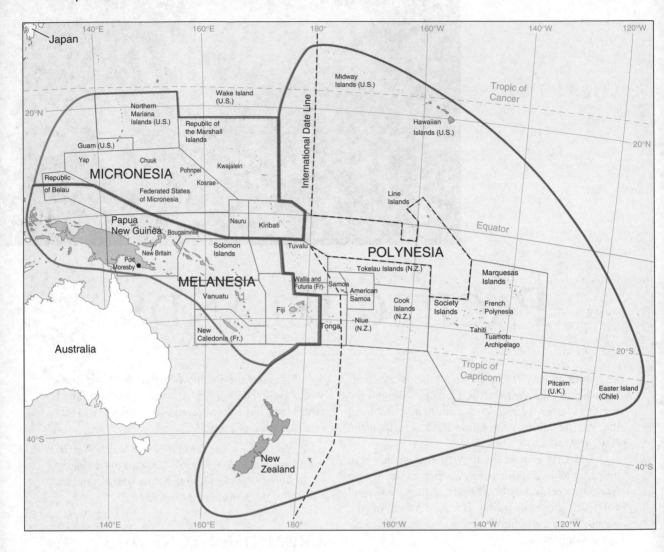

the calm ocean, which he called the *Pacific* ("peaceful"). However, for ninety-eight days his men sighted only two uninhabited islands. Provisions ran out, and the crew was forced to eat rats and leather. Finally the starving men reached the tiny island of Guam in the Marianas, where they took on fresh supplies. Over the next two centuries, few expeditions braved this forbidding "empty" quarter of the earth.

During three voyages between 1768 and 1779, the great scientific explorer Captain James Cook filled in many empty spaces on the world map. He charted the east coast of Australia and discovered New Caledonia and the Sandwich Islands (Hawaii).

Others soon followed. Traders came in search of coconut oil, sandalwood, and pearls. Afterwards came Congregational missionaries and Roman Catholic priests. The missionaries provided medicine and education, and they encouraged the natives to adopt Western dress and social norms. Although many islanders still worship their ancestors and believe in animism (spirits that indwell plants and animals), the professed religion on most islands is Christianity.

Tribal people use this spirit house in the Sepik region of northern Papua New Guinea.

to help the islands to recover from their losses and to develop stable governments. Most of the islands have since gained independence, although a few prefer to remain territories.

MELANESIA

Most of the Pacific Islands are small and uninhabited. The islands of interest can be divided into three broad groups—Melanesia, Micronesia, and Polynesia.

Melanesia is located south of the equator, near Indonesia and Australia. The name means "black islands" (*mela-* + *nesia*). A variety of short, black-skinned peoples settled Melanesia long ago. Over twelve hundred different tribes developed, each with its own language and primitive rituals.

With the rise of colonialism in the nineteenth century, foreign powers competed for control of the islands. During the 1930s imperial Japan extended its control over many of the Pacific Islands. American Marines later fought some of their bloodiest battles as they struggled to free the islands from Japanese control.

After World War II, the United Nations divided the islands among the Allied countries. They wanted

Skirmishes between rival tribes were once a normal part of life. A "big man" rose to power within a tribe based on his prowess in battle. Head hunting and cannibalism (the eating of human flesh) were common practices.

The Pacific Ocean separates Melanesia from the rest of Australia's continental plate. Like the

Pacific Islands Statistics

COUNTRY	CAPITAL	AREA (SQ. MI.)	POPULATION	NATURAL INCREASE	LIFE EXPECTANCY	LITERACY RATE	PER CAPITA GDP	POP. DENSITY
Melanesia								
Fiji	Suva	7,055	792,441	1.7%	66	92%	$6,100	112
Papua New Guinea	Port Moresby	178,259	4,496,221	2.3%	58	72%	$2,400	25
Solomon Islands	Honiara	11,500	426,855	3.3%	72	54%	$2,590	38
Vanuatu	Port-Vila	5,700	181,358	2.1%	61	53%	$1,200	38
Micronesia								
Belau	Koror	177	17,000	1.8%	71	92%	$5,000	96
Kiribati	Bairiki	264	82,449	1.9%	63	90%	$860	263
Marshall Islands	Dalap-Uliga-Darrit	70	60,652	3.8%	64	91%	$1,680	866
Micronesia	Palikir	271	127,616	2.2%	68	90%	$1,700	470
Nauru	Yaren (District)	7.7	10,390	1.3%	67	99%	$10,000	1,267
Polynesia								
Tonga	Nukualofa	270	107,335	2.1%	70	93%	$2,160	370
Tuvalu	Funafuti	9.8	10,297	1.4%	64	95%	$800	1,095
Samoa	Apia	1,097	219,509	2.5%	69	100%	$1,900	200

continent, these *continental islands* have a rich variety of soils, rocks, and resources. Heavy rains produce vast tropical forests. Yams and sweet potatoes grow well in the acidic soil. **Taro,** a potato-like root that can grow up to twelve feet long, is a favorite food.

White Europeans visited Melanesia last of all the Pacific Islands. Treacherous reefs and tricky currents fill the shallow waters near the shore. Good harbors are scarce. The first missionaries did not arrive until the 1830s, at Fiji. Even then, few missionaries attempted to reach the rugged interior.

Papua New Guinea

Two countries occupy **New Guinea,** the second largest island in the world. The western half is a province of Indonesia, called Irian Jaya. The eastern half is part of Papua New Guinea (PAP yoo uh), a young country that gained independence from Australia in 1975. Papua New Guinea has several other tropical islands, but 85 percent of its land area is on New Guinea.

Rugged Terrain   The most prominent geographical feature of New Guinea is the rugged mountain

Warriors wear ceremonial dress for a singsing near Mount Hagen in the highlands of Papua New Guinea.

There are forty-three species of birds of paradise. They display a colorful assortment of tails, plumes, crowns, and halos.

system that extends the length of the island and continues into the ocean. Although it is a tropical island, a few mountains, such as the 12,793-foot Wilhelm Mountain, remain cold year-round. Steep valleys lie between the mountain ranges. Numerous large, raging rivers flow through these ranges to the ocean.

New Guinea is a land of forbidding swamps and thick jungles. Tropical rain forest covers about 75 percent of Papua New Guinea. Swamps occupy much of the narrow coastland. The seven-hundred-mile Fly River—the longest river in New Guinea—flows south through an endless swamp, which is the only major flatland on the island.

A variety of animals flourish in the isolation of New Guinea. Like Australia, the forests host many kinds of kangaroos and other marsupials. The swamps have salt- and freshwater crocodiles, one species of which climbs trees! The Queen Alexandria butterfly is the largest butterfly in the world, as large as a small bird. The island's most famous faunas are its birds. New Guinea has 660 species of birds—more than the entire continent of North America.

Papua New Guinea has several offshore islands. The largest is the Bismarck Archipelago, named after a nineteenth-century chancellor of Germany. New Britain, the largest island, is the most developed area in the country. Its capital, Rabaul, is the nation's export center. Tragically, nearby volcanoes destroyed most of the city in 1994.

Coastal Settlement   More people live in Papua New Guinea than in all the other Pacific Islands combined. Over seven hundred tribes coexist, each speaking its own language. The tribes are divided into two main culture groups: the lowlanders on the coast and the highlanders in the interior.

The Dutch claimed the western half of New Guinea in 1828, and Great Britain claimed the southeast in 1846. But no settlers came. Interest in settlement changed when imperialist Germany laid claim to the northeast coast of New Guinea and its nearby islands in 1884. The Germans established a post at the mouth of the great Sepik River in the north. But malaria-bearing mosquitos made life difficult on the German plantations. After Germany lost World War I, their lands came under Australian supervision.

The first British settlers came in 1874 after Captain Moresby discovered a deep harbor on the south coast of New Guinea. The "settlers" were Protestant missionaries who hoped to preach to the local Motu people. Port Moresby is now the capital of Papua New Guinea, with modern buildings and paved roads. Although tribes near the capital speak Motu, English is the official language. To help communication between tribes, Melanesians speak a simplified form of English called *Tok Pisin*.

The Grand Valley For decades European explorers attempted to reach the interior of New Guinea, but difficult mountain ranges, torrential rains, and disease blocked their path. Everyone assumed that no peoples could survive in this inhospitable land. Then, in 1930, a couple of gold prospectors from Australia stumbled upon a "lost civilization" of one million souls. Hidden in the midst of the mountains of New Guinea was a Grand Valley, where Melanesian Highlanders lived and fought. Because these people did not travel far from the safety of their tribes, they thought they were the only inhabitants on earth.

At present, no highway system or railroads link the capital with the rest of the country. Most travel is by plane. Even today, few outsiders visit the remote villages. A new Highlands Highway connects some of the highland villages.

Cargo Cults

When first faced with Western culture, many Melanesians became fascinated with its great variety of riches. They desired the goods that began to arrive by plane and ship on their islands, but they had no idea how the goods were made or where they came from. They concluded that the goods or cargoes came from the spirit world. Late in the nineteenth century, their prophets promised a new age of plenty when tribal deities, ancient heroes, or dead ancestors would return with cargo for the Melanesians. Some leaders moved their tribes to the coasts where they built crude airstrips, docks, and outposts to prepare for the event. They built rows of warehouses to store the hoped-for goods. The tribes often imitated government flag raising ceremonies and the like, hoping that such magic rites would hasten the arrival of the cargo.

These **cargo cults** also arose as a revolt against White colonial rule. Melanesians were often mistreated as slaves on plantations and in mines, and they never received the freedom and wealth that Europeans had. So the cult settlements refused to pay taxes, would not allow visitors, and would not work unless they were paid outrageous wages. They abandoned their traditional wealth—gardens, pigs, and money—which they would not need in the age of plenty. Natives expected their strange worship to bring justice, freedom, and plenty of eating, dancing, and kava drinking. However, because the cults threatened the White economy and government, their leaders were arrested. The seventy or so cargo cults eventually died out.

Cargo cults rejected the gospel of Jesus Christ, which promises a time of eternal peace and plenty in heaven. Instead they lusted after the vain treasures of this earth.

But godliness with contentment is great gain. For we brought nothing into this world, and it is certain we can carry nothing out. And having food and raiment let us be therewith content. But they that will be rich fall into temptation and a snare, and into many foolish and hurtful lusts, which drown men in destruction and perdition. (I Tim. 6:6-9)

The Four Cs The economy of Papua New Guinea is largely subsistence agriculture, taro and other roots being the most common crops. Most land is owned by the whole clan; individuals cannot buy or sell property. Coastal tribes grow two cash crops, *cacao* and *copra*. Plantations in the high altitudes grow *coffee,* the nation's most lucrative crop. Unfortunately, the shortage of fertile land encourages fighting among the highlander tribes.

The nation is beginning to exploit its mineral resources. After the discovery of *copper* in 1965, a major mine opened on the easternmost island—Bougainville. But in 1989 the Nasioi natives staged an uprising and closed the mine. They resent the desecration of their sacred grounds, and they do not want to be a part of the new government.

The largest gold mine outside South Africa opened in Porgera in 1991. Recently a mountain of copper was discovered at Ok Tedi near the head of New Guinea's Fly River. Copper and gold account for two-thirds of the nation's exports. The nation is seeking to develop oil reserves too.

This Japanese biplane is one of many World War II wrecks strewn across the Pacific.

The hot and humid climate breeds several deadly diseases, including malaria and tuberculosis.

Between 1870 and 1911, infamous **blackbirders** used bribes or force to load their ships with Solomon Islanders to work on cotton and sugar plantations in Fiji and Queensland. To end these abuses and to protect the workers, Great Britain took control of the islands in 1893.

The islands became independent in 1978, but the islanders have not yet developed a strong sense of national identity. Although English is the official language, native tribes speak ninety indigenous languages.

Over one thousand miles of ocean separate the Solomon Islands from Australia. Because of their isolation, the islands do not enjoy the same diversity of wildlife as New Guinea does. The only mammals to colonize the islands were some marsupials and bats (which natives eat). Humans brought dogs, cattle, and rats. Sea birds, unlike mammals, thrived on the islands. The frigate bird, once considered sacred, is a national emblem.

Forests cover more than 90 percent of the land, supplying valuable wood for logging industries. In contrast, only 1 percent of the area is arable. Islanders clear land on a few narrow coastal areas and mountain valleys to raise copra and cacao.

Guadalcanal is the largest of the Solomon Islands and the second most populous (after Malaita). The capital city of Honiara is located on a deep port at the north end of Guadalcanal. Many tourists visit World War II battlefields on the island.

SECTION REVIEW

1. Define *acculturation.* Why has it been difficult for the Pacific Islands?
2. What explorer first discovered Hawaii and many other Pacific Islands?
3. What is the largest island in Melanesia?
4. List the four Cs of Papua New Guinea's economy.

💡 Based on population and language statistics, calculate the average number of speakers for each language in Papua New Guinea.

Solomon Islands

 The Spanish explorer Alvaro de Mendana first discovered the scattered Solomon Islands in 1568. In anticipation of the riches he expected to find, he named the islands after the biblical King Solomon.

Europeans never found mineral riches, but they did discover plenty of dangers. Four active volcanoes belch smoke and fire, and earthquakes pose a constant threat on the seven main islands.

Vanuatu

Southeast of the Solomon Islands is Vanuatu (VAH noo AH too), a chain of twelve volcanic islands and some sixty smaller coral islands. Captain Cook named the islands New Hebrides after the Hebrides Islands in Scotland.

Several islands have active volcanoes. In these unstable conditions, three-fourths of the people build rural homes made of bamboo and palm leaves. Bislama, a language that combines mainly English words with Melanesian grammar, is the most widespread of the hundred different spoken languages. The subsistence economy is based on copra, along with cacao, coffee, fishing, and cattle.

Fiji, Crossroads of the South Pacific

The Fiji archipelago has over eight hundred scattered islands, but only about one hundred are inhabited. Three-fourths of the country's population lives on the large volcanic island of Viti Levu (Big Island). Suva, Fiji's capital and largest city, lies on Viti Levu's southern coast.

Girl on Ovalau Island, Fiji

Before the arrival of the Europeans, warring tribes of cannibals inhabited the islands. Cannibalism ceased in 1854 when the high chief Cakobau converted to Christianity. Twenty years later, Fiji became a crown colony when Cakobau petitioned Britain for protection from the other chiefs.

Great Britain imported laborers from India to work on sugar cane plantations. Nearly half of the present islanders are descendants of these Indians.

Fiji has been called "the crossroads of the South Pacific." Airplanes fly constantly in and out of the airport at Nadi, and commercial ships dock at the natural harbors at Suva and Lautoka. Most of Fiji's money comes from agriculture, with sugar cane the major export. Since gaining its independence in 1970, Fiji has encouraged tourism and strived to develop the country's manufacturing and forestry.

The Mines of New Caledonia

James Cook discovered **New Caledonia** in 1774. He thought the islands resembled Scotland. Hence the name New "Caledonia," which is Latin for New "Scotland."

From 1853 to 1894 the French used the islands as a penal colony. However, they later discovered that one-third of the world's nickel reserves were buried beneath the mountains of the main island.

Conversion of a Cannibal King

Only 150 years ago, many tribes of fierce warriors lived on the islands of Fiji. Often the menus of their feasts included *bokolo,* another name for roasted enemies. One cannibal chief, Cakobau, who was born in 1817, gained power on the islands. He led his people to war against enemy tribes, murdered those who displeased him, and gave cannibal feasts. During his reign, however, Christian missionaries came to Fiji to preach the gospel.

In 1854 Cakobau accepted Jesus Christ as his Savior. He changed his ways, ended cannibalism on his island, and publicly told his people that he was a Christian.

Cakobau's power grew, even though he was no longer a fierce cannibal warrior. In 1867 he became king of Fiji, and his people lived in peace on the islands. Today most Fijians claim to be Christians. Many, however, have accepted only the form of religion. Like others around the world, these people need Jesus as their personal Lord and Savior—just as King Cakobau did.

Strip mines now dot more than half of the island's landscape. New Caledonia is one of the world's leading producers of nickel.

⊚ SECTION REVIEW

1. What sea bird is an emblem of the Solomons?
2. Name the main Solomon island, where many American soldiers died in World War II.
3. Compare Vanuatu's economy to that of the Solomons.
4. What people live in Fiji besides the native Fijians?
5. What mineral is mined on New Caledonia?
9. Calculate the total land area of the nations in Melanesia. What percentage of this total does each nation have?

MICRONESIA

North of Melanesia are the small, widely scattered islands of **Micronesia,** which means "small islands." Although Micronesia covers an area of ocean about the size of the continental United States, its land area is less than that of Rhode Island.

Unlike the continental islands of Melanesia, most islands in Micronesia are atolls. An **atoll** is a ring of coral on the submerged cone of a volcano. Since they rise only a few feet above the water, coral islands are called **low islands.** Coral sand, which lacks organic material, is a poor soil. Few plants grow well. The islanders rely on fishing to subsist. Coral islands lack fresh water, except for what they receive from rainfall. Most of the islands have little hope for a brighter future. They depend on copra, tourism, and foreign aid to survive in the modern world.

Micronesians are a little taller than Melanesians and have lighter skin and straight or woolly black hair. Only during World War II, when fighting devastated many of the islands, did Micronesia attract worldwide attention. Following the war, the United Nations gave most of the region to the United States to govern, aid, and defend. It was called the "Trust Territory of the Pacific."

New Caledonia

The majority of these islands are now self-governed in "free association" with the United States. Under this system, the countries control their internal and foreign affairs, but the United States has promised to defend them. In return for this protection, the countries have agreed to keep out foreign military forces. Micronesia contains three large island groups: the Caroline Islands, the Mariana Islands, and the Marshall Islands.

Caroline Islands

The **Caroline Islands** consist of more than 930 islands. In 1978 the Caroline Islands were divided into two groups—the Federated States of Micronesia and Belau.

Federated States of Micronesia
The federated states consist of Kosrae, Pohnpei (formerly Ponape), the Chuuk Islands (formerly the Truk Islands), and the Yap Islands. The Federated States of Micronesia gained the status of free association with the United States in 1986.

Kosrae, a high volcanic island on the eastern corner of the Carolines, is one of the few important islands among mostly coral islands in the east.

Yap stones were once used for currency. Each stone had a unique history.

Missions

Missionary Aviation

What do Arctic Eskimos, Amazon Indians, and New Guinea cannibals have in common? The answer is remoteness, primitive conditions, and hostile climates. Aviation missionaries use their planes to move people and supplies where they could not otherwise go, and they respond quickly to medical emergencies.

One of the newest pilot programs is located in the Chuuk (Truk) Islands. Jody Colson, a Fundamentalist missionary in Hawaii, got the idea from members of his congregation from Chuuk. They were burdened for their homeland because it had no gospel preachers and because it has horrendous medical problems. In 1997 Colson and two other missionary couples moved to Chuuk to begin their ministry. They all shared their money to run the plane—a "car" to get them from island to island.

Becoming a missionary pilot requires great dedication. The typical college program at a Christian school, such as Bob Jones University, includes five years of Bible and flight training. Fundamentalist mission boards require a commercial pilot certificate, an instrument rating, five hundred hours of flying time, and an aircraft mechanics certificate. Boards also demand that their candidates be debt-free—perhaps the hardest challenge because flight expenses add $12,000-$20,000 to the normal college bill. Once accepted, the missionary candidate goes through regular deputation, except that he must raise a larger sum of money.

Missionary pilots face many challenges. Landings on small and remote airstrips can be dangerous. Precipitous mountains and fogs have claimed the lives of more than one missionary pilot. A pilot often must stay many days away from home. His mechanical skills are often in demand. Such busy schedules can take a toll on his family, unless he takes time to provide spiritual leadership and family recreation. God's Word encourages aviation missionaries to remember that they are "earthen vessels" dependent on God to meet their daily needs.

But we have this treasure in earthen vessels, that the excellency of the power may be of God, and not of us. (II Cor. 4:7)

Congregational missionaries have made a lasting impact. The islanders reserve Sunday strictly for going to church. The women dress modestly, and bathing suits are not permitted—even for visitors. Known for its outstanding citrus fruits, Kosrae has the potential of becoming the vegetable and fruit basket of the Pacific.

The volcanic island of Pohnpei never suffered the ravages of World War II because armies avoided its forbidding terrain and heavy rainfall. The modern city of Kolonia on Pohnpei is the capital of the Federated States.

The Chuuk Islands and the Yap Islands are predominantly volcanic. Both Chuuk and Yap were sites of Japanese bases during World War II.

Belau Poverty-stricken Belau (formerly Palau) grows only enough food to provide for its rural population. Nearly two-thirds of the population lives in the capital of Koror. Half of these people depend on government work for their salaries.

Mariana Islands

The **Mariana Islands** extend 350 miles from north to south and are part of a partially submerged mountain range in the Pacific. Only four of the islands are occupied: Guam, Saipan, Rota, and Tinian. **Guam,** the largest, has the distinction of being the most populous island in all of Micronesia.

Guam is an independently governed territory of the United States. The rest of the Marianas are a commonwealth of the United States with Saipan as its capital. Their residents, as well as the residents of Guam, are U.S. citizens. Tourism is the major source of income on Guam, and American military bases are second.

Sports

Snorkeling and Scuba Diving

Two of the most popular ocean sports are snorkeling and scuba diving. People from all over the world fly to the Pacific Islands to enjoy these sports. Belau's reef, one of the "seven underwater wonders of the world," offers some of the best diving anywhere. Like Australia's Great Barrier Reef, its waters are filled with coral, exotic fish, lava tubes, undersea caves, and shipwrecks.

O Lord, how manifold are thy works! in wisdom hast thou made them all: the earth is full of thy riches. So is this great and wide sea, wherein are things creeping innumerable, both small and great beasts. (Ps. 104: 24-25)

Snorkeling is an easy sport that you can do in as little as a foot of water. Snorkelers require just a mask, flippers, and a snorkel. A snorkeler floats on the surface and

Scuba divers find a variety of life on the ocean reefs.

watches schools of colorful fish, crabs, eels, and other creatures moving on the coral floor. Scuba divers wear oxygen tanks that allow them to stay underwater for as much as an hour. But the equipment is expensive and requires special training to use properly.

Marshall Islands

The **Marshalls** lie due east of the Carolines. This island group has thirty-four low-lying islands and atolls, which split into two parallel chains. The islands were named for John Marshall, a British sea captain who explored them in 1788. Many of the people live in poverty.

The United States used Bikini Island and Eniwetok from 1946 to 1958 to test nuclear bombs.

Kwajalein Atoll was one of many islands where Americans fought the Japanese during World War II. They retook it in February 1944.

The residents of Bikini Island, who had converted to Christianity many years earlier, vacated their island after the military convinced them that the nuclear testing would benefit mankind. Although steps have been taken to rehabilitate the contaminated soil on these islands, the islanders are still waiting to return to their home.

Kwajalein, the largest atoll in the world, encloses a mammoth 839-square-mile lagoon. The United States rents the Kwajalein Atoll to use as a target for rockets launched from California over forty-five hundred miles away.

Other Micronesian Islands

Nauru Nauru (nah OO roo) is the third smallest country in the world—only Vatican City and Monaco are smaller. The oval-shaped coral island is a mere eight square miles in area. With over ten thousand people, it has the highest population density in the Pacific. The nearest neighbor, East Ocean Island, lies two hundred miles away. Nauru has no fresh water except for rainwater, and the soil is extremely poor. Yet in stark contrast to the Marshall Islands, Nauru is prosperous and financially independent. Four-fifths of the island sits on a deposit of high-quality phosphate, an important fertilizer used by farmers around the world. The country's ten thousand residents live solely off the royalties they receive from the government for the sale of phosphates.

Kiribati The Republic of Kiribati straddles the equator and the international date line. Located at the juncture of Micronesia, Melanesia, and Polynesia, it contains both Micronesian and Polynesian peoples. Most islanders live in rural villages of crudely constructed houses and are heavily dependent on the sea to supplement the bananas, breadfruit, and sweet potatoes they grow. The islands are overcrowded. To help ease this problem, some inhabitants are migrating to other Pacific Islands.

SECTION REVIEW

1. What is another name for a low island? Why is the soil so poor on these islands?
2. The Caroline Islands are divided into what two nations?
3. What island chain in Micronesia is a U.S. commonwealth? What island is a U.S. territory?
4. Name the largest atoll in the world.
5. What mineral compound made Nauru rich?
   💡 Which Micronesian island would you prefer to live on? Why?

POLYNESIA

Polynesia, which means "many islands," encompasses a broad triangle that stretches from New Zealand in the west to Hawaii in the north and to Easter Island in the east.

Despite being separated by thousands of miles, the inhabitants of these islands are remarkably similar in both appearance and culture. The Polynesians have lighter colored skin and wavier hair than the inhabitants of Micronesia and Melanesia. Their different language dialects are mutually understandable throughout all of Polynesia.

The beauty and natural wealth of the islands are the result of their volcanic origin. Volcanic islands, often called **high islands,** have beautiful hills and mountains. The rich volcanic ash provides fertile soil.

Polynesia has a complex system of hereditary chiefs. With the arrival of missionaries, Christianity spread quickly as the chiefs converted one by one. Many foreign countries vied for ownership of the islands. At the present time, three island groups are independent, and the rest remain closely tied to their mother countries.

Tuvalu

Tuvalu gained its independence from Britain in 1978. With a total land area of only ten square miles, Tuvalu is the fourth smallest nation in the world, just a little larger than Nauru. Nearly 97 percent of the adults belong to the Church of Tuvalu (a Congregationalist church).

Tuvalu is one of the most undeveloped countries in the world. The soil is poor, and the islands have no mineral resources. Copra is the only major export. The country relies heavily on foreign aid from Australia, Great Britain, Japan, and New Zealand.

Samoan Islands

The Samoan Islands are mostly volcanic. The soil near the coasts is fertile enough to grow bananas, taro, and cacao. Not much grows farther inland because heavy rains leach the soil.

The first missionary to set foot on the islands, the Reverend John Williams of the London Missionary Society, arrived in the middle of the nineteenth century. Within a few years, Christianity completely changed Samoan culture.

Native houses called fales *are common on the island of Savaii in Samoa.*

Geographer's Corner

Crossing the International Date Line

It is relatively simple to adjust a watch if you travel between time zones. Travelers must make another kind of adjustment at the **international date line,** an imaginary line where time on the east side is one day behind time on the west side. When crossing the line from west to east, a traveler "loses" one day on his calendar. Traveling west adds a day.

The line could have been drawn almost anywhere. But it would cause havoc in a populated area. So Europeans decided to draw the line at about 180° longitude in the Pacific, far from the populous continents. Few islanders are inconvenienced because the line zigzags to keep populated island groups united.

Look at the time zone map on page 303 and the map of the Pacific Islands at the beginning of this chapter. Find the international date line on both maps.

What would happen if you flew from Honolulu, Hawaii, to Auckland, New Zealand? Suppose it were 8:00 A.M. Tuesday when you left Honolulu. You would subtract an hour for each time zone you entered as you traveled west. Eight in the morning Tuesday Honolulu time would be 6:00 A.M. two time zones to the west in Auckland. But because you cross the date line, you must add a day. Therefore, it would be 6:00 A.M. Wednesday. Use the time zone map to answer these questions.

1. If it were 11:00 P.M. Friday in London, U.K., what time and day would it be in Auckland?

2. If it were 6:00 P.M. Sunday in Tokyo, Japan, what time and day would it be in Honolulu?

3. If it were 2:00 A.M. Thursday in Honolulu, what time and day would it be in Sydney, Australia?

4. If it were 3:00 A.M. Monday in the Cocos Islands, what time and day would it be in New York City?

5. If it were 10:00 A.M. Tuesday in Sydney, what time and day would it be in Los Angeles?

💡 Which nation is first to see the sun rise on a new day?

The island chain has two parts. The islands west of longitude 171° W form the independent country of Samoa. The islands east of this line make up the unincorporated territory of the United States called American Samoa.

Samoa Samoa has two large volcanic islands, Opolu and Savaii, and seven smaller islands. Most of the people live in small villages along the coast, raising their own food on small plots of land. Samoa became the first independent Polynesian state in 1962.

American Samoa Eastern Samoa, or **American Samoa,** is a United States territory. As nationals, but not U.S. citizens, Samoans are able to enter the United States freely. Of the territory's seven islands, Tutuila is the largest and most populated. The capital city of Pago Pago, located on Tutuila, overlooks one of the most beautiful harbors in the South Pacific.

Although American Samoa is less than one-tenth the area of Samoa, it is in much better economic shape. In 1961 the United States launched a program to bolster the economy. Many people left their villages to take industry-related jobs around Pago Pago. The local tuna canning industry continues to provide the island's primary source of income.

Tonga, the Last Island Kingdom

Tonga is the oldest and last remaining kingdom in the Pacific. According to tradition, the most powerful chief extended his control over all the islands during a civil war in 1845, declaring himself King George Tupou I. Converted by Methodist missionaries, he persuaded many of his subjects to accept Christianity. The present king still wields great power in the constitutional monarchy.

The Wesleyan Free Church of Tonga has strongly influenced the nation's culture. The country's constitution strictly prohibits all trade, games, and work on Sunday. Despite a need for money from tourism, the king and others discourage it for fear the nation will lose its identity: "We will become like Hawaii, where there are no more Hawaiians," warned King Tupou IV, who was crowned in 1965.

The royal palace of Polynesia's last kingdom is located at Tongatapu on Nukualofa, Tonga.

The calm waters of Tahiti Lagoon, Tahiti

Tonga suffers from overcrowding, especially on Tongatapu Island. As arable land runs out, the people currently have few alternatives for making a living.

French Polynesia

French Polynesia includes five major island groups: the Society Islands, the Gambier and the Tubuai (Austral) Islands, the Tuamotu Archipelago, and the Marquesas Islands. About three-fourths of all French Polynesians live on the Society Islands, the largest islands in the territory.

French Polynesia is scattered over an area about the size of Western Europe. It has strong cultural, economic, and political ties to France. Its residents vote in French presidential elections and elect representatives to the French Parliament.

A majority of the islanders reside on the island of **Tahiti**—the geographical, social, and political center of French Polynesia. Two giant volcanic mountains unite to form the island. A coral reef surrounds most of the island, giving it a protected lagoon. Chief exports include copra, pearls, and vanilla. Papeete, the capital of the territory, is a bustling port city on Tahiti. Because of heavy tourism, Tahiti's 130 miles of roads experience traffic jams that rival those of many Western cities.

Copra dries at a beach on Nuku Hiva Island in the Marquesas Archipelago of French Polynesia.

Mutiny on the *Bounty*

The most famous mutiny in naval history occurred in the Pacific on April 28, 1789. William Bligh, commander of the HMS *Bounty,* had been sent to Tahiti to gather breadfruit and take it to Jamaica, where the British hoped to transplant breadfruit as a healthful alternative to American flour. But Bligh's harsh discipline provoked the master's mate, Fletcher Christian, to seize the ship. Bligh and eighteen loyal crewmen were set adrift on a twenty-three-foot boat. The captain managed to sail 3,618 miles in forty-eight days to Timor, where he found a ship back to England.

Meanwhile Christian and seven mutineers left Tahiti with twelve island women and six island men to find a safe island on which to hide. Uninhabited, isolated Pitcairn Island proved to be the ideal spot. Surrounded by jagged rocks and reefs, the forbidding island rises steeply from the sea. After managing to land, the crew burned the ship. The colony remained undiscovered until an American sealing ship landed there in 1808. By then only one adult male remained with the many women and children. The volcanic soil proved highly productive. But soon the two square miles of land could not support the growing population, so in the 1830s and 1850s some of the people left. Presently a few dozen colonists live there under British jurisdiction.

The Mystery of Easter Island

Easter Island is an unusual volcanic island twenty-three hundred miles off the coast of Chile, far from the other inhabited islands of the Pacific. The Dutch admiral Jacob Raggeveen discovered the island on Easter Day, 1722. On the coast he found rows of mysterious stone heads, called *moai*. The massive heads had very long ears and flat noses. On the larger heads were red stones that looked like hats or crowns.

Most of the heads are ten to twenty feet tall and weigh up to fifty tons. The largest finished head is thirty-two feet high and weighs one hundred tons, but one of the unfinished heads is over sixty feet high and over three hundred tons. How did the natives carve the *moai* out of the volcanic rock at the crater Rano Raraku, transport them to the coast, raise the heads to an upright position, and place the red stones on top?

In 1774 Captain Cook visited the island and talked to the natives. They told him that their Long Ear ancestors had made the statues twenty-two generations previously—around the thirteenth century. They called their island *Rapa Nui* and considered it the navel of the world. By that time the statues had been toppled. The natives said it happened during wars with Short Ear invaders from islands far to the west.

Where did the statue-builders come from? Where did the invaders come from who toppled the *moai*? If South American legends are true, perhaps the statue builders came from Lake Titicaca. A legend from the Gambier Islands, twelve-hundred miles to the west of Easter Island, may explain the origin of the tribe that toppled the statues. The legend tells of a defeated chieftain who took his tribe in two large canoes to a solitary island in the east.

Easter Island has another mystery that has not yet been explained. It is the only Pacific island with a writing system. But no one has been able to decipher the rongo-rongo tablets. Many of these tablets are hidden in secret caves, along with idols and skulls. Long Ears, whose features are depicted on the *moai*, hid in these caves during the war with the Short Ears.

Moai on Easter Island

Other Polynesian Islands

The volcanic Hawaiian Islands are the most important islands in the Pacific because of their size and strategic location. The United States also owns the Midway Islands west of Hawaii. New Zealand is another advanced, prosperous region of Polynesia. It owns the Cook Islands, the Tokelau Islands, and Niue. Can you find any other Polynesian Islands on the map, page 616, that have not been mentioned in this chapter?

SECTION REVIEW

1. Describe how Polynesia differs from the other two Pacific Island regions.

2. What is the smallest country in Polynesia?

3. Why is Samoa less developed than American Samoa?

4. What is the last surviving kingdom in the Pacific?

5. What European country controls Tahiti?

💡 Should New Zealand and Hawaii be considered part of the Pacific Island culture region?

REVIEW

28

Can You Define These Terms?

acculturation	cargo cult	atoll	high island
copra	blackbirder	low island	international date line
taro			

Can You Locate These Natural Features?

Pacific Islands	Caroline Islands	Marshall Islands	French Polynesia
New Guinea	Mariana Islands	Kwajalein	Tahiti
Guadalcanal	Guam	American Samoa	Easter Island
New Caledonia			

Can You Distinguish the Characteristics of These Culture Regions?

Melanesia   Micronesia   Polynesia

How Much Do You Remember?

Choose the word or phrase that correctly answers each question.

1. Which is not one of the major Pacific Island groups: Polynesia, Malaysia, or Melanesia?
2. Which type of island is most likely to have an abundance of mineral resources: continental island, high island, or low island?
3. Which is a major export for many Pacific Islands: rubber, bananas, or copra?
4. Which activity is a result of acculturation in the Pacific: fishing, animism, or playing soccer?
5. You would be most likely to meet primitive tribal members on which island: New Guinea, Tahiti, or Guam?
6. Guadalcanal is found in which island group: Fiji, the Sandwich Islands, or the Solomon Islands?
7. Guam belongs to which island group: the Caroline Islands, the Mariana Islands, or the Marshall Islands?
8. Nauru has prospered because of which resource: copper, phosphate, or nickel?
9. Which country controls much of Polynesia: Britain, France, or Australia?
10. Which island is connected with the United States: Guam, Tuvalu, or Tahiti?

What Do You Think?

1. If a tribesman becomes a Christian, does he need to adopt Western styles of worship, or can he keep his tribal traditions, such as dances and music?
2. Papua New Guinea barred television broadcasts in 1986 (with fines up to $1 million for violations). The people demanded an end to the law in 1993. Do you think this kind of law is practical for Pacific countries?
3. Why did missionaries not always see true conversions to Christianity among the islanders?
4. Should Tonga and other undeveloped islands encourage tourism to bring in foreign money?

THE LAST FRONTIERS

The Lord planted in the human heart an insatiable curiosity that will never be quenched. Many places in God's vast universe remain to be studied and colonized.

He hath made every thing beautiful in his time: also he hath set the world in their heart, so that no man can find out the work that God maketh from the beginning to the end. (Eccles. 3:11)

During the twentieth century, modern technology opened three new frontiers for scientific study: Antarctica, the ocean depths, and the heavens. While scientists discovered a wealth of new knowledge, they also found new areas of competition for scarce resources and military advantage.

ANTARCTICA

The heavens are thine, the earth also is thine: as for the world and the fullness thereof, thou hast founded them. The north and the south thou hast created them. (Ps. 89:11-12)

At the bottom of the world is a remote region known as the **Antarctic.** The Antarctic Circle, located at $66^1/_2°$ S latitude, marks the boundary of the region. For at least one twenty-four-hour period each year, the sun never sets in "the land of the midnight sun."

Because sunlight in Antarctica is either very slanted or nonexistent, temperatures there are

Sundogs *appear in the sky as small suns on either side of the setting sun. The large halo around the sun is a* parhelic *circle. Both phenomena are caused by sunlight reflecting off ice crystals in the atmosphere.*

extremely cold. Huge packs of permanent floating ice defied all attempts at systematic exploration until the twentieth century.

In the open seas, icebergs can be a major hazard. **Icebergs** are jagged chunks of ice that have broken off, or "calved," from a glacier as it reached the sea. Icebergs have been measured as large as two hundred miles long, sixty miles wide, and a thousand feet deep. Because more than three-fourths of an iceberg lies hidden below the water, ships may crash into the underwater portion before the crew realizes the danger is there.

South of the Antarctic Circle is the forbidding continent of **Antarctica.** Technically, Antarctica is surrounded by three oceans—the Atlantic, Pacific, and Indian Oceans. Yet a band of polar water circling the continent is much colder and less salty than the subtropical waters next to it. A gigantic ice pack covers this band. Pieces of the pack that break off are called **ice floes.** The open water between floes is called a **lead.** In places, the ice extends as far as nine hundred miles from the coast.

Physical Geography

Antarctica is shaped like a pear. East (or Greater) Antarctica lies at the fat, rounded end. At the other end lies West (or Lesser) Antarctica. Dividing the two ends are the 1,900-mile-long **Transantarctic Mountains.**

East Antarctica

East Antarctica is a high plateau covered by a thick ice cap over a mile deep. In fact, the weight of the ice has pushed the land down to form a great basin that is 9,840 feet below sea level in one spot.

Hast thou entered into the treasures of the snow? or hast thou seen the treasures of the hail, which I have reserved against the time of trouble, against the day of battle and war? (Job 38:22-23)

The Antarctic Plateau is famous for its cold cyclonic storms that whirl almost endlessly from east to west. Gales can reach two hundred miles per hour. The average temperature of

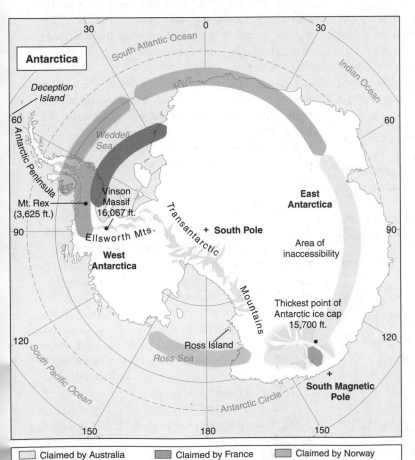

Antarctica

- Deception Island
- South Atlantic Ocean
- Indian Ocean
- Antarctic Peninsula
- Weddell Sea
- Mt. Rex (3,625 ft.)
- Vinson Massif 16,067 ft.
- Ellsworth Mts.
- Transantarctic Mountains
- West Antarctica
- + South Pole
- East Antarctica
- Area of inaccessibility
- Thickest point of Antarctic ice cap 15,700 ft.
- Ross Island
- Ross Sea
- South Pacific Ocean
- + South Magnetic Pole
- Antarctic Circle

Claimed by Australia
Claimed by Argentina
Claimed by Chile
Claimed by France
Claimed by New Zealand
Claimed by Norway
Claimed by United Kingdom

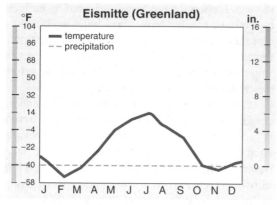

Eismitte (Greenland)

°F | in.
- temperature
- - - precipitation

The climate of Greenland's ice pack is similar to the climate of Antarctica.

An explorer stands among wind-blown sastrugi as he surveys the large, rocky nunatak.

the interior during the coldest months is -94°F (compared to -22°F on the coast).

The extreme cold of the interior prohibits life. Nothing lives here—not even a bush or an insect. However, the cold is a blessing. Because cold air cannot hold much moisture, the interior receives less than two inches of snow per year. The desert conditions prevent snow from building up and depleting the world's water level.

West Antarctica In West Antarctica the **Ross Sea** and **Weddell Sea** cut in on either side to form the neck of Antarctica's pear. Glaciers that flow into the Ross and Weddell Seas slide out onto the water to form solid **ice shelves.**

West Antarctica is mountainous rather than flat. The Ellsworth Mountains near the Weddell

The Ross Ice Shelf on the Ross Sea covers an area the size of France.

Sea—the highest mountains on the continent—peep up above the ice cap. Elsewhere, solitary mountains, called **nunataks,** stick up like rocky islands in an ice sea.

At the tip of West Antarctica is the **Antarctic Peninsula,** the most coveted piece of property on the continent. It is the only part of the continent that extends beyond the Antarctic Circle toward South America.

At the edge of this seeming desert, the coastal waters are teeming with life. Plankton forms the basis of the food chain. Small shrimplike krill and many different species of fish thrive in the ocean. Squid, octopus, whales, porpoises, seals, and dolphins are abundant. Penguins are the dominant birds.

Exploration

The ice-choked seas surrounding Antarctica are the stormiest known to man. Until the nineteenth century, the continent eluded discovery. Captain Cook circumnavigated the Antarctic region in 1773 in search of a fabled southern continent, but his ship could not penetrate the ice pack. In 1820, an American sealing ship, a Russian sealing ship, and an English sealing ship each claimed to be the first to sight Antarctica. Finally, in 1895, a Norwegian businessman named Henryk Johan Bull was the first to set foot on the continent.

The "heroic age" of exploration began in the twentieth century. On December 14, 1911, Roald Amundsen planted the Norwegian flag at the South Pole. At the same time, a British explorer named

Scott's Last Diary Entry

Scott set out for the South Pole on November 1, 1911. Five men reached the pole on January 18, but to their dismay they found a note saying that Amundsen had beat them. As they struggled back to the coast, they grew steadily weaker, carrying their own supplies on sleds because they had scorned the use of dogs. Even as their strength declined, they kept hauling thirty-five pounds of rock specimens among their gear. Two men had died by March 18. The last three men got within a few miles of supplies, but then a snowstorm struck. When searchers found their final camp, they discovered Scott's diary. He had scrawled these famous last words.

Thursday, March 29. Since the 21st we have had a continuous gale from the W.S.W. and S.W. We had fuel to make two cups of tea apiece and bare food for two days on the 20th. Every day we have been ready to start for our depot 11 miles away, but outside the door of the tent it remains a scene of whirling drift. I do not think we can hope for any better things now. We shall stick it out to the end, but we are getting weaker, of course, and the end cannot be far. It seems a pity, but I do not think I can write more.   —R. Scott.

Robert Scott was struggling to reach the site. He did reach it; however, his entire party perished on the return trip.

Other records followed. Admiral Richard Byrd flew a plane over the South Pole on his 1928-29 survey expedition. In 1958, Vivian Fuchs successfully crossed the 1,550-mile width of the continent.

International Cooperation and Disputes

Foreign powers began establishing bases on Antarctica in the 1940s. Once they started, no seafaring nation wanted to be left out. Scientists from the United States and other countries prevailed on their governments to reserve the earth's last great wilderness for pure science, unspoiled by the Cold War tensions. During an eighteen-month period from 1957 to 1958, twelve nations coordinated their efforts in building sixty scientific bases and in sharing all their findings. The following year twelve nations signed the Antarctic Treaty, agreeing to ban military bases and weapons testing on the continent, to freeze all land claims, to exchange all information freely, and to open all camps for inspection at any time. Many other nations later signed the treaty. In 1991 the "Antarctic Treaty Parties" extended the treaty indefinitely and agreed to ban mining for fifty years.

Scientists have studied all sorts of phenomena. Many of them are looking for evidence of rising world pollution. The discovery of an ozone "hole" above the Antarctic has raised fears that the atmosphere may be heating up. A warming of the earth could have serious consequences. More than 90 percent of the world's ice is locked in the ice cap of Antarctica. Were the ice cap to melt, the sea level around the world would rise two hundred feet, sinking many islands and every major coastal city. Such an event is apparently described in Revelation 16:20. An increase in heat from the sun may trigger the melting (Rev. 16:8-9).

Core samples and radio soundings provide tantalizing clues about what is under the ice cap. Extensive coal fields and mineral resources may lie under the ice, awaiting the development of economically feasible methods of mining. Some far-off nations have even set up sham research stations to ensure a right to participate in any bargaining over mining and land claims.

◎ SECTION REVIEW

1. What two large seas lie beside Antarctica's coasts?
2. What long, narrow peninsula extends from Antarctica?
3. What are ice shelves?
   ♀ Should the United States claim part of Antarctica?

THE OCEAN DEEP

He gathereth the waters of the sea together as an heap: he layeth up the depth in storehouses. (Ps. 33:7)

God created the deep (Gen. 1:2), broke it up in the great Flood (Gen. 7:11), and put boundaries on the new oceans and deeps (Job 38:8-11). For thousands of years the secrets of the deep have been hidden from human eyes. But new technology is finally allowing man to discover a whole new world of unusual life forms and valuable resources.

Undersea Landscape

The Bible says that God covered the foundations of the earth with the deep (Ps. 104:6). Only in the twentieth century did deep-sea explorers discover what this means. The continents are thick slabs sitting on a foundation of rock called *sima* (see page 20). The submerged edges of these slabs are called **continental shelves.** They slope gently down from the shore to a depth of about 650 feet. At the edge of the continental shelf, the continent drops off sharply. The steep sides of the continents, called **continental slopes,** descend to a depth of over two miles (about thirteen thousand feet). Here deep ocean basins stretch across the vast empty spaces between the continents.

Birds Who Wear Tuxedos

Penguins are curious birds whose dark backs and white fronts make them appear to be wearing tuxedos. These pudgy gentlemen look awkward on land as they waddle, and they cannot fly. But in water they are skilled acrobats, with flipper wings. They can even leap out of the water like flying fish or dolphins. They have to be fast. Catching fish is not easy, and eluding leopard seals and killer whales is even harder.

Antarctica's mainland has two species of penguins. The emperor penguin is the largest of all penguins, growing up to four feet high and weighing up to one hundred pounds. The Adélie penguin is named for the coast first claimed by France. A third species, the gentoo penguin, lives on islands along the Antarctic Peninsula.

Antarctica is not the only home of penguins. Over fifteen species exist, all in the Southern Hemisphere. Penguins live only in areas reached by Antarctic currents.

All penguins wear the same suit, but each species has a distinct head color, plume, and crest. King penguins have colorful cheeks that look like a beautiful sunset. They live on Macquarie Island, south of New Zealand. The Falkland Islands and South Georgia have two other species that are easily confused with gentoo and king penguins. Macaroni penguins have yellow-orange plumes that droop over their eyes, while rockhopper penguins display yellow tufts over their eyes. The blackfooted penguin has white-streaked sides and lives in South Africa. The fairy penguin in Australia is the smallest penguin, only one foot tall. The Humboldt penguin lives along the coasts of Peru and Chile next to the Humboldt Current. The Galápagos penguin lives the farthest north, near the cold currents that reach the equator at the Galápagos Islands.

(right) *An emperor penguin and its chick warm in the midnight sun near the Ekstrom Ice Shelf on the Weddell Sea, Antarctica.* (below) *A magellanic penguin swims at Sea Lion Island in the Falkland Islands.*

(left) *An Adélie penguin feeds its chick on Coronation Island in the South Orkney Islands, above the Antarctic Peninsula.* (below) *These macaroni penguins are incubating eggs on Livingston Island in the South Shetland Islands, near the Antarctic Peninsula.*

(right) *A gentoo penguin nests in Antarctica's South Shetland Islands.*

Features of the Ocean Floor

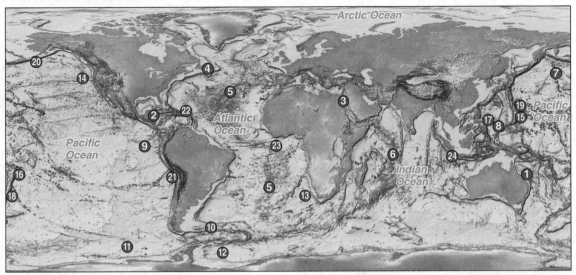

Continental Shelf Features
1. Great Barrier Reef
2. Belize Reef
3. Ras Muhammad Reef
4. Grand Banks

Undersea Mountains and Plateaus
5. Mid-Atlantic Ridge
6. Central Indian Ridge
7. Emperor Seamount Chain
8. Belau (guyot with reef)
9. Clambake I (deep-sea vents of Cocos Ridge)
10. Falkland Plateau

Undersea Plain Features
11. Amundsen Abyssal Plain
12. Weddell Abyssal Plain
13. Cape Basin
14. Mendocino Fracture Zone

Deepest Trenches	feet
15. Mariana Trench	36,198
16. Tonga Trench	35,433
17. Philippine Trench	32,995
18. Kermadec Trench	32,963
19. Bonin Trench	32,788

Other Trenches
20. Aleutian Trench
21. Peru-Chile Trench
22. Puerto Rico Trench
23. Romanche Gap
24. Java Trench

The sea creatures that mankind harvests live in the upper seven hundred feet of the ocean. This region is called the **photic zone** because there is enough light for photosynthesis. No plants grow below the photic zone. Some light filters down to two thousand feet—about the same amount of light that you see at dusk or on a starry night. This twilight region is called the *mesopelagic zone* (or midsea zone). Perpetual darkness reigns below that depth in the *bathypelagic zone* (or deep-sea zone). Here man has discovered some unusual fish. The angler fish, for example, has a light hanging in front of its mouth to attract prey.

The ocean floor consists primarily of deep **ocean basins,** which typically range from thirteen thousand to eighteen thousand feet deep. Soundings have uncovered a varied landscape, much more dramatic than the weathered landscape where people live.

Sediment from continental rivers and debris from landslides have caused a buildup at the base of the continental slopes. This buildup is known as the *continental rise.*

Like continents, the ocean basins have three major physical features: mountains, plateaus, and plains. The plains are known as **abyssal plains.** A few plateaus rise above the abyssal plains.

As you can see on the sea floor map, a number of deep canyons, called **trenches,** scar the ocean basins. The Pacific Ocean has more trenches than all the other oceans combined.

Undersea Surface Features

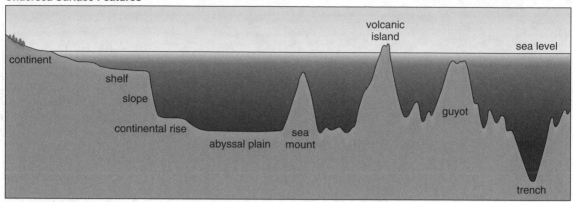

Less than 1 percent of the ocean floor descends below the ocean basin. The word *deep* refers to depths beyond eighteen thousand feet. The Milwaukee Deep, located in the Puerto Rico Trench, is the deepest point in the Atlantic. Can you find the deepest deep in the world?

Mountain ranges form along the **oceanic ridges.** Every ocean has ridges, but scientists have done the most studies on the Mid-Atlantic Ridge. This ridge of volcanic mountains divides the Atlantic Ocean in half. Occasionally the ridge rises above the surface to form islands. Iceland is such an island.

Isolated underwater volcanoes called **seamounts** dot the basins. Sometimes a new volcano breaks through the ocean surface, such as the island of Surtsey off the coast of Iceland.

Can you find the scarred areas on the ocean basin that are creased by numerous earthquake faults? These regions are called *fracture zones.* Sometimes hot springs, or **deep-sea vents,** spew hot lava and sulfur into the dark frigid waters.

Exploration

They that go down to the sea in ships, that do business in great waters; these see the works of the Lord, and his wonders in the deep. (Ps. 107:23-24)

Since even the best diver can hold his breath for only about two minutes, ancient exploration of the ocean was limited to about one hundred feet. Visits to the deep were not possible until the advent of modern pressurized crafts and suits.

Two Americans, William Beebe and Otis Barton, were the first humans to observe life below the photic zone, using a bathysphere (a steel ball with quartz windows) in 1930. Auguste Piccard of Switzerland designed an elongated bathyscaph, which in 1954 became the first vessel to reach the ocean basins.

Descent into Mariana Trench

The Mariana Trench is the deepest trench in the world. The deepest place in the trench, called the Challenger Deep, is 35,800 feet below sea level. It plunges a mile deeper beneath the sea than Mt. Everest rises above it. The first people to descend into this spot were Jacques Piccard, son of the engineer who invented the bathyscaph, and Don Walsh of the U.S. Navy. The trip took nine hours. During their twenty minutes on the bottom, they spotted a flounder, which proved that fish can survive the tremendous pressures of the cold, dark deep.

Sea Creatures at Each Level

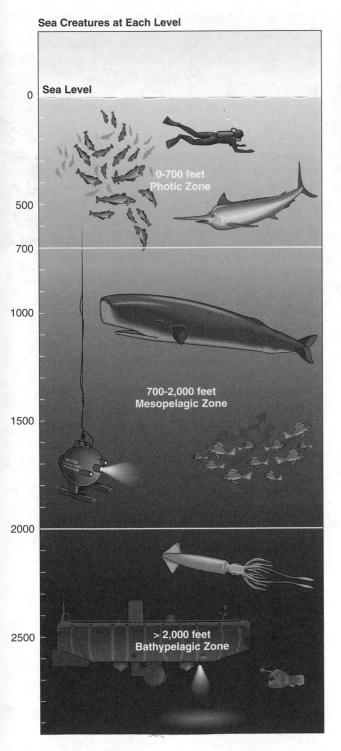

Sea Level

0

500

700

1000

1500

2000

2500

**0–700 feet
Photic Zone**

**700–2,000 feet
Mesopelagic Zone**

**> 2,000 feet
Bathypelagic Zone**

The American submersible Turtle *explores the ocean depths. The crew uses a mechanical arm to take photographs and to gather samples from the sea floor.*

Jacques Cousteau invented the Aqua-Lung in 1943, which allowed him to make deep dives. He later built experimental stations on the continental shelf.

Unlike the bathyscaphs, which were towed by cables, newer submersibles can move on their own power. Some unmanned crafts are operated by remote control and televise images to the surface. *Argo,* for example, discovered the wreck of the *Titanic* in 1985. Other crafts are manned. *Alvin,* for example, explored Clambake I, the first deep-sea vent to be found.

Disputed Waters

Almost every speck of dry land on earth has been claimed by one nation or other, but claims on water have always stirred controversy. The United States supports *freedom of the seas,* the belief that any nation can freely fish and trade on the ocean. But this position has become complicated. Modern high-tech ships compete for a limited supply of fish to feed the growing world population. The discovery of offshore oil has given waters a value they never had before.

During the seventeenth century, seagoing nations developed the concept of **territorial waters,** the right of a nation to exclude ships from other nations from a three- to six-mile-wide strip of water along its coast. Ships of other nations enjoyed the "right of free passage" only if they came in peace to trade. Beyond the territorial waters were the **high seas,** open to any vessel.

In the twentieth century, nations began extending their territorial waters to exorbitant distances from the shores. These claims often overlapped the valid claims of neighboring countries. One country's refusal to recognize the claims of another sometimes led to shooting. In 1958 nearly ninety nations agreed to limit territorial waters to a twelve-mile *contiguous zone.* However, narrow straits, such as the Strait of Gibraltar, were to remain open. Each nation was permitted to mine oil fields on its adjacent continental shelf, but the ocean basins were to remain free of claims. Disputes continued because some did not want to comply.

The United Nations drafted the Law of the Sea Treaty (LOST) in 1982 to address these problems. The treaty recognizes the previous twelve-mile zone and an additional two-hundred-mile **exclusive economic zone** (EEZ). Each nation that signs the treaty has exclusive rights to fish and drill for oil in its EEZ. The treaty went into effect in 1995 after sixty nations signed. But the United States balked because the treaty would undermine U.S. sovereignty. For example, "island nations" can claim an EEZ around their island possessions, but nations on a continent cannot.

Glowing nacreous clouds *float eighteen miles above Antarctica in the ozone layer of the upper stratosphere.*

outer space. But space flight has introduced new problems. Nations now have another "border" to guard from enemy warplanes, missiles, and atomic bombs.

The heavens declare the glory of God; and the firmament sheweth his handywork. (Ps. 19:1)

The Atmosphere

Psalm 147:8 says that God "covereth the heaven with clouds." This part of the heavens—the atmosphere—extends about six hundred miles above the earth. It has various layers defined by differences in temperature, pressure, and gases.

Lower Atmosphere The lower nine miles of the atmosphere, the **troposphere,** contain the air we breathe and the clouds that water the earth. The temperature drops about 3.5 degrees for every thousand-foot increase in altitude. (See lapse rate on page 51.) God filled the troposphere with just the right mixture of gases for breathing—78 percent nitrogen, 21 percent oxygen, and 1 percent other gases, including carbon dioxide.

Upper Atmosphere The upper atmosphere consists of three regions. The *stratosphere* extends from nine to thirty-five miles above the earth.

◎ SECTION REVIEW

1. Name the three ocean layers based on the amount of light received.
2. What are the three major features that the sea floor shares with dry land?
3. What is the deepest trench in the world?
   ❓ Should the United States sign the Law of the Sea Treaty?

THE HEAVENS

For thousands of years, the grandeur of the night sky has thrilled human observers. In the twentieth century man began to realize his dreams of exploring the heavens, both the atmosphere and

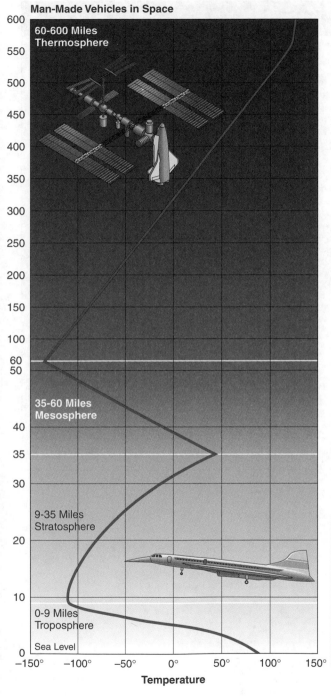

Man-Made Vehicles in Space

60-600 Miles
Thermosphere

35-60 Miles
Mesosphere

9-35 Miles
Stratosphere

0-9 Miles
Troposphere

Sea Level

Temperature

Unlike the troposphere, the stratosphere increases in temperature with altitude. This region contains most of the *ozone layer.* The *mesosphere* extends to about sixty miles from the earth. This region has decreasing temperatures; the coldest place in the atmosphere occurs at the top of the mesosphere. The *thermosphere,* extending to about six hundred miles from the earth, is so named because it retains warmth from direct sunlight. Its inner half, the *ionosphere,* protects the earth from harmful radiation and meteors. The outer half, the *exosphere,* reaches the limits of our atmosphere, where particles can escape into outer space.

Star Wars

In 1962 the first satellites transmitted television and telephone signals across the Atlantic. Since then satellites have become critical to world communications. High-tech spy satellites and military communications have given the United States a new edge in battle, which it wants to keep. Conservatives hope to build a defense system that will protect the United States and its allies from missiles. Space rights have become a volatile issue in international relations. Each nation can claim the right to limit airplane flights over its territory. But how high up does this right go? Can a country exclude satellites twenty thousand miles away in space? Can a country use its air rights to restrict radio waves or pollutants?

◎ SECTION REVIEW

1. How are the four main layers of the atmosphere distinguished?
2. In which layer is the ozone layer?
3. In which layer is the ionosphere?

💡 Based on how nations have solved disputes over territorial waters, how should they resolve disputes over space rights?

In the News

The Ozone Hole

As the earth revolves around the sun, a delicate blanket of atmosphere protects the earth's inhabitants from much of the sun's deadly radiation. Particularly important is the ozonosphere, so named because of the relative abundance of ozone. Ozone is a rare form of oxygen in which each molecule contains three atoms rather than the usual two.

The ozonosphere stretches from an altitude of six to thirty miles, but only six molecules in a million are actually ozone. Because air is so thin at that altitude, the total ozone would form a layer less than one inch thick were it brought to sea-level pressure.

As shortwave ultraviolet radiation from the sun passes through the oxygen in the ozonosphere, it produces ozone. Other radiation of a slightly higher wavelength then breaks down the unstable ozone. These chemical reactions help absorb some of the sun's dangerous radiation before it reaches the earth.

Recently governments have become concerned because laboratory experiments have shown that ozone is destroyed by nitrogen oxide from car exhaust and by Freon used in refrigeration and in aerosol cans. In 1985 scientists noticed that dramatic changes were taking place in the ozone layer above Antarctica. They discovered an "ozone hole" that appeared each spring and grew until November, when it started to shrink. The size of the hole steadily increased, raising fears that it was only the beginning of a worldwide catastrophe.

In the Montreal Protocol of 1987, ninety-three nations agreed to regulate or ban ozone-destroying chemicals and to search for less damaging alternatives. Citizens of the United States and other nations began paying hundreds of dollars to change their air conditioning systems. The estimated cost to the world economy could exceed four trillion dollars.

Yet the cause and significance of the hole is still uncertain. For one thing, no similar "ozone hole" occurs in the Arctic, even though continental air currents carry pollutants from temperate regions into the upper atmosphere. Theories about the culprits causing the ozone hole include volcanic eruptions, springtime upwelling of the air, and increased chemicals in the atmosphere (fluorocarbons, chlorine, and other trace gases). No one explanation is satisfactory. Is the hole a recent problem, or have holes appeared periodically throughout history due to weather cycles that we know nothing about?

💡 Should the government require families, such as yours, to pay large sums of money to use new substances because of an unproven environmental concern? Should taxpayers fund environmental research in Antarctica?

REVIEW

29

Can You Define These Terms?

iceberg	continental shelf	trench	territorial waters
ice floe	continental slope	deep	high seas
lead	photic zone	oceanic ridge	exclusive economic zone
ice shelf	ocean basin	seamount	troposhere
nunatak	`abyssal plain	deep-sea vent	

Can You Locate These Natural Features?

Antarctic	Transantarctic Mountains	Weddell Sea
Antarctica	Ross Sea	Antarctic Peninsula

How Much Do You Remember?

1. Describe two major differences between East Antarctica and West Antarctica.
2. How is an iceberg formed? an ice floe?
3. Which nations claim part of Antarctica? Why has the United States made no claims?
4. How thick is the Antarctic Ice Cap?
5. Why is it a blessing that the polar regions have very dry climates?
6. Based on a 1958 agreement, how far do territorial waters extend? Why has the United States refused to recognize a two-hundred-mile exclusive economic zone?

What Do You Think?

1. Other than raising the sea level drastically, how do you think the melting of the Antarctic ice would affect the world?
2. Some dry countries would like to tow large icebergs to their shores to provide fresh water. What difficulties can they expect?
3. Should Antarctica be open to tourism or remain a wilderness?
4. In what ocean was the first deep-sea vent found?

Cumulative Review

1. Name the seven continents. For each continent, give the largest mountain range, longest river, and largest lake.
2. Name the four oceans and the ten largest islands in the world.
3. Define primary, secondary, and tertiary industries. Which industry is most prominent in a developed country? in an undeveloped country?
4. List the eight culture regions of the world. For each region, give the most populous country, the largest country in size, the biggest city, the most-spoken language family, and the most common religion.
5. Pick the five most interesting countries that you studied. For each country give one important land feature, a famous man-made structure, and a famous person or a major event.
6. What country is most like the United States? List the basic elements of a culture region and show how your choice is similar to the United States in each area. Give the three best alternatives to your choice of a country, and explain why yours is the best choice.

Glossary of Commonly Used Terms

A

Absolute monarchy Rule by a monarch who has complete control of the government

Acculturation The process of adopting foreign values and practices

Alloy A mixture of two or more metals

Alluvium Sediment deposited by flowing water

Alpine zone The zone above the timberline that is too cold for trees to grow

Animism Religious beliefs that ascribe spiritual powers to animals and plants

Anthracite coal A hard coal with a high carbon content that burns with little smoke

Aquifer A layer of underground rock that yields water

Arable Able to be cultivated

Archipelago A large group of islands

Arid Lacking moisture

Atmosphere The layer of gases that surrounds the earth

Atoll A ring-shaped island formation built of coral on the rim of an undersea volcano

Autocrat A ruler with unlimited authority

Autonomous republic A self-governing republic

B

Barrier island An island that lies near the coast and is created by silt deposits

Bauxite The principle ore of aluminum

Bight A large bay formed by a long, curving coast

Biome A large geographic area that contains a particular group of plants and animals and has a specific physical environment

Bituminous coal Soft coal that occurs frequently and is of varying quality

Bog Water-soaked area covered with organic materials, particularly mosses

Buddhism An Eastern religion founded by Buddha that offers release from the suffering of the world through meditation and following the Eight-fold Path

Buffer state A neutral state between two rivals that serves to prevent conflict

C

Capital Money used to build or operate a business or industry

Capitalism A free market economy in which anyone may go into business in an attempt to make a profit; most businesses are privately owned instead of government owned.

Cartography The art of mapmaking

Cash crop A crop raised specifically for sale

Census An official counting of a population

Cirque A steep hollow in a mountain made by glacial erosion

Civil war A war between factions or regions of a nation

Climate The usual temperature, precipitation, and wind conditions of a certain area

Coalition government A government formed by the joining of two or more parties

Collective farm A large farm in a Communist country on which many farmers cooperate to meet production quotas set by the government

Condensation The changing of water vapor into liquid

Confluence The point at which two bodies of water join

Confucianism A Chinese philosophy that teaches harmony through proper treatment of others

Conifer A tree that produces its seed in a cone

Constitutional monarchy (or limited monarchy) A government that includes a ruling monarch whose powers are strictly limited by law

Continental divide A chain of mountains that divide the flow of river systems between oceans

Continental island An island, usually large and high, formed near a continent out of the same landmass

Convection precipitation Precipitation that occurs when an air mass warms and rises rapidly, then cools to the dew point as it gains altitude

Cordillera A chain of mountains

Core The central portion of the earth that lies below the mantle

Coup A sudden, illegal overthrow of a government by a military leader or government official (from *coup d'etat*)

Creole A language that mixes French and African words and is spoken by Haitians; or a person with Spanish ancestry born in South America

Crude birthrate The number of people born each year per one thousand people in the population

Crude death rate The number of people that die each year per one thousand people in the population

Crust The solid outer part of the earth

Cultural boundary Boundary drawn to separate people of differing cultures

Culture A people's way of life, including their political, economic, religious, social, intellectual, and artistic practices and beliefs

Cyclonic precipitation Precipitation that occurs along the line where two air masses meet

Cyrillic A modified Greek alphabet used for Slavic languages

D

Deciduous Plants that shed their leaves before a period of dormancy

Deforestation The cutting down and clearing of trees

Democracy Government in which people rule themselves

Demography The study of population characteristics

Desalination Removal of salt from water

Desert A dry area with little vegetation

Desertification The changing of arable land into desert

Developed country A country that has a wide range of industries that take full advantage of the people's skills

Developing country A country whose industries do not fully take advantage of its people's skills

Dialect A regional variety of a language

Dictatorship Rule by a person or group with the authority of military strength

Dissident A citizen who openly disagrees with Communist government policies

Diversify To give variety

Doldrums A permanent low-pressure area along or near the equator caused by the rising of warm air

Drumlin An elongated, smooth hill made of glacial debris

E

El Niño A slight warming of the water over a wide region of the Pacific that periodically affects the earth's climate

Empire Lands gained outside the national borders of a country

Equator The imaginary line that divides the earth into the Northern and Southern Hemispheres

Erosion The natural breakdown and removal of materials on the earth's surface

Esker A long, winding, narrow ridge of sand and gravel, probably deposited by a stream flowing in or under glacial ice

Evaporation The process of water changing into water vapor

Evergreen A tree that remains green throughout the year

F

Fault A crack in the earth's surface where two pieces of land have moved in different directions

Federal government The sharing of government power between a national government and a second level of government such as that of states

Federated republic A representative government that is also a federal government

Fertile Rich in nutrients that aid plant growth

Fold A bend in a portion of the earth's crust caused by pressure

Fossil fuel Remains of once-living organisms that can be used as a source of energy; includes coal, petroleum, and natural gas

Frontal precipitation Same as cyclonic precipitation

G

Gap An opening through a mountain

Geography The detailed study of the earth, especially its surface

Geometric boundary Boundary usually drawn as a straight line to connect specific points or to follow a line of latitude or longitude

Geothermal energy Power derived from heated water and steam beneath the earth's surface

Glacier A large mass of ice that forms at high elevations and flows downward

Grassland Region with plenteous grass but few trees

Great circle Any imaginary line that can be drawn around the earth to cut it into equal hemispheres

Gross Domestic Product (GDP) The value of all the goods and services produced by a country during a year

Groundwater Water that has seeped into the earth's crust and is held below the surface of the earth

Growing season The time from the last killing frost of spring until the first killing frost of fall

Gyre The circular pattern of ocean currents

H

Hemisphere Either of the two equal parts of the earth, as divided by the equator or a meridian

High island Volcanic island that usually rises above the sea, displaying hills and mountains

Hinduism The prevalent religion of India that emphasizes reincarnation and a supreme being with many forms

Homogenous Of the same kind; not varied

Horse latitudes Permanent high-pressure areas around 30° latitude caused by descending cold air

Humidity The amount of water vapor in the air

Humus A soil ingredient produced by the slow decomposition of leaves and other organic materials

Hydroelectricity Electricity produced by flowing water

Hydrologic cycle (water cycle) A cycle whereby water evaporates from oceans, lakes, the soil, and so on, to form clouds that in turn precipitate water to the earth

Hydrosphere All the water that exists on or around the earth

I

Iceberg A large chunk of floating ice that has broken off the edge of a glacier

Ice floe A large, flat sheet of floating ice that has formed from seawater

Illegal alien Foreigner who has entered a country illegally

Immigration The movement of foreigners into a nation

Imperialism The acquiring of an empire

Industrial country A country in which the majority of people work in secondary or tertiary industries rather than in agriculture

Infant mortality rate The number of infants per one thousand live births that die before their first birthday

International date line An imaginary line near 180° longitude to the east of which the calendar date is one day behind that to the west

Islam A Middle Eastern religion founded by Muhammad that emphasizes good works

K

Karst An area of water-carved limestone formations, such as caverns and rugged peaks

L

Landform One feature of the land, such as a hill, peninsula, or mesa

Landlocked Completely surrounded by land

Landscape All the land features that appear in a view of an area of land

Language family A group of languages that share many common characteristics

Lapse rate The rate of decrease in temperature with increase in altitude

Latitude Distance north or south of the equator measured in degrees

Leaching The dissolving of soil minerals by water and removal downward through the soil

Leeward Away from the wind; the direction opposite to that from which the wind comes

Lignite Brown coal with a high moisture content

Literacy The ability to read and write

Literacy rate The percentage of the adult population of a country who are literate

Lithosphere The area of solid matter on the surface of the earth

Longitude Distance east or west of the prime meridian measured in degrees

Low island A coral island that does not stand high above the water

M

Malaria An infectious disease spread by the Anopheles mosquito and common in wet, tropical countries

Mangrove A tropical tree with stiltlike roots that grows in dense thickets along swamps

Mantle The portion of the earth's interior lying between the crust and the core

Map projection A method of drawing features of the earth's surface on a flat map

Market People or businesses interested in buying a product

Marsh A wetland area with standing water, grasses, and small water plants

Martial law Law enforced by military troops

Mass communication Communication intended to reach a large number of people

Megalopolis A combination of several metropolitan areas that have grown together

Meridian A line of longitude

Mesothermal Descriptive of temperate climate regions

Mestizo Latin Americans of mixed European and Indian blood

Metal A substance that can conduct electricity and is usually shiny, malleable, and ductile

Metropolitan area A city and its outlying suburbs

Microthermal Cold or polar climate regions

Migration Movement of people from one country to another or from region to region within a country

Mineral A solid, naturally occurring, inorganic material with a definite chemical composition and crystal structure

Monadnock An isolated granite mountain

Monarchy A government with a hereditary ruler

Monsoon A seasonal wind caused by the heating and cooling of large land masses

Moraine An accumulation of stones, sand, or other debris along the side or foot of a glacier

Mosque Islamic place of worship

Mulatto A person with mixed European and African ancestry

Multinational state People of more than one nation united in one country

Muslim A follower of Islam

N

Nation A group of people with a common heritage, culture, and homeland

Nation state A nation with its own established government and political boundaries

Natural boundary Boundary drawn along prominent landscape features such as coastlines, rivers, and mountain ranges

Natural increase (rate of) The rate of population increase found by subtracting the number of deaths in a population from the number of births

Natural resource Any useful substance that can be found in the earth

Neutral Not joining either side in a conflict or war

Nomadic herding The wandering of stock and herdsmen from place to place to find new pastures

O

Oasis A watered, fertile area in the desert

Ocean current Basic path of water flow within an ocean

Oceanic ridge An undersea mountain range found along the edges of some tectonic plates

Orographic precipitation Precipitation that occurs as an air mass moves upward over mountains or mountain ranges

Ozone A form of oxygen that appears in the upper stratosphere and helps to shield the earth from harmful ultraviolet rays

P

Pacific Rim The countries that touch the Pacific Ocean

Pacific Ring of Fire A string of volcanoes that encircle the Pacific Ocean

Parallel A line of latitude

Parliamentary government A representative government led by a parliament and prime minister

Per capita GDP The Gross Domestic Product of a country divided by the number of people in the country

Permafrost Ground that remains permanently frozen even though the top few inches may thaw during a short summer

Petrochemical Chemicals obtained from petroleum refining processes

Petroleum Liquid fossil fuel

Physiological density The population of a country divided by the area of available land in the country

Plantation agriculture A large-scale agricultural operation, employing and housing many workers who help produce one product, such as rubber or sugar

Plates (tectonic) Large broken sections of the earth's crust

Political boundary Boundary that divides the territory of one country from that of another

Population density The population of a country divided by its area to reveal the average number of people per square mile or kilometer in the country

Portage Land routes used by traders to carry their boats and supplies around river obstacles

Prairie Rolling plains with high grasses

Precipitation Any form of moisture that falls from the atmosphere, such as rain, hail, snow, and sleet

Primary industry Work that makes natural resources available for use, such as agriculture, mining, and fishing

Prime meridian The meridian passing through Greenwich, England, which serves as the base line for determining longitude

Puppet ruler A leader who takes orders from another country or regime

R

Rain forest Dense forests found in tropical or temperate areas with heavy precipitation

Rainshadow Area opposite the windward side of a mountain that usually receives little precipitation

Raw material A material used in making manufactured items

Referendum A process that allows people to vote directly on new laws without going through legislators

Reincarnation A belief in a constant cycle of birth and death; each person supposedly lives one life after another

Relative humidity The percent of moisture the air is holding compared to the amount that it could hold at a given temperature

Relief The different heights and depths of a surface or region

Renewable resource Energy from sources, such as the sun, wind, rivers, and tides, which are unlimited in supply

Republic A government characterized by a representative system and operated according to a constitution

Reservation A portion of land set aside by the federal or state government for American Indians

Retail business A business that sells goods to the general public, usually in a small quantity

Revolution The orbit of the earth around the Sun

Ribbon development Building towns, farms, and industries along a narrow band of good land

River basin All the land drained by a river and its tributaries

Rogue nation A nation that ignores fundamental principles of international relations and uses any means to increase its power

S

Savanna The vegetation of tropical areas with a long dry season; displays grasses and scattered trees that are drought resistant

Sea A partially enclosed arm of the ocean

Secondary industry Manufacturing industries that produce products from raw materials or from manufactured materials

Sediment Particles of sand, silt, and clay produced by the weathering of rock

Shamanism The animistic folk religion of South Korea

Sharia The ancient religious law of Islam

Shintoism A Japanese religion promoting worship of many gods

Slash-and-burn agriculture The cutting and burning of a vegetation area to provide fields for temporary use; also called shifting agriculture

Sorghum A type of grass often cultivated for its grain, as a forage crop, or as a source of syrup

Specialized farming The raising of only one crop or one type of stock

Steppe A rolling grassland area, particularly of Cental Asia and eastern Europe

Stratosphere A region of the earth's atmosphere between the troposphere and mesosphere

Sublimation The process of changing ice directly into water vapor or water vapor directly into ice

Subsistence farming Agriculture that supplies only the basic food and material needs of the farmer and his family

Suburb A residential community outside city limits

Swamp Wetland area of standing water in which large trees grow

T

Taiga High latitude evergreen forests such as those in Canada and Siberia

Taoism Religion of China that promotes belief in two matched forces called *yin* and *yang*

Tariff Import or export tax

Technology The application of science for industrial purposes

Tectonic activity The movement of the earth's crustal plates and the resulting seismic and volcanic activity

Temperate zones The middle latitudes with seasonal changes caused by nearly direct sunlight half of each year

Terracing The building of level ridges along hillsides or mountainsides to reduce erosion and provide level areas for cultivation

Tertiary industry A service industry involving the distribution of goods and services rather than the manufacture of products

Thermosphere The uppermost layer of the earth's atmosphere

Till Deep fertile soil left by glaciers

Timberline The altitude of a mountain system at which trees do not grow

Topographic map A map that shows the topography of an area

Topography The shape and elevation of the land features of an area

Topsoil The surface layer of soil containing the most humus

Totalitarian government A government that totally controls the affairs of a country and limits the freedoms of its citizens

Trade Buying and selling between countries

Trade winds The common northeasterly winds of tropical regions

Transitional zone An area that lies between two other regions and has characteristics of both

Transpiration The giving off of moisture through the surface of the leaves of plants

Transportation network A system of transportation routes that links many points of a region with each other

Tribalism Strong identity with and loyalty to a tribe

Tributary A river that flows into and feeds another river

Tropics The latitude zone lying between the tropic of Cancer and the tropic of Capricorn with warm temperatures caused by direct sunlight

Troposphere The lowest layer of the atmosphere where continual changes occur in temperature, pressure, wind, humidity, and precipitation

Truck farming The raising and selling of vegetables and fruits for their special uses

Tsetse fly An African fly that spreads sleeping sickness

Tsunami A seismic sea wave

Tundra The vegetation regions of cold climates displaying little vegetation other than mosses, lichens, and similar small plants

Typhoon Name given to hurricanes that occur over the waters near eastern Asia

U

Uniformitarianism The belief that only those forces that are presently acting on the earth have shaped the earth in the past

Urbanization The movement of people from rural areas to cities and the growth of cities

V

Vegetation The plants in an area or region

Village A small group of dwellings in an isolated area

W

Wadi Usually dry streambeds in desert areas

Watershed An area of land that drains into a certain river or river system

Water table The level below which the ground is saturated with water

Weathering The degenerative process that contributes to the breaking up and alteration of rock materials

Wetland An area of stagnant water, such as a swamp, marsh, or bog

Wholesale business A business that sells goods in quantity to be sold by other businesses

Windward Into the wind or the direction from which the wind is blowing

Y

Yellow fever An infectious tropical disease transmitted by mosquitoes

Index

Index

Index

Index

Index

Index

Photo Credits

The following agencies and individuals have furnished materials to meet the photographic needs of this textbook. We wish to express our gratitude to them for their important contribution.

Phil Adams
Alabama Bureau of Tourism & Travel
Alaska Division of Tourism
Jeffrey Alford
Suzanne Altizer
American Iron & Steel
Ward Andersen
Aramco World Magazine
Argentina National Tourist Office
Arizona Office of Tourism
Asia Access
Bill Bachman
Chris Barton
Bob Bell
Alan Benoit
Tim Berrey
Mehmet Biber
Bob Jones University (BJU) Press Photo
  Collection
Mike Booher
H. Bradt
Dennis Bruckner
D. Donne Bryant Stock Photography Agency
George R. Buckley
Jim Buerer
Michele Burgess
California Division of Tourism
Canadian Government Office of Tourism
B. W. Carper
Maxine Cass
Bernard Chadenet
Charleston Area Convention & Visitors Bureau
Chicago Convention & Tourism Bureau
Kindra Clineff
George R. Collins
Consulate General of Japan, Atlanta,
  Georgia
Jeanne Conte
Corel Corporation
Creation Science Foundation
Danish Tourist Board
Terry M. Davenport
Beth Davidow
Grace Davies Photography
Tui De Roy
Naomi Duguid
Duke Power
Craig Duncan
EROS Data Center
Earth Satellite Corporation/Science Photo
  Library
Eastern National
Tor Eigeland
David Else
Victor Englebert
Jane Faircloth
Farm Bureau Management Corporation
Dave Fisher
Gene Fisher
Thomas R. Fletcher

J. A. Franklin
Winston Fraser
Richard Frear
Kenneth Frederick
Free China Review
Freer Gallery of Art
Carson Fremont
French Embassy Press & Information Division
French Government Tourist Office
Robert Fried
Andre Gallant
Georgia Department of Trade & Industry
GeoSystems Global Corporation
German Information Center
Penni Gladstone
Glen Canyon National Recreation Area
Joe Golden
James Gordon
Gospel Fellowship Association
Gospel Furthering Fellowship
Bob Grant
Thomas Gray
Greenville County Library
Yosef Hadar
Allen Hagood
Hammond, Inc.
Jim Hargis
Robert Holmes
Honda of America Manufacturing, Inc.
Edwin Huffman
Idaho Department of Commerce
Indiana Tourism
International Society for Educational
  Information, Inc.
Israel Ministry of Tourism
Italian Tourist Agency
Kenneth Jensen
Brian D. Johnson
Sivasankar Kumar Kande
Kansas Film Commission
Tim Keesee
William Keller
Stephen Kirkpatrick
Jason Lauré
D. Lazaro
Library of Congress
Louisiana Department of Culture, Recreation
  & Tourism
Louisiana Office of Tourism
Malaysian Tourism Promotion Board
Mammoth Cave National Park
Fred Mang, Jr.
Juca Martins
Massachusetts Office of Travel & Tourism
Jim McGuire
Jerry McKenney
Metropolitan Museum of Art
Mexican Government Tourism Office
Michigan Travel Bureau
Douglas R. Miller
Minnesota Office of Tourism
John Mitchell
Moscow Images & Recording (MIR) Agency
John Moss
David Muenker, Muenker Media
Nasco

National Aeronautics & Space Administration
  (NASA)
National Archives
National Oceanic & Atmospheric
  Administration (NOAA)
National Park Service
James D. Nations
New Brunswick Department of Tourism
State of New Hampshire, Office of Travel &
  Tourism Development
New York Convention & Visitors Bureau
New Zealand Tourism Board
John Nolan
North Carolina Travel & Tourism
Northern Territory Tourist Commission
Ohio Historical Society
Oregon Tourism Commission
Oriental Institute of the University of Chicago
Christine Osborne Pictures
Pacific Garden Mission
Pana-Vue
Embassy of Papua New Guinea
Ravi Kumar Pasupuleti
Penguin/Corbis-Bettmann
Walter Persegati
Photo Disc, Inc.
James Pickerell
Dan Polin
Portuguese National Tourist Office
Charles Preitner
Promotion Australia
Wade K. Ramsey
Glenn Randall
Reuters/Corbis-Bettmann
Ed Richards
Franklin D. Roosevelt Library
The Roving Tortoise
Royal Canadian Mounted Police
Simon Russell
Mike Sample
Peter Sanders Photography
Kevin Schafer Photography
Jay Schug Photography
Eugene G. Schulz
Tomas Sennett
Kay Shaw Photography
Bob Shelton
Steve Shimek
South African Consulate General
South Dakota Tourism
Tom Stack
Steve Strike
Ann Swengel
Patrick Syder
Ron Tagliapietra
Texas Oil Company
Transparencies Inc.
Travel Montana
United States Army
United States Department of Interior, Bureau
  of Reclamation
United States Geological Society (U.S.G.S.)
  Photo Library
United States Navy
Unusual Films
Vermont Department of Tourism

Victorian Tourism Commission
John A. Visser
Visuals Unlimited
Ward's Natural Science Establishment, Inc.
Washington D.C. Convention & Visitors Association
Washington State Tourism Division
Wei Family
Nik Wheeler
Wisconsin Dells Visitor & Convention Bureau
Ray Witlin
World Bank
Worldwide Slides
Wyoming Division of Tourism
Xinhua News Agency
Yellowstone National Park
Zion National Park

Cover: World Bank (lady in foreground); Kenneth Frederick (Neuschwanstein Castle); Jeffrey Alford/Asia Access (rice terraces); World Bank, by Edwin Huffman (Philippine girl); Zion National Park, by Allen Hagood (natural arch)

Title Pages: Terry M. Davenport ii(top left); World Bank, by Yosef Hadar ii(top right, bottom left); French Government Tourist Office ii(bottom middle); Chris Barton ii(bottom right); World Bank, by Spidle iii(top)

Contents Page: Corel Corporation v(background)

Reference to Maps Pages: Dan Polin vi-vii(background)

Pronunciation Guide Page: Corel Corporation viii(background)

Poem Page: Jay Schug Photography ix(background)

Unit I Opener: George R. Collins x, x-1(background), 1(top right); Brian D. Johnson 1(top left)

Chapter 1: George R. Collins 2; courtesy of The Complete Encyclopedia of Illustration, by J.G. Heck, published by Gramercy Books 4; Unusual Films 9; U.S.G.S. Photo Library 12, 15

Chapter 2: George R. Collins 17; Photo Disc, Inc. 18(bottom); Jim Hargis 18(top); National Park Service 19, 34(top); Corel Corporation 21, 30; Ron Tagliapietra 23(top); Nasco 23(bottom); U.S.G.S. Photo Library 24; Stephen Kirkpatrick 27, 28(top), 29(middle, right); Chicago Convention & Tourism Bureau 28(bottom); Louisiana Office of Tourism 29(left); EROS Data Center 32(top); Ward's Natural Science Establishment, Inc. 32(bottom); New Brunswick Department of Tourism 35

Chapter 3: NASA 37; Photo Disc, Inc. 40; B. W. Carper 49; Brian D. Johnson 52(all), 54(top); Corel Corporation 54(bottom left), 55; Terry M. Davenport 54(bottom right)

Unit II Opener: World Bank, by Yosef Hadar 58(left); World Bank, by James Pickerell 58(right); Farm Bureau Management Corp. 58-59(background); World Bank, by Bernard Chadenet 59

Chapter 4: Photo Disc, Inc. 60; Jerry McKenney 61(left); World Bank, by Yosef Hadar 61(right), 63(bottom); World Bank, by Ray Witlin 63(top); World Bank 66, 79; American Iron & Steel 67(top); Metropolitan Museum of Art 67(bottom); B. W. Carper 68(left); George R. Collins 68(right), 75; Texas Oil Company 69(top); Library of Congress 69(bottom); National Archives 70; Honda of America Manufacturing, Inc. 72; Jeanne Conte 73; Duke Power 74(top); U.S. Department of Interior, Bureau of Reclamation 74(bottom); Unusual Films 77; Free China Review 82

Chapter 5: Robert Holmes 86; World Bank, by Huffman 87(left, right); Gospel Fellowship Association 87(middle); World Bank, by Ray Witlin 91; John Nolan 93; Ward Andersen 96; French Embassy Press & Information Division 98; Mehmet Biber/Aramco World Mag. 100; Unusual Films, courtesy of Wei Family 101; Unusual Films 102; World Bank 103, 106; Creation Science Foundation 108(top); Corel Corporation 108(bottom); Aramco World Magazine 109;. Tim Keesee 111(top); New York Convention & Visitors Bureau 111(bottom); U.S. Navy 112

Unit III Opener: George R. Collins 114-15(background); Michigan Travel Bureau 115(top); George R. Buckley 115(middle); Terry M. Davenport 115(bottom)

Chapter 6: New York Convention & Visitors Bureau 116, 127, 129; George R. Collins 118, 119(top), 136, 139(top); Massachusetts Office of Travel & Tourism, by Kindra Clineff 119(bottom); Worldwide Slides 120; Robert Holmes 121; State of New Hampshire, Office of Travel & Tourism Development, by Bob Grant 122; Ron Tagliapietra 123(top), 125, 137; Vermont Department of Tourism & Marketing 123(bottom), 124; Corel Corporation 132; Eastern National 133; Unusual Films, courtesy of James Gordon 134; Metropolitan Museum of Art 135; Washington D.C. Convention & Visitors Association 138; Dave Fisher 139(bottom)

Chapter 7: George R. Collins 142, 150 (middle), 157(top), 165; Wade K. Ramsey 145; North Carolina Travel & Tourism 146; Mammoth Cave National Park 149; Unusual Films 150(left, right); Brian D. Johnson 152; Charleston Area Convention & Visitors Bureau 154; Mike Booher/Transparencies, Inc. 155 (left); Thomas R. Fletcher 155(right); Georgia Department of Trade & Industry 156(top); Photo Disc, Inc. 156(bottom), 161; Alabama Bureau of Tourism & Travel 157(bottom); Library of Congress 158; Terry M. Davenport 160(top); National Park Service, by Richard Frear 160(bottom); Louisiana Department of Culture, Recreation & Tourism 163; Corel Corporation 166

Chapter 8: Photo Disc, Inc. 168, 175(bottom); Ohio Historical Society 172(top); National Park Service, by Richard Frear 172(bottom); Indiana Tourism 173; Pacific Garden Mission 174; Chicago Convention & Tourism Bureau 175(top); Wisconsin Dells Visitor & Convention Bureau 178; George R. Buckley 180; Minnesota Office of Tourism 181; Brian D. Johnson 182; Kansas Film Commission 183; Corel Corporation 184; Joe Golden/NOAA 185; South Dakota Tourism 187

Chapter 9: Wyoming Division of Tourism 189; Yellowstone National Park, by William Keller 191(top); Worldwide Slides/Pana-Vue 191(middle); Photo Disc, Inc. 191(bottom), 209, 214(map), 215; Glen Canyon National Recreation Area 192(top); National Park Service, by Fred Mang, Jr. 192(bottom left); George R. Collins 192(bottom right), 193(bottom right), 206, 219; National Park Service 193(top left); Corel Corporation 193(top right), 203(bottom); Alaska Division of Tourism, by McBride 193(bottom left); Travel Montana, by Mike Sample 197; National Park Service, by Thomas Gray 198; Idaho Department of Commerce 199; Jay Schug Photography 200 (top); Terry M. Davenport 200(bottom); Ron Tagliapietra 202(top), 203(top); Zion National Park, by Allen Hagood 202(bottom); Alan Benoit/Arizona Office of Tourism 204(left); Travel Montana, by Steve Shimek 204(middle); Robert Holmes 204(right); California Division of Tourism, by Robert Holmes 210, 211; Oregon Tourism Commission 214(bottom); Washington State Tourism Division 216

Chapter 10: Robert Holmes 223; Canadian Government Office of Tourism 224; David Muenker/Muenker Media 225; Corel Corporation 226, 231, 237, 238(both), 239(bottom), 240; New Brunswick Dept. of Tourism/Andre Gallant 227; Eugene G. Schulz 228(top); Ward's Natural Science Establishment, Inc. 228(bottom both); Photo Copyright Winston Fraser 232; B. W. Carper 234; Royal Canadian Mounted Police 239(top); Photo Disc, Inc. 242

Unit IV Opener: Kevin Schafer Photography 245(top); World Bank, by Martin 245(middle, bottom), 244-45(background)

Chapter 11: Mexican Government Tourism Office 246, 250, 251, 252, 253, 255, 257; Kevin Schafer Photography 259(both), 263; John Mitchell/D. Donne Bryant Stock Photography Agency 260; David Muenker/Muenker Media 264; Library of Congress 265; Photo Disc, Inc. 266(top), 268; Michele Burgess 266(bottom); Kay Shaw Photography 267; John Nolan 269

Chapter 12: Ward's Natural Science Establishment, Inc. 271; Victor Englebert 274, 282(middle), 283(top); Photo Disc, Inc. 275, 285(top); Kenneth Frederick 276, 291; Kevin Schafer Photography 277; Kay Shaw Photography 279(all); Corel Corporation 280(left), 296; BJU Press photo collection 280(right); James D. Nations/D. Donne Bryant Stock Photography Agency 281; Michele Burgess 282(left, right), 295; Tui De Roy/The Roving Tortoise 284; Beth Davidow/Visuals Unlimited 285(bottom);

Photo Credits

World Bank 286; Glenn Randall 287; Argentina National Tourist Office 288, 290; Craig Duncan/ D. Donne Bryant Stock Photography Agency 289; Juca Martins/D. Donne Bryant Stock Photography Agency 293; Robert Fried/D. Donne Bryant Stock Photography Agency 294

Unit V Opener: French Government Tourist Office 298-99(background); Charles Preitner/ Visuals Unlimited 299(top); Danish Tourist Board 299(middle); George R. Collins 299(bottom)

Chapter 13: Kenneth Frederick 300, 302, 304(right); Corel Corporation 304(left), 308, 311, 312(top); Grace Davies Photography 312(bottom); Ward's Natural Science Establishment, Inc. 314, 322(top); Kay Shaw Photography 316, 318; Tom Stack 320; Danish Tourist Board 321; Photo Disc, Inc. 322(bottom)

Chapter 14: French Government Tourist Office, by Moatti 324; Ed Richards 326, 333; French Government Tourist Office, by Parlette 328(top); French Government Tourist Office, by Desazo 328(bottom); French Government Tourist Office, by Camille 330; French Government Tourist Office 331(both); Corel Corporation 335; German Information Center 337; Kenneth Frederick 341(top), 342; Phil Adams 341(middle, bottom); Ward's Natural Science Establishment, Inc. 344; Photo Copyright Winston Fraser 345, 346

Chapter 15: Gene Fisher 348; Dennis Bruckner 351; Photo Disc, Inc. 352; Victor Englebert 353; Link/Visuals Unlimited 354; Portuguese National Tourist Office 355; Jeanne Conte 356; Unusual Films 358(top), 362; Ed Richards 358(bottom); George R. Collins 359(top); Ann Swengel/Visuals Unlimited 359(bottom); courtesy of Bob Bell 361(top); Italian Tourist Agency 361(bottom left); Walter Persegati 361(bottom right); Ward Andersen 364; Corel Corporation 365

Unit VI Opener: MIR Agency 368(top); Naomi Duguid/Asia Access 368(middle); Kenneth Frederick 368(bottom), 368-69(background)

Chapter 16: Kenneth Frederick 370, 377; Tim Keesee 371, 375, 376, 382, 383, 384(bottom), 386(bottom), 389; Photo Disc, Inc. 378; Maxine Cass 384(top); John A. Visser 386(top); D. Lazaro 387(left); Penguin/Corbis-Bettmann 387(right); Franklin D. Roosevelt Library 391(top); MIR Agency 391(bottom)

Chapter 17: Corel Corporation 393; MIR Agency 398(top left), 400, 402(bottom), 404, 410(top), 411, 412; John A. Visser 398(top right); Kenneth Frederick 398(bottom); Library of Congress 402(top), 408; Eugene G. Schulz 407, 410(bottom)

Chapter 18: Christine Osborne Pictures 414; MIR Agency 416(both), 417(bottom), 420(top), 422; Jeffrey Alford/Asia Access 417(top); Tor Eigeland/Aramco World Mag. 419; Naomi Duguid/Asia Access 420(bottom), 421(bottom);

Aramco World Magazine 421(top); Victor Englebert 424

Unit VII Opener: World Bank, by Edwin Huffman 426-27(background); Michele Burgess 427(top); Jeffrey Alford/Asia Access 427(middle, bottom)

Chapter 19: Robert Holmes 428, 435, 444(top); Michele Burgess 431; Jeffrey Alford/ Asia Access 432; Ravi Kumar Pasupuleti 433(left); Photo Disc, Inc. 433(middle), 436, 444(bottom); Unusual Films, courtesy of Sivasankar Kumar Kande 433(right); Greenville County Library 434; Christine Osborne Pictures 438, 440(bottom); World Bank, by Tomas Sennett 440(top); Corel Corporation 442; World Bank, by Hadar 445

Chapter 20: World Bank, by Huffman 447; Michele Burgess 449, 460(top); Earth Satellite Corporation/Science Photo Library 450; Bob Shelton 451, 455(left); Kenneth Jensen 453; Robert Holmes 454, 455(right); Malaysian Tourism Promotion Board, painting by Simon Russell 456; Photo Disc, Inc. 457, 459, 460(bottom); Jeffrey Alford/Asia Access 461

Chapter 21: Photo Disc, Inc. 463; Free China Review 464, 470(top), 477(top); Xinhua News Agency 466; Carson Fremont 468, 469; National Archives 470(bottom left); Reuters/ Corbis-Bettmann 470(bottom right); Freer Gallery of Art 472; Michele Burgess 475(top); Jeffrey Alford/Asia Access 475(bottom); Nik Wheeler/Aramco World Mag. 476; George R. Collins 477(bottom); Consulate General of Japan, Atlanta, Georgia 481(top, bottom left), 483(left), 484(all), 485; International Society for Educational Information, Inc. 481(bottom right); Robert Holmes 482; Gospel Fellowship Association 483(top right); Corel Corporation 483(bottom right);

Unit VIII Opener: Christine Osborne Pictures 488-89(background); Chris Barton 489(top); Jeanne Conte 489(middle, bottom)

Chapter 22: Christine Osborne Pictures 490, 498, 499(both); Aramco World Magazine 494(left, bottom right), 495(both), 496(right); Corel Corporation 494(top right), 496(left), 502, 506(bottom); U.S. Army 501; Oriental Institute of the University of Chicago 503; Christine Osborne Pictures/Patrick Syder 504, 506(top); Photo Disc, Inc. 505

Chapter 23: Unusual Films 508, 515, 516(left), 524(top), 527(Dome of the Rock), 528(St. Stephen's Gate, Chapel of the Ascension, Garden of Gethsemane, garden tomb), 529(Pool of Bethesda, Church of the Holy Sepulchre, Golgotha,); Christine Osborne Pictures 510, 516(right), 530; Jim McGuire/Transparencies Inc. 511; Israel Ministry of Tourism 517, 525, 529(Golden Gate); Jeanne Conte 519, 533(bottom); Reuters/Corbis-Bettmann 521(top); Ron Tagliapietra 521(bottom), 522, 524(middle), 527(Wailing Wall), 529(Upper Room); Hammond, Inc. 523; Tim Berrey 524(bottom), 526(broad wall), 528(Hezekiah's

Tunnel, Pool of Siloam), 529(The Pavement); Peter Sanders Photography 529(Mount Moriah); Corel Corporation 531, 532(both), 533(top)

Unit IX Opener: Christine Osborne Pictures 536-37(background), 537(middle, bottom left); J. A. Franklin 537(top); Jane Faircloth/Transparencies Inc. 537(bottom right)

Chapter 24: Christine Osborne Pictures/Chris Barton 538; Reuters/Corbis-Bettmann 540; Christine Osborne Pictures 541, 545; Chris Barton 544, 546, 547; World Bank, by Ray Witlin 548, 549

Chapter 25: Christine Osborne Pictures/Chris Barton 551, 554; Jane Faircloth/Transparencies Inc. 552; Christine Osborne Pictures 553; World Bank, by Yosef Hadar 558(top); Corel Corporation 558(bottom), 559, 560, 561; World Bank, by John Moss 563; Jim Buerer 567

Chapter 26: Chris Barton 569, 578(top right), 580, 587(left), 589; Corel Corporation 572, 577, 579(bottom), 587(right), 590; World Bank, by Ray Witlin 573; Christine Osborne Pictures/David Else 575; Douglas R. Miller 578(middle, bottom right); Kay Shaw Photography 578(bottom left); Gospel Furthering Fellowship 579(top); South African Consulate General 582, 584(top); Jason Lauré 584(bottom); Reuters/Corbis-Bettmann 586; Christine Osborne Pictures/H. Bradt 591

Unit X Opener: Robert Holmes 594-95(background); Tui De Roy/The Roving Tortoise 595(top); Creation Science Foundation 595(middle, bottom)

Chapter 27: Jeanne Conte 596, 598, 600; Bill Bachman 601(left), 603, 605, 612(both); Promotion Australia 601(right); Victorian Tourism Commission 602; Corel Corporation 604; Steve Strike/Aramco World Mag. 608(top); Creation Science Foundation 608(bottom); Northern Territory Tourist Commission 609(both);Tui De Roy/The Roving Tortoise 610; New Zealand Tourism Board 611, 613

Chapter 28: Robert Holmes 615, 621; Embassy of Papua New Guinea 617, 618(both), 620; Photo Disc, Inc. 622(top), 628; Suzanne Altizer 622(bottom); Corel Corporation 624 (top); National Archives 624(bottom); Maxine Cass 625; Penni Gladstone/Robert Holmes Photography 627(top left); Dan Polin 627(top right); Victor Englebert 627(bottom)

Chapter 29: Tui De Roy/The Roving Tortoise 630, 632(bottom), 634(Adelie, macaroni, magellanic, emperor); Corel Corporation 631, 632(top), 634(gentoo), 638; U.S. Navy 637

Maps on the following pages Copyright 1998 GeoSystems Global Corporation:

x-1, 117, 143, 169, 195, 217, 218, 220, 224, 247, 260, 272, 301, 317, 325, 349, 372, 381, 394-95, 415, 430, 442, 448, 464, 479, 491, 509, 539, 542, 555, 562, 570, 582, 597, 611

All other illustrations not listed above provided by Precision Graphics